MARKING TIME

A Soldier's Story

by
Harry Foxley

Illustrations by **Trev Windsor**

© Copyright 2004 Harry Foxley. All rights reserved.

No part of this publication may be reproduced, stored in a retrieval system, or transmitted, in any form or by any means, electronic, mechanical, photocopying, recording, or otherwise, without the written prior permission of the author.

Printed in Victoria, Canada

Note for Librarians: a cataloguing record for this book that includes Dewey Classification and US Library of Congress numbers is available from the National Library of Canada. The complete cataloguing record can be obtained from the National Library's online database at:
www.nlc-bnc.ca/amicus/index-e.html
ISBN 1-4120-1587-1

TRAFFORD

This book was published on-demand in cooperation with Trafford Publishing. On-demand publishing is a unique process and service of making a book available for retail sale to the public taking advantage of on-demand manufacturing and Internet marketing. On-demand publishing includes promotions, retail sales, manufacturing, order fulfilment, accounting and collecting royalties on behalf of the author.

Suite 6E, 2333 Government St., Victoria, B.C. V8T 4P4, CANADA
Phone 250-383-6864   Toll-free 1-888-232-4444 (Canada & US)
Fax 250-383-6804   E-mail sales@trafford.com   Web site www.trafford.com
TRAFFORD PUBLISHING IS A DIVISION OF TRAFFORD HOLDINGS LTD.
Trafford Catalogue #03-1964   www.trafford.com/robots/03-1964.html

10   9   8   7   6   5   4   3   2   1

But meanwhile it is flying, irretrievable time is flying.

Virgil 70-19 BC

To *the Old Man*
who might have written a better book

to Mam
with fondest love

and to
Brum Barry, Alastair Gillan and Tony Watkin
three of II who shall not grow old

Prologue

Beginning
1941-1955

Service Beginning
1955-1969

Service Renewed
1969-1983

Service Ending
1983-1997

Epilogue

Introduction

Good reasons for attempting autobiography are hard to find. The prospect of making a pile of money is one (this manuscript seems unlikely to), whilst perhaps a loftier motive might be claimed in the hope of leaving an accurate record for one's children (I have none). Discounting these reveals the somewhat less attractive possibility that my motivation is merely self-aggrandisement, ego or vanity - vices I believed that I had jettisoned some years ago.

It is however possible that I have laboured to satisfy the curiosity of extant family and friends; the former having perhaps wondered what I found so difficult about a settled and secure life in a prosperous country, and the latter because they forever asked when I would publish my diaries. (The diaries, actually, proved unworthy of much other than blocking draughts in the loft, although they served to correct a faulty memory before I began to write the manuscript.)

It is true that in recent years I have become curious about my more immediate ancestors and the town in which I was born, and I have included the results of research which such curiosity provoked; although the product is merely a few hundred words among two hundred thousand of rather more egocentric study. Perhaps an autobiography should only seek to pay tribute to family and friends, whilst hoping at the very least that readers may be mildly diverted and entertained by the incidental humour of those experiences which seemed wholly bereft of humour at the time, although the humour was always present.

I have endeavoured to write honestly and objectively, but the latter is especially difficult and perhaps the more so where I describe some aspects of reservist service in very recent years. Opinions expressed are of course my own and I offer no evidence that they are either widely held or popular.

The 'interludes' may appear whimsical and perhaps are, but they represent thoughts and experiences that I wished to include, yet did not sit easily within the narrative. They may be altogether ignored.

I have divided the book into four segments, having discovered that the biblical 'three score years and ten' yields five periods of fourteen years, which fits my life to date rather conveniently. At fourteen I was newly arrived in Australia and at twenty-eight I had returned to England. At forty-two I was recently married and had just purchased my first house. At fifty-six I finally put off uniform and 'nailed boot', after a virtual lifetime in military service of one sort or another. At which point the narrative closes.

As to names: some appear and some do not. I excluded all names from the initial draft and this seemed, upon revision, to be very artificial. I have therefore included all names where it seemed natural to do so, although those that do not appear are nevertheless warmly recalled from time to time. (Others, a very few, are recalled with a degree of heat).

Marking Time? Well, the military connotation rendered a fairly apt title for that which mostly describes a life in uniform, but it is also intended to convey the sense of describing events and experiences that have marked one's progression through life - and time. I otherwise might have called it 'Chronicles of Wasted Time', a fragment of Shakespeare and an excellent title which has been used elsewhere.

Be advised that the bad language appears within a few chapters and that this may seem gratuitous, offensive and wholly unnecessary. Four-letter words possibly still qualify as 'obscene', although I have formed my own opinions as to that over the years. For example, several of the larger landowners in this country annually receive £1,000,000 in EU funds for *not* growing crops, whilst several thousands of children in other countries die each day of starvation. Perhaps that offers a better definition of obscenity, but it is maybe too large an argument to develop in a short introduction. Suffice instead to say that this is mostly a soldier's story that is sometimes written in soldiers' language.

The mistakes, whether in life or in the book, are my own, but then, so are some of the jokes.

   Harry Foxley
   Holywell Bay
   Cornwall

Glossary

AD	*Air Despatch*
AIG	*Assistant Instructor, Gunnery*
Askari	*Generic term for Arab irregulars*
APC	*Armoured Personnel Carrier*
AWOL	*Absent Without Leave*
Basha	*Field shelter constructed with Poncho*
Bivvie	*Ditto*
Bergen	*Generic term for most modern types of large pack*
BG	*Recruit Gunner*
CB	*Confined to Barracks*
CMF	*Citizen Miltary Forces - Australian reservist force equivalent to TA in UK*
CP	*Command Post*
CEFO	*Complete Equipment Fighting Order*
Compo	*Composite (Iron) Rations*
DPM	*Disruptive Pattern Material - camouflage clothing*
DS	*Directing Staff*
DSC	*Deputy Squadron Commander*
DZ	*Dropping Zone*
Endex	*End of Exercise*
EOD	*Explosive Ordnance Device*
FSMO	*Field Service Marching Order*
GDOC	*Ground Defence Operations Centre*
IG	*Instructor, Gunnery*
KD	*Khaki Drill; lightweight cotton uniform*
LSL	*Landing Ship, Logistic*
LZ	*Landing Zone*
MO	*Medical Officer*
MOB	*Main Operating Base*
NAAFI	*Navy, Army and Air Force Institute; services canteen*
OG	*Olive Green; lightweight cotton uniform*
PLF	*Parachute Landing Fall*

Poncho	Waterproof cape worn against rain or used to construct bivvie
PTI	Physical Training Instructor
PJI	Parachute Jump Instructor (drawn from PTI ranks)
PMC	Personnel Management Centre; administrative hub of RAF
RA	Royal Artillery
RAAF	Royal Australian Air Force
RCL	Recoilless Rifle
RAASC	Royal Australian Army Service Corps
RAP	Regimental Aid Post
RSM	Regimental Sergeant Major
RTU	Return(ed) to Unit
SOAF	Sultan of Oman Air Force
TA	Territorial Army; UK Reservist
U/S	Unserviceable

Prologue

The past is the only dead thing that smells sweet.

*Early One Morning
Edward Thomas 1878-1917*

Prologue

The birth of the town preceded mine by a century, and it would be a further half-century before I began to understand just how significant a town it had been and how great its contribution to the age of rail. Migrant town, railway town and new town. Crewe.

During the 1830s, the Grand Junction Railway Company operated the Birmingham-Liverpool line through a minor junction and station called Crewe. The name derived from the Earl of Crewe, whose adjacent estate provided employment for the occupants of a tiny hamlet, and whose sanction for the line had presumably been necessary. Perhaps some of his land was acquired for the line and it is certain that he was provided with a private platform at the station. In 1840 the GJR purchased the Chester-Crewe railway and the company then decided to build an engine repair shed to augment its works in Birmingham and Liverpool. Crewe was not the chosen site for this, but Nantwich, an ancient town four miles to the west. The Nantwich selection was not proceeded with and the reasons are obscure, although it may have resulted from opposition by the Nantwich citizens, or the fact of cheaper land around Crewe.

By the time of the final choice, the idea of an engine repair shed had been overtaken by the decision to build a locomotive works, and thirty acres were acquired about half a mile to the north of the existing station. Since the town would develop to the north of the works, it would not have the station, as is usual, at its centre, and the station actually remained beyond the town boundary until 1936, when it belatedly caught up. Until that time, the station, which lay on the Nantwich-Wheelock Turnpike road, remained in the parish of Barthomley, whereas the new town lay within the parish of Monks Coppenhall.

In addition to establishing the Works, the Railway Company

built the first of five hundred houses in an area that remains the centre of the present town, bounded by Market, Earle and Forge streets and Liverpool Terrace. Market and Forge are obvious names, whilst Liverpool Terrace may reflect the fact that the first two hundred employees of the Works were introduced from a railway works in Liverpool. None of the houses has survived and only Earle Street is intact. Market Street was successively truncated from the mid-Sixties onwards, whilst Forge Street deteriorated and was briefly reduced to the status of an unofficial car park before vanishing entirely in very recent years. Contemporary surrounding streets have endured, Prince Albert Street among them. Named, clearly, for Victoria's Consort, the street included a parade ground for the Railway Volunteers, a militia company that was disbanded at the formation of the Territorial Army in 1911. A railway veterans' club was built on the site of the parade ground and it also has survived. Prince Albert Street buildings included The Mechanics Institute, which fostered technical education for Works' apprentices, in addition to providing a library and reading rooms for railwaymen. The Institute, redundant for many years, was demolished in 1970, at a time just prior to a burgeoning interest in railway heritage that later served to rescue such historic buildings.

To the houses was added, in 1845, Christ Church to provide a place of worship which hitherto had taken place in the workshops. It was apparently well attended and this may have reflected the spiritual revival of the time, although it is equally possible that railwaymen deemed it prudent to worship at the 'company church'. Jobs might depend upon such things. Christ Church, whose severe architecture has been compared to that of engine sheds, was stripped of its roof in 1977 and the space where generations of railwaymen worshipped is now a walled garden. The church tower remains and services are conducted within it, doubtless on a much smaller scale than a century or so ago. The company built twenty churches in the town, including St Pauls, where I briefly attended services before precociously discovering religious scepticism.

The Works produced the first of thousands of locomotives in 1843, but there is no clear record of its name. For a number of years, it was believed that the Columbine, preserved at the York Railway Museum, was the first, but Columbine wasn't built until 1845 and she was merely the first of a new type; of radical design and greatly enhanced power. The record is further clouded by the fact that several locomotives were repaired at the Works before the first engine was built.

In 1846, the GJR was amalgamated with the London-Birmingham and the Manchester-Birmingham railway companies to form the London & NorthWestern Railway Company, which by 1851 was the largest joint-stock corporation in the world. Its Crewe possession would become the largest rail junction in the world. It was soon recognised that the Works would need to expand, but the building of the new town so close to the Works precluded expansion to the north. The new works was therefore sited along the Chester Line, about half a mile to the west, and this site would grow to cover a hundred and thirty-seven acres, with forty-eight of them roofed over. Turn of the century photographs show a forest of chimneys rising from sheds, foundries and forges; a number of them belching black smoke from the steelworks. Between 1864 and 1932 some 3,000,000 tons of steel were produced at the Works, which pioneered the large-scale use of the Bessemer process and, later, the Siemens-Martin open hearth steel-making process. The first rails produced by the Bessemer process were laid at Crewe station.

The new Works, in addition to lying alongside the Chester Line, was adjacent to the Valley Brook, an apparently insignificant watercourse yet one which nevertheless supplied the Works and town with 80,000 gallons of water per day. The brook also provided - presumably downstream - the dumping point for the town's effluent, until complaints were made in Nantwich that the River Weaver was becoming polluted. The Works then built a sewage treatment plant.

Sewerage was yet another Works' amenity to add to employment, houses, churches, schools, libraries, baths and parks, with water, gas and electricity developed for the Works and also serving the community.[1] For a century, the Railway Company was the only significant employer in the town and although it exploited its monopoly politically, and was guilty of intimidating employees, it was

---

[1] Interestingly, however, the Company neither built nor encouraged the building of public houses, although they mushroomed nonetheless. Perhaps the Company felt guided by the burgeoning temperance movement, unless drink-related absenteeism was already a feature of industrial life.

largely benevolent and the company was seen as a model of its time.

The town population mushroomed. The Monks Coppenhall Parish in 1841 numbered 747 and ten years later the Crewe population was 4,600 and rising. By 1858 it was 8,000. Crewe was very much a migrant town, attracting workers from the already industrialised industrialised North and the Midlands to the Cheshire Plain that had been wholly agricultural and thinly populated. The comparative remoteness of the area may be gauged from a contemporary description of migration to Crewe as analogous to departure for the American West. Four of my great-grandparents arrived in the town from Buckinghamshire. These were the Foxleys and the Emertons from the villages of Akeley and Leckhamstead, in the years 1872-77.

Buckinghamshire was greatly significant towards the mid-Nineteenth century with regard to population movement, following agricultural changes that affected three-quarters of the national workforce. A Royal Commission in 1832 produced several recommendations for the relief of poverty (to include the infamous Union Workhouses), and among the implementations was the sending of entire families, by canal boat, to fill the manpower shortages in the Manchester mills. The first such 'emigration', was from Bledlow, in Buckinghamshire. Results were mixed and although many of the migrants would achieve levels of comfort or prosperity, conditions remained hard for many others. Boys at the age of seven often worked a twelve-hour shift in factories, ironworks or mines.

I had supposed that the Foxley and Emerton families may have been seeking to escape from rural poverty, but research suggests differently. The villages of Akeley and Leckhamstead are five and six miles from the town of Wolverton, which was a GJR locomotive works that closed at some time after 1867. It seems likely that both William Foxley and David Emerton were railway employees at Wolverton and transferred to Crewe after the works closed.

There is a family story that William Foxley built the first brick kiln in Crewe and prospered, but in later life had to be supported by his sons. Sadly, only the latter part of this story appears to be true. There had been eight brick kilns feeding the Works' and town's voracious demands for bricks, and the Works' management decided to build its own kiln, in 1862. So successful was the kiln, that it reduced the price of bricks by almost forty per cent, driving the independent brick burners out of business. Census returns indicate that William Foxley arrived in the town 1873/74 and although the

1881 Census records his occupation as a brick burner, he was almost certainly a railway employee. His address at the census was 69 Richard Moon Street, which was built by the company in 1875 for employees and named for the company chairman. William Foxley may have been comfortable, rather than prosperous, but by the time of the 1891 Census his fortunes had declined. His occupation by then was 'General Labourer - Irregular Work', and at the age of 54 his future was less than secure in an era which long-preceded pensions and the welfare state. No photograph of William Foxley survives and he has vanished into the sands of time, yet his legacy includes g-g-g-grandchildren that are second-generation Australians likely to prosper in the 21st Century.

David Emerton, who was the father of my Gran'Ma Foxley, fared rather better after his move from Leckhamstead. He found Works' employment as a mechanic and a house in Ramsbottom Street, which was named for the chief engineer and which led directly to the Works' entrance at the imposing north wall. I knew that Gran'Ma Foxley ran a shop in the west end of Crewe where my father was born and raised, and in the Crewe Library in 1996 I found a Trade Directory which revealed that David Emerton had occupied the shop by 1896. The shop, together with the entire street, was razed during the Sixties, but a memento of it survives. A simple wooden box served as the shop till and Gran'Ma Foxley retained it for bric-a-brac for the rest of her life. A few years ago, I rescued it from dereliction and I have it still.

William Foxley and David Emerton had not travelled alone. The 1881 Census reveals that four per cent of the Crewe population originated in Buckinghamshire, doubtless numbering those who had been employed at the Wolverton railway works. The Crewe Foxleys were migrant and, briefly, railway families.

The vast Works produced not only great quantities of steel, brass, iron, coke and brick, but also a huge range of smaller products to include soap and grease. There was even a shop in the Works that devoted its effort to the production of artificial limbs, for the frequent victims of the notorious belt-driven machinery. For those victims who did not survive their accidents, a carpentry shop produced cheap coffins. It was a very different age.

Beginning
1941-1955

*"Where shall I begin, please, Your Majesty," He asked
"Begin at the beginning," the King said, gravely,
"And go on until you stop."*

*Alice's Adventures in Wonderland
Lewis Carroll 1832-98*

1

It was a troubled year and the events that shaped it have long since passed into record and history, accurately and otherwise. Mankind was at war and the time was of death; premature, violent and global, accounting for some 50,000,000 men, women and children. Yet life went on and births, mine among them, continued. Oblivious to the terrors it offered, I entered the world on 15 May 1941 at Number 4 Henry Street, Crewe in Cheshire.

I was delivered at home to Dorothy May Foxley, nee Lindop, and my arrival had been preceded by that of my brother Arthur, born three years earlier. My parents, Doll and Harry, were married at the church of St. Chad at Wybunbury, in Cheshire, in 1937. The church no longer exists, having in the Seventies to be demolished because of subsidence.[1] Only the tower survives, having been expensively underpinned, and it now dominates the church yard where my maternal grandparents, John and Margaret Lindop, are buried.

John Lindop was born 18 April 1885, at Willaston, Cheshire, and he was a son of George Lindop, a railway labourer. George married in 1872 at Nantwich and he was the son of Thomas, a farm labourer. At the time of their marriage on 14 December 1910, John Lindop was a twenty-five-year-old bachelor and a railway porter, and his bride, Margaret, was a twenty-seven-year-old spinster. Gran'Ma Lindop was born 8 May 1883, a daughter of William Meacock who

---

[1] The problem of subsidence was not new; the tower had developed a distinct lean in the mid-Nineteenth century and this was tackled by a local man named Trubshaw, whose solution was to sluice soil from the 'high' side of the tower, thus allowing it to straighten itself. His idea was more recently examined as a means to arrest the lean of the Tower of Pisa.

was a farmer at Hargrave, near Chester. William Meacock, who was born in 1858 and was twenty-one years old when he married Mary Fleet, a twenty-two-year-old spinster, in 1879, had a puzzling chronology that described him as a farm labourer at a much later period in his life. This seeming anachronism was solved for me by an older member of my family, who knew that William Meacock's dairy herd had been wiped out by anthrax. Presumably, it also wiped out his farm. William Meacock was also a widower before he was thirty; his wife Mary and new child dying during the birth. At the time of the 1891 Census, William and his three daughters, the youngest of which was seven and my future maternal grandmother, were living either with William's parents or those of his late wife.

My paternal grandparents were Arthur Malvern Foxley, born 3 December 1880, and Mary Ellen Emerton, born 7 March 1880. Both were born to migrant railway families living in the Monks Coppenhall parish of Crewe, a settlement that had long preceded the modern town, and neither family had Cheshire antecedents. Arthur was a son of William Foxley, born in Greenwich, Kent in 1838. William had married Elizabeth Adams on 30 April 1866 at Akeley, Buckinghamshire, which also was the county of origin of Mary Ellen's parents. It is of interest to me that various strands of my family had links with both farming and railway labouring. I do not know what survives within us of our ancestors, other than genetic codes, but I have always had a good resistance to cold weather and I wonder if that perhaps is something handed on by hardy forbears.

My birth had not been planned; a fact my father vouchsafed to me some years ago over a pot of lager at a Miners' club, in a dusty gold-mining town in Western Australia. I cannot recall the context of the remark and I doubt if I was very curious about it at the time. It is very easy, now, to comprehend the reluctance, in 1940, to plan children at the nadir of a black war. 1941 was doubtless the worst year for Britain, when unrestricted U-boat warfare so nearly cut the tenuous lines of supply from America and Empire. America had not entered the war and nor, in May, had Russia. It is nonetheless a late-twentieth century myth that England stood alone in 1940. The Empire was still extensive and Britain was backed by the immense resources of Australia, Canada, India, New Zealand and South Africa, in addition to a clutch of Far Eastern colonies that were not yet threatened by the Japanese. The fact, for example, that Britain was able to prosecute the aerial campaign against Germany was mostly due to the success of the

Empire Air Training Scheme, whereby tens of thousands of aircrew were trained in Canada. (The enormous cost of the scheme was mostly borne by the Canadian taxpayer.)

At this time, however, the future must have seemed very bleak to the ordinary people of England, with the prospect of German invasions much likelier than any attempt to reverse the debacle of Dunkirk. At the time of my conception there had not even been the victory over the *Luftwaffe* which we have ever since celebrated as the Battle of Britain. This was a single victory against a stunning record of German successes in Europe, and perhaps it convinced the Americans that England was worthy of support, thus underpinning the vital lifeline of lend-lease. Among the quotations from the era is a most perceptive one by Josef Stalin: "America provided the money; Russia provided the blood and England provided the time."

To this, as to every other aspect of war, I of course was oblivious. The war had imposed rationing upon me - and to virtually everyone other than the black marketeers - but I was well fed. My father once remarked that the British population was better fed during the war than in the years that preceded and followed it, and I do not doubt that he was right. It is a matter of record that rationing during the years 1945-48 was tighter than during 1939-45, whilst meat remained rationed for a decade after the war had ended.

Bombs fell but, with a single exception, they fell distantly and if I spent odd nights in a damp, cold and crowded bomb shelter, then I retain no memory of such discomforts. These I would have to inflict upon myself later. The war hardly touched the Foxleys but we had the merest brush with a major player at much the time of my birth. The Deputy *Führer*, Rudolph Hess, undertook a bizarre mission, flying an ME 110 to Scotland to propose peace terms to the Duke of Hamilton. Subsequently arrested, he was taken by train from Perth to Euston on the sixteenth of May and the train driver was Mel Foxley. Hess remained in prison to the very end of his days and thus his life was effectively over as mine was beginning

Until the war the Railway Company had been the only significant employer in the town, and at the age of fourteen my father had followed his father into the company, then of course privately owned, to train as cleaner, oiler, fireman and driver, but his job as a fireman did not survive the Depression. He eventually retrained as a bricklayer and he mostly followed that trade for the remainder of his life.

My maternal grandfather, John Lindop, also worked for the railway, rising from porter at the time of his marriage to an inspector by the time he retired. At the outbreak of war his only son, Arthur, was called up and he served with the Cheshire Regiment, training for D-Day in the Orkneys. *En route* for the landings, which he joined at D-Day plus four, he travelled through Crewe and managed to get word to Grandad of the movement. They exchanged a few words at Crewe station in the early hours of a summer's day and it must have been a poignant moment for father and son. Happily, Uncle Arthur survived both the landings and the subsequent slog through France and Germany, right up to V-E Day. He survives to this day and, like most old soldiers, he seldom mentions the war, but the action his unit saw is evidenced by the fact that three members of his rifle platoon were decorated. His unit also entered and witnessed the horror of one of the Death Camps.

Dad had tried to escape unemployment in the Thirties by enlisting in the army, but he was rejected on account of poor eyesight and rejected again when war broke out, by which time he was thirty-two. The war put him into the Rolls-Royce factory which was built in Crewe for the production of Merlin aero engines, and his occupation is described on my birth certificate as 'Engineer Turner'. The Air Ministry had originally selected Liverpool as the site for the factory, but the view of the management at the parent company at Derby prevailed. The factory produced the first engines seven weeks before the outbreak of war, and for the next six years worked around the clock and the calendar to make Merlin engines for Spitfires, Hurricanes, Mosquitoes, Lancasters and a dozen other war machines, including the Comet tank. There was similar effort at the Locomotive works, where hull plates for the Matilda tank were machined and complete examples of the Covenanter tank rolled off assembly lines. The Works also designed a thirty-ton tank, which however was not accepted by the War Department, in addition to out-shopping steam locomotives throughout the war.

Dad worked a lathe in Royce's (as the factory became known locally) but he had little affinity for indoor work. He was eventually transferred to work on some of the airfields that mushroomed on the face of England until they absorbed one per cent of the total acreage in the country. He also worked on bomb damage repair in London, from where he once brought a dog that had apparently been bombed out. I have the vaguest memory of the dog, which was named Togo, and it was the first of several animals that the Foxley houses would know down the years.

The war holds no memories, good or bad, for me since I was only four by V-E Day and hardly older at V-J Day. I may once have followed a file of marching American troops, importuning for chewing gum, but this may be a false memory or a real one but long post-war. Americans were certainly stationed in the area, and a local landlord achieved a degree of fame when approached by an American commanding officer with the view that white and coloured troops should not drink in the same premises. The landlord agreed and he promptly banned the white troops.

David & Elizabeth Emerton
nee Hurst

John & Margaret Lindop
nee Meacock

Arthur Malvern & Mary Ellen Foxley   Harry & Dorothy Foxley
nee Emerton   nee Lindop

2

It was during the years that immediately followed the war that I began to recognise the environment I was born into. Henry Street seemed to stretch into infinity and actually was several hundred yards long, but in my childhood it was more particularly the row of eleven attached houses that ran from 4 to 24. Number 2 is a mystery to me now since ours was the gable end which was separated by an alley from Middlewich Street, running at right-angle to Henry and, presumably, in the direction of Middlewich.

The houses were of the classic 'back-to-back, two up and two down' pattern of which Crewe had an abundance, many having been built for railway workers. The downstairs had a 'front room' which looked out onto the street and a dining room at the back, whilst the kitchen was hardly more than a passage to the enclosed back yard of about fifty square feet. A narrow flight of stairs led to the two upstairs rooms, where Arthur and I shared a bed at the front, with that belonging to Mam and Dad at the back. There was no bathroom and the lavatory occupied a corner at the end of the yard. No lobbies, halls, landings or porches existed to offer additional space and only the 'glory hole' - a panelled area beneath the stairs - provided storage space of sorts. It was to the glory hole where a pet mouse I had at one time went to live, presumably being fed up with its travelling companion. A galvanised tub hung in the yard and was the means of bathing when brought indoors in front of the fire, and filled with hot water from a succession of kettles and pans. The use of the lavatory was frequently a cold prospect and this doubtless did little to foster good bowel habits

If storage spaces about the house were few, then there was in any case little with which to fill them. Number 4 had a sparse inventory of beds, wardrobes, tables and chairs and the house, during our occupancy anyway, never saw a refrigerator, a freezer, a microwave oven, a washing machine, a tumble drier, a stereo system, a video recorder, a television set or a dozen other appliances that today would seem quite ordinary. A vacuum cleaner would have been wholly redundant since we had no carpets beyond simple rugs, and linoleum covered the floorboards. The houses were small and that may have derived from the fact that they were intended to contain little, other than children.

Mam did the washing in an iron tub, plunging clothes in the water with a 'dolly peg' that looked like a stool attached to a pole, and wringing out the excess water with a cast-iron mangle. During inclement weather, the washing was left to dry on a rack which lowered on pulleys from the ceiling of the back room, catching the heat rising from the coal fire, and it is likely that such methods did little for those who suffered from bronchial complaints. It is interesting, however, to note that such racks - or replicas of them - may now be ordered from trendy home magazines as the perfect complement to a period kitchen.

The house seemed large in boyhood but we moved out when I was ten and I did not see it again for eighteen years. On the later occasion I was astonished at how tiny it was, and it seemed as if I might almost reach up and touch the bedroom window I had slept behind, or sometimes awake listening to trains clattering across the adjacent Cumberland Bridge. I was unsentimental about the house though and I did not grieve when the entire row was demolished just a few years later.[1] Nor did I hear of any spirited petition to save such relics at a time when the wholesale demolition of Crewe's Victorian heritage was in hand. These houses, in the main, were cold, damp, crowded and insanitary and only a fool would mourn their passing. In later years, however, I was pleased to note that some of the original railway houses were preserved when they, too, might have met the bulldozer. 'Gaffer's Row' stood close to Crewe Square and had been built for railway foremen in the nineteenth century. These were renovated, whilst preserving original features, and continue to provide an interesting example of the time.

At some point in the Forties I would discover that Henry Street led past a row of allotments towards an expanse of open ground called 'The Razza', and that on the far side of this stood the Borough

---

[1] The houses were immediately replaced by a row of 'maisonettes' that seemed to offer little more living space than the original houses, but doubtless were much better equipped.

School, later termed the Brierley Street School. I believe that I remember being taken there by my mother for the first day of attendance as an infant, and dissolving in tears as soon as she left. School, however, had to be adjusted to, as was an acceptance that the stencil blocks and paint in the infants' class would yield to the more structured forms of primary school classes. I soon learned that I was not a natural scholar and my preferred pursuits were the noisy games in the schoolyard, where I tried to amaze Heather Tinsley with my gorilla impressions. Heather I had taken a considerable shine to but she remained aloof to my attempts to attract her attention.

During our primary school progress, the regular staff was briefly augmented by student teachers, one of whom encouraged us to write a play. From some inspiration, I wrote of John Brown's bids to emancipate the American Negro, and the play was selected for a class production. I modestly cast myself as the eponymous hero and in the concluding scene I played the now dead John Brown in a coffin which was an upturned table. Having also used my producer's clout to cast Heather Tinsley in a prominent role, she now upstaged the entire cast with a histrionic display of weeping and wailing at the funeral scene. Heather reserved no such affection for the living Foxley, however, and my attempts to secure it utterly failed.

Evanescent success as a writer did not reflect achievement across a broader spectrum of subjects. In a class of about twenty-five I usually lay at twenty-three or twenty-four, sometimes alternating with my friend, David Vickers. He lived around the corner in Middlewich Street, had an elder brother much the same age as my elder brother and, in time, would have younger brothers of much the same age as my younger brothers. The Vickers' family later outstripped ours and they also had a disabled child of whom we were fiercely protective. She had what is now referred to as Down's Syndrome but we knew her, and not unkindly, as simply somehow different.

David displayed an early entrepreneurial flair that manifested itself when the Razza was excavated to lay sewerage pipes. The Razza now proved to have been the site of a domestic rubbish tip in the past, when the spoil of the excavation threw up dozens of ceramic jam jars from an earlier age. Whilst most of these were lined up to become the target of stones, David persuaded me that we might cart these from door to door and sell them as dripping jars. Since I had a trolley cart, which Dad had made for me out of some scrap, I had the necessary transportation and we made some sales, although we did not pursue the idea for long. The Razza was another minor mystery that I solved about forty-five years later via the Crewe Library. 'Razza' was a corruption of reservoir and reservoir, in Victorian usage, referred simply to any pit. Such a pit existed near New Street that ran parallel to the future borough school. It had originally been excavated and mined for the clay that made bricks for the new town, and later was used for the dumping of builder's rubble and household detritus. The Town Corporation acquired the pit in 1911 for such use, but the pit, pre-sewers, attracted less salubrious waste. Health concerns arose, particularly when the school was built, and the pit was closed and sealed in 1929.

Elsewhere, money was to be made periodically by drowning the frequent litters of Mrs Yoxall's fertile cat. These would be sewn into a sack by Mrs Yoxall and dropped into a washing tub half-filled with water. My job was to hold the sack under with a boiler stick until the bubbles ceased, having been assured that kittens felt no pain until their eyes opened. For this unwitting cruelty I received the sum of sixpence. At much the same time at school, our attention was drawn to the message of cruelty to animals implicit in Anna Sewell's book *Black Beauty*, and we were urged to join the RSPCA. This I did, failing to appreciate the irony of my occasional duties on behalf of Mrs Yoxall.

At primary school I succeeded only in the field of horticulture, growing a bean in a jam jar lined with pink blotting paper, and my academic results remained poor. At eight or nine I opened a school report on the way home and remembered forever the single line which summed up my scholastic year: 'Inclined to dream, could do better.'

Perhaps dreaming was essential in an austere decade when money was not plentiful in any of the houses that we knew. Sweets were still rationed and fruit was seldom seen. Butter remained a rarity and powdered egg frequently replaced the farmyard variety, although some of us preferred it to the original. Entertainment in the home then centred upon the wireless, and the nightly exploits of *Dick Barton: Special Agent*. Between 1946 and 1951 the thrilling music of *Devil's Gallop* heralded another fifteen minutes in which the hero, assisted by Snowy and Jock, punched the lights out of assorted, and usually foreign, thugs. When the series ended it was replaced - a recent discovery - by *The Archers*, which has endured for much longer, albeit with little appeal for small boys.

The first TV set appeared in a neighbour's house and Mrs Fewtrell would sometimes allow a row of suitably silent children to sit in front of the tiny screen. A considerable novelty, yet it seemed to offer no great threat to our principal treat, which was the Saturday matinee session at the Kino cinema, which stood just off Market Street towards the town centre. Once past the imposing figure of the commissionaire, resplendent in greatcoat, brass buttons and peaked cap and largely intolerant of small boys, we could form anarchic knots in the seats immediately below the huge screen, the better to hiss the 'baddies' and cheer the 'goodies'. The serial heroes were Batman, in baggy tights, Flash Gordon, in wobbling spaceships, and Tarzan, whose echoing jungle call was greatly admired.[1] The Three Stooges were a firm favourite, as were Laurel and Hardy and the Bowery Boys. A list of cowboy favourites would occupy half a page, but we were not keen on Roy Rogers, since he wasted so much screen time singing when he might have employed himself more usefully by blasting the baddies to death. It was the cowboys who made the lasting impression at the close of the screening, as we galloped down Market Street slapping our backsides as if we rode fine horses, and firing imaginary revolvers at anyone who had the temerity to stand in our path. I once varied this routine when Aunt Bess gave me a pilot's outfit for my birthday. This comprised a silvered helmet, goggles and a compass and for some time I ran dementedly about imagining that I was at the controls of a Spitfire.

Xmas might bring the gift of a No 1 Meccano Set or a John Bull Printing Outfit, to make wonky constructions or blotchy letters, but games were simple and required no expensive equipment, for which no money would have been found. We played Conkers, in a season, and at other times of the year relied upon ingenuity. A passable game was to fire rubber bands, produced by cutting an old innertube

---

[1] In later life I read that the aged Johnny Weismuller lost his mental faculties and had to be confined to a home for old people. Some remnant of his celluloid existence clearly remained with him, however, since he was prone, from time to time, to startle the other residents of the home with his famous call.

into strips, at matchboxes along a pitch of about six feet. If you hit the matchbox, you kept it, whilst the pitch owner retained the bands which missed. We collected cigarette packets and a fertile search area for these were the bins at the back of the Cumberland Arms. I was prospecting one day when a drunken neighbour gripped me about the throat. I was not alarmed, since I recognised him as a member of the Gaffney family who lived a few doors from us. Nor did I report this to Dad, who likely would have gone around and thumped the man. The cigarette packets of the age seem, in retrospect, to have been of superior design and of greater variety. The rarity of the more expensive cigarettes in our neighbourhood put a due premium upon such finds as Kensitas, Dunhill and State Express cigarette packets, whereas the open paper packets that enclosed just five Woodbines were on nobody's collection list.

We were doubtless ignorant of the fact that the Cheshire Plain stood on a great raft of clay, but clay nevertheless featured in our play. It was dug from some bank and fashioned into a small oven that we stuffed with cotton waste and lit. Running about with the open end held forward produced a satisfying stream of smoke from the top aperture. Whether this was intended to simulate a steam loco, I do not recall, but it is fairly certain that the cotton waste originated from the Loco Works. (As did 'Foreign Orders', which included a couple of brass horses in Gran'Ma Foxley's house. In time, they came into mine.)

Such were the games, but, less innocent, I was once persuaded by Michael Wood, who lived in Audley Street, to entice the butcher's daughter to the area of the Cumberland Bridge embankment, where an open drain lay behind a fence. She was slightly younger than we were and agreed to accompany us to hear a joke. The joke, it transpired, was when Michael raised her frock and pulled down her knickers to inspect her private parts. I also looked but was little wiser, since she appeared not to have any private parts. The girl did not seem offended, but for some time afterwards I was beset by the greatest anxiety that she might complain and point an accusing finger. Mr Dixon seemed a large man - a very large man to a seven or eight years old - and on my errands to his shop I had noted the lethal array of knives he had, one or other of them usually gripped in his large, red hands.

On some other occasion I was sworn to secrecy and invited into a tent to witness a ceremony where an older boy anally penetrated another older boy. I do not recall being particularly shocked by this, but it did seem a very odd thing to. This view, at least, has not changed substantially in the near half-century since. School lessons held few clues as to this sort of behaviour, and nor do I recall references to it in the brief period we attended church. Although both of my parents had strong lines of Methodism in their upbringing, and my mother's family remained churchgoers all their lives, only nominally were we Church of England. Dad's politics now ruled out religious beliefs of any kind, although he may once have encouraged us to join the choir at St. Paul's. He had sung with a choir as a boy and he possessed a fine voice. Perhaps he had hoped that choir practice might develop similar ability in Arthur and me. I did attend some practises at the church in the evenings, but was shocked when the choirmaster slapped the face of a boy for deliberately singing a shrill note in some paean to God. I did not return, although I liked to sing as a boy and only discovered in later life that I was among those who could not carry a tune in a bucket.

The area to the rear of the houses was known as 'The Backs' and it featured a small piece of open ground and the bomb shelter. The shelter was a marginally interesting place to play, since it made a passable 'pretend' submarine, but it smelled of urine and even excrement, and perhaps was occasionally used as a transit urinal by patrons going home from the Cumberland Arms pub. An abandoned yard off Middlewich Street provided a fort to enact the fantasies fuelled by the Saturday matinees, and I formed my own gang there. We were just three: myself, David and Dennis Walker. Dennis was about eighteen months older but he was a small child who simply never grew. Later he became a jockey who had some success at steeple chasing and, like me and some members of David's family, he would emigrate to Australia.

'Gangs' were the focus for all children from ages of about six to twelve, but we were a fairly innocuous crew. We were once questioned and sternly reprimanded by a policewoman, for scattering the feathers from a pillow in the street (and made to collect them; there was certainly respect for if not fear of the Law then which seems no longer a feature of British life), but the general behaviour was seldom more egregious than door-knocking in the early evenings. Playing in the dark held no terrors and we clearly enjoyed an era that was relatively free of child molestation, to say nothing of children brutally killed by slightly older children. We ranged a little and once went to the golf course at Haslington, catching a snake there and discovering, when we cut it open in the improbable and unrealised dream of making snakeskin belts of it, that a recently-consumed frog lay inside. These were simple and innocent pursuits and it seems, in retrospect, to have been a happy time. We lived in austere times, but children had little sense of that. The future was infinite, the world without limits and all things seemed possible. Only later would we understand how disappointing family, friends, lovers and life may prove, that the world can be a cruel place and happiness elusive. Happiness in any case, for a boy of eight or nine, was probably a new pair of pumps (plimsolls) on an endless summer's day. Or bottles of Dandelion & Burdock. Or packets of Smith's crisps with the salt in a twist of blue paper.

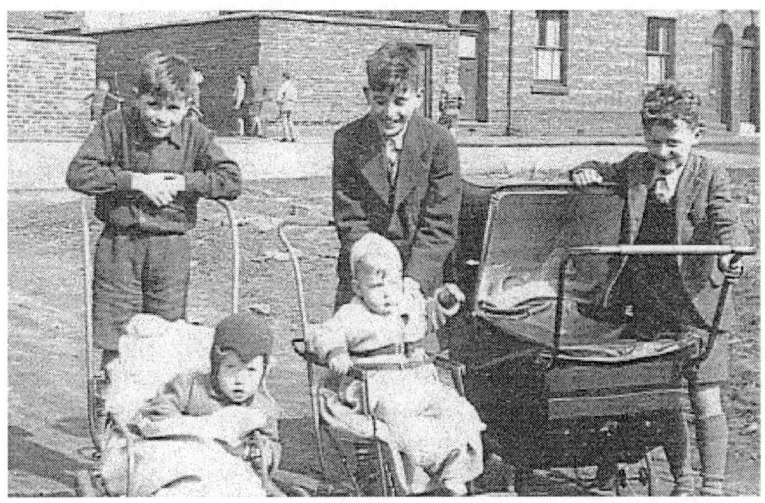

Sibling Pride 1949
Henry & Middlewich Streets Crewe
Photo: Harry Lloyd

3

A late event at Henry Street was the birth of my brother Jack in 1948. Arthur doubtless understood this rather better than me, but we were greatly thrilled by the arrival. We seemed to conform to some pattern of working class life and if our comforts were few, then we did not feel especially disadvantaged. If some families were doing better than ours, then surely we were doing as well as and better than a few others. I remember a visit with Mam to relations of her friend, where we were offered tea in jam jars. There was certainly no impression of our being poor.

Emigration might have taken us away from the town in the immediate post-war period, for Dad was keen to seek a new life, but Mam had reservations which were compounded by her reluctance to leave her parents for what probably would be the last time. When I was ten, we moved to Adelaide Street, in the west end of the town, and I spread the word that we were moving to Adelaide, Australia. This led to odd enquiries at the door from neighbours who wanted to know if any household goods needed a new home.

Dad bought the house at 35 Adelaide Street for, I think, £100 and he may have bought it from Gran'Ma Foxley. She certainly owned some properties in Crewe at the time and was relatively wealthy. It was a Victorian dwelling and a few streets from where Dad was born and raised. It was another gable end house and it still featured gas mantles on the walls, although Dad already had renovations in hand. It was larger than our former house and the bathroom had piped hot water, although the lavatory was still in the yard. The lavatory bowl was a vertical piece that was entirely boxed in to form a 'throne'. I thought this very grand and I etched my initials in it with a screwdriver. Tiled surround fires soon replaced iron grates and a modern gas cooker had pride of place in a fairly spacious kitchen, which served the dining room through a wall hatch that Dad devised.

The street was laid to a gradient which led to the school I was now enrolled at, and that had the distinction of being the first in Crewe which was built neither by the railway company nor the church. The change in house and school now marked a change also in an academic record, for I joined a class of strangers and without the distraction of friends I began at last to pay some attention to lessons. By midterm I was placed thirteenth in the examinations and this improvement led to some speculation that I might follow Arthur into Grammar school.

I again attracted notice as a writer, having seen the facsimile of an eighteenth century newspaper that detailed the hanging of a thirteen-year-old boy for stealing bread. I wove this account into a story and the class teacher, Mr Kearney, read the story to the class, praising it lavishly. I responded to such interest and wanted to do better. By the end of the term I was placed third in the class and I was by now determined to pass the 11-plus examination.

Within the lengthy school holidays we found the time for simple breaks, often travelling to a property owned by Dad's employer. Years before he had purchased a redundant railway carriage and he installed it in a field in Shropshire, a few miles below Market Drayton, intending to use it as a base for fishing trips or rabbit shooting. We would travel down in the firm's motorcycle and sidecar and spend a weekend or a week in 'The Hut'. The sidecar was actually a rectangular wooden box, we termed 'The Coffin', and Arthur and I once shared it with the dog, by this time an Alsatian, which was sick over both of us. A greater discomfort, though, was in having to wear sandals that were made out of hemp. They itched abominably.

Tibberton featured not only the hut, but also an adjacent wood with a well at its edge. The well was dry and had long exceeded its function of supplying water to a tiny hamlet that had hardly grown with the twentieth century, but it had immense novelty for a town boy. Another excitement was the river Meese which flowed nearby, and a rusting mill wheel that was a picture of benign neglect. The hut was lit by paraffin lamps whose fumes lingered attractively on the evening air, as we awaited the return from the local pub of Dad and his mate, Arthur, bearing pop and crisps.

It was a magical place and when I returned to it after an absence of fourteen years I greatly feared that it might be occupied by a housing estate. Happily not so: not a single new building encroached and only the well had changed, with its wall demolished and the void boarded over. Happy days.

By the time we had moved into Adelaide Street I had learned something of birth and something also of death, although both were difficult to comprehend. Dad's twin sister, Aunt Phyl, had three children and the eldest girl contracted polio and died. Grandad Foxley also died, when I was five, but he at least had seemed to be very old. I could just remember both of them but I was too young to experience grief, life's later lesson.

Death also visited the famous and into our Adelaide Street classroom one day came the headmaster, Mr Furber. King George had died, he told us, and we would be given a day off in mourning. This provoked a tremendous cheer that made the headmaster furious, and the day off was promptly cancelled. We observed a disappointing two-minute silence instead.

In the year at the school I made few new friends, other than a casual friendship with a classmate who also lived next door. We lived on the town side of the west end, Adelaide Street being one of about a dozen which lay at right-angle to West Street, which ran from Hightown to the very gates of Royce's. The west end had a reputation for roughness and some of its streets certainly looked meaner than most. Some of the inhabitants, too. A number of them wore clogs without socks to school, whatever the weather, and others sported haircuts which hadn't been popular since about 1914 - a tuft of hair at the forehead and everywhere else 'shaved to the wood.' I walked down a neighbouring street once and noticed a boy of about six hanging from the roof guttering by his fingertips. He had apparently climbed up the drainpipe for some reason or other.

I succeeded at the 11-plus and when the notification arrived I rode to Middlewich Street on the bike which Dad had largely built from scrap a year or two earlier. Disappointingly, David had not passed and we would not therefore renew friendship in the classroom. Although Crewe had a grammar school, Arthur had gone to the one serving Nantwich and Acton. Nantwich was a town of some history, as indeed was the school, and it was picturesquely set on the River Weaver.

Arthur had been at the school for three years by the time of my arrival in the autumn of 1952 and he belonged to the house of Hodgkin, the others being Thrush and Wilbraham. As a sibling, I should have followed him into the same house, but through some oversight I was installed in Wilbraham. Although this counted for very little, it may have been an early signal that my brief time at the school would not be marked by academic achievement. I made a poor start in the third form at Nantwich and by the close of the first term I had failed to do well in anything, including sports. I was perplexed by French and Algebra as new studies, and I fared equally badly in more familiar disciplines. At the end of the first year I scored 6% in French and 12% in maths, and although I made strenuous efforts in the school holidays to reverse this trend I remained at the bottom of the class, shaken by this failure.

Greater alarms at home centred upon Jack, who contracted what we believed to be encephalitis that paralysed him for a time and nearly killed him. He escaped with a very slight disability but the illness seemed to have taken the joy out of him. Life could be very worrying at times.

If I was learning little at school, I was persuaded by a friend to learn something about sex, purchasing tickets for a matinee performance at the Crewe Theatre. Top of the bill were Jimmy Jewel and Ben Warriss, heroes of the *Radio Fun* comics and a comic double act that had started in the Thirties but was now fading. What the show also offered, though, was a nude show that provided a frozen tableau at the very end of the performance. The performers for this had to remain absolutely still on the stage in order to meet very stringent criteria established by the Lord Chamberlain, and it was no feast for prurient eyes. In truth, there was very little to see and our sexual education did not advance at all. Meanwhile, the theatre and cinema audiences continued to desert in droves to the new entertainment medium of television, and my precocious friend and I had possibly been witnessing the death throes of variety acts on the live stage.

Crewe had six cinemas that in their heyday played to packed houses and even sold tickets for standing room at the back. In the Sixties they died and were variously turned into supermarkets, tyre sale outlets or bingo halls. Only the Odeon, whose art deco facade looked out upon Crewe Square, survived into the Eighties. It eventually was replaced by a beefburger vendor.

I had been from an early age a voracious reader, beginning no doubt with the *Dandy* and the *Beano* and progressing to the mature heroes of the *Hotspur* and *Wizard*. To a pantheon occupied by the creations of Richmal Crompton and Captain WE Johns, was added Rockfist Rogan, scourge of Jap airmen whenever he was not otherwise engaged in knocking seven bells out of putative contenders for his heavyweight title. A busy man, Rockfist. Such stories and similar were doubtless jingoistic tosh, but they at least drew me from pure comics to the printed word and helped to establish a lifetime reading habit. Better stories, and fact, would follow.

More precociously, I read *'The Ragged Trousered Philanthropists'* by Robert Tressell, which Dad believed was too deep for me, and it may well have been, but I was much absorbed by it. I also found interest in the newspapers and these included the *Daily Worker*, since Dad was a member of the Communist Party. I particularly remember a campaign mounted by the paper to win a reprieve for Ethel and Julius Rosenberg, an American couple sentenced to death for Soviet espionage. How much support the campaign gathered I do not know, but the Rosenbergs went to the electric chair in 1953.

Interestingly, I have no recollection at all of a petition at almost exactly the same time to reprieve Derek Bentley, sentenced to death as an accomplice to murder. Bentley, a nineteen-year-old epileptic with a mental age of seven, had taken part in a warehouse break-in with an accomplice, Craig, who was only sixteen. Bentley, unarmed throughout, was already in police custody when Craig shot and killed PC Miles. After the briefest of trials and the swift dismissal of appeal, Bentley was hanged. Craig served a ten-year sentence.

The pages of the *Daily Worker* also introduced me to atrocity, when they pictured a row of North Korean heads severed and lined up along a bank, with a row of severed hands propped against them in mocking salute. Nor was it merely the *Daily Worker* that tried to highlight atrocity occurring in the Korean War. A respected journalist, James Cameron, and his photographer, Bert Hardy, sent ample evidence of atrocity and execution visited upon captured North Korean troops by their southern brothers, but the proprietor of *Picture Post* suppressed the publication of it.

In later years, I wondered why my father, patently a good and a hardworking man, had believed in a system of government which was clearly underlined by massive suffering and cruel death, under such brutal dictators as Josef Stalin, Mao Tse Tung, Kim Ill Sung, Enver Hoxha, Nicolae Ceausescu and a dozen, blood-drenched others. We did not discuss his beliefs, and I regret that, but I now know that the ogres were not confined to the politics of the Left. Central and South American dictatorships were equally bloody, but the Somozas, the Stroessners, the Trujillos, the Duvaliers, the Pinochets, the Batistas and a score of that ilk were considered to be safely right-wing and heaped with millions of dollars in foreign aid.

I believe now that my father had some faith that Communism might be a key to the future, if only it could be practised without interference (cf Cuba and nearly forty years of American embargo) by men of principle. He perhaps saw it as the solution to our continuing experience of 'have' and 'have not' which was anathema to him. Whatever his beliefs, I admired his courage, which was as physical as it was moral, for he did not conceal his beliefs even at a time when much distrust settled upon those even slightly left of centre. (His physical courage may be gauged from an accident in which a circular saw severed his thumb at the joint. He wrapped the stump and went home to his dinner, keeping the injury concealed before walking to the surgery to have it stitched)

4

Dad's fortunes changed somewhat when the only son of his original employer succeeded to the business without taking much interest in it. He soon relinquished it entirely in order to better devote his time to spending his inheritance, and the business passed to Dad and his partner, Duncan. A telephone was added to the house in Adelaide Street but business was not good. In addition, both Dad and Duncan suffered some health problems that affected their work. Dad was prone to blackouts of which there was very little warning, and this was not a handy ailment to suffer in the building trade.

Occasionally I would accompany him about building jobs during school holidays and some of the houses we visited provided an education of sorts. At one in the west end, the walls were entirely decorated with Xmas wrapping paper, and in another, in an upstairs room, we encountered a tin bath half-filled with urine. Dad once remarked that he could fill a book with such gems and I have often wished that he had done so. Empty houses sometimes turned up a treasure or two and we had half a dozen musical instruments about the house that came from such sources. A violin, a guitar, a zither and a banjo among them, but neither Arthur nor I ever mastered them. Dad's blackouts did not improve and he eventually abandoned the partnership, taking work in Royce's. Things seemed to get tight for a time, with the television in the front room being replaced by lodgers, Derek and Doreen.

For school I had to be outfitted with a uniform, and for one year at least I had to wear for gym classes a pair of girl's shoes handed on from somewhere. These drew some stares but no obvious remarks, and it was an experience I would have preferred to miss. School was by now sufficiently distressing as it was. Unable to leave my academic failure at the school gates, I became, at home, a sulking, fretful, tearful and difficult child for a time. I consider it likely that later problems of self-confidence began as a result of three years of classroom failure, after a single year of success.

Girl's shoes or not, I failed to star at games or sports, and my appreciation of cricket was little improved when I was knocked out by a ball at nets' practise one day. On some other occasion I took a chunk out of a finger with a chisel at woodwork, and nor was I even safe at dinner, where I got a plum stone lodged in my throat. I was rushed to the cottage hospital and whilst I awaited attention the stone appeared quite spontaneously, earning me further reproof.

At school I was happiest when I did the X-country runs which took us around local fields and home along the banks of the Shropshire Union Canal which still had the odd working 'butty' plying the opaque water. I was not particularly swift, but a steady runner and running would become a later and an enduring interest.

Dad referred to the canal as 'The Cut', a term handed on, I imagine, from the very early days of canal construction. He had often taken Arthur and me fishing along local reaches of the water and in the summer months we would take trunks for a dip. I could not swim and had little confidence in water I could not see the bottom of, but Dad, with typical ingenuity, fashioned a life jacket from an inflated inner tube which he twisted around my narrow chest.

Canal fishing was also experienced with my cousin Trevor, actually the son of Mam's cousin, during visits to Hargrave, from where Gran'Ma Lindop had originated. Brief holidays with Aunt Gertie and Uncle Arch were a great novelty, as their cottage featured an earth lavatory and a water pump in the yard. Fishing with Trevor, I learned how to immobilise eels with newspaper. Visits to Hargrave were especially welcome when I was doing so badly at school, which was virtually all of 1954.

Following the death of her daughter, Aunt Phyl and her family moved into Adelaide Street and Gran'Ma Foxley left her comfortable house at Gresty, just outside the town, to move into a house in Beech Street, also in proximity to ours. Aunt Phyl was dad's twin but there was little physical resemblance between them. Nor had Aunt Phyl any of Dad's easy good humour and she was also less than robust, having suffered from asthma and bronchitis for a number of years. The illness frequently confined her to bed and she had long nurtured a dream of migrating to Canada where her husband, Jim, had relatives. Gradually, this dream translated into plans for migration to Australia instead, and the plans moreover began to include me.

My failures at school had by now turned me into a chronic worrier. School was an ordeal that I could only escape if I was ill and

I therefore began to invent illnesses. Headaches or biliousness was the usual, if limited and unimaginative, resort until Aunt Phyl at some time suggested that I was suffering from asthma. I was happy to accept this diagnosis and had no difficulty in believing that I was indeed short of breath on occasion, although the family doctor seemed less than convinced. I was, however, short and light for my age and the idea of the sick child gradually took root. When Aunt Phyl applied to emigrate, my name was added to the list and I think it is very likely that Dad saw this as the first step to emigration for the rest of the family.

The Fifties were the peak years of emigration, as thousands sought to escape austerity and make a prosperous new life in Canada or Australia, where the economy might be developing a better pace. The assisted passage scheme meant that adults paid just £10, with the Australian government defraying the balance. This was the 'Ten Pound Tourists' scheme under which we proposed to travel, except that the wheels of selection now proved a little slow, whilst a downturn in Aunt Phyl's health sounded new alarms.

This matter was resolved by Gran'Ma Foxley, who had decided also to join the emigration. She was a woman of some means, having inherited the shop in Alexandra Street that her father had opened and her mother ran for a good number of years. Although Great Gran'Ma Emerton had been known to be illiterate, she obviously had business acumen which gave her prosperity. Having run the shop in her turn, Gran'Ma Foxley invested in bricks and mortar, owning several houses in the town at some time.

The full adult fare to Australia amounted to £120 and Gran'Ma paid for four of them in addition to two child fares. By March 1955 my misery at Nantwich and Acton Grammar had ended and I had exchanged school uniform for a smart jacket and long trousers. We were about to sail from Tilbury Dock on the P & O liner Orcades.

5

I like to think that a steam locomotive bore us overnight from Crewe to Euston for the boat train, but it may have been a diesel engine. Steam had largely begun to pass with Mel Foxley and the nationalisation of the railways in 1948, although it would take two decades to replace all the steam locos on British lines and the last of the type would not be out-shopped until 1958.

At Tilbury I was seasick even before Orcades had slipped her moorings, and I continued to be so for several days afterwards. Uncle Jim and my cousin Malvern, who was of the same age as Arthur, were disparaging of my condition, but I had the satisfaction of seeing them succumb to it long after I had recovered - although their illness may have been related to an excess of alcohol which was cheap aboard. The three of us shared a cabin with a fourth man I have no memory of, whilst Gran'Ma, Aunt Phyl and my cousin Phyllis shared another cabin.

We were almost a month on the water and the daily routine was fairly agreeable. Orcades displaced 28,000 tons, could make twenty-two knots and she was doubtless making a lot of money, along with her sister ships of the line, from emigration. We sailed through the Suez Canal just a year before Anthony Eden tried to flex atrophied imperial muscles against Colonel Nasser, and prior to the Canal we had made stops at Gibraltar and Naples. Other stops were at Port Said, Aden and Colombo.

At such stops I acquired some useful experience of human nature. When the 'bum boats' at Port Said and Aden plied the passengers with novelty cigarette lighters, flick knives and a hundred sorts of bric-a-brac, some of the passengers would haul up the ordered goods then vanish from the ship's rail without paying for them. Stealing, apparently, was not theft if you merely stole from an Arab. There was also the matter of the baths on board that could not be used because someone had defecated in them. Clearly, any scheme that offered global travel for just ten quid did not always attract 5-star passengers.

Children seemed to me to be tolerated rather than welcomed aboard and there were endless attempts to corral us into exhausting games of table tennis, which I had neither patience nor talent for. I preferred to wander into as many parts of the ship as possible to observe its working and was eventually left alone to do just that. In the warmer waters, the adult passengers seemed intent on burning themselves to a crisp on the open deck, or working their way through as much of the unrestricted and duty-free alcohol and cigarettes[1] as possible. One adult, however, stood apart from all of this and he usually attracted a small gang of boys. Ralph had war service in the Royal Navy, possessed a very powerful pair of binoculars and had the answers to recondite naval questions about Plimsoll Lines, pennants on the mast or the distance to the horizon. Ralph was also apparently a homosexual.

Learning that I was unable to swim, Ralph offered to teach me and he suggested that I call at his cabin before breakfast when the swimming pool would be uncluttered. Before I could take up this offer I was intercepted on my way to the dining room by another adult and advised to stay away from Ralph who 'was not a nice man.' Uncomprehending, I informed Gran'Ma and she made me sit with her on the boat deck until Ralph next approached. Gran'Ma then rose and stood directly in his path, without saying a word. Ralph faltered a greeting then turned and walked away. He did not approach me again. In a photograph of Gran'Ma taken at the turn of the century, she displays a strong, intelligent face and she clearly had considerable presence. She had it still at the age of seventy-five.

Shipboard entertainments were mostly aimed at the adults, but at Port Said an Egyptian conjuror came aboard and he dextrously produced day-old chicks from unlikely places. It is likely that he just as dextrously wrung their necks after the performance, too. Fancy dress competitions were organised for children but I avoided those and also a 'crossing the line' ceremony when we passed the Equator.

---

[1] Twenty cigarettes costing 4/5d in the UK at this time yielded 3/6d in duty to the Exchequer, whilst a 1/8d pint offered 10d. to the Chancellor.

Even the Ancient Mariner was not cursed with that.

As the nights grew hotter I took to sleeping on a rope locker on deck in order to avoid the stuffy cabin which was buried somewhere in the depths of the ship. I continued my roaming wherever I would not be challenged and I kept a diary, which has not survived. It would be another seven years before I acquired the regular habit of a journal.

Our final port of call was at Colombo, now Sri Lanka and then a fragment of Empire that had served as a coaling station for the Far Eastern Fleet. We had ample time to stroll about and absorb the poverty and the smell, also taking in the few tourist attractions. Among these was a giant statue of Bhudda that was wholly covered with pieces of glass, although Uncle Jim was adamant that these in fact were diamonds. I did not know it at that time, but Uncle Jim actually was not at all worldly.

I had risen sufficiently early to catch the first glimpse of Australia, and I mostly stayed at the ship's rail as the port of Fremantle became focused, and a tug guided us through the Gage Roads to F Shed, the front wall of which bore the greeting: Welcome to Australia. We had arrived in the new land.

*Service Beginning
1955-1969*

The chief attraction of military service has consisted and will consist in this compulsory and irreproachable idleness.

*War & Peace
Leo Tolstoy
1828-1910*

1

We were met at Fremantle by Reg Astbury, a former Crewe man who had emigrated immediately after the war and was now a resident in the Goldfields town of Boulder, to which we were bound. Reg had trained as a fireman at much the same time as Dad but had survived the Depression layoffs to become a locomotive driver. Asthma had led to his emigration, also, but he had remained in touch with Crewe relations that led to contacts with Aunt Phyl.

We had arrived on Thursday 21 April and the seasons were reversed. Instead of spring we faced the Australian autumn, but the shade temperature that day rose to seventy-one degrees Fahrenheit and that seemed a pretty good exchange. Jackets and long trousers certainly seemed superfluous as we made sweating progress through the Customs and Immigration controls in F Shed.[1]

Boulder lay at the end of a railway line that ran three hundred and eighty-five miles north east of Perth; the overnight train departing at 5pm. It was a fourteen-hour journey, which yielded an average speed of about twenty-two miles per hour and the swaying of the 'Rattler' carriages was only briefly arrested by the numerous stops at towns *en route*. Most travellers opted for the sleeper carriages but we occupied seats instead, emerging bleary-eyed at the Kalgoorlie station at 7am on the following morning.

By then there had been the opportunity to gaze through the windows for a couple of hours and survey the passing landscape. This was mostly an unrelieved scene of Eucalyptus trees - the native Gum

---

[1] F Shed had ceased to throng with immigrants by the close of the decade; now it is packed from time to time with visitors to the maritime museum it houses.

- as far as the eye could see, and odd, remote, properties studded against the red soil that deepened its hue as we approached the town. In the station forecourt a stone statue depicted a Digger to commemorate the dead of WW I and WW II, and it would shortly be festooned with wreathes to mark ANZAC Day on the 25 April. I suppose that my later army service fixed the occasion and the date firmly in my mind, for I have never since forgotten what the 25 April represents, although I do not always recall that the 23 April is St. George's Day.

ANZAC Day itself commemorated the day in 1915 when Australian and New Zealand troops were landed at Gallipoli against huge odds and entrenched Turks. The slaughter matched that of the Western Front and the landing utterly failed. Australian casualties during the eight-month campaign were not even eclipsed by the carnage on the Somme a year later. Its architect had been Winston Churchill, who bore most of the blame and lost his portfolio, but it was the vacillation of the Royal Navy that laid the foundations of the catastrophe.

The ANZAC parade was held three days later in Kalgoorlie and it was led by a holder of the Victoria Cross, won in the Second World War. Ironically, the VC holder was killed in a motor accident just a few months later.

Our acquaintance with Kalgoorlie was brief, however, since we had been booked into a Boulder hotel at the junction of the town's principal streets. We spent just one night there, having used the day of arrival to select a rented house which lay about five minutes' stroll from the town centre. Five minutes' further stroll in that direction, I discovered, put one onto the very edge of the town and a fringe of Gum trees. Boulder, we learned, was not merely small but actually shrinking, and along a street just one down from the principal thoroughfare, Burt Street, were several abandoned shops. The towns of Kalgoorlie and Boulder (which at one time had styled itself as 'Boulder City'), had grown out of the gold discoveries made in the late-nineteenth century and had prospered for decades, but the Gold Standard, which fixed the price of gold at £17 per ounce, had not been raised since 1935 and mining was becoming increasingly uneconomical.

Gold was first discovered at Coolgardie, which lay twenty-five miles to the southwest along the road and rail link to Perth. Although the Coolgardie gold was mined to early extinction, a modern town that featured some handsome buildings in stone was established and it remained. It was largely a 'ghost town' by the mid-fifties until a burgeoning interest in the mining past helped to make the town into a living museum.

Ranging beyond Coolgardie in 1892 was an Irish immigrant named Patrick Hannan, and at the site of the present Kalgoorlie he went looking for a lost horse and found a gold nugget instead. The first Goldfields shaft was sunk quite close to where Paddy made his find - the exact site of which is today marked by a tree - and it was named Mount Charlotte after the hill just to the rear of the shaft. The Mount Charlotte shaft pulls gold to this day, being the sole survivor of hundreds of shafts, successful and otherwise, in a century of mining in the town. Since 1893, thirty-five million ounces of gold have been produced by this one shaft.

Today, many of the old shafts have been subsumed by the 'Super Pit'; a switch of some years ago to open cast mining. The pit is expected to produce eight million ounces of gold in a period of twenty years.

In 1955, however, the super pit was doubtless beyond the wildest imaginings of even the most optimistic of townsfolk. The prevailing opinion held that the mines were finished and that Perth or the coastal towns held the keys to future employment. This was not of great concern to me, although I was keen to get a job. I was approaching fourteen, which was the legal age for school leaving in Australia, and I had no wish to return to school. In this I was supported by Aunt Phyl, who perhaps welcomed the idea of another wage, however small, coming into the house, although I remember that Gran'Ma had expressed an opinion about renewed schooling. She believed that I had been 'clever' enough to attend a grammar school and should therefore continue to seek academic qualifications that would secure for me a 'good' job.

In the meantime, I had the opportunity to examine our new environment, and there was much that was interesting. Few buildings in either town were actually built of brick; these generally being the municipal buildings of courthouse, post office (actually termed 'Telegraph Office') and railway station, in addition to the commercial premises such as banks, large shops and hotels. The latter seemed to me to be particularly elegant, with elaborate filigree of wrought iron adorning their upper balconies and bull-nose corrugated iron verandahs to span the pavement width below, offering screens from the blazing heat of the summer sun. As I write, I can glance at four plates on the wall that depict hotels in Queensland. They could as easily represent four of the hotels I noted four decades ago, and which were built four decades before that time.

Little elegance attached to many of the houses, which were wooden-framed and lined internally with asbestos sheets, clad externally with sheets of corrugated iron. The roofs also were ironclad and frequently painted red, although some were silvered to reflect the heat. The houses were basic and had few refinements. The lavatory stood in the yard, which was no great surprise, but these lavatories stood in splendid isolation, being connected neither to water supply nor sewer. The boxed lavatory seat was arranged over an iron bucket of about ten gallons capacity, and it stood before a hinged access that was visited once per week. The exchange of filled buckets for empty ones was effected by the 'Shitties', whose 'twenty-eight door saloon' made a lumbering and malodorous progress along the lanes that divided the rows of houses. This system of sanitation seemed to me a touch archaic, although Dad mentioned some years later that there were plenty of them still in use in Crewe until just before the war.

If our eliminations were removed at the rear of the house, then at least our daily bread arrived at the front door, and it was delivered by a bread carter driving a pony and cart. We seemed to have arrived in the nineteenth century. Bread carting - by horse and cart anyway - was soon to become an extinct trade. Perhaps it was an early example of health and safety at work, where someone decided that the propinquity of fresh bread and fresh dung was not especially salubrious.

In retrospect, the pony and trap appear to be a perfect metaphor for the pace of the town, notwithstanding the obvious industry of the mines which operated at full blast. Boulder, particularly, had the quality of timelessness, and I was fascinated by its empty shops and utilities that had simply ceased to function. At the top of Burt Street, along the road that led to the mines, stood a railway station which once had carried miners on a daily basis and which now was redundant. Its modest but enduring brick buildings stood ready for use, as did a steam locomotive which had been shunted into a siding to gather rust in silent retirement. On the street side of the station was the Town Park, whose grass struggled against the heat, and whose bandstand had probably seen its last performance pre-war. That war was remembered in the park with two artillery field pieces, although in later years they were removed to a Burt Street museum.

The town was less frozen in time than melting away though, and it would take the visits of more than thirty years later to bring that message home to me. The railway station became a museum and the fire station became a Chinese restaurant. Billiard halls became boutiques and town halls became empty. Hotels became hostels then became empty and derelict. Some were destroyed, leaving a pitiful remnant, and others vanished without trace. Four hotels had stood side by side and back to back at the Boulder Block for many years, but the super pit replaced all of them with a yawning hole five kilometres long, two kilometres wide and half a kilometre deep (Australia by then having adopted metrication). Shops became other kinds of shops or remained empty. The Masonic Hall - another fine, brick building - preserved its secrecy and no one but Masons knew if the membership waxed or waned. The auctioneer's became an estate agent and the cobbler's became a cafe. The cafe became a tourist information office, something that would have puzzled the residents in 1955. Among the many changes, two services remained wholly unchanged. The Kalgoorlie brothels continued to sell sex and the 'Hotspot' hamburger bar continued to sell hamburgers. Perhaps this says something about the more enduring nature of some human appetites.

2

Our stay in the rented house was brief, lasting just long enough for Gran'Ma and Aunt Phyl to agree upon the purchase of a house. Gran'Ma's agreement was essential to this process since she was providing the money for it. (I think that the house cost £800.) The chosen house stood at the far end of Burt Street, almost a mile from the town centre, and the area, known as Victory Heights, had once formed a suburb of the town. By now, the houses were diminishing, few buses served the area and only one shop remained open. It, too, closed a year or so later. Opposite the house, which was built in 1928, stood the grandstand of the former Boulder Racecourse. Long redundant, the grounds were now occupied by a golf club, although the 'greens' were the by now familiar red soil which characterised the area. Even the golf club was on borrowed time, but happily, rather than being another example of degeneration, it became the site of a brand new housing estate, subsequent to the renewed prosperity of the Goldfields in the late Sixties.

265 Burt Street featured four usefully sized rooms with verandhs on three sides of the house to offer additional living or sleeping space. My cousin Malvern and I initially shared a bed in a small room on the front verandah, until Uncle Jim boxed in another area of it to create a bedspace for me. The yard space to the front, sides and rear magnified the area of the house four or five times, and a couple of large Gum trees stood close. These were invariably filled with screeching Galahs - a distinctive native Australian species of parrot - in the early morning and the late afternoon. The yard was unremarked by much else, save for a water tank of about five hundred gallons capacity. Most houses had them, for garden watering purposes if not for the occasional filling of kettles, and they clearly recalled a day when water was scarce and all rainwater was carefully husbanded.[1] By

---

[1] At the turn of the century a pipeline had been laid from the Mundaring Weir, north of Perth, to ensure a regular supply of water to the

this time, Uncle Jim, Malvern and myself were employed. Uncle Jim was a Fitter and he had found no difficulty in being taken on in the Fitting Shop at the Great Boulder Gold Mine. He would be known as 'Pommy Jim' for all of his working life and I believe that it grew from his penchant for disparaging most things Australian - a trait shared by Aunt Phyl, who seemed to be not wholly thrilled by the new life she had dreamed of for so long.

The average Australian wage for a Fitter in 1955 was £16.1s.6d[2] for a flat week of forty hours, although I did not know then what wage was in the packet Uncle Jim turned up, unopened, to Aunt Phyl. The wages earned by Malvern and me were turned over in exactly the same way, in return for an allowance and a sum set aside in savings. We had been offered employment by a concrete worker from Merredin, a farming town about halfway between Kalgoorlie and Perth, who held a contract from the Kalgoorlie council to provide several hundred septic tanks. The council decided to address the sanitation problems posed by the 'bucket brigade' with an offer of septic systems to householders in the towns. The cost of the septic system was £100; a considerable sum at that time and leading the council to offer installation against a loan whose repayment was spread over ten years at a fairly modest 3% interest rate as an incentive to potential buyers.

I joined a gang of three or four youths of about Malvern's age, and each day we mixed and cast sufficient concrete to make five septic tanks. The workplace was in a Lamington yard that once had a house in it and, in time, would have another in it. I think that Malvern earned nine pounds per week and I earned seven, which seemed to be a good sum. I confirmed this later with a piece of research that revealed that the accepted wage for someone of my age was more commonly four pounds and ten shillings, with trade apprentices earning much less. I did not retain much of that, however, since Aunt Phyl remitted five shillings per week to me and put a pound into savings, leaving me with a few coins in my pocket that seldom lasted the weekend. 5/- doubtless bought rather more in 1955 than 25 pence or fifty cents might today, but it actually bought very little, and I acquired the early

---

Goldfields.

2 A penny represented 1/240th of a pound.

habit of thrift that would prove useful later in life.

What a pound, or several of them, might have bought was revealed to me much later in a perusal of newspaper files at the Library of West Australia, during a visit in 1995. A four-bedroomed house at Cottesloe, a popular Perth suburb, was available for three thousand pounds, whilst one thousand would pay for an example of 'Australia's Own Car', the Holden. Those without that sort of cash might settle for a 1934 V8 Ford, with radio, at 275 pounds, whilst the more musically-minded might opt for a 2-button accordion at two pounds, ten shillings, or a mouth organ at 4/6d. For those reluctant to entertain themselves, tickets to the Capitol Theatre in Perth for the Terrence Rattigan play *The Sleeping Prince*, at one pound or 7/6d. Sybil Thorndike and Ralph Richardson, pre-damehood and pre-knighthood were starring in a production thought likely to have a good run.

The *West Australian* in the month of our arrival was devoting many column inches to allegations that the Labor Party Opposition Leader, Dr Evatt, was being funded by the Communist Party (later revealed as a clumsy smear job), and to reports that the English Prime Minister, Winston Churchill, was seriously ill and would stand down from office. (Churchill was in fact seriously senile in his last years in office, and he would be replaced soon by Anthony Eden)

The *West Australian* also reported that the government contemplated sending conscripts to join the fighting in Malaya (reporting also that 49 Communist Terrorists had been killed there during March), but did not do so. (Although the same government would, contentiously, send conscripts to the war in South Viet Nam a decade later). 216 *Mau Mau* Terrorists died in Kenya in the same month, but that had rather less prominence in the news than the report of a truck driver 'who smelled strongly of drink' knocking down a one-legged man at the city junction of Stirling Street and James Street, causing the man's remaining leg to be amputated. The truck driver was fined £10.

The Goldfields had its own news organ, the *Kalgoorlie Miner*, and the big news the day we arrived was the announcement that the Kalgoorlie-Boulder bus would henceforth turn at the Piesse Street junction, rather than in Burt Street. Some bean counter at the Eastern Goldfields Transport Board had already calculated that this would cost an extra £200 per year in fuel costs. Also in the pages of the *Miner*, Mandrake the Magician was in deep trouble, Lana Turner was advertising Lux soap, a 2lb loaf cost 1/3d, winceyette pajamas were being offered at 27/6d a pair and the ten top selling gramophone records included several by Glenn Miller, one by Bill Haley and the Comets but none by Elvis Presley (Elvis would make up for this omission shortly).

**The steely-eyed concrete worker
Boulder 1955**

3

Although by the time we began work the season was edging into winter, the days were beautifully warm and I really thought that working outdoors was the life. After five days, however, I got the sack. The Contractor, Ted Pellew, was a kindly man and he explained that he believed the work too strenuous for me, although I had thought that I was swinging a number four shovel with the best of them. That appeared to be that, and I began a fruitless round of seeking alternative work, until it was realised that lids and baffles for the tanks also had to be cast, and this was considered a suitable job for me. I resumed work and the job lasted for nine months, taking us into 1956 and close to my fifteenth birthday.

The winter start had served to acclimatise us to the Australian summer, which proved blistering. The Goldfields was invariably hotter than the coastal area, but it was usually a comfortably dry heat without the humidity of Perth. The temperature one particular day rose to a hundred and fourteen degrees in the shade, of which there was none in Pellew's yard. We were sent home early on that occasion. At Pellew's yard I grew as brown as a nut and I added some useful muscle, although I did not appear to be adding much height. I seemed destined to remain short, whereas Dad and Arch were both around six feet tall.

When my deferred savings out of wages totalled £17, I bought myself a bike from a fellow worker. The bike offered the considerable novelty of cable brakes, whereas most bikes observed around the town seemed to depend upon the sharp application of heel to tyre to arrest them. I now cycled the three miles between the towns and I moreover had the means with which to explore the local area, although it was well isolated from other areas of habitation. On a summer's day I cycled to Coolgardie, then somewhere between ghost town and museum status, but *en route* home I gratefully accepted the offer of a lift on a lorry. The tyres of the bike were black with melting tar. Gran'Ma had meanwhile extended her largesse to the purchase of a '48 Ford V8 which Uncle Jim now learned to drive. He succeeded only after several attempts at the test and he remained an execrable driver all his life.

I biked and walked about every square foot of the two towns - something which I would not do again for forty years - and I noted some of the recent changes. Trams had only recently been entirely replaced by petrol-engined buses (themselves long replaced by diesel-engined variants by the time of my later examination), and the tramlines still ran between the towns and the length of Hannan Street and Burt Street. Power poles studded the centre of the streets to power the trams and also carried the domestic lighting and streetlights. Several of the trams were acquired by properties around the town and pressed into service as chicken coops or the like. I noticed in 1995 that one such had been retrieved by the transport board with perhaps a view to restoration, but it looked to me to be a basket case.

Hannan Street commemorated Paddy himself (although the town itself had originally been called Hannans) and at the lower end of the commercial section, in front of the town hall, sat a bronze statue of the old miner, usefully dispensing water from a pipe concealed within his bronze water bag. Every New Year's Eve some wag would paint footprints from the statue to a nearby urinal, and legend had it that the footprints had once led to an address in Hay Street, where the town brothels were located.

Although prostitution was illegal in the State, the Kalgoorlie brothels had been uniquely tolerated since an era when it was believed that some form of sexual release for a predominantly male population was required to protect the town women. The brothels were controlled to a degree by discreet police supervision and by regular medical examination of the 'ladies'. Some thought this hypocritical, but it was a system that appeared to work.

If the brothels conveyed a wildwest image of the town, then there was little else to substantiate it. The hotels, although open all day, closed promptly at 11pm (with the notable exception of the Westralia which lay close to the Boulder mines and catered to the afternoon shift which came out of the shaft at 11pm), and on Sunday they hardly traded at all. The cinemas, three in Kalgoorlie and one in Boulder, were not then open on Sundays, and the dance halls at the Railway Institute, the Caledonian and others ejected their patrons at midnight. An attempt to turn a redundant pub, the Duke of Cornwall in Hannan Street, into a nightclub failed in a matter of weeks. Even the streetlights were turned off after midnight.

There were some scandals though. An entire family in Boulder was charged with incest and the details were thought to be so shocking that the case was heard *in camera*, much to everyone's disappointment. Suicides were fairly common and the preferred method was by using *Fracteur*, the sticks of Nobel explosive which the miners used, and which, it seemed, were easily smuggled out. A miner in Burt Street chose the method, having first doused the house in petrol and ignited it to deny it to his wandering wife, but the blast of the explosion blew the flames out. Some you win, some you don't. I cycled to work one morning and noticed a line of policemen armed with sacks and litter sticks, prodding away at a piece of waste ground. They were collecting the pieces of a chap who had wasted himself.

Such occurrences, one felt, made the policeman's lot not a happy one since they literally had to pick up the pieces, but a worse case was a man who got an underage girl pregnant and drove out into the bush to end his problems with a hose pipe and carbon monoxide. It was the height of summer and a few days elapsed before the vehicle was sighted, by which time the corpse was pretty ripe. The policeman who had the job of transferring it to a metal container subsequently walked into a town pub for a drink and the bar cleared in seconds.

Pregnancies occurring outside marriage were minor scandals that were mostly dealt with by the girls 'going below' (to Perth) for the term of the pregnancy, the birth and the adoption of the child. The contraceptive pill had not yet arrived, nor a more willing acceptance of illegitimate births, and this unwillingness contrasted with the fact of the brothels. It was an aspect of hypocrisy that by no means was confined to Australians, although it is certain that conservatism was a much stronger facet of Australian life than might generally have been acknowledged. It certainly stands in stark contrast to Australian mores of today.

Unwanted pregnancies revealed a seamier side of town life when the proprietress of a Kalgoorlie hamburger bar, a popular call after pub or pictures, was sent down for six months for procuring abortions. The demise of the burger bar was much lamented.

I made no friends in my first year since my workmates were practically adult and everyone of my age appeared to be still at school, and sensibly so. This did not seem to me to be a particular disadvantage at the time, but it meant also that I had no opportunities for developing relationships with girls, and this would be a later difficulty when I felt paralysed by shyness in mixed company. The situation also bore the early seeds of a partial dependence upon alcohol, later, in order to feel at ease with women.

    I had settled to life with the Parker family and it offered no traumas. It was not an especially cheerful family, I learned, and one which placed great faith in laxatives - a routine which I was not keen to embrace. Aunt Phyl's asthma was not much arrested by the benevolent climate and she still took to her bed for days at a time, although occasionally we would all go to the pictures on a Friday or a Saturday evening, and sometimes both. Because there were no female relationships in my life at this time, I now wonder why my preparations for an evening at the Palace theatre included smearing Californian Poppy on my short back and sides. This unguent was a thinly greasy, yellow liquid purchased for 1/3d a bottle at Coles' Store, which was the Australian version of Woolworth's. I would grow out of Californian Poppy, if only to acquire, just as uselessly, the Old Spice and the Brut habit for a time.

    The cinema, the Palace, reversed the Kino tradition by putting the expensive seats at the front of the house and the cheap seats at the back. We invariably sat at the back, anyway, since the best seats, called 'decks', were exactly like rows of deckchairs down to the striped fabric, and Aunt Phyl considered these to be very bad for one's back. The films were screened indoors in winter and outside during the summer and there were usually two features, unless a particularly long film was offered. Long films were just coming into vogue and *The Ten Commandments* was one of them. Otherwise it might be Doris Day or Mario Lanza warbling along to a barely-existent story-line, but it passed a couple of hours when alternatives were few.

    A wireless had been among the secondhand purchases at Billy Smythe's auction rooms and we discovered commercial radio. Broadcasts were received from 6KG, which was the locally broadcasting station, in addition to 6GF that provided the commercial-free station of the Australian Broadcasting Company. I soon learned that neither had anything to compete with the Goon Show broadcasts to which I had run each Friday lunchtime from the Adelaide Street school. Australian humour appeared to be something else, and I never discovered anything even remotely funny in the routines of either Jack Davey or Bob Dyer, who reputedly were the country's top comedians. Some of the commercial radio shows were so bad that they were almost good. I shall not easily forget 'The Taubman's Paint Show', in which the presenter, Mr Dunn, attempted to cheer up contestants whose lives had been blighted in some way or other. Prior to walking away with some prize, plus a big tin of Taubman's paint, an account of misfortune seemed mandatory and competitors frequently broke into great, wracking sobs as they described their truly rotten lives. It was, as someone once observed of the story of Little Nell, impossible not to be moved to shrieks of laughter. The Barry Humphries' personas of Edna Everage and Les Patterson were somewhere in the future and in the meantime the nightly dialogue of Dad & Dave was about as funny as it got - which meant not very.

Towards the end of the Pellew contract Gran'Ma announced the purchase of another house, three doors along at 271, where she and I would now live. This was a surprise to me, but it became apparent that my own family was preparing to emigrate and it was intended to occupy a house for their arrival. 271 was a smaller dwelling, with just four, small rooms and an open verandah, but adequate. I now turned my wages up to Gran'Ma, but the job ended in February 1956 and I was out of work. Malvern, who had trained as a Fireman at Crewe, left the town to work on the state railway at Perth and I began a dispiriting round of job interviews. These seldom progressed much further than my lack of qualification for anything other than shovelling sand, cement and stone, and although I believed that I had done well at a post office entrance exam, I failed to get the job. Several weeks of unemployment followed and engendered in me such a feeling of uselessness – guilt, even – that the experience came immediately to mind forty years later, when I contemplated the possibility of long-term unemployment.

I found temporary work in the cordial factory that took on extra staff to meet the summer thirst, but lost it when I turned fifteen and was thus eligible for a small pay rise. I did not mourn this loss since the work was a brain-numbing routine of transferring crates of empty bottles from one conveyor belt to another. The work force looked like an advertisement for frontal lobotomies, and despite the heat we worked in we were only allowed to drink the cordials from bottles which came through the washer with blobs of dirt still in them.

The owner of the local shop to which I ran errands eventually pointed me out to a salesman from his wholesalers, and he came to the house to offer me a job as a junior storeman. The firm, George Wood

& Son, was the Kalgoorlie branch of a Perth firm and they took me on at £5.00 per week. My job, working under a senior storeman, was to fill out orders for tinned commodities of all kind, and to weigh out brown paper bags with tea, sugar, rice, raisins, flour etc. and box it for delivery. We supplied about a hundred shops, with even the largest of them not approaching supermarket status. If the corner shop was everywhere else a threatened species, then its future seemed secure on the Goldfields.

The job generated some friendships at last. Another junior storeman, Charlie Pridmore, was of my age and his younger brother, Stan, also later joined the firm. I discovered too that a rival grocery wholesaler in the town employed a lad who lived at 259 Burt Street. He was the son of Welsh immigrants and we struck up a friendship, cycling to work and home together. I now went with these friends to the cinema, rather than with family, although I could not yet accompany them to Patroni's billiard saloon in Kalgoorlie, where the minimum age for entry was sixteen. Both friends could pass for that age but I could not, although I tried it on a few times. Clarrie's billiard saloon, in Boulder, was much less scrutineering of age, but Clarrie's cues were like coathangers and the baize had more shine than the balls. Through Terry Ace, the lad in Burt Street, I met a much wider circle of lads my age and I found an easy acceptance among them. I was duly noted as a 'Pom' but no rancour attached to the term, although some offence was offered in another quarter at the time, leading to a fight that I lost.

To cycling about the town or in the bush was now added the excitement of cycling off the tops of the slime dumps which lay adjacent to the mines. These were great plateaus of solidified slime that was the residue of the crushed ore in the treatment plants. They rose to a height of sixty or seventy feet and had acutely angled sides, which provided either a thrilling ride or an abrading fall, depending upon nerve and talent.

Another voyage of discovery was a ten-shilling ride in an Avro Anson aeroplane from the aerodrome that lay about half a mile from the house. The Anson dated from 1936 and the thirty-minute flight offered an aerial view of slime dumps, poppet heads and vast acreage of bush. It led me to a fascination for aircraft that has not entirely faded.

Hannan Street Kalgoorlie
The last of the trams on a street laid out for bullock carts

Photo: Battye Library Ref 3545B/7

4

After a year or so in the job I appeared to have impressed the manager sufficiently to be offered a position in the office as a junior clerk, with the prospect of rising to a sales' position. Four girls worked in the office and since there was insufficient space among them, I was sandwiched instead into a room behind the office where the tobacco stocks were held. It was small, windowless and stifling in summer and I further discovered that my daily duty was an endless round of checking the figures on sales invoices. The sums had already been worked by the office girls, and would be checked again by the girls at the head office in Perth, and my role seemed therefore to be somewhat nugatory. Terry had enjoyed a similar promotion with his firm and we began to attend night school together, to learn book keeping and typing.

Gran'Ma was very pleased with this development, believing that I now had a job with 'prospects' and she forecast a bright future for me as some kind of sales executive. I found neither the 'office' nor the classroom congenial, however, and soon joined Terry in simply registering at the classes and slipping quietly off to the billiard saloon or the cinema. This deceit was uncovered when Aunt Phyl spotted me at the latter one evening, swiftly reporting the fact to Gran'Ma. At breakfast the next day I was chastened with a stern admonition about deceit and I cycled off to work feeling badly about it, but I did not resume the lessons. To complete my fall from grace, I also began to smoke, although I concealed the habit until I joined the army.

In the middle of August Dad, Arthur and Jack arrived at Fremantle on the Moreton Bay, a ship that was quickly turned around since she was headed for the breaker's yard next trip. She, and all aboard her, had been detained in the Suez Canal since the sailing had coincided with Colonel Nasser's grab of De Lesseps' engineering masterpiece, followed by Anthony Eden's bid to reclaim it.

Only Aunt Phyl had travelled down to meet them, and I saw them briefly at the house before setting off to work when they arrived from the Kalgoorlie station. Mam had not accompanied the move since she was by this time carrying my youngest brother and planning to arrive in the following year.

Dad had hoped to return to bricklaying, as had Arthur since he had followed that trade after leaving school, but it was a poor time for the construction trade and both sought local jobs in vain. At length, Dad accepted a job as a Fettler on the Trans-Australian railway line which connected Western and South Australia. The line spanned the vast emptiness of the Nullarbor Plain and Dad was stationed at a remote spot some hundreds of miles from the town. It was heavy, manual work, offering Spartan living conditions, and the work mostly attracted Italian migrants. Dad was then approaching fifty and I wonder now, at an age little greater, how I might view the prospect of having to swing a hammer or a pick under those conditions. Not joyously, I imagine. It is a measure of Dad's commitment to the new life in the new land that I wholly failed to appreciate at the time. To his few possessions he added an Italian-English dictionary and he got on with it. His home visits were few and brief. At one time he was returned to the town to have gallstones removed and I visited him at the St. John of God Hospital, which was a Catholic establishment staffed by nuns. I do not know if Dad advertised his Communism there.

Arch remained in the town for a few weeks, working at the Boulder electrical power station, but there seemed no chance of resuming his trade. He decided instead to enlist into the army and was soon inducted, serving after training in Queensland before being posted to Malaya for a period of three years. His move aroused my interest, since Boulder already seemed to me to be quite confining and I was alert to new possibilities

Jack was enrolled in the local school and he swiftly assimilated, making friends of his age in the neighbourhood, generally settling in and rapidly acquiring an Australian accent. Gran'Ma remained at the helm at 271 and would not return to 265 until Mam arrived from England a little over a year later. At work I became increasingly dissatisfied with the confining office - and careless with my sums - and I eventually asked the manager if I might return to the warehouse. He agreed but I was transferred to the smallgoods section, learning how to bone sides and shoulders of meat and to slice them into bacon. Several hours each week slicing and packing bacon gave me the world's softest pair of hands, which I did not appreciate at all. For the women out there who spend hundreds of pounds pursuing soft hands, I have the cheap and guaranteed solution: get a job slicing bacon.

Access to the billiard saloon, at sixteen, was something, but limited pocket money meant that the time spent in Patroni's or Clarrie's would never amount to a misspent youth. A game cost 2/- and any game taking longer than twenty minutes tended to draw frowns from the proprietor. I also had a smoking habit to support, although this was not the heavy habit it swiftly became when I joined the army. Friends and I would frequently bike out along the Coolgardie road in the evenings just for something to do and this at least was a healthy activity.

During the Easter that I was sixteen I decided to bike as far along the Perth road as I might, by way of escaping the fact of four days off work and having nothing very much to do with it. I wound up in the small, farming town of Southern Cross, about a hundred and thirty miles from Kalgoorlie, and on arrival I parked the bike to stroll the length of the street. At the end of it was a fat policeman leaning against the fence of the station and he beckoned me across.
"Where you from, Son?" He wanted to know.
"I've just ridden my bike from Boulder." I responded, and not without a measure of pride.
"Well, Son," He advised, "best you get on your bike and ride back. We don't want any hoodlums around Southern Cross."
This, I now recognise, was Australian conservatism at work.

Friendships with girls failed to materialise, partly because I had not the financial means of sustaining them, and this also contributed to my desire to tread new pastures. The town still appeared to be in terminal decline, although there were attempts to generate renewed interest in its future. A community fair was organised to prove that there was plenty of life in the area, and I attended the inaugural one. Several competitions were held, to include demonstrations of sheepshearing, whilst 'boggers' from the mines shovelled tons of gravel into trolleys, or loggers used a flashing axe to fell substantial logs in a few minutes. There were also demonstrations of boomerang and spear throwing by Aborigines from the Kurrawang

Mission, although the enthusiasm for such displays cooled slightly when an incautious spectator was speared through the chest - fortunately without fatal result.

The 'Coolgardie Picnic' was another annual attraction, when a substantial proportion of the town population boarded a train at Kalgoorlie some Sunday in November, travelled to Coolgardie, and got off the train to stroll about for a few hours before boarding the train for the home journey. This was less than thrilling.

In November 1957 Mam arrived with Malcolm from England. She had sailed on the Castel Felice of the Shaw Savill Line and had been ill for much of the journey. The day she arrived, the temperature rose to eighty-eight degrees Fahrenheit and she faced a journey of nine hours or so, by road to Boulder. Dad had borrowed the Ford from Gran'Ma and I accompanied him to Fremantle, travelling overnight and sleeping in the car when we had some hours to fill.

Years later, Mam described the journey as one she thought would never end, as we drove through the baking heat along the single ribbon of tarmac which was the Great Eastern Highway. She never confided her impressions of the house at 271, but it can only have been a shock after the comfort of the house in Adelaide Street. There, the house had gradually been modernised with a range of appliances and made cosy. Here, she had a wood-burning stove to cook on and a copper in the yard to wash clothes in. A straw broom was the chief weapon with which to attack the results of the frequent summer dust storms, which left a thick coating of red soil over the entire household. Now past forty and with a baby to look after, it cannot have been easy, and it was another degree of commitment that I utterly failed to appreciate. At a surprise party to mark her eightieth birthday, I was asked by my youngest brother, Malcolm, to say a few words. I was happy to do so and I tried to convey my late understanding and recognition of the sacrifices she had made in those years.

Dad by this time had succeeded in returning to his trade with a job at the power station and we were pretty much a family again, but in the New Year as I approached my seventeenth birthday I began to harbour ideas of enlistment. Dad opposed them but when Mam saw that I wished to join, she added her persuasion. There being no recruiting office in the town, I acquired enlistment forms from the employment office and sent them off. In due course I was instructed to present myself at Perth for examination and since this necessitated two days off work I requested it of the manager. He got very angry at this, claiming that I was taking time off to find another job, and that instead of two days I could have as many as I wanted, with no prospect of return. I left feeling that I had let him down, since I had admired his record of service flying bombers from England during the war.

I travelled on the sleeper from Kalgoorlie, reporting to Swan Barracks in the city and soon finding the process quite demoralising. Of more than a dozen candidates, only one - also from Kalgoorlie - was of my age and he was much bigger and heavier. The rest were adult and in their conversation they appeared worldly.

Stripped at the medical, I stood five feet and four inches and I weighed one hundred and twelve pounds. Two doctors examined me and one muttered something about flat feet whilst his colleague referred to 'congenital deformity'. They hardly spoke to me at all.

The written tests were for IQ, mechanical aptitude and academic levels and no scores were announced. I had no reason to feel confident about any of it and I took the Sleeper back to Kalgoorlie quite convinced that I had failed. I began to look for new employment and when my former boss heard about this he offered me my job back. Two days later I was notified that my application was successful and I was invited to enlist on 6 November 1958.

The coat I wore by this time had been given to me by Terry, and he had acquired it from an elder brother, who may have got it from his uncle. Whatever the truth of that, it had been intended for broader shoulders than mine, a fact I am reminded of whenever I look at the photograph which was to adorn the inside front cover of my Record of Service, AAB 83. For the photo I stood beside a graph which recorded my height - or the lack of it - and I displayed across my chest a number, in the manner of a convict. I was ordered to memorise the number, 5/410792, and I am now unlikely ever to forget it, although I would add two new ones in time. I was obedient to such commands for the closed society of Boulder had suddenly opened up to an entirely new world, and I wanted to succeed in it.

Two of us were attested in a short ceremony at which we swore a bible oath of allegiance to the Crown, and my companion was a much older recruit who in fact had served in the Australian Air Force towards the end of the war. The bible oath gave me no problems of conscience, although I had no belief in God, and it had seemed prudent in my enlistment application to describe myself as a

Christian. I had also carefully avoided referring to Dad's membership of the Communist Party in responding to a political question.

We were issued with a rail warrant which took us and our few possessions out to a personnel depot at Guildford, about thirty minutes' travel from the city, where we would receive initial kitting and form a draft to the recruit training camp in New South Wales. Other recruits were already at the camp and others followed us, including a couple, Tony Coles and Daryl Howden, with whom I struck up an immediate friendship.

The stay at Guildford was for almost a fortnight and we were required to carry out duties there. These were not onerous and might involve working in the kitchen or cleaning the camp surrounds. I was at some time put to work tending the wood-burning boiler that supplied hot water to the kitchen and I kept a good fire going. Unfortunately, no one told me that the boiler was *not* to be stoked after the evening meal, and I continued to heap the wood on. Later in the evening the pipes began to rattle and vibrate in an alarming manner and the keys to the kitchen had to be found, in order to drain the hot water pipes. Only steam issued from them for a while and the next day other duties, less incendiary, were found for me.

We were issued with a full set of uniform at the depot and also allowed to proceed into Perth wearing it, although we had little notion of what was correct and what was not. Daryl at least had completed a three-month camp as a national serviceman prior to his regular enlistment, and therefore had a fair idea of how we should dress.

The uniform wasn't quite enough to gain me admittance to a pub, where the drinking age was twenty-one, but I did gain admission with some older recruits to a sly grog known as Ma Black's in West Perth. Homemade wine was served there in cordial bottles and I unwisely accepted a challenge that I could not drink a full bottle of it. Whichever of us was the more stupid, the one who issued the challenge or the one who accepted it, is now moot, but I was unconscious for seventeen hours. It was an early lesson in the consequences of drinking to the point of stupidity, although I failed to extract much benefit from it.

When a sufficient number had assembled, we were entrained at Perth, in uniform, for the journey east that would span four days. We were in the charge of a Lance-Corporal recently returned from Malaya and now returning to his battalion. After the overnight journey to Kalgoorlie we had about half an hour on the platform before departing on the Trans train and Mam and Dad came to see me off. By the time I had transferred my kit bag to the new carriage we did not have long together, which I preferred since I suddenly felt awkward. I pressed some money upon Mam and then we were boarded. The Goldfields fell behind me at a gathering pace and ahead of me lay some sort of a military future.

"Best you get on your bike, Son….."

5

The Trans train took a night and the thick end of two days to cross the Nullarbor Plain, whose Latin name meaning 'no trees' was pretty accurate. The view from the window, hour upon unremitting hour, was of a table-flat expanse as far as the eye could see, unremarked by much other than saltbush and spinifex. For three hundred miles of its length the line ran without a single bend and it was not an exciting journey. At its terminus we continued the process of exchange in trains since each of the states, prior to Federation in 1901, had built its own railroad and built it moreover to a different gauge to its neighbour. We changed at Port Augusta for the relatively short haul into Adelaide, then at Adelaide found the train that would take us overnight to Melbourne.

In Victoria we had a break, being taken from the train by army lorries to Watsonia Barracks for a couple of days. We were to await another draft here and we spent the time on minor duties, but were also given some tuition in saluting by a member of staff. The time passed swiftly and we were by now developing a degree of apprehension as to what might await us at our next destination, 1 RTB.

The recruit training battalion was (and remains) at Kapooka, which lay a few miles out of the celebrated town of Wagga Wagga in NSW. It was in fact just about halfway between Melbourne and Sydney, although that geographical fact meant little to us now: we might as well have been on the other side of the moon.

We were again met at the train by lorries and dropped at the main gate of the camp, where we were marshalled into ranks to march up to the lines, which were formed by endless rows of green Nissen huts. We passed by those already occupied and from many of them issued a roar of **"YOU'LL BE SORRY!"** which seemed disconcertingly like the voice of experience. I tried to feel cheerful but failed, wilting in the early December heat under my load.

Halting at the designated Nissen huts, we were told off to occupancy and ordered to drop our bags, then to fall in again. Despite the plethora of kit issued at Guildford, we had to receive another mountain of it, to include bedding and webbing equipment. A knife, fork, spoon, plates and a mug were also issued, but before we were fed, in a cavernous mess hall, we were submitted to a short back and side's haircut (pretty much the fashion of the day in any case) and Smallpox vaccinations. The wisdom of receiving jabs last of all was revealed later in the evening when arms began to ache abominably.

Stood down at last to contemplate the bewildering pile of kit, we began to be visited by more senior recruits - which is to say anyone who had been at Kapooka for a week already. Some of them would jocularly ask if anyone wanted a punch in the arm, and others offered a brass rolling service for 2/- a set. The brass keepers on our webbing belts were issued flat, and rolled brass caught the light much better to reflect a shine. We quickly availed ourselves of this service and the brass rollers made money.

There were twelve occupants to each of the huts, with two rows of facing cots exactly aligned on a specific floorboard. Each bedspace, about five feet from its neighbour, was equipped with a large locker, a small locker and a bedside mat, which also aligned on a floorboard. Among the new issues had been two strips of wood, about two inches wide and twenty inches long. These, we learned, had to be folded inside our sheets when they were made into a bedpack, sandwiched between blankets and wrapped around with the counterpane, very shortly after the 0600hrs reveille each morning. When not in use, our assembled webbing, blanco-ed to matt green perfection and with glistening brass, was laid out on the cots. Underneath, spare boots, shoes and plimsolls were aligned with millimetric precision, having first been spit-polished to mirror perfection. Whatever our individual religious beliefs might be, here, we soon learned, the great God was uniformity. I thrived on it.

We were 5 Platoon, A Company and we numbered forty something. We included five Smiths, three Jones and two Wilsons, two Germans, a Dutchman and three, like me, who were English. We additionally included a New Zealander and representatives from each of the six states, but no Aborigines, who would prove to number very few in the army although I noted a fullblood in an adjacent platoon. Our training would take three months and we would then disperse to units of choice, either the 'teeth arms' of armour, artillery or infantry, or the supporting arms of engineers, signals and others. We had enlisted for either three years or six years and the system allowed for no renege on that, although a member of our platoon, one of the Germans and a former member of the Hitler Youth, would desert about halfway through the training.

Training began immediately, although the battalion was shortly to stand down for the Xmas break, and it began with long hours on the parade ground. We were blistered by the sun and the instructor in about equal parts, and discipline began here as we learned to remain perfectly still although the flies crawled about our faces and sweat trickled everywhere. Faces turned red, then brown, exempt the strip of flesh covered by the narrow leather chinstrap of our Slouch hats. This was known as the 'Kapooka Stripe', and it was sometimes matched by a blistered left ear lobe, since the brim of the Slouch hat was turned up on that side to permit the sloping of arms with our .303in Lee Enfield rifles.

The Lee Enfield was a venerable weapon, having been in service since 1900. My own at Kapooka was dated 1915 and might have served at Gallipoli, thus nicely combining historical interest with lethal purpose. Its nine-pound weight was an amalgam of machined wood and blued metal, and its bolt closed with a satisfying click, especially when it chambered a gleaming brass round of ball (live) ammunition when we had advanced sufficiently in preparation for the 25 Yard Range. When we progressed to weapon handling, other than for arms drill, we also met the .303 Bren, which was another long-serving weapon. This had been adapted from a Czechoslovakian design by Enfield in 1936. The 36 mil grenade also had been around for quite some time (and would be around for some time yet) and in addition to throwing live examples of it at a much later stage of training, we would also fire inert versions of it from the EY Rifle. EY derived from Extra Yoke, which presumably was the wire binding on the upper woodwork of a .303 rifle, which was fitted with a discharger cup. A powerful blank cartridge known as a ballastite hurled the grenade up to two hundred yards.

Shortly before the Xmas break I was surprised to see cousin Malvern arrive in the camp. He had decided upon service in the catering corps and he joined 6 Platoon that was a fortnight in training behind mine. Since I was selected for Xmas duties, we came to an agreement where I gave him practically my entire fortnight's wage to accompany his leave, and he reciprocated when I took late leave early in January.

In the week or so of the break from training I mostly drew guard duty, which was not arduous, although I learned the early lesson that the hours of the night between about 0200 and 0500 are utterly leaden and each seeming ninety minutes long. There were two guard posts in addition to the main gate and one of these was the magazine, which was a fifteen-minute march from the Guardroom. Several piles of empty cartridge cases lay about and in an attempt to relieve boredom during a duty, I practised loading and ejecting cases from my rifle. Boredom fled, to be replaced by horror, when one of the cases jammed in the breech and would not eject. It took an age for me to prise it free with the tip of the eighteen-inch bayonet we were also armed with. The other post necessitated a patrol through long grass from which we learned the existence of a weed called Paspalum. The weed deposited sticky, black seeds on the gaiters, making the job of blanco-ing even more laborious.

Apart from guard, I was once rostered for duty in the Sergeants' Mess kitchens and I determined to avoid future mess duties if at all possible. It was an early start and a late finish, with mountains of plates or dixies to wash between mealtimes. A companion recruit, named MacAllister, was put to work on the vegetables and left to top and tail a large sack of runner beans whilst the cook went off on some errand. When he returned, he was confronted with a tiny dish of beans that Mac had carefully extracted from the edible pods, which by now were floating in the wet garbage bin.

For the deferred leave I joined a group in a visit to Melbourne, where we stayed in a service hostel. I could still not get served with beer in the pubs, although I was allowed to drink squash in the bars, and eventually came up with the idea of drinking gin squash, which the older recruits ordered for me.

Local leave was possible in Wagga and we availed ourselves of it from time to time, being minutely inspected at the Guardroom before we were permitted beyond the gates. We were just as likely to be inspected upon return, though more for reason of sobriety and attempts to smuggle alcohol aboard than attention to detail of uniform. Such visits to the town were not riotous, however, and we would form small groups for a quiet beer, a trip to the cinema or merely a stroll about the streets to examine shops, or to stare at the opaque waters of the Murrumbidgee River. Wagga was somewhat less than exciting.

When training resumed, we added education lessons to our syllabus, and by the end of the training I had passed the Third Class certificate of education. It is probably up in the loft somewhere. We underwent PT in the gymnasium and the classes included boxing. I was matched against a recruit who was even smaller than I was but who had time in the Australian navy. I lost the bout, decisively.

Less structured fighting tended to be a feature of billet life after hours, as tensions surfaced. A recruit named Francis in my platoon was invited into the scrub behind the hut on a number of occasions, but he usually emerged victorious. I once had a go at him when his behaviour had landed the entire platoon with extra drill after a particularly hot session, but he fortunately did not respond to it. Francis later elected for 'teeth arm' and was posted to dental duties, which perhaps reflected a sense of humour somewhere.

Each day began with a formal reveille parade at which we stood in three ranks to answer our names, after which we were required to shave, make our bed packs and clean the hut before being marched to the Mess. Anyone reporting sick had to rise even earlier than 0600hrs and be marched by the duty NCO to the Regimental Aid Post, carrying overnight kit in the small pack in case of being turned in. I reported sick just once, learning that the interminable wait, feeling wretched, was more than likely to be rewarded with a couple of pills and the curt instruction to 'get on with it'. The procedure may have been designed to discourage malingerers and it was an early lesson in ignoring minor ailments and 'getting on with it'. In the following six years I reported sick only twice.

Our instructors represented the teeth arms of the service and they had considerable experience. Lance Corporal Baird had served in the Eighth Army in Africa, retiring as a warrant officer from the British army before enlisting in Australia. He was a barrel-chested Scot whom we easily imagined as having wiped out whole platoons of Germans with the Bren that he handled with consummate ease. A corporal instructor on Malvern's platoon wore the ribbon of the Distinguished Flying Medal on his breast, having completed fifty operations over Germany as an air gunner.

The company commander was Major Dennis who, I think, was a holder of a Military Cross. He was reportedly a reformed alcoholic, which, if true, may have accounted for the obvious pleasure he took in a ritual enacted each Saturday morning. In front of the assembled Company, Major Dennis would hold aloft bottles of alcohol confiscated from recruits who had tried to smuggle them into the camp. He would then pour the contents into the dust, often to the accompaniment of audible groans from deep within the ranks.

As the training progressed, my fears that I might not achieve good results diminished. I performed well at the timed tests and my weapon handling was better than most, although my results on the range with them were not outstanding. With my very first shot on the 25-yard range with the .303 I smashed the concrete post which supported the target frame, watching with mortification when the target frame slid slowly sideways and crashed to the ground. I also had some difficulty controlling the recoil of the weapon, and when I fired from the squatting position I often fell over backwards. Left-handedness put me to some disadvantage when trying to sight the Bren, but this was not a personal weapon and I passed the rifle practices on the longer ranges easily enough.

We ran about the camp to improve our fitness, and we crept about it at night to improve our fieldcraft. The parade ground continued to provide for a considerable chunk of our military education, and we began to march, wheel and form with a degree of precision and even pride. Long hours of notionally free time were devoted to the spit-polishing of boots and shoes and even the leather scabbard of the long bayonet which the Australian army had retained after the war, having gained a fearsome reputation in the use of it.

Sundays were also notionally free, once we had returned from the obligatory church parade, but in practice much of it had to be devoted to the cleaning of kit and the billet. The full webbing assembly that comprised Field Service Marching Order was a considerable array of canvas and brass, which had to be blanco-ed and polished once per week, and Sunday morning provided a useful opportunity. It was first stripped to its separate components then hauled to the tables that stood outside the Nissen huts. The task required a tin of blanco, a dish of water and a brush, and we had already discovered that the issue nailbrush formed an admirable tool for the job. When the blanco dried, preferably to a smooth and uniform finish, the blanco which had dried on the brass fittings was carefully scraped off with a matchstick and the brass then polished, also carefully to avoid white stains on the webbing. '37 Pattern webbing, so called because it was introduced in 1937, had about forty separate pieces of brass and we usually sat out on the grass to polish it. With any luck, someone might have a portable radio - about the size of a small suitcase - (and to which size portable radios appear to have reverted) and we might listen to the latest offerings by the Everly Brothers or Slim Whitman. Country & Western music had a good following although it was known to some, pejoratively, as 'Queensland Opera'. Among the brass to be polished was the 'rising sun' cap badge of the Australian Military Forces, which had been issued with a gilding finish. At a very early stage of training we were ordered to remove the gilding and polish the brass which was underneath it. This looked like being a laborious job until an older hand advised us to soak the badges overnight in CocaCola. Suspecting a legpull, we did so and by morning the badges were stripped to naked brass. I doubt if I have ever drunk Coke since.

Meals were filling rather than sumptuous and we ate voraciously. Bread was not provided on the tables but actually issued, two slices per man per meal, with a slim rectangle of butter. The latter usually began the long journey across the first slice of bread, giving up about halfway. In the light of this, together with the fact that the milk was often powdered, it was difficult to believe that we lived in a dairy country. To augment such meals we would often toil up the hill to the Canteen and buy a pound block of Neapolitan (three flavours) ice cream, then take it back to the Nissen hut and sit on the cot to spoon the lot of it down in a sitting.

The Canteen wet bar was available to all of us, irrespective of age, and we all received the adult wage, which was fifteen pounds per week. This seemed an enormous sum to me, but I was thrifty and made a regular allotment into my pay book, which thus served as a savings account. From what I actually drew each fortnight I would go early to the Canteen to buy eight ounces of Champion Ruby tobacco for my hand-rolled cigarettes. This measure was intended to keep me in smokes even if I had spent the remaining cash, although I more than occasionally offered the tobacco to less provident mates and was as smokeless as they towards payday. I was by now already a heavy smoker.

I was not yet an accomplished drinker and when I tried to match the pace of the more experienced I usually fell asleep at some early point. I did so at the end of training party, on a pile of greatcoats, having first listened to the platoon commander's speech. His punch line turned on a piece of Latin, *thermos excreta*, in which he suggested that although we had been so much hot shit on arrival, we were now 'shit hot', an expression then meaning terrific. In 1993 I would write to the Commandant at 1 RTB to comment upon a BBC 1 TV programme I had seen which featured current training at Kapooka. In the letter I mentioned my former platoon commander, 2Lt Kleinig. The Commandant responded and mentioned that the retired Colonel Kleinig was a good friend of his.

On 12 March we assembled to march out of Kapooka and I was photographed in full marching order beside my kitbag, and was thus pictured with everything that I actually owned in the world. I had given my bike to Jack and the clothes that I was rapidly growing out of had been dropped off on the way through Kalgoorlie. I wore a wristwatch that I had bought secondhand for a fiver from a recruit named Guse. It had a transparent case through which it was possible to view the workings. This became no longer possible after a week when the watch stopped, but Guse and my fiver had moved on.

Swan Barracks Perth 6 November 1958
Australia's newest – and perhaps shortest - recruit

6

Virtually the entire product of 5 Platoon travelled north, with the eight or nine of us who had expressed the wish to serve in the infantry due to disembark at Liverpool, some twenty-five miles from Sydney. We had travelled overnight from Wagga, crammed with marching order and kitbags into seated compartments, and we emerged unrested and unshaven at about 0700hrs the following morning. Khaki Drill uniforms which had been crisply starched and carefully ironed for the departure, and webbing that was immaculately blanco-ed and boots which gleamed were by now comprehensively stained, soiled, wrinkled and scuffed. We struggled from the carriage under our loads, assuming that we would make a swift transition to lorries despatched from 4 Battalion, the Infantry Training Centre at Ingleburn.

What we encountered on the platform instead was every Digger's worst nightmare made flesh. It was RSM MacDonald, the much-feared 'Ronnie the One', and he now met us with terrifying shouts which appeared even to make the city commuters cringe. We were, he swiftly informed us, the scruffiest, idlest, most undisciplined draft he had ever had the misfortune to set eyes on, and when he had corralled us sufficiently to his satisfaction he put us to ten minutes of close order drill along the length of the platform. What the commuters or the railway staff made of this, I have no idea, but to us it did not bode well for life at 4 RAR.

Released at last to the lorry and clumsily rolling cigarettes as we jolted the few miles to the new camp, we were pretty much alone with our thoughts, but uppermost in mine was the desire to do as well at Ingleburn as I believed I had at Kapooka. I had originally corps-enlisted for the Engineers, and was advised to stay with that choice by Major Dennis when interviewed as to corps choice, but I had at Kapooka developed a liking for infantry training and now wanted more of it.

Training actually began quite slowly, for we had to await other drafts from 1 RTB, and there also appeared to be some problem with instructors. At a later stage of training, those among us who had previous service, including a couple with wartime experience, were pressed into the role of assistant instructors. The training also made a couple of false starts, adding a month to our stay, which was to have been for twelve weeks only. Within a week or two of arrival in the camp a letter from home informed me that Aunt Phyl was dead. She was just fifty-one.

We had observed the usual routines of drawing bedding and finding hut accommodation, with the latter being somewhat superior to those of Kapooka. We no longer occupied Nissen huts in groups of a dozen, but lived in wooden huts in four-man rooms. We were issued with more kit to include two sets of khaki protective dress, comprising a blouse and trousers, which was intended to be worn for training and duties and to preserve our three sets of KD for guard duties or walking out.

The sets of PD had simply been pushed across the Q Store counter against signature without the opportunity to try them on, and I discovered in the hut that the waist of the trousers reached my armpits, with plenty of leg trailing beyond my feet. Mustering as much indignation as a recruit is entitled to - which isn't much - I returned to the Q Store to invite comment from the Quartermaster.
"Hmm," He said, after studying me for a moment or two. "What you've got there, Son, is a pair of Victor Sylvester trousers."
Victor Sylvester?
"Yair. Plenty of ball room."
I wore my 'Victor Silvester' trousers for four months and although they did not shrink an inch, I did grow into them a little. I also personified the old joke: 'I **am** standing to attention, Sir, it's the uniform which is standing at ease'.

Delays in the training syllabus yielded plenty of duties in lieu and I soon learned to avoid kitchen duties, by volunteering for guard if necessary. Kitchen duties could include washing up to three thousand plates by hand after each meal, and no sooner was the last of them on the drying rack when the horde arrived to fill them again. Scraping the remains of meals into the wet garbage bins was another fun job. TE Lawrence once observed, during his time as an RAF recruit, that 'each service throws away enough food to feed the other two'. He was right and probably still is.

The worst possible combination of duties was to work in the kitchen by day and on fire picquet by night. Fire picquet was supposed to be a sleeping duty but it often wasn't and a week of that particular routine was wearing. I recall going to bed one Friday evening and not waking up until Saturday evening. Everything about the camp appeared to be carried out by trainees, with the exception of the civilian who tended the boilers, and we would learn that this practice extended also to the regular battalions. Even the Canteen staff wore KDs and badges of rank.

To no great surprise, we had to clean a number of latrines each day and the principal tools for this job were a tin of Phenyl, which arguably smelled worse than the urinals, a bog brush which was the size of a mature hedgehog and a tin of Brasso with which to polish several yards of copper pipe and brass unions to perfection.

When our training finally gathered momentum, we revised the weapon and fieldcraft skills learned at Kapooka, and added minor tactics, mapcraft and new weapons. We learned the drills for the Owen submachine gun, an Australian design from WWII, and operated wireless sets of perhaps the same era. We operated for a time from a 'bush camp' but I do not recall precisely where that was. I do recall that I was awarded a penalty guard for allowing a taxi to penetrate too far into the camp when I manned the picquet post barrier one evening.

Penalty duties were at least preferable to a formal charge, which invariably resulted in a fine and the award of confinement to barracks. £2 and seven days or £5 and fourteen days' CB were the going rates. The confinement aspect of the award was no great hardship, but the routine that was its concomitant certainly could be. CB meant rising early to don Field Service Marching Order and report with a rifle at 0600hrs for thirty minutes of drill under the Orderly Sergeant, and again at midday and finally at 1800hrs, before undergoing duties prior to a last-parade inspection by the Orderly Officer. The FSMO of course had to be blanco-ed and Brasso-ed to perfection, and the packs were filled. The drill not infrequently included being doubled about the parade ground with the rifle held high above the head, which felt every inch the punishment it was intended to be.

Lateness for CB parades or an unsatisfactory standard of kit or turnout usually meant an extension of CB, and a few unfortunates seemed to be parading continually. When I read today of a female soldier awarded tens of thousands of pounds in damages for sexist remarks in a training camp, or of similar awards to former recruits for ill-treatment, I am tempted to bring a suit for a million pounds for the 'trauma' induced by CB. Perhaps not.

I did more than a dozen Guard duties at Ingleburn but these were not particularly onerous, although the mounting guard was inspected by Ronny the One himself and not the Orderly Officer, as was traditional. Among the RSM's idiosyncrasies was his refusal for KDs to be starched and ironed, at half a crown a set, by the canteen service. He termed this 'artificial soldiering' and we had to learn to do this ourselves, making a terrible mess of early efforts. Packet starch had to be dissolved and stirred into boiling water, and the KDs when ironed had about as much flexibility as plywood sheets.

A guard corporal on one occasion was of the Ordnance Corps and I learned that he was actually the battalion cobbler, responsible for resoling and heeling the steel-shod boots we wore. Since a battalion then comprised eight hundred and fifty men, it worked out to nearly three and a half thousand boots. "How do you manage to stay ahead of that lot?" I asked him. He replied that he was allowed to send a fair few to a civilian cobbler in Liverpool. "So how many do you actually do?" I then asked. "Two pairs," He replied, "mine and the RSM's".

Ceremonial drill had little prominence in the syllabus until it was learned that the Australian wars dead were to be commemorated in a weekly ceremony, and that 4 RAR was to find the inaugural guards. The guards were to be mounted in Martin Place, in Sydney, where the Cenotaph stood, and at the Shrine in Hyde Park. Four Diggers would be posted at each, having marched there to a band, and the thirty-minute vigil would be punctuated by slow marching to drum beats. Victoria Barracks, a mile or so from the city, would provide the assembly and dispersal point.

I was by now good at drill, which of course requires no great intelligence, nor any ability other than to remain perfectly still or to move with alacrity, and I was pleased to be selected for the guard. I was less keen when I learned that Ronnie the One would personally train it. I had already fallen foul of him on several occasions, and most recently for having failed to present arms to an armed party, when I had been the main gate sentry.

"DIDN'T YOU *NOTICE* 50 SOLDIERS MARCHING PAST YOU?" screamed Ronnie, his puce face just inches from my pale one. Actually, no one had informed me of such a requirement, but in the circumstances it seemed wiser to say nothing. Another mistake. **"ARE YOU *DEAF* AS WELL AS *BLIND*?"** Screeched the RSM, who by now might have been ready to impale me against the sentry box with his gleaming pace stick. For days afterwards I would turn and flee if my path appeared to converge with that of the RSM, and I would willingly have walked around the world to avoid him.

A putative guard was selected and put to intensive drill in addition to the lessons that meanwhile prepared us for onward postings to Australia's defence. The guard received an advance issue of the 7.62mm Self-loading Rifle that was just coming into service to replace the venerable Lee Enfield. An entirely new drill had to be learned with the SLR although the RSM, doubtless suspicious of novelty, had us for a time performing the old drill with the new rifle. When it became obvious, however, that the cocking handle raked the collar bone in a particularly unpleasant manner when Ordering from the Slope, and that the extended magazine of the SLR offered insuperable problems to the second movement of the Present, the RSM agreed to the new drill. We learned the new movements, added funerary drill to perfect our slow marching and learned how to reverse arms. We bruised our hands hitting the rifle to the RSM's satisfaction and we sweated despite the winter weather. Arms ached from the constant repetition of the rifle drill, and legs ached from the balance step of the slow march. And I upset Ronnie again.

In order to preserve our Slouch hats for best wear, Routine Orders instructed us to wear the issue cotton beret for training instead. Since we had not previously been required to wear this item, mine had briefly stood service as a boot cloth before vanishing entirely. I now learned that the Q had none in stock, and I thus turned up for guard training under my Slouch hat. Ordered by the guard corporal, with the RSM hovering menacingly nearby, to wear a beret, I turned up after lunch wearing the dark blue woollen beret we also were issued with. The corporal ordered me on this occasion to wear my steel helmet in future, until such time as I might acquire the proper headdress. The RSM was again in attendance and also the following morning, when, due to a chinstrap which had lost its elasticity at about the time of El Alamein, my helmet would fall off with a ringing clang and roll away whenever I prescribed a halt or an about turn.

The veins in Ronnie's neck were again beginning to stand dangerously out and I had a good view of them as I received another blast. **"NOW THAT WE'VE SEEN YOUR COLLECTION OF**

HATS AND YOUR MUSIC HALL TURN, FOXLEY, DO YOU SUPPOSE THAT WE MIGHT GET ON WITH SOME DRILL?" Fortunately for me at that moment, another member of the guard made the mistake of laughing at this witticism and I was forgotten for the moment as Ronnie whirled on the offender with a blistering tirade. As if this were not sufficiently egregious, on guard duty a few days later I was required to give the RSM an early call, and I woke him up an hour too early. There were times when I felt like emulating the example of a recruit interestingly named Albert Hall, by marching through the camp gates and never returning.

We performed the guards at the Cenotaph and Shrine on four or five occasions and the ceremony attracted dense crowds. We awaited the lorry at Victoria Barracks for the return to Ingleburn and the guard corporal approached me. "I heard the RSM saying that you were the smartest there," He said. It was an accolade I floated on for weeks, although I continued to avoid Ronnie the One for the remainder of our time at 4 RAR

Time has greatly modified my view of drill, and there is a quotation on my office wall that I culled from a book about military incompetence. The quotation is of Albert Einstein:

> "The man who enjoys marching in line
> and file to the strains of martial music
> received his great brain by mistake.
> The spinal chord would have sufficed"

Quite. But there is no doubting, even at this span of time, that when we turned to march down Martin Place and the band struck up with Waltzing Matilda, it was a moment of proud emotion. I felt nine feet tall.

"What you've got there, Son, are Victor Sylvester trousers"

7

As Spring approached, we completed our training and received posting notices. To my bitter disappointment I was not to accompany the major draft to 1 RAR, in Queensland. That battalion was shortly to relieve 3 RAR in Malaya and eighteen and a half was the minimum age for operational service. I was a couple of months short and was posted instead to 2 RAR at the nearby camp of Holsworthy. It was particularly disappointing since Arch, who had gone from training to join 3 RAR would now stay on in Malaya with the relieving battalion.

It is a cliche that one never forgets the earliest of friendships within the service, but it is nevertheless true. I saw few of the 1 RAR draft ever again, and where Daryl Howden, Tassie Graham, Rocky Dreezens and all may now be, I hope that their gods go with them. Bernie Smith died as a sergeant in Viet Nam a few years later, and Tony Coles, tragically, by his own hand. These are the more sobering milestones in life.

I heaved my kit aboard a Studebaker lorry and travelled the few miles to Gallipoli Barracks, home of the Second Battalion, the Royal Australian Regiment. At the Guardroom I noticed a large brass badge which I now wore in miniature on the upturned brim of my Slouch hat, whilst awaiting directions to the lines of 2 Platoon A Company, that obviously would be my home for the next couple of years.

Some changes in uniform were made. KDs were replaced by Olive Greens, and the blanco-ed anklets, web were swapped for mud gaiters which attached to the tops of boots and came halfway up the shin. These were not blanco-ed but treated with boot polish. Only the '37 Pattern webbing belt, rifle sling and bayonet frog got the blanco treatment from this point on. The remainder of the webbing, and its brass, was given a coat of dark green paint to render it a more tactical hue in the field, although this had the unfortunate side effect of making it even more uncomfortable to wear than it naturally was.

On our best OG shirts we were now entitled to sew the scarlet flashes which proclaimed: **Royal Australian Regiment**, and underneath them the field force formation sign which crossed gold sabres over a boomerang against a red shield. Best summer dress was completed with the addition of a green lanyard, worn on the left shoulder, although all other corps wore them on the right. The transition from KD, which we associated with recruit and trade training, to OG uniform had been impatiently awaited, although I now learned that *faded* OG was the desired dress. I was soon making repeated trips to the steam boiler in the rudimentary laundry facilities, in an attempt to hasten this natural process. Issues of bush kit included a second-hand Slouch hat to be worn during field exercises, and we were instructed to weave a leather bootlace about its brim and insert a razor blade in the headband. This was intended for use as tourniquet and treatment in case of snakebite or that of a poisonous spider, of which several species abounded.

I soon met the members of my platoon and discovered that they included another man from Kalgoorlie. My section commander was a Taswegian named James Windermere Carne, although he was known to everyone, including the company commander, as 'Shagger'. He had served in Korea with 3 RAR and he wore on his upper arm the blue and gold badge of the Presidential Citation that his battalion had won for extricating the Americans from some disaster during that war. There were three veterans of Korea in the platoon, one of them being a Scot who had served in the same rifle company of the King's Own Scottish Borderers as Bill Speakman, who won the Victoria Cross. Another had been decorated with the Military Medal for subsequent service in Malaya, and a second holder of the MM in A Company was the Staff Sergeant in the CQMS, a WWII recipient of the award. A good number in the company wore the mauve-green-mauve ribbon of the General Service Medal for recent service in Malaya, and the platoon sergeant, Jack Cramp, had a whole row of ribbons for service in New Guinea during the war, fighting the Japanese. Medal identification was another legacy of 4 Battalion and Ronnie the One, who had insisted that we learn to distinguish the ribbons of the eight campaign stars awarded for WW II service and other, associated, medals. The platoon commander, bereft of medals, was a recent product of the Royal Military College, at Duntroon.

Among the surprises was the news that corporals were no longer, as in training camps, minor gods. We were on first and nickname terms with each of the platoon NCOs, and even the platoon commander was seldom addressed as 'Sir'. He was 'Skipper', in or out of the Bush. I was allocated to the support weapons element of the platoon, which was no tribute to my skill with specialist weapons but merely the means of identifying someone to carry the 3.5in Rocket Launcher. This was a cumbersome device of dubious efficiency, normally carried in two pieces that assembled into a tube more than six feet long. It was believed that no rockets for it existed anywhere. Issues of the new SLR were made and they arrived covered in green tape and heavily greased. This could only be removed by employing the steam hoses that were more normally used to clean the wet garbage bins at the Mess, and a fair bit of grease continued to exude from the weapons during the summer months.

I was measured up for issue of 'blues' that formed the ceremonial dress. It was a heavy woollen uniform with a broad red stripe down the trouser legs and worn with white shirt and black tie. This was put to early use when the battalion performed a Trooping of the Colour ceremony for minor royalty at the Sydney Show ground a few weeks later. The uniform trousers were also worn for a tattoo where we re-enacted the Battle for the Plains of Abraham, which had been fought and won exactly two centuries earlier. For tunics, a number of white stewards' jackets were dyed red and for 'muskets' our not-quite demobbed .303s were carried. Maybe they looked realistic from the grandstand. For the tattoo we had to perfect the 'perfect volley' which apparently had won the battle for General Wolfe, and we devoted some hours on the parade ground firing blank rounds to get it right.

Towards the close of the year, and with summer well advanced, the entire battalion deployed to Puckapunyal Camp, about sixty miles from Melbourne, to undergo a major Armoured-Infantry exercise, called, unimaginatively, Sabre Foot. Pucka was the home of 1 Armoured Regiment (the *only* armoured regiment, we infanteers liked to sneer) and we travelled the 600 miles in the backs of Studebaker lorries. At the end of the first day of travel we stopped at Gundagai, where the dog sits on the tuckerbox, and we marched through the town, led by the CO. We were then made very welcome to drinks at several of the town pubs and at the club that was the watering hole of the Returned Servicemen's League.

The Studebakers leaked fumes into the passengers' compartment and I felt moderately sick from them for the entire journey, but everyone was sick after Gundagai - a consequence of the hospitality.

At Pucka I ran across cousin Malvern, now serving as a cook, and we went out for a drink one evening. I overdid the drink by a considerable margin, being sick over my OGs, which accounted for my appearance the following day in a pair of KDs with catering corps flashes on the sleeves.

We worked up to a series of exercises that culminated in the final effort, the highlight of which was to be a move up to the 'battle area' atop Centurion tanks. At a given signal we were to emerge from cover and scramble aboard the tanks, and rehearsals had already taught us that there were precious few handholds or perches. The 3.5 launcher now proved a formidable impediment as I tried to juggle it and my rifle whilst grasping for a secure piece of Centurion, and what I actually grabbed was a cowling which covered the manifold exhausts. While not as hot as the exhausts themselves, they proved to be very hot, and I fell back to the churned earth with a howl. 2 Platoon went to war without me.

We returned after a month to Holsworthy and prepared for Xmas leave, which was usually taken in a single lump and collectively on account of the distances involved. My journey to Kalgoorlie attracted four days of travelling time and this was a weary stint. Only the Trans-train offered sleepers at second-class prices, although there were lengthy breaks at Melbourne and Adelaide to break the routine a little.

By now we were allowed to wear civilian clothes, but I had not yet bought any and I quite liked wearing uniform off camp. A good many of us did, although we had to be careful of the 'Meatheads', the Provost Corps policemen who lurked adjacently to the railway stations and the town and city pubs, ever alert to failures of sobriety or dress. The civil police also had to be reckoned with and a drinking mate named David Rose came up against the law after we had left a Liverpool pub one evening. Rosie had been caught by the police urinating in an alley, and promptly carted off to cells for the night. He made a subsequent appearance in the Magistrate's Court, was fined a hefty fiver and also admonished by the beak. "You can take the word back to your battalion, Private Rose," Said the magistrate, "I'm new here and I intend to clean up this town."
"Oh, I've heard about you," Responded Rosie, "you fucking must be Wyatt Earp." He promptly was done for a tenner for contempt.

With about nine hours to fill at Melbourne, I had a shower in the station facilities and joined some Diggers for a drink at the Prince's Bridge Hotel, better known as Young & Jackson's and famous for 'Chloe', a nude study which hung above the bar. I was by now having no difficulty in being served with alcohol, and in Victoria your drinking had to be during the day since the bars closed at 6pm. This was the infamous 'six o'clock swill', introduced as a wartime measure in 1915 to get the war workers home sober and fit for the next day at the factories, and never repealed. Finally arriving at Kalgoorlie around 2000hrs, and not having advertised it, I caught a cab home and surprised Mam and Dad. Part of the surprise was that I had grown four inches since they had last seen me. The Goldfields seemed little changed since I had left, but I felt like a new citizen. I mostly remained in uniform, although I spent a good sum at the Ardagh Brothers' Emporium in Burt Street acquiring new duds, which did not include a fashion in trousers which was unique to the Goldfields. At that time, males anywhere between the ages of twenty and forty sported trousers that flared to twenty-two inches at the turn up. This was a decade and nearly two before the fashion became worldwide, and perhaps it killed the Goldfields predilection, for I never saw them again. The uniform guaranteed pub access, although I once felt on my shoulder the hand of the 'liquor john', an angular man named Slater who affected trilby hats and double-breasted suits in midnight blue cloth. It is possible that his heroes included Dick Tracy. I brazened out his challenge and he let it pass, but I saw the doubt lurking in his eyes.

My friends Terry and Stan had recently been fined for underage drinking and much envied my access. It may have had some bearing on the fact that both followed me into the army within a few months. Stan's solution to the problem of drink was novel. He drove a '34 Ford which had a keg of beer on the back seat. We would go to the recently built drive-in cinema to be suitably refreshed between reels, and afterwards would often drive into the bush with an assortment of .22 rifles. The selected game was kangaroo and it is a mystery to me now that we did not succeed in shooting each other. We certainly shot no kangaroos. Awakening in the Ford at dawn, throats thick with alcohol-induced dehydration and reluctant to attempt cigarettes, we potted a few parrots at a property dam. This was mindless slaughter to no purpose at all.

The leave, twenty-three days of it, expired at midnight on the third of January, by which time I had returned to Holsworthy. I was unable to retrieve my Soldier's Box from the *Q* and since my mosquito net was in it I got eaten half-alive all night. Perhaps that was a return blow from the wildlife.

8

The Fifties were over and Summer marked the new decade as we moved into the hottest months of January and February, adding an extra dimension of hardship to our frequent excursions into the bush where we exercised the techniques of advance to contact and counter-ambush. The axis for these was invariably the Old Coach Road whose gravelled surface cut a red swathe through the relentless landscape of eucalypt, and which had served the coaches of Cobb & Co. a century before. Many of the gum trees bore evidence of the not infrequent bush fires in summer, and their charred limbs provided an expedient means of blackening hands and faces for camouflage purposes as we embarked upon training.

Bushfires sometimes intruded upon leisure time and one Saturday I was spending a quiet day in the lines when a member of the guard entered and ordered me to the Guardroom. From there I was taken with others in a Studebaker to the site of a fire and we were equipped either with knapsack sprays or fire beaters. The spray was a simple tank of about two-gallon capacity, fitted with a pressure pump and a spray nozzle on a short length of hose. With furious pumping, it was possible to direct a thin jet of water at a point about six feet away, and it was not an appliance to inspire much confidence when the advancing wall of flame was six or twelve feet high. The beaters comprised a six-foot pole with strips of leather or canvas attached, but it seemed a more useful tool to attack a swarm of flies with, rather than some raging inferno. We fire fighters were swiftly reduced to a sorry spectacle of smoke-blackened, scorched Diggers whose eyebrows were missing and whose OGs were everywhere holed by sparks.

We returned to camp late in the day, scorched, tired, thirsty, hungry and not a little curious that so many of the platoon were now in the lines which had earlier seemed so empty. "You missed the fire." I remarked to a mate.

"Too bloody right I missed the fire." He retorted, leading me to his bedspace where a blanket hung from his cot to the level of the floor.

He pulled it aside and revealed his camp stretcher, which was a portable bed, set up beneath the cot frame and having sufficient space for the occupant to sleep or maybe read a paperback. I checked the other huts and found several such arrangements, all belonging to platoon members who had once been called out to fight bushfires. Just the once.

A new man was posted in from 4 RAR and I had little difficulty in persuading Shagger that the new bloke looked like a natural operator of the 3.5 launcher. I in turn inherited the 2" Mortar from a Digger who may well have persuaded Shagger that I was a natural mortarman, but this at least, although heavy, was compact and easily carried. It was thought that no bombs existed for it anywhere.

Having qualified as a Group One private when I completed recruit training, I now looked forward to promotion to Group Three, which brought an increase in wages. Eighteen months service was required and passes on a number of tests to include weapons and fitness. None gave me any problems and I felt secure in my job.

The platoon underwent some changes and the Kalgoorlie man returned to mines employment. I last saw him roaring down Hannan Street on an unsilenced, and probably unlicenced, motorbike, wearing a battledress blouse with the red flashes still at his shoulder. He was replaced by a chap who, to my expert eye, looked like a born mortarman and I gave him the good news. Unlucky.

I now became the Number Two scout for my section, having undergone a short course at the Old Holsworthy camp a mile or two down the road. This aimed to put a gloss on basic tradecraft and we broke twigs over a succession of days to observe the changes in them. We learned to inspect spider webs - often a metre wide - for signs of disturbance, and discovered that a man's feet tend to splay out when he carries a load. I returned from the cadre convinced that I was the reincarnation of Kit Carson, but in truth probably had great difficulty in following a cinema queue.

The lead scout in my section was a laconic veteran of Korea, Jeff McNamara. Mac was quite old - 28 - and upon his arrival had solved a minor mystery which attached to a major in one of the other rifle companies. The major was known as 'target arse' and Mac revealed that 'target arse' had been a subaltern platoon commander in Korea, much given to testing his sentries' alertness by sneaking up on them at night. This was presumably a useful method until the night he tried it on a bushman named Ned Sparkes, who did not bother with a challenge but simply let fly with the Bren, which was his personal weapon. The efficiency expert was taken to the casualty clearing station with two rounds in his buttocks, and Sparks was later asked by the company commander to account for the failure to challenge. When it was also pointed out to Sparkes that he had wounded his platoon commander, and where, Sparkes reportedly remarked that he would have to re-zero the weapon, since he had "definitely aimed at the bastard's head."

Mac and I shared hootchies in the bush and we got on well. He was tolerant of my early mistakes (once leading the entire company in a virtual circle in some untypically close country) and he offered good advice on a range of topics.

Our frequent exercises had elements of hardship which are recognisable only in retrospect, since the conditions then seemed ordinary and thus accepted as the norm. We had, for example, a standard cotton uniform for field wear, summer or winter, with just a thin pullover to augment it when the temperatures dropped - occasionally to freezing. We might have taken our greatcoats into the bush except that they were too bulky and heavy to carry in the large pack. On sentry-go for two hours in every six at night we would simply man the Bren pit with a blanket draped about our shoulders, and we learned to accept a margin of cold discomfort. Shivering also helped to keep one awake, when the effort of the day pulled the eyelids down, but I preserve a sharp memory of trench vigil; yearning in the dead hours of the night to be somewhere distant or at least ten feet away and cocooned in the largely illusory warmth of a single blanket.

Sleeping bags were not issued and most of us took a single blanket to sleep under, since more simply added to the weight we had to tote. I did modify a blanket by string stitching down one side and the end of it to form a rudimentary bag, but the cold, generally, was something to get used to. I recall also that, in the lines and in a wooden hut whose warmth in winter depended solely upon four, naked light bulbs which were strung the length of it, I took to sleeping with a bare minimum of blankets on my cot, in order to develop hardiness. Perhaps my resistance to cold weather now actually is more acquired than genetic.

A mate on another platoon in A Company once complained to me that his section commander insisted on cold shaves all around and that iron rations were to be eaten cold, as a means of developing toughness. This seemed extreme, although any doubts there may have been about the toughness of the section commander were dispelled a few years later. He was Kevin 'Dasher' Wheatley and he was awarded the first of three Victoria Crosses for the Viet Nam campaign. I ran across him in Sydney a few months before his posting and he confided that he had 'wangled a job as an adviser.' I never saw him again for Dasher's VC was posthumous.

During the months of training at 4 Bn we had improved our knowledge and practice of fieldcraft and minor tactics at the bush camp whose name I have forgotten, but much of the routine at Ingleburn had been classroom-based. There were hints, however, that life within a regular battalion held more than a cushy routine of loafing about and awaiting WWIII. I knew the truth of that by now and although I was young and fairly fit, I often felt stretched by the short-term exhaustion of section battle drills or the longer attrition of 72-hour patrols through rough country. We were in the Bush for three or four days each month and each of these opened with an hour of 'standing to' in a battle trench, if dug, or a shell-scrape. After Stand To, unless we were remaining in a defended position, we usually had very little time, possibly as little as twenty minutes, in which to execute the ritual of folding bivvies (collapsed at stand to), cleaning weapons and boots, shaving, packing extraneous kit and sorting out a brew and some scoff before being ready to move. The routine was followed as a strict priority and only the brew and scoff was considered expendable, although Shagger had emphasised the importance of not attempting to soldier on 'a Dingo's breakfast', which he helpfully defined for us as ' a piss and a look around'.

Advancing to contact along the Old Coach Road, and the alternatives of seventy-two hour patrols thus required a high level of fitness, and I devoted spare time to it. I often went to the assault course during the weekend to improve my confidence and reduce the time it took to complete the course. I ran sporadically, but was yet to develop the habit that in later years would be the mainstay of my fitness. Adjacent to the Battalion HQ lines was a large shed which served as a gymnasium of sorts, although it was ill-equipped save for some Indian clubs and coconut matting which hadn't seen the coconuts in some time. What the 'gym' also had was a lurking band of psychopaths known as the regimental boxing team, who invariably lay in ambush for the unwitting visitor. A casual invitation to 'join in a bit of sparring' usually meant being laced into a pair of sixteen-ounce gloves which henceforth remained in pristine condition, whilst the unfortunate wearer was thumped into oblivion. Only the congenitally stupid went there twice.

Each of the four rifle companies and the Support Company that acted as signals or mortar specialists undertook battalion duties, which cropped up every few weeks and ran for a week at a time. I avoided Mess duties whenever I could see them coming and particularly the Mess-related job of cleaning the grease traps. These lay adjacent to the kitchens, collecting a foul-smelling and disgusting scum, which had periodically to be scraped off and carted away. The simple tool for this was a large tin with a few holes punched into it, nailed to an old brush stale. Cleaning the grease traps was easily the world's worst job, especially if you were somewhat ill from drink of the previous night. If Mess duties represented unrelieved drudgery, they might occasionally offer a salutary lesson on the possible consequences of abused authority. On some occasion I was employed in the Officers' Mess as a steward and had virtually cleared the tables one evening when a lieutenant entered from the bar and demanded a meal. I conveyed the order to the cook, who responded succinctly: "Tell him to fuck off," He snapped. I conveyed an edited version of this to the officer who promptly strode into the kitchen and informed the cook that he could dish up a meal or spend the night in cells. The cook nodded acquiescence and the officer returned to the dining room. The cook then carefully ignored several unused cuts of meat and vegetables, selected ingredients instead from the floating detritus in the stinking wet-garbage cans, gave them a quick burst on the stove and strode into the dining room to present the meal with a flourish to the unwitting officer.

I mostly did guard duties, finding the routine easier than most jobs, although the cycle of two hours on and four hours off over an entire weekend was tiring. I also discovered that the battalion operated a 'Stick Orderly' system on guard as an incentive to excellence in turnout. The Guard mounted with one more man than the posts required and the best dressed man was appointed Stick Orderly and allowed to return to the lines as a replacement guard, should someone go sick.

Having willingly accepted at Kapooka the spit-polishing regime, I now became completely obsessive about my kit. My boots and best pair of mud gaiters were spit-polished from top to bottom, my brass gleamed and I mixed batches of starch you could have plastered a wall with. I even made special brews of a starch paste for epaulettes and pocket flaps and my OGs were like armour plate. In order to preserve the razor creases, I used to seek assistance when I dressed for the guard mount, standing on a chair and lowering myself into the trousers that a mate held. My hat puggaree was also starched and I had replaced the small, painted eyelets in the crown of the hat with some large, brass ones that I could polish. The brass eyelets in my boots were polished, and the steel heel plates buffed to a chrome-like shine and I even discovered how to polish my leather bootlaces to a shine by stropping them on the metal end of my cot. This demented behaviour persisted for some years but I am quite cured now.

Although I won release from a considerable number of guards, my aptitude with the iron and a tin of small circles also landed me with the job of batman to the platoon commander, by now a Portsea graduate replacing the Duntroon man. This meant twice as much kit to wash, iron, polish, etc. but at least I could do it, mine included, in the Firm's time and I was also exempt some company duties.

Guard duty by day meant acting as the ceremonial sentry at the entrance of Gallipoli Barracks, patrolling fifteen paces or waiting, at ease, to spring to attention and pay compliments to passing officers. At night, the main gate sentry checked access and two additional posts were manned with roving sentries. The four hours in the Guardroom not devoted to sleep might be spent reading a paperback or playing cards. I once lost a fortnight's wages in a few hands and was forever cured of gambling by the experience. A supper tray for the guard was provided by the Mess, and I do not remember it being anything other than cheese and onions. Raw onions were a terrible snack option at about 0300hrs but the cheese never lasted very long. It is likely that the cheese was eaten *en route* by the sentry who collected the tray.[1]

I stood sentry at the gate one day when a car pulled up and an old chap requested directions to Old Holsworthy, which was a mile or

---

[1] At 4 RAR, the battalion mascot, which was a dog of indeterminate breed, used to live at the Guardroom and it was the job of a sentry to collect the dog's meal with the supper tray. It often happened that the sentry ate *that* as well.

two further down the road. He turned out to be a former German National who had been interned at the camp during 1914. I have ever since wondered if the man was *Herr* Resch, founder of the brewery whose product I was partial to.

We also had to find ceremonial guards occasionally to mount at Victoria Barracks. These tended to be popular for the proximity of city delights that could be sampled during the entire day off between duties. We were no strangers to Sydney in any case, often leaving Holsworthy in a group on Friday evening and not returning to the lines until Sunday. For just six shillings a night a bed could be had at 'Johnnies', which was an Australian naval hostel in the heart of the city. The beds were two-tiered bunks in large dormitories and your chance of finding yourself in your numbered bed was actually quite small. It was more usual to lurch to the nearest bed, strip and slump into it.

We generally eschewed drinking in the public bars, where uniform seemed to act as a magnet for scroungers and hard luck stories. We drank instead in the lounges where groups sang and played the popular songs and tunes of the day. The lounges also attracted women whose company might be secured for the evening, if not the night, and many of these 'lounge lizards' were semi-professional prostitutes. This was no way to meet a nice girl, even if I had not still been paralysed by shyness unless I was drinking, and I eventually satisfied my sexual curiosity with a visit to the Kings Cross brothels. The encounter cost me £2, was less than satisfying and led me to conclude that resort to prostitutes was hardly more than an expensive form of masturbation. I did not become a regular customer at Palmer Street, which was just as well since it was also a proven method for meeting Provost Corps policemen or members of the vice squad.

The scroungers referred to above were thick on the ground in Sydney. In the city some day with a mate and wearing battledress, we were confronted by a gaunt figure wrapped in a tatty greatcoat. "Have youse got a couple of bob for an old Digger?" Croaked the apparition. The mate answered him in flash: "Fuck off, Sport," He snapped, "*we're* working this side of the street."

Victoria Barracks Guard Sydney 1961

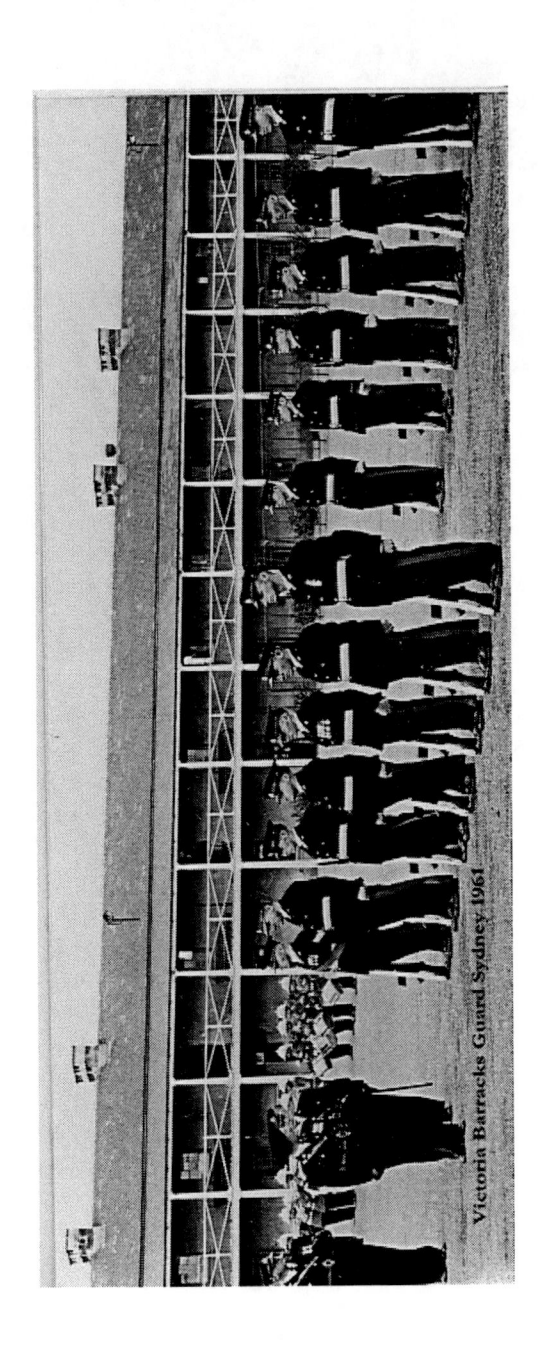

"Have youse got a couple of bob for an old Digger?"

9

    Habitually going about with a small crowd of mates, or having a particular close mate, is something that no longer exists in my life and I regret that. Perhaps it does not quite fit with middle age and sober habits. It certainly fitted at the time and doubtless was the basis of the camaraderie that is a pearl beyond price among uniformed companions. We probably drank too much and on occasion behaved egregiously, usually as a result of the drink, but we seem, in retrospect anyway, to have observed common decencies. Closing time in city hotels, of which our favourites included the Town Hall, the Civic and the Bognor, might be the signal for a fight, or several, to break out, but fists were the preferred weapons and I cannot recall ever seeing a bottle or a glass used.

    The Sydney pubs closed between 1830hrs and 1930hrs - apparently another unrepealed wartime idea - and a meal was the means of filling that time, although some of us were less than imaginative in our choice of food. My idea of a 'Chinese' meal was to enter a Chinese restaurant and order a T-Bone steak. An alternative was to sit in one of the newsreel theatres and have a quiet sleep, or choose the theatres that ran a continuous cartoon show.

    As an occasional break from the pubs we might visit Luna Park, which was a funfair adjacent to the Harbour Bridge. I once visited with a mate and he succeeded in picking up a girl who was attractive. She had a friend who could have been Yasser Arafat's twin sister and I was obliged to accompany her in order not to spoil the mate's prospects of improving his new friendship. We eventually wound up in a boat that was being cranked around the tunnel of love, although I had not been at all keen on the ride. I studied the damp walls, wondering how I might quietly detach from the group outside, when the Arafat lookalike gave me a hefty push. "Oi, Mate!" She wanted to know, "are you the captain of this fucking boat, or what?"

Life in 2 RAR proceeded pleasantly. Our advance to contact drills along the Old Coach Road continued to provide the staple exercises, which we alternated with training within Gallipoli Barracks. A battalion parade was held on the last Friday of each month and it was usually a two-hour affair, immediately followed by a church parade. For the latter we were called out to three groups: RCs, CEs and OPDs [1] and I attended services at all three in the hope of finding one which might be shorter than the rest. Eventually, I summoned my nerve and refused to fall in with any group, being put to work cutting grass ineffectually with my bayonet for such temerity.

Routine training was broken when I was selected to attend an air loader's course at an Australian air force camp at Richmond, about forty miles out of Sydney. The RAAF had recently acquired examples of the Lockheed C130 aircraft and since these were likely to be used in any trooplift, small groups of battalion personnel were now to be trained in the techniques of loading the capacious fuselages with vehicles, kit and bodies.

I was astonished at the size of the Hercules, wondering how it could ever get off the ground, and greatly pleased when the course included a number of flights. We spent a week at Richmond, where I was astonished also by the quality and choice of food, and learned how to prepare cargo, how to load and secure it, and also how to work out complex weight and balance sheets to ensure that the aircraft flew within its centre of gravity limits. I did not know it at the time, but this course was to prove very useful to me a couple of years later.

Back at Holsworthy I contrasted the food in the Other Ranks Mess which invariably ran to just two choices: take it or leave it. The food was seldom inspiring and perhaps not least because a number of our cooks were not of the catering corps, but actually regimental cooks. These were simply Diggers who had little enthusiasm for infantry work and therefore escaped to the Mess, having undergone a brief course. They were generally referred to as 'bait-layers'. For a time we were fed on compo rations for one day each week, and on that day received neither fresh milk nor bread. In lieu of bread we were given the incredibly hard Biscuits, Service, said to be weevil-proof since no weevil could possibly bore into them. Only one choice existed at meals

---

[1] Roman Catholics, Church of England, and Other Protestant Denominations.

and if you could not stomach the army version of curry and rice well, tough. (A mate once queued at a field kitchen where the Cook stood behind a large dixie that appeared to contain stew. "D'you want stew or curry?" asked the Cook, whereupon the mate opted for curry. The Cook ladled out a portion of stew then liberally sprinkled it with curry powder.) The limited menus came around in a swift and steady rotation for those who lacked calendars and Friday was always the signal for fish - otherwise known as 'a Catholic steak'.

We nevertheless queued for the food and the queue usually formed half an hour before the meal. The last six in it were called forward to serve up the food, the cooks having banged it onto the servery and often having departed to the Canteen for a pint and a meat pie. The boredom of queuing for meals might be enlivened by the minor sport of knocking a chunk of enamel off someone's mug with the handle of one's knife.

A new man arrived from 4 RAR and we became mates. Danny Wright was a couple of years older than I but we had a number of shared interests, including the Goons. I actually knew him as Bob Williams at this time, since he had enlisted under an assumed name. A Sydneysider, he had tried to enlist in NSW and was turned down when he revealed a conviction for fighting. He subsequently borrowed a birth certificate and enlisted in Victoria. Dan was in another section, where he insisted on carrying the Bren, but we saw plenty of each other when not actually in the bush.

Danny was then beginning to develop an interest in sports parachuting, which he would eventually develop to a total of some eight thousand descents and an Australian championship, and he persuaded me to try it. We went one Saturday to the Camden parachute club and I spent the morning undergoing ground training, learning the exit drills and how to roll when landing. The aircraft was a biplane of about 1935 vintage, a De Havilland Dragon Rapide, which boarded five parachutists and a despatcher when the ground trainer, an RAAF warrant officer named Bob Milligan, deemed we were ready.

Two of the other novices were drivers from an Australian Army Service Corps transport platoon, also at Holsworthy. We had met and had a chat and the odd thing was that I would serve on the same platoon as both of them a couple of years later. It was an early example of how small the military world really is.

The Dragon had clearly not been designed with parachuting in mind, for its door was quite small and the drill was to first place a foot on the small step that projected from the fuselage below the door sill. In trying to do this, I slipped and was suddenly out of the aircraft and upside down, until the static line developed the canopy and brought me upright again. No other problems presented themselves and my descent from some two and a half thousand feet provided a marvellous, circular view as I pulled a toggle on the lift webs to rotate the canopy. At one point I believed that I was not descending at all, a fallacy which was corrected when the final eighty feet or so came rushing up to knock the wind out of me. A fine experience, although at a fiver a time not one I was about to become addicted to.

Platoon, company and battalion training continued to run along familiar lines. Deployment into the bush was almost on a monthly basis, at a duration of three to five days. The Advance to Contact which inevitably led to anti-ambush drills, and which doubtless was the staple of training for a tour in Malaya, was occasionally varied with patrol or defence exercises. Patrol exercises were arduous, as we stuffed three-day's worth of compo rations into our packs then toiled across some of the more daunting terrain within the training area. This was uncomfortable in any of the seasons, but the more so in high summer when a raging thirst was added to the distractions of fatigue and flies. Another disagreeable aspect of training in high summer was the stench of bodies when we flocked to the shower block on return to camp after a few days. We were often subjected to water discipline, which meant that our single bottles of about a pint capacity would be filled early in the day and late in the day, and refreshment for some ten hours in between depended upon very careful conservation. Watercourses, where a quick refill might be possible, were few at any time and mostly of the non-perennial variety. Tobacco was often shared; water bottles seldom were.

The rigours of the day were compounded by the necessity of sentry duties each night, when we took turns on the Bren during the silent hours. The best arrangement of shifts offered no more than two hours of duty followed by four hours of sleep, until the duty came around again. First and last shifts were popular, since they followed or preceded the hour for which we all stood to at last light and first light, whilst the leaden hours between 0100hrs and 0500hrs were least favourite.

Water shortage was remarked in a different way when 2 Platoon was selected to trial a new type of ration pack, in which packets replaced tins and all of the food was dehydrated into powder or biscuit form. We had deployed for a seven-day exercise and for three days of it would eat the new ration. For comparison, 1 Platoon fed on fresh rations prepared in a field kitchen, whilst 3 Platoon ate the normal, tinned, compo.

We learned that a team from the Commonwealth laboratory that had designed the food would accompany us into the bush to monitor results, and interest quickened when it was learned that a Miss McNaughton was among the team. There was distinct effort to comb hair and generally appear more presentable than was usually required in the bush, until it transpired that Miss McNaughton was a flinty object of about sixty summers. Combs became redundant again.

We were obliged to strip naked in the back of a lorry each morning to be weighed, and this was a chill prospect in midwinter. We were also urged to visit the latrines prior to the weigh-in, but since the latrine was nothing more than a slot in the ground in a totally exposed position, it made rather more sense, if at all possible, to let the day develop a bit of warmth first.

Learning that Miss Mac was to pass among us, canvassing opinion on the food, some effort was made to brief Burry Cullen, a platoon member whose language was so foul that even the rest of us noticed. Burry was briefed to nod or shake his head if questioned, which he duly was.
"Are you enjoying the food, Private Cullen?" Miss Mac wanted to know.
A vigorous nod from Burry.
"Are you eating everything?" Asked Miss Mac.
Another vigorous nod from Burry.
"Anything you don't especially like?" Persisted Miss Mac.
End of restraint for Burry. "Yair," He replied, "fucken cabbage is fucken crap!"
Exit Miss Mac.
The food actually was filling and tasty, but its preparation required about a quart of water and we did not see it again.

Some equipment changes were effected. The venerable '37 Pattern webbing was withdrawn and we were issued with an American design. It was light and fairly capacious, although the snaphooks which held the assembly together were all too prone to do just that. We also were issued with the American GI helmets of WW II vintage. These arrived in boxes that bore the legend: A Gift From The American People, a sentiment we were not entirely persuaded of. We now wore the helmets all the time in the bush, which clearly was going to be a sensible operational practice, but we greatly missed the soft Slouch hats, complete with bootlace and razor blade which had no place on the helmet. I do not recall being told what we should now do in case of a snake or spider bite, but the emergency did not arise.

The new issues included an inflatable mattress for bush use, and this novelty was much appreciated until it was discovered that one or more of the three inflatable panels had a tendency to deflate during one's precious four hours off, tipping one onto the familiar soil.

No clothing updates took place and we continued to wear the steel-shod ammunition boot when the rest of the military world appeared to have switched to rubber soles. Some of the boots still being issued at this time were clearly stamped with the date 1942. A good year to be making boots, obviously.

Route-marching was another staple of training[1], and also one of the annual tests which secured Group Three pay and preserved it. The increment was welcome since, although I still maintained savings through deferred pay and actually had a healthy bank account, I was profligate with that which I drew each fortnight.

Pay parade was conducted on alternate Thursdays and we lined up alphabetically and by state enlistments. Regimental numbers were prefixed by a number that denoted the state of origin, beginning

---

[1] 4 Battalion had provided our introduction to what then was still the principal means by which infantrymen, and their equipment, travelled from A to B. At an early outing, the corporal in charge of our group had offered the advice that 'singing was an excellent means of maintaining cadence and morale on the march', whereupon one of our number began a reedy rendition of *A White Sports Coat and a Pink Carnation*. He progressed little with this however before being angrily ordered to shut up by the corporal, and we continued in sweaty silence, surmising that Marty Robbin was not among the pantheon of road-marching heroes.

with Queensland as 1 and Tasmania as 6. West Australia was 5 and any West Australian named Zuppar (I later knew one) was destined to spend a lot of time on pay parades.

In addition to pay we were also issued a bar of soap and two razor blades ('7 o'clock to beat that 5 o'clock shadow'), although this scale was never explained to us. My bar of soap was quickly used but the razor blades lasted forever. Impatient to grow a beard, this did not happen until I had passed twenty-one.

Payday signalled a clandestine event for which the Guardroom gambling merely whetted some appetites. Late in the evening of a pay Thursday some sort of bush telegraph would pass the word of a gathering at an ablutions block within the lines of one company or another, where a fortnight's wage might be wagered and lost on the turn of dice on a Crown & Anchor board, or the spin of a pair of pennies at Two Up. I went along as a spectator a time or two but kept my wages in my pocket.

Route-marching assumed greater importance when it was announced that we would march from Sydney to Singleton early in the New Year, and prior to the Xmas break we went on frequent marches of increasing distance. It was intended that we would cover a hundred miles in the space of four days.

When December arrived I did not travel home, having volunteered for Xmas duties in return for leave deferred until February. I managed to avoid all mess duties during the month by doing guard, twenty-four hours on and twenty-fours hours off. Unfortunately, the Stick Orderly system was suspended for the period, or I might have won some extra days off. By this time I was a walking advertisement for Kiwi polish, Reckitts starch and Brasso. I was alerted from home that Arch would be making a Xmas Day broadcast from Malaya, but I had been drinking to excess on the night before and slept through the programme.

The guard duties passed easily enough but the camp was unnaturally quiet in the period and I was glad to see the mates return from leave. We swapped stories sprawled on our cots, with boots carefully perched on the bed end to preserve the counterpane from polish, smoking endlessly and discussing new forays into Liverpool or Sydney. Life seemed good and doubtless was.

Marching resumed and early in February we set off into the Blue Mountains, following a bush road where the dust soon rose into our throats. It would prove to be a record summer and this the hottest month. A routine of early starts was soon established, whereby we might rise at 0230hrs and complete the twenty miles or so before the sun was at its zenith, but there simply was no escaping the heat. By early afternoon, with marching ended, we would rig our poncho hootchies to provide shade, gasping with thirst until the water bowsers of the company echelon caught us up. On the third day a platoon commander from another rifle company died, and it was variously speculated that he had died of heat exhaustion, snake bite or spider bite. A week or two later the battalion commander, a hulking veteran of WW II and known as the 'Brahma Bull', ended the speculation with a single line in Battalion Routine Orders. '2nd Lieutenant Smith died,' it ran, 'because he wasn't fit.' That's OK then.

Under our hootchies on the last day of the march, mail came up with the water and I received a letter from Mam. Gran'Ma Foxley, she told me, was dying. I felt my throat constrict and my eyes burn and it had little to do with marching or summer heat.

Because my leave was due, I returned to Holsworthy ahead of the battalion move and I entrained for home. This time I was expected and met at Kalgoorlie by Dad. At the house I went to see Gran'Ma in her bedroom and was shocked by her appearance. She had been a robust woman and now cancer had reduced her to a few stones. She could hardly speak and I could not speak at all. While I had been growing she had been shrinking, and was now almost nothing. She died the following evening and I knew for the first time the meaning of grief.

10

We buried Gran'Ma in the Boulder cemetery a mile or so east of the town on a sweltering day. I wore uniform and stood among the small knot of mourners at the brief ceremony. We did not attend a church service, although Gran'Ma had been raised a Methodist and perhaps retained her religious beliefs. Thirty-three years would elapse before I saw the grave again.

I had eighteen days' leave and it was a fairly subdued time. Dad taught me to drive the Ford, but I did not take the driving test before the days ran out and I was again boarding the Trans at Kalgoorlie. I looked forward to returning but there were now changes in the air as the battalion prepared for a two-year tour in Malaya towards the end of the year.

Danny Wright was no longer about, having volunteered for the Special Air Service and now undergoing a tough selection course. A few others had left 2 Platoon and newer faces replaced them, among them a lad quickly nicknamed 'Orbit', since that was where his brain appeared to reside. One Sunday morning, another platoon member was lying half-asleep under his mosquito net when he saw Orbit help himself to money lying on the locker top. A fight quickly developed and when those who intervened learned the reason, Orbit was dragged down to the latrine block and comprehensively thumped by anyone who cared to. He was eventually carted off, in a bloodied state, and held in the Guardroom for his own safety. An ugly incident to witness but no one questioned the rough justice meted out to a thief caught in the act.

Another new member of the platoon was an early return from 1 RAR and he brought news of Arch. We had then yet to develop the habit of a frequent exchange of news that we have maintained since.

Promotion moved Shagger out of the platoon and in his place we got a corporal who had spent a good deal of time as an instructor with a national service battalion. He had few clues as to bush work and tactics, but he was a good bloke and the section worked for him. Shagger was missed, if not for his practical jokes. A recent example had been to lurch from the Railway Hotel in Liverpool and order sixty hamburgers at an adjacent counter. He then slipped away, leaving the platoon sergeant to sort out the problem. We also got a new platoon sergeant (Jack Cramp perhaps having gone off to have a nervous collapse) and there were various changes at company and battalion levels.

On the basis of my recent driving experience, I bought a '52 Singer Tourer from the CQMS, a man named Swampy Johnson. It cost £100 and a condition of the sale was that I should retain a spider that lived in the hood. I evicted it at an early opportunity. For a time I became Mr Toad, illicitly zooming about the local area until I sold the car on to a Lance-Jack named Hank Snow, whose driving would have put Mr Toad into a trauma unit.

I was by now having to come to a decision about signing on, for my three-year enlistment was entering its final months. This I found difficult for although I doubtless enjoyed the life, I occasionally found it somewhat confining and also repetitive. On a recent exercise I had actually dug my trench only yards from a site I recognised from two years before, and I wondered if I might find another three years simply emptily recurring. Another thought, despite the certainty of a trip to Malaya, was that army life seemed to offer less travel prospects than a platform ticket, whereas I had the urge to discover.

The company commander, Major Hone, who was another WW II veteran, interviewed me at the time and urged me to sign on, but I felt undecided. A week or two later I was transferred out of A Company to the Australian component of 1 RAR, whose new home would be Holsworthy. My companions turned out to be those who were either too young to serve in Malaya, or, like me, whose time was expiring. We were not a prepossessing crew, which hardly mattered since we did no training and merely carried out endless duties about the camp.

To escape at least some of the duties, I volunteered for a fortnight at the Royal Military College, Duntroon, where a Senior Officers' symposium was to be held. The college was close to Canberra, in the Australian Capital Territory, and I had not been there before. To my disgust, instead of the guard duties I had volunteered for, I was dragooned into stewarding at the Officers' Mess along with a dozen other blokes.

Canberra in our time off proved to have an excellent war museum, and I spent considerable time there, although I was not immune to the more usual pursuits. A mate and I were lifted by the police one evening for a piece of drink-related egregiousness, but allowed to return to camp with a warning. The time ran out and we returned to Holsworthy, where the time also ran out. I handed in my Soldier's Box and sundry kit and prepared for discharge. The military career appeared to be at an end.

When I returned to Boulder it was to 265 Burt Street. In the last months of her life Gran'Ma had decreed that our family would live there, and that Uncle Jim, who now had only his daughter at home, would live at 271. In the event, Jim declined and bought a house closer to the town centre. We saw little of him for some time.

At Xmas Arch arrived home for the first time in three years. He looked lean and fit and he complained about the cold, although December was not a noticeably cool month on the Goldfields. He had been promoted to Lance Corporal but soon relinquished it in order to volunteer for service with the Special Air Service.

I saw little point in seeking a job until after Xmas and in truth had no idea of what I might do. I was by now old enough to work on the mines, but had little enthusiasm for that form of work although nothing in the service had provided any sort of a basis for civilian prospects.

What was slightly dispiriting to me was that after three years of service I was still too young to either vote or drink, and I could not risk the pubs without the armour of uniform. I had continued to grow and to fill out a little, but I still had no need to shave and preserved a youthful appearance at a time when it was not at all appreciated by me. I was at this time also still quite under-confident of my social abilities, although service had endowed me with a degree of confidence in my performance as a soldier. I continued to mask my shyness with alcohol and consequently often drank far more than was good for me.

Little stigma then attached to a scale of drinking which today would be considered quite unacceptable, and hard drinking often went with a particular territory, be it soldiering or mining. My father drank heroic amounts of beer and he was known to shift twenty and more pints in a session. I do not believe that he was an alcoholic, but he was certainly a heavy drinker and drink doubtless contributed to the cancer that killed him. At that time, however, and in many places heavy drinking was an accepted fact of social life.

I became a member of the Mines & City Worker's Club in Boulder, a men only facility which thronged with workers at the end of the day, and again in the summer evenings after the men had returned briefly home for a meal. Its walls were hung with staid portraits of past presidents and committee men, who looked sternly down as the pack at the long bar queued for foaming pots, glasses or jugs of Hannan's Lager, brewed in Kalgoorlie. I went there with Dad, learning to enjoy his conversation and company, and setting a periodic routine for what remained of the decade. Occasionally we would go home late at night to bed, only to find, when the alcohol had worn off, that it was too hot to sleep, and we would sit together over cigarettes and a brew of tea in the kitchen, discussing this or that. In a diary note from that time, I counted myself lucky to have a father who also was a companion.

By New Year's Day I had been almost two months out of the service - and out of a job - and still with no clear idea of what I wanted to do. Inexorably, I was drawn to the idea of another term of enlistment and I duly applied, expecting to be summoned in a matter of days. Inexplicably, I was not required for medical until March and it was apparent by then that I had wasted not just time but the product of my thrift over the previous three years. I had saved £440 at the time of my discharge, which would have bought a fairly recent car or even a house of sorts.[1] Instead, I had largely squandered the cash on frequent and late drinking, in addition to wasting my days with late sleep.

The delay was never accounted for and clearly it derived from no press of recruits, since few were at the medical I attended and the personnel depot, when I arrived there in April, was virtually empty of recruits.

The Guildford camp had by now closed, or was transferred to other purpose, and I reported to Karrakatta, which stood on the Perth-Fremantle railway line a few miles from the city. I took the 'Rattler' from Kalgoorlie, found my way to the camp and reported to the Depot Sar'Major, Andy Anderson, who was a long-serving warrant

---

[1] The house at 271 was sold at this time for £350, having been rented for a time to a tenant named Stubbs who inconsiderately used the internal doors for firewood.

officer of the artillery. My papers were stamped: 'Recruit Training Waived' but I was informed that my onward move to trade training was deferred a couple of weeks since the receiving camp was not yet ready to assemble a course.

This time I had elected to join the Service Corps as a driver, fearing that reenlistment in the infantry might see me patrolling the Old Coach Road again, rather than being sent to the exotic attractions of the Far East.

Karrakatta in the autumn was pleasant and the duties were not onerous. I renewed acquaintance with Danny Wright, now serving with the SAS in the nearby Campbell Barracks, at Swanbourne, although I did not see a great deal of him since he was doing fourteen day's CB (Confined to Barracks) for allowing a civilian to enter the barracks. I thought it very likely that Danny's guest had been a female.

Among my duties was to collect a prisoner from the Guardroom and escort him about the tasks we were both given. Les Musgrave was from the North of England and a former member of the Parachute Regiment. He had enlisted in the UK specifically to serve with the SAS but was told upon arrival, in Sydney, that he would first have to complete a year with an infantry battalion. Les promptly walked out of the Sydney camp and hitchhiked across to the West to plead his case directly to the Campbell Barracks CO. He was now awaiting court martial, and was eventually sentenced to the term that he had already been confined for, prior to being posted to the SAS. A victory for common sense.

Les had abundant good humour and a fund of amusing stories about his previous experience in the British Army. Occasionally, we were able to slide away from the job in hand and seek refuge in the kitchen. The cook there was prepared to hold bottles of beer for us in the fridge, in return for payment in kind, and after one lengthy session we were caught at it by the Provost Sergeant. He, too, however, was a good bloke and he joined us for a drink without a word.

I sometimes had to work under the direction of an engineer corporal, Ken Colbung, known as Darkie, since he was an Aborigine. I do not suppose that he is known by the nickname these days, since he rose to prominence as an Aboriginal Rights man in the Seventies. We did not hit it off immediately but I came to recognize him also as a good bloke.

I also found Orderly Room employment on the camp

switchboard, but this proved brief since I seldom succeeded in transferring any calls. The Orderly Room was run by an elderly corporal who was so deaf that his responses to questions were wholly unconnected, lending an even more surreal atmosphere to proceedings.

The Depot was commanded by Captain Marshall, who was an ex-ranker and a Military Medallist of WW II service. He was an affable man but slightly less so with me when I nearly succeeded in gassing him and his HQ staff. Late one Friday I was despatched to clean the HQ latrines, armed with little more than a mop, a bog brush and a tin of chloride of lime. I mixed the entire contents of the tin and spread it copiously about before rushing off for a 'happy hour' drink at the Canteen. By Monday morning the autumn heat had developed fumes from the concentrate and the entire building could not be used until it was thoroughly ventilated.

Having arrived at Karrakatta with just 25/- remaining from my savings, I looked forward to my first payday with considerable anticipation. Life until then had to be very sober, although I was rediscovering the simple delights of lying on the cot with a hand-rolled cigarette, reading a paperback or listening to the wireless. Patsy Cline had a hit record with '*Crazy*' and she would repeat it, posthumously, thirty-two years later.

An occupant of the block was a member of the artillery known to all simply as 'Gunner'. He had served since 1942 and had not risen above the rank of private. He also had an elder brother who had served before and since the war in the same rank. Gunner was distinctly odd, and I sometimes speculated that he might in fact be an escapee from a mental home which was adjacent to the camp, and whose occupants were not only dressed in khaki protective dress which was identical to ours, but who also tended to shuffle about as aimlessly as we.

Just about the time that life in Karrakatta was becoming tedious, my draft notice came in and I prepared for the journey to Puckapunyal, last seen during the Sabre-Foot exercise. Pucka was also home to the Royal Australian Army Service Corps and I was to undergo basic and driver training there. I boarded the train at Perth for the overnight journey to Kalgoorlie and shared a compartment with three jockeys, which at least relieved the usual problem of crowding. At some low point of the night during one of the interminable stops, one of the jockeys stuck his head out of the window to identify the station. "We're at some place called Bovril." He announced.

Andy Anderson had allowed me to break my journey briefly at Kalgoorlie and I had two days at home before continuing the journey. The break coincided with Anzac Day and I went with Dad to attend the Boulder RSL. I happened to be the youngest there whilst the oldest member was ninety-three. He still possessed a fine baritone voice and he sang several songs.

When I boarded the Trans, the company seemed good and it included a chap who owned a piano accordion and a tape recorder. Unfortunately, he turned out to be a homosexual and I invited him, less than cordially, to find new quarters.

Breaks in Adelaide and Melbourne were welcome, particularly since only the Trans offered sleeping accommodation at second class prices, and I did some drinking at Young & Jackson's, where 'Chloe' still adorned the bar. I got drinking with an elderly Italian migrant who had worked on the Goldfields before the war, and who recalled Walter Lindrum. Lindrum was a native of Kalgoorlie and in later life he held fifty-seven world billiards' titles. Kalgoorlie's other famous person was Eileen Joyce, concert pianist and slightly less well known. Possibly because she held no world billiards' titles.

11

Having arrived at Puckapunyal in the evening and spent the night sharing the picquet hut with the Guard, I reported to the RAASC Centre and learned there that my trade training would not start for a week or two. In the meantime I was to be employed as a steward in the Sergeants' Mess bar. This was a piece of unwelcome news, since I felt that my renewed service had suffered sufficient delays already, and nor was I enamoured of the prospect of becoming a 'boozer's labourer'. The job quickly proved to be characterised by early starts, late finishes and very little of interest in between. There was some excitement one evening when a fight developed between two sergeants and I took advantage of the commotion this caused by gulping down two glasses of beer.

When I became really fed up with the job, which took days only, I began to drink quite overtly behind the bar. One of the SNCOs frowned at me one evening, saying, "Don't you think you ought to pay for one of those occasionally?" I shook my head and poured another. As a strategy to get myself thrown out of the job, this worked but I only got thrown as far as the Officers' Mess to do the same job. Some you didn't win.

I celebrated my twenty-first birthday on duty in the Officers' Mess and doubtless was the only sober member there. The Mess had a good number of ex-rankers, who were the best of the bunch from a steward's point of view, and some Duntroon men who were completely up themselves. I tried to lose the job by wildly varying the drinks' prices and adjusting the barrel gas and the cooler to serve the flattest and warmest beer in the world, but to no avail. The trade course eventually assembled though and I made my escape. I have not worked in a bar since and I don't suppose I ever shall.

Kapyong Barracks was newly built in brick and provided comfortable accommodation. As trainees we were subjected to reveille parades, bed packs and room inspections, but I quickly sensed that the Centre JNCOs had little enthusiasm for such duties. The food was good although we still spent plenty on rolls and pies in the Canteen after duty, along with fairly inordinate amounts of beer.

I was smoking again, having stopped entirely in the last nine months of my previous service, and I now embarked upon a fitness campaign that put me in the camp gymnasium a few nights each week. This zeal did not extend to sports' afternoon, however, where a few of us found little interest in the organised games. We soon learned that tennis was among the options, though, and one which did not appear to be closely supervised. A growing number of us began to turn up at the Wednesday afternoon parade sporting a tennis racquet, prior to a quick double back to the block to practice some Egyptian PT. This deception only lasted until an observant physical training instructor noticed that, whilst every available racquet had been signed out of the store, not a single ball had. On the following Wednesday the 'tennis players' were invited to board a lorry which then dumped us at the foot of a long hill, some fourteen miles from Pucka. We were invited to practice our lobs and volleys on the walk back and the lorry rumbled away. A fair one.

The basic trade training was neither lengthy nor particularly enlightening. We learned that the Corps motto was *Par Oneri* (Equal to the Task) and what RAASC establishments existed in the recently established Pentropic Division. We paraded often and at inspection the RSM pronounced my boots the best he had ever seen. This was gratifying until the RSM's boots appeared before me with the instruction to perform a similar miracle upon them. I did get 15/- for this work, however.

A score of trainees had assembled, mostly from Kapooka but also including two UK enlistments. One of these was Dave Armstrong, a former National Serviceman with the 1/3 East Anglians, who had completed a tour in Malaya at much the same time as Arch had been there. Following demob, Dave had returned to his job as a Fitter in the Dagenham Ford plant, but was unsettled and decided to enlist. The other UK man was a Scot, Dave Grubb. Dave was incredibly scruffy in virtually every aspect of his dress, but the Korea and United Nations ribbons on his battledress breast appeared to divert criticism. Dave Armstrong was a few years older than I but we struck up a friendship immediately. Four decades later, and despite living half a world apart, we still meet from time to time.

With the trade training over, we were again in limbo until the driving course might begin, and another round of duties appeared. What passed for social life ran in the same familiar groove, with much drinking on the 'pay' weekend, followed by a fairly lean week. The lean week might be augmented by collecting empty bottles for return of deposit at the Canteen, and several of us vied for the title of 'Bottle Baron' at the time. It was considered entirely ethical to pinch your mate's bottles if he was insufficiently protective of them. On some other occasion, a group of us picked a load of mushrooms in local fields and swapped them at a town pub for beer. I wonder if soldiers do that sort of thing now?

The news from home was that Arch had bought a '59 Holden, which he would drive across from the East for his SAS service, and that I had inherited £35 in Gran'Ma's will. I have no idea how I spent the money, but I suspect that it was unwisely.

During a weekend off I stayed with a group at the 'White Ensign Club' in Melbourne, another version of 'Johnnies' in Sydney. I walked into the ablutions one morning and there encountered Colin Keoskie, who had been one of the training team on my platoon at Kapooka. It was an early example among very many since of unlikely meetings.

An unpopular corporal was the duty NCO one evening and he borrowed my alarm clock. I somehow neglected to tell him that the clock lost an hour overnight and no less a person than the RSM discovered the lack of a reveille parade. The Orderly Corporal got a huge bollocking from the RSM, but so, subsequently, did Private Foxley. Worth it, though.

The preliminaries to the driving course included a colour perception test, where we identified numbers that were buried in fields of coloured dots. A dozen of us failed this test and were taken down to Melbourne to undergo another sort of test at Watsonia Barracks. We were all cleared this time by a puzzled examiner, and it turned out that the bloke who administered the test at Pucka was himself colour blind.

The driving course began and we were grouped in four or five to a number of Ford and Chevrolet Towing Tractors. These were squat V8-engined vehicles of wartime vintage, designed to tow twenty-five pounder artillery pieces into battle. Each student took a turn at the wheel whilst the remainder huddled in greatcoats at the largely open cab at the rear of the vehicle, as we toured the wintry environs of camp and beyond.

I discovered that the students included two named Quail and Partridge and these proved to be birds of a strange feather. Either of them had the ability to bore for Australia, as I learned when it was my misfortune to be wedged between them in the arty tractor once.

The course, designed to run for seven weeks, was abruptly suspended in the second week in order that some of the students could undergo an air dispatcher's course. This sounded very interesting and Dave Armstrong and I were among the first volunteers. We learned that a new air despatch platoon was to be formed near Sydney and trained crews were required for it.

The AD course was to run for three weeks and about a score of us had elected for the training. We were to learn how to pack a variety of stores for dropping from aircraft, how to rig them with parachutes and how to calculate the correct weight and balance for aircraft loading. I had some advantage here, having a year or two before attended an air loader's course while serving with 2 RAR, and the cargo manifest was a lot less daunting than it might otherwise have seemed.

We were taught G Factors and restraint criteria, and how to calculate the safe working stress for the manilla and hemp cordage we used to bind the loads. We also had a formula for calculating the strength of steel wire rope (twelve times the diameter squared, expressed in hundredweights, should you be dying to know) and for a while we were walking compendia of calculations.

The Centre had the fuselage of a redundant Dakota (DC3) aircraft, and also a mock up of a C130 fuselage, to allow practice in loading, lashing and despatching. It was heavy but agreeable work and we had the prospect of live despatching from Dakotas to look forward to in the second week of the course.

We added Drop Zone recce, selection and marking to other skills which included knots and lashings, and we manned and cleared the DZs when the dropping programme began. The flying programme was the best of it, as we sat aft of the load looking out through the open space where one half of the port loading doors had been removed. A crew of four operated; two to drag the load down to the despatching board which was roughly the size of a kitchen table, and two to tip the board and despatch the load on a green light signal from the pilot. Again, this could be heavy work, with some of the packs weighing three hundred pounds (and more than that if the pilot was pulling 'G' just when the load was being manhandled to the door), but it was exhilarating work.

Although we did not work with the C130 Hercules during the

course, we had to pass an examination on weight and balance problems, and this might involve some serious long division and multiplication in a day when pocket calculators did not exist. Conscious of my limited schooling, I devoted some extra evening hours to such problems since I had no wish to fail at any aspect of the training. The air despatch platoon now looked infinitely more attractive than some transport company.

Whereas the Dakota had a payload of just five thousand pounds, the C130 increased that to thirty-five thousand pounds and the range of the load was astonishing. A Dakota could carry a Jeep (although not a Land Rover), but the C130 could comfortably carry a couple of four-ton lorries and a mound of equipment besides. This meant, however, a fairly complicated loading programme according to centres of gravity stations aft of the aircraft nose, ensuring that the aircraft flew within safe limits. The optimum Centre of Gravity for the Hercules was 525.2 inches from the nose and the safe limits forward and aft of this figure had to fall within a few inches. Hence the extra study to get this aspect of the exam right.

At the close of the third week we completed final practical exams and a ninety-minute written paper. I was subsequently most pleased to not only pass the course but to record the highest marks. This looked a good augury for the future. We put aside our course notes and prepared to resume the driving course.

Our memories were now required to cope with the types and grades of oil used in engines, gearboxes and differentials, and each Friday we de-greased the Tractor engines, replaced the oils and greased the steering linkages. We had about forty minutes of driving each per day, and the routes took us variously through Bendigo, Benalla and Ballarat. We added Nagambie and Shepparton and drove through Bandiana to Glenrowan - made infamous by the Kelly gang a century before.

I was by now beginning to manifest some problems with my driving, being less than confident in control, although I could think of no good reason why. This did not improve when we switched to Austin Champs for some inner city driving around Melbourne. The Champ was a Rolls-Royce-engined equivalent of the American Jeep, and very nippy, but my nippiness through two red traffic lights in succession did not earn approbation from the instructor. The Champ was also good for a small joke, since it had no reverse gear, but a lever that reversed the entire box. The trick was to engage the driver's attention whilst an accomplice quietly engaged the reverse lever, with the result that the driver might rev up and vanish at a rate of knots - backwards.

My humour was poor, however, when I was warned for the 'chop ride' with the senior instructor. Four of us were so warned and all four of us were duly chopped, being asked in fairly short order whether we preferred postings as stewards or storemen. Two requested steward jobs, one requested discharge and I asked for a corps transfer back to the infantry. In the meantime we were detailed to mess duties, where we worked from 0600hrs to 2000hrs, under the supervision of a corporal who read Superman comics all day.

News from home included the information that Arch had topped his parachute course, and in an Army newspaper report I read of a terrorist action in Malaya which included the names of former comrades. The Malayan Campaign had officially ended at the close of 1960, but clearly there was activity there still. I felt utterly out of everything and wondering what else might go wrong. The following day I learned that I was posted to a supply depot.

12

Changing trains because of different rail gauges was still a necessity and a nuisance. The change between Melbourne and Sydney was at Albury, near the border, and Albury shared with Kalgoorlie the distinction of the longest platforms in the country. It came as no surprise to half-asleep Diggers that the carriages they vacated were just about as far as it was possible to be from the new carriage.

At Sydney I made the short journey to Randwick camp and renewed acquaintance with Dave Armstrong and Co. since Randwick was also where the new air supply platoon was to form. That had not yet happened and I was somewhat mollified to learn that the product of the recent course had done nothing yet but mow lawns and sweep up litter. I found a bedspace in the same lines, which were a small assembly of wooden huts, and I settled in.

The supply depot was about four hundred yards down the road and I reported in with a corporal who also lived in the lines. His conversation made clear his view that supply work was the most exciting of all challenges, and I thought that he was a complete tit. I discovered that the depot had a staff of twelve, commanded by a captain, and that I was one of three privates, but the only storeman. The others at my rank were the driver and the clerk.

Among the discoveries was that we hardly wore a uniform at all, simply dark blue overalls - although the brass buttons on the blouse polished up nicely - and that my first job each day was to clean the latrines. The rest of the job was depressingly similar to duties I had done until four years before, and I soon submitted a new application to corps-transfer, complaining that my job was fit only 'for tired, old gentlemen'. This proved a touch inflammatory, but I would not change the wording.

Stacking sugar or despatching bully beef became the deadly dull routine somewhere between cleaning the bogs and lowering the metal roller doors at 1700hrs. Elsewhere, global, nuclear warfare might have been averted by the withdrawal of Soviet missiles from Cuba, and Marilyn Monroe had just died, but these events seemed of very little consequence to me and I distinctly lacked spring feeling.

Two major exercises, 'Springtide' and 'Nutcracker', arrived and since there was a large amount of air supply involved in both of them 40 Air Supply Platoon suddenly blossomed into activity. I felt envious as the mates now spent a lot of time putting their qualification into practice and accruing a healthy number of hours on dropping sorties.

The exercises were to provide also something of a lifeline for me, when the officer commanding 40 heard of my qualification at a time when his platoon was undermanned. I was summoned to interview and advised to apply for a posting to the platoon, and in the meantime representation was made to the supply depot OC to detach me to 40. This was agreed and I believed that my problems were now resolved.

I joined the crew of a corporal, Gary Cole, with whom I had shared the cabin of the De Havilland Dragon a couple of years before. His companion on the same descent was Ray Harvey, now the platoon sergeant on 40. We deployed to the RAAF Station at Richmond, where I added parachute packing to my skills and flew a number of sorties.[1] Renewed happiness was punctured a fortnight later when I was ordered back to the supply depot with no immediate prospect of posting.

I now made an application for SAS selection, although I doubtless overrated my fitness, but made little progress. At the Ingleburn interview my admission of being a non-swimmer precluded further interest and I was advised to try again when I could swim.

The supply depot got busy feeding the exercise troops and issuing fuel. It was sending two thousand, four hundred Jerricans per day to a camp at Singleton, and I worked out the cost of nearly ten thousand gallons of petrol at commercial rates of 3/8d per gallon.

More interestingly, I accompanied an articulated lorry to the Sydney wharves to load stores aboard some ship. My presence was necessary to keep an eye on the lorry whenever the driver might have

---

[1] Arch was in the field at this time and I tried to airdrop him a bottle of Rum, but never drew his particular DZ.

to go in search of someone or other. During a wartime strike, the army had manned the docks and the Wharfies had a long memory of this. It was known for unattended army vehicles to be vandalised or the loads looted.

Between mundane duties and toiling around the sports' field, I embraced the social scene. The city was close but we usually drank in the beach pubs dotted about Coogee or Malabar. I often spent my restricted drawing rate of £16 per fortnight before a new payday appeared, even though it was possible to take change out of a pound home after a lengthy session at the pub.

Camp duties had not entirely gone away and I drew some kitchen chores in the Officers' Mess. The cook there was notable for having had two nervous breakdowns, and he had to be dragged away one evening for threatening the Orderly Officer with a breadknife. The Orderly Officer had made the mistake of turning up late for dinner and demanding a meal.

Dinner was announced by gong in the ante-room and, having had a few drinks in the afternoon, I struck it with such violence one evening that it broke from its suspension and rolled, badly dented, towards the startled, putative diners. I was duly regarded with some apprehension, and probably thought to be a mad brother of the mad cook, but no one terminated my duties.

Another duty was to man the camp back gate and control access each Sunday. The Canteen tended to be popular with civilian visitors, since the wet bar traded when all hotels remained closed. I had already noted that there were sometimes no glasses - and hence no beer - available on Sundays because so many civilians were in. When on the gate I resolutely refused to allow any civilians in at all, which proved controversial, and I never did the duty again.

The latrines seemed to be the fief of an Area Command Digger named Jack Higgins, who was the camp 'Blowfly'. Jack had many years of service but no rank to speak of, although he appeared to be a highly educated man. He was also an alcoholic who went on occasional binges, which would put him into a terrible rage, threatening 'to kill all you bastards'. These rages did not seem especially worrying, although it sometimes appeared prudent to lock the door of the hut if Jack was performing, and he was usually affable. "I don't suppose you've got a rusty old quid you could let me have, Scholar?" was his most frequent conversational gambit.

Since I was so proficient at cleaning bogs, I took a spare time job at a nearby oil refinery, doing just that for 30/- per night. The Boral Refinery boardroom sometimes left unfinished bottles of spirits on the table and finishing them seemed the tidy thing to do. Boral also had an impressive copying machine, the first I had ever seen. My supply depot corporal used it to reproduce some lewd photographs, the mere possession of which in Australia at that time was a gaoling offence.

By Xmas I had amassed £200 in savings but I was not about to blow much of it on leave, having drawn picquet duties over the leave period. This proved exceedingly dull toil, enlivened only by listening to 2UE on a huge Kreisler wireless – gifted by the Women's Guild in 1942.

I sent £50 home to Mam and a bottle of Jamaican Rum for Dad. Some time later Mam wrote and asked me not to send more rum; Dad had a Xmas session in the Mines & City Workers' then went home and drained the bottle. On Xmas Day I was served with dinner by the Officers and SNCOs, and I had received a greetings telegram from home. Otherwise, it seemed not at all festive.

13

The New Year brought me a reprieve, for I was re-posted to 40 Air Supply Platoon, conditional upon passing the driving test. I began a one-to-one course of instruction on a Dodge three-quarter tonner with Tony Dowd, a corporal on 40, and I suddenly acquired confidence which had been wholly absent from my vehicle handling at Pucka. After a week or so of suburban and city driving, I progressed to the Studebaker that I would have to master for the driving examination. The Studebaker was a venerable lorry of wartime design, employing six-wheel drive and actually having ten wheels, although its carrying capacity was not great. It was a left-hand drive vehicle and none of its five forward gears was synchronised. This meant that smooth gear changes were greatly dependent upon the driver's ability to match the road speed with the engine speed, particularly when changing down. I was not adroit at this and reckoned that the grinding noises I produced might just as easily be emanating from the instructor's teeth.

Some months later I was dropped at an Ordnance Depot with instructions to collect a replacement Studebaker for the platoon. I was directed to a shed where stood a large crate and within was the Studebaker, in several pieces. A packing note revealed that the crating had been carried out in 1942 in, I think, Michigan. I had to get a lift back to Randwick and the lorry was collected some other time.

The Studebaker did not convert much of its engine power into road speed, which was just as well since the brakes had to be pumped quite frantically to achieve anything which approached emergency stops. The vehicle also had a very narrow steering lock, as I came to appreciate when I drove the wrong way into Lower Pitt Street, in Sydney one evening.

Rather than continue down the narrow one-way, I decided on a **U** turn and now understood what limited lock really meant as I wrestled the lorry through something like a twenty-three-point turn.

The worst of it was that a pavement drunk watched my efforts and broadcast the event as if it were the Melbourne Cup. **"AND HE'S COMING THROUGH ON THE INSIDE. AND HE'S GOING TO DO IT. NO. WAIT. HE'S LOST IT. HE'S DONE HIS DASH, HE'S SHIT IT. OH, NO. HE'S SHIT IT THIS TIME. HE'S GOING BACK. HE'S GOING BACK AGAIN. HE'S STUFFED IT"** When I finally escaped, it was a question of which burned the most; my face or the clutch.

I completed the short course, was issued a G11 (licence) and gratefully joined a crew on 40. For the moment, there was little prospect of flying duties, after the major exercises at the end of the year, but I was simply glad to be free of confining duties.

Randwick was the home also to 101 Transport Company, which operated domestic supply lorries and the Holden staff cars which serviced the nearby Victoria Barracks, and 42 Company, a water transport unit which was equipped with the amphibious DUKWs of WW II design. In the absence of air supply duties, we were often detached to 101 as relief drivers and this brought some useful trips delivering rations to camps at Singleton or Kapooka. 101 also had a high proportion of WRAAC drivers but although many of these were good-looking girls, we formed few relationships with them. Possibly this was because their quarters were on the far side of Sydney Harbour, and somewhat off-limits even if you made the trip. journey.

40 Air Supply was still quite small at this time, comprising about a dozen from the course I had undergone, together with another dozen from 39 Air Supply Platoon, which was now a wholly CMF[1] unit. Additionally, there were a couple of blokes arrived from 1 Company RAASC, at Holsworthy, which provided transport for the infantry brigade. In the space of a year, however, new arrivals would take the platoon strength to about fifty, and we included a cook, a storeman and a couple of clerks. The platoon was led by a captain, with a 2nd lieutenant as the 2ic.

Australia had maintained the techniques of air supply after having gained considerable experience in them during the New Guinea campaign in WW II. Britain had resurrected air supply units when the Malayan Emergency, which endured for twelve years, produced the

---

[1] The Citizen's Military Forces; the equivalent, in Australia, of the Territorial Army in the UK.

need to re-supply antiterrorist patrols which might be combing the jungle for three weeks at a stretch. In the meantime, much of the heavy drop technology was being pioneered by the Americans.

At the conclusion of our AD course at Pucka, the Commandant, Colonel Blake, had told us that we were in on the ground floor of a developing application, and could go far with it. This did not mean much at the time, although we began to realise the implications when half a dozen of us from that course were selected for promotion training, with every prospect of promotion before the year was out.

This training was conducted at Randwick and we had four separate subjects to pass. In addition to purely trade ability, we also had to demonstrate an understanding of administration and military law, and, not least, an ability to function as a section commander in the infantry role. Irrespective of corps, all promotion had to be underpinned by infantry skills which, potentially at least, put every one of us behind a bayonet. It would be a few years before I was to encounter service where this did not apply, and I would be a witness to some of the problems that the deficiency produced.

We completed the course and returned to a mix of driving duties and the odd stint of despatching, slowly building hours and sorties to brevet awards. Forty sorties entitled one to the winged AD badge which was worn on the left sleeve, and only the members who had arrived from 39 Platoon presently wore them. Operational sorties, we learned, counted as double, and we had some prospect of acquiring such since a detachment to Malaya was pending.

Air supply to jungle forts and patrols within Malaya was conducted by the Royal Army Service Corps, based at RAF Changi, Seletar and Tengah on Singapore Island. The 39 Platoon men had already undergone a three-month detachment, whilst one which included members of my AD course had gone to Singapore at about the time of the promotion training. We were scheduled to go in August, during the Australian winter.

The weeks to this passed agreeably enough since the platoon duties were varied and interesting and the social life was good. Members of the platoon struck up friendships with nurses from the local hospital and we were frequently invited to parties, although some of us were not sober guests. I went to one in the early evening having had a lengthy session during the day, and realised, as I sat down, that I was already quite drunk. Applying a drunk's logic, I decided that eating a few handfuls of crisps off a plate before me might help me to sober up and I tucked in. I was coming to the conclusion that the crisps were not at all tasty when one of the nurses put a question to me. "Why," She wanted to know, "are you eating peanut shells?"

I had achieved good scores on the promotion course, assisted no doubt by previous experience, and although the pass was not particularly distinguished I was now interviewed by the OC, Captain Howes, with a view to commissioning. This surprised me but I promised to give it some thought, realising that I would first have to address my lack of academic qualifications. This was something that had occurred to me from time to time, irrespective of promotion, since I often keenly felt disadvantaged by the premature termination of my schooling.

For the moment, however, training went on and I was more than happy with it, especially the flying side. The Australian air force then operated a score of Dakotas and these provided the usual mount for our exercises, where the hard work and long hours in the packing sheds produced a couple of hours flying to some DZ to despatch dummy loads of food, water, fuel and ammunition. The Dakota was a noisy bird and conversation without a headset was quite impossible. We therefore depended upon slick drills and a few hand signals to achieve the despatch of the door bundles. Rubber-soled boots were still not an issue item and to protect the aluminium floor of the aircraft we were issued with a boot that had a canvas and rope sole. Since we also wore them about the packing sheds, to avoid constant changes of footwear, it soon looked as if we were strolling about with a couple of mops tied to our feet.

In August, about ten of us boarded a Boeing 707 at Mascot and flew to Singapore on a secondment to 55 Company RASC at Seletar. We mostly wore suits and these were really useful to us as we trudged across the apron at Paya Lebar airport, feeling as if we had walked into a Turkish bath.

55 Coy made us welcome, issued us with hose tops, puttees, OG shorts and Bush Jackets with a Dakota badge sewn on the sleeves, and allocated us to crews to learn the new ropes. Specifically, we were to add some experience of heavy drop techniques, which was the way forward in air despatch, but there was still plenty of door bundle work to do with smaller aircraft.

The platform for the heavy drops was the Blackburn Beverley, a huge aircraft that had been in service with the RAF about ten years. If I had once marvelled that something as large as the C130 could fly, I was now astonished that the Beverley could even lift itself off the runway. It had been memorably described as 'a block of flats with wings', which summed up the cavernous fuselage. The flight deck was thirty-five feet above the ground and flat out the aircraft could make about a hundred and eighty knots. More impressively, it then held the record (and possibly still does) for the heaviest single airdrop - some twenty tons.

The Bristol Freighter (or 'Frightener' for its ungainly appearance that suggested anything but a flying machine) was a smaller, twin-engined aircraft and originally designed as a cross-channel car ferry operating between England and France. We also flew sorties in the Handley Page Hastings, which was a close relative of the wartime Halifax bomber, and were disconcerted by its take-off run, which seemed to last forever.

Despatching door bundles, by parachute or free-fall, was also conducted on the Scottish Aviation Twin- and Single-Pioneer types. The single-pin was reputedly based on the German Feisler *Storch*, a wartime design that had incredibly short landing and take-off characteristics. At full flaps, the single-pin seemed to double its wing surface and it flew extremely slowly, whilst the despatcher, seated behind the pilot with the bundle balanced across his knees, waited for the nod to heave it out. I am reasonably certain that I once glanced over the side of the cockpit as we 'ran in' and saw a man running parallel to our flight path along the DZ and gradually overtaking us.

Singapore was hot and humid but some allowance was made for this in our working routine. We paraded at 0700hrs and ceased at 1300hrs, unless a late sortie was being flown, and we were intended to rest during the heat of the afternoon. In practice, we usually went directly to the midday meal - which never once failed to serve chips during the detachment - and from there to either the NAAFI or the Malcolm Club (an all ranks facility) for several pints.

The draught beer was a Singaporean brew, Tiger or Anchor and tasted greatly of chemicals, although that did not inhibit our drinking, particularly in view of the fact that it was duty-free and cheap. Cigarettes also were duty-free and we normally bought tins of Player's at 2/6d for fifty. Apart from the low cost of just about everything, our wages were at least double that of the British Other Ranks we worked with.

We had been made welcome by the BORs but in our

enthusiasm to be accepted we doubtless adopted some of the more egregious aspects of their behaviour, especially in their treatment of the locals. During drinking runs to the local village of Jalan Kayu it became our practice to steal a bicycle to ride home, whereas others might catch a taxi then disappear without paying on arrival. The various people who worked within the lines, boot boys, *dhobi wallahs* etc., were seldom the recipients of much kindness and occasionally swindled. We had already noticed that BORs seemed not to be greatly loved by their officers - and occasionally not even acknowledged - and perhaps the psychology of this was that the BORs felt obliged despise someone else. We regrettably emulated this to some degree and became the ugly Australians for a time.

Among our early discoveries were the brothels of Singapore and districts that offered the availability and variety of sex at a range of prices to suit the soldier's pocket. The lower end of the scale might be commensurate with a high rate of the venereal disease that we were frequently warned of - and VD was the reason that the brothels were out of bounds - but we seldom remembered such advice until *after* a brothel visit. Tattooist's parlours proved to be out of bounds for the same reason (dirty needles possibly spreading VD), yet we just as cheerfully visited those establishments as well. We were clearly conforming to traditional images of troops abroad.

We added the Vicker's Valetta to our flying logbooks, learning that it was known to ground crews as 'the Pig'. It could also be a pig to despatching crews as well, since the main spar ran through the fuselage to a height of about eighteen inches. All cargo stowed forward of the spar had to be lifted over it for despatch, and this was a real problem if that act happened to coincide with the pilot pulling 'G' as he banked the aircraft for a subsequent run along the DZ.

At about the middle of the detachment we were split into two groups and I was appointed to the command of half and take them to Penang, where we would fly sorties from the RAAF base at Butterworth. We were released from Seletar early in the day, paid and dropped at the railway station with several hours to fill before the overnight train left.

This combination of circumstances meant that we were very drunk by the time the train actually pulled out, and although we had sleeping accommodation we lacked the sense to go to it. At a late stage of the evening I decided to take a walk along the top of the carriages and might have been wiped off them by some bridge or tunnel, had I not been spotted by a conductor and brought down. This was drinking to, and beyond, the point of stupidity, but I was not yet cognisant of this. New lessons awaited.

At Changi we operated in the familiar Dakotas, flown by Australian crews, and we added some operational sorties, red-inked in the logbooks. British and Australian forces were currently suppressing the Brunei Revolt, which had broken out in the previous year, and we supplied some of the ground units. Malaya, formerly a British colony, had sought a Federation of Malaysia, incorporating Singapore, Sabah, Sarawak and Brunei. This was opposed by the Indonesians, who harboured expansionist ideas, and they fomented insurrection. Indonesian activity and infiltration increased after Federation in September '63, and British and Commonwealth troops combined to meet the threat. Geographically, the affair was of more than academic interest to Australia, and confrontation continued until the Indonesian president, Sukarno, was ousted in a coup in 1966. We also routinely supplied the jungle forts, which were manned by Malay policemen, and these sorties might have us in the air for three or four hours. It was a relief to escape the humidity on the ground in the cooler air at a few thousand feet, gazing through the doors at the apparently endless vista of an olive-green jungle canopy. We could only guess at how hard a slog it might be for the troops on the ground.

Among the troops were Ghurkha units, who had to be supplied with live chickens for some religious reason of food preparation. This was achieved by nailing together simple wooden boxes that were strapped to other drop items on the afternoon prior to sorties. On the day itself, the chickens were taken to the packing area and stuffed through the box slats. It happened that some of the slats were more generous apertures than recommended, and occasionally the slipstream at the moment of despatch would blow a chicken clean out of the box. The chicken then had about five hundred feet in which to learn how to fly, although I never saw this achieved.

Early in the detachment I was promoted to corporal, which was gratifying. I now ran a crew of my own and began to add sorties to the magical forty, although it was apparent that we would not achieve this in what remained of our attachment to 55 Coy. When it was time to return to Seletar we again drank unwisely and a number of us dived off the Penang ferry as it neared the Georgetown dock. This was a particularly stupid act for a non-swimmer. We then compounded this by jumping off the train as it left the station, returning to the detachment lines. I lost my bush jacket during this escapade and the next day had to wear one belonging to Dave Armstrong, who had about three stones on me. As ill luck would have it, our own OC was visiting from Brunei that day and I was paraded to him. He was not greatly amused by the example his new JNCO was setting for the troops.

Having returned to Seletar, we were further detached to RAF Changi, an airfield just a few miles away, to proceed with training sorties of the door bundle type. The camp also contained a squadron of RAF Regiment and there had been a history of fighting between their lads and the BORs. We saw little reason for this and neither had any desire to get involved, but nevertheless became embroiled in a couple of fights in the NAAFI simply because we wore the distinguishing badges of 55 Coy. The fights usually ended when the RAF Police put their German Shepherds through the door.

We noted some water shortages that meant that showers and even lavatory flushes were turned off. Forty-four gallon drums filled with seawater were substituted, although we also noted that few of our hosts ever bothered flushing the lavatories.

RAF Changi included a school of land air warfare, which trained parachutists, and since a few of my detachment were para-trained the school invited me to fill some seats on a training descent. Since no one in authority appeared to know who was qualified and who was not, I added my own name to the list, although two of the trained men declined. I then quietly haunted the parachute training hangar for a few days, gleaning clues on aircraft and exit drills, although I had some idea at least about how to land.

The whole stick had to undergo ground training prior to the jump, and I was nonplussed when the parachute jump instructor called me out to service the equipment container we would be jumping with. I hadn't the first clue and simply fumbled about with straps and pins until he took over the task.

The aircraft was a Hastings and we were grouped in threes to exit simultaneously from the port and starboard doors. I was in the second stick on the port side, but my group was sent back from the door twice because low cloud was obscuring the DZ and the jump markers. We were eventually despatched, with a Royal Marine leading the stick. When I lowered my leg bag, it actually landed atop his canopy, but eventually slid off and we separated to make unremarkable landings.

This might have been a good note to end the detachment on, except that I joined a group in a brothel visit after a film show one Sunday evening, and we were arrested there by the RMP. I spent a night in cells at Seletar, was duly charged and reprimanded and advised that my OC would be notified. I had the uncomfortable feeling that I would be due for interview when we returned to Randwick. I was not wrong.

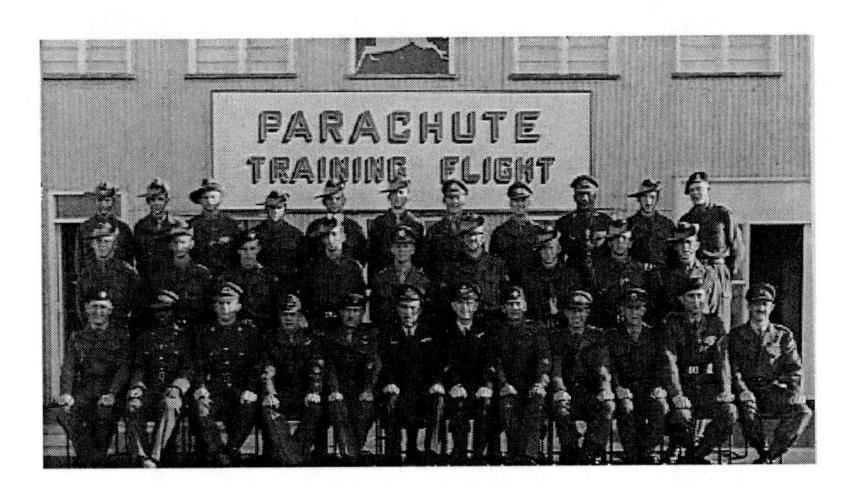

Basic Assault Parachutist Course RAAF Williamtown

40 Air Supply Platoon RAAF Richmond 1963

14

At an interview with Captain Howes I was simply informed that the incidents in Penang and Singapore were two strikes; I would be out on a third and bound for some supply depot or transport company. Commissioning was not mentioned again and I fear that the brothel escapade had convinced the OC, who I believe was a lay preacher, that I was not, after all, fit material for the Officers' Mess. At the same time, and somewhat to my surprise, I was selected to undergo promotion training to qualify in the rank of sergeant. This suggested to me that my egregious behaviour socially had not entirely eclipsed my work record, and I resolved to work hard at redemption.

We ended the year upon the note of a lengthy exercise that added more sorties to the total. John F Kennedy was assassinated at some time during the exercise although I recall no particular sense of shock at the news. It is certainly another twentieth century myth that everyone remembers exactly what they were doing at the time.

When I went home to Boulder I took Dave Armstrong with me. He had made one trip home to his folks in the UK but was at a loose end for this particular Xmas. Arch was also home, although he was making more frequent visits in view of the SAS posting within the State. My cousin Phyllis now worked as a nurse in Kalgoorlie and I met and struck up a relationship with Val, her friend. This relationship, although it lasted for eighteen months, was destined to remain platonic. Val had, she told me, seen too many of her friends go 'down below' and had no intention of following their example. The contraceptive pill was not yet freely available, and it would require the AIDs problem a couple of decades later to make the condom an acceptable accessory to sex. Val was good company though and we maintained a steady correspondence after the leave. I actually felt quite guilty whenever I exploited sexual opportunities elsewhere at the time, recognising that for some of a certain age in the supposedly 'Swinging Sixties' there remained a legacy of uncertainty from the Fifties. If some of us were sexually repressed, at least we had not invented the condition.

Upon return to Randwick I volunteered for everything and consequently was detached alone or with a small team to various exercises. The infantry battalions were in the process of expansion and 4 RAR formed in South Australia. I took a team down and we were intended to supply the battalion by air using only Cessna 172 aircraft, which carried under-slung loads on each wing.

Our preparation was complicated by an absence of packing crates and when I requested these we received instead a pile of timber and a couple of pounds of nails. We also lacked the thread which had a specific breaking weight, and which was used to secure the petals of the parachute packs until the load fell free of the aircraft, paying out the static line which deployed the parachute. I experimented with some strands of nylon from the core of parachute cord, believing that I had found a usable substitute. A day or two later, one of the pilots returned reporting that the twenty-eight-foot diameter canopy had inflated whilst still firmly attached to the wing, changing his heading by ninety degrees pretty quickly. Until that time it had been speculated that such an occurrence might tear the wing off a Cessna. Happily not so.

We were under continual pressure to meet supply deadlines, and took some pride in doing so, even when late additions to loads were requested. On one occasion I kept adding to an existing wing load until even *I* felt uneasy about it. The frontal area of such loads was not supposed to exceed two hundred square inches - about the end area of a forty-four-gallon drum - nor two hundred and fifty pounds in weight. The load this time was beginning to assume the proportions of a grand piano.

The grass strip had a mound about half way along its length that the Cessnas usually cleared at take-off. This time, the engine roared and the kite rocked against the brakes then sluggishly rolled down the strip. The Cessna crossed the mound, vanished beyond sight and eventually lurched into the air, narrowly missing some trees beyond the edge of the clearing. The pilot, whom we had already noted as something of a 'line-shooter', looked particularly thoughtful when he returned and thereafter seemed to take more interest in the loads we strapped to his aircraft.

Continually packing supplies, re-packing 'chutes and meeting the deadlines put us to an eighteen-hour day and it was a week before I felt able to visit the mobile showers which had been erected in the Echelon. I chose a time of day when it was likely to be quiet and there was just some old bloke under one of the canvas buckets when I stripped off. He asked me how I was going and I took the opportunity to have a really good whinge. A few days later we attended a barbeque to mark the end of the exercise and the 'old bloke' turned out to be the 4 RAR Commanding Officer.

Things were quiet at Randwick and I did the promotion subjects in addition to attending a Class 2 education course. All of this went well and I felt that I was retrieving my reputation somewhat. Other detachments followed and I did some more work with Cessna, greatly envying the pilots of these.

At Easter we manned a display at the Sydney Showground, but it had little appeal for visitors, being mainly a display of heavy drop items which did not compare with artillery field pieces or small arms on view elsewhere. One of our exhibits was the 'Storpedo', a WW II air drop container made of compressed cardboard. It had a pointed nose, designed to crumple on impact with the ground and absorb the shock, and a Hessian parachute in the tail. It was painted red and looked a little, to small boys anyway, like a bomb. I manned the stance with a Lance-Jack named Chook Fowles, whose tolerance of small boys was pretty slim. A couple of them approached the display and regarded the 'bomb'. "What happens if I kick this bomb, Mister?" Asked one. "What happens?" Repeated Chook. "I kick your arse. That's what happens."

We were no longer drinking in large groups, as the blokes began to develop relationships which led to engagements and a couple of marriages, and nor was I particularly in tune with some of the newer blokes who joined the platoon. I drank alone for a while until I began to worry about the direction this might be taking me in. I had recognised by now that I mostly drank to mask a crippling shyness, socially, and I decided at last to consult a psychologist. I had a number of sessions with him in Sydney, usually arranging them for sports' afternoon, and these helped although they were costly. A two-hour session left little change out of a week's wages.

Whether it was attributable to the sessions, or merely a natural progression, I had the sudden sense that I had matured and problems of self-confidence evaporated. I felt that this should have happened much earlier in my service, but better late than not at all. Unfortunately, I continued to base my social life upon alcohol and it would take a number of years to see the error of that. In the meantime, my fears of personality defects were put nicely into perspective when, in the foyer of a city theatre, I struck up a conversation with a New Zealand couple who subsequently invited me to their North Shore flat.

It had been a pleasant evening and towards its close my host invited me to examine a genealogical chart which 'proved' that Queen Elizabeth of England was directly descended from Moses (of the Promised Land). I expressed polite interest in this revelation whilst quietly eyeing the door, and my host went on to explain that he and I were actually the true Jews from the Lost Tribe of Israel, whilst the present Israelis and assorted Jews elsewhere were actually a gypsy strain of no Hebrew connection. I was persuaded to attend a meeting with the couple and other friends and the meeting proved to be a religious gathering, attended by about forty people. The service was short on hymns, psalms, the common book of prayer and sermons, being replete instead with cries of **HALLELUJA! PRAISE THE LORD!** among shrieks of unintelligible noise from several of the congregation. The latter, my host had forewarned me, was 'speaking in tongues'. Whilst my companions were absorbed in a communion which had left me untouched, I quietly left the hall and strolled down to Circular Quay. I reckoned I had no problems at all, really.

To our list of aircraft we added the De Havilland Caribou, a short take-off or landing aircraft which was intended to replace the ageing Dakotas.[1] In order to establish just how 'STOL' the new aircraft was, landing runs of successive brevity were attempted at an RAAF base, until one pilot managed to smash the undercarriage on a ridge of earth short of the runway sterile strip. We acquired the fuselage of the aircraft for loading practice. It's an ill wind etc.

At the end of April a dozen of us were returned to the RAASC Centre at Pucka to undergo a month of advanced air despatch training. This introduced us to the techniques of heavy drop, briefly met at Seletar, and qualified us to rig one-ton containers for despatch from C130 and Caribou aircraft. Heavy drop lacked the small team intimacy of the C47, but this clearly was the future of air despatch, and if we now spent far less time stuffing straw into sandbags to make percussion bases for water jerricans, we had the satisfying experience of seeing sixteen one-ton containers go out of a Herc like an express

---

[1] The 'ageing' Dakota continued for another decade in service with the RAAF, which, at this time of writing, preserves four in service. At this time also, air forces world-wide, from Argentina to Zaire, operate some two hundred and fifty C47s.

train.

Weekends were nominally free during the course, although a good deal of homework was required for a **B** pass. We did not neglect the social life entirely but Melbourne proved to have little appeal for us. Barry Humphries, yet to develop his Edna Everage persona, once expressed it pretty concisely. "Melbourne is well placed," He said, "you can be somewhere interesting in six hours."

The army had a ski lodge at Mount Bulla and we elected for a skiing weekend although none of our party actually had any experience. In the event, the early snow did not materialise, but we had the foresight to take several crates of ale along. Also, there was a group of WRAAC that just about matched our number, and we made a convivial crew. Among the WRAAC was a Kalgoorlie girl I had known slightly when she worked for the grocery wholesaler which rivalled my own. I had been quite struck on Norma, but she took a shine on this occasion to the bloke in our crowd who drew women the way a magnet attracts iron filings.

We had travelled to Pucka in an assortment of private vehicles, which included a VW Beetle that broke down. A tow was hitched by a bloke who drove a V-8 Mainline Ford, and was noted for his nerveless driving. He proceeded to tow the VW at speeds in excess of ninety miles an hour, and since the roads were wet the Beetle windscreen was soon totally obscured by mud. It was a most relieved Beetle driver and passenger who eventually were dropped off tow at a garage.

We completed the course and I was pipped for first place by Dave Armstrong, although the **B** grade was welcome. We returned to Randwick and the news that we were to relocate at Holsworthy camp, which was not welcome to our ears. Sports' afternoons at Coogee Beach and a friendly pub at the end of the street were not likely to be replicated at the Holsworthy that I remembered, and we looked forward to the move with some gloom.

Before the move I was visited by Danny Wright, who stayed in the lines for a few days. Danny had been involved in some fight and as a punishment sent back to a battalion for a year. We did a fair bit of drinking and on his last evening had to finance it out of a jar of sixpences I had saved. We then had spaghetti bolognaise to follow and paid for the meals entirely in pennies and halfpennies. The proprietor was really pleased by this.

I also saw Arch in the period, whilst he was over from the West on a course, and our conversation in a Coogee pub was cut short when I was unceremoniously ejected for having responded to an assault gratuitously offered by some patron. Another visitor, and astonishingly so, was Derek Vickers, elder brother of my boyhood friend David. Derek had emigrated and was living in the Randwick area.

If we missed the attractions of the inner suburbs, we at least did not miss the big city, being by now infrequent visitors to it. I had for a time attended a city gymnasium to augment the running programme, but it became apparent that most of the clientele were rather fonder of eyeing their oiled bodies in the tinted mirrors than actually training. If I had a drink in Sydney at all, it tended to be at the dock pubs, which had a reputation for roughness although they seemed to me to be full of character. The Sunday papers were on the streets by Saturday evening, and it became my habit for a while to collect a copy to read in some pub on the Woolloomooloo Docks, where 'Harry's Cafe de Wheels' offered very decent bacon sandwiches for supper.

Kings Cross held few attractions. The area had a distinctly sleazy atmosphere and to walk alone in the Cross was to invite being trailed by a homosexual, or a posse of them. I preferred to drink at the pubs in the adjacent area of Taylor Square, which seemed to be the hub of the pawnshop world. I have a recurring dream in which I am striding the streets of an unfamiliar city, looking for somewhere familiar. I think that it is Taylor Square I am looking for.

"What happens if I kick that bomb, Mister?"

15

Our move was to Kokoda Barracks at Holsworthy and the camp was on the opposite side of the road to the familiar Gallipoli Barracks, my erstwhile home with 2 RAR. Kokoda housed the Royal Australian Artillery, whose assets mainly were pack howitzers of fairly recent design, and field pieces known as 'Long Toms', which were much heavier weapons of WW II origin. We moved into a remote corner of the camp which had until recently been occupied by an antiaircraft battery.

It was a return, for some of us anyway, to the familiar ten-man huts and these were in a poor state of repair. I was allocated the NCO's room in one of them, noting that there were large holes in the lining walls and that the door lock was broken. I pasted cardboard over the holes, chucked some paint around and solved the lock problem by stealing an entire, lockable, door from neighbouring lines. A couple of weeks later we were reshuffled and I was moved into a similarly derelict room in another hut. Some you don't win.

It was a return, also, to the Railway Hotel in Liverpool, where I soon encountered Shagger Carnes, by now a sergeant with the resident infantry battalion. If I had forgotten Shagger's fondness for practical jokes, I was reminded of it when he introduced me to the group as 'the famous boxer, Billy Can' then adding, "I reckon he could take on any two of youse blokes at the same time." For the remainder of the session I was uncomfortably aware that a couple of the meaner-looking blokes were quietly sizing me up.

I was still living largely out of my kit bag, volunteering for odd jobs and detachments. I took the overnight train to Amberley in Queensland for Cessna wing bundle work, and was returned on the next train when the unit professed no knowledge of it. Signals flew and I was on the next overnight train from Sydney to try again.

40 Air Supply was deemed to have a parachuting capability, and in the winter Dave Armstrong and I were among half a dozen of the platoon sent to RAAF Williamtown to undergo the basic assault parachutist course. This was an exciting prospect and at least half the reason I had been working on the fitness. The course formed some

twenty-five strong and we were a mix of corps, to include the boss of the New Zealand SAS and a couple of Papua New Guinean officers - one of whom who became a general in fairly rapid order.

The course was designed to cover ground training and eight parachute descents within three weeks, and we made an early start in the hangar, learning the PLF, or parachute landing fall, which was designed to roll the body across its fleshy parts and thus reduce the landing impact. We did a great deal of these, rolling from a standing position and progressing to runs up short ramps. We were also hoisted off the floor in dummy harnesses, given a good shove to simulate oscillation and dropped again to make the best of it with a sideways, forward or back landing.

The school had several devices to simulate parachuting and I found none of them much to my liking, although you might make a small fortune renting them out these days to people who spend large amounts of money to make bungee jumps. The Fan Trainer was intended to perfect aircraft exits and to confirm PLFs. The harness was attached to a wire cable that wound off a drum connected to fan blades. The jumper stepped off a platform about twenty-five feet off the ground and as he dropped the fan blades developed resistance that arrested the fall.

Outdoors, the Polish Tower dominated the training area. Its platform was sixty feet above the ground, and the dummy harness was clipped to an overhead frame before the student stepped off. He then practised canopy check, all-round observation drills, avoidance drills, release of the leg-bag equipment and selection of the correct lift webs to counter drift imparted by the prevailing wind. The student was eventually released under hydraulic control to perfect his side, forward or back landing and roasted from on high if he made a balls of it. The climb up the Polish Tower was a less than jolly occasion.

We were taken aloft, fully kitted with main and reserve parachutes, for an air experience flight and we watched the parachute jump instructors clowning about before they stepped, with studied casualness, out of the aircraft. Another course reported that one of their PJIs rode a bike off the ramp of a C130, presumably lowering it like a leg bag at some point. This was done to strike a light note in what might be a lethal practice, and we landed from the experience flight knowing that the next flight was a one-way journey, insofar as the aircraft ride was concerned.

Initial descents were made from the Dakota, which could carry twenty-one parachutists, who could be despatched in a single stick. For our first descent, however, the Dak would orbit the DZ twenty-one times with each student doing a solo equipment check and a shuffle to the door.

I had done two descents already but I have preserved a better memory of the first jump from the C47 for some reason. I was about halfway down the stick and thus had already witnessed nearly a dozen exits that I would now emulate. With a shout and a gesture the PJI ordered: "**PREPARE FOR ACTION! STICK, STAND UP, HOOK UP.**"

I stood up, positioned myself in the centre of the fuselage facing aft, and I hooked my static strop onto the steel wire rope that ran the length of the compartment.

"**CHECK EQUIPMENT!**"

The equipment check had been learned like a mantra on the ground and it was chanted aloud as the fingers ran over the kit to physically check: Helmet, Reserve Handle, Reserve Hooks, Quick Release Box, Two Shoulder Ties, Centre Pack Tie. Static Strop. In a stick, I would be checking the shoulder and centre pack ties of the man in front, whilst the man behind would check mine. If we were jumping with equipment, then the checks would include Quick Release Tape and Pin and Suspension Buckles.

"**ACTION STATIONS!**"

With the static strop gripped in my left hand and my right arm folded across my reserve 'chute, I hunched slightly and began the rhythmic shuffle down the fuselage to the door, sliding my left foot flat along the floor and only raising my right foot to place in check behind the left, calling the time as I went, and by now oblivious to the remaining students. I continued until I was turning towards the door and held there by the PJI. There was nothing beyond the door but space.

"**RED ON, STAND IN THE DOOR!**"

I relinquished the strop, advanced a pace to put my left foot on the door sill and lay the palm of my left hand against the side of the door. I felt the slipstream fluttering my fingers and I could now see the horizon, apparently motionless. I knew that in seconds I would have to hurl myself out into the slipstream, folding my left arm over the right and concentrating on keeping my legs together until the static line and parachute paid out. Lack of control over one's legs was to 'ride Pegasus' and invite the scorn of the DZ officer.

"**GREEN ON, GO!**" Bawled in my ear and accompanied by a clap on the shoulder, and I was gone, rushing away into sudden silence that was broken only by the snap of the deploying canopy and, moments later, by loud hailer advice from the DZ. There was a moment of pure exhilaration in every descent I subsequently made, but there was nothing quite like that first one from the Dakota.

We progressed to the C130, jumped in ever-increasing sticks and completed simultaneous descents from port and starboard on the Herc. We completed seven by day and one night descent, got a couple of extra ones in and duly qualified. I was adjudged 'nervous but controlled' and thought that a fair comment. We added parachute wings with a degree of pride to our dispatcher's brevets and returned to Holsworthy. (Returned slightly ahead of us had been Graham Hay, a member of the platoon. On the threshold of the final, and wings qualifying descent, Graham learned that his brother had been very seriously injured in a motor accident. The staff at PTS, as keen as Graham for his qualification, arranged for him to appear at the aircraft in best uniform, put a pair of flying overalls on him and duly despatched him from a Herc before sending him home. His brother survived) A fortnight later we were returned to Williamtown for a refresher course of four descents. No one quite knew why, but we were not arguing.

Towards the end of the year four of us were selected to undergo training as helicopter crewmen, and we entrained for RAAF Fairburn, near Canberra. The Bell Iroquois helicopter had recently been accepted into service by the RAAF and it was operated by one pilot, although the controls were duplicated. The RAAF employed air loadmasters on C130s but for some reason had elected not to provide crewmen for the UH1B; hence our training which raised in us some expectation that we might be elevated to aircrew status and regular flying pay.

The course was of eight week's duration and we spent a fair amount of time 'up front' with the pilot and even assisting with the navigation. The Iroquois could carry a small internal load, although it more commonly carried half a dozen passengers, and the logistics of these gave us no problems. We also learned to act as winch men and to talk to the pilot through headsets from the cargo compartment whilst doing underslung loads. We took part in a couple of exercises and gradually completed the training tests that qualified us as crewmen.

Life at Fairburn during off-duty hours was pleasant. RAAF food (and choice) was excellent, whilst in the accommodation we discovered such luxuries as bedside reading lamps. We struck up some relationships with WRAAF personnel and I was particularly smitten by a girl who hailed from Newcastle, although the relationship failed to develop.

Return to Holsworthy was a hefty dose of reality. The food

was simply terrible in the combined mess. Our accommodation had not been improved and when a hut burned down one evening, due to a fan which had been left running for some days, our efforts to save the building were not wholly enthusiastic.

As we approached the Xmas break I had arrived at a decision to leave the army in April, although I had recently been asked to sign on and knew that my promotion prospects were again excellent. The decision to leave had nothing to do with poor food or rough accommodation. I simply recognised a restless spirit that sought something beyond predictability. It was true, too, that the character of the platoon was changing as we expanded and the tasks become all-embracing of heavy drop doctrine, to the virtual exclusion of door bundle work. When a group of us returned from a minor exercise on the back of a Studebaker, the conversation turned to how a similar, forthcoming exercise might be avoided. I surprised the group, and myself to some degree, by rounding upon them in anger for their attitude.

I took Dave Armstrong home again and we spent much of the leave drinking to excess. I was still courting Val and borrowing her father's utility for limited passion at the drive-in theatre. The leave was generally a quiet time and I began to consider the fact that my term of enlistment was again drawing to a close.

By the time we returned to Holsworthy, Captain Howes had been replaced by Captain Bryant, who had recently undergone an exchange tour with the US Army. Captain Bryant proved to have assimilated some irritating Americanisms, and he further upset most of us with some barbed comments about our performance. With sober reflection, however, these were recognised to be home truths.

A three-month detachment to New Guinea was announced and I was to lead a crew, until the CO learned that I was not extending my service. I was removed from the draft, which was disappointing, but I could not fault the logic behind it. I was sent instead to Broken Bridge to work on low-level container extraction with Caribou aircraft, then spent some more time at RAAF Richmond enjoying the food and the change.

At this time I had stopped drinking altogether, a discipline I would maintain for about six months. During the crewman course I had formed a good friendship with a Lance-Jack named Bob Green. Bob had been one of the founder members of the unit and a fierce drinker who eventually suffered a breakdown. I didn't know the half of it, but Bob had been raised in a house where a succession of 'uncles' came and went, giving Bob a fairly rough time of it in the process. It never occurred to me at the time, but, given Bob's implacable hatred of homosexuals, I think it likely that he had also been the victim of sexual abuse.

Bob was now alcohol-free and I simply decided to join him in that. My own drinking had given me pause for thought on occasion, and abstinence was suddenly very appealing to me. I was also working quite hard at fitness at this time, although to what end I could not say.

Bob left the army in January and asked if he might accompany my return to the West in April. He had heard that good wages might be earned in the North West and that seemed a fair idea. He moved back to Randwick in the meantime, having friends there to stay with for a few months.

I spent a whole week on a map-reading course, which culminated in a two-day exercise in the area of the Woronora Dam. For that we were simply dropped off and left to get on with it. There was no sign of any safety vehicle or emergency drill, other than initiative and common sense, and I wonder if that would be allowed today. Probably not.

The chance of parachuting presented itself and I took a group in a Studebaker off to Williamtown. We got four descents in and they included equipment and night drops. Learning that the Herc was returning to Richmond at the conclusion of the descent programme, I had a word with the Loadie and he arranged for all of us, Studebaker included, to ride with them.

The venerable Studebaker was by now on borrowed time, being replaced increasingly by an army-designed vehicle that was built by International Harvest. It looked very businesslike and was equipped with air brakes, which were extremely sensitive. Having done the familiarisation course, I took one out on some errand and picked up a Digger who was looking for a lift. He sat at the tailgate, but only until I treated the brake pedal as if I still had a Studebaker underneath it. The lorry seemed to stop in about point-five of a second, which was about all the time it took for the Digger to travel from the tailgate and arrive, with a thud and a howl, at the back of the cab. When I dropped him off, he was less than effusive with his thanks.

I was summoned to Area Command and interviewed by the RSM, who wanted to know why I would not sign on. He pointed out that I was certain of promotion and that the chance to be a sergeant at twenty-three was not to be lightly dismissed. I was not persuaded, but I was by now beginning to have very serious doubts about the wisdom of leaving the service.

With virtually all of the platoon absent on one detachment or another, I was again packed off, this time to assist in the running of an air despatch course for the CMF 39 Air Supply Platoon. Reservists were not held in the highest of esteem by the regular forces (although it would be another twenty-seven years before I realised the extent of it), but I had a fairly open mind about 39, having met some of its members before. In the event, they were a hardworking crew, and since the course dealt exclusively at the level of door bundle despatching, it was a welcome return to the Dakota.

When the course was over there were still less than a dozen blokes at Holsworthy and I went off again. This time it was to Singleton camp to rig one-ton containers for despatch from Caribou. I ran across a couple of blokes I had served with in 2 RAR and joined them in the canteen, drinking lemonade. At some other table a battalion man bet his mates ten shillings he could drain a bottle of rum. He won the 10/- but never collected it, dying on the way to a hospital.

When I returned to Holsworthy I seemed to have exhausted the exercise list and was detached down to Randwick to drive with 101 Coy. I led a packet of four vehicles off to the Blue Mountains, but the lorry I had chosen proved to be a thirsty brute and I ran out of fuel at midnight. I curled up in the cab until one of the other drivers ferried a jerrican to me.

I caught up yet another exercise at Tianjara, and actually was never happier than when I was so employed at this time. I had to borrow maps from the artillery, and no one in the exercise area seemed to know quite what was going on but it was a stimulating period.

Along with Bob Green I made a visit to Goulburn Gaol to see a former member of 40, serving six months for a break-in at some garage. He seemed in good spirits, but the gaol looked an entirely cheerless place.

I did one more exercise, travelling to Singleton camp again to advise an army unit on DZ marking, and my time simply ran out. I handed in the drip-dry non-iron KD uniform that had only recently replaced cotton OGs and prepared to be a civilian again. At the same time I was advised that my application to become an Australian citizen had been approved. Soldier and Citizen, I packed my kit bag and entrained West.

16

Bob left the train at Kalgoorlie and I continued to Perth to complete the few procedures of discharge. I made a visit to the parents of Arch's fiancee, Jan, whom I had first met on the recent leave, but had little time to fill since my service had actually expired during the rail journey. Arch was by this time a sergeant and apparently serving in Malaysia, although, given the nature of the SAS, it was not certain. (I would not discover until 1989, via a history of the Australian SAS, that Arch at this precise time was leading the longest patrol in the annals of the Australian army. It totalled 89 days, during the Confrontation when Australia conducted cross-border patrols into Indonesian territory).

A few months of sobriety had done little to redress the lack of thrift during my second term of service, and an early job was a priority. Bob and I duly secured chest X-rays and applied for underground work with the Lake View & Star gold mine. We were teamed and put to work with shovels, clearing the track of spillage from the loco-hauled trolleys that conveyed ore from one part of the mine to another. This proved to be cheerless and backbreaking work, and nor did it offer an exciting wage. A week's money was just £15.10s, which was actually less than we had earned as Diggers, with no food or accommodation to find from it. The real money in mining - apart from owning a mine, of course - lay in contract drilling, but we were not intending the sort of lengthy stay necessary to develop that sort of expertise. We were actually awaiting a response to enquiries we had made about working in the distant north of the state, utterly ignorant of the fact that the only place to enquire about jobs up north was actually up north.

In the meantime, we continued with the mine work with little variation in our duties. We worked in a particularly slimy and rotten drive at three thousand feet, and were less than impressed when a chute that fed ore from a higher level collapsed on us. We escaped with cuts and bruises, although Bob went on compensation for a few days, and it did nothing to encourage our staying on. After six weeks we took a job with an engineering works in Kalgoorlie, where pump housings were cast. Our job was to grind the slag off the castings with carborundum wheels and it was noisy, dirty work in a shop that recognised no tea or smoke breaks. This job ended quite abruptly on the second day when Bob took exception to rough words from the foreman and thumped him. Bob's psychological problems were far from resolved at this time, and he had been seeing a psychiatrist right up until our departure from Sydney.

We accepted a job as trainee shunters at Merredin, a country town about half way to Perth, and we caught the Rattler. Both of us happened to be afflicted with a touch of the 'flu at the time and we were disgruntled to learn upon arrival at Merredin that nothing would happen until 0800hrs. It was 0330hrs when we gleaned this piece of intelligence and the town was quieter than an abandoned anthill. We tried to get a fire going in the ladies waiting room, then went in quest of a hotel for a bed. Drawing a blank, at 0500hrs we started hitchhiking to Perth

In the city we renewed our bid for northern jobs but nothing materialised. Bob then quietly confided that he felt the need of more psychiatric counselling, offering to return to Sydney alone, but I countered that the prospects up north appeared dim and elected to return to NSW with him. We duly purchased tickets, broke the journey briefly at home, and were back in Randwick by the end of May.

Randwick was probably a mistake since although 40 had departed to Holsworthy, we knew plenty of Diggers at the Randwick camp and we found ourselves in their orbit quite often. We were not drinking but the company over a glass of squash at the Royal Hotel inevitably recalled the happy times on 40, and fostered twinges of regret for having walked away from the life. I was beginning to realise that I had failed to see how happy I had been in the service, and that I had jettisoned a secure career. For the moment, however, I simply had to make the best of it.

We occupied a flat and found a job in a foundry at the suburb of Alexandria. The foundry smelted enamel products and we were employed as general gofers on three shifts, among a work force of about twenty. The average weekly wage was £24, which was an improvement upon the mines, although the work was endlessly boring. There were some interesting characters in the job though. One was a Greek who had virtually no English and the foreman was at his wit's end to keep the migrant usefully employed. He eventually gave him a stencil, a brush and a tin of paint and demonstrated how to stencil some batch details on about three hundred bags of produce. When he later went to check the job, he discovered that the Greek had held the stencil the wrong way around, achieving quite a Greek-like effect. "Fucken A-rabs," fumed the foreman, whose geographic knowledge was somewhat defective.

Another bloke talked endlessly about making a Scuba kit out of two fire extinguishers he had got hold of. For weeks afterwards I scanned the papers for a report of the mysterious drowning of a body with two fire extinguishers strapped to it.

After five weeks, and in anticipation of a driving job, I packed the foundry in. I did not get the driving job. Bob also left the foundry and seemed assured of a job with Qantas as cleaning staff, with a view to promotion to cabin crew. He seemed intent on a period of stability and I had no wish to persuade him otherwise, although I now wondered what direction I should take. In the midst of my deliberations Bob suddenly took an overdose and spent some time in a hospital. I visited him but he was well sedated and hardly aware of whom I was. This was a depressing turn of events and wholly unexpected.

I decided to cash in an insurance policy whose surrender value was a considerable £100, and I moved out of the flat, spending a few cheerless nights in the People's Palace in Pitt Street. People's it might have been; palace it wasn't, although it was very cheap. A few days later I presented myself to the recruiting office and applied to re-engage, expecting to be inducted within a few days. I made a trip out to Holsworthy to see the OC on 40 to assess the chances of returning directly to the platoon, and he promised to make efforts on my behalf.

At this point a hiatus set in and at the worst possible time since the insurance money would not arrive for a month and I was meanwhile running out of cash. Things got so tight that I eventually moved into a room at Randwick camp and became a phantom digger for a couple of weeks, taking meals in the mess and trying to blend unobtrusively with the crowd.

I returned to the flat to arrange the removal of Bob's kit and to square the outstanding rent, in the sum of seven quid. I had raised exactly that sum by selling off the clothes I had mostly bought with my army severance pay a few weeks earlier. The market for secondhand clothes was clearly none too good, unless of course it was implied criticism of my dress sense. I was not greatly distressed by the loss, since I intended to travel light, but I could not bear to part with a red waistcoat that I had bought in Melbourne for £7.10s. I have it still. During the visit, I was invited to coffee by the landlord and whilst we were chatting he made a homosexual overture. Life in the big city was suddenly looking very shitty and I reckoned that it was time to move on.

I continued to visit Bob and I felt bad about his condition, wondering if I should not have noticed his deterioration and done something about it. He seemed to be making a recovery but I could only guess at what demons might be driving him.

At Randwick camp I renewed acquaintance with Curly Nelson, formerly a corporal on 40 and now a driver with 101 Coy. Having by now reverted to drinking, I joined Curl for a pint one evening and when he suggested hitchhiking up to Tamworth for a few days I readily agreed. My insurance cash had arrived and there was still no word from the recruiting office, although more than a month had elapsed.

Curly was as anxious to leave the army as I had recently been to rejoin it, although he had not actually undergone the formality of discharge. His marriage had come apart, he had recently been reduced to private from the rank of corporal and he was now simply walking away from it all. This perhaps did not make of him the most reliable of companions, but I did not see this at all quickly. We spent two days in a boarding house in Tamworth, where the work prospects were less than exciting, and we hitched up to Brisbane. I believed that we needed to go a good bit further north in the sunshine state, to find work in areas suddenly prosperous with bauxite discoveries and mining, but Curl evinced little enthusiasm.

We spent a night in the Brisbane YMCA and I wandered down to the TV in the evening. The few chairs were filled but I leaned against a wall and became engrossed in some programme. The screen suddenly went blank with a click and to a man the audience rose and left the room. I inspected the TV and found that it was a coin-operated job, and since the programme had captured my attention, I fed a two-bob piece into the slot. The instant the TV clicked back into life, there was a stampede back into the room and the few chairs were filled again almost before I had turned around.

We occupied a flat at Kangaroo Point for ninety shillings per week, which the insurance cash defrayed, along with our modest eating requirements and less than sensible drinking habits. We secured a job in a bottle-washing plant and it was so exciting that we stayed there for nearly four hours before sacking it.

Curl remained immune to my suggestions that we push on and his counter-suggestion was that we hitch down to Melbourne. This had no particular appeal to me and I considered going north alone, but what I now also had to consider was a commitment to reserve training which I had made before leaving the army. I had joined the Emergency Reserve for four years and a fortnight camp, annually, a requirement which was shortly to fall due. Melbourne was in no great proximity to Perth, but a fair bit closer than Brisbane and points north.

We hitchhiked south in foul weather, occasionally encountering those jovial drivers who halt about three hundred yards along the road and roar off, laughing, when you arrive, panting, at the car door. We made a brief halt in Sydney and I went to visit Bob Green, still in a hospital but looking marginally better.

In Melbourne we located a cheap flat in Prahran, which appeared to be a Greek suburb, and I briefly found work with a security firm. At some point I shared the inside of the van with £2,000,000 in postal wages whilst I had about five shillings in my pocket. When I began the job, a loaded 7.65mm Webley & Scott pistol was handed to me, with the instruction not to shoot anyone. No holster was provided and I fretted for a while that the heavy pistol entirely spoiled the line of my remaining (unsold) suit.

It had transpired by now that Curl had a girlfriend at Puckapunyal camp and this formed the motive for the journey south. We spent a weekend at Pucka and Curl's girlfriend turned out to have a friend who was simply stunning. I was instantly smitten and when Maggie appeared attracted to me I believed that life was perfect, despite the absence of job, money and a sensible plan.

Curl now decided to uncomplicate his life by turning himself in at Watsonia Barracks, where he was subsequently court-martialled, fined and returned to Randwick to soldier on. He was doubtless also eating; a practice I was losing touch with. Chasing casual work, I put some days in at the railway marshalling yards, where the putative workers lined up daily to be selected for however many jobs there happened to be. Waiting for The Man one morning, I discarded a cigarette end and was startled when two blokes dived for it. We worked one day when a line of flatcars loaded with Chrysler Valiant cars were being loose-shunted (against policy) and the engine driver managed to shunt four of them off the flatcars into a heap. We heard later that his mates now referred to him as 'Prince Valiant', which was a lot funnier than Bob Dyer or Jack Davey had ever been.

I got a steadier job in some galvanising works where I appeared to be the only worker, apart from the foreman, who could speak English. Smoke-o and meal breaks were a barrel of laughs. The job did not last and paying the rent became a problem again, until I solved that one by pawning a watch I had bought in Singapore. I might have moved on except that the lovely Maggie was just a couple of hour's hitchhiking away and I was disinclined to leave just yet. It was, however, a chaste relationship, since she was devoutly Catholic.

The reserve camp was now pressing and I had to make the move. With about two thousand miles to cover and just £3. 10s in my pocket I caught an early train to Footscray then got out on the highway. Good lifts put me into Adelaide by 0200hrs, where I shaved and spruced up in the railway lavatories before striking off again. I was twice stopped by police patrols, but it was friendly enough and included some advice on lifts, although I thought it prudent to keep moving. Some police were not slow to apply the vagrancy act to anyone who could not produce a minimum of ten shillings in cash, and I was rapidly approaching that status.

I achieved it at Port Augusta where I bought two large packets of ham sandwiches to stuff into the pockets of an old parachute smock I was wearing. This modest provision was intended to be my food across the Nullarbor Plain, and it left me with just a few shillings.

The hiking initiative had mostly succeeded in putting me on the wrong road prior to daybreak on the second day. At daybreak I had to backtrack a few miles, wishing that I had added a map to my few possessions. I selected a new route from the rising sun to put me nor-nor-west, but it was likely more luck than solar navigation which put me back on track. At Augusta I also had a shower, sneaking into the railway staff ablutions with a rehearsed line about mistaking them for public facilities, should someone ask what the fuck I thought I was doing.

By 1700hrs I was heading for the Eyre Highway but almost immediately pounced upon at a police roadblock, since a hitchhiker had pulled a knife on some driver further north. Fortunately, he had bright red hair and I was soon released, although it was an anxious moment now that I was virtually broke and patently heading across the

Plain. By 1000hrs on the following morning, having secured short lifts between long stands, I was dropped at the town of Penong, which was the last town on the South Australian side of the Nullarbor. The wait here could be a long one indeed, since it would be the big lift or none at all. Kalgoorlie suddenly seemed a long way off and it was too depressing a thought to dwell upon. I had five ham sandwiches and six shillings.

I stood at the dusty roadside for ten hours the first day. It was Spring and not excessively hot, but the flies were aggressive and I fashioned a swish from the branch of a nearby Pepper tree. Its pungent aroma trailed about my nostrils each time I waved the flies away, and I had to replace it from time to time as the leaves batted off against my head and shoulders. Nothing much seemed to be moving in the tiny community and time stood still, although I gauged the passing of it from the arc of the sun. My watch was presumably keeping good time in the pawnbroker's window.

My roadside pitch was adjacent to the fence of a small school, from which a group of children would emerge occasionally to play noisily in the yard. A number of them gathered where I stood and stared up at me. They included a little girl who had a question for me: "Are you a tramp, Mister?" I certainly felt like one. When the class was recalled, the schoolmaster also approached, inviting me to drink from the yard water tank whenever I needed to. I thanked him and immediately took up the offer. The water was warm and brown in my cupped hands and the tank, of about five hundred gallons capacity, likely had a foot of dead budgies floating at its top, but it was as welcome a drink as anything I've had since.

When the school released its few pupils, the area was briefly lively as the children noisily dispersed but it swiftly reverted to quiet. Few sounds emanated from the tiny town, where people brewed tea, ate meals, chatted and went to bed obliviously of the stranger on the doorstep. As the sun sank out of sight and as I pulled on the smock against the developing chill, even the flies abandoned me, the absence of their day-long buzzing accentuating the silence.

I stood for two hours, a sentry without patrol orders, looking in vain for headlights to penetrate the night sky. I might have been the last man on the planet and I did not even need to turn out the lights, for they vanished one by one. At last, I stepped over the school fence and entered an open shed that had a bench along its back wall. I made a pillow of my bag and stretched out to sleep cold, stiff and fitfully until the rising sun and the newly-discovering flies drove me out to the water tank to drink, sluice my face and examine my lift prospects for the day. Time also to breakfast upon one of my sandwiches. The bread was now quite dry and yellow where the butter had melted into it.

The hours until midday were some of the longest I had known and absolutely nothing moved; I might have been on a road to absolutely nowhere. A little after noon I was considering whether or not to eat another sandwich when a semi-trailer halted at a fuel pump along the road. I decided to ask the driver directly, rather than risk his driving by, and I confronted him. He was not immediately enthusiastic, curtly pointing out that he'd had his quota of deadbeats who ate his tucker, drank his water, smoked his fags and got in his way. This was disconcerting and not least since this description sounded uncannily like mine, with six shillings, three stale sandwiches and some brown dust at the bottom of my tobacco pouch, but the driver took me on. I doubt if I shall ever quite forget the wave of gratitude and relief that I felt at the time.

Solving the big problem of the lift left me with the minor one of concealing my indigence for the length of a journey that would span forty-eight hours. The driver's routine, I learned, was to stop for one hour at midday and in the early evening for fuel and food, and at midnight for two hour's sleep. He was taking pills of some sort to sustain twenty hours each day at the wheel, but I was in no position to criticise his chemical habits. We jolted off down the unmade road, conducting conversation at a shout above the roar of the engine between us.

When we stopped for the evening meal, I made a show of reading the menu before expressing a lack of appetite, and ordering a mug of tea. The driver meanwhile tucked into a **T** - bone steak that overlapped his plate by a good margin, and I hoped that the rumblings of my stomach were not audible above the chatter of the few patrons. At midnight the driver stretched out in the cab for his two hours whilst I rested on top of the trailer load, which was timber. Before I nodded off I ate one of my sandwiches, which by now had the taste and texture of ham-flavoured plywood. They were delicious.

The Eyre Highway was at this time entirely unpaved and the gravel surface took a heavy toll of tyres. By way of earning my ride I assisted with the changing of half a dozen tyres - his record for this particular stage was an even dozen - and when we were rolling I endeavoured to maintain a flow of conversation. During the second night I noted with some interest a gang of road workers, scores of miles from anything remotely resembling habitation, and knew that I was hallucinating a little later when I saw crocodiles crossing the road. Crocs were not indigenous to these parts, and the chance of a travelling reptile house seemed as remote as the parts we travelled through.

Later that morning we passed through Coolgardie and I dropped off to hitch the few miles to Boulder. I arrived home at midday and it was the last day of October. When I strolled into the house, the Sunday joint was browning in the oven. I had a single ham sandwich left in my pocket and that was browning, too.

"Are you a tramp, Mister?" she asked

17

After five days at home I assembled my uniform and caught the Rattler down to Perth. I had again missed Arch since he was now posted to Puckapunyal as an instructor with a national service battalion. I had also just missed his wedding, which Jan and he had advanced due to the posting. I saw something of Danny Wright, now returned to the SAS from his 'punishment' posting, but for the moment I was busy with the reservist camp.

Having neglected to have a haircut for three months, I now addressed the matter, borrowing the price of it from the CSM who gave me also one of his long-suffering looks. The course was about forty strong and it turned out to include Stan Pridmore of junior storeman and keg in the back seat days. Stan had done three years as a Tanky but was now married and settled in a Perth suburb.

We began, predictably enough, on the parade ground with close order drill but soon moved on to revise tactics, navigation, weapons and range work. A group of SAS SNCOs was attached from Campbell Barracks and they included Arch's best man. We were kept very busy for a few days and the second week featured an exercise that made a reasonable outing. We combined a plethora of corps and my group was eventually attached to 90 Transport Coy to get some driving in. An officer attached for instruction was none other than Captain Howes, lately of 40 Air Supply, and when he heard of my difficulties in trying to enlist in Sydney he immediately offered to arrange enlistment in Perth. I was briefly tempted by his offer, having recognised that the months since discharge had been an utter waste of time, but I felt that the moment had passed. At the same time, however, I noted a newspaper item that claimed that a West Australian recruiting campaign, conducted at huge expense, had failed to attract a single recruit. At this I wrote a mildly sarcastic letter to Dr Forbes, the Minister for the Army, wondering why the army had found it so difficult to reenlist a recently discharged, trained Digger, whilst throwing quite so much money at the recruiting problem elsewhere. The slightly tart response pointed out that the delay had occurred because representation had been made to reenlist me in the rank of corporal, and this had required special authority. This, and subsequent instructions to report for attestation, had been advised to my Randwick address and when no reply was received, it was assumed that I was no longer interested. Good old Ron, the pouf.

For the second week of the course we were attached to 90 Transport Coy, engaged on city and bush driving to re-familiarise ourselves with the new lorries, the Mk IV which I had briefly met in the last days of service with 40 Air Supply. The time passed agreeably and at the conclusion of the camp I returned to Boulder to seek work.

I picked up a job as a surface labourer on the Great Boulder Gold Mine, where Dad by now worked as a bricklayer. Occasionally, I worked as labourer for the Old Man, which was pleasing, and we usually met to eat our crib - sandwiches - in the shed where he kept his tools. The shade was welcome since we were into December and the summer was well advanced.

No two days seemed to be the same, which offered welcome variety, although some of the jobs were less than welcome. One day I had to shovel a railway truck free of the cast iron balls which were used in the ore treatment plant and there were sixteen tons of them. Frankie Laine sang about sixteen tons in a slightly different mining context, but I can tell you that sixteen tons on the end of your shovel is pretty bad news whatever the context.

I worked for the electricians, fitters, riggers and platmen, all for the same sixteen pounds per week, then caught up some steady employment in the magazine, mixing explosives. For years the mines had relied upon sticks of Nobel for blasting, but lately a much cheaper alternative had been found. An industrial fertiliser, prilled ammonium nitrate, was mixed with diesel fuel in a cement mixer to make a potent explosive. The mix, if you are interested in blowing somebody up, was about twenty-five pounds of fertiliser to a pint of diesel, but you'll have to sort out the detonator yourself. An old Polish chap called Joe was the man in charge and he set a very steady work pace. Apart from the heat bouncing off the corrugated iron shed, the diesel fumes and old Joe's penchant for interminable stories and terrible tobacco, it wasn't a bad job at all as I ticked off the days to the New Year.

I spent New Year's Day unloading 450 bags of lime from railway flatcars; another joyful job in the process of extracting gold from the ground in order that it might be stacked, in bars, underground somewhere else. Saving was a laborious business and not least since I tried to match the Old Man's drinking when we called after work each day at the Mines & City Worker's Club, where the bar thronged three and four deep at this time of the year. It was at this time that I established the easy companionship with the Old Man that would resume intermittently over the next four years, and endure for the following ten. The scale of the drinking was later to be regretted, but the time spent in the Old Man's company makes a warm recollection on wintry days.

A day or two into the year a shaft on a winder broke and since that immediately stopped production at that particular mine, twelve-hour shifts were imposed to get the repair effected. I laboured for the fitting shop - carrying tools for Uncle Jim at some point - and the happy result of all this was a net wage of thirty pounds per week. Reunion with Maggie now seemed an earlier possibility than had formerly been the case. When not working or drinking I had been writing voluminous letters to Maggie, fearful that she might mistake my continuing absence for indifference. I also wrote her reams of bad poetry. Happily, none of it appears to have survived.

In the first week of February I packed a few things in a kit bag again and set off across the Nullarbor. Saving the train fare seemed wise and hitchhiking with money in my pocket no great hardship. I made swift progress to Coolgardie and Norseman, then hit the inevitable wait for the big lift. When it came there was no room in the cab but I was invited to climb atop the load, which was Jarrah timber, a hard redwood. I accepted but found it a cold ride at night, despite snugging as far down as possible, wrapped in a blanket that the previous trip had taught the value of.

The lorry had seven flat tyres during the trip and at one time the compressor valve failed and the driver had to roll the huge wheel five miles to get it inflated, whilst I kept an eye on the load. I couldn't see anyone stealing the Jarrah, but I suppose the driver was more concerned about his remaining wheels. Australia was - and perhaps still is - a bad place to leave an unattended vehicle.

I left the lorry at Port Augusta and secured another lift just as rain began to hammer down. My relief at the lift was short-lived when I discovered the absence of a window or even much of a door on my side of the vehicle, and I was dropped off miles later absolutely soaked to the skin. The train, in retrospect, seemed a fine idea.

Having walked six miles into Adelaide in the early hours of the morning, I got a quick lift through the city and then was picked up by a Digger who was going all the way to Puckapunyal. I dropped off in Seymour and in one of those odd coincidences the first people I saw happened to be Jan and Arch, just bound for Pucka where Arch was now serving. Less happily, Maggie was no longer at the camp, being by now posted to Singleton in NSW, but it was good to spend a few days with Jan and Arch, and also to renew acquaintance with Dave Armstrong, by now a sergeant on the staff of the RAASC Centre.

Arch was serving as an instructor at 2 RTB, a recruit battalion formed at Pucka to train national servicemen for Australia's commitment of troops to fight in South Viet Nam. It was believed at this time that the Americans had formally requested assistance under the terms of the ANZUS Pact, a mutual defence agreement between the US, Australia and New Zealand. It would be a couple of decades before it was revealed that the Australian Prime Minister, Robert Menzies, had actually offered the troops, although requesting that the offer be disguised by a formal bid by the US to make it politically more acceptable.

That stratagem did not work particularly well, since the idea of conscripts generally, and the Viet Nam war especially, was not popular with Australians. The decision would ultimately cause the collapse of a Liberal (ie Conservative) government for the first time in nearly two decades, and keep it out of power for another decade.

Conscription was by lottery, which was at least the fairest system, and it called up the eighteen-year olds for two year's service. This represented part of the unpopularity, since the voting age was still set at twenty-one, but rather more was made of the fact that Australia had found sufficient volunteers to join the Colours in campaigns from the Boxer Rebellion onwards. It seemed that there was no great enthusiasm to join the American crusade in Viet Nam, scene of French humiliation a little over ten years previously.

In 1966, however, I was applying no great thought to the morality of all this; simply, I expect, accepting the current wisdom of the 'Domino Theory', which held that if one Asian country fell to Communism, then the rest would follow. This argument was extended to the reasoning that it was better to fight the Communist threat in South-East Asia, rather than on Malibu Beach/Bondi Beach, depending upon American or Australian points of view, and at twenty-three I swallowed this as well. Today, it looks the specious nonsense it always was, to anyone with even half a brain.

At his Inaugural Address in 1960, John F Kennedy said:

"Let every nation know, whether it wishes us well or ill, that we shall pay any price, bear any burden, meet any hardship, support any friend, oppose any foe to assure the survival and success of liberty."

In Vietnam, the price (in American lives), the burden (of a host ally unwilling to fight) and the hardships (of American veterans stigmatised by the war and despised by their fellow Americans) proved too costly. $141,000,000,000 and 60,000 American lives were part of the price, as was a disturbing incidence of US Veterans' suicides post-war. The Americans had learned nothing from the French and their costly lesson at Dien Bien Phu in 1954. The Americans achieved nothing useful in Viet Nam and they carry the burden of their failure to this day.

Dissenters apart, it was all then accepted on the premise that nothing in this world could be worse than living under Communism (Cf 'Better Dead than Red', a slogan of the time). Actually, there was and anyone who doubts it should read accounts of life for Cuban peasants under Batista before Castro ousted him, or life under Somoza before Ortega, or even life *after* Allende, in Chile, where the American CIA engineered the coup which brought General Pinochet and a military dictatorship to power for thirteen bloody years. The list of Central and South American dictators, supported by US dollars simply because Fascism was an acceptable substitute for Communism, is a lengthy one.

At this time, however, my thoughts centred upon Maggie and political arguments would not have troubled me in the slightest. It is doubtless the sort of political apathy which politicians and governments thrive on.

Karrakatta Camp 1965
Tapping the CSM for the price of a haircut

18

I caught the train to Sydney and was met by Maggie on the platform. We had a cup of tea and a shy chat in the railway buffet then took the train up to Newcastle to spend the weekend at her home. Maggie's parents were Polish and they proved very hospitable, although they were naturally curious to know what I now intended to make of my life. It was a good question to which I had no easy answer. Renewed military service seemed no longer among the options, but I had no good ideas for a career, other than to recognise that manual work held out no great prospect for either security or prosperity. For the moment, though, life seemed good.

When I returned to Sydney, I once again looked for accommodation in the Randwick area, eventually renting a flat on the Coogee Bay Road, a stone's throw from the Royal Hotel. 'Flat' puts it a bit grand, since it was a single, small room with a tiny annex for the 'fridge, sink and a gas ring.

Whilst I had trekked from the West, the country had adopted decimal currency and the dollar was based upon the former ten shilling note. Bob Menzies, in another of his wizard ideas, had wanted the new note to be known as the 'Roil', pronounced 'royal', but several van loads of mail persuaded him that no great consensus existed for this, and dollar it was. Prior to finding the flat, I had spent a night at the Peoples' Palace where the tariff was $1.30, formerly thirteen shillings. My flat rent was $9 per week.

I had decided to try my hand at commission selling and pored over the *sits vac* in the *Sydney Morning Herald*, ringing a few of a wide selection which promised rich rewards to determined young men. I made application and was short-listed by a firm that sold hairpieces for gentlemen, and a rather better known firm that wanted the world and its brother to fill the bookshelf with a set of encyclopaedia. A suitcase full of wigs seemed a marginally lesser risk of a hernia than a suitcase full of reference books, but this speculation proved entirely academic when neither firm offered me a job. What I actually got was a start with a firm called 'Glamour Homes', selling brick veneer.

At this time virtually every house in the Sydney suburbs was timber-frame and clad with asbestos, and it was the mission of Glamour Homes to turn every one of these into 'brick' houses by adding our product, which itself was asbestos backed. The 'bricks' were a raised pattern of some synthetic or other and the finished job, at a cost of several hundred dollars, looked authentic, provided that you stood no closer than about forty yards. I probably lacked any real faith in the product but I made a bold start, and tried to make a success of it. The job paid no wages except commission on sales, although a weekly retainer of $9 was paid. This at least paid my rent.

About twenty of us reported to a North Shore building and were put to work learning a script. ('Good evening. My name is Harry Foxley and I am a representative of Glamour Homes. My company is currently looking for houses in this area which may be suitable as display homes for our product, which is an exciting range of brick veneer finishes....') This sort of drivel ran on for a couple of pages and was clearly designed to mesmerise the owners of suburban asbestos boxes, filling them with dreams of a brick house, free of charge. We were rehearsed in the script by Mal, who allegedly was a top salesman, and he wore a bow tie whose effect was slightly spoilt by the fact that his Glo-weave bri-nylon shirt had a dozen holes burned in it by sparks from his incessant cigarettes. Within days the score of applicants had shrunk to six but I lacked the wit to join the intelligent fourteen.

When we were turned loose in the suburbs of Sylvania, Marrickville and Gladesville, my first door opened to reveal a middle-aged man whose expression I should have read much quicker. He allowed me to complete the pitch then replied, "I don't like your pointy shoes, Son. Now piss off." At the next doorstep, that actually was next door, my knock was answered by a well-stacked lady who wore only a bikini. I mumbled something then wandered off without even asking if she was interested in brick veneer. I should have quit right then.

Commission on sales is all very well if you are actually selling, but too often I wasn't and I ran through my slender capital at an alarmingly rapid rate. Within a matter of weeks whilst I persisted with Glamour Homes, I was reduced to a single, daily meal and even that eventually went. Transport by the firm was supplied intermittently and one evening I walked home ten miles in pouring rain from Canterbury Station. Among my problems was that I was unable to visit Maggie at Singleton camp and she evidently began to interpret this as disinterest.

My wristwatch, redeemed by mail from the Melbourne pawnbroker, now went to live with a Taylor Square proprietor, and it was shortly followed by the portable radio I had borrowed from Maggie. Eking out the retainer between too few sales led to some interesting dietary habits, such as living exclusively on home-fried chips for a month, followed by four days of eating nothing at all. In Marrickville one evening I knocked upon a door which opened to frame a former member of 40 Air Supply Platoon. He was not interested in brick veneer, but he invited me to stay for dinner, which was greatly appreciated.

Glamour Homes mounted a display at the Parramatta show and we were invited to man the display, on the assumption that it would lead to great interest in sales. It did not and to relieve the boredom I took a stroll around to view the army display. It was manned by none other than Chook Fowles, noted child psychologist.

Letters from Maggie abruptly ceased and after three weeks I hitched-hiked up to Singleton to see her. This journey proved both late and fruitless since the relationship was now foundering. I felt bad about that and not least since it seemed to derive wholly from my ineptitude. I returned to Randwick and considered what now to do.

Two guitarists, Dylan and Segovia, came to town but I hadn't the freight to see either of them at the Sydney Town Hall. I was finding a degree of entertainment however at a folk music venue called 'The Lime Juice Tub' (a reference to sailing ships and scurvy, as the audience were perpetually reminded). The folk club was in an old warehouse near the docks and it was occupied for a peppercorn rent by a disparate group of poets, singers and musicians. The modest entrance fee entitled patrons to as much coffee as they wished and caffeine became my staple diet for a time. Bus rides between Randwick and the city were replaced by thoughtful walks, and during one trek through Taylor Square I noted a group of policemen clustered about a shattered pawnshop window. Maggie's radio was on the other side of it.

I enjoyed a number of the acts at the club, although the proportion of posers appeared quite high. These were easily recognised since they tended to be the guitarists who came on stage and lit a cigarette. The fag was then immediately impaled upon spare string outside the tuning keys and allowed to smoulder, uselessly, whilst the guitarist embarked upon a lengthy dissertation about the short piece to follow. They also usually played and sang 'The House of the Rising Sun' - badly.

The poets might also prove a bit hard to sit through. The product of garret toil was incomprehensible to about 85 per cent of us, although an old chap easily beat that by reading his work in Esperanto, thus defeating 100 per cent of us. The old chap actually was a German Jew who had survived the Death Camps. I longed to ask him about the experience but it was not an easy subject to introduce conversationally. ('Terrific that piece called '*Lavabo mano lachcryma*,' Jake. Er, by the way, Jake, how was Dachau?')

More attractively, a pretty girl picked at her guitar and sang what I now recognise as Bessie Smith blues numbers, although these were frowned upon by the club committee who perhaps were closet Morris Dancers. My interest in the girl was not merely confined to her musical talent and she seemed to reciprocate my interest, until she discovered that my invitation to walk her home was quite literal. She lived on the North Shore and the Harbour Bridge was a mile away, just for starters. There were few of the audience to strike much rapport with. Over interval coffee one evening, a chap introduced himself as a painter and - knowledgeably, I thought - I asked him if he worked in watercolour or oils. He replied that he mostly worked in houses, being a painter and a decorator.

I had a visit from Dave Armstrong, up from Pucka for some reason, and we had a few drinks at the Royal that I could hardly afford. Even the retainers were being paid sporadically now, as Glamour Homes experienced cash-flow problems, and my existence was becoming precarious. In the flat I had become adept at hanging about on the landing whenever another tenant was under the shower, in the hope that there might be credit on the gas meter which provided the hot water. Cold showers now that winter had arrived were an additional hardship I could do without. So adept did I become, in fact, that I could shower, shave and wash out socks and shreddies on as little as three penn'orth remaining on the meter (which had not yet been decimalised). I could transform ten cents into seven potatoes that yielded four plates of chips, but I occasionally splurged fifty cents on a small loaf and four eggs, which I consumed at a sitting.

The other tenants were a charmless lot and I took particular offence at the landlady's son, who lived upstairs with his wife. To judge from the noise late at night, he knocked her about a bit and I tried without success to interest the local police in this. Unless the victim was prepared to complain, it remained a 'domestic incident' and of no concern to the police. I was at the same time firmly advised not to get involved, on the grounds that I would be the likeliest candidate for arrest.

I renewed acquaintance with the nurses first met a couple of years earlier, and paid sporadic court to one of them who was a dead ringer for Miss Jones, in the TV sitcom '*Rising Damp*'. She seemed hardly better funded than I and we would spend an evening sitting on her bedsit sofa, exchanging rather passionless kisses.

A financial lifebelt in the form of annual bounty payment for my emergency reserve arrived shortly before my twenty-fifth birthday, as good a present as I could imagine. It seemed, in fact, a huge sum in the light of recent constraint. I proceeded to spend it with little regard for the future, although I made a priority of redeeming Maggie's radio and sending it off with some money I also had borrowed from her. I received a terse note in reply and that appeared to be that.

Against all expectation that brick veneer offered me any sort of realistic employment, I continued for a while and by this time I had struck up a companionship with two other salesmen. One was a recently arrived French-Canadian migrant, Marcel, and the other, Graham, was a native of Melbourne. Both had come to conclusions similar to mine that prosperity was elsewhere, and we had talked a little of taking a look at Queensland.

A battalion returned from Viet Nam and marched through the city. When it was dismissed, many of the blokes dispersed to the city pubs and I got chatting with a bloke I had served with in 2 RAR. It was a vaguely unsettling experience and I wondered if I was leaning towards another term of service. Concurrently, I finally abandoned Glamour Homes, Glamourite and door knocking for all time, and instead found some casual work at a car wash. I also found a roll of brand new carpet and tried, without success, to sell it. I simply was not cut out to be a salesman.

My newfound wealth was rapidly draining away. It had financed some meals with Noelene, the Miss Jones lookalike, but even these failed to generate much other than some ineffectual fiddling with her foundation garments. I eventually appeared on Noeleen's doorstep with the suitcase only recently retrieved from the care of Ron, the pouf, asking her to look after it for me whilst I was 'up north' earning a fortune.

    Despite her violent son and his late-night rages, the landlady had impressed upon me when I moved in her absolute insistence on quiet tenants. In deference to her wishes in this respect, I left the flat very, very quietly and very, very early one morning. The wander bug had bitten again.

Interlude

TENANT'S LAMENT

Home from the pub on Sunday morn, it's going on for three,
lazing on my cot at ten, I'm lost in reverie.
Now there's a whining at the door; oh Christ, it's Mrs D.
Dusting, bustling Landlady at her morning industry.

She's brought me a brand new dustbin, that's lined in polythene
and cautions me before she goes, "Be sure to keep it clean."
The old bag's bloody barmy. Now what the hell's she mean?
But I'm wrapping my potato peelings in an old Pix magazine.

Through the gate goes Mrs D. in her Sunday finery.
Wearing her hat and polished boots, for off to church is she.
Gone to genuflect and pray and recite a Hail Mary;
but I reckon it's in a coven is where she ought to be.

The upstairs tenant, Arnold Twit, such simple likes has he,
watching 'Wrestling from Great Britain' on his portable TV.
Home to his wife next Saturday night, he'll show her the best of three;
Home again is the wrestler, home from his weekend spree.

There's a mantrap living in Number Two, she's angular and pale,
she always has time to exchange a word with any passing male.
She was once a wartime nurse, she told me of the tale;
I'll bet she was at Sebastopol with Florence Nightingale.

The bloke I'm always shunning is the Conductor from Number Four,
no sooner does he spot me than his foot comes through the door.
At the mental age of seven, he's a bloody awful bore,
with his talk of clipping tickets on a daily city tour.

I start each day with a cup of tea, but there's trouble yet in store.
The meter's an armless bandit, sitting on the kitchen floor.
I've tried to sate it with pennies, but it swallows them by the score,
and I cannot boil the kettle till I feed a shilling more.

Home again is the wrestler, I can hear it from the yell,
"You can stick yer bloody sausage, yer bloody mash as well.
You can pack yer bags, I'm telling yer, and go to bloody hell."
Home is the drunken Arnold, home from the RSL.

We're all sharing one small copper and the situation galls,
to me the fate of last in line invariably falls.
Last week I tried before it dawned, but Mantrap ups and calls:
"You can't do your's yet, Mr F. I'm doing out my smalls."

No gentle Sorbent tissues grace the door of our WC,
instead, a book of numbers supplied by the PMG.
Two hundred and ten pink pages, suspended on a string,
and nothing short of dysentery with see Smiths out 'fore Spring.

The plaster off the ceiling keeps flaking in my tea,
the springs within my innerspring are springing into me.
But I've a plan for a life of ease that's evermore carefree,
I'll move lock, stock and barrel to the nearest monast'ry

I'll gladly join the Brothers (such a quiet little club),
and work from dawn till sunset for a modicum of grub.
I'll hoe and rake and dust and sweep, their flagstones I shall scrub,
provided I'm free on Friday night to pop down to the Lime Juice
Tub.

Coogee Bay Road
April 1966

19

Graham had recently bought a new mini, which he now proposed to drive to North Queensland, taking Marcel and me along to share costs. Unfortunately, he had bought the car on credit and had not made any payments for a month or two. We were at his place one evening when I happened to notice a bloke climbing behind the wheel of the car. Alerted, Graham dashed out to confront the bloke, and when Marcel and I also turned up the bloke decided to level the odds by producing a small automatic from his pocket. I reckoned that there was a pretty good chance that the automatic was nothing more lethal than a starting pistol, but a small voice asked me if I cared to be proved wrong over someone else's bad debts, and the answer was no.

We made a formal complaint to the local police, but the incipient interest in the desk sergeant's eyes died at the mention of 'credit company'. "That's between you and the company, Mate." was the advice Graham received, and I wondered if the sergeant was related to the domestic violence experts at Randwick.

Having assessed the situation, we decided to pool our cash to buy a secondhand vehicle for the journey, and we toured the numerous car sales on the Parramatta Road. The selection we made was not actually on the forecourt at all, but around the back and obviously traded in after a long life on the road. The salesman had not quite been contemptuous when we named our price, reserving that for our request for a testdrive. The car was a '52 Vauxhall Velox and the price was $60. You wouldn't buy much reliability for $60 now, and nor did you then.

The car had a pronounced sag to the rear and the brown corrosion of the body was swiftly overtaking the original grey paint job. Three of the tyres had about as much tread as a bandaid, with just one showing any meat on it, and when the engine was fired up it became obvious that the muffler didn't. We bought it.

The first of many problems manifested itself as we drove across the Harbour Bridge in the early evening. It began to rain and as soon as the windscreen wipers were turned on, the headlights went out. Switching the wipers off again restored the lights, but the windscreen was quickly made opaque with rain. Wipers on, lights off. Lights on, wipers off. Queensland suddenly seemed very distant.

Pausing to raise the bonnet offered no great insights into the problem, although hitting the voltage regulator appeared an effective means of restoring both wipers and lights for brief periods. We moved on.

The firewall of the vehicle was so corroded that abundant heat from the engine flooded the passenger compartment. Unfortunately, what also flooded in was carbon monoxide fume from the exhaust manifold that was cracked at the side of the engine block. This ingress made it prudent to drive with a window open, despite the rain, which was handy since the passenger's window had been wound down earlier for some purpose and now refused to wind up again.

The car employed column change for the four forward gears and it became apparent that the top gear selector was worn, necessitating holding the gear lever hard to keep top gear engaged. The gear linkages were also quite sloppy and during a late evening gear change some of the linkages fell onto the road. We had to make a flaming torch of some old newspapers in the back to go looking for them.

Also late in the evening, there was a suddenly alarming **THUMP-THUMP-THUMP** at the rear of the vehicle. We stopped to investigate and learned that the 'good' tyre had in fact been a retread, and probably a reject retread, which had now completely stripped and lay a few yards back, like an exhausted snake. The tyre itself now showed more canvas than a circus, adding to the illegality of the muffler, which was getting noisier by the minute.

The real problem, however, and one which we were as yet unaware of, was the failed suspension at the back of the Vauxhall. It was so bad that the underside of the body was actually resting against the spinning prop shaft, setting up a whine that we had mistakenly attributed to the differential (which actually was none too good). The friction set up by the contact between shaft and body eventually produced sufficient heat to cause the newspapers in the back to smoulder, although this smell was masked by the monoxide fumes leaking from the manifold.

I happened to be driving when Graham announced that something was burning.
"That's the monoxide you can smell." I replied. We continued for a few minutes until Graham repeated the claim. "Monoxide." I said. At Graham's third complaint I pulled off the road and as soon as Graham opened his door a great draught of fresh air ignited the papers under the back seat. Throwing handfuls of burning newspaper onto the road kept us all busy for a time, but the delay allowed the prop shaft and floor time to cool down, and for the monoxide fumes to disperse a little. It was also good to rest the left arm from the strain of holding top gear in. I additionally used the halt to try to wedge the muffler more effectively, reaching under the diminished space between the car floor and the road. At this precise moment Marcel, who had taken scant interest in the firefighting, chose to climb back into the car. His weight further reduced the gap, nicely pinning my head to the ground whilst coincidentally trapping my hand against the hot muffler. I spent a few moments demonstrating my fluency in Anglo-Saxon to the bi-lingual Marcel before extricating myself. It had been a wholly wasted effort, since the muffler fell off entirely a few miles along the road. Thereafter, we tried to coast through small towns in order to avoid drawing attention to the fact that the noise generated by the engine under acceleration was roughly that of a medium tank.

It took us two days just to reach Toowoomba, no great distance, and by then it was impossible to maintain top gear. We found ourselves on the edge of town and coincidentally alongside some car wreckers. My knowledge of car maintenance extended little further than checking the fuel, oil and water, but Graham had a degree of mechanical skill and he now proposed that we buy a scrap gear box and effect a roadside repair. As unlikely as this sounded, the alternatives were few and we duly purchased a box.

At this point we had a piece of luck beyond credence. Opposite the scrap yard was a house in large grounds and the owner proved to be a retired mechanic. Learning of our problem, he offered the use of a barn on the property and a box of tools. This was good fortune indeed, although the run of luck proved very short.

With the prop shaft, clutch and gearbox removed, we discovered that the replacement box, although a Vauxhall type, was the wrong fit, being mounted with six studs instead of the four on ours and with none of the holes aligning. The good news was that the gears were identical, so we began the laborious job of stripping them out to exchange for the worn set.

Another problem was food, since we were by now conserving every penny for fuel, and after dark I did a bit of foraging in local fields. All I managed to acquire was pumpkin, which I had never been fond of and which I have since hated, since all we ate for three days was boiled pumpkin.

As if life was insufficiently trying, I had now to deal with the embarrassment of a mistake by the old man whose property and kit we were using. He came down to check on progress on the second day and he suddenly looked keenly at the parachute smock I was wearing. "Were you serving at Ingleburn?" He suddenly asked me. I confirmed that and was about to tell him about 4 RAR, when he slapped me on the shoulder. "I thought so!" He exclaimed, "Inf Div Workshops, 1943!" It took me a moment to realise that the old bloke's mind perhaps wasn't quite as sharp as it had been, but the moment was lost as he embarked upon some lengthy reminiscence about mechanical problems at a time when I knew nothing more mechanical than a pram.

Worse was to come. In the evening, when we had eaten our boiled pumpkin, the old bloke came down to collect me and take me to the house to meet his wife, having told her about his 'old mate' from Ingleburn. I cringed at this since his wife would patently see a bloke in his mid-twenties and perhaps accuse me of conning her husband. Somewhat to my relief, it transpired that the bloke's wife was also senile and over a cup of tea I had a conversation with the couple which was surreal and also quite sad.

A cannibalised gearbox and a diet rich in carbohydrates did not solve all of our problems. In reassembling the box we fitted the clutch plate the wrong way around and the first gear change as we waved goodbye to the old couple stripped the springs out of the plate. We renewed acquaintance with the couple and trekked down to the scrap yard for a second-hand plate, although by this time we had no cash. Stealing a plate marked for an Austin A40, but looking about right, solved that particular problem, but the renewed journey was anything except brisk.

We encountered some dirt roads and the car wallowed very badly on the rough surface, making any speed above thirty MPH inadvisable. Renewed rain reminded us of the problem with the wipers and/or headlights, and we were still trying to freewheel through built-up areas to avoid drawing attention to the unmuffled engine. As if we hadn't sufficient problems, the 'new' gearbox also began to present symptoms of failure identical to the original. So far as the ride was concerned, it was difficult to know which was worse: coping with the wallowing car on bad roads as the driver; sitting as passenger where the rain shafted through the permanently open window; or sitting in the back where the vibration set up by the prop shaft and body contact threatened to loosen your fillings, and where the odour of incinerated newsprint persisted.

Four hundred miles north of Sydney we hit the Queensland town of Gladstone, and we had been on the road - or at the side of it - for almost exactly five days. That yielded an average speed of slightly less than three and a half miles an hour, which was a good strolling pace. The gearbox was rapidly failing, our petrol reserve had expired and the Vauxhall just didn't seem to want to go any further. I knew how it felt.

20

The journey had imposed strains upon the comradeship and we soon went our separate ways in Gladstone, which, if not exactly the far north, at least looked a good employment prospect. The town possessed a natural deep harbour and an aluminium refinery was being built to process for export the bauxite discoveries in the state. There was a good deal of associated work and there was even the prospect of worker's accommodation with some of the contracts. Unfortunately, the principal contractor, the Kaiser Corporation, was an American firm and there had been frequent strikes because of differences in American and Australian management methods. Just such a strike was imposed at this time and no firms were taking on.

Winter was well advanced by now and although the days were warm and even fairly hot, the nights were very cold. I slept for a night or two just outside the town under a large tarpaulin and a tree, but this had little to commend it. I then found what appeared to be an abandoned caravan on an open piece of land and gratefully moved in, only to be hastily moved out by the irate owner an hour or so later. My explanation of, 'Sorry, Mate, I thought it was derelict', doubtless sounding more like an insult than apology. I next discovered a large shed on a newly-cleared strip of bush, which perhaps had been intended as a building store, and I spent a couple of nights in it. Other occupants arrived, among them a bloke in his early forties and who had little in the way of conversation. A nod and 'G'day' seemed the extent of it, but perhaps you haven't much to say when you're in your forties and still on the road. Where everyone came from is anybody's guess, although at much that time I had read a piece which claimed that in the state of Victoria alone there were no less than 10,000 maintenance dodgers. A few of those were likely on the road. A group of Abos, with several dogs, also discovered the shed but there was still plenty of space for visitors and I had no fears for my kit. I was sleeping in most of it.

An early visit to the town employment office revealed about fifty blokes sitting in the street outside, clearly awaiting jobs. Periodically, a vehicle would draw up and the driver, without even bothering to enter the office, would say how many labourers he needed. The scramble this produced was impressive and the lesson I swiftly learned was that sharp elbows and a loud voice were the principal job qualifications here.

To provide the large quantity of water required by the refinery, a dam was being built on the River Boyne, about twenty miles from the town. I succeeded in being taken on as a labourer and although no accommodation was offered, I managed to get a lift in and out daily, on the promise of sharing fuel costs on payday.

Foundations for a pump house were being dug and it was the task of about twenty of us to carry chunks of rock blasted by a drilling and firing crew. Why the firm did not employ some sort of mechanical device for this was beyond me, unless plant hire was more expensive than wages. We were certainly earning no fortune, and we were monitored all day by a 'standover' man, who was not slow to chivvy us if he detected slack effort. At the end of the first day I asked him for a sub on wages but what I received in lieu was half a loaf of bread, two tins of bully beef and a packet of tobacco. This of course was manna and gratefully accepted. My nocturnal foraging at this time was producing paw paw (a sweet fruit which I haven't eaten since), sweet corn and, naturally, bloody pumpkin. I had also tried my hand at fishing off the Gladstone jetty but never grew quite hungry enough to eat the several pounds of seaweed that I caught.

The workers at the refinery were accommodated in a hostel and I took to nipping into it for a shower. I also used the laundry facilities until I was challenged by someone, but I made no attempt on the dining room since it was well policed.

I took to nursing a very small beer in the Young Australia Hotel, since I was keen to learn of other employment options. The hole in the ground offered no long-term prospects and it represented hard yakka for poor wages. The recent shortest day of the year had been plenty long enough for me.

Within a week or so I got a start with the firm which was laying the pipeline from the dam to the refinery, and the job was on a jackhammer. This was noisy and dusty but the job also offered food and accommodation in a bush camp and this package looked very attractive to me. Among the stuff I did not take with me to the camp was a sack containing about twenty pounds of paw paw. I had also by then been ejected from the hostel when discovered by authority in the showers, and that clearly was no longer an option.

The pipeline job offered $40 per forty-hour week, although overtime was possible, but an alarming discovery was that gangs seemed to be sacked quite arbitrarily, and apparently just to keep the rest on their toes.

I found myself working with an older man, Alan, who was rumoured to have once been a foreman fitter with the firm and sacked because of his drinking problem. Alan certainly *had* a drinking problem, and when we arrived at the site each morning he would be in such poor shape that his first act was to introduce air into the fuel lines of the diesel compressors that powered the jack-hammers. We would then flag this problem to the 'pink slip guy' who regularly cruised the line, and it might be an hour or two before the fitters arrived to diagnose the fault and bleed the air out of the line. Alan repeated this daily when I worked with him and no one ever seemed to cotton on.

Alan and I also shared a hut at the camp and I once offered him a mug of tea I had brewed on a small spirit stove. He declined, saying he had some errand to do, and after he had gone I discovered that he had drunk my bottle of methylated spirits. There were plenty of others with drink problems and they included a bloke who drank bottles of beer for breakfast. Another chap whiled away his time in the food queue by filling his pockets with cigarette ends. This was not the Ritz Hotel.

There were about a hundred blokes in the camp and drunken fights were not infrequent. When a man got stabbed over a card game dispute, it seemed a good time to be looking elsewhere for employment (about fifteen blokes not at all involved in the game or the fight simply vanished when the police visit became obvious). This decision was unexpectedly accelerated when the 'pink slip guy' came down the line a day or so later and peremptorily sacked the gang I was working on. Rumour had it that the sacking was because petrol had been stolen at the camp, and our gang was the only one in which a bloke had a private car. It was academic; I was out of a job, food and accommodation again and I wondered if the shed and the tarp were still on offer - to say nothing of a sackful of paw paw.

The refinery was taking on again and I secured a job as a builder's labourer. No accommodation went with the job but I struck up an acquaintance with a couple of glaziers and they in turn had a mate who was living in a caravan. The mate told me that a fire-damaged caravan in the same yard might be available at a modest rent, and this proved to be the case. For $2 a week I had a roof over my head and after a while you noticed neither the black walls nor the powerful smell of carbon. 'Fire-damaged' had proved to be something of a euphemism, since the van interior had been virtually destroyed. There was a shed in the yard with a water pipe and a shower rose and it became something of a joke between the other bloke and me to race home for the 'hot' water. The sun during the day took a little of the chill off the water where the pipe ran above the ground.

I began working a sixty-hour week that spanned six days, and laboured for the spectrum of trades on the site. Only the bricklayers employed their own labourers - possibly having noted the poor quality elsewhere - and most of the tradesmen were agreeable to work with. Whenever I needed a tool, the foreman would invite me to 'find' it on an adjacent site, and I noted with some amusement that I was eventually given the job of painting identifying marks on our by then considerable range of 'found' tools.

I equipped the van with a kerosene lamp, whose fumes were not unpleasant, and a small stove that burned bottled gas. I generally bought a box of canned food each payday and augmented that fare with odd meals out. I once bought a cheap job lot of canned spaghetti and used it in my site sandwiches day after day, to the obvious puzzlement of my companions, whose lunchboxes provided by the hostel were of Fortnum & Mason proportions. There was no form of heating in the van and I tended to get under the blankets quite early most nights.

I did some weekend drinking with the neighbour, Bob, but he proved to have a short fuse if provoked in the bar and a drinking session in his company was seldom dull. We left the pub one Sunday, carrying bottled beer, and were accosted by a policeman on some account. Bob calmly handed his armful of bottles to me, decked the policeman and retrieved his bottles almost without pause. We stayed out of town for a lengthy spell after that.

Staying in his caravan was his mother and sister and we sometimes drank a bottle of rum over games of Euchre. I also combined with Bob on his plan to fit a six-cylinder engine into a four-cylinder car he had acquired. Since the engine mounts did not match up, we pushed the car to a nearby garage and asked the Greek proprietor to weld the engine in. This he began to do on the garage forecourt near the petrol pumps, using oxyacetylene equipment. The disconnected fuel line to the engine had been stowed away against the firewall and during the welding it dropped forward, spraying fuel that immediately caught fire. Bob laughed uproariously at this development, whilst the Greek danced about, shouting incomprehensibly. The risk of the vehicle tank and the pump tanks going up must have been considerable, but we eventually quelled the blaze and the project died with it.

The sixty-hour week paid $60 but strikes remained frequent and pulled the wage down to $40 more often. I was saving quite hard though and my overheads were not great. Bob bought a '51 Humber Hawk and we made trips to Bundaberg and Gin Gin, suffering considerable damage when we collided with a large kangaroo on one evening return. The 'roo was maimed by the collision and I had to despatch it with blows from a jack handle.

After three months I sacked the job and prepared for return to the West. Before the journey, however, I planned a three-day stay on Heron Island, which was about the southernmost inhabited island of the Great Barrier Reef. I paid $32 for three days, then extended it for a week since it was such a lovely setting. The island was only about a quarter of a mile in diameter, but the coral perimeter extended that by about a mile at a low tide. When the sea retreated, it revealed deep pools where the coral had collapsed, and each of these would teem with brilliantly coloured tropical fish. These would swim unconcernedly whilst one snorkelled among them. It was mesmerising.

During the evenings I would drink at the bar until the generator was turned off at about 0100hrs, and the companions included a cousin of Barry Humphries, who I had never heard of. By day I would loaf on the sand, explore the coral pools or wander about. One day I picked up a shell which was clearly marked with a number, and I deduced that it may have migrated from a distant shore. In some excitement I took it to the bloke who manned a small Commonwealth Scientific and Industrial Research Organisation station on the island. The CSIRO man shook his head, "Naw, Mate. I labelled that one yesterday."

21

Returning to the mainland after a happy week that I determined to repeat some time, I hitchhiked to Brisbane and then, untypically, bought a first-class ticket for a sleeper to Sydney. The American president, Lyndon Johnson, was also in town and the subject of a noisy demonstration by protesters against the war in Viet Nam. I spent a week in the city, staying at the Peoples' Palace, and I collected my case from Noelene. I didn't rule out a return to the city, but nor would I put much money on it.

I spent a week with Jan and Arch at Pucka, and Arch was now studying for a commission. I met a few former members of 40 Air Supply at the camp, and I also spent some time with one in Adelaide as I passed through. These breaks were pleasant although they rapidly drained the product of my recent thrift.

A few days at home preceded a fortnight in November on the second reserve camp, which was conducted partially at Karrakatta and included a week at the Bindoon training area, a good stretch north of Perth. I noted on this occasion that few of the instructors had an infantry background and seemed to have no great knowledge of working in the bush. It was also quite obvious that they were entirely lacking in the enthusiasm displayed by the SAS instructors at the first camp. Noting that reservist success depended in no small measure upon regular infrastructure and enthusiastic support, would be more fully brought home to me more than twenty years later.

After the exercise at Bindoon ended, we spent a fair bit of time plucking sheep ticks out of various parts of ourselves, then organised a party at the Ocean Beach Hotel, at Cottesloe. I arranged a later date with one of the barmaids, taking her to see '*The Sound of Music*' in the city. It was a film I would certainly have walked out on, had I not been harbouring carnal hopes of ending a lengthy period of celibacy. We spent a few days together in Perth then my cash ran out. I had a rail warrant for Kalgoorlie and passed the day until the evening train strolling along the embankment that flanked the Swan River. I was hailed by a passing lorry driver and it was the bloke I had visited in Goulburn gaol.

I fronted the Great Boulder again and upon learning that no surface work was available I accepted an underground job as a fitter's mate. Workers blew in and blew out of the town and the mines attracted a fair proportion of transient labourers, who would work for a week or a month or two then finish up. 'Finishing up Friday' was known on the mines as 'doing a Robinson Crusoe', another piece of Australian humour which I appreciated.

The fitter was a bloke named Jim Fraser. He was about fifty and had lost an index finger and an eye in separate mining accidents. This possibly contributed to his bleak view of just about everything connected with the mines, and our crib breaks underground were punctuated by lengthy whinges from Jim. He also had a ritual that consisted of minutely inspecting the crib his wife had prepared for him, then dumping it in the bin and getting on instead with the first of several cigarettes. I soon learned to grunt assent during Jim's monologues without really listening to them, and I learned also to carry a paperback in the tool bag, for we were often stranded between levels with time to kill.

The cages began to lower the miners and other workers at 0800hrs and they serviced the deepest shafts first. On the Boulder, this was five thousand feet. At 1500hrs the cages would pull from the lowest shafts and between those times only the shift bosses had any guaranteed travel - unless someone rang out twelve bells for an accident, which would put a cage straight to that platform. Once when ineptly swinging a spoiler (a sledgehammer) I caught a finger against protruding rock, opening it to the bone, and the shift boss insisted on ringing twelve bells. This was embarrassing in a week during which a miner had crushed his pelvis and was some time in being recovered, and when another had gone down about fourteen hundred feet of shaft without a cage. The latter, of course, was quite beyond pain.

We might have to service or repair equipment on several levels and the options were reduced to two. We might climb up or down a series of ladders in a secondary shaft, or we could ring out and secure a ride on an ore skip. This meant standing on the top edge of the skip and clinging to its frame whilst the timber-plated walls of the shaft rushed by at sixteen feet per second. This routine doubtless broke several mining regulations, but it was a damned sight easier than climbing ladders. The ladders in any case, often slimy with damp, accumulated dirt, were not that safe. The alternative routes for travel between levels, whenever a cage or a skip was unavailable, could also be confusing. Sent off to the surface to collect a replacement part one day, I emerged from a totally different mine, the Lake View & Star, although no one appeared to find this strange.

I never heard of any death resulting from riding the skip, but rock falls accounted for a few, and a number of miners simply fell down shafts through some negligence, if not design. The unseen killer, however, was silicosis and it killed very many more in the longer term by paralysing the respiratory system. There were a number of 'dusted' miners among the membership at the Mines' and City Worker's Club and they provided a thoughtful study for anyone who contemplated a working lifetime underground.

Water ran continually through the ground and it was conducted into underground reservoirs, from where it could be pumped to the surface. At some point, I was required to man such an underground pump when the regular attendant went on holiday. There proved to be little to do, except check the mercury tilt-switch floats in the dam, or to re-pack with greasy hemp the pump glands which might blow out periodically. It was a soft job and actually reserved for older blokes who yet had a year or two to run before a pension might be paid. I had no need for the lamp on my helmet, for the pump chamber was both spacious and well lit, and it was a fine chance to catch up on some reading. The chamber boasted a small library of paperbacks that mostly ran to Westerns. There was also the Book of Mormon, which possibly had been left by a visiting disciple of Joe Smith, but I have to say that it was not a thrilling read.

On New Year's Eve I was invited to a party in Kalgoorlie and was loaned someone's car. After the party I tried to see in the New Year horizontally by visiting the brothels, but they had closed. I drove home and I cannot imagine what sort of state I was in.

Drinking with the Old Man, invariably at the Mines' & City, whether just after work or later in the evening, produced marathon efforts which were good for neither health nor wallet. The Old Man was good company though and he attracted an interesting circle about him.

The news from Pucka was of a nephew, Ian Michael, and at much the same time we heard from England that Gran'Ma Lindop, Mam's mother, had died. We were reflecting the cycles of life and death. I also heard from Danny Wright, who had been a civilian for some months, and who shortly would return to the army. I wondered anew if this was the sensible thing for me to do, being by now none too impressed with my lack of progress after nearly two years of civilian life.

When my reservist bounty of $300 was paid in April, I bought a '57 Holden Station Sedan. The urge to move was growing and I thought that I might attempt to bring some style to my travel this time. This purchase almost exactly coincided with a visit by Danny Oates and George Whitty, the glaziers I had met at Gladstone. They were bound for Port Hedland, in the north of the state, where there apparently was a fair bit of work, and they wondered if I was interested. They stayed for a few days at the house and, no mean drinkers themselves, were greatly impressed by the prodigious amounts that the Old Man shoved away. They moved on and I arranged to follow them in due course.

The Holden needed some work on the lights, muffler and brakes, and the Old Man, who had a good working knowledge of engines, did some work on the tappets. I gradually built a small cash reserve and set off one morning, driving initially south before swinging for Geraldton and the coast. The consumption was twenty-three miles per gallon at a steady fifty, although the car was good for about seventy-five. On the mostly dirt roads north of Geraldton, however, much more modest speeds were advisable.

From Geraldton I had a hitchhiker aboard, a red-bearded itinerant folk singer who was hoping to busk his way to Darwin. He proved to have no tucker in his swag, no money, very little in the way of conversation and he moaned bitterly when I cannoned across a creek bed culvert that bounced his guitar (and us) quite severely against the roof of the car. That's the trouble with hitchhikers, of course. Bludge your tobacco, eat your tucker, pain in the arse, etc etc.

I had covered the seven hundred miles to Geraldton with an overnight roadside halt, but made much slower progress on the seven hundred miles to Port Hedland. The gravel surface reduced my speed to twenty miles per hour on long stretches, and the road had been washed out by floods in some parts. New sections had been hastily graded and I lost my direction on one of them, ending up nearly a hundred miles off route at the town of Exmouth. I elected to spend the night there, setting off early the next day and almost as quickly getting bogged in a swampy section of track. A passing police vehicle towed me out and the remainder of the trip passed uneventfully, except that taking a creek bed too quickly had removed the exhaust tail pipe.

Danny and George had fixed me up with a job as a carpenter's labourer and the job included board at the Esplanade Hotel. I had a bed on the verandah among a dozen others and sleep was frequently interrupted by fights erupting on the street below. Many of these were between Aborigines, who nominally at least lived in a housing development on the edge of the town. They apparently were in receipt of some form of a state pension, which they tended to blow in the bar as soon as it was paid. Their existence appeared to be apartheid without written rules, and I was among the very many who saw without seeing the sad plight of the Aborigines. Thirty years on, I have written as a member of Amnesty International to enquire of the Australian Prime Minister why more than a hundred Aborigines have died in police custody in the last decade. I have received no reply. Thirty years ago I firmly believed that I was living in the land of 'the fair go'. Today I am not so sure.

I struck up a bar acquaintance with an English bloke and it is interesting to me now that in my diary I referred to him as 'the Pom'. The job was all right and it paid $84 for a fifty-hour week. The muffler fell off the Holden but few cars about the town appeared to have them and I took my time about replacing it. Fights in the bar proved a staple of entertainment, although they were usually brief and confined. I challenged a loudmouth on some occasion but generally avoided trouble.

After a few weeks in the 'Nade, I found a job on a motel construction outside the town and moved my kit into the marquee which served as accommodation. It was fairly basic, as was the food that was cooked by the foreman's wife. Standing in the queue for my first meal I heard someone complain that it was fish, yet again. "Get a lot of fish, do we?" I asked. The chap turned around to face me. "You get so much fucking fish here," He said, "that your stomach goes in and out with the fucking tide." The food took a turn for the better when the foreman left quite suddenly, taking the fish cuisine expert with him. It transpired that the foreman had been guilty of some creative accountancy, paying wages to several labourers who didn't actually exist.

I found it easier to save now that I wasn't living in a pub, and I reckoned on saving about $800 before moving on. Danny and George had already left for Darwin and that sounded a reasonable place to visit.

There were some wild men on the site and one of them had actually managed to overturn a full size billiard table during a disturbance in the town. It was reckoned by a witness that the arriving police had seen this and each of them simply grabbed the nearest man for arrest purposes, rather than tackle the big man. There were also some characters. I laboured for a Scots bloke who had been sacked from another job in the town but told to hang half a dozen doors before he left. He spent the day carefully checking in the hinges and planing to size before hanging the doors - from the top of the frame. He had also acquired some letterheads from the previous firm, which was a major American contractor, and he asked me to type up some glowing references for him that he then signed with a flourish.

The motel was being built to hacienda style and since all the walls were painted white, I graduated to brush hand and then a painter, usefully increasing my wages. When that work expired I got a job driving an REO tipper for a bloke in the town who had various contracts for asphalting.

The year was wearing on and a delay in travelling to Darwin might mean a wait of some months, since the Fitzroy River could not be forded when the wet season began. In mid-November I loaded the Holden and prepared to travel in tandem with two Irish lads who until recently had the brick-making contract for the motel. They too were keen to see what Darwin had to offer. We waited for the heat of the day to fade a little and we set off, hoping for an uneventful journey. I probably should have known better.

"D'you get much fish here" I asked

22

The journey began badly and failed to improve. Within a few miles of travel out of Hedland I noted that the radiator was running hot, but I pressed on in the hope that this would not manifest a more serious problem. I was distracted from that late in the evening when I cannoned across a creek bed culvert (again) which completely stripped a tyre off and also removed a relatively new muffler. I fitted the spare wheel, left the remains of the muffler in the creek bed and pressed on until the dirt road degenerated into what was hardly more than a couple of wheel ruts.

Alec and Rob had been following me at a couple of mile's distance to allow the blinding dust to settle, and they caught me up when I stopped to deal with another problem. The culvert had also damaged a steering drop arm and we pulled off the track to sleep until daylight provided the opportunity to arrange a temporary repair. I had been reluctant to waste the hours of darkness resting, since the relative cool of the evening alleviated the overheating of the radiator, a problem which was undiminished.

We effected the repair and got under way again, only to stop a few miles along when my fan belt stripped. I had a comprehensive pile of spares, which the Old Man had assembled for me, and a fan belt was prominent among them, but it was an irritating delay. Fitzroy Crossing was four hundred miles from Hedland and it seemed to be getting little closer.

The track failed to improve and as the sun rose I had to make increasingly frequent halts to cool the engine and refill the radiator, fortunately having plenty of water aboard. I was also carrying a twenty-gallon drum of fuel aboard, which caused another small problem when the car went into a four-wheel drift in soft dust, and the edge of the drum smashed the rear window. I then hit a large 'roo which chose a bad time to cross the road during the night hours, although the damage arising was confined to the bodywork. The journey was beginning to feel like that of a year or so previously.

It took twenty-four hours, mostly travelling, to reach Broome, the former pearl-fishing town, and we spent a night on the beach there hoping to get a good run at the journey on the following day. I had the drop arm inspected at a local garage but no quick repair was possible. Since the temporary repair seemed to be holding up, I decided to continue, although the boiling engine was of rather more concern now.

We left Broome at 1700hrs, again having let the sun lose most of its heat, and at midnight we crossed the Fitzroy River at a fording point. This would not be possible in a week or two, when the rains of the wet season would turn it into a deeply swirling barrier to late traffic.

Eighteen hours later we arrived in the former gold-mining town of Hall's Creek, and it was more than obvious to me now that the Holden would not complete the journey. We had covered eleven hundred miles but were not yet out of West Australia and had another six hundred miles to cover.

I guessed that the engine block had cracked and there was no quick fix for that. Actually, there was no fix of any kind at Hall's Creek, which was hardly more than a refuelling stop on the track between West Australia and the Northern Territory. The Irish lads offered to tow the vehicle, but this offer, although generous, was impractical. Their own vehicle, which was a '59 Holden utility, was pretty loaded and likely to become another victim. I gave them my kit, other than the bag that had done roadside duty before, and waved them off. I hoped to catch them up in Darwin and in the meantime I was awaiting the big lift.

At least, I had put the Fitzroy behind me, although there remained the uncomfortable possibility that nothing else might appear on the Hall's Creek side of it until the wet season ended. The heat was already well into the century and at the roadside I fashioned a shelter from some forty-four gallon drums and a piece of tarp which was lying about. This might be a lengthy wait.

A pub survived in what remained of the town and I made an early visit. The request for a beer produced a quart bottle on the bar top and no glass. The beer was not chilled and the price would have bought three bottles elsewhere, which was fine if you were elsewhere The Landlord proved also to be a stickler for protocol. **"No bare buff in here!"** He bellowed one day when I strolled in without a shirt on. He was also short on jokes, political views, football analysis, opinion on current affairs, chat, smiles, advice or any form of social intercourse, but he did own the only pub in about three hundred miles.

My roadside shelter attracted another tenant, an Abo, who was in residence when I returned from a hot bottle of beer one lunch. Since his drinking habits appeared to be no worse than mine, I did not object.

I counted the days in hours and there had been seventy-one of them by the time a semi-trailer drew to a halt and my plea for a lift was accepted. The journey to Darwin would occupy a further three days, and seemed much longer since I wholly failed to strike any rapport with the driver. Despite willing attempts to assist with numerous blown tyres, I seemed only to annoy him. His name was Angus and in a slip of the tongue I once called him Agnes, at which point I thought I was about to be turfed into the bush.

Angus' load slipped at some point on a bad piece of track and we spent some hours in the noon sun re-stacking it. The 'roo bar on the front of the vehicle was hung with half a dozen canvas water bags, and we drained half of them whilst at the work. We also bathed in the Katherine River during a pause and I was fairly stinking by then. Perhaps that was the basis of Angus' antipathy, although I have to say that he was no rosebud, either.

We arrived in Darwin towards midday and I found Alec and Rob simply by touring the few hotels. They were staying at a Salvation Army hostel and I joined them there. Neither had yet found a job, but it was early days and a rest after the rigours of travel seemed desirable.

An effect of the 'wet season' was to curtail bush work, driving workers into Darwin to compete for the few jobs. Employment prospects proved none too good, when we did get around to looking, and it appeared that only casual work, and low-paid at that, was on offer. We picked up a few days in a cordial factory, humping crates of bottles around, but saw little future and no money in it. One of my companions was a woman who turned out to be more usually employed as a prostitute, using the cordial factory job as a cover, and to avoid vagrancy charges. The short time fee was $10 and since she had no upper row of teeth, was covered in crudely executed tattoos and was built like a forty-four-gallon drum, I wondered who actually got the ten bucks. I did not ask. She was referred to, if not very directly, as 'Oddjob'.

We usually drank at the Don but the other two or three pubs took it in turns to remain open until 2330hrs, an hour later than usual. We would therefore drink up - sometimes having spent the entire day in the pub - and move around to the late bar. Drinking was about the only way to ensure sleep, for the humidity was oppressive.

Via a contact at the Don, where I also ran across a bloke I had known in the army, we got a job on the wharf, stacking cement that came in from Japan. It paid $1 an hour and was filthy work. The heat in the iron shed was ferocious and the cement dust blinding and choking. To protect mouths and noses against inhalation of the dust, we were issued with what looked suspiciously like sanitary towels and they were of little use. Cement burns on the skin were quite common and no one in his right mind should have worked there.

There actually were a number on the gang who were not in their right mind; these being the 'alkies' of which Darwin had a good proportion. Whereas most of us brought in a sandwich or a meat pie for the midday break, the alkies would bring a newspaper-wrapped bottle of cheap wine. Rather than await the midday break, they would frequently retire behind the cement stack for a restorative swig, and a number of them slept in the shed each night.

Darwin was 'top of the track' and psychologically the end of the line for a number of arrivals. The town suicide rate was something like ten times the national average and it was not hard to see the reasons, with just a casual glance about the bar or the workplace. I was not greatly surprised to learn, three decades later, that the Northern Territory had been the first state to legalise euthanasia.

In the Don one day we noticed an Abo whose fingers and thumbs were missing at the first joint, and we speculated that this could have been a tribal punishment. We invited him into the group, buying him beer until we felt able to broach the subject, asking what had happened to his hands. "Leprosy." He replied and we were suddenly less enthusiastic for his company.

We attracted some other company and equally bizarre. One was a recently released convict and another was a dwarf who would from time to time leap onto the bar top, via a stool, to perform a little dance. Neither of these companions endeared us to the bar staff, but both, however, were welcome one night when we were caught up in some fight at which we were outnumbered. The ex-convict swung a bar stool to terrible effect whilst the dwarf ran continually at people's legs. It did not seem in the slightest bizarre at the time.

Fights at the 'late pub' were endemic and one such involved us in a fracas with a group of Thursday Islanders. The island was in the Torres Strait, off the north coast of Queensland, and the natives were traditional railroad workers in various parts of the mainland. On this occasion, we were about to march out of the pub with a small group of challengers when we noticed that about thirty more were standing outside. We called the police instead and had to be ignominiously escorted out.

An exchange of accommodation was effected and we moved into a Commonwealth Hostel, where bed and board came at modest rates, just sixteen dollars a week, all found.

The rates had to be modest since the cement stacking was intermittent and nothing else was offering. By coincidence, I loaded a semi-trailer one afternoon and discovered that the driver had lifted me across the Nullarbor the year before. I happily bought him a beer.

Our four-man gang shifted thirty tons of cement in ninety minutes one day, for the same dollar, and we reckoned that it was time to move on. Alec and Rob were keen to try Mount Isa, across the Queensland border, but I was none too distant from another reserve camp commitment and the West beckoned. In the meantime, we thought that we might take a look at Alice Springs.

Whilst I drank warm beer in the pub, another tenant arrived

23

We left Darwin at 0800hrs on a Saturday in the first week of January, heading directly south. Katherine was two hundred miles down the road and we paused there only briefly in order to cover six hundred miles by midnight. It had been an uneventful ride, apart from 'bottoming' the Ute a few times in potholes which were deceptively filled to the rim with dust as fine as talcum powder. When we hit three of them in very short succession, bruising ourselves against the cab, Rob allowed a faint note of annoyance to enter his voice. "D'you think, Alec," He asked, "that you might miss those once in a while?"

At midnight we slept at the roadside for some hours then continued to Tennant Creek and breakfast. We completed the journey, of eight hundred miles or so, in the early evening at Alice where we made early acquaintance of the barmaid at the Stuart Hotel. Her prognosis of local jobs proved discouraging, although we were not staying long in any case.

We slept in the bush a mile or two out of town for a few nights, being somewhat plagued by mosquitoes, while we confirmed the barmaid's opinion of local work. We tried for a job as 'desert wharfies'; the term given to labourers who transhipped freight from one rail gauge to another, but were unsuccessful. I also applied for a position as a road sweeper, but the job went to the only other applicant who was a university graduate. It was a powerful demonstration of the advantages which tertiary education confers.

Alec and Rob soon decided to move on to Mt Isa and I found accommodation in a small hostel in the town, believing that I might as well pass a few more days in pleasant idleness. I struck up a drinking acquaintance with an American who was passing through, and he asked me where he might procure 'grass' locally. I assumed that he meant Marijuana and told him that his chances of finding grass of any description in the Alice were pretty slim. I suppose that the drugs' scene was happening somewhere in Australia at this time, but neither the 'top of the track' nor the 'dead centre' seemed a likely venue. During my unintended diversion to Exmouth on the drive to Hedland, I had been drinking with a couple of American sailors from a US communications facility in the area. They had invited me back to the base to 'sniff some glue', which was an invitation I found easy to resist. I left the pub wondering if they did any important sort of job at the base.

I stretched out in the sun for a few days, read a copy of *'War and Peace'* that had been in my bag for some time, and tried without success to cultivate the interest of the barmaid. In the middle of the month I caught the train to Port Augusta, assuming that I would make a quick connection with the Trans for the journey to Kalgoorlie. I really ought to have known better.

The news in Augusta was that a stretch of the Trans line had been washed out and that no trains were departing until repairs were effected. It was possible to buy a ticket and sit on the train in the meantime, but the view through the window was pretty bad at eighty miles an hour; at the halt it really *was* boring. I booked into a hotel where the mattress was like a slab of granite, although I didn't really notice after several hours in the bar, and it was the bar I went to each morning, having first established that the train was going nowhere.

The delay lasted for three days and it was a relief to get moving. On the Nullarbor we passed the washaway and a derailed train. The carriages were quite crumpled although, amazingly, no one had been hurt. Ours arrived in Kalgoorlie at much the usual time of evening and it was a short progression to home and to the Mines' & City with the Old Man.

Although I had thought that I was cutting it fine for the reserve camp, a letter awaiting me at home advised a delay in the camp of some weeks. This put me back into the job-seeking game again and I thought that it would be the mine again. As it happened, a new railroad was being built between Perth and Kalgoorlie and the firm was taking on labour. I applied and duly got a start.

Prior to Federation, in 1901, each of the states, which had grown from colonies, built railways to service the towns but without much regard for neighbouring states. The result was railways of varying gauges and the need for train transfers on long journeys interstate. Travel from Sydney to Perth necessitated half a dozen such transfers and the decision had been taken in the early Sixties to lay a standard gauge track across the country. The section from Perth had now reached Southern Cross - country town of my eviction some years before - and I secured a lift to the camp.

The working week was of sixty hours that paid $50, with food and accommodation thrown in. The work itself would prove to be physically demanding and the turnover of labourers was very high, some leaving within hours.

The core of the eighty or so at the camp proved to be Thursday Islanders, but if I had any reservations about these as a result of the Darwin encounters, then they were quickly dispelled. This lot was tough but friendly and accepting of anyone who could swing a hammer without much complaint.

The hammer was a fourteen-pounder and I made the early acquaintance of it, being put to work driving anchors onto the railway line flange. The anchor was a piece of spring steel which had to be 'sprung' onto the flange with an accurate blow from the hammer, and its purpose was to prevent movement of the wooden sleeper. It was pretty much like a large paper clip. The problem was that the man with the hammer had to balance on the railway line in order to bring the hammer to bear properly, and this was not easy. It was also quite easy to miss the anchor entirely and drive the hammer shaft against the rail flange in a spine-jarring swing. This usually took a chunk out of the handle and it was not unusual for beginners to fit a new handle three or four times each day. There were days when I arrived at the site and deliberately snapped a worn handle in order to buy some minute's respite fitting a new one.

It was backbreaking work and quite relentless. A Ganger hovered all day and even smoking was only permissible provided that you continued to swing the hammer. Sackings seemed quite arbitrary and there were a good few blow-ins who had no intention of working. The blow-ins caused some problems in the camp, usually in the canteen, but that was not my problem since I usually went directly from work to the shower, then to eat and to bed. On the few occasions that I entered the canteen, I got some hard looks for ordering lemonade but nothing physical was offered. I had also helped myself to a hickory shaft from the abundant pile of them and took to carrying it about the camp with me. I wasn't looking for trouble, but nor was I about to suffer any.

No one offered the Islanders any trouble, but they got a fair bit of it when they made Saturday visits to Kalgoorlie. I don't doubt that it was racially inspired. The Islanders had huge reserves of stamina and liked nothing better at the end of the day than to play football for some hours. They also were quite immune to heat and usually did not strip off their outer layers of clothing until midday, whereas I went out in just shorts and boots at 0500hrs, when we had breakfast before riding in the lorry to the line.

Another joyful job was in dragging sleepers up the embankment to roughly position them for the line-laying gang. At a mile a day, this was a lot of sleepers, but the best of them was me, rolling into my cot before even the sun had gone down.

One of the older white blokes on the gang failed to appear for work one day and was later found in his hut. He was sitting cross-legged on bare bed springs, with a towel around his head and otherwise clad only in a loin cloth that he fashioned from a torn sheet. This Mahatma Ghandi impersonation was unexplained, other than that the bloke had gone quietly mad, and he was duly carted off to hospital. He did not return.

Membership in the Australian Workers' Union was compulsory, but we were not well served by it. The water truck that cruised the line was a former petrol bowser and the water tasted terrible. I collared the union rep when he next appeared to levy the joining fee on another batch of new arrivals, and he was clearly affronted that anyone should suggest he do his job.

The breakfast and evening meals were good, but the crib was always rubbish. We had peanut butter sandwiches for several days in succession, and the cook became a target for some richly deserved abuse, although his sheer size deterred any physical threat.

$300 went missing from the canteen and the Southern Cross police were brought in. It soon transpired that the theft was by the canteen manager and he had to be taken into protective custody. Several of the workers had other reasons to fear police interest and they were not appreciative of the manager's act in drawing police attention.

During this period I was reviewing the three years since leaving the army, and it was not an encouraging retrospective. Some extremely crap jobs on crap wages had led inexorably to the latest crap one, where I felt completely whacked out within an hour of starting each day. I was working in considerable heat - a hundred and eight in the shade and there was no shade - with about three hundred flies in close attendance, and I reckoned that swinging the hammer for ten hours meant that I was lifting about fifteen tons per day. That worked out to about ninety cents a ton. Given the nature of the fag packet calculations and even the faultiest arithmetic, I reckoned that a dollar a ton would be poor reward. I had been a victim of the heat on the very first day, when I stripped off my shirt and laid it on a flat car that subsequently was towed up the line. My back was burned and blistered by the noon heat and I was sleeping on my stomach for a couple of nights.

I acquired a new roommate, but only until I discovered that he wanted to play Slim Dusty records all night. I invited him to fuck off and he went away to conduct his soirees to a more appreciative audience. After six weeks I felt that I had contributed more than enough to Australia's industrial progress and I returned to Boulder. It was time to remove the beard, acquire a haircut and resume the uniform.

24

The camp in March proved very different to those that had preceded it. No attempt was made to revise us in basic infantry skills and nor was there any revision of trade training. After a few days I was detached to Northam Camp, about sixty miles north of Perth and joined with a small team of SAS instructors, Hank, Jim and Brian, to instruct to a CMF annual camp. I had enjoyed the small amount of instructing I had found in regular service, and the Northam experience was equally satisfying, with the exception of an incident in one of my classes. There was more than a suspicion that some of the CMF reservists had signed up to avoid a term of national service, under a deferment programme, and it seemed likely that avoidance of a year in Viet Nam might be a factor in it. Whatever the truth of that, a member of a weapons class I held was openly contemptuous of the instruction and he made no attempt to learn. Enraged, I had a go at him then tried to take the matter further at Battalion Headquarters. BHQ didn't want to know and that ended the matter.

An exercise in the second week proved more rewarding and there were obviously CMF Diggers who were prepared to lend plenty of effort. I also appreciated the bush week as a break in what had become a succession of hard social evenings in Northam. Hank and Co. knew a pub owner in the town and he frequently locked us in at closing time, making the 0600hrs reveille an unhappy experience.

Before the camp ended, I sought an interview with the Command RSM and discussed with him my intention to apply for regular service on reservist terms, something for which a precedent seemed to exist. Specifically, I asked if I might undergo a tour in Viet Nam and I mentioned that I saw a resumption of regular service as the logical outcome. A formal application was subsequently submitted, but the idea came to nought. There was no especially good reason for my application, although I recognise now that active service -irrespective of the morality of the particular fight - will always prove attractive to young men who wish to be weighed in the balance, whilst putting their courage to sterner tests than those which are offered by routine training. It is doubtless a form of curiosity which has killed a good many young men down the years.

Arch had by this time returned to the SAS, with Jan and their son occupying a married quarter at Campbell Barracks. I made a visit and was invited to stay with them for a while. The offer I was delighted to accept since I had recently experienced a desire for a more ordered life. Refreshment in the pools of libraries, museums, bookshops and theatres which the city offered seemed a good and timely substitute for rough companions and employment uncertainties.

Not that I was about to find work immediately. I had saved a good quid at Hedland, shortly had another bounty to look forward to and was happy to loaf for a bit. I was also happy to avoid drinking, exempt for a Saturday stroll of a mile or so to the Ocean Beach Hotel for a solitary evening. Elsewhere, I found a folk music venue in the city and although it was not particularly good, it passed a couple of hours each Friday. I bought a guitar and some lessons on a weeknight and learned to strum seventeen chords. This was probably about fifteen more than Elvis Presley, but he obviously had something else going for him. A good manager, perhaps. I possibly dreamed of owning a Gibson guitar - or at least learning to play identifiable tunes on the anonymous instrument I actually owned - but this did not eventuate.

I also bought a secondhand typewriter, since I had some illusions of writing at the time, but the machine was also useful for producing legible letters. I briefly worked in the Drapery and Manchester department of David Jones, a large city store, but the work was utterly dull. Some fine looking women worked on the same floor but they were, without exception, married. It occurred to me then that it might be a most pleasant thing to be married and leading a settled life, although I had no one even remotely in focus. I left the store after a fortnight and took as job as a builder's labourer on a small apartment block at Shenton Park. By this time I had acquired another vehicle, a '57 Volkswagen Beetle for $220. At least, having an air-cooled engine, I wouldn't face any radiator problems with it.

At the folk club I began to meet a girl who made pleasant company. Her older brother turned up one night - presumably to look me over - and I recognised him as a bloke who had served on the Airborne Platoon at RAAF Williamtown. More 'small world' proof in the same place was when a visiting folk singer turned out to be a chap I had once tried to flog Glamourite with.

Life at Swanbourne was pleasant. Jan set a good table and I had the vicarious enjoyment of watching my nephew grow. I occasionally baby-sat and even mastered the technique of changing nappies, although I was uncertain of how much future value this might prove. I attended a few job interviews, seeking the unusual, but nothing came of them.

The labouring paid $40 for a forty-five-hour week and in July four of the eight labourers were laid off. I happened not to be among them but the job was in any case running out. A carpenter on the job was one I had met in Port Hedland and the meeting set me to think anew about a spell up north. Then, right on cue, Alec and Rob appeared.

They had found little work at Mt Isa and swiftly travelled through the state before heading back to the West. On the motel I had worked on, Alec and Rob had managed the fairly lucrative brick-making contract, and they now heard that another motel was being built by the same firm. They spent a couple of days in Perth and I met them one evening at the Shiralee, the folk club off Hay Street. Just how badly the performances had deteriorated there may be judged from the fact that Alec and I provided the first half of the evening bill. The lads duly set off north and I agreed to follow them, having decided to first visit Boulder.

The Beetle had no fuel gauge and the guard against running out of fuel was to fill the tank, then close a tap which preserved about half a gallon in reserve. Unfortunately, I was forever forgetting either to open this tap on fuelling the car, or to close it after I had done so. I must have been a very familiar sight around the Perth suburbs, walking around with a fuel can. On the trip home I ran out of fuel at Southern Cross, a town which seemed to have few happy associations, and it was an inconvenient hour. I made a note to buy a jerrican, against future needs.

It was fully Winter and I was glad of a sleeping bag I had acquired for roadside halts, making two of them on the trip north. It was gratifying to note that some stretches of road were now sealed with bitumen, but there were still many miles of dirt road and potholed surface. The journey took a little less than forty-eight hours and I had no problems, other than two flat tyres.

The 'Nade Hotel was doing a brisk afternoon trade when I

arrived and I struck up a conversation with a fellow drinker. When I asked him about Max, the asphalter I had briefly worked for, the bloke glanced theatrically over both shoulders and advised me to forget Max. Max, it seemed, had vanished owing a parcel of money and his many creditors were anxious to speak to anyone who knew him.

Alec and Rob eventually wandered in and they were now working as electrical linesmen. The new motel, they had discovered, was being built at Mt Newman, where iron ore was being mined, but there had been no chance of getting back into the brick-making game, which a Perth team had contracted for. I learned, however, that the motel was in need of a driver and labourer and I got in touch with the Pearce Brothers, the builders, by wire. In the meantime, I had a few drinks in the 'Nade, avoided the frequent fights and camped each evening at Pretty Pool, a bathing spot on the edge of town. I also managed to bog the VW there, being towed out by the ever-obliging police.

Word arrived that the job was mine and I set off for Newman along two hundred and fifty miles of gravel. Incautious steering on a tight bend put me through one hundred and eighty degrees of skid and it deflated another tyre. The simple job of replacement suddenly became very difficult when the ratchet jack stripped and I could find no means of raising the car to get the wheel off.

With no other vehicles in sight, I began to dig away the ground underneath the wheel, with no more efficient tool than the wheel brace, and the hole got ever deeper as the suspension lowered the flat into it. The job took an hour and I was soaked in sweat despite the fact of it being midwinter. I pulled into Marble Bar - which has the reputation of being the hottest town in Australia - an hour or so later, only to learn that the pubs had just closed. I managed to refill my water bag and I moved on, arriving at Newman after dark.

Having no idea where the worker's camp was, I simply identified the motel site and, having fallen into a footing trench whilst looking for a place to spread my bag, slept in some corner of it until the various gangs arrived at 0600hrs. The foreman, who was a youthful Londoner named Nick, showed me around and within the hour I was carting bricks to one of the brickie gangs, who also were Londoners and whom I recognised from the Hedland motel job.

The labouring gang was a dozen strong and it included two Irish, two Spanish and half a dozen Yugoslavs. I had an early go at the latter when I discovered that two of them had stacked only fifteen hundred bricks in the same period that one of the Irishmen and I had stacked six thousand. It would not have occurred to me then to wonder if the Yugoslavs were Serbian or Croat Yugoslavs, or even Serbo-Croat Yugoslavs. What mattered was that they were lazy bastards. It was all that mattered in Australia then, and I would hope that it is all that matters in Australia now.

The accommodation was 5-Star, comprising air-conditioned cabins, and the food was excellent. A typical breakfast was fruit juice, fruit, scrambled eggs, sausages, bacon, tomatoes and toast, and the variety and the portions of the main meals were impressive. I had a brief problem with the chap I shared a cabin with, since he was a middle-aged Italian whose footwear stank. I solved the problem by throwing them into the bush some evening and he shortly found new quarters.

The driving aspect of the job occupied little of my working day, which was a standard ten hours. Sand for the bricklayers and the brick-makers was scooped out of a local creek bed, where the firm left a bucket loader more or less permanently, and I would occasionally drive out to the bed with a 7-Yard Toyota tip truck. Filling it was the work of minutes with the loader, and tipping it a similarly painless task. Another truck on the site, a 10-Ton Albion Reiver, was constantly travelling between Newman and the railhead at Meekatharra, collecting building supplies. The driver of that had also worked on the Hedland job.

After a few weeks I got the job of leading labourer, then actually became acting foreman while Nick went below on leave for a couple of weeks. This didn't change my job dramatically, since only the labourers worked directly for the firm with everyone else contracted. It did however allow me some scope for initiative, and this was put to an early test when the brick-making gang suddenly decided to quit, and at a time when the brick reserves were down to a couple of day's worth.

The bricks were handmade in moulds, four at a time, with a sand and cement mix and then simply laid out in the sun to harden. These were quite a rough product, although this suited the architect who was striving to produce the effect of an ancient Spanish building. I saw a good opportunity for Alec and Rob to take on the contract and I wired the Pearce Brothers to this effect, although they never acted on it. In the meantime, I organised a brick-making gang by using the best of the labourers, working with them from Midnight until 0400hrs.

We then had a brief sleep and breakfast before returning to the more ordinary forms of labouring. This clearly was not a routine we could hope to sustain for very long, but it at least kept the brickies going until a new gang arrived from Perth.

I also hired some casual labourers to assist with brick stacking in the period, and was not greatly surprised to discover that the gang included a bank manager and the post office manager from the small township which had sprung up to meet workers' needs.

A readymix truck arrived at the site one day, asking if we had any need of concrete. It had been ordered for an adjacent site that proved unready for it and the driver proposed to dump it in the bush if there were no takers. We happened to have some footings ready and took the concrete, which was paid for by the other firm. I also hired out our bucket loader to one of the larger firms, Bechtel, for $120 a day when their own broke down. A problem I could do nothing about, however, was a newly arrived carpenter. He used a power saw to cut the butt end off a roof joist and took off three fingers at the same time.

It tended to be a thirsty day and the first call after work was to the wet canteen. The bar did not bother selling beer by the glass, and simply sold it by the jug, which held about two and a half pints. It was normal to drink two jugs then clean up for the evening meal. The canteen remained orderly and unremarked by fights for the simple reason that the Mt Newman authority swiftly ejected any troublemakers. The working population was a lot less transient than that of Hedland, with most seeming to want to knuckle down to hard work for three months or six, and then move on.

Keeping various bits of machinery going proved another test of initiative in an area where the usual facilities did not exist. When a battery terminal on a dump truck broke off, we fashioned a new one by cutting a piece of copper water pipe to act as a mould, and melting lead into it. Carburettors had to be stripped and cleaned frequently because of the iron ore dust which blanketed the site; generator brushes were cleaned and replaced and oil changes and greasing carried out at a regular interval. It made a nice change from carrying timber or stacking bricks.

When the Albion driver returned to Perth I succeeded to his job and now faced a steady routine of driving between the site and Meekatharra, about two hundred and sixty miles to the south. It was a day's journey, after which I would stay overnight at the Meeka hotel then load in the morning before returning to Newman. It was entirely a dirt road and the journey was sometimes unrelieved by the sight of a single vehicle going in either direction. Flat tyres were frequent and I carried a good selection of spares, but once had to return to Newman on nine wheels, when the spares ran out. I occasionally made a 'double run' to Meeka, when the demand for materials was high, and sometimes slept at the roadside when the hotel or the camp proved too distant. I once forgot to take the sleeping bag and wrapped myself instead in a painter's drop sheet. Its insulation proved inadequate on an uncharacteristically cold night and I gave up the sleep as a bad job.

At this time, an old bloke who was known as 'Walking Jimmy Wadsworth' was amiably filling out his retirement by walking around Australia, pushing a wheelbarrow and trailed by a couple of dogs. I had narrowly missed meeting him when he put up at the Meeka hotel, and a TV crew who had hoped to record his arrival at Perth some weeks later also missed him when Jimmy decided to stop off and have a beer with an old mate. I admired his independence, his lack of vanity and, perhaps most of all, his one-wheel mobility whenever I sweated over multiple wheel changes.

The standard week was of sixty hours, although we sometimes worked up to eighty in response to demands of the job. We were being paid $2 an hour and this was really good money. Most of my wage packets went straight to the bottom of my kit bag, since daily expenses were few.

A snake about four feet long was lying in a trench one morning. I didn't know if it was of the poisonous variety, but after a hefty whack with a shovel it was certainly of the dead variety. It also caused some alarm to the Slavs, whose phobias about work clearly extended to snakes.

The architect made one of his periodic visits and decreed that the site needed dressing with a number of coloured rocks. These, apparently, were available at Wittenoom Gorge and I was despatched with the tipper to collect them. Finding that the stones lay on the slope of a hill whose gradient was quite stiff, I sought to reduce my effort by reversing the tipper as far up the slope as it would go, then rolling the stones down to it. I had left the tipper in gear and when one of the stones rolled into the rear duals, the tipper engine bump-started and off the tipper went. I charged after it with visions of seeing it wrecked or disappearing over the horizon, but it fortunately stalled within a few yards. Wittenoom Gorge was rather better known for its asbestos mines, to which I had once written seeking a job. The failure to get it was just possibly a life-preserving act, in view of much later discoveries about blue asbestos and lung cancers.

Resuming my runs to Meekatharra, I was asked at the hotel if I minded sharing a room for the night. I didn't and the room companion turned out to be a chap from Kalgoorlie I had undergone the medical examinations with when I had first joined the army. I hadn't seen him since Kapooka, a decade earlier.

The swimming pool at the motel was completed and it made a welcome dip at odd times of the day. Even as early as October the daytime heat was well into the centuries and it grew hotter as the days wore on.

Motel supplies began to arrive, and several bottles of champagne were diverted by the unloading crew. We drove back to the site one evening to sample this out of drinking mugs and it ought to have been a jolly evening. Somehow it wasn't and several fights erupted between blokes who had been working together amicably for months. I tried to stop two fights and was landed with a punch in both of them. When I drove the tipper back to the accommodation later, I engaged the hoist and dumped everyone on the road. They do say that revenge is a dish best eaten cold - if not cold sober.

Female staff began to arrive and most of us made a play for them. I was turned down in swift succession by a receptionist, two barmaids and three waitresses, having generously offered to sleep with any or all of them, although the cook smiled upon me. She was comely but served good portions. We had by now left the main camp and were living on the site.

The job ran out towards the end of the year, and all that was left was to return the two lorries, loaded with machinery, to Perth. I drove the Albion and the Toyota followed. I had a minor panic when the air brakes failed, but it proved a minor repair only and effected at the roadside. The Toyota lost the windscreen to a flying stone and this was unfortunate for the driver, since the nights had turned suddenly cold, although it was less than a week to Xmas.

On a late night stop, I slept at the wheel since there was no way to stretch out in the cab, and I came suddenly awake, believing that I had fallen asleep whilst driving. It gave me such a fright that I could not get off to sleep again.

We completed the journey to Perth in a little less than forty-eight hours, handed over the vehicles and were unemployed again. I was also without wheels again. The foreman had been driving the Beetle down for me and a piston came through the block at Meekatharra. The car is perhaps there yet. Having arrived at Newman with just $10, however, I now had $2000. The good times seemed to be back.

25

I went home for Xmas then returned to Perth in response to a message from the Pearce Brothers that there might be some follow up work at Newman. Within a day or two I learned that nothing had come of it and I made a visit to Swan Barracks to ask if I might undergo the reserve camp earlier than usual. It was and my instruction was to report at the end of the month.

When I reported to Karrakatta I was immediately sent to Northam, where a cadet camp was in process, and it transpired that I was to be employed for the fortnight simply as a driver. The Emergency Reserve, which had commenced only in the year of my leaving regular service, appeared to be running out of steam.

Whatever the truth of that guess, I meantime was not at the cutting edge of the Australian army. My daily routine consisted of collecting civilian workers and the newspapers and driving the garbage truck, before taking the civilians home again. A large group of WRAAC was also engaged on camp and driving duties, and I was assiduously courting one of them. Sadly, the SNCO WRAAC was a dragon who imposed tight curfews on her charges.

When the camp ended, I made a quick visit to Jan and Arch then caught a 'bus to Port Hedland; hitchhiking and second-hand cars suddenly having little appeal as a mode of travel. I arrived at the town in a little more than twenty-four hours and found Alec and Rob at the 'Nade, which now featured a stripper to vie with fights as entertainment.

I had been intent on some general labouring, but learned that Alec had represented me as a carpenter to his boss. The boss had bought a piece of land on a new light industrial site, had a slab of concrete cast on it and now wanted someone to build him a house of sorts. Just about all the material was assembled at the site and I simply got on with it, erecting a wooden frame and roofing trusses, then cladding it with asbestos sheets. Whenever I became stumped for the way forward I took a run into one of the numerous building sites in the town and found the answers there.

Work of all sorts was slightly delayed when the town received thirteen inches of rain in twenty-four hours, a by-product of Cyclone

Gladys, and I had some difficulties sawing waterlogged wood for a while. The 'house' was taking shape and I sheeted the roof with tin then fitted door and window frames. Hanging the doors provided a moderate challenge, but I got there.

Between times I worked with Alec and Rob erecting light poles and stringing cable, but my enthusiasm for Hedland was dimming. There appeared no chance of a lucrative job for the moment and I decided after a couple of months to return home for a spell.

The Goldfields at this time was beginning to boom again, thus vindicating those in the Fifties who believed that renewal of prosperity was simply a matter of time. It came from nickel.

Huge deposits, second only in size to the enormous reserves in Canada, had been discovered in close proximity to the 'Fields and it was now merely a matter of time before mining operations began. Several firms were still carrying out nickel exploration surveys, and I now got a job with one of them, Broken Hill Proprietary.

We operated from a bush camp about forty miles from Boulder, working and living there from Monday to Saturday noon. I would then catch a lift home and pick up the easy routine with the Old Man at the Mines' & City. At the club one afternoon I got talking to an elderly Scots migrant and he had a good story to relate about nickel. As a brand new migrant in his youth, Scottie had found gold worth several thousands of pounds, and with the money he learned to fly and bought his own aeroplane. He could never understand, he said, why the aircraft compass spun crazily whenever he flew over the area of Kambalda. Now he knew; Kambalda was the principal area of the nickel finds.

With the exception of the weekend drinking excesses, I was living the quiet life again. I stopped smoking for a while, began running along bush tracks in the early evening and did not frequent the wet canteen. After running I would remain in the caravan, reading by a paraffin lamp.

The job consisted of collecting soil samples from an area pegged out by geological surveyors. These lines would be five thousand feet long and at every hundred feet it was necessary to dig a hole about six inches deep and place a scoop of soil into a marked envelope. Later, we would sit in a tent and sieve the soil down to a fine powder for analysis. The work force was a mix of local lads and the usual blow-ins, few of whom stayed for long. One of them was a bloke who could regurgitate his stomach contents at will, and did so with depressing regularity.

I went home one weekend and found Rob there. He and Alec had apparently had a bit of a rift, which was sad in view of the fact that they had been travelling together since leaving Co. Antrim three years earlier. He stayed for a few days, resisted my invitation to get him a job with BHP and duly moved down to Perth.

I was upgraded to driving a Land Rover that collected soil samples and delivered steel to drilling crews. This was easy, if slightly dull, and only enlivened when I chased an Emu one day. It easily outdistanced the vehicle. I also chased a dingo on foot, but this was such an unequal contest that it turned around to laugh at me a few times.

In a Boulder pub one Sunday afternoon I ran across Val, whom I had not seen for three years. We had a chat and it was an affecting meeting. I subsequently wrote to her but there was no response, and I should not have been surprised by that.

My final bounty, to the tune of $350, arrived, and I now had a decent sort of bankroll. I also had a reasonably wellpaid job and one which I might easily have continued doing. I also had the chance of some preferential shares with the firm, but lacked the wit to see the potential in them. My brother Jack had just such an offer from the nickel firm which employed him, and he subsequently made a useful sum out of them.

I was simply unsettled again, and I decided at last to try a visit to England. I booked a sea passage at $816 return and the sailing was set for August. I filled in a few more days with BHP then prepared for the move down to Fremantle and a month on the water. I made a final visit to the Mines' & City one Sunday afternoon and bought a round of drinks for everyone. There were about two hundred blokes in. This was not thrifty.

By this time, I suppose, I was an accepted member of a close and friendly community, but I wore it lightly. It would take the longer perspective of later years to bring home the realisation that I had walked away from this happy situation just as casually and as thoughtlessly as I had left the army.

In Perth I visited Jan but Arch was now serving in Viet Nam, which was slightly worrying. I also ran across Rob and thought that I might see him in the UK, since he also planned a visit, and he saw me off at Fremantle. The sailing was in the late afternoon and I watched as the coast diminished, remembering that I had risen early, fourteen years before, to see it grow on the horizon. The light faded and I went below to see what sort of companions I might find, conscious of having broken threads.

*Service Renewed
1969-1983*

Yet a man's enlisting is his admission of defeat by life.

The Mint
TE Lawrence 1889-1935

1

The cruise, which I had greatly anticipated as a holiday afloat, soon proved to be utterly boring. Avoiding the dubious attractions of deck quoits, learning Italian or attending fancy dress parties, I too easily fell into a routine of drinking late and sleeping late. The ship, the *Achille Lauro*, of the Lauro Line, had a fair percentage of Italian passengers aboard, in addition to the Italian crew, and these were a noisy lot. The English passengers included several of the 'whingeing Pom' variety, who presumably were going home for a good feed of fish and chips. Better company was a woman I met at dinner, who was travelling home with her parents and three daughters. Her husband, who worked in textiles, had flown home to England to organise the house. I spent a fair bit of time in her company on the boat deck, where knowing glances from other passengers seemed to assume that we had developed an intimate relationship. It was not the case and nor did I seek elsewhere to change the celibacy which I had maintained for a year or so.

We made port calls at Singapore, Capetown and Tenerife for a few hours. In Singapore I tried to drum up some enthusiasm for visits to places remembered from the 55 Coy detachment of half a dozen years earlier, but in retrospect the social side of the time looked suspiciously empty, and only the work and the flying now seemed worthwhile. I bought a Rolex Submariner for $96 Australian and I still have it although I seldom wear the watch these days. Then, it was the hallmark of timekeeping accuracy, which is why I bought it, but nowadays its accuracy is left standing by a quartz watch for about a Fiver in Woolworth's. It is still a Rolex, however.

At Capetown, I rode the cable car to Table Mountain and the stunning view it offered, and dined in a restaurant that served a steak the size of a saddle. Tenerife offered little more than volcanic rock and hordes of European tourists and I soon returned to the ship, impatient by now to be in England.

It was a beautifully clear Sunday afternoon when we sailed into Southampton, and the Solent was alive with small yachts, whose white sails reflected the sunlight. It was also hot and the process through Customs and Immigration was slow and sticky, triggering a sharp memory of arrival in Fremantle fourteen years earlier. It had turned midnight when the boat train off-loaded at London, where a considerable queue formed for too few taxis. I eventually found my way to a small hotel at Kings Cross and the amenities, upon daylight inspection, proved remarkably similar to those of the People's Palace in Sydney, although the tariff was about five times higher. This was an early lesson that tourists in London tend to be viewed by some locals as prey.

  I spent two weeks in the city, dividing my time between the museums of Kensington and the theatres of West London. Live theatre, musicals particularly, I had experienced only in Sydney previously and none too often. In London, there was an entire district devoted to theatre - more than a hundred shows - and I was delighted with it. I easily resisted, though, the cast invitation to dance on stage at a performance of 'Hair'. I drank very little, finding the beer unappealingly warm, and I smoked the last of the duty-free cigarettes, which had cost just 8d for twenty aboard ship. The local price for twenty Senior Service or Player's Weights added six shillings to that.

  I shopped around for a second-hand car, having decided upon a 1.5 litre Riley. The car appealed to me, although the firm had long been taken over and the '62 model I acquired was a product of the British Motor Corporation, itself shortly to be acquired by new owners. I bought the car for £180 from a chap in Dagenham, who assured me that he wanted a 'good home' for the car, having lavished much care upon the vehicle. In fact, what he had been most lavish with was body filler, as I came to discover when chunks of it dropped out from time to time. It was quite lively, though, and the car secured my affection.

  The journey to Crewe proved surprisingly short, and I also broke it with a trip to Coventry, where my boyhood friend, David Vickers, now lived. He was married and had gone into partnership with another schoolmate from Brierley Street who also had lived in Henry Street. The business was sheet metalwork and it was flourishing.

  In Crewe, I found digs half a mile from the town centre and began a round of family visits, beginning with Mam's sister, Aunt Bess. She and Uncle Reg would become the regular port of call for the next twenty years and unfailingly welcoming.

  The Old Man's oldest friend was Arthur Podmore, who now lived in a council flat mere yards from the demolished street where he and the Old Man had been born and raised. They were of much the same age, had attended school together and gone into the building trade, Arthur as a carpenter until back problems forced him into Royce's.

I also looked up the Old Man's cousin, Alf Brockley, who had been his best man in 1937. Alf was a retired locomotive driver and on one call he said that he was taking me to a Crewe pub which was a favourite among railwaymen, and included a few of Grandad's era. When we entered the Woodside, Alf took me across to a couple of old blokes and asked them who they thought I might be. "Is he a grandson of Mel Foxley?" Asked one. I was surprised at that, having then seen no photographs that suggested a good resemblance. Mel Foxley was of course long gone, and Mam's parents had died earlier in the Sixties. Over a pint with Alf on some other meeting, he mentioned that the Old Man and he had toured England and Scotland on motorbikes in their youth. I did not press him for details and have regretted ever since that I did not do so.

I made an early visit to Henry Street and was astonished at how diminished it seemed. Since I had lived there, it appeared that someone had demolished the area and re-built it half-scale. The length of Henry Street that contained number four actually was demolished a few years later, and a row of maisonettes replaced it. Scores of similar houses within the town went under the bulldozer at the same time, and the process continued into the Eighties. There was little to be regretted about the wholesale demolition of such houses, but I have wondered since if something of the town character and community spirit passed with them.

Among the visits was a trip to Cumbria to represent a family now living in Boulder at the wedding of their niece. The family owned a farm and a pub, which was a pleasing combination, and I was cordially welcomed. The patriarch of the family was a man who had left the village to serve in France for the duration of the Great War. He returned to the village and never again left it. We had some chats although I found the dialect difficult to follow. "Ay mickle peths thee shoon?" apparently translated as: "How much did your shoes cost?"

The digs in Hungerford Road were run by a Polish woman, whose husband had been killed during the war. She had family still in Poland and they would occasionally send her cigarettes, which she would press upon me. Smoking them, even without inhalation, was a terrible ordeal. The digs cost £6 per week and I was quite comfortable. I had some difficulty in persuading the landlady that a daily bath was desirable, and I periodically had to take one at the Flag Lane swimming baths, at 1/- a time.

The year, and the decade, was swiftly running out and so was my reserve of cash. A new hospital was being built at Leighton, on the outskirts of Crewe, and I took a job as a labourer on the site. It was a bad choice, since the weather was now beginning to bite and nor was the wage at all good. Little overtime was available and the flat rate of £12.16s.4d. per week offered little prospect of savings. The weather deteriorated into frost, and I quickly discovered that a patch of ice could put me into a one hundred and eighty-degree turn just as easily as a patch of gravel on an Australian track, fortunately without injury or damage.

Economies seemed the order of the day and I soon reduced the smoking to occasions only when I was having a pint, which was not often. I would meet Arthur Podmore each Wednesday evening and Saturday morning, and we might drink three or four pints, followed by fish and chips at the flat, with his wife, Ida. A pint of Bitter cost 1/10d at the Delamere Arms - better known to its patrons as The Blazer, which was short for blazing cat, itself a reference to the red lion rampant on the pub sign, and presumably a bit of Lord Delamere's heraldry. The Blazer featured an autocratic landlord who would refuse to serve anyone who was known to be unemployed and on the Dole. "You're not coming in here and drinking *my* bloody money." Was his emphatic retort on these occasions.

The Riley yielded 32 MPG and petrol was selling at 6/8p a gallon. Of rather greater concern was the cost of spares or repairs, which began to feature with the car. Brakes and battery set me back £30, and when I closed the boot one morning a hole suddenly appeared in it. I reopened the boot to find a plug of nicely painted Polyfilla resting inside. It would not be the last I would find. I had joined the AA, and I eventually had to stage a couple of 'breakdowns' to secure mechanical assistance for problems that were beyond me.

Learning that I was a voracious reader, the landlady offered me a selection. These included '*Sexual Experimentation in Marriage*' and 'A *Study* of *Sexuality and Pornography* in *Nineteenth Century England*', and I began to wonder why she did not replace boarders who left. In a matter of weeks I was the only one. Rather more worrying though were the boxes of cigarettes arriving from Poland.

I found a new job, working in a textile factory at Winsford, half a dozen miles from Crewe. The town there had been much expanded and heavily settled with arrivals from Liverpool, as slums in that city were cleared. I appeared to be the only non-Scouser in the work force of about thirty, and I soon noticed a strange phenomenon. Work mates would go sick for a few days, almost as if by rota, and when they returned to work they not only looked well but actually quite sun-tanned. It seemed that cheap, off-season visits to the Canaries had something, if not everything, to do with the mysterious illnesses that afflicted the factory.

I was working the afternoon shift that began at 1400hrs, and when I walked by the Crewe Square one morning I noticed a recruiting van for the Royal Air Force. On impulse, I stepped in and asked the sergeant if he had any information about the RAF Regiment. He handed me some brochures and I examined them during the meal break at the factory. I was particularly struck by the fact that the RAF Regiment had a parachute squadron, and by the time I drove home I had decided to pursue further enquiries. I had also made an enquiry about enlistment into the Royal Marines, but was flatly informed that, at twenty-eight, I was too old. There would be a sequel to that.

The Riley continued to be a joy and a burden in about equal parts. A corroded exhaust and muffler added to the running costs, and even parking it posed somewhat of a problem. It seemed to me that whenever I pulled into the kerb adjacent to the digs, someone would rush out and claim that I was stealing 'their' space, whether they owned a vehicle or not. On some other occasion, I drew to a halt and watched the car aerial disappear into the wing, and this was puzzling since I could not recall fitting a retractable aerial. Investigation revealed the aerial lying under the wing, with a great chunk of Polyfilla aggregated about its base. Dagenham Man had
struck again.

Thoughts of renewing military life recurred and the oddest reminder of previous service was in a TV programme about the burgeoning Aboriginal Rights Movement in Australia. The programme featured an interview with Darkie Colbung, last seen as a Sapper corporal at Karrakatta and now a leader in the West Australian Aboriginal rights movement. I took a day off work, motored to Stoke on Trent and furthered my RAF Regiment enquiries at the RAF Careers Information Office. I was invited to take the application tests, without obligation, and I did so, being subsequently informed that I could enlist in any trade. I repeated my interest in the Regiment and the recruiting officer smilingly suggested that the Regiment did all of its recruiting in the Gorbals. I responded with the view that it was as good a way as any to meet Scotsmen.

Having no evidence of my army service, I learned that a check on it would be a necessary requirement and it could be undertaken whilst I considered enlistment. I agreed to this, feeling by now that a three-year term of engagement upon something that I undoubtedly enjoyed was infinitely better than any of the jobs I had attempted since discharge.

Apart from plying me with terrible cigarettes and dubious literature, of which the latest offering was Krafft-Ebings *'Psychopathia Sexualis'*, where all the descriptive paragraphs were in Latin, the landlady began to appear in my room with a cup of tea the instant I was out of the bath. She eventually appeared in my room very late one evening, requesting assistance with the fastening on her dress. It was definitely time to be moving on.

I responded positively to a letter from the Stoke CIO and was requested to appear on 17 March to be attested, thus adding St. Patrick's Day to those I can remember without difficulty. There was fog, snow and ice that morning and I arrived late, without feeling that it might be a poor augury. I was duly attested, making a solemn oath rather than swearing on the bible, since I had this time declared myself as Atheist, was given an advance of wages and instructed to report to RAF Swinderby, in Lincolnshire. I was also instructed to take with me two padlocks and a set of collar studs. I still have the padlocks.

Interlude

The 'Swinging Sixties'...

....is another of those myths that irritates me. I do not know who originated the phrase, although it probably emanated from within the pop music industry, for which the word 'hyperbole' may well have been invented. The same industry proved also a focus for the drugs culture that has exerted some lethal damage upon youngsters who followed bad examples, since too few good ones were provided. Drugs of the hallucinogen variety were the basis of the cliche that 'if you remember the Sixties, then you really weren't there.' Perhaps not, but life went on in all of its forms, not least the brutal and cruel, and many of those who were *there* in the Sixties are not *here* because they became the victims of random or organised violence. A swift reprise, alphabetically, of just ten per cent of the world's nations in the decade, by way of striking a balance.

ANGOLA: A Portuguese colony in 1960 and one which in earlier centuries provided a million slaves. Insurrection in 1961 was savagely repressed by the Portuguese dictatorship, using 70,000 Portuguese troops and 30,000 African troops.

BOLIVIA: Elected government overthrown by military coup in 1964. General Ortuno suppresses, with great brutality, guerilla campaign. Victims include Che Guevara.

CAMBODIA: Massively supported by US Dollars until President Sihanouk breaks relations with the US, and is deposed by a CIA-inspired coup. A new political group called the Khmer Rouge forms in 1960 under its leader, Pol Pot. Khmer Rouge launch the armed struggle in 1968 and its policies after winning control result in the deaths of 2,000,000 Cambodians.

DOMINICAN REPUBLIC: Ruled for thirty years until 1961 by General Trujillo, recognised to be one of the most brutal dictators in the region.

ETHIOPIA: Denied Eritrean demands for independence in 1962 and opens warfare that persists for two decades. A 'proxy' war for the major powers and massive death by famine.

FRANCE: Having fought and lost, in the early Fifties, a costly and bloody war to preserve its colony in Indo-China, France fights and loses an even costlier and bloodier war to preserve its colony in Algeria. Over a million deaths by the time of independence in 1962, and more of it in the fratricidal war which followed independence.

GUATEMALA: A country that was largely run by the American United Fruit Company, reflecting dollar support for dictatorships. *Amnesty International* reported that 20,000 Guatemalans were murdered by government forces during the Sixties.

HAITI: The oldest black republic (1874) in the world and one of the saddest. Francois 'Papa Doc' Duvalier declares himself president for life in 1964, and retains power with brutal repression by police death squads and troops.

ISRAEL: Launches a pre-emptive strike against Egypt and Jordan in 1967. 100,000 casualties.[1]

JORDAN: By the close of the decade, Jordan is home to 800,000 refugees of Arab-Israeli wars. These live in utter squalor, entirely dependent upon foreign aid.

KOREA (North): A so-called 'People's Democratic Republic' which actually is a dictatorship. Led by Kim Il Sung, to whom a slavish personality cult is organised. Radio sets can only be tuned to the government channel. Could be a model for George Orwell's '1984'.

LAOS: Decade opened with fighting between left-wing and right-wing

---

[1] The Sixties proved briefly swinging for Adolf Eichmann, who swung from a Tel Aviv scaffold in 1967 for his complicity in the industrial-scale murder of 6,000,000 Jews.

factions. Bombed by the Americans and invaded by the Vietnamese.

MALDIVES: A British Protectorate until Republic formed in 1968. During a dispute with Britain over an RAF base on a southern atoll, a secession attempt results in suppression by the Mali government and castration of the secessionists.

NIGERIA: Independence from Britain in 1960 and its government overthrown by a violent military coup in 1966. Attempt by the country's eastern region to secede as Biafra leads to war and massive death by the close of the decade.

OMAN: Ruled in the Sixties by Sultan Said Ibn Taimur, a despot who permitted no schools, hospitals, radios or bicycles. A UN report stated that the Sultan retained an entourage of one hundred slaves, including eunuchs, at his royal palace.

PARAGUAY: Throughout the decade, a military dictatorship under General Alfredo Stroessner, an admirer of Hitler. One of the poorest countries in the region, despite massive foreign aid.

QATAR: A British Protectorate but ruled by the Al Yamani family, which permits no political discussion.

RWANDA: Independent in 1962. Tutsi population is 10 per cent and previously had been installed by British as overlords of the Hutu population. Fratricidal strife produces 100,000 Tutsi refugees (and massive death in the Nineties).

SPAIN: A European dictatorship led by General Franco who, assisted by Hitler and Mussolini, overthrew the elected democratic government in the Thirties. Under Franco, no political parties, no trade unions and no free press allowed. The United States (champions of democracy) supports Franco with millions of dollars in return for American air bases on Spanish soil.

TOGO: Suffered a military coup in 1967 that abolished the constitution and dissolved the elected assembly. Political parties banned and a military dictatorship imposed.

USA: Learning nothing from French experience in Viet-Nam, begins major military build up in the mid-Sixties. 60,000 American dead and more than a million Vietnamese dead. The US also supports, with arms and cash, several Central and South American dictatorships. 'Land of the free, home of the brave.'

VENEZUELA: Democracy overthrown in 1957 by Colonel Marcos Jiminez, whose secret police practice torture on a huge scale.

WESTERN SAMOA: An oasis in a riven world. Independent in 1962, it had a stable population, abundant food and the government ran the country like an extended family. (The major powers presumably didn't know of its existence)

YEMEN: A British Protectorate until 1963, when independence is marked by bitter fighting and atrocity.

ZAIRE: Independent in 1960 and immediately consumed by a bloody war. Power seized by General Mobuto in 1965 and free elections declared - with Mobuto as the sole candidate, and subsequent dictator.

2

1970 had begun and was little advanced when I reported to RAF Swinderby. I had availed myself of a free rail warrant for the journey, since finances were at crisis levels again. Swinderby was only a hundred miles and that represented just three gallons of petrol, but a pound was a pound, however little it might be buying at home or abroad.

The train was met by a suitably sarcastic drill NCO, and the arrivals were herded aboard a coach for the short journey to the camp, or station, as RAF establishments preferred to be styled. We would prove to be sixty strong, with several other recruit flights ahead of us in training.

My previous service had not won me a single day off the recruit syllabus, but it landed me the appointment of Senior Man, a position I had little enthusiasm for. There were several other ex-servicemen and these were appointed as room leaders. One of them came to me with a problem after training one day, explaining that one of his room occupants resolutely refused to bathe or shower. I promptly organised a cold bath for the bloke and it nearly caused my service to cease at Week Three. The unwashed one was a Jamaican and he claimed that he was being treated with racial prejudice. The matter caused some concern and I was subsequently put to some hard questioning, but the matter eventually was quietly dropped.

Swinderby was the Recruit Training Depot for all male entrants to the RAF, except apprentices and commissioned ranks, and the course was of six week's duration. It began, predictably enough, with long sessions of drill and PT was also heavily featured. I was now twenty-eight years old, I was five feet, ten inches tall and I weighed one hundred and sixty-eight pounds. I was healthy and I felt fit. The

PT presented no problems, but it occurred to me that I might face a harder regime at the RAF Regiment Depot, which would be the next step, and I began to train in my own time. Swinderby, which had been a wartime fighter station, had a dormant airfield and I took to running five miles, then ten, about it each evening.

Because every airman was regarded, primarily, as a defender of his station, ground defence training was the focus of the recruit course. The Self-loading Rifle was no mystery to me and, apart from drill, there was little else to the syllabus. Registering as an Atheist failed to preserve me from numerous 'Padre's Hour' sessions, where the topic usually was either sex before marriage, morality of,[1] and the importance of religious faith within the service. Contributions from the floor, especially those of a dissenting nature, were unwelcome, and I again made the round of the different faiths to see which might be the shortest.

The starting wage was £7 per week, which of course was the remainder when food and accommodation charges had been deducted. It was, effectively, pocket money since we had no travelling expenses, but it did not go a long way. I was still compromising on cigarettes, only smoking when I had a pint, but as an element of boredom with the training began to prevail, I would accompany a team to some local pub rather more often than was either wise or economical.

The Riley, that I had collected from Crewe at an early opportunity, proved popular for such runs, since taxis were generally out of the question. A pub none too distant from the station was a useful venue for a couple of pints and darts, or a game of fives and threes dominos, and such excursions helped to move the time along. Evenings and weekends were mostly free and it soon occurred to me that the easy routine might have been intended to discourage 'opt-outs'. At this time, it was possible to secure a free discharge in the sixth and twelfth week of training. Discharge by purchase, at a later date, could prove very costly.

---

[1] The tone was exactly that of Padre's lessons at Kapooka, although, unlike the earlier experience, the Swinderby version was not augmented by presentations of the horrors of VD by a gloating corporal of the medical corps, who accompanied his lecture with graphic film of victims, and promised for an inflamed uretha the medieval treatment of the 'umbrella needle' for those who ignored his advice.

The flight was passed off parade early in May and I was sent on two week's leave; the reason given was that the course at the RAF Regiment Depot was not yet ready to assemble. This two weeks was then extended by another fortnight, and I began to wonder if the 'system' was not simply trying to use up the opt-out period. Whatever the reason, I began to become very bored in Crewe, having little money left after digs' rent. I spent a fair bit of time rowing on the park lake, before even that modest expenditure became prohibitive.

The time, and another birthday, passed and I drove up to Yorkshire, wondering if the petrol in the tank would suffice for the one hundred and fifty-mile journey. It did - just - but the road fund licence was also running out and when I parked the car it remained idle for the three months of the basic Gunner course.

I renewed acquaintance with Alec Fraser, a former Brickie and prison warder who had been on the same recruit course. The reason for the delay became apparent when we learned that our course was only a dozen strong. There was not exactly a flood of applicants for the RAF Regiment. We also learned that Gunners were pejoratively known as Rockapes, or Rocks, and a terse introduction to this was offered by one of our instructors, a squat Scotsman. "You have perhaps heard the expression 'being caught between a rock and a hard place'; well, this is the hard place and I am that Rock." An encouraging welcome. The Regiment, we also learned, had somewhat of a poor reputation for mayhem and violence, of which there was some evidence in the NAAFI on pay nights. Rockapes were generally regarded as thick and belligerent, it seemed.

The Depot was also home to four squadrons, which mostly were equipped with Bofors antiaircraft guns, the RAF Regiment Band and the Fire School. Firemen at that time also wore RAF Regiment Flashes (shoulder titles) on their uniforms, although this distinction never seemed too popular with at least some of them, who tended to remove the flashes after their graduation from training.

When our training began, I was slightly dismayed to discover that the webbing assembly was none other than the '37 Pattern I had once blanco-ed to cream/green perfection. I was now required to blanco it to blue/grey perfection, then add a coat of floor wax to it. We were, however, spared the detail of polishing the brass, which was painted black.

We wore a single garment of grey overalls for all training and were seldom required to wear either the Number 1 or Number 2 uniforms that were woollen. Another slightly archaic feature of the uniform, and one that explained the instruction to report bearing collar studs, was the fact the issue shirts had no collars attached. Three shirts were issued with six collars in a detached roll. I borrowed boiling water from the Depot kitchen to starch my collars, since the 'hot' water in our ablutions was frequently stone cold, although there was no great insistence upon such attention to dress detail.

Weekends were free but there was pressure to attend adventurous training activities organised by the Depot staff, and I saw no good reason to avoid these. Hill-walking in the Yorkshire Dales was at least preferable to loitering about the camp, and I also joined a group which completed the Lyke Wake Walk. This apparently celebrated some Viking ritual and it included a forty-mile hike overnight across the Moor. I saw such opportunities as extra training for the parachute squadron, being by now under no misconception that acceptance by that unit would be at all easy. A recruiting team from II Squadron visited the Depot and their explanation and slides of the parachute selection course indicated a high failure rate. For the moment, however, this was not a concern, with twelve weeks of basic training to push. Again, there were no great surprises, since we were training to standard infantry techniques. Among the weapons, only the 84mm Carl Gustav anti-tank device was new to me, and that proved remarkably simple to operate, if heavy to carry and reprising something of my experience with the 3.5in Rocket Launcher. Rockets *were* available for the Carl Gustav, as I subsequently discovered when required to fire a live HEAT (High Explosive AntiTank) round during a live-firing exercise towards the end of basic training. Firing the HEAT round produced an effect that was like being simultaneously kicked in the head and chest.

When my flight commander, who had until recently served with II Squadron, learned that I had qualified as a parachutist in Australia, he invited me to undergo a balloon descent with a Territorial Army unit at Gateshead. This appealed to me and during one Wednesday sports' afternoon we travelled to the TA Centre for the necessary ground training. This began, disconcertingly enough, with a run in a large group around the streets of Gateshead, although the locals seemed to find nothing odd in this.

On the following Friday we travelled at cease-work to the

Gateshead DZ, which actually was a small sports' field in the town. As guest jumpers, we had to await the last cage, and by the time we were winched up to the jumping height of eight hundred feet it was practically dark. The dispatcher and a stick of four jumpers filled each cage and I was the fourth man out. The descent produced a few moments of terror when I dropped about two hundred feet before anything much began to happen with the parachute. This turned out to be normal with balloon jumps, which lacked a 100 MPH slipstream to assist the inflation of the 'chute, but no one had actually told me that. A bad start was compounded by a bad landing which knocked the wind out of me, also bestowing a slight head whip, and I was groggily sorting myself out when a Geordie kid ran up. "Canna carry yer helmet, Mister?" He wanted to know. "You can carry me, if you like." I wheezed.

Towards the end of August we embarked upon a final, confirmatory exercise, much of which was conducted on the Catterick Training Area, with an Internal Security phase on the Depot airfield to follow. At some bleak hour of the morning I was 'guarding' a redundant Hastings which was awaiting destruction by the Fire School, when a student from the concurrent officers' course dodged about the perimeter, offering taunts which were straight out of some Ealing Studios B-movie script. After about ten minutes of this I scouted around for a large stone then hurled it in the direction of the voice. When I next heard from 'Charlie Chan' he was on the opposite perimeter.

I tried to improve my social life with a meeting at the NAAFI disco one pay night, overlooking the fact that acquaintances struck up after half a dozen pints and in dim surroundings are seldom wise. I met the girl on the following Saturday in Darlington and was staggered to discover that she had somehow put on about four stones in three days. Worse, proximity to her in the council house we retired to revealed a case of BO that was of chemical weapon proportion. The incident served to remind the truth of the admission: 'I never went to sleep with an unattractive woman, but I certainly woke up with a few.'

RAF Swinderby 1970   Service Renewed

3

At the conclusion of the Basic Gunner course, we were briefly paraded in Number 1 uniforms which were adorned with RAF Regiment shoulder flashes and despatched to our new units in the rank of Leading Aircraftman, which was signified by a two-bladed propeller on the tunic sleeve. Six of us had opted for service with II Squadron, in Wiltshire, but the posting would not be confirmed until we had successfully completed the parachute selection course, known as 'prepara' and closely based upon the 'P' Company selection course run by the Parachute Regiment.

I had managed to husband sufficient cash to tax the Riley and fill it with fuel, although I could do little for the moment about the numerous holes in the bodywork caused by the expansion and contraction of metal, allowing lumps of Polyfilla to drop out. *En route* to the new station, I experienced fuel pump problems and I diverted to Crewe for the night, putting up at Aunt Bess' and wondering if my late arrival at RAF Colerne might prove contentious.

Having aimed to arrive in a neatly-pressed Number 1 with gleaming brass buttons and sparkling boots, the Riley suffered a flat tyre a mile short of Colerne and by the time I had changed it on a boiling day I was about as crisp as a wet cornflake. Fortunately, no one at the General Office seemed to take much notice, whilst I was issued with a 'blue card' which was the concomitant to arrival procedure everywhere in the RAF.

When I had completed the calls around the domestic site, I was pointed in the direction of II Squadron, which occupied a hangar on the distant side of the east-west runway that bisected the station. The hangar proved to be open but mostly devoid of life, until I found a flight sergeant who explained that half of the unit was in the Gulf and the other half was on leave, having just returned from the Gulf. I was therefore to be sent on two week's leave, fortunately with an advance of wages. I retraced my route to Crewe, stayed with Aunt

Bess and spent some time drinking and playing darts with my cousins.

The pre-para course formed at a dozen strong and it included two officers and two Gunners from the Queen's Colour Squadron, which was a ceremonial unit based near London. The members of QCS appeared to be particularly despised by the pre-para staff, although none of the remainder of us felt especially loved. We were certainly offered no welcome by the members of the squadron, now returning from leave, and it was plain that we would not even be acknowledged by them until we had passed the course. This smacked of elitism, but I reckoned that I could live with that.

I had no qualms about the four-week course, believing that I had prepared for it adequately, but nor was I complacent. Among the early sights in the PT hangar was a large board covered with photographs of pre-para courses covering a period of about eight years. Some seventy-five per cent of the faces were scored with a red cross, indicating that they had either entered a 'VW' - Voluntary Withdrawal - or had completed the course without achieving a pass. There were far more VWs on the courses than failures and these were most marked among candidates who had made little or no attempt to get fit.

The course was entirely physical, ranging from minor games to circuit training in the gymnasium, and some permutation of assault course, confidence course and road runs with and without pack about the local, and steep, roads. Days tended to begin with a circuit of local road known as 'The Short Mile'. The short mile was actually closer to two and the route included a lengthy stretch of a hill whose gradient was 1:10. Candidate morale on the run was seldom improved by the sight of an instructor, a very fit man named John De Rosario, who usually ran up the hill backwards. The training was designed to develop fitness to the point where we would complete a dozen different tests of stamina and confidence, rounding off with a three-day programme of climbing in the Snowdonia region of North Wales. The course itself, in addition to proving fitness, was aimed equally at severely testing the endurance and the commitment of each candidate.

Assault and confidence courses offered me no problems, since I had once devoted weekend time to such courses during 2 RAR days, in order to produce faster times over them, but the sheer saturation of the programme required a fair bit of adjustment. VWs began and rapidly developed momentum, reducing the course to half a dozen in a matter of days.

I began to experience some problem with my right ankle, which I believe dated from a sprain I had incurred when jumping out of a lorry a couple of years before. My real problem, however, proved to be my left knee, which suddenly became very painful and stiff. I was allowed a couple of days to rest it and one of the officers on the course, who would later be my flight commander, offered to take me to see a chiropractor he knew. Since the chiropractor lived at Bournemouth, this was a most generous offer that I was happy to accept.

The treatment gave some relief and I was able to undertake the selection tests, meeting the stipulated 'bogey' times for the assault course, steeplechase and road runs. The confidence course required nerve rather than stamina, and the milling was simply a matter of standing toe to toe with a candidate of roughly equal size and slugging it out for a minute. The Milling was a popular spectator sport for the squadron members, who would line the 'ring' that was formed with gymnasium benches. Pre-para candidates were matched roughly by height and build, but officer candidates found themselves milling against a member of the squadron boxing team. The hapless officer would be duly battered by some hulking neanderthal and by way of adding insult to injury, the audience would shout such helpful advice as: "Hit him with your handbag, Sir!"

Less humorous was the Log Race and the Stretcher Race. The log was carried suspended on toggle ropes by four candidates, who were then sent at the double across rough ground and stiff gradient, with the log bouncing awkwardly and seeming to rip out one's arms at the socket. The stretcher was a variation, in that the four candidates carried the stretcher, laden with two hundred pounds of canvas, on their shoulders for a route which seemed to last forever. Put simply, the log race wasn't much fun and the stretcher race was a complete bastard.

Four of us got to Wales, where we embarked upon climbs by day and lengthy road runs by night, huddling in ponchos at the edge of a stream when we were not required. Heavy rain flooded the stream overnight, forcing us out of the ponchos and into the notional shelter of some rocks, until bleak daylight offered the dubious attractions of a cold shave and some compo food.

I completed two of the climbs with increasing knee problems, hacked the night twenty mile speed march but made a miserably slow progress off the hill when we had climbed the *Devil's Kitchen*. I was withdrawn on the following morning, to my bitter disappointment, and sent to my hootchie whilst the course completed the programme. One more VW followed, on the final day and with only the last run of about eight miles to push, and that was that. Two candidates added to the squadron strength.

Medical examination diagnosed torn ligaments and I was offered a posting to RAF Wittering. I declined and asked if I might stay on II in any capacity until I was able to try again. This was agreed, and I was told to report to the Squadron Warrant Officer, who would find employment for me. I was not greatly surprised to learn that I would be cleaning the bogs and sweeping the hangar floor. Anything else was a bonus.

The Warrant at this time was Charlie Eyles, a veteran of WW II who had been among the defenders of Kos, a neighbouring island to Crete, during the war. The Germans took the islands after a short and costly campaign, putting Charlie and his surviving comrades 'in the bag', as Charlie ruefully expressed it in one of his rare and later references. He was taken to a *Stalag Luft* for the duration, being something of a rarity among downed aircrew, and he witnessed the harsh treatment meted out to Russian POWs in an adjacent camp.

When it was decided, in 1959, to form a parachute squadron within the RAF Regiment, it was decided also that the nucleus of the new unit would have to undergo selection by P Company at Aldershot. Charlie was by then a flight sergeant and over forty years of age, yet he nevertheless completed the selection to Parachute Regiment standards. A tough man, and it is my privilege, these days, to buy him a pint at Depot reunions.

Sweeping the hangar floor was a task that had few rivals for utter boredom. There was a lot of it and my brush was about a foot wide. The squadron vehicle fleet was parked down one side - and the MT detailer would obligingly move them so I could sweep that space also - and one end of the hangar was rigged with parachute ground training equipment. On the floor there was also what appeared to be an abandoned football, and few new arrivals to the hangar could resist taking a kick at it. What they were actually kicking, though, was an old, punctured ball that had been carefully placed over a lump of steel that projected from the floor. New arrivals were easily identified; they were the ones in best uniform, clutching a blue card and limping.

The MT fleet was painted RAF blue at the time but about to undergo repainting in matt green (and later still in camouflage green and black). Among my bog-cleaning duties I scored the task of rubbing down the gloss with emery paper, before the vehicles were driven to REME workshops at Warminster for spraying. Another welcome variation was to accompany the squadron to the nearby station of RAF Hullavington, where a balloon-jumping programme was often arranged. I was not permitted to jump, but handing out or recovering 'chutes passed a few hours agreeably. During the programme, I encountered some members of 55 Coy RASC, last seen in Singapore in '63. I was meanwhile impatient to resume the course - another one having formed and dispersed by now - but it was December before I was deemed ready for it. Wales promised to be bloody cold.

Early medical advice from the MO had been to give the knee plenty of exercise, and that baffled me. The MO actually hanged himself a few months later, and I can only hope that he did not feel unduly burdened by my problems. For three months I had done no exercise at all, and I feared that this would put me at considerable disadvantage for the new attempt.

On the eve of the course, the squadron detachment returned from jungle warfare training in Malaysia and had a solid session in the NAAFI, getting stuck into flagons of Cyprus sherry when the bar closed. Fighting erupted late in the afternoon and everything in the NAAFI that was made of glass, including the light bulbs, was broken. The CO was carpeted by the station commander early on Monday morning, and the arse-kicking duly handed on to the squadron, which pre-para was now miraculously a part of. The punishments included being barred from the NAAFI for two weeks, and this also extended to pre-para, as I discovered that evening when I fronted for a mug of tea. Rejection by the NAAFI may have intimated a degree of acceptance by the squadron, but it was too complicated to work out.

Ten of us began the course and five were on light duties at the close of the first week. I was not among them and was so far successful in a determination to finish first on all of the runs, marches and assault courses. The knee twinged periodically, but it was holding up. My morale took a boost when I was told that my time for the Eagle House March - a course of about eight miles and featuring stiff gradients - was one of the best for pre-para. I had run most of it.

The selection tests came around and light relief was added when we went to the Soundwell Swimming Baths in Bristol. We were required to go off the ten-metre diving board in a variety of attitudes;

the least favourite being to remain stiffly at attention and fall forward off the board. The theory was that one would enter the water as cleanly as a knife, but this did not work in practice. Another departure was to step off the board backwards, and when one of the group went he had second thoughts, grabbing the board on the way down. This duly bounced the 'despatching' NCO, who unfortunately was not wearing swimming togs, into the deep end.

Five of us made it to Wales this time, but one burst into tears climbing *Tryfan* on the first day and two more opted out as we toiled up the *Pyg Track* on Snowdon, leaving just two of us to complete a twenty-two-mile road march that evening. My companion was a corporal who had just returned from a three-year tour in Cyprus. His teeth chattered incessantly and I felt quite warm by comparison.

We completed the night tab mostly at the run, returning to the bivvie site long before we were expected to. Our hootchies were in a sodden patch by a watercourse, whilst the pre-para staff lived in some comfort in the back of a Bedford RL which was parked nearby. When it was obvious that the staff had gone off somewhere, and probably for a pint, I climbed into the Bedford to see what food might be proffed, and I also made a pot of tea on the gas stove. It was the foulest cup of tea I'd ever had, and much later I discovered that the teapot I had used was an old one reserved for filling the paraffin lamps.

We slept, if we slept at all, cold and wet, bereft of sleeping bags and anxious for daybreak and the final run from Lake Ogwen, where we camped, to Swallow Falls. When we ran, our overalls were soaked and the webbing was stiff. The DS, a tough Brummie named Mick Chittem, urged us to keep up but he soon vanished into the curtain of rain. I paused just once, consulting my map to find Swallow bloody Falls, and completed the run. A lorry never looked so good.

"Hit him with your handbag, Sir!"

4

The return to Colerne proved the briefest of respites, since the following Sunday saw us back in Wales for a fortnight of field-firing and exercise at Sennybridge Camp, near the Brecon Beacons. I had been posted to C Flight and was not greatly surprised when someone saw me as a natural for the Carl Gustav anti-tank weapon, which weighed thirty-eight pounds. I signed the cleaning kit for it out of the flight stores, idly wondering when the next pre-para might be sending a man to C Flight. Whenever and whomever that might be, I already felt that he was a natural for the anti-tank weapon.

Among the assortment of ranges where we fired the SLR, the Sterling sub-machine gun and the larger General Purpose Machine Gun, we also did grenade and anti-tank stalks. At the latter I had the dubious privilege of firing two HEAT rounds after an exhausting crawl along a quarter-mile of ditch. The 'kicks' in the head and chest were added to the more obvious discomforts of being soaking wet and cold. At the conclusion of the tank stalk, I was debriefed by a squadron SNCO who was enveloped in a huge parka, and who was sipping at a steaming mug of tea as he stood over a blazing fire created from broken up ammunition boxes. I decided right then that his was a crap example to set for the new man, although the SNCO was not typical of II Squadron.

The fortnight culminated in an evasion exercise, where I was selected as one of the screen troops. It was perishing weather and I would have much preferred to be making my way across the area, rather than laying about. The ends of my moustache froze.

We recovered to Colerne with a few days to fill prior to Xmas leave, which I planned to spend in Crewe. I moved my kit from the pre-para accommodation into G Block, where I shared a sixteen-man room with seven other occupants. We were from a mix of flights, which seemed to me to be a sound idea, and we got along.

On parades I wore my squadron stable belt with a degree of pride. It was only awarded at the successful completion of pre-para and it was of a different design to the RAF Regiment stable belt. The latter separated the dark blue and dark red colours of the navy and the army - signifying the Royal Naval Air Service and Royal Flying Corps origins of the RAF - with a thin light blue stripe. The II Squadron belt was thinner and of a uniformly bright blue colour. This distinction was of uncertain origin and the source of some irritation to other squadron's members, and also to authority. The wearing of the belt was actually prohibited a couple of years later - and about a fortnight after I had bought a new one.

Colerne proved to have an Airmen's Mess that routinely won catering prizes, and the food was simply excellent. The wet bar in the NAAFI was usually lively with members of the squadron, although we had our 'own' pub in the nearby city of Bath. This was 'The Beefeater', a stone's throw from the 'bus station, which was handy for all those who did not possess a set of wheels. Mine, by now, was beginning to resemble a motorised colander, and it was surely a matter of time before my request at the local garage would be: "Two gallons of Super, a pint of oil and a packet of Polyfilla, please."

Colerne had been one of the last of the Thirties Expansion Scheme airfields to be built, actually being completed after the war broke out. Several aircraft types had flown from the station, and they included a Hurricane squadron manned by Poles, who defended the Bristol docks from German bombers. The ghost of a Polish pilot was reportedly haunting one of our blocks, but the only ghostly figures I ever encountered were those who had overdone the cider the previous night.

Cider was a popular tipple since the rough stuff - scrumpy - was available locally for a few pence a pint. Some of it actually looked green in the glass. Drinking was part of the territory of being a gunner, which was no surprise, but there was some quaffing of fairly epic proportions. A group into which I strayed from time to time was known as 'the Mandatory Gallon Men'. These recognised no one who did not drink at least eight pints at a session.

I soon noted the high proportion of Celts on the squadron, and I later formed the view that an RAF Regiment devoid of Scots or Irish would probably have had trouble manning a single squadron. They probably also featured a high proportion of the drinkers and/or fighters, but they also provided some of the better soldiers. The squadron also had about a dozen Jamaicans, and when these went about the station together they were collectively known as 'the oil slick'. This was jocular but today doubtless would be interpreted as unacceptably racist.

No aircraft were based at Colerne, but the C130 Hercules' from RAF Lyneham, which lay about twenty miles away, were routinely serviced on the station. As they climbed away from the airfield after maintenance, the pilots would occasionally chop an engine to simulate failure and practice the emergency drill. On one occasion, an engine on the same wing cut out simultaneously and the aircraft spun into a small copse adjacent to the married quarters. The crew perished.

The news from home was that brother Jack's nickel shares were now worth $12,000, which put into perspective my wage of £9 per week. I would not begin to draw parachute pay of 7/6d per day until I had re-qualified, although it would be backdated to the completion of pre-para, which was something to look forward to. I also had a letter from Dave Armstrong, who was by now a warrant officer serving in Viet Nam. I reckoned that he probably paid his boot boy nine quid a week. Arch also was by now promoted to warrant rank, and returned from Viet Nam.

The Xmas leave was a pleasant break and I spent some time with my cousins, the children of Aunt Bess, in local or district pubs. One evening we had been drinking and playing darts at a pub in the country some miles from Crewe, and at closing we found that a thick fog had descended. It being too cold to kip in the car, we set off cautiously for home. I had my window down to monitor the white line in the road and I advised cousin Pete to keep a watch through his window. Some time later the white line disappeared and I found myself staring at a hedge from about ten inches. "What's on your side, Pete?" I asked.
"A hedge." He replied. I stopped the car and got out, discovering that we were in someone's drive.

Returning to Colerne, I requested a driving test with the squadron MT, but when they learned that I was driving on an Australian licence they made arrangements to detach me to RAF St. Athan. I thought this a bit extreme, and subsequently found that I was being taught to drive from scratch. I actually began the lessons in a Link trainer, which I could not get the hang of at all. I was forever stalling it and I also had frequent 'crashes'. Fortunately, we soon moved on to Land Rovers and there were few mysteries there.

The social life took an upwards turn when I met a WRAF who was undergoing training as an armourer. She was actually being courted by another student, but I discovered that he was married and promptly revealed the fact. Another Rock on the same course warned me that the bloke was planning a late-night visit to me on a particular night, so I sat up awaiting him. He did not loiter, however.

The majority of driver trainees were directly from Swinderby and it was irritating that we were all treated in the cavalier manner that they were. Even more irritating were the frequent PT lessons, where we were too often regarded as dummy classes for the trainee physical instructors, whose school also was at St. Athan. "With a jump, feet together, **PLACE!**" and similar was definitely not for the big boys, and I eventually approached the PT flight sergeant. I asked if I might go for a long run in lieu of PT classes and he happily agreed.

The relationship with Bonny took an agreeable turn when she announced that she wanted to sleep with me, and we secured a hotel room in Cardiff. The room cost £6 per night and I financed this by pawning my Rolex at a nearby establishment. We were at the seedier end of the city, and the hotel facilities were so poor that we actually returned to St. Athan for showers.

I completed the course, passed the test and was retained at the school to undergo Heavy Goods Vehicle training. I now ploughed the same routes in Bedford TKs and RLs, for a couple of weeks before the tests. I failed the first one, when I tried to bluff a Geest banana wagon along the side of the Cardiff Docks, but passed a subsequent attempt and went back to Colerne. I had been away for two months and the squadron had gone off to some trouble spot in the meantime.

A ten-week postal strike precluded news from home, but the news in Britain included decimal currency. A pound containing two hundred and forty pence, became a pound with one hundred new pence, and I thought that was cumbersome. The ten-shilling note, as in Australia, would have been a smarter idea, but the decision perhaps reflected sentimental attachment to the pound.

Pounds, decimal or otherwise, remained in short supply. Running a car and a girlfriend was proving expensive, and I usually found the gap between paydays at least five days too long. Pay parade was still a time-consuming ritual, as we lined up alphabetically and received our due. When presenting oneself at the pay table, the money was counted out by the paying officer, and picked up and transferred to the left hand by the recipient, who then saluted with his right hand. Elsewhere at this time was a Gunner named Coulson, who had tattoos on the palms of each hand. On Coulson's left palm was tattooed: **THANK YOU** and on Coulson's right palm: **FUCK YOU**. Coulson was easily recognised on pay parades; he was the one wearing gloves - whatever the weather.

Going back to Colerne with a 4 Tonner qualification coincided with the need of the squadron canoeists for a driver and general gofer on weekend practices. The teams were in training for the annual canoe marathon that was the Devizes-Westminster race, a paddle of some hundred and twenty-five miles. I did not object to this, since my spending at St. Athan, mostly on drink but additionally on carnal pursuits, had drained both the wallet and the post office savings book to new depths. Some financial restraint was called for.

The canoe club did not provide such luxuries as wet suits, and I considered the teams to be a hardy breed. Actually, they were simply adept at remaining inboard of their craft and I was subsequently falsely lulled into trying my hand. This was a big mistake, since the canoes were strictly racing craft - Moonrakers, I think - with a keel about the width of a comb. If paddling and chewing gum at the same time, it was wise to chew the gum in the centre of the mouth. At my ninth or tenth capsize on some stretch of the Avon on a bleak, March day, I gave up and retired, shivering, to the 4 Tonner to brew a pot of tea which did not taste of paraffin.

Inexpensive habits became the order of the day for a while and included the Astra Cinema on station, where admission was a modest 20p. Service cinemas by this time were the only examples where the national anthem was still played, although at the beginning of performance rather than at the conclusion, which had been the practice elsewhere and usually the signal for a stampede for the exit. I was ejected by the manager on some occasion for failing to stand for the anthem, having little respect for the royal family about twenty-five years before it became fashionable.

There was also a small, but fine, collection of vintage aircraft in a hangar adjacent to that which was occupied by the squadron, and I was developing an interest in such specimens. St. Athan also had a collection, but these were not generally available for viewing, being usually in some state of restoration.

Our own hangar was quiet, since the squadron was presently split between detachment duties in Bahrein and Salalah, both in the

Gulf and the latter a somewhat secretive operational duty. I had to drive to RAF Lyneham one day to pick up a member of the Salalah detachment returning early, and subsequently learned that he had been running about with a loaded rifle, threatening to shoot someone.

I had expected to join one or other of the detachments but suddenly was ordered to RAF Abingdon to undergo the assault parachutist course. This was expected to take two or three weeks, depending upon how the weather might effect the programme of descents. I packed my bag, fired up the Riley and drove up to Berkshire. At the camp gates, the policeman was a chap I had undergone recruit training with, which appeared to settle the matter of social evenings.

The course was about fifty strong and was overwhelmingly formed by recruits from the Parachute Regiment. The remainder was a sprinkling of Royal Marines and independent parachute units that still existed at this time. I was the only RAF man on the course. Although the course was conducted by the physical training branch of the RAF, there was a strong Parachute Regiment presence on the station, and a Parachute Regiment RSM took us for lectures from time to time. He was Knobby Arnold and he made the national newspapers a few years later, when he challenged some strangers at the Aldershot depot he had by then transferred to. The strangers proved to be very important people - or so they supposed - and Knobby was censured, despite the very recent bombing of the Officers' Mess by the IRA. Knobby chose to leave the service on that note.

Ground training began and contained no surprises, except that there was an additional piece of ground training equipment that the Australian school had not featured. This was the Exit Trainer, where the dummy harness was clipped to a cable and the student despatched from a platform at thirty feet or so. The cable was rigged to spin the student through ninety degrees before he hurtled down the cable to a landing. The device was known - with justification - as the 'knacker cracker' and I soon added it to the list of ground training equipments I did not like.

The prospect of renewed parachuting stirred old fears of incapacitating injury or death, and the nights before descents were the anxious time. Such fears fled with the first of the emplaning drills however, when repetitive routine took over the mind, obscuring negative thoughts. The descents began with a balloon programme at a DZ called, picturesquely, Weston on the Green, and we completed four descents there before tackling a clean fatigue jump from a C130. 'Clean fatigue' had nothing to do with the laundry of one's kit, and merely indicated that no leg bag equipment was carried.

The balloons, briefly encountered in my case with the jump with the Geordie TA, were of the type designed to tear the wings off Hun bombers over England during WWII. These were underslung with an open 'cage' which offered an expanding view of the very pretty countryside as we were winched up to the jumping height of eight hundred feet. Four student parachutists were aboard, along with the despatching PJI, usually a sergeant of the physical training branch. The initial descent on Weston offered an amusing moment as a consequence of the first student out anticipating his landing by extending a foot, rather than keeping them tightly pinned together in the prescribed drill. The landing broke his ankle, which of course the remaining students remained unaware of. Since the second student was obviously very nervous, the PJI held his harness very firmly and invited him to look out on the DZ as he positioned him at the gate. The student did so and was rewarded by the sight of an ambulance, red cross well visible on its roof, speeding towards the injured student. Several degrees paler, he nevertheless went on command.

I had the considerable advantage over the rest of the course in having trained before and having a score or so of jumps behind me. This did not prevent me from making some terrible landings, however, and I spent as much time doing press-ups as anyone for such errors.

Easter split the course and we had a four-day break. The police mate, Neil O'Brien, mentioned that he and a Parachute Regiment corporal were attempting the Devizes-Westminster race, and he wondered if I would support them. I agreed to this and also took Bonny along with me. Bonny had abandoned armourer studies and remustered as a kennel maid at the RAF Police school at Debden. Relations with Bonny were actually becoming a bit tense by this time. She had demonstrated a capacity for foul tempers and black moods, which did not augur for a happy relationship, and she also appeared to be reading more in the relationship than actually existed. For the moment though, it was mostly sweetness and light and particularly since we had access to a spare bedroom in the married quarter occupied by friends of Bonny.

Promotion to senior aircraftman brought some welcome back pay and I was able to redeem the Rolex from Cardiff. The Riley, meanwhile, was becoming a sorry sight and I considered selling it to reduce my costs. Vehicle ownership on an airman's wages did not seem to add up, without even considering drinking costs. I reckoned that what I really needed was a stint of overseas detachment.

Neil and his mate, who had jumped at Suez, completed all the exhausting portages on the canal sections of the race, and had just hit open water when a leaking hull forced their withdrawal. We retired to Abingdon and devoted what remained of the weekend to the bar. I was quite relieved to pick up the training on the following Tuesday, although it was another session of the dreaded knacker cracker. We duly completed the jumps' programme, including the night descent, got in a couple of extras from the Andover aircraft and were dispersed.

The chance of a detachment seemed as remote as ever. There were just a dozen Rocks on the rear party and we were despatched to RAF St. Athan to form a Regiment vehicle handling team for the Royal Tournament. An RAF team was already under training, and we learned that each of the three services was to field two teams at matinees and evening performances of the tournament in July. This sounded as if it might be a pleasant diversion and a social opportunity, and there was also a strong WRAF element in the RAF team. Thoughts of Bonny, who had taken to delivering strong hints of marriage, were discarded.

The teams trained at St. Athan for a couple of weeks then moved to Borden, an army camp near Aldershot. We were finally lodged at RAF Uxbridge, which was no great distance from London, and this would be our base for the ten days of the tournament. It soon became apparent that the Regiment team was destined to become the gallant losers in the daily competitions. We twelve had been selected from the available twelve, whilst a good many had tried for the other teams. We were not distressed by this, feeling that we gave it our best, and that someone had to lose. In the meantime, we were making the most of social opportunities.

I had moved in on one of the WRAFs, an MT driver named Pamela. Pam had an uncomplicated attitude to sex and she was not dismayed by the lack of hotel facilities that my persistent lack of funds precluded. The sports' field at Uxbridge proved suitably remote, and we actually found a tent on the field one evening. Life seemed good.

Among the squadron team was a Geordie named Terry Pemberton. We had formed a drinking partnership and he was good company, if sometimes difficult to understand. When he left the service, he held a NAAFI party to which he invited all the members of his flight and I also went along. At the end of the evening, Terry returned to the block and thumped all those of his flight who had failed to attend.

As the tournament came to a close, and I wondered what prospects remained for a Gulf detachment, we were visited by my flight commander, Flying Officer Gillan. He informed us that we were 'off to the land of the green'. "Should be nice in Hawaii." I remarked. Actually, he meant Northern Ireland.

Coulson was easily recognised on pay parades…

5

Anglo-Irish hostilities began somewhere in the middle of the twelfth century, but the reason for our detachment was rooted at the end of the seventeenth. James II of England was a Catholic who sought to repeal many anti-Catholic measures in Ireland that his predecessors had implemented. English Protestantism was against him and England was invaded by an army of 14,000, led by the Dutchman William of Orange. William, who would rule England as William III, was actually a son-in-law to James II, who was overthrown by the 'Glorious Revolution' in 1688 and obliged to flee to France. James, with French assistance, landed in Ireland to organise the defeat of William, but the latter marshalled Protestant allies in Ireland and defeated James on the banks of the River Boyne, west of Dublin, in 1690.

The Orange Order was formed in 1795 as a secret society devoted to Protestantism, and its lodges were in England and Ireland. It was suppressed for a time in the nineteenth century and later regenerated as a less closed organisation, but no less committed to Protestant supremacy. In the modern day, its members celebrated the Protestant Ascendancy with a summer marching season, culminating on the 31 August, which was the anniversary of the Apprentice Boys' defence, and holding, of Londonderry. The Battle of the Boyne, a definitive defeat, provided another anniversary to be celebrated with a major parade, on 12 July. (The battle actually was fought on 1 July, but the date was changed with nineteenth century change to the Gregorian calendar.)

In 1967 the Catholic minority of the six counties of Protestant Ulster formed a civil rights movement to work for equal rights for Catholics, who were discriminated against in virtually every aspect of their lives, and not least with regard to jobs and housing. A 1968 march by Catholics through Londonderry led to violence and bloodshed, and the British army was moved in to protect the Catholic minority. The violence escalated and the troops were eventually used to seal off with barricades and barbed wire the separate communities within the towns and cities. The troops, having initially been warmly welcomed by the Catholic communities, began increasingly to be seen as allies of the Loyalists and targets for Nationalist violence. In July 1971 we were still a few months short of what would be the most violent and death-ridden years of the 'troubles', but the violence was nonetheless widespread and serious. Police stations were coming under bomb attacks and the police had the prime responsibility for containing violence at the Orange Order marches, which the Stormont government steadfastly refused to prohibit. A newspaper of the day condemned the marches as 'provocative nonsense', which they were but also quite lethal nonsense. Elsewhere, Protestant clergy defended the marches (and still do) as 'little more than young girls playing accordions and making their way home from church'. This roseate view entirely overlooked the hundreds of Orange bands dressed in quasi-military uniforms, thumping the huge Lambeg drums and parading, if not flaunting, their Protestantism through purely Catholic areas. It was the task of the squadron to reinforce a number of police stations during this inflammatory period.

A small advance party had been assembled and I drove the 4 Tonner from Colerne to Liverpool. We were there loaded onto a Landing Ship, Logistic that was crewed by the Royal Fleet Auxiliary. Confusingly, it was also crewed by the Royal Corps of Transport, who concerned themselves with cargo, and their number included a demented RSM who made us all rise at 0400hrs to polish floors. One of our group had raised a smile among the army team by grandly inscribing his baggage with the chalked legend: **NOT REQUIRED ON VOYAGE**. It was all of twelve hours to Belfast.

The LSL proved to have much the sailing qualities of a rubbish skip and we were somewhat relieved when it tied up at the Belfast dock. A glance from the deck revealed a large sign which proclaimed: 'PREPARE TO MEET THY GOD', which was immensely cheering, and a small knot of Rocks from the Regiment squadron which currently was undergoing a three-month roulement tour in the Province. When we disembarked, this team equipped us with flak jackets and a small amount of 7.62mm ammunition for our rifles, then they escorted us to HMS Maidstone for an overnight stay.

The Maidstone, which later would achieve a degree of notoriety as a floating prison when the measure of internment without trial was introduced, had served as a submarine supply ship during WWII, and she was now providing floating accommodation for sundry visitors such as we. She smelled powerfully of diesel oil and BO and would not have been a natural choice for cruising. Her galley served what easily was the worst food I had ever eaten.

When the squadron main party arrived, it was quickly detached at section level to a number of police stations in the city and the suburbs, but I remained with squadron HQ briefly. Among the tasks there was that of escorting the Warrant on a round of visits to the police stations, and we were often pressed with cups of tea by householders during such rounds. The donors were Protestant; Catholic gratitude having by now evaporated.

I joined a section at the Musgrave police station in the city, standing duty in a sangar at the rear of the building and adapting to encouragement or abuse, according to tribe, from late-night passers-by. A sangar companion one night, himself an Irishman, proved less than philosophical about some insult and strode across to fell its author with a single blow, and make an arrest. I met him at a reunion a year or two ago and we chuckled at the memory of it. The shift system at Musgrave was two hours on and two hours off, which promised to be a wearing routine over the space of a fortnight, but after a couple of days I was transferred out to the suburb of Glengormley. Section strength here meant that we could work two on and four off, but when we discovered that we had a squadron cook in our midst we absorbed his shifts so that he could devote his efforts to the cooking. This in any case would be less than *cordon bleu* since we were feeding on composite (iron) rations.

Glengormley was Protestant and quiet - although the police station was destroyed by a bomb in later years - and boredom seemed the likely enemy. We stood duty on the roof and in a sangar to the front of the building. It rained occasionally and our only defence against it was to wear a poncho, which was inconvenient. Since it remained warm, a preferred option was simply to get wet and dry out during the four hours off. The neighbours were friendly and during an early sangar duty an old lady pressed a bag of fruit upon me. 'For the boys', she said. Bugger the boys, I thought, demolishing the fruit during my shift. Later in the day we received word from HQ not to eat any gifts of food, since a Squaddie had been poisoned in the city. I felt psychosomatically and deservedly ill for a few hours.

The local Orangemen duly paraded through the suburb, wearing their orange sashes, their bowler hats and brandishing their banners, their brollies and the occasional sword. To my eyes, they merely looked foolish, but such foolishness in the city resulted in three dead; two civilians and a soldier.

The deaths, of civilians and servicemen alike, would escalate and they continue to this day. England had been forced to defend its bigoted child, Ulster, and this drew the line for the IRA. The truth is that England's record down eight centuries in Ireland is simply appalling, as has been the treatment by Protestants of Catholics in Ulster since partition in 1922. It is also true that there will be no acceptance of Catholics in Ulster by Protestants, and those who would have you believe that the troubles have nothing to do with religion have a nice line in bullshit. I do believe that the violence will end one day. Perhaps when we have ceased teaching religion (and bigotry) in our schools. And I believe the violence in Ulster will end when the people of Ulster, ordinary people, say that they have had enough. They will make it happen despite all of the mealy-mouthed platitudes by generations of devious and self-serving politicians on both sides of the water. One day.

The brief detachment ran its course and we prepared for home, with most of the squadron flying out. That was not an option for me, since I had a 4 Tonner to drive and I also had to put another night in on the malodorous Maidstone. I refuelled the wagon at a camp occupied by 1 Para, whose duty was in the worst areas of sectarian violence, chatting briefly with some lads I had met at Abingdon. When I rolled onto the LSL, I learned that no bunk existed for me and I curled up in the back of the Bedford. This offered the considerable advantage of escape from the ship's RSM, who clearly had shares in floor polish.

At Liverpool, a police escort had formed to expedite the move through the city of a Royal Artillery unit that had been aboard. I was travelling alone but smartly tucked myself into the convoy until its direction was no longer the one I required. By the time I arrived at Colerne, there had already been a pretty general exodus to leave, and I soon joined it. My parachute back pay, in the enormous sum of £90, had been paid and I was further saving money by having finally given up cigarettes. A habit of up to forty a day - when I could afford them - I had managed to break during the stint at Glengormley. I would never touch cigarettes again.

After the leave, which I again spent in Crewe, I returned to preparation for a guard of honour. The Queens' Colour Squadron fielded most of the major ceremonial for the RAF, but was presently over-stretched. A German general was visiting and for a five-minute guard the entire squadron was issued with a brand new Number 1 uniform. I noticed that mine had gilt buttons and I promptly cut them off and sewed the brass ones on. Old habits, to say nothing of stupid habits, died hard. We were also issued with new shirts, which had the collars firmly attached to them. We seemed to be advancing from the Thirties, in this respect anyway, at last.

Other uniform changes included the issue of a disruptive pattern combat dress to replace the former OG combat suit. We still wore boots with puttees, however, and there was yet no sign of the waterproof clothing that apparently was somewhere in the supply chain. '37 Pattern webbing had thankfully been left behind at Catterick (although for a number of years afterwards I continued to notice it being worn by army units which were not 'teeth arm'). The 'new' webbing was '58 Pattern, and it was a useful assembly which distributed load much better than its predecessor. It had, however, an entirely useless large pack and many Gunners bought Bergens.

Having drilled to a degree of competence, if not perfection, we rode in coaches to RAF Northolt, which was close to London. Upon arrival, we were told that the visit was off and we immediately returned to Colerne. At Colerne we were told that the guard was on again and we returned to the coaches, this time spending a night at RAF Uxbridge.

Back at Colerne, blue uniforms were returned to the lockers they seldom came out of and we settled to an intensive programme of parachuting. The downside of these lay in the fact that very few of them were straight up and down jobs. After emplaning each day we were usually flying at low level for two hours prior to the descent. Low level invariably was turbulent and this combined with a stuffy atmosphere in the Herc fuselage upset most stomachs. A 'spew bag' was always tucked behind the reserve 'chute for low level, and the first use of one usually triggered a rash of them. I was never sick in the air, but on a couple of occasions only held onto my stomach contents until I hit the DZ.

My social life was much the same as anyone else's at the time. I joined the 'mandatory gallon' men, hung out in the squadron pub and moved in on a group of nurses who seemed to favour us. An attempted relationship proved short-lived when I visited a flat and the girl put a selection of classical music on the record player. "Do you like Dvorak?" She asked. "Oh yes", I replied, "I've got all his records at home."

If attempts at developing relationships with the opposite sex were occasionally disappointing, there was a rich vein of comradeship in the barrack to be enjoyed. Particular mates were Fred Morrow and John Walsh. Fred drove an Austin Westminster which was in even more dubious shape than my Riley, and he had wisely joined the RAC recovery service. Every single attempt to drive to his native Barrow in Furness on leave ended with the Austin being hoisted aboard a recovery truck. Fred believed that his fuel consumption figures would prove a valuable selling point whenever he got around to disposing of the car. John hailed from Waterford in the Irish Republic and was that great rarity among Rockapes - a highly educated one. This did not impair his sense of fun, however, and his guaranteed method of securing quick pints in a crowded bar was to turn his eyelids inside out and affect gross deformity. A path to the bar would immediately open.

Between parachuting, or being sick waiting to parachute, we underwent an intensive programme of Nuclear, Biological and Chemical training for a forthcoming Germany exercise. NBC was beginning to assume a greater importance in our routines of defence or patrolling, simply because the Warsaw Pact Forces led by the USSR reputedly had such vast NBC resources (chemical particularly) and had apparently advertised their intention to use it in any large-scale operations. We soon discovered that running around in a 'Noddy suit' - made of a carbon impregnated, chemically-resistant material - on a summer's day was no fun, and the temperatures in Germany were likely to be much stronger than in the UK. Not much fun, either, in wearing the S6 Respirator for hours at a stretch.

We began the exercise, which had imaginatively been entitled 'Summer Umbrella', by emplaning in three Whitworth Argosy aircraft at RAF Lyneham. The Argosy was known to groundcrew as 'The Whistling Wheelbarrow' for the twin booms of its fuselage and the high note of its turbo engines. We knew it as 'The Flying Tit' because of the bulbous shape of the nose, which had a nipple-like projection on it which was the radome. We emplaned at 0800hrs and, unusually, were allowed to remove our 'chutes until the order 'prepare for action' came down the fuselage at 1020hrs. Also unusually, I fell asleep until the order arrived.

I had drawn the Number 1 position in the starboard stick, and this was highly desirable since it avoided the shuffle-cum-gallop that inevitably ensued whenever a large stick had to be despatched. Stick leaders merely advanced to the door and were cleanly away on the green light. Not so cleanly on this occasion, unfortunately.

We were by now equipped with a leg bag that comprised of nylon straps which secured our webbing and weapons which were wrapped in a lightweight sheet. This arrangement was known as Container, Straps & Personal Equipment Pack, and it replaced the bulkier canvas leg bag of WWII design. A fault with the CSPEP was that the nylon straps had a tendency to slip, which is precisely what had happened to mine as we went to 'action stations'. At the door, I had a bit of time on the run in to take a new hitch on a strap, but this happened to coincide with the aircraft hitting turbulence. Without a hand to steady myself against the side of the door, I was caught unawares when the aircraft pitched and I went out. I banged against the fuselage outboard as I went and the sloppy exit doubtless contributed to the very severe twists I found in my rigging lines when my canopy blossomed above me. I was still kicking out of the twists - having first lowered my leg bag - when I hit the ground. By then I had already watched the Argosy drone on with no further figures falling from it.

At least, I knew the direction of the DZ and when I had 'daisy-chained' my rigging lines and stuffed the canopy into a carrying bag, I had merely to trudge off in pursuit of C Flight. With about a hundred and sixty pounds of kit, it was slow progress and the DZ reorganisation phase was all over when I arrived. I got a swift bollocking from the flight sergeant for 'farting around', and found a seat on the coach. We then had a five-hour journey to RAF Wildenrath, where we would continue to work up to the exercise, which consisted of defending Harrier sites.

The Wildenrath training consisted of yet more NBC, which clearly enjoyed a higher profile in Germany than in the UK. We were then deployed into the field and dug trenches within flight defended areas, at a site that had already been prepared for the 'jump-jet' Harriers. Although these aircraft required no take-off or landing run, steel decking was laid to prevent some forty tons of aircraft sinking into the ground. The sites, usually in woodland, were also extensively camouflaged.

A large number of RAF groundcrew deployed on such exercises and we soon noticed two unusual features. One was that the largest of the tents within the perimeter was actually a beer tent, and the other oddity was that groundcrew had an alternative to the use of night vision after dark. This was a torch with about eight batteries, and most effective at blinding those of us who were getting along quite nicely using the bits of the eye which best cope with darkness.

The 'enemies' were Belgian paras, but although a reputation for toughness preceded them, their skills were not that impressive. We saw a good few of them off, and some contacts degenerated into fist fights when it could not be determined exactly who had shot whom with blank ammunition. Tempers in this respect were not improved by spending up to six hours in complete NBC protection. It was high summer and, soon, so were we.

We passed a couple of days at Wildenrath when the exercise concluded, and the RAF Regiment reputation for aggression which was not entirely confined to training got an airing with some fights in the NAAFI. Charges followed us to Colerne. Prior to departure, we made a trip to the Airborne Museum at Arnhem, where I noticed that the field dressing on display was newer than mine.

6

The exercise theme continued, with a deployment to RAF Odiham to work with helicopters of the Wessex Mark V variety. There was much speculation at the time that this was the way forward for the RAF Regiment. A quarter of a century later, this appears to be the 'new' idea.

The autumn days ran down and we deployed to Sennybridge for another intensive package of field-firing ranges and exercise. Sennybridge seemed to be forever cold and wet and the ambush ranges were interminable. Waterproof clothing had arrived, but it proved to be as useless as the poncho it was intended to replace. The material was rubberised on the inside and body heat was unable to escape, which resulted in condensation forming, and cooling, and the net result was in being cold and wet.

I spent some leave in Crewe again, much of it ferrying Aunt Bess to a hospital to visit Uncle Reg, who had lung problems caused during the war. He recovered and I had a couple of quiet days with him. The leave was in lieu of Xmas, since we were due to undergo a detachment in the Oman for three months.

The training for the Oman, in addition to all of the usual routines, was based upon Mortars, General Purpose Machine Guns in the Sustained Fire role and, new to us, a man-portable radar, called ZB 298. We underwent training in cadres on the GPMG (SF) and the radar, which was swiftly christened 'Zebedee' after a character in a children's TV programme. GPMG SF was impressive, since the tripod added one thousand metres to the light role range of eight hundred metres, whilst the inclusion of an optical sight with the kit (identical to that which was fitted to the 81mm mortars) meant that targets could be recorded and later engaged in conditions of target obscuration, such as nightfall or smoke. The GPMG itself was a proven weapon and largely derived from the German MG42 of WW II vintage. The mortars were strictly the province of the Support Weapons flight of the squadron. The field flights were equipped with the light 2" mortar, but it had no sights, was of indifferent range and was not regarded as a useful defence weapon in the context of Oman operations. There also appeared to be no HE ammunition anywhere available for the weapon.

Zebedee weighed about a hundred and twenty pounds and was powered by batteries. It could detect movement out to six thousand metres, provided that it had line of sight, and although it had no audio component some boffin had arranged things so that a detected vehicle actually 'sounded' like a vehicle, and a walking human betrayed a 'footfall'. We learned how to set up and operate the system, how to plot 'dead ground' traces, and how to relay the information to the SF teams, who had the means of applying the radar information in terms of azimuth and elevation to the GPMGs. Interesting work.

Winter was biting hard again, and a number of us were less than pleased to be posted at the camp perimeters one evening in response to a threat by a gang of 'skinheads' who had been ejected from the NAAFI dance a week previously. Incredible as it seems now, there was at this time very little control of people entering RAF stations (a neglect which saw a bomb planted at RAF Uxbridge some years later), and we had to be specially organised. In the event, the skinheads stayed away, which seemed a pity since most of us would cheerfully have cracked heads with our pick helves just to get warm.

Another unwelcome piece of work was in manhandling a piano from the Officers' Mess up three flights of stairs at the NAAFI for the squadron leaving party. The same crew was assembled to manhandle it down again, which was probably a mistake. We struggled with it to head of the stairs then simply gave it a push.

Between the revision of old skills and the acquisition of some newer ones, we were given some background to the place we would defend for three months. Specifically, we were charged with the ground defence of RAF Salalah, in the country of Oman, formerly Muscat and Oman.

The Oman was a Sultanate and a province in the Arabian Gulf. Its land neighbours to the north were the recently federated United Arab Emirates and Saudi Arabia, while to the west, and less than friendly, lay South Yemen. The Yemen provided the conduit than friendly, lay the South Yemen through which arms and advisers flowed to foster an Omani rebellion that had begun in 1969. The Sultan at that time was Ibn Said, an elderly despot who permitted no schools, hospitals or any sort of civic infrastructure. Even bicycles and radios were prohibited, since the Sultan's view was that this sort of progress was harmful. His was a medieval outlook, and a United Nations report at the time accused him of having a personal entourage of two hundred slaves, which included eunuchs.

When his people began to agitate for a progressive regime, Ibn Said responded by destroying the centuties-old irrigation system that fertilised the Salalah Plain, reverting it to a virtual desert. When armed rebellion erupted, Ibn Said requested British assistance, and a good card in his hand was his ownership of the island of Masirah, which was an important staging and refuelling station for RAF aircraft travelling to the Far East. Masirah also featured an important BBC link to the world. How keen the British government was to be seen supporting an act like Ibn Said's is debatable, but what is certain is that we were told to say little of our detachment. The war in Dhofar Province was to remain unsung virtually until the British presence ended with the end of the war in the mid-Seventies.

The problem of Ibn Said was partially resolved when his son, Qaboos, mounted a coup against him. It was thought then that the coup was mounted with British complicity, and it would be two decades before it was revealed that the coup was entirely organised by the British Foreign Office, with the complicity of Qaboos. Ibn Said, slightly wounded by his own Mauser pistol during the coup, spent the rest of his days in a suite of rooms at the very swish Dorchester Hotel in London. How many slaves or eunuchs accompanied him is not recorded.

Qaboos was Sandhurst-trained and, by Arab standards at least, a progressive. He declared amnesty for the Dhofari rebels - the *Adoo* - and there were many acceptances of this. There was, however, a hard core of some two thousand *Adoo*, firmly in the grip of Yemeni 'advisors' and the fighting continued. A degree of their effort was directed against the Salalah airfield, which remained under the control of the RAF, although the Sultan's air assets also operated from it. The country was twice the size of England, but the population was well under a million, being mostly nomadic.

Late in November we flew from RAF Lyneham to RAF Akrotiri, on Cyprus, and continued late that night to Salalah. The seating in a C130 was a canvas arrangement which was bright red and looked very jolly, but was anything but jolly in about the tenth hour of travel. Apart from the refuelling stop at Akrotiri and the inevitable urn of tea in the transit lounge, we had sixteen hours in a fuselage that was packed to capacity with bodies and baggage. The older hands had wisely carried aboard their sleeping bags, and thus were able to stretch out on the rear ramp of the aircraft, which was otherwise too cold for comfort.

Midmorning and Salalah met us with some heat, and we were quickly allocated to several huts; these dispersed and all but enveloped by forty-four gallon drums that were filled with sand and stones. These 'Burmoils' were a staple of defence against ground attack, and we would spend a fair bit of time extending their use.

We had left England under frost and here it was a comfortable eighty degrees Fahrenheit. This was something I could live with for three months, having yet to discover in the UK anything that really approximated summer. KD shorts were produced and when I found the Arab who operated a barber's shop, I had my hair reduced to half an inch on the top. Apart from the heat, it was already apparent that this was a dusty place, and short hair seemed a partial answer to the problem of clean hair.

The hut I moved into had sixteen occupants with hardly a bed's width between beds. Since half of us would be on duty at any given time, this crowding represented no real hardship. Of rather more pain was the fact that the bloke in the next bed to mine was a fan of Johnny Cash and 'spittoon music', and he had about a suitcase worth of cassette tapes. Fortunately, he was moved to a shift other than mine, and I was subjected to *San Quentin Prison Blues, Folsom Prison Blues,* or any other bloody prison blues no more than a score of times.

Support Weapons deployed out of the camp with their mortars, and they would remain out, working a twenty-four on, twenty-four off pattern for the next three months. The field flights were split between duties in the Command Post on the camp, and duties on the external defences where the mortar line was. Within a day, we had assumed the defences from a sister squadron and we were up and running. It also took just about one day for several of the detachment to acquire the red-checked *shamaq* head dress that the Arabs wore. "Bloody hell," Muttered the CP shift NCO, as an LAC strolled in sporting an example, "six hours in Salalah and he thinks that he's bloody Lawrence of Arabia."

"Six hours in Salalah and he thinks he's Lawrence of Arabia"

7

The detachment opened upon a note of minor disappointment, when projected patrols to dominate the Salalah Plain were abruptly terminated. The Plain was overlooked by the Jebel, the mountain range that stretched to the north and from which raiding parties appeared, usually under the cover of darkness. It had been the CO's intention to field fighting patrols to counter such incursions, and the planning and rehearsal for them was implemented. We believed that the cancellation of the intended patrols originated at high level, although it may simply have emanated from the Salalah station commander. It may also have been the case that we were seen to be exceeding our defensive role, and this sat uneasily with us. Some of us began to wonder why we practised such offensive capabilities on the major training areas within the UK, if we were not permitted to exercise them in reality. Others, including talented NCOs, began to think of taking their abilities to other arms (and armies) where they might find wider expression.

We otherwise shook out to our new duties and were too busy for a time to dwell upon disappointments which seemed to reflect upon professional ability. The daytime task in the CP seemed a staple of improving the camp defences, using the ubiquitous Burmoils. We cut the tops out of these, using a lump hammer and a pick head and taking about twenty seconds to do it, then manoeuvred them into position before filling them with sand and stones. Most of the camp buildings were screened by a double row, stacked to the height of two drums. The shovel work was pretty endless and we were often joined at it by the CO. He claimed that he merely joined in to keep his waist trim, but we reckoned that he liked to keep in touch with the squadron at all levels. He was a much-liked and respected figure.

Routine runs were made out to each of the Hedgehogs, which formed the depth defences to the airfield. For these the CP operated a standard Bedford RL which had been somewhat modified. The cab had been entirely removed and a steel shell fitted from the chassis to the level of the steering wheel. This offered protection against fragmentation from mines, although the passengers riding in the back, which also was quite open, had to rely upon a double row of sandbags laid on the floor.

The combined weight of steel and sand made the Bedford a fairly ponderous vehicle to drive, but the routes to the Hedgehogs necessitated slow driving in any case. Few roads existed and these were out of bounds because of the risk presented by mines. Among the occasional raiders from the Jebel were mine laying parties, who had the odd success against patrol vehicles driven by the *Dhofar Gendarmerie*. We were encouraged to free-range each trip and sometimes became slightly lost in the twisting wadis.

Four Hedgehogs had been created at a distance of about six kilometres from the airfield perimeter, and each stood about six Ks from the foot of the Jebel. The exception was Delta, which was so close to the mountain that frequent attacks upon it had caused it to be abandoned. Of the remainder, Bravo and Charlie were jointly manned by an element of the Royal Artillery and the RAF Regiment, whilst Alpha was manned by some combination of *Dhofar Gendarmerie* and surrendered enemy, who were generically referred to as *Firkat* or simply *Askaris*.

I had accompanied a familiarisation run out to 'our' Hedgehogs on the day of arrival, but failed to become properly oriented to the area. On my first run from the CP a day or two later, I headed off in the general direction but was soon wallowing about the beds of wadis whilst the escort, riding 'shotgun', stood on the steel carapace looking for landmarks. We eventually sighted the Hedgehog and drove in, only to discover that it was the abandoned Delta. Since Delta was alleged to have been heavily booby-trapped after evacuation, we did not loiter.

Driving problems were exacerbated by the swirling dust, a legacy of Taimur Ibn Said's annoyance with his people and the smashed irrigation system. Driving goggles seemed necessary but none existed at the camp. We made representation to the Suppliers and in due course a box of them arrived. Upon closer inspection, these proved to be the 'gas goggles' which probably dated from the Twenties. Any thoughts I might have entertained about looking like Rommel (The Desert Foxley) swiftly evaporated when I checked the mirror. The goggle lenses had greatly discoloured, and peering through them gave one the appearance of a myopic Japanese aviator.

In the evening, when shorts had been exchanged for long trousers and shirtsleeves rolled down as a simple protection against mosquitoes, the CP crew, which was at section strength, manned three towers on the camp perimeter. These were equipped with a GPMG in the light role and Zebedee. They were dull duties where nothing ever seemed to happen, and sleepiness in the dead hours of the morning was hard to resist. A free-fire zone existed outside the wire, which meant that boredom might be relieved by taking a pot shot at a native dog. This practice ended when a sentry loosed half a belt of 7.62mm GPMG at one, which resulted in a general stand-to within the camp which clearly believed that a major attack had developed.

The day on, day off routine proved agreeable. I ran about the perimeter until I shone with sweat, did some simple routines in the equally simple gymnasium and worked my Bullworker programme. I was off drink for the duration and not missing it at all. Entertainments were few but included an open-air cinema - built, inevitably, from Burmoils - which received all the standard *Astra* programmes to include the children's matinees. I greatly enjoyed *'Bedknobs and Broomsticks'* and *'The Jungle Book'*, although I drew the line at *'Mary Poppins'*. The admission fee was a hundred Baiza, or 10p, but some of us were not above sneaking in when the lights went down. Detachment saving could become an obsessive exercise in frugality that made Ebenezer Scrooge look like Lord Nuffield.

The camp also had a small library of incredibly ancient books, which had accumulated from long-disbanded RAF stations of the Middle East. Among these I was delighted to discover *'Deep Waters'*, a collection of stories by WW Jacobs. I carefully rationed this reading to last the detachment, then I sent the book to the Old Man.

After a fortnight, the shifts were rotated and I joined a four-man team manning the SF and Zebedee at Bravo. The mortarmen were by now well established and their shifts were varied only by the routine of twenty-four on and twenty-four off. Field flight Gunners would continue to rotate about CP and Hedgehog duties, on a weekly basis.

The Hedgehogs rose from the plain stark and foursquare, seeming to need only the draped bodies of dead Legionnaires to fit the *Fort Zinderneuf* image. Burmoils were again the principal means of construction, with a central tower to accommodate the Royal Artillery officer who acted as forward observer, and who could call in fire from the gun line at Salalah. Another tower had been devised for the SF and Zebedee, and only the mortarmen seemed to prefer life below ground, having fashioned pits lined with sandbags and of about eight feet diameter for their 81mm 'tubes'.

Sandbags formed the overhead protection and it appeared to be the job of each successive detachment to renew the bags, which were 'lifed' at about six months. It also gave us something to do during the day, other than practice our weapon drills or carry out 'hazard firing' tasks which were intended to discourage any form of movement on the Plain between the Hedgehogs and the Jebel. This activity was much more frequent at night, when we would fire either on fixed lines or at radar targets, and the fire might be from 25 Pounders, Mortars or GPMG SF.

Incoming fire was much less frequent, being usually confined to attempts to hit either a Hedgehog or the camp with a recoilless rifle. The intelligence briefings we had received listed RCLs among the weapons held by the *Adoo*, without specifying calibre. These may have been anywhere between 94mm and 120mm, with an effective range between four hundred and four thousand metres. We assumed that it was the RCL of greater range that was used for random pots at the Hedgehogs or the camp.

The first of the RCL attacks occurred within a fortnight of our arrival, and the last a few days before we handed the detachment over. There were several in between, but none of these proved to be sphincter-loosening exercises. The RCL round was designed to disable armour and it was not the fragmentation weapon of the HE type, such as was fired, daily, from the gun line or the mortar line. The RCL round might be seen to explode in a cloud of grey smoke, but it was heralded by no ominous whistle and the event was over before the threat was perceived.

However slight the threat, the response was swift and heavy. The gun line on the camp also operated a radar device, Green Archer, which detected the trajectory of incoming fire, thus offering targets for the guns or ground attack aircraft. The aircraft were Strikemasters, better known to us as the *ab initio* Jet Provosts which RAF pilots trained on. Painted in camouflage colours and equipped with rocket pods of French design, the Strikemasters provided a formidable reply to raiders. An early weakness in them, however, proved to be the absence of self-sealing tanks, and an aircraft hit by small arms fire ran out of fuel and had to belly-land on the Plain. The stripped shell remained for a couple of years where it had ground to a halt, a considerable coup for the *Adoo*.

The *Adoo* were also extensively equipped with the ubiquitous AK47[1], of which several examples were in evidence. Those *Adoo* who had accepted the amnesty offered by Qaboos were allowed to retain their weapons, and a trip to the local *Souk*, or market, usually brought the sighting of an AK worn casually on some Arab's shoulder. Copies were also brought in by British Army Training Teams (a euphemism, since they tended to be detachments from the Special Air Service) who were looking to trade for some ammunition they might be short of. Several thousand rounds of the 7.62mm short ammunition, which was incompatible with our own rifles, was included in the trade and most of us had the opportunity to fire the AK, which appeared to be a very handy weapon.

Our own weaponry was augmented by the arrival of some .5in Browning heavy machine-guns. The paperwork suggested that these had last been employed by Bomber Command, circa 1945, but the weapons were in pristine condition. The ammunition included armour piercing, tracing, incendiary and explosive, but all natures were in very short supply and for a time we could merely admire the weapon, or take it to pieces to clean and oil it.

Cleaning and oiling weapons was a staple of the morning routine on the Hedgehogs, particularly those weapons, like the SF, which remained on site for the new shift. I had been appointed in charge of the SF/Zebedee crew and had early occasion to muster it for a bollocking when I discovered that the GPMG, which had fired several hundred rounds on a hazard fire tasking, had not been cleaned for the shift handover. After that, we understood each other.

In addition to the routines of fire tasking, improving defences or cleaning weapons, we also devoted considerable amounts of time to improving our living conditions. A cement mixer was briefly

---

[1] Whilst recovering from wounds in 1943, Mikhail Kalashnikov, a tank crewman, designed the assault rifle which would bear his name. Some 20,000,000 examples of 'the weapon which armed Warsaw Pact' followed, although Kalashnikov never received a rouble in royalties. He was, however, raised to the rank of major general from his retired rank of colonel, on the occasion of his 75th birthday, which must have cheered him up immensely.

'borrowed' from camp and used to cast a concrete floor in our kitchen, which was an important focus of activity. The food was merely compo, unless it might be augmented with rations filched from the camp, but the duty 'chefs' vied in their attempts to make it as appetising as possible. Some of it defeated even the best attempts, and the Chicken Supreme, which was a pale, gooey and tasteless mess, brought little festive cheer to the table on Xmas Day. Some you didn't win.

'Finding' things on camp which were of use to us on the Hedgehog was virtually a fulltime occupation. Vehicles left unattended were likely to be quickly stripped of taillights that could be rigged to a twelve-volt battery to illuminate the kitchen for vital, early morning brews. Another useful acquisition was a length of thick hosepipe, with which we rigged a voice pipe from the radar position to the gun bay, thus facilitating the swift dissemination of target information.

Lavatory arrangements were of the 'bucket and chuck it' variety, whereby a pail was used then taken out into the wadi and dumped. A quantity of fuel and perhaps some augmenting cartridges from the mortar rounds would be scattered over the excrement, which was then burned. The job attracted an extra payment of fifty pence a day, which was worth having, and there was some competition for it. The Arabs who sometimes were posted to the Hedgehogs as night sentries had a much simpler routine, whereby they merely left their wadi eliminations to the attrition of wind and rain, obviously regarding our method as a mysterious ritual. They also managed without the use of toilet paper and it was suggested that flat stones were the alternative. In the interests of research, I once tried this. I do not commend it to you.

Each of the Hedgehogs possessed a kitten - known on Bravo as Ali Cat - and these were sometimes killed by feral cats that roamed the Plain. I surprised one in the kitchen in the early morning and it was twice the size of any domestic cat I had ever seen. We succeeded in trapping it and despatched it with a firing squad. The squad NCO delivered the *coup de grace* with half a magazine of Sterling submachine gun fire.

A member of my crew, Taff, was taken into the camp hospital for an emergency appendectomy and I visited him. In the next bed was a member of the SAS whose kneecap had been smashed by small arms fire in an action on the Jebel. I chatted with him and speculated that his career might be over, but he was optimistic, having been told that new surgical techniques offered him a good chance of soldiering on. Ironically, the new surgery was the result of study into the victims of the IRA's penchant for drilling holes through the kneecaps of those who displeased them. On a second visit to Taff, I passed a stretcher where a *Firkat* lay with half of his head missing. He was alive, barely, and died in the night. He had arrived in one of the periodic helicopters that made dusty landings at an LZ adjacent to the medical facility, having extracted casualties from fire fights on the Jebel. It was a sober reminder that the real war was being fought up in the hills, and that ours was a Butlins holiday by comparison.

We continued to alternate CP duties with stints on the Hedgehogs, with the latter being preferred. The CP was by far too much the focus for odd jobs and the night routine was dreary. We were also experiencing difficulties with Zebedee and the camp towers were the first to be denuded of the kits to replace problem sets on the Hedgehogs. Whenever this happened, we reverted to being merely visual sentries. Late in December I observed a series of flashes on the Jebel between 2100-2200hrs, and these proved to have been strikes against Charlie, although no casualties resulted. At much the same time, another amnesty offered by Qaboos resulted in acceptance and a night approach to the camp. Zebedee proved its worth by not only tracking in the surrender party, but also a following group, which was ambushed.

Recreation runs were sometimes made to Rayzut beach, which offered either a swim or surf canoeing. The more adventurous might opt for water skiing, although for some of us it was no more than the opportunity to be dragged off the skis and towed, half-drowned, through the water. Such runs had to be accompanied by an *Askari*, armed with .303 rifle, and we once persuaded him to shoot a coconut off a palm. He may have been the same *Askari* who, on gate duty, fired at a British army captain who was not only breaking the night curfew, but also failed to stop when challenged. He was shot in the arse for his neglect.

A visit to the *Souk* usually concluded the beach runs, although there was little on offer. Some of the lads had rings made and the gold source for these was George V sovereigns. I wondered if some of these had perhaps been circulating since TE Lawrence disbursed several thousand of them in the area, but this was doubtless fanciful. The locals seemed to regard us with disinterest, although the children would approach us in a display of curiosity. The children were lovely, with deep, liquid eyes and shy smiles.

The .5 ammunition state did not improve and I was incensed when a VIP party inspecting Bravo was invited to fire the weapon. The group burned off a hundred rounds at a time when the Hedgehog reserve totalled less than two hundred. I entered an official complaint but it died the death. The crew was left with the job of cleaning the gun and visitors remained unpopular for a time.

Although no routine training was attempted during the detachment, other than for promotion qualification, a local course was conducted on the 81mm mortar. I attended this and enjoyed learning the drills, although I was not especially keen to join the Support Weapons Flight on return to UK, as appeared to be the intention.

New Year's Eve was marked in the conventional manner and also by the theft of six crates of beer from the NAAFI store. The culprits were traced to the squadron and these spent a fair bit of their free time improving the security of the store. The CO was a believer in punishments that fitted the crime. The incident may also have provoked a lecture on security by another of the squadron's officers. I do not recall if he was a convincing lecturer, but some months later he was gaoled for the theft of cheque cards.

Zebedee continued to detect contacts on the Plain, and these were usually fired upon, although follow-up patrols by day revealed little. It was possible that the contacts were animals.

The RCL attacks also continued but we were fairly blase about these. The annoyance was in having to respond, whatever the hour, and I became the minor casualty of one when I ran headlong into a fire trench, whilst sprinting to the Armoury on camp.

The detachment wore on. I got fitter and tanned and I was saving well. Salalah pay was an extra £3 per week and I lived entirely within that, saving some £200 during the detachment. There was little to spend on. The NAAFI shop had a selection of cheap cassette tapes but I was not much attracted by pop music. I could listen to Carol King or James Taylor but my burgeoning interest in New Orleans jazz met with nothing on the music shelf. Taff was enthusiastic about Leonard Cohen and urged me to listen to his material. I thought that Cohen was the most depressing singer I'd ever heard, and I was not greatly surprised when Taff attempted suicide a couple of years later.

8

Late in February, the advance elements of No 51 Squadron had arrived to begin the process of a handover, which we duly completed and boarded the Herc for the flight home. Leave beckoned, as did termination of my alcohol drought, and we spent a couple of nights at the squadron's pub prior to leave. Drinking at the Beefeater, as elsewhere, was by candlelight because of a Miners' strike that resulted in power cuts. I spent some time in Crewe again, drinking with cousin Pete and various of his friends from York University.

Back at Colerne, we learned that the expected six months of training routine before the next round of detachments had in fact been reduced to three. Problems on the island of Malta had resulted in No 15 Squadron, which shared RAF Wittering with No 51 Squadron and should have relieved the latter at Salalah in May, was now earmarked for the Mediterranean.

Malta, which had been independent within the British Commonwealth since 1964, under the National Party had aligned with the West. Now, and under Dom Mintoff's Labour Government since 1971, non-alignment was preferred and Mintoff himself was seeking a special relationship with the People's Republic of China. This sat uneasily with Britain, which retained a substantial presence on the island in the form of a naval dockyard, and troops were despatched to Malta; a modern and faint echo of Palmerston's 'gunboat diplomacy'. Meantime, training continued.

A parachuting programme was arranged, by way of justifying our 37p per day para pay, but of no less than seven C130s that were available for a descent, not one proved serviceable on the day. Instead, we did a series of night descents from a tethered balloon at Hullavington. Little went wrong with balloons, although it was known for one to break its cable and drift away occasionally.

Night descents added to the apprehensions associated with parachuting. Just how dark naturally depended upon the degree of ambient light, and some 'night' descents could be very light indeed. It usually required a cloudy night to present a black void beyond the paratroop doors, where the sole illumination other than a briefly red or green light was provided by the alarming amount of flame flickering from the engine exhausts. PLFs from a night descent could safely be boasted about, since no one ever saw them, but they were generally hard ones.

Awaiting court martial at this time was a Gunner on B Flight which had been on a detachment in Hong Kong, whilst the remainder of the squadron was in Dhofar. A parachuting programme had been arranged using Whirlwind helicopters, but the Gunner in question, who had served previously with the Parachute Regiment, had refused to draw and fit his 'chute, claiming a premonition of disaster. His flight commander gave him some time to think about it, and when a second refusal was made the Gunner was arrested and returned to the UK within a few days.

I knew him as a decent bloke, having been on the Tournament team with him, and I went to the Guardroom a couple of times to see if he needed any dhobi sorting out, or whatever. After his court martial, he was sent to the military nick, at Colchester, for a month and he was posted.

Training became dull for a while and occasionally nonexistent. The morning administrative parade was often followed by the instruction to 'hang about in the lecture room or the flight store', and when I was interviewed by the flight commander on the subject of annual assessments I took the opportunity to comment. I felt, I told him, like some sort of firefighting appliance.

The quality of instructors varied very greatly when we were revising tradecraft. Some of the SNCOs were keen to make the work realistic and interesting, and others were not. One of the JNCOs, Corporal Knobby Clark, had no interest in making out lesson plans and he merely read directly from the weapons pamphlets, whilst comfortably seated and usually with a cigarette on the go. Knobby was no instructor, but he had some interesting service, having served with the Black Watch in Korea and in Kenya. Knobby had turned twenty-one in Kenya and had been invited, he told us, to celebrate his birthday by shooting a *Mau Mau* terrorist brought in by a patrol. Knobby duly did so, and he seemed untroubled by this casual atrocity.

A pre-para course formed and I offered to accompany it to Wales as driver and Gofer, an offer that was accepted. The Spring weather was delightful and I joined all the day climbs and runs. An evening in some local pub was preferred to the night marches and it made a pleasant break. At Swallow Falls, with the last of the students yet to run in, the course commander, who was also the Deputy Squadron Commander, fired up his Land Rover and said that he would see us back at Colerne. It happened that the Bedford had been stripped of its engine governor and I passed the DSC on the M5 at seventy miles an hour. He was not best pleased.

A member of the pre-para, passed and now awaiting the parachute course, had been a coach builder prior to enlistment, and he offered some assistance when I next tackled the disappearing bodywork of the Riley. I was by now tempted to simply sell the vehicle, particularly in view of the forthcoming detachment which would take another three months out of the year. Money spent on Road Tax for such absences was simply wasted. I had just renewed the Third Party insurance at £20, and I put another dent in my Salalah savings by ordering a tailor-made suit for £35. Money problems were endemic on the squadron, and not just at the level of Gunner. We were paraded for pay and at the end of it the paying officer discovered that he was £28 short. It was not discovered who received the bonuses that day, and the officer was the chap who was later done for cheque card theft. Not a lucky man.

We were briefly placed on standby for Northern Ireland again, although nothing came of it. The province was now in its bloodiest year, when the death toll would double that of any other to date. We had heard, in January, of 'Bloody Sunday' when men of the Parachute Regiment had fired at an unarmed crowd in Londonderry, killing thirteen apparently unarmed demonstrators. There were to be bitter legacies of that.

At the squadron's pub, I took a shine to one of the barmaids, Veronica, who was busty and attractive. Unfortunately, she was being courted by Tim, a matelot of about sixteen stones and volatile moods. Tim duly learned of my interest in Veronica - which clearly was reciprocated - and in the pub one evening he invited me to the lavatories for 'a chat'. The chat was short and Tim aimed a kick at my testicles, fortunately missing. I then hit Tim with my best punch and was dismayed when he appeared not even to notice it. We were separated before much else developed, and I went home with Veronica but the relationship was clouded and failed to develop greatly.

Towards Easter, the squadron celebrated its 50th anniversary. The RAF Regiment had not formed until 1942, but II Squadron, which was the senior, claimed lineage from II Armoured Car

Company, which had formed at Heliopolis, Egypt on 7 April 1922. It had equipped then with Rolls-Royce armoured cars, armed with Vickers and Lewis machine guns, and it served in the Middle East continually until 1959.

RAF St. Athan preserved an example of the period Rolls-Royce armoured car, (Although its 'armour' was in fact plywood) and this was later transferred to the RAF Museum which was opened at the former RAF Hendon. The Rolls was borrowed for display during the 50th celebration, and two visitors on the day were founder members of II Squadron with some interesting accounts of action against the desert tribes in the Twenties.

For the parade, I was despatched to RAF Cosford, adjacent to Wolverhampton, to borrow seating from the indoor sports arena, and I was contacted whilst there to divert to an army camp to collect some Zebedees. A long day resulted in which I clocked three hundred and sixty miles, and an interesting moment occurred when the engine, which was cab-mounted, caught fire as I negotiated a busy roundabout. I subsequently halted and put the fire out, finding no apparent damage and continuing the journey, only to run out of fuel a few miles short of Colerne. Not a good day.

In the run up to the next round of detachments, we deployed to Sennybridge for a fortnight of field firing and exercise. This was made more interesting by a series of survival lectures by a couple of SAS instructors from Hereford, who may have been looking for recruits. It had recently been made possible for RAF Regiment Gunners to apply directly for selection, rather than have to transfer initially to an army unit.

I was promoted to acting, unpaid corporal for no better reason that the forthcoming detachment required it. I was off to Hong Kong with a composite flight and saw that as a pleasant change, since Salalah would doubtless feature again. We flew in a VC10 from Brize Norton and I took little interest in the flight, having a stinking head cold. The pressure changes at each landing drove nails into my ears and I was relieved to see the Kai Tak airport. I noted the considerable novelty of looking into apartment windows as we crossed the threshold of the airport, since Hong Kong was nothing if not densely populated. It was my thirty-first birthday.

9

The Kai Tak international airport also formed the runway for RAF Kai Tak, and it was a fair assumption that the former had developed from the latter. The RAF station was flanked by an incredibly busy six-lane highway that led to Kowloon, and one of the first difficulties we discovered on the detachment was to actually break into an almost incessant stream of traffic. The traffic actually ceased for a couple of hours around 0300hrs and the sudden quiet was apt to wake everyone up.

We were relieving No 51 Squadron and we observed the usual familiarisation handover before they departed. I also had the opportunity of a drink with a couple of mates who were serving with the outgoing unit. We settled into our accommodation, which had once housed Japanese occupation troops, and picked up the routine. KD was the dress and since we had brought none with us it had to be issued. The RAF KD at this time was a fairly smart affair in polyester, and we were somewhat surprised to be issued with cotton kit that looked as if it may have been lying in a Rangoon warehouse for the last thirty years. The 'shorts' flared to about thirty inches somewhere below the knee, and the cotton weave was of windjammer sail strength. It took very little time to locate the camp tailor and get him to knock up something that wouldn't cause the locals to fall about in hysterical laughter.

I already had sufficient problems with the locals, having lately affected waxed ends on my moustache. The 'wingspan' on this was twelve inches and it drew amazed stares from the local Chinese, who are generally a beardless race. I got used to the idea, during jaunts beyond the gates, of attracting a following of children, like the Pied Piper.

Duties, it transpired, were not arduous. The CP, called the

Ground Defence Operations Centre, was co-located with the Guardroom, which was manned by locally employed police levies. We had no defence duties on the camp and the only other tasking was external. This was at a radar installation atop a mountain called Tai Mo Shan. At three thousand feet, the installation, whose housing was of the 'golf ball' type, peered out over the New Territories and it presumably also had some interest in the airspace above the Republic of China. Not that anyone ever told us, and nor did we ask. 'Need to know?' was the firm principle.

The only hardship attaching to the Tai Mo Shan duty was the act of breaking across the traffic stream at the camp gates. The duty began at 1400hrs and ended at 0800hrs the following morning, and virtually all the section was required to do was to check identities of the coach passengers at shift changes. Since all of these were RAF, the check seemed a touch nugatory, and the more so when we noticed that the Chinese workers passed to and fro without hindrance.

The access road to the mountain top conformed to a stiff gradient, was extremely narrow in the last mile of it and featured a number of hairpin bends. Our detachment managed to tip two Land Rovers off the road in quick succession, fortunately without injury, and some wag posted a notice. **'Beware of Falling Rocks'**, it ran. Even getting to the access road could be a problem, since our familiarisation had been nothing if not fleeting. At the first attempt, my section wound up in the Walled City, where even the police reputedly went in not less than platoon strength. We did not hang about looking for postcards.

We were at the edge of the New Territories, with Kowloon as the nearest focus of interest. A visit to Hong Kong meant a ferry ride, which we soon experienced, but we were shocked to learn that beer sold at four times the UK price. Bar girls and brothels offered the usual troop comforts, but at £10 for a short time, which was the thick end of a week's wages. Prices were also prone to rise steeply whenever the American Pacific Fleet hit town, and Hong Kong was also a major Rest and Recuperation centre for the American forces then serving in South Viet Nam. They simply priced us out of the game and we soon learned to drink our fill at NAAFI prices before venturing downtown.

We were given some advice before leave ashore was permitted. This began, naturally enough, with lectures and films to detail the horrors of VD, then pointed out that armed muggers were a local fact of life. These would stop the small buses that plied, packed to capacity, around the conurbation, and demand money or valuables from passengers. Their preferred weapon was a sharpened bicycle spoke and they would often stab a passenger, in the arm or leg, for having insufficient cash. We were advised to travel in sizeable groups and generally we took the advice. An exception was Mick the Nutter, who invariably travelled alone. We did not fear much for his safety, since it was Mick the Nutter's habit to complete his ashore preparations by casually dropping a cutthroat razor into his pocket. Anyone attempting to mug Mick was likely to lose his ears.

When I had a set of KD that meant I no longer had to flit about under the cover of darkness, I sewed white chevrons on the sleeve and prepared to run my section. The acting rank was no big deal and neither was it a guarantee of obedience. II Squadron fostered a worthy tradition of leadership by example, and the rest of it was an amalgam of persuasion and coercion. We got along.

We had arrived at the onset of the monsoon season, and a swift consequence of that was in being flooded out of our accommodation, which was on the ground floor of three other levels in the block. One of the crew refused to budge and he lay unconcernedly on his cot reading pornographic books, with detritus floating about him, until the waters receded. The entire area remained under water for a day or two, and produced the idea that it might be novel to swim down to Kowloon. This idea faded when the swimmers took a closer look at some of the objects that were floating around them.

An idea that took root came from Mick the Nutter. He proposed that we form a boxing team and issue a challenge to one or other of the resident army units. I was asked to manage the team, simply because it was believed that my rank might facilitate the use of service transport. The detachment was accompanied by the Squadron Warrant Officer, who had done some boxing in his time, and he proved very supportive. We duly set up a training programme that I joined in with, being on another fitness campaign.

The resident infantry battalions were from the Black Watch and the Irish Guards, and Mick and I approached both. The Jocks pleaded intensive exercises but the Irish agreed and we made a provisional date for a novice tourney. We then spoke to the Hong Kong police, having heard that they operated a swish gym and wondered if we might use its facilities. The police not only agreed that, but they also offered to set up arrangements to stage the tourney in the

China Fleet Club. This sounded good and we had further meetings. These had an exotic flavour since an interpreter was present, although this may have owed more to Mick's Norfolk accent.

We had drenching rain most days and I mentioned this in a letter to the Old Man. By return he remarked that it had barely rained in Boulder since I left - two years before. I was by now wondering what to do when my service expired in less than a year, and the possibility of extending service was a recurring thought. For the moment, however, I was content to drift until a decision had to be taken.

The Education Officer had asked me to contribute a series of articles about the boxing team to the station magazine. I sweated over these during the Tai Mo Shan duty and they appeared, almost verbatim, in the *South China Mail*, but under someone else's name. Tai Mo Shan offered plenty of free time and I usually filled mine with the gleanings of the station library. 'The Arms of Krupp' spanned a few duties. Scrabble was a popular game in the standby room, although I soon opted out of the games. I had a fit section that included half of the boxing team, but spelling was not its strong suit. Heated arguments raged over any entry that had more than about four letters in it.

I had greatly eased our transit problems by appointing Mick as the driver of the lead Land Rover. Mick's driving terrified even the Chinese and traffic began to clear as magically as if we had a siren and a flashing blue light on the cab. His aggression knew no bounds and when he became annoyed by some driver he believed had carved him up, Mick deliberately rammed the vehicle at the next set of traffic lights. We happened to have an RAF policeman in the back, who groaned and told us not to bother calling him as a witness. He would claim that he had been sleeping at the time. I had to appear before the MTO and lie heroically on Mick's behalf.

Mick was also running raffles to finance a dinner for the boxing team, and seldom went anywhere without huge quantities of tickets. The raffle prize invariably was a car radio, and since these came without a box and usually with wires hanging out of the back, it was wise not to enquire into provenance. Mick's routine with the raffle tickets prompted a memory of the 'Nade Hotel in Port Hedland a few years earlier. I struck up a conversation over a beer at the bar some evening and compared hard times stories with another blow-in. "I usually drummed up a few bob by raffling chooks (chickens) around the pubs." Said my companion. "Where d'you get the poultry from." I asked. He gave me a sidelong look. "No poultry, Mate. Just a suitcase full of raffle tickets."

I had negotiated with the Warrant for some boxing training in the Firm's time, and he acquiesced. This took the form of sweltering runs about the camp perimeter, followed by circuits in the small gym on station. Sparring and ring work took place after hours at the police gym. I began to suffer the delusion that I might be a contender myself, a notion which evaporated after a sparring session with one of the Jamaican lads who was extremely good with both hands. I decided to cultivate the managerial style instead.

The airfield pan where visiting aircraft parked was occasionally interesting. A camouflaged Dakota, looking for all the world as if it had just flown in from WW II, was an American visitor from South Viet Nam, as was a New Zealand Air Force Bristol Freighter, which recalled to me the RAF Seletar days. Kai Tak also sported a fine example of a Spitfire, which presumably was the legacy of post-war service on the island.

Towards the midpoint of the detachment, we staged the tourney, fielding eight boxers at a spread of weights against the Irish Guards. By this time, the only management required of me was to manage the sponge bucket as a Second, but it at least offered a ringside seat. Our success was almost total. We lost two of the bouts on points, but the remaining six boxers won their fights on knockouts. I had a pint with the Guards' team trainer afterwards and he expressed rueful reluctance to parade the next day, knowing that a summons to his CO would follow. We had a good drink with the team, planning a follow up tourney just as soon as we might arrange it.

A day or so later, the *South China Mail* carried an account of the tourney, together with the allegation that we had fielded open class boxers against novices. This was untrue and I angrily 'phoned the *Mail* office, threatening to take the boxing team around unless they printed a retraction. This duly appeared, but the damage was done and I had a call from the Guards' trainer, advising me that feelings were running high and that it might be prudent to avoid the Fleet Club for a couple of weeks.

As it happened, we were suddenly busy with a parachuting programme to occupy some of what would normally be our free time. We were to do a series of descents from helicopters at the Ghurkha camp at Sek Kong. We underwent ground training, insofar as the limited facilities permitted, and we expected to complete up to a dozen descents.

Older hands described helicopters as 'noisy balloons' and the comparison was fairly obvious; no slipstream and simply a straight drop of about two hundred feet until the canopy had fully developed. Since the cargo door of the Whirlwind was so small, we did not exit from the standing position, but simply shuffled on our bottoms to the door sill and pushed ourselves off at the Despatcher's command. The DZ proved to be a football field, which was denuded of goal posts prior to use, and looked to be about the size of a postage stamp from a thousand feet. Given the limited steerability of the canopy then in use, it was not surprising that we drifted off it. I landed in the dhobi lines on one occasion, and another in the same stick, unluckier, landed in the sewage farm which flanked the camp. The detachment officer, yet to be caught for cheque card theft, landed on concrete and was unable to walk for a couple of days. Definitely an unlucky man.

If beer and sex had proved expensive, there was at least a cornucopia of tax-free and therefore relatively cheap consumer goods to be had on the island. Watches, cameras and stereos began to appear in the accommodation, along with some exotic choices of clothing via the camp tailor. I had a suede suit made for £35 and I wore it with some pride in the UK, until I discovered that it was attracting entirely the wrong sort of sexual interest. It ended up doing ignominious service as windscreen cloths for the Riley.

Towards the close of the detachment, we challenged the Guards to another tourney, but their short reply referred us to sex and travel. We then sought opponents from the Chinese and managed to stage another event at the China Fleet Club. We were just as successful and followed the tourney with a sit down dinner at the club. It had become obvious during the bouts that a high proportion of Irish Guards was filling the hall, and I was approached by the trainer and warned that his lot was looking for trouble. We were advised to move on, but there was no way of cancelling the dinner.

I happened to be visiting the lavatory when trouble sparked between one of ours and several of theirs, and I was suddenly trading punches with a couple of them. The other squadron man was Andy Ritchie and we were seriously outnumbered until a flight sergeant from the squadron forced his way in. "One against one, you lot" He ordered. "Fuck off, Dad's Army!" Was the response from a large Guardsman. The flight sergeant, Charlie Younghusband, may have appeared old but he was nimble and he decked the surprised Guardsman.

The fighting erupted throughout the club and into the street, and I suppose that some forty fights were in progress at any given time, although I was a bit too busy to actually stop and count. A lorry load of riot police arrived, sitting impassively and giving no indication that they were about to intervene. We gradually disengaged and returned to Kai Tak to compare injuries. By the next morning I had a fat lip and a black eye, but there were no serious injuries anywhere on our side. We reckoned that honours were about even and Charlie Younghusband was the local hero.

The bruises had barely faded when the advance elements of No 15 Squadron arrived to take over the detachment from us. Their number included Rocky Roxburgh, a mate I would run into from time to time over the next twenty-five years. We had a few pints.

China Fleet Club Hong Kong
After the boxing tournament and before the fight

RAF Sek Kong
Landing in the dhobi lines

10

The squadron reassembled at Colerne and the respective detachments traded experiences over pints at the Beefeater. The Salalah crew was deeply tanned and sported healthy savings, whereas most of our lot had bar room tans and little money. What *we* had was stereo equipment by the yard, transferring rooms in the block which formerly had shared a single radio into wall to wall sound systems. Listening to the music of one's choice usually resulted in a battle of the amplifiers, and bedlam the outcome.

My meagre savings sufficed to tax and insure the Riley, but it would have taken the genius of Archimedes to establish what proportion of the bodywork was metal and what was Polyfilla. I resolved to get rid of the car and duly acquired a '67 Morris 1100 for £160. The Riley traded in for just £10.

I bought the Morris in Crewe, where cousin Peter was also on holidays from university. We went fishing and four hour's worth of angling effort secured for me a two-inch Gudgeon. I also put some time in on the Crewe park lake, rowing the length of it repeatedly. I then cut the leave short in order to drive up to London, where my brother Jack and his wife had arrived for a late honeymoon and an extended stay. Their news was that Mam was not enjoying particularly good health, and it was felt that my lengthy absence might be a contributory factor. I felt bad about this and passed an uncomfortable night.

September brought an extensive parachuting programme, but I missed most of it. 4 Tonner drivers were suddenly in short supply and I was mostly required to drive the wagon which carried the 'chutes. This was annoying, for I was enjoying parachuting by now and we missed sufficient descents because of poor weather or aircraft unserviceabilities as it was. Enjoyment apart, parachuting would ever remain a curious amalgam of deep apprehension and marvellous euphoria.

My acting rank had evaporated on return to the UK, but this was entirely painless since the promotion had attracted no extra pay. I continued to lead a section, which was satisfying, and when my annual assessments were read to me I had picked up a strong recommendation for a promotion course. For the moment, though, I was not that keen. Apart from my ambivalence about signing for another term, promotion would mean a certain posting and I was reluctant to leave II.

Another Germany exercise beckoned, but I was not due to jump - or fall - in with the remainder of the squadron. A small advance party which comprised two 4 Tonners was required to drive to the exercise area, and I was detailed to it. Due to sail overnight from Hull, we were briefed to travel via an interim stay at RAF Wittering, and we duly rolled.

At Wittering, we drank an unconscionable amount of beer and were in poor form when the Orderly Officer turned us out at 0400hrs the following morning. We had been recalled to Colerne for some unspecified emergency that would not even await breakfast. The wagons had been parked on the far side of the airfield and when I led the move from the compound I became disoriented. What should have been a relatively narrow perimeter track suddenly became an expanse of bitumen, and it dawned upon me that I was actually driving up the runway, normally the preserve of Harrier jets. An irate air traffic controller despatched a vehicle to sort me out. My co-driver, who was in even worse shape than me and comatose in the passenger seat, was a bloke named 'Shovel' Hill - so called because he once hit another Gunner with one during a trench argument.

The 'flap', we learned, was in connection with Uganda. Idi Amin had decided to eject the Asian population and many of them held British passports. 16 Parachute Brigade, to which we were attached for airborne operations, had been placed on standby for Kenya, a neighbouring country of Uganda, and the squadron was now working up to it.

The work consisted mainly of fitness training and we were put to an exhausting regime of runs, marches, assault courses and anything else that the DSC could come up with. He stated later that his express intention had been to weed out the unfit, and he certainly put a few in the queue at sick quarters. The squadron had no great problems with shirkers, although notice of a parachuting programme might flush a couple. There was at this time a Gunner named Talbot on the unit. He went sick so often that he was known instead as 'Tablet'

We waited, and trained, for a couple of weeks but no detachment followed. Germany exercise and Asian exile proceeded without us. We resumed the social life and my drinking returned to its previous, and wallet ruinous, levels. I occasionally woke up in the mornings to find my bedspace littered with the foil cartons of Chinese takeaway food, obviously having bought an armful after the pub but having no memory of it. It was clearly time to return to the discipline of a Salalah detachment.

In October I was again detailed for advance party duties, this time to Singapore. The squadron was to undergo the jungle warfare training course in Malaysia, and the advance party was deploying to draw vehicles and exercise kit. The advance party was also to form the rear party and we would spend two months on the detachment. I had no problems with that.

Singapore and Malaysia were by now countries working to quite separate agendas and earlier attempts at federation had failed. The UK had combined with Australia and New Zealand to provide for the continuing defence of the island, but even ANZUK appeared to be in its twilight. There was at this time, though, both a Kiwi and an Australian battalion based on the island, and I fleetingly wondered if I might encounter someone I knew.

This happened within days. I was collecting a lorry from a base ordnance depot in Singapore, when I ran across a bloke named Shufti Fraser. Shufti had served with 101 Tpt Coy at Randwick and he had been a particularly good mate of Bob Green, although he had no recent news of Bob. What he was able to tell me was that there were no less than three former members of 40 Air Supply presently serving on Singapore, and I duly looked them up. The first I found was Curly Nelson, whose brief desertion I had financed almost a decade before. Curl had survived the court martial and was now a sergeant.

Another sergeant was Dinger Bell, who had once rejoiced in the title of 'the tightest man in the Australian army'. Among the stories told of Dinger's carefulness with a quid was that related by a bloke who once tried to borrow a razorblade from him. "Sorry, Mate," Replied Dinger, "I've only got new ones."

Whilst collecting stores at RAF Tengah, I ran across Gary Cole, with whom I had shared the experience of leaping out of a De Havilland Dragon. Gary was now a warrant officer, but he later was commissioned and retired in the rank of major. All of these former comrades seemed faintly surprised that I was serving in the RAF Regiment in the rank of baggy-arse.

Our accommodation was in the jungle warfare camp at Kota Tingii, on the mainland, and we spent a few days simply ferrying vehicles up from the island. A coach was among them and when it was discovered that no one held a coach licence, I acquired one with the stroke of a pen. That was II Squadron initiative in practice. On the eve of the main party arrival, I was ordered to make the beds up for all of the officers and the SNCOs. I did so but I short-sheeted every one of them.

In the run up to the training programme I was informed that I would not be returning to my flight, but would form part of the demonstration group. This was mysterious, since my knowledge of the jungle was based upon a day trip with 55 Coy in 1963 and several Tarzan films a few years before that. I did however have a good knowledge of contact and anti-ambush drills, which had been practised to the point of exhaustion along the Old Coach Road some years before, and the rest of it somehow fell into place.

The squadron shook out with a number of navigation exercises and a mate and I manned one of the RVs. After a time the more usual jungle noises were augmented by a crashing off to our flank somewhere. "That must be B Flight," Offered the mate, "we'd better intercept them and give them a steer." We made for the noise and eventually located its source. It was a large and none too friendly-looking elephant, accompanied by her calf. We turned and bolted. Bloody B Flight.

Minor tactics at flight level were interspersed with demos and one of them was the technique of crossing a river using a flotation pack, rigged with pack and poncho. Two of us were selected for this and the lead man was chosen for his swimming abilities, since his was the job of crossing the river with a light rope. This man was Brum Barry, a fine swimmer and rugby player, and a parachutist of about sixteen stone who always landed first, irrespective of his order in the stick. Brum was a fine character and greatly liked by all. Sadly, he was killed in a gun accident in Germany a few years later. I was the number two, an indifferent swimmer at this time, and when I had tied on the heavy rope for Brum to haul across and anchor, it was my job to demonstrate the knack of propelling self and flotation pack across the river. The flotation was supposed to be made from twigs and foliage, and by trapping air inside the poncho, but as a 'belt and braces' I augmented mine by inflating a polythene bag. I soon realised that this was a mistake, for the pack hardly settled in the water and it became unwieldy and difficult to control.

The real problems began in midstream when the rope, insufficiently tensioned at the anchor point, actually dipped below the surface. Pretty soon, I was dipping with it and by now also contending with a powerful current. We happened to have chosen a tidal river and this was some tide. For tactical reasons, my rifle was held atop the pack and my great fear was that this would be lost. I was by now desperately trying to retain a grip of the pack, my rifle and the rope, whilst simultaneously attempting to breathe underwater. The far bank looked very far indeed.

Just when I was ready to believe that everything that could go wrong *had* gone wrong, a great pile of elephant shit came swirling downstream to smash itself around my head. This went down exceptionally well with the observers on the bank, who by now doubtless believed that I was the comedy act which preceded the serious business of river crossing. It took an eternity to complete the crossing and by the time I crossed I had swallowed an inordinate amount of water which probably also held a fair measure of elephant piss. This was not a good beginning.

Learning nothing at all from this, we chose the same stretch of river and the same swirling tide for our demonstration of how to handle pontoon craft, which might be bolted together to form a bridge or simply used as boats. Rowing as mightily as the tribesmen in the film *Sanders of the River*, we made about three knots - backwards.

Another slightly less than successful demo was arranged by the sergeant whose preference on field-firing ranges was to debrief over steaming mugs of tea and a blazing fire. He apparently had some kind of demolitions qualification and he now proposed to demonstrate to us how detonating cord might be used to transform a growing tree into a portable tree. We watched the setting up, which appeared even to the untutored eye to account for a great deal of explosive, then we retired some distance. The earth presently shook, the jungle wildlife screeched even louder than usual and we trooped back to inspect an impressive, smoking crater. The tree was by now certainly portable, since it had been reduced to several thousand wood slivers of about matchstick size. Because the sergeant was also on the demo team, we shared a hootchie when the squadron camped on Panti Ridge, but he moved out when he found a scorpion in his sleeping bag two days in succession. He was convinced that I was introducing them, since there was no way of 'short sheeting' a sleeping bag.

At the conclusion of the warfare course we drew and fitted 'chutes for a parachute assault, eventually emplaning in a Herc and being despatched in 'sim sixes' (simultaneous despatch in groups of six from both port and starboard paratroop doors). The DZ was obviously quite small and precluded larger sticks. Having made my exit and watched the canopy develop, I performed the all-round observation drills and watched with interest as a leg bag headed for the DZ a good minute ahead of its owner. The rifle it contained was a write-off and the unlucky owner, whose inexpert roping had caused the loss, was fined to the equivalent of a month's wages.

The heat and humidity were fierce and even the simplicity of folding and toting the 'chutes off the DZ reduced us to dripping forms. What followed was an arduous toil up sixteen hundred feet of Panti Ridge and the seven-day exercise suddenly seemed a very long prospect indeed.

For the exercise I was attached to one of two small enemy groups which would harass the flights in three separate locations. One of the groups was under the command of a young officer who was attached to the squadron from RAF Tengah. He led his group out on day one and was not seen again until day seven. Unluckily, the 'lost patrol' had omitted to take more than a day's rations with them.

My group was choppered up country and we made a base adjacent to a pleasant strip of beach where the film *South Pacific* had been filmed some years before. The sea, with its bathing prospects, was welcome, and nor did our routine seem especially arduous. This changed when it was learned that the ration replenishment of the flights, intended to be conducted by helicopters, was changed. Chopper unserviceabilities ruled the option out, and it suddenly became the enemy responsibility.

Each of us was given a box of rations, which weighed about forty pounds, and sent off to find a flight. Since I was working from a sketch map and having no knowledge of the area, I thought that, like Captain Oates, I might be gone for quite some time. I found the flight though and the reward for this upon return was to be given another box for a repeat trip. High ferns and knee-deep water made the chore less than attractive, but there was also the feeling of doing something useful. I also had to bring in three injured Gunners at various times, including victims of snakebite and the bite of a scorpion.

The officer in charge of our enemy group also became the victim of a scorpion, suddenly leaping up with a howl as he was issuing orders one morning. We were puzzled until we found the scorpion *inside* his trousers. It had obviously crawled in whilst he was performing a bowel movement. He was casevac'd out.

I almost became another sort of casualty when I practised my jungle survival, eating the flesh of a plant which looked like a pineapple and tasted like the nut of a cabbage, without first carrying out the prescribed checks. After about half an hour I began to vomit and I continued to do so all the way to the endex RV. What I had eaten was clearly neither fruit nor vegetable of an edible variety. I was at this time in the company of a JNCO, Josker Smith, who also had been with the enemy group. The extent of Josker's sympathy, as I continued to vomit, was to ask if he could have my Rolex when I died. Josker, who earlier had organised the feral cat firing squad in Salalah, left the squadron soon after. He was later reported to be working as a mercenary in some troubled outpost, but, given the predilection for colourful rumour in the Mob, it is equally likely that he was working as a window dresser in Milton Keynes.

During the detachment I had been exploring the possibilities of a trip home, and there appeared to be some chance of an indulgence flight. The RAF ran a courier flight through Singapore to Perth each week, and, with the backing of the DSC, I stood a good chance of securing a seat. I had enough cash to pay for a flight back from Perth to Singapore, which was a precondition for all indulgence flights, and plans went apace.

The main party flew out and the rear party dwindled to just two, Brum Barry and me, before Brum also left. I was due out on the courier the next day, only to learn that it had gone unserviceable *en route* and would not complete the journey. This was a blow, but all proved not yet lost when a chap at Movements learned that the Australians had chartered a Boeing 707 to bring some troops home from South Viet Nam for Xmas. I had a chance of a ride and I swiftly fronted up for it. I was only marginally bothered by the fact that the flight was to Sydney, which was about five hundred miles further from Singapore than Perth was.

The aircraft loaded at Paya Lebar in the evening and we disembarked at Mascot airport at Sydney around 0800hrs. Having cleared the terminal, I quickly 'phoned RAAF Richmond to enquire if any aircraft might be flying to the West, or in that direction, but the base was rapidly closing for Xmas. In the lavatories, I changed into OGs and got out on the highway with thumb extended. Shortage of cash dictated some hitchhiking. At least, I knew the way.

A brew prior to demonstrating underwater breathing

Safer, probably, than tidal rivers

11

Two months in the Far East had provided a useful acclimatisation for the Australian summer, which moreover was free of the Singaporean humidity. This though was a lesser problem as I stood on the Prince's Highway swatting flies and awaiting the first lift. The uniform, which was an illegal amalgam of jungle greens, desert boots and a bush hat, proved a good draw and I soon left Sydney behind. It might have been good to spend some time there and note changes, but time was a commodity I had too little of. The leave clock had begun to tick even before I left Paya Lebar and I had little more than a week before I was due to begin the return to UK. Lengthy hitchhiking simply wasn't among the options, either.

I secured good lifts but at daybreak on the following morning, again at the roadside, I was still in New South Wales, with Victoria, South Australia and West Australia somewhere before me. It was an unwelcome reminder of just how large Australia was, and how insignificant we are against such a landscape. A semi-trailer eventually took me across the state line to Benalla, where I had a wash and a shave in park lavatories. I found something to eat and had just resumed my roadside pitch when a police car drew alongside. I briefly wondered if perhaps hitchhiking had been made illegal in Victoria, until a police inspector told me to jump in. He was heading into Melbourne and when he learned that I was over from the UK on a very limited leave, he radioed ahead and ordered his station to hold a car which was heading south of the city. It was a nice gesture.

By 0100hrs on the third day I had arrived in Adelaide and I went to the railway station. I had a wash and shave in the lavatories then stretched out on a bench to sleep until the station came alive. I had decided to price a ticket to Kalgoorlie, recognising that my time was running out. I made the fare and relaxed until I caught the connection to Port Augusta. On the Trans, I had dinner then immediately went to bed, there having been little opportunity for sleep since leaving Paya Lebar. The train arrived in Kalgoorlie at 2000hrs and I arrived home, unannounced, shortly after. Mam and the Old Man were watching TV, something that had arrived since my departure. I had just $10 in my pocket, which bought a couple of rounds at the Mines & City Workers', that we immediately made for.

Xmas was just days away and a round of parties was in progress. Between parties we drank at the Mines & City or the RSL and I had to borrow from the Old Man to support this routine. The air ticket from Perth back to Paya Lebar had cost £100 and there was no prospect of a service lift, although I had made enquiries on the 'phone to a West Australian RAAF base.

On New Year's Eve the temperature rose to 113 degrees and that was warm enough for anyone. That night we attended a party at Geordie friends of the family, and I was given a piece of coal and asked to 'first foot' in order to bring some luck to the house. Later, I learned that Geordie's wife had left him and his son was gaoled. Some luck.

I spent just a week at home then felt that I should be making a move, being already a few days adrift. I had intended to hitchhike to Perth but the Old Man quietly bought a rail ticket for the journey. I found it difficult to express a farewell to Mam, having by now told the folks that I had decided to extend my service to nine years. The Rattler rolled out of Kalgoorlie and I wasn't sure when I might see the town again.

Perth brought anticlimax and hiatus when I learned that fog in the UK had delayed the outbound flight. I was fixed up with a bed in a city hotel but there was little to do in the city since I had refused to accept more money from the Old Man. When the flight eventually boarded, I had to reject the offer of headphones, since the hire of them was a 'nominal' £1, but the film proved to be a foreign production with English subtitles. Some you win. At Paya Lebar I connected with a VC10 and by midday on 4 January I was at RAF Brize Norton, gripped by winter. Having travelled half way around the world in about a day, it then took me nine hours to get to Bath. I went to the squadron's pub and borrowed a pound from a mate, had a couple of pints and went up to Colerne wondering what 1973 might have in store.

I was almost a week overdue but the DSC merely wished to

know if I had gotten home all right. He was known to us all as 'Barney Rubble' for his resemblance to a cartoon character, but he was greatly respected and liked by the squadron. He was also about to leave us to command his own squadron.

I rejoined the cider drinkers - a 'pint of apples' in the current idiom - and noted that the NAAFI was still a popular arena for fights, but I mostly looked forward to the training which would put us into the next round of detachments, and the scope for saving which these offered. Among the minor tragedies was the fact that the squadron's pub was bulldozed and a car park created where it had stood. We mourned its loss then found a pub that was equally scruffy but serving a good pint. The Salamander also had a host who appeared none too bothered that his new clientele were a rowdy crew. Perhaps he was distracted by the noise emanating from his till.

Another piece of grief was the loss of the squadron's distinctive stable belt. Although its origin was obscure, the squadron had worn it for a dozen years and the right to wear it was seen as a distinction for having completed pre-para. The Air Board now decreed that it was unacceptable and we were invited instead to wear the standard stable belt, which moreover was now permitted to be worn by all RAF personnel. No one did.

It seemed to be the season for fights in the NAAFI and on some occasion I succeeded in stopping one between a squadron man and my former adversary, Tim. Another fight between two squadron members resulted in just one of them being locked away in the Guardroom, although he had merely defended himself against a bottle attack. The bottle wielder, who was simply reprimanded, was black, and I counted this as an example of reverse racism.

I had again been promoted to acting, unpaid corporal and I went to the Guardroom to visit the prisoner, by now sentenced to fourteen days in cells. 'Boots' Barlow was a Scouser and a complete fitness nut. I had gone to see if he needed any dhobi doing, but he asked instead if I might sign him out for some decent exercise. This was agreed and we set off to run the cross-country course, which was about seven miles through local woods.

Since I could not hope to match Boots' pace, I told him to run the course at his own speed and wait for me on the road for the short stretch back to the Guardroom. Boots nodded and vanished and when I emerged from the wood there was no sign of him. I eventually ran up to the Guardroom, just as the Station Warrant Officer appeared at the door. "Ah, Corporal Foxley," He said, "where's the prisoner?" Believing that my acting rank might now be the shortest on record, I shook my head. "I dunno, Sir, but I reckon he might be halfway up the M5 to Liverpool by now." Actually, Boots had tired of waiting and he was behind the Guardroom doing a few hundred press-ups.

The routine of signing out the prisoner had featured another squadron member who had been AWOL for some months and had eventually been arrested on a Midlands building site. He spent some weeks in the Colerne Guardroom and was actually put to work behind its counter during the day, being locked in a cell at night only. At this time, the TV set in the NAAFI had twice been stolen and the solution for the third installation was to keep the TV room key within the Guardroom, where it might then be signed out by a responsible Airman. Just such an issue was effected by the Squadron man awaiting court martial, but he adroitly arranged for the signature to appear in the prisoner's signing-out book, before walking out of the Guardroom with the unsuspecting airman. When the airman returned the TV room key later in the evening, he was naturally asked where the prisoner was, and duly locked up himself when he expressed bewilderment. The prisoner fell out of a taxi outside the Guardroom at midnight, having enjoyed a visit to Bath.

Training got under way and it again featured heavy revision of GPMG SF and the Zebedee, although we were accomplished at such drills by now. Of rather more interest was a day and night parachuting programme, although this was plagued by strong winds and we were seldom despatched. This was particularly annoying since there was no prospect of parachuting during the Salalah detachment.

In mid-February we emplaned at Lyneham and this time I had a sleeping bag under my arm, subsequently smirking from within it at the new chums who were allowed to learn the hard way. Apart from the halt on Cyprus, at RAF Akrotiri where a paper cup of gopping tea in the transit lounge awaited, I mostly slept and only stuck my head out of the bag to search for something resembling food in the white cardboard boxes which the Loadie had distributed among us.

My crew deployed directly to Hedgehog duty and we were surprised to learn that a new Delta had been built. No mortars from our own support weapons flight operated from it, but we shared the duties with *Askaris,* whose armament included a 4.2in mortar of WWII American design

I was not happy with the target information recorded for the

SF by the previous detachment, and we used a couple of boxes of ammunition - some four hundred rounds - to re-register the targets. More alarmingly, when I checked the orientation of the radar head I found an error of two thousand mils, which at one thousand metres range would have yielded a lateral inaccuracy of two thousand metres. About twenty mils error was acceptable. However unlikely the threat of ground attack, the prospect of my team missing its targets by more than a mile was somewhat less than attractive. There had furthermore been little effort to either maintain or improve the site and it kept us busy for a while.

The first RCL round arrived as I was driving the 4 Tonner down to Rayzut beach for some recreation. As usual, we knew nothing until the round exploded on open ground off to our flank. I braked sharply and we bailed off the wagon looking for cover, soon realising that there wasn't any and that the wagon itself probably offered the best protection, despite the proximity of a fuel tank. No rounds followed though and we returned to camp for the inevitable Stand To, whilst Strikemasters screamed off the runway to punch rockets into the firing position. Room occupants could be more dangerous. I was sharing with an artilleryman and I awoke to a smoke-filled room in the early hours of a morning. My companion had fallen asleep with a cigarette and his mattress was smouldering nicely. Not as much as me though, as I dragged it and him outside. I then moved into a room with another squadron NCO, Mel Bonfield, whose companion until that time had been a pet chameleon he had acquired from somewhere. I never tired of watching its camouflage change whenever it moved to a differently coloured background.

I was not drinking and I had embarked upon the latest fitness programme. Having been a non-swimmer and a poor swimmer for too long, I now resolved that I would swim a mile by the end of the detachment. The camp had a pool of about twenty-five metres length and I went directly to it as soon as I came off shift. It actually took only a month to build up to a mile and then I concentrated on swimming underwater, although I never managed more than a length of that.

I thought that I might soak up spare time by polishing a couple of brass twenty-five pounder cases from the gun line. I approached the RA officer one morning as he sat reading a paperback alongside a small mountain of the fired cases, asking if I might have a couple. "Certainly not," He retorted, "these are all accountable." I returned after dark and accounted for two of them myself. They are currently on the mantlepiece among sundry other brass, representing a monthly cleaning chore.

A pistol and a rifle were stolen from the Armoury and they were left, stripped and neatly laid out, on the steps of the RAF Police Section. It was widely believed to be the handiwork of Mick the Nutter, and we lost a fair bit of free time to questions of the Special Investigation Branch, who flew in from Cyprus. The culprit was not identified.

Minelaying parties were still active and a Sultan of Oman Air Force vehicle was blown up outside the camp perimeter. It was just possibly an old mine, but we had a fair bit of activity on Delta as a result, being the closest position to the site. A patrol was led by an RAF Regiment officer who was on a secondment to the SOAF. Such secondment, like that of the RAF pilots who flew Strikemasters, was an acceptable form of mercenary service. An earlier attempt at minelaying had ended in failure when the mine exploded, reducing the inept layer to a bloodied torso. Rumour had it that a pair of excrement-filled shorts was also found a few yards from the corpse, indicating the presence of a surviving, but very frightened, companion.

My crew was switched to Alpha, which was predominantly manned by Dhofari troops whose weapons also included a 4.2in mortar. On the strength of my local mortar course during the previous detachment, I was required to check the azimuth and elevation bearings before the mortar fired its night taskings. Finding the bearing off by a few mils on one of the checks, I attempted to traverse onto the correct setting, but found the mechanism against the limit of traverse. I managed to convey the problem to the *Askari*, whereupon he lifted the aiming post out of the ground and replanted it within the arc. I resigned myself to the fact that we were unlikely to kill any friendly troops with illuminating rounds and I simply let them get on with it.

We continued to operate Zebedee, although it gave us problems from time to time. The radio code for an unserviceable radar was 'Magic Roundabout', which was the children's programme the name Zebedee had derived from. When Zebedee went down we stood on the sandbagged roof and employed the Mark I eyeball, although the *Askaris* reputedly had catlike night vision and were usually pressed into service on such occasions, whatever the truth of their reputation. We were also just receiving into service a device called the Individual

Weapon Sight, which made night vision entirely redundant. It magnified ambient light many thousands of times and although it made a weapon cumbersome when fitted to it, it was a marvellous piece of kit. Today, they are about the size of a pocket torch.

A member of my crew was a Pakistani who spoke Arabic, and he spent a fair amount of time with the *Askaris*. Hussein maintained his cheerful good humour throughout the detachment, and it was much later that I discovered his cheerful good humour derived in no small way from the hashish the *Askaris* supplied him with.

Salalah was beginning to change. A modern port was under construction, as were hospitals and schools. Qaboos was clearly determined to create a modern state, and even the war was winding down. RCL attacks notwithstanding, it was a much quieter detachment, and the turning point had probably been the battle at Mirbat, a year earlier. A force of some forty *Adoo* had mustered for an attack on the town, and they were repulsed by a handful of SAS men and a few troops of the *Dhofar Gendarmerie*.

Iranian troops began to appear, apparently as a result of some arranged marriage between the family of Qaboos and that of the Shah. The Iranians appeared to be entirely armed and equipped by the Americans, but we had no idea what their fighting qualities might be. We soon learned that they employed considerable political clout.

A 'revue' had been staged by the squadron in the cinema on the day that a Cup Final victory was especially appreciated by the Geordie element. A fair bit of drinking followed and fights began which drew in the Iranians. At the height of these, a brick was bounced off the head of an Iranian warrant officer and this looked like developing into an international row. The squadron was briefly placed on stand by for evacuation to Cyprus until a sensible compromise was reached. This was in the brick-thrower - none other than Mick the Nutter - being sent to cells on Cyprus. He was also banned from further service in the Oman, which left some of us wondering what sort of punishment this was supposed to be.

Also destined for cells was a Gunner who thumped the Padre at a function, claiming that the Padre had made improper advances. The court martial chose not to believe him. We had a new CO at this time and he now publicised his intention to rid the squadron of troublemakers when we returned to the UK.

On a slightly different note, a member of my crew approached me at a very early stage of the detachment, requesting compassionate leave. He was very recently married and I asked him what the problem was, supposing that it was a case of young wife not coping very well. It transpired that his wife had just been sentenced to three month's gaol in Bath for Grievous Bodily Harm. He did not get the leave.

We got on famously with the *Askaris* and found the CP duties a poor substitute. The *Askaris* had a .303in Vickers machine gun on a tripod and we were invited to fire this. They also had HE rounds for their 2" mortar (which I had never seen before) and we added these to our routine firing.

I had begun to experience some moments of rich contentment on Alpha. Although the Plain was generally drab, there was the odd profusion of wildflowers whose scent was remarkably strong in the early evening. Excepting the noise of hazard firing, evenings had a quality of stillness that was hard to define, yet distinctly beautiful. I began to have the merest glimmer of understanding why writers such as TE Lawrence and Wilfred Thessiger had found Arab lands so compellingly attractive. Time here seemed to mean something else.

I stood at the tower one evening when a young camel strolled unconcernedly in to drink at the Burmoil we used for washing. It drank its fill, gazed aloofly about, then strolled out again. Less lucky was another, a few days later. The *Askaris* tethered it overnight then slit its throat in the morning. We were invited to share the subsequent camel curry and it beat Chicken Supreme by a considerable margin.

12

Intelligence reports had it that a major attack would be launched against Salalah to commemorate the birthday of Karl Marx. This failed to happen on 4 May and I cannot recall anyone being especially alert. Perhaps the *Adoo* got the date wrong or maybe they had a party instead. As the detachment drew to a close, there were three separate RCL attacks, but none caused injury. We emplaned and my acting rank vanished, but this caused no pain, either. I was a far better swimmer, was tanned and fit and I had a couple of hundred pounds in deferred wages. We were returning to the English summer and life seemed good. In fact, life *was* good and although I did not know it then I would never again know quite the degree of contentment and the job satisfaction engendered by those particular detachments.

We flew out to the island of Masirah for an overnight stay and the NAAFI there was like something out of Dodge City. When the bar closed, we filled the tables with drink and although bar closing was theoretically bar clearing time, the Orderly Officer and the Orderly Sergeant prudently left us to get on with it. We continued drinking until the early hours and, for a change, it was entirely amiable. I broke my alcohol abstinence again for the occasion, but by the time we had returned to Colerne I had begun to think quite seriously about giving up drink totally.

We were sent on two week's leave and I spent mine at the Union Jack Club in London. I was keen to revisit the museums of Kensington and the Imperial War Museum at Lambeth. The RAF Museum at the former RAF Hendon had recently opened and I spent a day there. Theatre tickets could be picked up free at the Nuffield Centre on the Embankment, and these were for some of the best shows in town. I saw '*Oh, Calcutta!*' among others. Lord Nuffield's gifts to the services were numerous and generous, but he also donated tens of thousands of pounds to Oswald Mosley's Fascists in the Thirties.

The time in London filled pleasantly and when I returned to

Wiltshire I continued the museums theme with a visit to the restoration of the *SS Great Britain*, in the dock from which she was launched in 1845. Brunel's great ship had recently been rescued from dereliction in the Falklands Islands - which then were virtually unknown to everyone in England - and it was thought that it might take five or six years to restore the ship. A couple of decades later, the restoration continues.

Returning to duty, I was detailed as an escort for the Geordie who had thumped the Padre in Salalah. He had drawn twenty-eight days in cells and was to serve them at RAF Innsworth, in Gloucester. NCO, escorts, driver and prisoner stopped *en route* for a pint and had several. The driver was unable to and the prisoner actually drove the Land Rover for the remaining journey.

I was interviewed by my flight commander and informed that I had been selected for a D Course at the Regiment Depot. Successful completion of the D Course meant promotion to corporal, but promotion also meant posting. I turned the course down. The flight began ground training again for a series of parachute descents, but when we were half way through them, I went sick, feeling as if something had dropped on me from a great height. It was thought to be malaria and I was given penicillin and turned in at Sick Quarters, feeling too ill to regret the missed descents. When I was more or less normal, I was visited by the flight commander, Flying Officer Neame, who later transferred to the Parachute Regiment, and urged to accept the D Course. I turned it down again.

The flights were undergoing annual range qualifications by the time I caught up with mine, and I was detailed to drive the wagon that carried the Hay Boxes of stew. The duty cook was a bloke named Nat Davis, a Londoner with a sharp sense of humour. Nat had presided over the stew and bread issue on the range and he had noted that the Adjutant, somewhat of a faddy eater, had passed down the line without taking any of the stew. Nat then placed a very small square of cake in the larger of the two mess tins proferred by the Adj and both regarded it for a moment. "Would you like two pieces of cake, Sir." Asked Nat, eventually. "Oh, yes please, Corporal Davis." Replied the Adj.
"Then cut that bugger in half." Said Nat.

I usually drove a 4 Tonner whenever we went to the range, and slow progress home might mean a missed evening meal. Returning on some occasion, I thought that I might trim thirty minutes from the journey by cutting along a road that led through a hamlet. In it, I found the street diminishing in width to the point where the nearside wheels rode along one pavement, and the offside wheels along the other. The locals were less than complimentary.

Postings out had usually been at a trickle and suddenly developed into a flood, as entire lists of names appeared on Orders, with Germany the usual destination. It appeared that the CO was making good his promise for a major reshuffle of Gunners. We also had a new Warrant and he had declared war upon indiscipline. Whilst I neither regarded myself as one of the hard men nor one of the indisciplined, it occurred to me that three years on the squadron might now put me in line for a posting.

Since I had no particular wish for a Germany posting, I responded to a call for volunteers to serve on the Queen's Colour Squadron, at RAF Uxbridge. I had long lost any enthusiasm for purely ceremonial duties, but I was attracted by the idea of service at a unit in close proximity to the big city. I entered my application and learned within four days that it had been accepted. I drew my rifle and cleaned it, performed the blue card routine and had a farewell party in the NAAFI that wrecked me. I loaded my kit and drove down the M4 taking two other volunteers with me.

We three joined volunteers from several other squadrons to form a training flight a dozen strong. We learned that a fortnight course would assess our suitability for drill and ceremonial on a unit that routinely provided guards of honour for Royal and State occasions. At an early stage we were marched down to the sports' field to watch the squadron performing a Sunset Ceremony. I looked out over the field, reflecting that Pamela and I had performed a very different ceremony on it a couple of years before.

RAF Uxbridge had been the original RAF Depot, after the new service formed from the amalgamation of the Royal Naval Air Service and the Royal Flying Corps. Among the recruits who sweated where I now sweated was TE Lawrence, in his *persona* as Aircraftman Shaw. Lawrence had described his experiences in '*The Mint*', which was only recently available since its publication had been suppressed for half a century. Notwithstanding Lawrence's dim view of the camp, I found it very attractive. Mature chestnut trees lined the parade square and many of the camp roads, and the whole station had the aspect of a country estate. It had actually been that, since Hillingdon House, a major communications facility at the top of the camp, had been built originally as an eighteenth century hunting lodge.

More recent history was noted by the pole-mounted Spitfire[1] just inside the main gate and a deep bunker within the station which was a perfectly preserved time capsule of the important fighter HQ it had been during the war.

The River Pinn bisected the camp and it was pleasant to stroll about during the mid-evening of summer and autumn. I retained a great fondness for Uxbridge and it was always a pleasure to visit in later years.

I retain also a fond memory of the NAAFI bar and not least on account of the cheap, rough cider that was dispensed for just nine pence per pint. This was poured from a barrel that sat on the bar top and when it became too cloudy to see through, it would be given away. On the 'off' pay week the cider drinkers were prone to nurse their pints until the 'free' stuff came on line.

Payday was slightly less welcome for one of the volunteers who had accompanied me from II. This was the bloke whose wife had been gaoled for GBH in Bath. She would travel up from Colerne on payday and wait until Rocky received his wages. These she would then confiscate, exempt a pound, and return to Colerne until the next payday. A fierce woman.

New issues included two pairs of Boots, Army Pattern, which

---

[1] There was at this time almost a score of these aircraft serving as 'gate guardians' in various parts of the country. A decade and a half later, the RAF, perhaps realising that such examples were quietly rotting away whilst a pristine Spitfire might fetch as much as £300,000 at auction, withdrew all of the type and replaced them with fibre-glass replicas. The funding for them was defrayed by selling a couple of the original aircraft, and the Uxbridge type, a Mk XIV, was the first to be restored to flying condition. A year or so later it went to an American owner and, sadly, was destroyed in a crash whilst returning from an airshow, killing the pilot.

is to say leather-soled and iron-shod. The upper leather was deeply pimpled and this had to be reduced to a flat surface which could be 'bulled'. The traditional method of doing this was with a candle and a hot spoon, but a modern and more efficient means was to use an electric soldering iron, borrowed from the Armoury. This had to be used with some care, to avoid shrinking the leather to the point where the boots would not fit.

A long day in the heat on the parade square, performing close order foot and rifle drill proved just half of the course content. Much effort, elbow grease and midnight oil were the ingredients which transformed clothing and equipment to parade acceptability, and, naturally, there were always the bogs to clean. A 'tin of small circles' was the means of completing the job begun on boots with soldering iron and beeswax. Razor creases were required in the stiffly unsuitable serge of 'Hairy Mary' battledress, and 'shaving' on the outside and soaping on the inside were the discovered tricks to achieve them. Shirt collars, and anything which might be seen of the shirt, were starched to a glass finish, and belt brasses were rubbed in pools of Brasso on newspaper until they gleamed. Hours of effort with Emery cloth polished bayonet blades until they shone like chromium plate, and the scabbards were sprayed with gloss paint to reflect more shine. Despite my cynicism, I found myself again warming to such routines.

Some proved less adept at these, and none more so than the hapless Rocky. At the end of the first week, we were paraded for inspection by the course SNCO, a stocky Welshman who looked as if he had stepped out of a recruiting poster. Rocky stood at the end file of a rank which glittered in the afternoon sun, but he reflected none of it. His uniform held more wrinkles than a pound of tripe and his collar was creased and singed. The peak of his cap was scratched, his brass was dull and little brilliance radiated from the toecaps of his boots. Indeed, there was a matt surface on one toecap, which on closer inspection proved to be his sock. In his zeal with the soldering iron, Rocky had managed to burn a hole straight through the leather. The sergeant inspected Rocky in silence, from head to (literally) toe. The silence grew. Finally, the sergeant had a question for Rocky: "And who the fuck are you, Son. Davy Crockett?" 'Davy Crockett' was soon posted to another squadron, or to some wild frontier.

The Colour Squadron was at least notionally divided into flights, but it was more routinely split into equal halves; the Left Division and the Right Division. This grouping reflected a 'bread and butter' role of the squadron whenever it was not providing guards of honour at Royal or state occasion. The squadron was nominally RAF, rather than RAF Regiment, although it was entirely manned by members of the latter, and it comprised about one hundred and ten all ranks. Since a Royal guard required ninety-six, it was imperative to maintain the unit manning levels which accounted for the frequent hijacking of the product of successive basic gunner courses at the Depot. A trickle of volunteers from one or other of the fifteen squadrons that the Regiment then fielded topped up the numbers, and repeat or extended tours by those who enjoyed the role were common.

The squadron had formed in 1959, at much the same time and for exactly the same reason that II Squadron had acquired a parachuting capability. That reason was to stimulate recruiting at a time when National Service was ending and the ready supply of 'pressed men' about to dry up. The purely ceremonial role, which previously had been conducted on a much smaller scale by a unit of the RAF at Uxbridge, usefully took some pressure off RAF stations up and down the country whenever they exercised their Freedom rights in local towns and boroughs. QCS would routinely be despatched to provide the major parade presence, and the station role would not be seriously disrupted. In addition, QCS trained to provide drill displays at town and county shows and at tattoos at home and abroad. The thrust of these was continuity drill, where squads of various sizes performed arms and foot drill without spoken words of command, accompanied by a band or taped music. I had seen this performed once prior to my posting to the squadron and it was quite impressive. On the drill course we were briefly introduced to it, learning that the sequence depended simply upon counting paces on the left heel and performing a drill movement each time the heel struck the ground. The squads might be as few in number as two dozen, or as large as six dozen, whilst the routines lasted anywhere between five and twenty minutes.

I was posted to the Left Division, along with a fellow trainee who was Brummie and a natural comic, and my room mate who had gone briefly AWOL during the training course in the hope of being posted back to his former unit. He was merely fined, instead. The Right Division was absent, doing a drill show with a thirty-six squad at the Birmingham Show. Within days of joining the Left, we relieved the other half to continue the same show with the same sequence. The newer members, however, were not required to perform, being deemed untrained insofar as continuity was concerned. The Division was quartered at RAF Cosford and the non-performers drew the job of cleaning the ablutions and latrines, and providing rifle guards at the showground between shows. It was an idle week and my greatest difficulty was in finding enough cash to keep up with the frequent opportunities for drinking. An occasional drinking companion was another member of the recent training flight. He was married with two children and the service wage at this time was so poor that he was actually qualified to draw supplementary benefit from the Department of Health & Social Security. Our daytime duties proved anything but onerous and we soon discovered that we were being left to organise ourselves for the cleaning duties and the rifle guards. Since there also were more than a few of the perpetually 'sick, lame and lazy' which the Squadron appeared to have a fair component of, we arranged shifts and found plenty of time to explore the local area, which was quite pretty. Neither Birmingham nor Wolverhampton offered a compelling attraction and I devoted much of my free time to quiet strolls.

I learned the drill show sequence by watching it and offered to take part, but I was not required until the squadron undertook a selection of very minor shows as the season ran down towards winter. The continuity season ran from April until the end of October, and the winter months, apart from ceremonial duties, were reserved for more conventional training since QCS also had a war role to fill.

Within a few weeks I had taken a good look around me and was not impressed with what I saw. There was little of the camaraderie that was self-evident on II Squadron, and too many of the Gunners seemed interested only in time off and more time off, despite the very generous amounts of free time given. In summer, unless a guard was required, the unit seldom worked after midday, and nor were there any exercises or lengthy detachments to contend with. I began to wonder if I might seek an early posting and I ruefully considered that dodging Germany had been a bad idea.

As the season ran down, we travelled via Dover to Zeebrugge and then to an air force base operated by the Belgiques. The squadron was to provide a continuity show at the Europalia Stadium, and a finale that was the re-enactment of the Battle of Waterloo. The base was mostly occupied by Belgian national servicemen, who looked fetching with their collar-length hair, and the creature comforts did not run to hot water in the showers. The huts were heated by a coal-burning stove, which was stoked until it glowed red, and those who slept in close proximity to it sweated all night, whilst those nearer the door froze. The meals were very basic but we were given bottles of beer with them, which was very civil. The price of beer beyond the camp gates was frightening.

We had taken a 4 Tonner with us and it became my job to drive it between the base and the showground. Having no idea of the local area and no map, I clung grimly to a light vehicle that led and clocked up no less than ten red lights on one run. This produced shouts that may have been French or Flemish, but certainly were less than complimentary.

I was in the drill squad and we performed our routine then stooged about until the finale, for which we dressed as Redcoats. This was the second time in my career I had been a Redcoat, but this time I drew a tunic which had three stripes on it. A sergeant on QCS who apparently envied my waxed moustache and regularly gave me a hard time, albeit in a jocular manner, drew a tunic without stripes. As we filed into the arena each night I made a point of belabouring the sergeant and telling all and sundry what an idle bastard he was. "Christ," Muttered the sergeant, "he's got a speaking role now."

We had been issued with period muskets for the battle enactment and each day received a handful of blank cartridges, which produced a good deal of noise, flash and smoke when they were fired. The firing was choreographed to a musical programme by the band - in much the manner of the 1812 Overture - and a director high in the balcony signalled the volleys and the cease-firing with a torch. Day by day, we each saved a few cartridges for the final performance and turned Waterloo into Rorke's Drift with endless firing. The auditorium filled with smoke and the balcony man jumped up and down in a demented rage.

After the final performance we drove to the docks and boarded an LSL of the Fleet Auxiliary. I was still driving the 4 Tonner and I had made a priority of arriving first in the queue of vehicles that had to be crane-lifted aboard. To my chagrin, the lifting slings had been laid out for the Bedford Rls in the packet, whereas I was driving a TK and it was 0400hrs before I got the vehicle lashed down in the hold. I was also still wearing my Number One uniform, which had gathered a fair bit of grease from the tie-down shackles as I performed the task. There were no bunks left by the time I arrived on the accommodation deck and I curled up in the bar area. I had no sooner done so than bells rang stridently throughout the vessel. This was a boat drill, but almost to a man the squadron appeared clutching their knives, forks, spoons and mugs. They thought that it was breakfast being announced. Following this failure, I dived into a recently vacated bunk and slept soundly whilst we appeared to sail, somewhat aimlessly, off the English coast for some hours before docking.

Back at Uxbridge there were just two remaining jobs before the season ended. The first of these was the Festival of Remembrance at the Albert Hall, which mainly commemorated the dead of WWI. The service itself was preceded by a tableau by different units and ours provided a continuity show, which proved to be a new, if short, offering which we rehearsed for a day or two on the Uxbridge square. Elsewhere on the same bitumen, representatives from several other stations were drilled by the QCS NCOs for other roles at the ceremony. On the evening the arena was filled by representatives of all of the services and veteran's organisations. They filed down the steeply banked stairs and were led by two pensioners from the Royal Chelsea Hospital, who marched to the tune of *'The Boys of the Old Brigade'*. On this occasion it was two veterans of the Great War and as they stepped off the stairs into the arena one stumbled. His companion seized his hand and they continued, hands clasped, across the arena and expressing comradeship more beautifully than a thousand words might. It was an affecting moment whereas much of that which had preceded it looked suspiciously like entertainment masquerading as remembrance. Scarlet uniforms, glittering braid, musical pomp and floor shows conveyed no hint of immense sacrifice, no whiff of disgusting death and never the word 'futility' breathed anywhere.

I noted too that many of the 'celebrity' presenters appeared to be those whose show business career was well faded, causing me to wonder, and perhaps uncharitably, if these were more motivated by recaptured limelight than displays of contrition.

On the Sunday that fell closest to Armistice Day, November 11, we paraded with the Royal Navy and the British Army in Whitehall, flanking Lutyens' monument to the Great War dead which was the Cenotaph. At the inaugural parade, in 1920, one hundred holders of the Victoria Cross had led the parade. Half a century later it still attracted hundreds of veterans, and I noted how shabbily dressed some of them were, contrasting the bright medals on their jacket lapels. We never did build the 'land fit for heroes' and I don't suppose we ever shall.

Continuity was behind us, at least for a few months, and we

paraded at flight level to revise basic tradecraft and put some time in on ranges. I also began to think about fitness again and I mapped a set of runs that took me across the Uxbridge Common and along the banks of the Grand Union Canal. I ran five, nine or twelve miles and made a point of sticking to the routine in order to offset the lack of physical training within the squadron syllabus.

The cider was still proving attractive and I endeavoured to combine social interests by pursuing a succession of NAAFI barmaids, although such pursuits seldom progressed to intimacy. One that did was a liaison with the manageress, but after some weeks she confided to me that she experienced no pleasure from coitus, which was deflating.

Late in November I was summoned by the DSC, Flt Lt Chadwick, and advised that I had again been selected for a promotion course in January. He was aware that I had previously turned the course down, and he quietly invited me to consider my age and my remaining service before turning the course down again. This made sense suddenly, and nor was I overlooking the posting prospect which promotion offered. I accepted the course.

Three candidates had been nominated from QCS and we were withdrawn from the normal training syllabus in order to undergo intensive preparation for the D Course. This was organised by a corporal, Ray Hughes. Ray was already a drinking acquaintance and we would serve together at home and abroad on a number of occasions. He later became the QCS Warrant Officer.

The Morris had mostly lain idle since I had arrived at Uxbridge and I had begun to consider getting rid of it. This was resolved for me when I loaned the car to one of the Guardroom staff during the Xmas break. He wrote the car off, and almost himself, on icy road. I had only insured for Third Party.

I took a shine to a WRAF at a NAAFI dance but was too late in following up. She was soon courting a JNCO on the squadron and they married in fairly short order. I resumed the relationship with the NAAFI manageress, guiltily overlooking the fact that the sexual gratification was entirely one-sided.

The preparation for the D Course included a lengthy navigation exercise in the local area, and I was making good time when I cut through a bridle path. About half way down it I encountered five or six horsemen galloping my way, and I was caught on the knee by a flailing hoof. I had to arrange a lift back to Uxbridge and was sent to my bed with a knee that was unbroken but the size of a football. That evening I had been intended to take the manageress to a Catering Section dinner dance, but clearly was not up to that. In the early hours of the morning, she came to my room and got into bed. This was promising, but all thoughts of passion fled when her perfectly good knee connected with my extremely tender one.

13

I spent the Xmas in Crewe, travelling via Luton where I attended the wedding of Rocky Roxburgh and Jan. I didn't actually get to the wedding since the chap I was riding with to the church smashed his car into a parked vehicle. We arrived at the reception instead, picking bits of broken windscreen out of our suits. The loss of my own vehicle was meanwhile not proving entirely painful. The recent oil crisis had virtually doubled the price of petrol and petrol coupons had already been issued for an expected fuel shortage that did not eventuate. Meanwhile, a fifty miles per hour speed limit was imposed upon English roads and motoring became something less than a joy for a time.

The D Course was due to assemble in the first week of January and I was concerned that the knee injury might now keep me off it. The loss of fitness was irritating and particularly in the light of canal runs which I had built to a distance of sixteen miles, in order to be fit for the course. In the event, the knee seemed all right and I joined the two other QCS students on the Tube to Kings Cross to connect with the train that would deliver us to Darlington and a waiting 4 Tonner. A jolting ride delivered us in turn to the RAF Regiment Depot and a receiving member of the Directing Staff who clearly had styled his act on Marlon Brando. The DS, the weather and the immediate future seemed uniformly bleak and seven weeks began to look like a slice of eternity.

The course was about forty strong, subscribed from the spectrum of units and I encountered members of II Squadron. Their news was that the 'reign of terror' had moderated at last but a lot of the old faces had gone - mostly to Germany. Germany, and overseas allowances, was actually looking pretty good to me right then. We mustered into squads and occupied hutted accommodation on the edge of the airfield. This was of the dormitory type and the facilities were even more rudimentary than the brick-built barrack blocks that were little changed since they were built in the Twenties. We had also returned to bed packs, locker layouts and room inspections, and the latrines, whatever their sanitary efficiency happened to be, were a mass of gleaming brass and copper. We soon developed the routine of cleaning our ablution areas and latrines to the required standard of excellence, and then preserving this by using the facilities in a neighbouring block for which we had no responsibility.

We spent a day being put through elementary weapons and trade tests, and any student who failed these was returned to unit. One such RTU had travelled from Singapore for the course and he looked quite relieved to be escaping a sharp dose of the English winter. With those preliminaries dispensed with, we were issued with a mountain of training pamphlets and another mountain of amendments to them. This represented a considerable amount of work after hours and an infuriating aspect to it all was that some amendments were amended by other amendments. Much handwriting and scissors and paste effort was thus expended quite uselessly.

Since every Regiment NCO had, at least, to qualify as a Weapons' Instructor, the early days weredevoted to instruction by the DS, who mostly had been trained as weapons' instructors at the School of Infantry, Warminster. This aspect of the course I found most agreeable, being fairly adept with weapons and having, I believed, some ability to teach. The squads contained about eight students and we would either take the class on a nominated weapon or we would form the class.

The classroom work was welcome at a time when the weather was filthy and likely to be even worse on the Moors, where we would undergo much of the tactical leadership training and exercises. Lessons in navigation, minor tactics and internal security formed some of the class work and our notebooks grew thick. Not least of the later hurdles was three hour's worth of written exams which would closely examine our knowledge across a broad spectrum. Reading such notes was often sandwiched into odd minutes of the day, such as the back of a 4 Tonner *en route* to ranges or training areas, in the queue at the Mess, in bed at night or even in the bogs. Failing any component of the final tests was to fail the course itself, and we figured that seven weeks of slog was not to be lost lightly through some failure of application. This forcing of the brain produced oddities of behaviour. My roommates, returning from a bold trip to the village pub one evening, reported that when they entered the room I sat bolt upright in my sleep and announced: "**Attachments and Detachments, Nil!**" This was a reference to a paragraph in the NATO Orders Format, which had become another bible for us.

I was off the drink for the duration, merely strolling across to the NAAFI sticky bar at about 2100hrs each evening for a mug of tea. This was intended to relax the mind and forget the lesson preparation for half an hour, yet when more than one student sat down a quiz inevitably developed, or some discussion of difficulty being encountered with the preparation of a particular lesson. I was not finding the time to do any running and whereas most students reported a loss of weight, I was actually putting it on. I was eating so much at meals that even the other students noticed.

Our weekends were nominally free but the homework load was such that few ventured much further than the village or Darlington. I made a point of reserving a couple of hours each Sunday for a relaxed perusal of the *Observer*, but the pamphlets were the more usual reading and I barely looked at a book in the period.

A stroll around the airfield revealed a large number of Shackleton aircraft that had been flown in for stripping before their fuselages were destroyed in rescue exercises for the Fire School. The type, a near relative of the wartime Lancaster, was to remain in service for another twenty years yet, clocking about forty years of operational service. The Hastings that I had 'defended' on the basic gunner course had managed to avoid destruction and did so for a number of years. About twenty years later, an aircraft preservation group in Yorkshire decided to build a Halifax bomber - an extinct type - virtually from scratch, and they discovered that the Hastings had an identical wing spar. The Depot Hastings was sold to the group for a purely nominal sum towards the ultimately successful replica.

Within a week or so we deployed to the first of the field exercises, at Gandale Camp on the edge of the Catterick Training Area. We lived in twelve foot by twelve foot tents and were exercised in a series of navigation 'leads' as section commanders. We soon discovered that features on the area shown as 'houses' or 'farms' were in fact nothing more than piles of indistinct rubble, and that if we did not stick religiously to the compass and count paces, then we were likely to become very lost, very quickly. Having learned, vicariously, from the leads of others, I navigated my first quite successfully, only to encounter a very different problem. I halted the patrol and whispered some instructions to the man behind me to pass along. The DS, who had been trailing along at the rear, became impatient at this unscheduled and unaccountable delay and he moved up the line to establish the reason for it. "Where's Foxley?" He wanted to know. "Gone for a shit." He was told.

The Gandale outing ended upon a mutinous note. The Duty Student reported to the DS, who were living in some opulence in a tin shed on the area, for the morning instructions. When these were given, he was also given the course commander's boots and ordered to have them cleaned by the course. The Duty Student was Vic Eastman, who also was from QCS, and he brought the news to the course. We, in turn, gave the news to Vic that the course commander could shove his boots up his arse, which was pretty much the message Vic returned to the DS. This, predictably enough, led to a swift reprisal that had the course crawling backwards and forwards the length of the field, which was liberally coated with sheep shit. On the first couple of passes, we crawled around the shit but when exhaustion set in we crawled through it.

The Duty Student roster was alphabetical and I had the job of reporting the following day. I was given a very tight, not to say impossible, time scale for packing and stacking the dozen tents, and I duly failed to meet it. For this omission we struck and re-erected the tents half a dozen times before doubling around the field under them. This provided us with a great laugh. Later. About twenty years later.

Back at the Depot, in the relative luxury of the huts, we added the study of range management to our skills, since we would have to qualify as competent to conduct 25 Metre Ranges as junior NCOs. This instruction was illuminated by a DS playlet on the station range that was very funny and had us howling with laughter. The DS had an occasionally human side, although they mostly kept it pretty well concealed.

As the final exercise approached, we devoted much discussion as to what to wear. It was the familiar problem of too much or too little, with few good compromises. Too much and movement simply generated sweat which soaked then cooled; too little and you were cold from the start. We all accepted that we would get very wet at some point. The poncho was the sole means of remaining relatively dry, but it was a useless garment when patrolling or digging. The boots we wore were similarly useless in more than three inches of water and wet feet were a given.

In the quest for good ideas, I heard that women's tights provided excellent insulation for the lower trunk and legs, and I duly fronted up at the NAAFI Families Shop. I presented my packet of

Pewter, micromesh one-size tights to the lady behind the till, trying desperately not to look like some sort of transvestite. "Out on the Moors, Dear?" She queried, obviously knowing the score better than me. Having heard on the grapevine that our sleeping bags for the final exercise would be confiscated, I smuggled out a large plastic bag that had covered a new mattress. This would prove very popular. I also added a flask of Brandy to my contraband and several slabs of cooking chocolate. I guessed that time to prepare compo food might not be accorded a high priority by the DS.

For the move out, I drew the appointment of flight commander, and this offered the very considerable bonus of being a major lead whilst one was completely fresh for it, together with the luxury of preparing Orders in the comfort of the accommodation. The deployment took place during the day, which obviated navigation problems, and it seemed to go well enough. I put the flight, which naturally was the course, into predesignated positions and we began to dig in. Orders began to come in for various of the students to prepare for patrols and I got on with my trench. Around midday, the appointments changed and I was sent off to a section where no trenches had yet been started. I began my second trench. I next accompanied a very brief recce patrol and when we returned I was attached to another section since mine had gone off on some other mission. To no great surprise, I found that I was required to start another trench, although I was digging less enthusiastically by now.

With the short days of winter, it was obvious to me that we would be standing to by 1600hrs, and that there would be no prospect of hot scoff or even a hot wet after that time, because of the betraying flames from the Tommy cooker. I therefore began to dig into my pack for the appropriate materials. At this point I seemed to be the only student left on the site, and therefore the natural target for a figure which appeared from the DS tent.

This was a pilot officer who had recently failed the J Course that would otherwise have qualified him to command a flight. His failure clearly had not been of an order to terminate his service, and he was now 'holding' with the DS until another J Course formed. He was a very short officer and presently there was little of him on view since he wore an arctic parka that enveloped him from the top of his head to the tops of his puttees. The parka furthermore had a wired hood that projected forward about a foot, giving him the appearance of a tiny animal peering from a burrow. He had perhaps wandered out of the DS tent of his own volition, or perhaps he had been sent out by the DS to exercise his authority. Whatever the case, I was not best pleased to see him, for my brew prospects were diminishing by the minute.

"Ah, Foxley, isn't it?" the voice from within the depths of the parka hood offered, perhaps because he had read the name on my combat jacket. I affirmed that it was. He then went on to say that he had been inspecting our preparations to date, and had noted a major omission. I could hardly wait to learn what this might be. "There's no latrine dug yet. Very important aspect of living in the field, sanitation." He looked at me expectantly and I refrained from mentioning how important a hot wet of tea was in the life of SAC Foxley right now. My silence was probably misinterpreted as a failure to understand just how vital latrines were, and the pending J Rock chose a more direct method. "There's just enough time before the Stand To; I think you should go and dig the latrine." This was decision time, I recognised, if not a particularly tough one. Aiming for tactfulness and probably hitting truculence, I answered: "Sir, why don't you fuck off?" then thinking that I was now very likely to be RTU'd to Uxbridge. He digested this and eventually nodded. "Well, I'll leave you to get on with it, then." I got on with my brew and the area did not acquire a latrine pit. (Nor did the exchange seem to blight the life of the young officer; he later attained the rank of wing commander.)

We were put to a crash move by night and ordered to dig in anew. The fog had the visibility down to a metre and I shared a piece of ground with Vic, trying to dig a trench in earth that had frozen solid and our efforts over some hours with a pick resulted in a pockmarked surface, but nothing remotely resembling a fire trench. It was at this time that the smuggled plastic bag proved to have been a stroke of genius; it being abundantly clear by this stage that our sleeping bags held in the Echelon were not about to be made available.

We found a small mound with a depression at its rim and we took turns in the bag, which kept the wind out and trapped body heat. It could also have been a giant asphyxiation kit, except that a good queue formed for the use of it and a turn in the bag did not exceed thirty minutes. It was Spartan comfort, but the best available. The ineffectual labour with the pick was the only alternative, and the real misery began when we Stood To in anticipation of daybreak. I had learned at some time that shivering was the body's own method of stimulating warmth, and if that was true then we should have generated enough heat for an auditorium. We were shivering so badly that we looked like a convention of epileptics. It was clearly time to bring on the Brandy, although I also understood that extremes of cold and alcohol do not mix. My 'trench' companion by this time was Amos Marshall, a Jamaican Gunner on II Squadron. Amos was quite grey with cold by now and his shivering made mine look like an exercise in still life. I uncorked the Brandy and we both took a hefty swig. It put some of the black back into Amos' cheeks and the red into mine and life for a time became a little more bearable.

Later in the day I was summoned to the DS tent to receive Orders for my night patrol lead. I went around the positions to issue a Warning Order for the patrol and with the fog down to a metre again I strayed beyond the perimeter and got lost. My relief at finding another Gunner was short-lived when he informed me that he also was lost, and it took us two hours to find our way in again. By this time, I was due to issue Orders to the patrol in the DS tent, and there was no way of avoiding this by admitting that I had been lost for two hours. I therefore opened my section commander's aide-memoire and, using the format as a guide, I made up the Orders as I went along, hoping to Christ that neither the members of the patrol nor the DS would question me too closely at the conclusion of the Orders.

None did and we proceeded to task, got lost for a while and eventually accomplished the mission. I breathed again and went off to boot someone out of the plastic bag. The four days passed and some combination of cooking chocolate, Brandy, plastic bag, good fortune and perhaps a little effort seemed to have brought me through it. The course was mustered and told to shave before the return to the Depot. We were so wet by now that I simply stripped off my jacket, pullover and shirt and waded to my waist into a pond to shave. We were then offered a mess tin full of 'all in' stew which looked dubious and lacked takers. I had three helpings of it, drawing incredulous stares from the DS. Exercise SOB (Shit or Bust) was over and real life beckoned.

Like some small animal peering out of its burrow

14

The final two days of the course had consisted entirely of practical tests and written exams. I had a bad moment when I misread the programme and turned up twenty minutes late for a map-reading lesson I was to deliver. The examiner was a Warrant Officer of WW II vintage and he merely invited me to achieve my lesson aim in half the stipulated time. I reduced the lesson to its essentials and had another bad moment when I confirmed the lesson. The class, formed of Gunners from the Training Support Flight at the Depot, had neither paid attention to my instruction, nor did they remember the lesson from basic training. I achieved a grading, however, which saved me the job of hunting the class down with vengeance later.

The experience, at an early stage of the tests' phase, reinforced my determination that seven weeks would not be wasted and by some fortune, which did not entirely preclude hard word, I finished at the top of the course. This was rewarded with the Commandant's Prize that was an inscribed copy of '*A Short History of the RAF Regiment*'. It is, unfortunately, a dull account, although I have it still, and a definitive history of the Corps has only recently been attempted.

John Steel, who was the other QCS student, ran second and Vic was in seventh place, so we had some good news to take back to Uxbridge. At Darlington, we made directly for the buffet on the train and remained there for the entire journey, putting a serious dent in their stock of beer. We then struggled with packs and kit bags to the Tube for the brief journey to Uxbridge, where the NAAFI bar beckoned.

We were promoted within days and told of our postings. John was off to one of the newly forming Rapier missile squadrons and Vic and me were staying on QCS. This was a surprise, but for the moment at least I was content to take stock before examining anew the postings' prospects. I had chevrons sewn onto my uniforms and noted in the diary that I appeared to have arrived at the point at which I had been eleven years earlier.

Having put on nearly two stones during the course, I now resurrected the canal runs and ran eleven miles a day until the surplus weight fell off. Spring was on the way and the squadron began to shake out for the continuity season, bringing the discovery that corporals had few duties. Having qualified in what presumably was state-of-the-art section leadership, I was now a JNCO with nothing more vital to arrange than the morning issue of rifles or urns of tea for the numerous coach journeys to guard or continuity venues. I most needed a section to command, but there seemed to be no early prospect of it.

The NAAFI manageress had moved on and her replacement might have served buns at Benghazi. I developed a relationship with Trish, a clerk in the General Office, and this was greatly enhanced when I moved into a room of my own in the block.

I continued to appreciate the novelty of a town just outside the camp gates, although it occasionally offered facets that were less than attractive. I returned from the Tube station some evening and was approached for assistance by a Pakistani who was being trailed by three thugs. I was keen to take them on, which may have been the beer talking, but they dispersed, thus proving that at least some racists are gutless bastards. I was also beginning to understand then that we are a much more racist nation than we care to admit.

When the continuity season got under way, we had early proofs that the squadron, or whomever spoke for it, was reluctant to turn down any venue, however inappropriate or small. Perhaps this was linked to anxieties about the Defence Spending Review, which shortly was to pronounce on RAF cuts. We travelled to Staffordshire for the agricultural show, where our billing was between 'The Junior Farmer's Comedy Football Match' and 'The Grand Parade of Beasts'. Following anything in a field which was by now liberally coated in wet mud and even wetter manure, did little for the boots, whilst the announcement: "Ladies and Gentlemen, the Queen's Colour Squadron of the Royal Air Force", was clearly a coded signal that the beer tent was now giving away free ale. We noted the stampede from the arena, performed our routine in dejected isolation and wondered what we might be doing for recruiting.

I had been looking at the possibilities for a trip home again, but the hike in oil prices had a severe knock-on effect for airline ticket prices. I was not best pleased to learn later that airlines paid no tax on the prodigious amounts of fuel they burned. I had also hoped that I might qualify for free travel, under Commonwealth arrangements, but I had invalidated myself for this scheme by working in the UK prior to my enlistment. Pity. I explored instead the possibilities of taking an extraordinary period of absence, and discovered that I could take up to a month's leave without pay. I arranged to take such leave in conjunction with the thirty days which was the normal allocation, intending to go home for Xmas.

The fitness training was concomitant to a period of abstinence from drink, although I found myself in the bar on occasion. (Among the memories of Uxbridge that has preserved more sharply than others is that of leaving the bar at closing time for the short stroll to the block. The night air, although odourless, always smelled sweet and clean after the fug within the bar and I would inhale great draughts of it as I walked.) I was experiencing knee problems, which may have stemmed from the recent kick or perhaps had an earlier origin, although I did not discontinue the running. One Sunday, I became preoccupied as I ran along the towpath and I missed my usual turn off it. I eventually emerged at Watford Junction and by the time I returned to Uxbridge I had covered twenty-two miles. I missed the evening meal, went to the NAAFI and, having had five pints, went to bed. I ignored the pebbles that Trish pitched at the window.

QCS proceeded on block leave that I did not take in view of the Australia trip. I was sent to work in the Guardroom and for the Station Warrant Officer, a holder of the Distinguished Flying Medal and an Air Gunner veteran of fifty operations over Germany during the war. A good man. I also struck up a friendship with a member of the Guardroom staff and shortly attended his wedding in Northamptonshire. When he was posted we exchanged regular letters but did not meet again for twenty years.

The SWO also went on leave in the period and when a squadron leader died I was given a chunk of the funerary drill and a random collection of station personnel to train to it. I opened the squadron and dug out a copy of the drill manual, and anything which the manual did not address I simply invented. No one appeared to notice.

Whilst the squadron was on leave, a signal arrived requesting a volunteer JNCO for a ground defence posting on the island of Gan. I had no idea where Gan might be, but I submitted an immediate application and destroyed the signal, although it would have been copied to various units. In short order, my application was accepted, although it would not be implemented until March of the following year. Before then I would have to acquire some additional instructor qualifications.

The squadron was earmarked for the Royal Tournament, a venue it performed at every other year. When the leave ended, a sixty-four squad was assembled and it began to rehearse a continuity show of about fifteen minute's duration. I was neither required in the squad nor to have much to do with the training of it, and my time instead was devoted to running a cadre for students listed for the next D Course. This was agreeable and at least represented a better use of the time I had spent at Catterick than anything since.

When the Tournament began, I had the familiar job of arranging tea urns and rifle collections, with a long day at Earls Court to follow. The matinee performance was followed by a long wait until the evening performance and finale, and we seldom returned to Uxbridge before midnight. We drew some overnight guard duties and I watched with interest one morning as a matelot and a Royal Marine rolled down a long flight of stairs, locked together and swapping punches on every other step. Since this did not appear to constitute a security problem I did not intervene.

Exploration of the local area revealed a pub called the Coleherne, where exotic perfumes frequently turned our heads from the bar. It took little time to realise, however, that the clientele was exclusively male. My assessment of Earls Court - which was also known as 'Kangaroo Valley' for the density of Australian visitors - was that it was about fifty per cent tourist and fifty per cent parasite. The parasites were the ones selling ice creams or whatever at extortionate prices and clearly dependent upon the visitors' ignorance of exchange rates.

A sixty-four drill squad did not permit a 'spare' man for all of the spots within the sequence, although most of the blokes got a relief for at least some of the shows. My former roommate, Clive, mentioned to me one day that his girlfriend was coming to watch the evening performance, and I asked him if he had someone to do his spot. When he said that he had not been able to identify anyone, I immediately volunteered, brushing aside his concerns that I had done none of the training or rehearsals. I figured that I would simply follow the bloke in front and do what he did; simple enough. On the night, this worked fine until the bloke in front became me and when the squadron executed a turn in mid-arena, sixty-three went left and I went right. I marched about the empty end of the arena for a while, performing rifle drill in splendid isolation, then eventually grafted myself onto the rest of the squad for the march off. Dismissal outside was rapidly followed by a summons to the CO, Sqn Ldr Hawkins, who later became the Commandant-General of the Corps, and he was less than amused, although he expressed the view that my motive had been laudable.

The Tournament was worth watching for the spectacle of the Naval Gun Teams, where huge matelots hurled several hundredweight of cannon over a series of obstacles. Their training not infrequently broke limbs and severed the odd finger. Less impressive, although the punters seemed to like it, was the musical drive of the King's Troop Royal Horse Artillery, where four teams, each of four horses, towed cannon and limbers around the arena. This event preceded ours and we had already observed the amount of time the troopers spent polishing leather and brass. The process continued even at the arena doors, with troopers applying a coat of linseed oil to the horses' hooves, but I reserved my fascination for the specific duties of the troop sergeant. He went deliberately to each horse and raised its tail, then wiped its arse with a towel. Suddenly, the tea urns and the rifles job was no problem at all.

The Tournament was followed by a spate of guards at Heathrow or Gatwick airports, and some shows at minor venues. Life was only enlivened by the prospect of being caught with a female in the block, although the Ministry of Defence police, whose remit this was, seemed to observe a hands-off policy. This may have had something to do with the fact that whenever they were called to disturbances in the NAAFI, they could depend upon QCS lads for assistance in controlling unruly civilians, who tended to drift in for the discos and the cheap beer from time to time.

Autumn and the continuity season ran its course and the chestnut trees which flanked the parade square littered it with golden leaves. We were then warned for Public Duties that entailed relieving the Brigade of Guards at their usual task of finding the guards in London. We were to mount duties at Buckingham Palace, St. James's Palace, the Tower of London and the Bank of England. For these we learned army drill and rehearsed the duties on marked portions of the Parade Square. For some reason, the Queen's Colour that was conventionally escorted by an SNCO on either side of it, was escorted on PDs by JNCOs. I was selected for the duty, together with another JNCO who was not only of similar height and build but who also had a similar moustache.

The guards were transported early in the day to Wellington Barracks, on the Mall, to change into uniform for the guard mount and dismount procedure on the forecourt of Buck House, a stone's throw away. The Colour Party accompanied this ceremony then marched down the Mall to Jimmy's for a slightly less formal ceremony. The guard duties were of forty-eight hours duration and we carried enough Gunners to provide double sentries on a two hours on, and four hours off roster. If the Royal family was not in residence at either palace, however, we reduced to single sentries and a much lighter workload. Corporals were merely required to post the reliefs every two hours and we worked on a six-hour rotation.

We found several guards then returned to a field training routine which I escaped by attending the first of the courses I was required to do. This was at a tri-service Nuclear, Biological and Chemical warfare centre in Wiltshire. Three weeks at Winterbourne Gunner would qualify me as an assistant NBC instructor and an NBC Cell plotter. The camp looked every inch a sleepy hollow when I got off the train to report, and it seemed as if the liveliest thing in the area was Stonehenge, just up the road. The course was busy, though, and a fair bit of study in the 'free time' was required to keep abreast of the instruction. The first two weeks were devoted to the NBC instructor qualification and the last week was the cell plotting. I soon learned that I had no talent for nuclear and chemical prediction, and I probably could have gotten better results by studying the entrails of a chicken, rather than the complicated tables we worked with. I fluked some sort of a pass at the end of the week and returned to Uxbridge briefly before travelling to the School of Medicine at RAF Halton, in Buckinghamshire, to acquire another instructor qualification that was mandatory in ground defence duties, wherever the station was located and whatever its role.

This requirement was to qualify as a first-aid instructor and the course lasted for a fortnight. RAF Halton was the home of the Boy Entrants, whose training scheme had been originated by Lord

Trenchard, and the camp was nicely set in rural Buckinghamshire. The Officers' Mess was originally a country house owned by Baron Rothschild and he had presented it to the nation after WW I. Duly qualified and returned to Uxbridge, the news was that another dose of Public Duties would interfere with my home leave plans. I would now be unable to travel until the twenty-fourth of December, which was cutting Xmas a bit fine.

I had toured the 'bucket shops' for the cheapest ticket available and the result was a meandering journey home that took me via Brussels, Tehran and Kuala Lumpur, mostly in Boeing 707s. At KL I was obliged to observe a twenty-four-hour hiatus and although a posh hotel was provided at no extra cost, I felt unable to avail myself of the bar at local prices. They charged like wounded buffaloes. On a sweltering Xmas Day, I sat in the hotel lounge reading a paperback, and when I had heard *'Frosty the Snowman'* played for perhaps the thirtieth time I was about ready to strangle someone.

When we flew out, the trip to Perth was relatively brief and the landing was at 0200hrs. After I had cleared Customs and Immigration, I headed for the lavatories and changed into OGs. The 'Rattler' would not depart for a further fifteen hours and I had wasted enough time already. I got a couple of short lifts which put me clear of the city area, then settled to await a longer lift.

It rained a little during the night but I was none too concerned at that. When the sun came up and illuminated my oddly pleasing anonymity, I breathed in the characteristic smell of the damp soil, and smelled also the fragrance of wood smoke from somewhere close. The highway and the day unfolded before me; the cackle of a Kookaburra split the peace and a screeching flock of Galahs descended upon an adjacent Gum. I was warm and I was happy. And I was home.

RAF Uxbridge 1974

15

I arrived home at midday and was greeted by a pair of German Shepherds, of which breed there seemed to be at least one at any time in the house. Jan and Arch were also at home and I had not seen Arch for five years by this time, although we regularly exchanged letters. Their children, Ian and Lisa, were growing fast and it was another reminder that time moved on. The whole family was together for the first time in some years, and it would prove to be the last time.

It was approaching high summer and I was content to loaf about on the lawn for a couple of weeks, soaking up the sun, and spending some time at the Mines & City or the RSL. I then got a job on the nickel mines at Kambalda, through the family friend I had first-footed on the last visit. He clearly bore me no grudge. The nickel finds had rescued the Goldfields from extinction for, although the principal finds at Kambalda were thirty-odd miles away, the town infrastructure served the new industry. There was a distinct air of renewed prosperity in the town.

I had expected employment as a general labourer on the mine but was in fact employed as a 'shitty', cleaning the surface lavatories and showers each morning then strolling underground to assemble the lavatory pans for collection. Such strolling was made possible by the fact of no vertical shaft accessed by cages, but a gently declining slope through a passage sufficiently high and wide to accommodate front end loaders. The work was easy and in fact reserved for miners whose better health lay behind them, and who needed a soft routine towards retirement. I had relieved one such who was on holiday and his absence nicely coincided with the month I intended to work.

The Old Man was still working, although he was sixty-eight by now. This recalled to me a comment made by a member of the family I met, when I had first returned to Crewe. "Your father," She said, "didn't have an idle bone in his body." It was a nice tribute and his capacity for work was clearly undiminished by age. Nor was his capacity for drink, as I was to discover in several lengthy sessions in the clubs.

A surprise visitor was a chap named Andy Williams, with whom I had served both on II Squadron and QCS. Andy had left the RAF after a short engagement and went to South Africa, but found apartheid repugnant. He went on to Australia and was making a call on my folks entirely unaware that I was home. He also was found work on the mines and he remained in Australia for some time. When I next ran across him, twenty years later, he was a beat policeman in a Cornish town.

It was good to be home and particularly good to be in the Old Man's company. I worried about the size of his drinking, but it was temperedby the knowledge that he always remained affable and nor did I ever see him suffering from the effects of a hangover. He was obviously well regarded at the Mines & City and the RSL, where his circle of friends included Australians and migrants old and new. Someone once asked him why he did not routinely take a holiday in Perth, which was the annual habit of just about everyone else. "I take my holiday here, every weekend." was his reply.

The regular 'shitty' returned a little ahead of schedule and I became the assistant shitty, until I realised that the 'boss' was an utterly idle bastard. I 'did a Robinson Crusoe' and the Foreman expressed regret, telling me that I was welcome back anytime. I appreciated his remark and I had appreciated the job, giving it my best efforts even when it entailed hauling buckets of shit to the surface. I had remarked to a companion at the time that I had once done such a job under fire, which was stretching it a little.

I resumed a running programme in what remained of the leave, although there didn't appear to be a cool time of the day for it. Temperatures were well over a ton and reached a hundred and eight one day. The days inexorably ran out and I made another difficult farewell from Mam. I had intended to travel to Perth on the Rattler, but a line problem stopped the service. The Old Man dropped me out along the Coolgardie Road late in the afternoon and I hitchhiked to Perth. I put in a couple of days with Jan and Arch at their house in the suburb of Girrawheen, and the family accompanied me to the airport to see me off.

I had not shaved during the two months of leave and when I was back at Uxbridge I reported to the MO with a tale of skin disorder and shaving agonies. He gave me an excused shaving chit for a couple of weeks and when it survived scrutiny by the Warrant, I wondered if I might preserve the beard for the Gan posting. This was barely a fortnight away, and I had few duties with QCS before packing the bags and observing a short tour with a blue card. The relationship with Trisha was renewed and despite warnings that the MOD Police had finally targeted Struma Block, we threw caution to the winds. By the time of the posting, I was quite looking forward to a period of abstinence. At an assembly of mates on the eve of departure, I chucked a tenner over the bar - which demonstrates either that I was careful with a quid, or that ale was still very cheap - and got very drunk. I caught a train to Swindon the next morning and I had a quiet evening in the Gateway House prior to flying from Brize Norton early on the following day.

We landed at RAF Gan at 0300hrs and I was met by my new boss, Flying Officer Pete Moralee, who also had been my flight commander on II Squadron three or four years earlier. We were the only RAF Regiment personnel on the island (with the exception of the RAF Firemen, who also at that time formed part of the RAF Regiment branch), and he gave me a quick run down on the job, which primarily consisted of maintaining the ground defence skills of RAF tradesmen. He told me not to report for work that day, but he invited me to join him for a run around the island. I did so, being nearly creased by the humidity, despite the acclimatising effect of the recent time in Australia.

Gan was an island in the Addu Atoll, which was a part of the Maldives chain. The islands lay off the West Coast of India, with Sri Lanka the nearest neighbour, and we were just below the Equator. The atmosphere was tropical and steamy, and to allow for it the station worked from 0700hrs until 1300hrs, thus leaving plenty of time free for leisure until the light failed at about 2000hrs. The island was a refuelling stop for the aircraft that serviced Far East assets, although the writing was on the wall both for them and the island itself. Gan was scheduled for closure under the edicts of the 1974 Defence Spending Review and a minor distinction of my job was that I would be the last RAF Regiment corporal to serve on the island. This, however, was not uppermost in my thoughts at the time. I was a relatively new JNCO in my first Ground Defence Training tour, and I was keen to get it right.

My accommodation was in a line of bashas occupied by the Fire Section, a good crowd of lads I instantly got on with. Several of them, I learned, were on repeat tours. The runway that bisected the island had its southern threshold just yards from the basha, a fact of which we were reminded whenever VC10s - the most frequent visitors - landed or took off. Four Conway jet engines being revved for a take-off were not easily slept through. The island had a perimeter track of almost exactly four miles length and I decided that I would run it every day. Some fag packet calculations told me that I could clock a thousand miles fairly easily during my tour, and I therefore made that my target distance. I usually timed the run for sunset, not merely for the advantage of relative coolness, but mostly to enjoy the spectacular loveliness of a sight I had seldom witnessed since leaving Australia.

Gan in the afternoons was like a giant sports' club, with every conceivable sporting and recreational activity. I was attracted to the idea of joining the sub-aqua club, but at the medical attention was drawn to my right ear that had recently been troublesome. The MO opined that pressure changes might well exacerbate the problem to the detriment of further service. I took up snorkelling instead.

Another afternoon, and later an evening, activity was study. I had decided to teach myself German from books and tapes, and I then added O Level classes in English Language and the Structure and Working of British Government. I had by now been twice advised to consider applying for a commission, but a first step in that direction was in remedying my educational deficiencies. Grammar school was a good few years back by now.

My predecessor in the job, and his predecessor, had formerly served with II Squadron, and I was therefore not greatly surprised to discover that I had inherited a smoothly efficient system. The work was not onerous and consisted mainly of running arrival courses, and continuation weapon training to include range firing for everyone else. In the mornings for six days of the week I lectured on First-Aid and the care and maintenance of the S6 Respirator, and in the afternoons the Boss and I ran range practices on the 25 Metre facility. I also, and for some reason never explained to me, screened films on flight safety and security. The latter was covered most laboriously by a sixty-minute film that depicted an RAF officer seduced by some tart and obliged to steal secrets. Most of the classes sensibly regarded this epic as a golden opportunity to catch up on some sleep. After the screenings, the reels had to be carefully rewound on a device, and carelessness with this might enliven the next showing, when the characters appeared walking backwards or upside down or both.

I acquired a running mate on the daily circuits of the island.

This was Phil Mutton, a JNCO Supplier. Phil was a much better runner though and my view of him at about the halfway point tended to be a receding one. I also acquired a bike - rare treasure on Gan - which greatly facilitated my errands about the island and to the range to either set up or to clean up. Carrier boxes were fitted to the handlebars of the bikes and it was customary to decorate it with art that was appropriate to the job. That of the Boss had a fine representation of King Kong on it, whilst the Padre's was simply: 'Maker's Rep.'

Gan, idyllic and serene in aspect, had some sad history. In the Sixties, the locals, who received little of the largesse which RAF rental disbursed to the Mali government, attempted secession. The ringleaders were castrated as a condign example to the rest and the matter of UDI was forgotten. At some other time, one of the Pakistani policemen employed on a contract by the RAF was intimate with a local child and was found chopped in pieces in the vicinity of the range. Some two thousand of the locals worked on the island in menial capacities, but they lived on neighbouring islands. They commuted in *dhonis* - native boats - and the *dhoni* lines were busy morning and afternoon.

En route to my studies at the Education Section one afternoon, I encountered a very pretty girl and took the rare opportunity for a chat. She was off a ketch that was briefly visiting the island. No women served on Gan and if a visiting WRAF Loadmaster from a transient Hercules decided to take a stroll around the island, she might find herself accompanied by a couple of hundred blokes who 'just happened to be out for a stroll.' This absence of females was addressed in a jocular manner annually, with the RAF Gan Drag Queen Competition, where each section vied for the honour by dressing up a candidate in the finest clothing sent from family at home. I sportingly offered to represent the Fire Section, attracting the withering comment that bearded ladies weren't exactly in demand, even on Gan.

Other entertainments included a chariot race the length of the runway, during the Easter Break, and my efforts were appreciated here. I joined the Operations team and we won. That apart, a four-day break at Easter was not appreciated and by the time it ended I was ready to start digging a tunnel to Sri Lanka.

Volunteers operated a radio station that broadcast on the airwaves, and fan mail was received from South Africa. A regular programme featured jazz and I became an avid listener. I was again observing strict sobriety and anything that filled the odd half-hour was welcome. The radio programmes included *'Bushey Island Discs'*, whose format was not a million miles from Roy Plomley's BBC programme, *'Desert Island Discs'*. I was a later guest and for my luxury item I chose an entrenching tool, on the premise that an island paradise was unlikely to remain so without a latrine. I *had* learned from the D Course.

Despite the steamy heat of the evening, the Airmen's Mess served hot cocoa at 2100hrs each night and I was always in line for it. The pin-up board in my room was bereft of anything save my own version of a 'chuff chart'. Mine simply noted the progress of the runs *'herum die insel'*.

I had remained in touch with Trish and within weeks I was penning mildly erotic letters to her and then, unbelievably, I met her on my birthday. She had been posted to Singapore and spent a couple of hours in the transit lounge in the early hours of the morning. I began to wonder what the possibilities might be for a quick trip to Singapore during the tour.

Working with Pete Moralee was never dull, since he came up with new ideas almost every day. These sometimes led to an excess of zeal and his idea for floating targets, to be engaged from the decks of air-sea rescue launches was a sample. One of the Maldies - locals - who worked in the ground engineering section had been taught rudimentary welding skills, and Pete got him to weld together some foam drums, which would provide the floating platform for the targets. I happened to go to the section on some other errand, just as the Maldie was about to gas-weld some drums. These, however, were not foam drums but those which had lately contained aviation fuel. The vapour content in that heat made a pretty good bomb of each of them, simply awaiting the torch.

Another idea was that we should be the first and last Rockapes to parachute onto Gan, simply by utilising one of the Hercs that routinely passed through. The Loadie was qualified to despatch, and the idea seemed a goer, until we learned that we would need a suitably qualified DZ officer. When this idea foundered, we secured places on a free-fall course on Cyprus, but on the eve of departure a signal advised us that the aircraft, a Beaver, had gone terminally sick. By now determined to do something, Pete secured several places on a jungle survival course at Kota Tingii, and we duly embarked for

Singapore.

We arrived as a team of seven, to include Pete and another officer, my running mate Phil, a PT instructor, a Fireman and a member of the medical staff. We were initially stationed at HMS Terror, on the island, and this was also where Trish was serving. Early attempts to renew the carnal relationship failed when a sentry saw me enter the female accommodation, and I had to make a hasty exit via a window.

We moved on to the former transit camp at Nee Soon and were equipped for the course. We spent a few days on basic navigation and survival techniques then were choppered up country for the exercise. The course was about twenty strong and predominantly made up of naval personnel. (I was initially assumed to be one of them, in view of the beard). Two of the naval party were officers and one was a singularly inept character who succeeded in hacking bits of flesh off himself each time he drew his machete. This provided the rest of us with useful first-aid practice and enraged his colleague, who obviously found it very disagreeable.

The jungle work was agreeable and I managed to avoid poisoning myself on this occasion. We were provided with a python to eat and I greatly regretted the death and carving of it. It was beautifully marked and we were in no danger of starving. We were in rather more danger from the machete-wielding Tar and soon learned to avoid his activities until he dropped the machete with a howl, whereupon we pressed forward to see which bit was bleeding this time.

When the course dispersed, I arranged to remain in Singapore on leave and moved into a rented room with Trish for two weeks. This bliss was slightly spoiled when I promptly went down with symptoms similar to those experienced at the end of the II Squadron tour, and thoughts of carnality were extinct for a time. I eventually returned to Gan, suddenly realising that my runs about the island were somewhat in arrears and that I would have to increase the daily distance. Since I always ran in boots, this activity had attracted some attention and a number of other were also building towards a thousand miles. I felt honour-bound to do the tally now, although four miles a day in the heat seemed plenty. It was by now also raining for much of the time and so heavily that the visibility was usually down to a few yards.

If I didn't have sufficient problems with the runs, I was now informed that I had been selected for promotion to sergeant, subject to successful completion of the C Course in November. I was therefore to be short-toured on Gan by seven weeks. I made some more fag packet calculations that suggested that I now needed to run sixteen miles each day. A brainwave was to run in the evenings, long after the sun had gone down. This lasted for precisely one run, during which I was chased by an enormous German Shepherd of the police flight. These dogs were trained to equate running figures with guilty bastards fleeing the scene of the crime. I took to running before breakfast instead, which invariably meant that the bullet catcher at the 25 Metre range became a latrine stop, and fitting the rest in when I could. With a few days remaining before posting, I completed the thousand miles and was met by the station commander with a bottle of champagne. This was a nice gesture, although it was like trying to drink syrup at the time.

Tidying a mountain of '37 Pattern webbing in the War Reserve Store (reserved for God knows what), I found a basic pouch which contained a packet of letters. They had been written to a National Serviceman in 1955 and had remained in the pouch since. I was able to contact the owner via the RAF News and I posted the letters on.

RAF Gan had provided the perfect opportunity to reflect upon my life. I had begun to believe that in the previous year at Uxbridge I had actually undergone a change of personality. I was uncertain as to the precise nature of the change, except that I feared that my sense of humour was somehow impaired and that I was finding life less amusing. I maintained this belief for some years and it is quite recently that I have recognised the real change. In that year, I had finally bid goodbye to youth, long deferred, and the progression to maturity doubtless impeded by my refusal to marry. I had lately and for the first time begun to consider a future beyond a week or a month or two, and to think seriously in career terms. On Gan, I evaluated my adult life to date and recognised the squandered years, whilst planning a better use of those which remained. At some point, too, I considered the eclipse of the younger Foxley. He had some attributes that I regret losing.

16

However welcome the prospect that I might enjoy an unexpectedly early promotion to sergeant, it was surpassed by the news that I was posted back to the parachute squadron. Even within my limited means of comparison, I believed that the camaraderie on II Squadron was without equal elsewhere within the Regiment, and I felt fortunate to be returning to it.

Arriving back in England in October, I passed the couple of weeks remaining until the C Course by continuing the tradecraft revision I had begun on Gan, when I was first advised of the course. II Squadron, upon closer inspection, proved to have undergone a radical change in a little more than two years. The average age of the unit had dropped quite noticeably and there was no more than a handful of familiar faces, whereas tours stretching to four and five years had previously been quite common. The character had changed but character still existed. II was also still defending its reputation as the fittest of the squadrons, and that was good to see.

Seven months of Equatorial heat had done little to prepare me for a winter course and I suffered for a while, along with the students who arrived from Singapore and Cyprus. My results on the ranges were abysmal, simply because I shook so badly with the cold that I could not control the rifle. I was not looking forward to the exercise phases at all. Fortunately, quite a large portion of the early weeks of the course was devoted to classroom pursuit of weapons tuition and minor tactics. For the latter I had devoted much time on Gan to Army Code 9624,[1] that was the tactics bible of the day, and it

---

[1] The Infantry Platoon in Battle. Each section of the pamphlet was prefaced with a quote that sought to convey the gist of the lesson. My favourite was from platoon attack and gave a Spartan mother's reply to

put me usefully ahead of the course. Prior to beginning training, we had to complete a series of lead-in tests, but these I had practised assiduously and they presented no problem. My companion on the pairs tests also knew his stuff but, for other reasons, he entered a VW after a couple of days and returned to unit. Those of us who stayed were issued with another mountain of amendments, in order that we should not get bored between planning weapon lessons, boning up on tactics, navigation, range procedure, battle exercises, internal security and drill, and life became very busy again.

On Gan prior to departure, I had reduced the illegal beard to an equally illegal handlebar moustache, which I did not expect to long survive the scrutiny of the course DS. Each morning, the course was marched to Building 159 and we were stood at ease outside the DS office window, whilst the Duty Student reported indoors for the detail. Whatever the detail, it began to be followed by an instruction that would not vary for the five weeks of the course. The Duty Student would be ordered to inspect the course and to that order would be added: "And tell Foxley to get that moustache off." The Duty Student would reappear, inspect the course and when he got to me would order: "Get that moustache off." To which I would reply: "Get stuffed." I thought that it was worth putting to the test of a direct order from the DS, but such never arrived. The handlebar went back to Colerne with me, although it would not survive later challenges.

During the weapons training phases, each student was given two different lessons to prepare each night, and since each student gave only one lesson each day a guessing game developed as to which might be the likely lesson. Time - always insufficient - could then be devoted to the lesson that mattered. The 84mm antitank weapon was one I had drawn, but since I had already delivered two lessons that week I was convinced that I would not have to conduct another. I spent the time on something else and was therefore dismayed to be called out to do the lesson. I had in fact forty minutes to revise the 84, whilst another student in the squad did his lesson, but it was insufficient to get to grips with the trigger mechanism of the Carl

---

her son's complaint that his sword was too short. "Add a pace to it." She retorted.

Gustav, which I hardly knew. I had a stab at it whilst the squad grew little wiser and the DS sat noncommittally in the corner. The latter did not bother with the usual verbal and lengthy debrief on this occasion. He merely handed me a folded slip of paper and left the room. I unfolded the paper to read his summary: 'Your brain is like a crow's nest; all shit and twigs.'

We moved out onto Catterick Moor for the battle handling exercises and it was predictably frozen. I was the student on a tank stalk and had to wade seventy yards through waist-deep freezing water. By the time I had arrived at the 'kill' position, I was shivering so much that a round fired from the weapon could have struck at anything between five and five hundred yards.

At the mid-course interview, I was surprised to hear the course commander say that I had something of a reputation within the Regiment. He followed this by saying that I was presently playing the 'grey man' on the course, and there was some truth in this. Handlebar moustache notwithstanding, I had been quietly getting on with my studies and trying to keep a low profile. The course commander had recently returned from a secondment with Omani forces, and he had distinguished himself by extricating a *Dhofar Gendarmerie* force from an ambush, acquiring a gong from Qaboos as a result. This gave him a great deal of credibility with the course, and he also obviously preferred to clean his own boots, so mutinies were not on the agenda this time.

I had not packed the Pewter, micromesh, one-size tights on this occasion, since the previous course had persuaded me that their thermal qualities were much exaggerated. They were also a difficult garment when it was necessary to urinate. I had improved upon my footwear though, by trading some duty-free liquor during the Singapore trip. On the island I had run across Boots Barlow, now serving with a helicopter squadron at Tengah, and he introduced me to a supplier from a Kiwi battalion at Kangaw Barracks. Among other treasures, a bottle of whisky secured a pair of high boots. These were immeasurably better than our own issue, although I had to disguise them on the course by winding my puttees around the upper leather. Students were supposed to get their feet soaked, it seemed. The theory prevalent at that time was that all forms of instruction and testing on the D and C courses was actually quite secondary in aim. The real object was to sharpen the feet of students, drive them into the ground and see who was still upright at the close of the course. There may have been an element of truth in that, and no one I knew had any argument with it.

In mid-December we began the final exercise (another SOB), and I again added cooking chocolate and brandy to my provisions. The weather was perishing and there was no opportunity for sleep at all in the opening twenty-four hours. There was very little to be had in the forty-eight hours that followed, and between the effects of cold and lack of sleep, I had some interesting hallucinations on day three. The 'leads' varied from section command to command of the flight, and I drew a couple of fairly routine ones early. On the second night I was summoned by the DS and appointed flight commander, then given five tasks to execute. One of the most important of these, I was told, was the digging of a trench for the GPMG SF. This task had already been given to several 'flight commanders' but none had actually achieved it. Dire consequences would follow, it was intimated, if the trench was not prepared.

I returned to the defence site confident that the SF pit and the other jobs were no big deal and that I would accomplish the lot in no time, but it was at just that moment when the site was virtually denuded of students. A load of patrol leads were required and it seemed that the members of the course were either leading or being led for the next six or seven hours. I sat down and considered the priorities and soon decided that the SF trench was the one to go for. I then went to see what the manpower situation might be. Not good, as it happened, and it actually had shrunk to the handful of Gunners provided from the Training Support Flight based at the Depot. TSF fielded drivers and gofers for the spectrum of courses and the Gunners were not always of a quality you might want to hit the beaches with. It is entirely possible that the Gunners on TSF were selected for their innate truculence, and very probable that they were additionally briefed by the course DS to be none too helpful to students. Whatever the truth of that speculation, I most certainly faced a degree of hostility when I found the senior TSF Gunner, and had explained my requirements to him, finally extending an entrenching tool.

He folded his arms across his chest. "Call yourselves fucking corporals," He expostulated. "You fucking lot couldn't organise a fucking fart in a fucking baked bean factory. You can fuck right off." Through the fog of fatigue, I recognised that this was a leadership problem that I now had to resolve with firm control, hedged about with tact and diplomacy. I shifted my grip on the entrenching tool and brandished it in the Gunner's face, announcing: "If you don't get a move on, I'm going to wrap this fucking shovel around your fucking head." The Gunner moved off, muttering darkly, and I counted this a success, although the trench never did amount to much.

I survived the exercise phases with a mix of scores, did badly on a navigation exercise and worked hard on weapon lessons to redress the balance. I had another bad moment with the drill exam, which was a classroom lesson teaching squadron in review. I had elected to use a metal board and magnetised figures for this, seeing the advantages this offered in frequent moves of the 'flights' and 'parade executives'. I learned the lesson verbatim and conducted several rehearsals with the board and training aids, confident of success. On the day, I was provided with a board that had been thickly repainted, and I watched aghast as the 'flights' and even the 'executives' became a load of deserters when the magnets failed to hold. Notwithstanding this, and the sniggers of the class, I scraped a pass. The final theory exam lasted for three hours, but I had poured plenty of revision into that and it held no terrors. Overall, I was beaten into second place but I did not feel too bad about that. Before the course dispersed, I won a small bet by strolling into the Sergeants' Mess and ordering a pint, although we would not be promoted until the New Year. I got some strange looks, but I got the pint. In the Airmen's Mess at Colerne, I was served Xmas Dinner by the officers and SNCOs for the last time, and in January moved into the Sergeants' Mess. It would not be a long stay in that particular mess, since Colerne was being closed and the squadron was about to take up duties in Northern Ireland.

17

I was posted to A Flight and soon learned that this was the least popular with the CO, the DSC and the WO, among others, for a series of cock-ups on the training front and indiscipline on the domestic front. The flight commander was a flight lieutenant and thus not a 'junior' officer, but relatively new to the Corps and not markedly 'streetwise'. He was keen to improve our standing within the squadron, and the general picture improved with the arrival of Tony Watkin, who would be the flight-sergeant. I knew Tony from the first tour; he had formerly served with the Royal Marines and he was a tremendously fit man who had conducted the pre-para courses from time to time.

The matter of fitness had also preoccupied my thoughts upon promotion, wondering how a thirty-four-year-old sergeant might set the example for Gunners in their late teens or early twenties. This preoccupation had bordered upon a crisis of confidence for a while, that was largely resolved by a squadron run where I beat about sixty-five per cent around the course. For the rest of it, I soon became far too busy training for the imminent detachment and the fears melted away.

The matter of flight indiscipline had to be addressed and I put my authority to an early test. I had inspected the flight one morning and ordered haircuts for half a dozen of the Gunners. When none chose to have them, I charged them all then briefed the flight that postings were available to anyone who didn't care for my methods, which were not about to change. No one actually applied for one and we began to develop a rapport that was based upon hard training and the desire to be a little bit better than anyone else on the squadron. It never became necessary to repeat charges, which I did not like as a disciplinary tool, preferring instead to make the punishment fit the crime.

Detachment-specific training was conducted by the squadron for a few weeks, then honed by the visit of the Northern Ireland Training Advisory Team, or NITAT. The NITAT package included photographs of recent victims of bombs and bullets in the Province; postmortem glossies which showed bodies with wires through them to depict the path of bullets. Other photos offered evidence of disgusting brutality but none of these ever found their way into newspapers or the TV. They ought to have been plastered on billboards the length of the country.

Since the detachment would offer no opportunities for parachuting, we completed an intensive programme before we embarked. I was supposed to have undergone refresher training at Abingdon, but there was too little time available for this. I instead accompanied a ballooning programme and refreshed by doing four descents in one day. This also served as an introduction to a modification to the PX parachute, which was now fitted with a net skirt. The net skirt served to obviate the 'blown periphery' that occasionally reduced the canopy area and could put the parachutist on the ground a good bit ahead of schedule. We did the balloon programme at Hankley Common, which imposed considerable travelling time loss upon on already limited winter's day, but the weather was beautiful. Winched up to eight hundred feet, the Surrey landscape swayed beneath us and I was at peace with the world. My anxieties about the job had evaporated, and I was happy to be back with the squadron we simply knew as the best.

We followed the parachuting programme with a three-day internal security exercise based at Imber Village, on Salisbury Plain. Imber had been a real village that was acquired by the War Office at the outbreak of WW II, and it was supposed to have been returned to its original inhabitants at the end of the war. This never happened, and the former locals staged protests each year on the anniversary of the evacuation. Little of the former village now remained except sad shells of the manor house and more modest dwellings. New works abounded, but these were the functional concrete structures created for fighting and clearing drills. I rested with my section within what remained of the old manor one night when moonlight and shifting cloud sent shadows stealing along the walls. They suggested to me the former servants who likely had served just as silently, although such fanciful thoughts did not long delay sleep after an arduous day.

The social life remained quiet, although I visited Uxbridge on odd weekends. Eddie Martin and Mick Austin were representative of the friendships I had struck up during the QCS tour, and they were still serving with the unit, although now keen to move on. Uxbridge, since the opening of the M4 a few years earlier, was no great journey and I was now driving a '65 MG B. This had cost me £500 and the Third Party insurance, at £60, was exactly four times that which it cost to insure the Riley. The merest hint of sunshine was sufficient for me to drop the canopy, and as a result I ended a number of journeys quite frozen. Even with the top up, the MG was none too warm, since the heater was *kaput*. I also discovered, long after the dealer had pocketed my banknotes, that the engine burned almost as much oil as petrol.

We completed a night range at a late stage in the training and shortly after return to Colerne a Tannoy announcement recalled the squadron to the hangar. I missed the Tannoy, since I was under the shower at the time, but later learned that we had left the range without a comprehensive check of weapons. The result was an L42 Sniper's rifle left on the firing point, along with a night-vision sight and two hundred rounds of Green Spot (sniper's) ammunition. I held my breath until I learned that it was no fault of A Flight, but all of the SNCOs were wheeled into the CO's office the next morning for a gentle roasting. The CO was known to the Gunners as 'Derek the Weed' for his slim build, but he had served with the SAS in the Oman and was nobody's fool. He administered his rebuke in a soft voice and with dry wit, and the reprimand was felt all the more keenly for that.

We got some more descents in, again on Hankley Common but this time from C130s. On a night descent, my rigging lines were severely twisted and I was still kicking them out when I hit the ground. Fortunately, I did not suffer any injury, other than to pride. Bad exits were thought to contribute to twists, but they mostly appeared to be caused by slipstream. On another night descent, I landed in a deep pool of water and was soaked from head to foot. The two-hour coach journey back to Colerne was fairly wretched as a result.

I continued to visit Uxbridge, usually taking with me a coloured lad, Lee Lewis, who had recently served on QCS and was preserving a relationship with a WRAF. Lee appreciated the lifts, if not the absence of heating in the car. Upon arrival at both ends of the journey he often looked quite grey. A firm drinking companion by this time was Tom Jones, whose acquaintance I had made through a mutual friend. Tom had a wicked sense of humour but he was an entertaining character.

The training culminated with some helicopter work on Pumas from RAF Odiham, preparing us for tasking out of RAF Aldergrove, which operated Wessex Mk Vs. Time was short now and some of it had to be devoted to the packing of personal belongings into boxes. RAF Colerne would cease to function as an RAF station in our absence, and the new home would be at the Regiment Depot, Catterick. We viewed this uncertainly, but it was not an immediate concern. Late in March, we drove in a convoy to Liverpool to board the overnight LSL for Belfast.

We relieved No 51 Squadron, whose members quickly showed us the ropes, then I took my section directly to duties. We were equipped with
a pair of Series III Land Rovers that had a carapace of Macrolon sheeting. This was intended to absorb fragmentation from bomb attacks, but it also made the vehicles slow and unwieldy. We soon abandoned any pretensions that we might find ourselves in hot pursuit of anything except, possibly, a milk float. The hub recess of the spare wheel, which was bolted to the bonnet, had a dustbin lid strapped over it, thus adding to the general air of inelegance that the vehicles displayed. The function of the lid was to prevent grenades or other hand bombs lodging in the wheel cavity, although the risk of this in rural Antrim seemed rather less likely than in, say, West Belfast. Each Land Rover was frame-fitted with a C42 radio set; cumbersome equipment that required patience to tune it accurately, but it provided a reliable and vital rear-link to HQ and to neighbouring patrols.

Within the first duty of twenty-four hours duration, we also completed a brief foot patrol - to which we were deployed by helicopter - and a number of Vehicle Check Points. VCPs were a useful means of controlling traffic in the vicinity of the Aldergrove airport, which had been mortared a few weeks earlier. On standby between the tasking, we rested at a former married quarter on the far side of the airfield. This was known as 'Hector's House' – more piracy from Children's TV.

Support Weapons flight had been detached to RAF Bishops Court, a few miles distant, and the field flights were organised into two shifts to defend Aldergrove. This produced a day on, day off routine and each of the flights divided into four patrols for the day on duty. Two of these duties were vehicle-mounted patrols, but included foot patrols, whilst a third provided security duty at the civil airport and the fourth was on standby to augment the first three. No training was intended during the four months of the detachment.

A permanent VCP had been established on the approach road to the airport and we were required to man this occasionally. It had been allocated to units of the Ulster Defence Regiment, which was the only reservist unit operated by the British army to serve on active service, but it was not a popular duty and we found ourselves being called upon to fulfil it more and more frequently. It was not seen to be a dangerous duty, unless one actually could die of boredom.

Airport duties were also a bore, albeit a welcome occasional break from the wet, cold and windy duties which we got in no small measure on VCPs, foot patrols and the odd search of some area buildings
for arms caches. The airport lounge was no great ambush site, unless you were an autograph hunter, although I never noticed any great queue for the signature of the Reverend Ian Paisley, cleric, Orangeman and world-class bigot. He had recently been photographed at the funeral service at some victim of violence and the brass commemorative plate read: **MURDERED BY THE ROMAN CATHOLIC IRA**. It expressed the Ulster problem more succinctly than any politician or newspaper editorial ever did.

Whenever an aircraft movement took place, we were obliged to put a man or two out on the Pan for local defence, and if we were remiss in doing so for any reason, the pilots would often 'phone a direct complaint to the RAF Aldergrove station commander. We dismissed them as overpaid and windy bastards for this, but the cabin crews were good to us. When they cleared the aircraft, they would press upon us any unconsumed goodies, and they even had a whip round for a flight party we mentioned that we were holding.

New to the detachment, we made mistakes at all levels. The DSC and the flight commanders operated from the isolation of a command post that combined with the RAF Police and the Intelligence Cell. They provided both the routine tasking and short-notice demands, being of course in radio contact with each of the patrols. We were thus routinely despatched to carry out vehicle checks in pub car parks one Sunday, when it was obvious to all except the CP staff that pubs did not open in the Province on Sundays. County Antrim was staunchly Protestant and it seemed that a good vein of Puritanism ran through the creed. Less routinely, we were despatched as fast as our Macrolon shells would allow to investigate a series of explosions on the patch. We duly arrived at a quarry, which was being peacefully, if noisily, worked. My section was also sent to the scene of suspicious activity that led us to the fence of Muckamoor Abbey, now the home of the mentally disturbed. The numerous patients behind the wire were certainly acting oddly, but not suspiciously. These were CP errors, but we were not immune. I responded to gunshots during a Mobile Patrol and swiftly deployed my section into a loosely wooded area. The farmer who was potting rabbits nodded affably at us and went on his way.

    VCPs could be terrifying for quite different reasons. Late at night, and particularly during the weekend, we would stop a car and find that the driver was quite literally too drunk to stand up. We had no powers of arrest in such cases and it was not within our remit to summon the Royal Ulster Constabulary. Provided that the personnel and the vehicle excited no alarm from the police computer we radioed our information to, we had no option but to watch the car continue its erratic and dangerous journey.

    The enemy continued to be the Provisional Irish Republican Army, or PIRA, although their activities centred on Belfast or the border with Eire. Nor, however, did we discount the activities of the Loyalists' terrorist gangs, such as the Ulster Freedom Fighters or the Ulster Volunteer Force.[1] Their activities were the bloody equal of anything that PIRA could produce, although there was little evidence, other than the odd arms find, that they were active locally.

    The Sergeants' Mess at Aldergrove was predictably lively, with so many SNCOs, apart from our lot, undergoing unaccompanied tours of duty. At an early stage of the detachment, I was prevailed upon to accept a blind date, and was pleasantly surprised when Patti turned out to be a very attractive twenty-something. She spoke with

---

[1] Late in 1993, there seemed to be a fresh mood for peace in the Province, with new overtures by Sinn Fein politicians and talks with Ulster leaders, but almost immediately the talks seemed doomed by fresh outbreaks of violence on both sides, although predominantly by Loyalist gangs. The English Prime Minister repeatedly condemned the PIRA violence without reference to the UFF or UVF, and I wrote to him to enquire if his reluctance to condemn Loyalist violence owed anything to his slender majority in the House of Commons. After all, the recent Maastrict Bill had needed the Ulster vote to get it passed. Mr Major passed my letter to the Northern Ireland Office, which produced a predictably anodyne reply.

a marked American accent, having an American father and an Irish mother. Patti had lived in the States for a number of years and was now living in Belfast. We sat over a quiet drink in the Mess and she agreed to visit the camp again on the following weekend. I wasn't sure how the relationship might proceed, in view of the considerable constraints we were subject to, but I wanted to see her again.

The action continued to be anywhere but at Aldergrove and although we were frequently warned against complacency, it was fairly obvious to us that this would be a quiet detachment. Every once in a while I had to relieve Tony in the CP and the boredom level there was even greater, although the intelligence reports which arrived late in the evenings made interesting reading. One of them reported that a severed penis had been found on waste ground in the city, although it was never clarified whether or not this was sectarian or domestic violence.

The CP also featured a large-scale map of Belfast, with its areas boldly coloured in green or orange to reflect the religious divide. This was the tribal map and it perfectly expressed, for me anyway, the problem. There are still those around us who write learned leaders in respected newspapers, arguing that the problem in Ulster has nothing to do with religion. Doubtless there are still plenty of Snake Oil salesmen around, too.

The relationship with Patti progressed to intimacy and she invited me to her parents' home, which was in a quiet suburb and adjacent to the Stormont Parliament. Stormont had been prorogued in 1972 and seemed unlikely to open. Patti's parents were currently in Tehran, where her father, an engineer with Lockheed, worked on defence contracts. The house was large, comfortable and a pleasant break from a crowded Mess. Slightly less comfortably, I was breaking the walking out rules, and I was duly reported by an RAF Policeman one morning when we returned to Aldergrove. I avoided disciplinary action, but had to operate a bit covertly thereafter, being dropped and picked up by one of the mobile patrols at a predesignated RV. Life seemed good.

I had been in consistently high spirits since the detachment had begun, and not least since I had a good section that worked very well together. Leadership, even at such a modest level, had its own rewards and I genuinely looked forward to each duty, although some of them contained a fair bit of boredom. The Mobiles were occasionally enlivened by escort duties between the station and the

Belfast docks, and we also carried out ammunition runs. One such sent us to Dundrum Bay, which I happened to know something about. Brunel's *Great Britain* had been aground there for some months in the nineteenth century.

In May, I went on three days of R&R to the UK, choosing to stay at RAF Uxbridge. As it happened, QCS were doing a tattoo at Tidworth so I had a fairly quiet time. I visited the city museums and the *Cutty Sark* at Greenwich. Three days evaporated and I went into the CP for three days whilst Tony took his R&R. Summer broke early upon us and the sun was welcome, if it made the flak jackets uncomfortably warm. The cold, night mobiles were not missed at all.

June arrived and with it the end of the tour. We escorted No 15 Squadron from the LSL and I had the opportunity of a brief chat with Ray Hughes, not seen since the QCS tour. The same LSL took my group home, and we were bound for Colerne to collect private vehicles. Leave, and what remained of summer, beckoned.

Suspicious activity had been reported at Muckamoor

18

The MG used no more than half a gallon of oil on the journey North, and I arrived to find the Depot a busy place. Since the inhabitants included the Fire School, the RAF Regiment Band and three other squadrons, at a time when there had been no major rebuilding since the Twenties, RAF Catterick was actually quite crowded. The other squadrons were Nos 37, 58 and 66 and were, respectively, formed as Bofors, Field and Tigercat missile units. The Tigercat system was obsolescent and about to be replaced by the Rapier missile system which would equip half a dozen squadrons. A long period of isolation for II Squadron, in an era when Regiment squadrons had been grouped in pairs or multiples at home and abroad, was ending and we had the uncomfortable feeling that this was not entirely to the good. We had long been aware that II was not unequivocally admired by the rest of the Corps, and that at least some of the resentment stemmed from pre-para, which eliminated some seven out of ten applicants for the unit. The lost distinction of the blue belt had perhaps seemed to be elitism flaunted, and even the styling of the squadron number in Roman numerals, rather than Arabic, had its detractors.

We now learned that the Depot Commandant was prepared to be none too impressed with our distinctions, and he made an early start by prohibiting the wearing of parachute smocks about the station. This was especially irritating since he affected one himself, apparently without qualification to wear it. The antipathy was stoked up a few degrees when the squadron assembled for a run out of the camp, and the CO's 'phone rang with a rebuke from the Commandant. He wanted to know why we were not uniformly dressed in standard PT kit, rather than a selection of sweat tops or tracksuit tops. Some of us wondered why he did not see fit to congratulate the squadron on the physical example it was setting for the remainder of the squadrons, instead. There was also a great willingness to blame the squadron for all the fights in the NAAFI and problems in the village. Some were justified and the landlord at the Oak banned II for a while, although the landlord at the Angel made us welcome and his tills rang accordingly.

We settled to training and I added inventory holding to my responsibilities by acquiring that of Gillan Block, where the squadron's single Gunners lived. Whilst any inventory was bad news and an incursion into free time, a barrack block was particularly bad news, and a barrack block full of Rocks was a nightmare. Inventory holders were advised to maintain monthly checks, but mine could have been dismantled in a week, and I learned to keep a close eye on it. Appliances such as radios and TVs had to be monitored since there now appeared to be a worldwide shortage of electrical plugs, as I discovered when I found such appliances connected to outlet sockets with bare wires held in place by matchsticks. Some appliances also tended to come through the windows from time to time, shortly preceded or followed by owners who had upset other occupants with late-night musical choices. I did not have a problem with this, provided that they first opened the window. Window replacement was expensive.

Within days of acquiring the inventory, a Gunner complained to me that there were no plugs in the sinks, and I duly entered a work service for rectification of the problem. This was speedily expedited, and just as speedily I received a bill for £27. Outraged, I protested this to the Accounts Flight, who blandly pointed out that plugs were an inventory item and that I should have made a more careful check before signing the acceptance. I did some swift homework, then levied a collective charge on the occupants that ran at a couple of shillings per man. Most paid this without protest but the Gunner who refused to pay was the one who had played endless 'spittoon' music in the Oman. He paid up when I threatened to throw *him* out of the window. I next went around the block and removed all of the plugs, storing them in my room. I got an old innertube from the MT yard and directed a Light Duties' Gunner to cut it into two-inch diameter circles of rubber which I then issued to each of the Gunners as their personal 'plug'. The real thing stayed in my room until I handed over the inventory a couple of years later.

The squadron went on block leave and I spent a week of it at Uxbridge, drinking with Eddie and Tom and eating corrosive vindaloo curries in the high street. We also attended a bizarre party at Notting Hill Gate, where the sacrifice of a live chicken appeared to be on the agenda. We were not actually invited to remain for the performance, and nor had we much desire to. For the second week of the leave, Patti flew over from Belfast on the Shuttle and we had a week in London. It was ruinously expensive and when Patti flew home I had just about enough in my wallet to fund the oil for the drive up the A1.

A parachuting programme opened and we completed some C130 descents onto Hankley Common by day and by night. The summer was glorious and it would be among the best for the century. We had no para cancellations for weather reasons and even the Hercs seemed to be holding up. It was disappointing to complete ground training and draw and fit 'chutes, only to be told that the aircraft had gone U\S. The back of a 4 Tonner made a poor substitute.

The flight commander led us out on a twelve miles run on a particularly hot day, and by the time we had turned towards camp but were still some miles short of it, it became apparent that we had some incipient heat exhaustion. The flight commander halted the flight in the shade and turned to me. "Run on ahead, Sgt Foxley, and bring out a 4 Tonner." Sgt Foxley ran instead to the nearest 'phone box and summoned the 4 Tonner. Sergeants were paid to think.

I was despatched to the School of Infantry, Warminster to undergo qualification as a GPMG SF instructor. This held no terrors since repeated detachments in the Oman had developed slick handling and firing drills, and we had routinely learned to strip the feed pawl and trigger mechanisms in pursuit of elusive sand. I set my mind upon a skilled pass and upon arrival I looked for a tests' partner who also was adept with drills. I duly found one, a Coldstream Guardsman, and he became additionally a lively drinking companion in the Mess. Also in the Mess, I encountered a WO2 of the Australian infantry who was doing an exchange tour. We had a pint and I learned that he had served with Arch a few years earlier.

A lot of time was devoted to ranges, but not much of it to firing on one particular day. I had quickly mounted and loaded my gun and had decided to check my range estimation, by firing at a distinctive yellow patch about a thousand metres forward of the gun line. As I pressed the trigger, I heard some DS saying "…….and *don't* fire at the yellow patch." The yellow patch now proved to be tinder-dry grass that ignited with my first tracers. These were the first and the last rounds fired that day, which we spent the remainder of fighting a huge grass fire. Another hardship was in each of us having to carry off the hill some three hundred pounds of ammunition it had been intended to fire from the weapons. When we returned to Warminster, there was no great rush at the bar to buy me a pint.

The mid-course weekend was free and I felt no great need to sit in my room swotting. I visited Stonehenge and the *Great Britain*, both crawling with tourists. When the course ended, we dispersed and at Catterick I drove directly to the married quarter occupied by my flight commander for Orders. We were to deploy the following day to the Otterburn Training Area, in Cumbria. The thrust of the exercise was live-firing on a number of close-quarter battle ranges, with minor exercises at flight level interposed. We received Orders on the final night for a Navex which would cover sixteen miles and had to be completed, at section level, between last light and first light, which gave us about six hours. The distance was not great but we faced climbs up to sixteen hundred feet, and the navigation proved a matter of sticking closely to the compass. I pushed my section hard, with few stops, and we made the deadline comfortably ahead of time. So did all of A Flight and it was a matter of some satisfaction to us that other flights had Gunners out on the ground until midday. A Flight appeared to be retrieving its reputation and there was satisfaction in that.

When another opportunity for leave arose, I applied for permission to visit Belfast. This was rejected, but I went anyway, describing myself on arrival forms as an employee of Rolls-Royce at Crewe. Patti's folks were home on leave from Iran and were welcoming. Patti and I filled the days with trips to Bangor, Strangford Loch and the Ulster Folk Museum. It was a pleasant week and I looked forward to renewing regular meetings with Patti during the detachment which by now was growing near.

The squadron was warned for a Harrier defence exercise in Germany and we trained to its specific requirements. When the syllabus ran out with a day or two to fill, I suggested to the flight commander that we teach the newer blokes on the flight how to make life comfortable in the field with **A** frame bashas and suspended beds. He agreed to this and we worked in a wooded area on the far side of the airfield. On the eve of departure, I went early to a bar session in the Mess and I left it late. It was not until we had deployed to the exercise area, where we would live in the field for twelve days, that I discovered my neglect to bring either my basha or my sleeping bag. I then went frantically about the Harrier site to see what I might improvise, helping myself to a canvas tilt off a Land Rover trailer that had been left unattended, and creating a bed from a pile of evilly-smelling sandbags. I augmented this arrangement with some scraps of polythene which were blowing about a neighbouring field, and soon had constructed something which might have been transplanted from downtown Soweto. It proved both dry and warm, but it drew a lot of curious glances from the Gunners of A Flight, who doubtless wondered what the fuck I was trying to prove.

When the Harriers arrived, we were given a cordial welcome by the wing commander whose unit flew them. This cordiality swiftly withered when one of our more enterprising sergeants, now in charge of the 'enemy', persuaded a German armoured unit to crash into the site. The wing commander, who doubtless pictured his Harriers being reduced to the recyclable value of beer cans, was enraged and told *all* of us to get off his site. You just couldn't please some people.

When the exercise ended, we remained in the woods for a night before returning to RAF Wildenrath, and took the opportunity of a visit to a local pub. This was a chance to practise my Gan German, but although *"Ein grosse bier, Bitte."* worked very well, my attempts at conversation with the locals drew little more than mystified looks. Someone offered us a lift back to the site and about a dozen of us clung to the outside of a Land Rover, whose driver seemed then determined to wipe us off against trees when we drove down a lengthy fire break in the woods. I felt considerably more sober when we arrived.

Fighting erupted at the Wildenrath NAAFI on the eve of return to UK, and I learned of this at the Guardroom when I returned from a drink in the local village. When I further learned that twelve of the squadron Gunners had been locked up, but no RAF or army who also had been involved, I called out the Orderly Officer to point out to him how strange this was. He seemed to consider my attitude impertinent. Charges followed us to Catterick and courts martial were convened, but all except one of the charges were thrown out. A considerable waste of the taxpayers' money.

We sailed overnight from Zeebrugge and I had dinner with Mick Tobin, who was the SNCO Fitter on the squadron and a man who had made more parachute descents during repeat tours than most of the Gunners. We got chatting with the table steward who invited us down to the crew's bar later in the evening. We accepted this, having first had a few drinks with the lads in the passengers' bar, and we tried not to appear dismayed to be met by 'Wendy', now wearing makeup and a pretty dress.

Met by 'Wendy', now wearing a pretty dress

19

The days remaining before the Aldergrove detachment that would take us through Xmas were swiftly running down. The training load lightened a little and I squeezed in some leave, meeting Patti at Newcastle airport and taking her to a rented 'castle' near Brough. We did some walking and also visited the Saul family at Asby. The village, farm and pub seemed utterly unchanged since I had first visited in '69, and I doubt if they have to this day.

A ballooning programme put a few more descents our way and we jumped on the Depot airfield, whose only other use was to receive aircraft condemned to the fire school. I managed to complete four descents before being dragged off to solve some minor crisis somewhere. A personal crisis was the MG, which now threw a piston, and I traded it in with £1300 to buy a Datsun 100A. This was of recent make and provided reliable motoring, although it sounded as if it ran on a boot full of torch batteries.

To fill some time, I was instructed to produce a fourteen-day cadre for half a dozen SF students. This I was happy to do, although there was no application for the skills in the Province. The Province was something we all heartily looked forward to by now, since the Commandant's poor opinion of us appeared not to have changed. At least in Ulster we *expected* to be sniped at. I vented my frustration by repeated runs about the airfield, laden with kit, and also by firing off the odd letter to the RAF News on the subjects of dress, deportment and discipline. I was by now forming the view that these were in sad decline in the RAF, and that the RAF Regiment was only just hanging on to such standards.

I varied my runs at four, eight or ten miles and I also sent on them those Gunners in my flight who committed some transgression or other. The Form 252, for charges, I did not resort to again, and nor was there any requirement for it. A Flight was doing all right and seemed secure in the knowledge that its effort was recognised. The squadron had a new Warrant and the CO was soon to change. Life went on.

The final exercises prior to the December deployment centred on the Stanford Training Area, in Norfolk, and made cold comfort. We were to have parachuted in and I had drawn a Number One stick position. I was standing in the door when the drop was aborted, because of inability to see the DZ, and we transferred to the inevitable 4 Tonners for the move in. During the exercise I had to visit an RAF hospital in the area for an audiometric test, which revealed that I had a degree of hearing loss. This was worrying, although my revised medical category did not affect Regiment employment for the present. At the hospital, I ran across the Gan medic who had accompanied the survival course at Kota Tinggi.

The exercise included the final scores for the inter-squadron competition for best section and flight, and it was gratifying that A Flight took it and that my section, on a narrow spread of points, won the section trophy. It was a good note to open the new detachment on. Before we went to Aldergrove, I took a team of runners to Bedfordshire to compete in the RAF Henlow 'Ten' - which was a ten-mile road race from the airship hangars at Cardington (built for the R100 and the ill-fated R101) back to Henlow. I was nowhere in the prizes, being beaten by a hundred and eighty-nine other runners, but I ran the distance in sixty-three minutes, which I thought fair. Among the runners was Pete Moralee, now serving at Henlow, and Phil Mutton, Gan running mate.

I had been intended to fly out to Aldergrove with the advance party, but fog scrubbed the flight and I joined the road and LSL move instead. We again relieved No 51 Squadron and our first task was to escort it to the docks. We then swiftly settled to routine, examining what changes had been implemented in the six months since we had left. Little *had* changed, but the less welcome included much longer stints on the Delta checkpoint that controlled access to the civil airport. We now appeared to have the lion's share of this duty, with the UDR appearing only for a late-night duty of about two hour's duration. Sometimes they did not appear at all, and although the task was necessary it had the feel of Securicor.

Intelligence gathering at section level was another unwelcome development, since this consisted of touring our area of responsibility - about seventy square kilometres - and knocking on doors to ask questions of the occupants. Some genius in the Int. Cell had dreamed up the questionnaire pro-forma, and we soon learned that householders did not much care to be quizzed on their religion by flak-jacketed, armed strangers on their doorsteps. On my own initiative, I took to leaving my flak jacket and rifle in the Land Rover, under the watchful eye of the Signaller, but the questionnaire remained greatly unpopular. On a lighter note, our patch included a long stretch of road known as 'Seven Mile Straight', which ran from Muckamoor to the southeast. A fish and chip van was usually parked on the 'Straight' and it was thought to be a cover for PIRA surveillance. The radio code, when referring to the van, was 'Codpiece'. Someone in the Int. Cell had wit at least.

Since the mortar attack on the airport a year previously, no further attacks had been attempted, but some other genius decided to seal off all of the alternative approach roads. This was quietly planned and executed overnight, when low-loaders and cranes appeared and blocked each of the roads with huge blocks of concrete. It was only then realised that a fair bit of local traffic was sealed in and that there might be a few problems for householders living within the 'quarantined' area. My section was given the job of interviewing these and we encountered even more belligerence than the 'house checks' had produced, and for good reasons. The hardship cases ranged from the farmer, who now had to licence for road use agricultural tractors driving several miles to fields he could see from his window, to the blind, elderly woman who now had to be driven some miles to the church which was only a few hundred yards from her cottage. A suggestion was made to me that lockable barriers be installed, and locals provided with keys, and I quickly passed this on. There was some resistance at higher authority, because of fears of coerced locals and proxy bombs, but the idea eventually was implemented. The interviews took some time and I produced a report that ran to about three thousand words. Some months later, whilst preparing for new duties, I was given relevant files to read and the style of one enclosure caught my eye. It was my report, appearing over the signature of some squadron leader of the admin branch.

It was good to resume regular contact with Patti, and even better that the walking out rules had been relaxed, allowing me to visit her home quite openly. I had even begun to form the view that our relationship might be heading for some permanence, but there were strains. The day on duty was a very long day indeed, and when I was off I was ready for little else except sleep, although I was trying to preserve a fitness schedule. Patti's folks were home again and I visited for Xmas, but at about the thirty-four hours without sleep point I was not the world's most scintillating conversationalist.

The fitness training was essential, for I had been nominated for the Parachute Regiment Battle School, usually referred to as Senior Brecon, in March. This was of two month's duration and it was known to be a tough course. Fitness training elsewhere on the squadron resulted in eight successes against the Black Watch in a novice boxing tourney. This was fortunately without the attendant mayhem of the China Fleet Club somewhat earlier.

We wore out the days with the familiar routines of Mobiles, VCPs, Foot Patrols, Helicopter Patrols and less frequent duties such as Escorts, and we again learned to dread the dead hours of the night on Delta Checkpoint. But another spring and summer was fast approaching by the time we handed the detachment over to No 15 Squadron. It was time to find if our fortunes at Catterick had improved. No one was taking bets.

20

I had spent a final night with Patti and left Belfast the following day. A day later I was back at the Depot and among the faces at the Angel was Eddie Martin, now posted to a Depot squadron and just returned from a detachment in Central America. The former British Honduras, now independent as Belize but under territorial threat from its neighbour Guatemala, was still being defended by Britain and this formed a detachment for squadrons which did not share the Ulster roulement. The Angel had rapidly become the focal point for drinking off camp, but I had little opportunity for it on this occasion. Within days I had loaded the Datsun and set off for Brecon and the course.

The arrival day was Friday, rather than the more usual Wednesday, and it briefly raised hopes in me that I might arrive to a relaxed weekend before the course opened. This proved fatuous and upon arrival I was instead ordered to double down to the 25 Metre range to check-zero my rifle, then be ready for Orders at 1530hrs. Since at this point I had not been issued with bedding, nor even allocated to a room, the pace looked ominous indeed. Between the range and Orders, I gleaned the information that the course, some sixty strong, was to undergo a weekend exercise that would determine our tactical leadership ability. So it proved, although we first were put to lead-in tests which examined our ability on section weapons, mapcraft and the A41 Radio, which was the principal tool of communication at section level in the RAF Regiment, although the army also used a smaller set, the A40.

We eventually deployed and if some of us wondered why we had not included sleeping bags in our kit, the reason was manifested by virtually incessant activity from the moment we arrived on the Sennybridge Training Area, to the moment we left it, two days later.

The course was quickly organised into two platoons and further subdivided into sections, and, in a scenario which recollected the promotion courses, we rotated through command appointments in a variety of minor tactical situations

I coped with the appointments but felt increasingly ragged by fatigue as we approached the exercise completion. I was particularly stretched by a road run we were put to, unfortunately being the custodian of twenty-eight pounds of GPMG by then and finding no takers to share it, and just as we shook out to clear a piece of ground I went down in a heap. I was mortified by this, and the curt instruction to get in the back of a Land Rover, and my morale plummeted when I later had to line up on the verandah outside the Commandant's office with half a dozen other students whose performance had invited scorn. The Commandant's advice was succinct: "Get fit." was all he had to say and I resolved to. I had eight weeks to achieve it, although I doubtless had other things to do in the period.

The students represented virtually every infantry regiment in the British army, although the course had once been reserved exclusively for members of the Parachute Regiment. I was the only member of the RAF Regiment (and the first from the Corps in five years), and my presence excited some curiosity among my fellow students, who seemed incredulous at my presence. During the infrequent breaks, when we chatted among ourselves,"What the fuck did you volunteer for?" was the most frequent question put to me, although I had not exactly volunteered. Most of the students, I learned, were actually only corporals in the acting rank of sergeant, and they needed the course qualification for substantive promotion. Moreover, some regiments insisted upon a high grading for such promotions. There would be much discussion, over tea or pints, of the feared **D** grading, the desired **C**, the elusive **B** or the impossible **A**.

Training began in earnest and each day we deployed to the training area to exercise at section or platoon level. Each of the eight weeks of the course had a slightly different focus, to include patrolling, defence, counterinsurgency, internal security and fighting in built-up areas. The programme stretched ahead and there appeared to be few gaps in it that I might exploit with some fitness training.

I enjoyed few advantages over the rest of the course, but among them were NBC and GPMG SF. I was especially surprised by the generally poor level of NBC knowledge among the students, and the fact that on the course it seemed almost to be regarded as a separate subject, rather than, in my own experience, as contiguous with more conventional tradecraft. SF also seemed generally unknown, although in later years, and notably after the Falklands War, the SF role was the means of virtually reinventing machine gun platoons in army units. Ironically, the RAF Regiment largely abandoned the weapon at much the same time.

Among our issues for the course (saying nothing about a pile of training pamphlets and a pile of amendments for them) had been neatly packaged bags of sand. Our Complete Equipment Fighting Order had to weigh no less than forty-five pounds at any time and was subject to random checks. At the end of any of numerous days in the first three weeks, when we had devoted virtually all of the day to dashing, diving and crawling into cover in umpteen section attacks, I thought that I could feel the weight of every single grain. The long days were followed by incredibly short nights and I did not spend much of them in the bar. The drinking was best left to hardier souls.

We did the first of the battle fitness tests within a few days of arrival, and I was heartened when I finished in the first twelve. My CEFO was then check-weighed by Captain Chibnall, a Royal Marine instructor, and discovered to be a pound under the mandatory forty-five. For this breach, I was subjected to a withering blast, addressed then and from that time on as 'Biggles' and made to run the course again immediately. I was less than heartened to arrive first on the rerun.

The month which was supposed to go out like a lamb came roaring back at us like a lion instead, and even much of April was marked by torrential rain and bitterly cold winds. We were so often soaked that our boots tended to dry out white, all the black dye having been bleached out of them. Prior to leaving Catterick, I had been issued with a pair of high boots as part of a squadron field trial, but I was not permitted to wear these at Brecon. Similarly, those students who had equipped themselves with wet weather and cold weather kit from specialist suppliers were forbidden to wear it. Service issues, useful or otherwise, was the inflexible rule.

The squad I joined for classes at Brecon, and which became a section for the fieldwork, included a mix of regiments: The Duke of Edinburgh's Royal Regiment, the Queen's Own Highlanders, the Green Howards, the Parachute Regiment and a man from 22 SAS who did not appear in the course photograph. Another was from the Irish

Guards and he became a particular friend. I had not expected to know anyone on the course but in another squad was the Coldstream Guardsman who had been my SF partner on the SF instructor's course. There were several guardsmen on the course and, cap badges apart, they were instantly recognisable. To a man, their DPM clothing, which was only intended for field wear, featured sewn pleats in the jackets and sewn creases in the trousers. Our squad instructor was a staff sergeant of the Parachute Regiment, which Corps appeared to find most of the instructors.

The RSM also wore the maroon beret and on one of the rare parades he singled me out and ordered me to get rid of the handlebar moustache. I stoutly claimed that handlebar moustaches were traditional in my Corps, then walked in terror for some weeks, fearing that he might check the veracity of my claim, which of course was bogus. The RSM was much feared by all of the students, and not a few of the instructors, and he was best avoided, if this proved not always possible. Our weekends were nominally free, but the homework and lesson preparation load precluded much other than work in the hootchie. We had to write a complete exercise during one of the weekends and it was reckoned that this alone might absorb some sixteen hours. I had determined to complete mine on the Saturday and at about 2200hrs I thought that I might reward myself with a pint in the Mess. I made it through the door and about three yards beyond it when a screech from the RSM halted me in mid-stride. "Get out of my Mess," He ordered, "you've been drinking in the town and now you want to drink after hours in the Mess." This happened to be untrue, but I was soon persuaded that argument was futile. Even unluckier were two students who *did* return from town, bringing with them two women they had met. **"GET THOSE WHORES OUT OF MY MESS!"** roared the RSM. The RSM may not always have been right, but he was always the RSM.

Students were at least allowed to use the Mess, although its dining room remained out of bounds to us. We dined instead in a separate wing of the Other Ranks facility, which was no great hardship. We were more concerned with the quality and quantity of the food, rather than ambience, and it actually was quite good on both counts. Slightly less pleasing were the 'bag rats' (sandwiches) which accompanied us every single day onto the training area. Every single day also, the sandwiches were filled with processed cheese. There was a complaints and suggestions book in the dining hall, and at some point one of the guardsmen on the course offered a bold suggestion: 'How about,' He wrote, 'less fucking cheese in the fucking sarnies?' And that was precisely what we got: less fucking cheese.

Our accommodation was in wooden huts that dated from WW II and possibly earlier. These were poorly lit and under-heated, although welcome enough as we dragged ourselves in, again soaking wet and utterly pissed off, from another gruelling session on the area. I made a point of spending at least some time each night reading up on the work which would feature the next day, but sleep was not resisted for long.

Other nights were not marked by sleep at all, as we underwent night patrols or defence exercises. Spring seemed unconscionably late in arriving, whilst the total immersion in some river for a tactical crossing at midnight convinced us that this exercise had been deliberately sprung on a cold night. We were some two hours about it and the discomfort was only slightly relieved by the humour of audible intakes of breath, as sixty pairs of testicles met with freezing water. This activity, in common with most night activities, ended at about 0200hrs, with weapon cleaning and kit cleaning to precede bed back at Dering Lines. My appointment for the crossing had been that of platoon sergeant, and it had produced no insuperable problems. At some quiet point of the process I had reflected upon the occasion of my last river crossing, and being half-drowned and bombarded with elephant shit seemed marginally preferable.

Less arduous, although no easier, was a session where we fired the GPMGs from pintle mounts at model aircraft controlled by radio. This was to exercise the role of the weapon against live aircraft, notionally as that might be, but our successes were very few. Each encounter usually ended with the operator making his unscathed model perform victory rolls, although I tried to bring one down by firing a fifty-round burst, succeeding only in enraging the instructor who was rightly concerned about likelier damage to the GPMG barrel.

At a mid-course interview, I was informed by my great friend, Captain Chibnall, that my performance to date was well below average and that I should get a grip. This might have been discouraging, until I compared notes with the rest of the squad. No one, it seemed, was doing well. I at least felt good about the runs by now, for I was consistently finishing in the first ten, if not better, whereas a good number of students seemed not to be improving at all.

Apart from reserving some time each Saturday and Sunday to

read the *Guardian* and the *Observer*, I did not get about much and the Datsun mostly remained on the car park. I made one tour through the quiet valleys one Sunday and found myself passing through the tragic village of Aberfan, where a collapsing slag heap in the Sixties took a school in its path and many young lives with it. The recollection put my trivial problems entirely into perspective.

The odd trip for a pint at the Sarah Siddons in Brecon could not always be resisted, but I was reluctant to form a habit of it. In contrast, the Jock student in my squad contrived to spend *all* of his time at the Siddons, where the attractions included lots of camp followers. He apparently managed this by doing without sleep entirely, save for the lengthy periods we spent in the back of a 4 Tonner *en route* to the area and return.

Warminster provided a welcome break, although I was completely unfamiliar with the techniques employed by mechanised infantry, which was the reason for our visit. The opportunity to drive an armoured personnel carrier arose, and I thought that a joy, bucketing about the range areas. My section, which had been bouncing about in the back, was less enthusiastic about my driving. The AFV 432 was a lightly armoured vehicle that was designed to deliver a section's worth of infantry to the point of battle, and they were surprisingly nimble. Elsewhere, we learned how to direct artillery fire on a simulator, which was interesting, then did the real thing with live-firing 105mm howitzers, which was about a hundred times better.

We deployed to an APC-oriented exercise and at some point I was posted as the perimeter sentry. The 'platoon sergeant' had provided me with a length of communication cord that connected my position with platoon HQ, and he insisted that I wind it around my wrist. The cord actually was D10 signals' cable, which combined copper and steel wires, and its strength was put to an unusual test when one of the APCs was crashed out of the site in response to some threat, dragging the cable, and me with it. The sight of the perimeter sentry, now vanishing at high speed and apparently in hot pursuit of the roaring APC, provoked a good bit of mirth elsewhere, but it was alarming from my perspective. Fortunately, the APC tracks soon shredded the D10 and I slithered to a halt, even wetter, muddier and more pissed off than usual.

We recovered to Dering Lines at Brecon then embarked upon a three-day counterinsurgency exercise. This included digging in and it was my misfortune to be paired with the course idiot. At some moment of low morale, I actively considered laying him out with the entrenching tool, which I otherwise used to dig to depth the entire trench. The appointments changed at daybreak and I was switched to another trench that to no great surprise of mine was only half dug. At this point, I considered laying *myself* out with the entrenching tool. I progressed through the appointments to platoon sergeant and in the early evening I became the platoon commander. We had been without sleep for about thirty-six hours by then, and I reckoned that my principal job, short of emergencies, was simply to keep the platoon on the ball and progressing the defences. Late in the evening, I was ordered to prepare for a withdrawal under fire and I reckoned that my final grade would likely be decided on this one. I wrote my Orders, issued them to the section commanders and we were pulled out at 0200hrs. Subsequent to the withdrawal, I received my new appointment - platoon runner.

We returned to Brecon and the weekend off was largely consumed by the writing of another exercise. By this time I had discovered that some of the students had brought their exercises with them, purchased from the students of earlier courses. I thought that Jock might be among them, but he clearly could not afford such purchases, given the scale of his drinking. He now appeared to forgo sleep entirely, and wrote his exercise in the back of the bouncing 4 Tonner.

We began another three-day exercise and when it concluded we were dropped at the foot of Pen-y-Fan, a granite feature that stretched vertiginously upwards. This was the venue for Exercise *Fan Dance*, and it consisted simply of climbing its three thousand feet in the shortest possible time without the tactical considerations which had characterised every other activity we had contemplated during the preceding weeks.. I clung to the heels of the squad instructor and was the first of the section to the summit, only to be told to go back down and encourage the others. I felt, however, that I had redeemed the failure of the first weekend. When all of the students were in, we were told to retrace our steps to the 4 Tonner and I made a point of running back down, leaving as many students behind me as I could.

The final exercise began with twenty-four hour's worth of internal security, during which we were repeatedly soaked with fire hoses then 'stoned' by a mob of Parachute Regiment lads drafted in for the occasion, and who clearly took inordinate delight in the opportunity to abuse and batter senior NCOs. We then moved into a forestry block and operated for two days in counter-revolutionary warfare. At night, the canopy of the trees rendered the light to virtually nothing and we were greatly dependent upon comms cords for navigation to and from the fire trenches and our bivvie positions. Going in search of my sentry relief after two frozen hours on the gun, I stumbled and the cord broke, leaving me to fumble around in the dark. Having spoked both of my eyes on pine branches in short order, I dropped to my hands and knees and began to search for the broken cord. Minutes later, I grabbed a human hand and this proved to belong to another lost sentry. We compared ideas on location and eventually went separate ways, mine taking me to the relieving sentry's position two hours later. I never did catch up that particular sleep.

When we returned to Brecon, we were given two hours to clean the encrusted mud from our kit, clean personal and section weapons, shave and then ordered to return our bedding. We were dog tired but there was no question of remaining in the lines overnight, since another course was due in at midday, although they seemed unlikely to occupy our beds at all quickly.. They began to arrive as we dispersed and we had no sympathy for any of them. Prior to dispersal, we were told what our grades were. Mine was a **B** and I prize it to this day.

21

Having left Dering Lines and stopped briefly for a kip in some layby, I made the relatively short journey to Crewe and stayed overnight with Aunt Bess. On Saturday, which also was my birthday, I met Patti at Manchester airport and we motored up to Yorkshire. I paused at the Catterick Guardroom to hand in my rifle, which had been stored somewhat less than securely since leaving Brecon, then we travelled the couple of miles to the Scotch Corner Hotel. Two nights' stay there was alarmingly expensive, but I balanced it against the recent memory of three hours laying in an ambush position and shivering like a dog crapping nuts and bolts. We then drove to Heathrow Airport, where Patti caught the Belfast shuttle and I boarded a Malaysian Airlines 707 for the flight to Australia, having again negotiated a lengthy period of leave.

The flight was via Kuwait and Kuala Lumpur and at the latter I was obliged to hold for twenty-four hours under the conditions of the ticket. The hotel was free but the evening meal cost me the equivalent of a week's wages, and left me thinking that I should have gone instead in search of a street Makan stall. The final leg put me into Perth at 0330hrs and I again fished a uniform of sorts out of my bag and hitchhiked home. It was autumn, edging into winter, but there was still a very welcome warmth in the days. I loafed about home for a few days then renewed my chest X-ray certificate with a view to employment on the mine for a month.

The nickel boom was over and jobs had actually become fairly scarce. The Old Man had ceased work by now, and simply because he felt that he should not be in work when youngsters were out of it. He appeared to have lost none of his fitness, though, and his capacity for drink was little diminished, however much he might claim that 'he could no longer put it away as he used to.'

For the first time, the job raised questions about my legitimate claim to work, since as a holder of a British passport, and despite Australian citizenship, I now required a work permit which I had not applied for. Since the work was for a month only, I simply described myself on the job application as a recently discharged member of the Australian forces, and that appeared to satisfy bureaucracy. The Old Man's mate secured a job for me on the Kambalda mine and I began a round of tasks which earned me a net wage of $40 a day. Not for the first time, I wondered why I persisted in serving for a fraction of that.

I mostly worked with a gang of Timbermen, occasionally finding myself 'babysitting' for miners who were working in bad ground. My job, if the roof caved in, was to extricate the miner or, failing that, run for help. It was never explained to me what happened if the roof fell in on both of us, and some questions were best left unasked. I had a daily lift between Boulder and Kambalda, having just the mile walk to and from the town each day. It provided useful time to reflect upon changes, not all of which seemed necessarily for the better. The tables in the bookshop which I had scoured for stories by WE Johns now groaned with pornography, and it was difficult to accept that this represented a worthwhile advance from the 'wowserism' of the Fifties and earlier. (Also somewhat later: when I had returned from Singapore in '63, Ian Fleming's *The Spy Who Loved Me* was confiscated from me at Mascot.) Boulder had changed and so, irrevocably, had I. It was apparent to me now that Boulder was no longer my home, although I reserved for the town some measure of affection. I could not claim it as my own, and doubtless it would have no cause to claim me, but we rubbed along somehow.

In my final week at home I found myself having long chats with the Old Man, noting in my diary at the time that I was glad to have had this opportunity. There was, I think, no prescience in this, but I must have recognised that such opportunities were receding. The Old Man was pushing seventy by now.

We took the 'Rattler' to Perth together, staying with Jan and Arch in a new home at Duncraig, among the new suburbs of the city. We had a quiet couple of days before Arch drove me to the airport, and the Old Man accompanied us. I never saw him again.

From Heathrow I went briefly to Uxbridge to look up Tom Jones, then I 'phoned Patti to confirm my visit to Belfast. We had arranged this prior to my trip home and I had reserved the last week of my leave for it. To my dismay, Patti now vetoed the trip and it became apparent that strains had entered our relationship. I returned to Catterick, devoted some time to runs on the airfield and prepared for a return to squadron duties after an absence of four months. The next detachment to Ulster was by now none too distant and I welcomed it.

The new CO had arrived in my protracted absence, and we also had a new Warrant, who was non-para for the first time since the parachute role was bestowed. The squadron had been recently under great pressure to reduce the severity of the pre-para selection process, and the training at Catterick had been taken out of the squadron's control and given to the Depot PT staff. The dozen selection tests also went, with just the stretcher race being retained as a grim test of commitment, and, finally, it was decided that anyone might be posted to the squadron in a non-volunteer capacity with no obligation to undergo either pre-para or parachute training. These were very significant changes.

A Flight also had a new flight sergeant, Dave Bryant, whom I had served under when he was a sergeant on QCS. We got along fine but my time on the flight was by now running out. At an interview with Sqn Ldr Bremner, a future Depot Commandant, he informed me that my instructor abilities were now required to serve a wider audience than just A Flight, and that I was therefore posted to HQ Flight as the Training NCO. I had mixed feelings about this, but it was clear to me that there was no alternative, and I got busy assessing the job.

Routine training was then suspended for a few weeks, in view of the Silver Jubilee celebrations, which were to be held at RAF Leeming, which was about an hour's drive from the Depot. I was given a small team and ordered to set up a GPMG SF position on the airfield, among a variety of 'sideshows' which were really intended to serve no purpose apart from dressing otherwise vacant space. We established the position on day one, then had to appear over a succession of days for interminable rehearsals until the day itself. Arriving on day two, I discovered that all of our camouflage nets were missing and duly tracked them down. They had been appropriated by some squadron leader in charge of the vital job of screening all offensive buildings from the Royal gaze. The 'offensive' building in question was an external lavatory.

It seemed to be the season for regal duties, for we were no sooner free of the jubilee when we were told to prepare for a fortnight's duties in the Province. The Queen was making a surprise visit and we were among a few thousand troops mobilised to ensure that no nasty surprises were sprung during the visit. We flew out on this occasion, which was a pleasant break from the tubs of the 'Grey Funnel Line', and we were of course based at RAF Aldergrove. It was a station we then saw very little of for six days as we completed a strenuous round of foot patrols, heli-patrols and VCPs, whilst the roulement squadron held the fort. VCPs continued to provide valuable insights into the local solutions to the 'troubles'. "Youse should get rid of all them Catholic bastards." was one view, and: "It's them Protestant bastards that's the cause of all this." was another. I would gladly have passed this intelligence to any House of Commons Select Committee, but somehow was not asked to. A variation at VCPs occurred when the driver, fuming at the delay, listed for us the important, nay, the *very* important people he knew, including high-ranking officers, as my section 2ic, Colin Kelly, checked the man's details. "Your problem, Mate," Said Colin, in an infuriatingly breezy manner, "is that you *didn't know* Colin Kelly."

In my telephone calls since return from Australia, Patti had remained distant and unresponsive to suggestions that we meet, but she knew that I was at Aldergrove and she agreed to meet me at the Mess. It was the only opportunity for a meeting before we returned to Catterick, and I proposed to her that we get married. She would not answer immediately, however, and I returned to England feeling that the relationship might be terminally ill.

Within a few days of return, Patti 'phoned with the news that she had some free time, and would I meet her? I drove to Dumfries to meet her off the Stranraer Ferry and we again stayed at Appleby in the 'castle', which in fact was a Victorian folly but pleasantly secluded and quiet. We seemed to be back on track again and I looked forward to regular meetings during the detachment that was now imminent.

When we deployed, I learned that my training duties were suspended for the duration and that I would be employed within the Intelligence Cell that worked closely with the RUC and Special Branch. I was to wear civilian clothes and this sounded as if it might be interesting work, but the reality soon proved otherwise. Having been given a heap of files to study for a couple of days, I was introduced to an RAF Police sergeant who took me across to an office within the Aldergrove airport. Two things happened here: one, we were shown where the coffee machine was and, two, we were shown nothing else. In the space of a few days, I noticed that earnest conversations dried up as soon as we entered the office, to be replaced by bland chat about football, and that we were soon left alone with the coffee machine. My companion was clearly regarded as the RAF equivalent of a 'woodentop', whereas I was merely a soldier and completely beyond the pale. I swiftly reported the facts to the CO and a day later I was back in uniform, putting together a training programme. Some inessential tasks were deleted from the tasking sheets, a minor adjustment was made to shifts and I had a section's worth of Gunners each day to train.

Life became very hectic for a time and I found myself working a six-day week that comprised some very long days. I was determined to make the training both interesting and competitive, in case it was seen simply as training for the sake of it. I also got involved with the production of a fortnightly newsletter we called '*Slipstream*', and this proved greatly absorbent of time. I was also making far too many calls at the bar, drinking virtually every night and usually until after midnight. This was far from sensible and only just balanced by a punishing routine of runs that were intended to keep me fit.

At the midpoint of the tour, I was advised that I was to be posted as an instructor to the Depot, with immediate effect. This news was unwelcome to the CO and myself alike, if for different reasons. The CO tried to affect a replacement with a volunteer sergeant from one of the flights, but he succeeded only in having my posting deferred until the tour ended, just before Xmas. This at least was something, and I got on with the job. I had known that I might be due a posting and had tried to preempt it by volunteering for loan service in the Oman. I had seemed to have a good chance of that, but it was now clearly off the agenda. The Depot spoke with a powerful voice to the personnel management centre.

The workload increased and my humour was little improved by having such useless jobs to do as chaperone repairmen to the barrack block. '*Slipstream*' was a great success, but a rod for the backs of the very few producing it, working after midnight on some occasions. I began to feel more tired than on either of the previous tours, and became somewhat unresponsive on the occasions when Patti visited the Mess. This renewed the strains.

Late in November, my R&R became due and Patti joined me for the flight to Heathrow. We were booked into the Union Jack Club for five days and we looked forward to a round of theatres, musicals and museums. The leave began well but Patti's mood deteriorated by the day, and she suddenly announced that she was returning to Belfast early and alone. I remained at the UJ a little longer, but had no enthusiasm for the empty room and I too returned early. I had just one pound in a wallet that had held one hundred when we had arrived, and the trip had been expensive, as well as painful. There would be some 'phone calls, an exchange of letters and a failed attempt to arrange a meeting in the months to follow, but we were finished.

22

My return was about ten days ahead of the squadron move and I took a Land Rover back for some reason. My former flight commander, Flt Lt Gritten, had recently been appointed DSC and he also returned early, in order to set up a range-firing programme for the New Year which was now very close. Since my new duties were not due to begin until January, I assisted with this. The Depot was busy for reasons other than Gunner training, resulting from a national strike of firemen which had begun a few weeks earlier, and the Fire School was training crews for the 'Green Goddesses' which were being deployed to meet the emergency. These were Bedford RLs, equipped with water tanks, hoses and ladders and actually part of some mothballed fleet intended to meet national disasters.

Among the familiar faces in the camp was that of Eddie Martin, again newly returned from Belize, and we quickly picked up the routine of pints at the Angel. It was perhaps too frequently a watering hole between detachments, but the crowd, and the pint, was extremely good. My imminent posting wasn't about to cause me great upheaval, since I would remain on the camp and in my room in the Mess, but I was already beginning to regret the demise of parachuting, parachute pay and detachments in my working life. Camaraderie, too, of a kind which seemed not abundant elsewhere.

Before the Xmas Grant began, the traditional Xmas Dinner was served in the Airmen's Mess and I went along to assist the serving of it. The meal was preceded by a sherry in the Officers' Mess, where the Commandant asked me what I thought of my new posting. I replied, diplomatically, that a change was not entirely a bad thing, and he went on to remark that this posting was something that the Corps had been seeking for quite some time. When he continued in this vein, I realised that we were not discussing the same thing at all, and I was astonished later to learn that I had been selected for an exchange tour with the Royal Marines.

No previous such exchange had existed and I was immediately conscious that eyes might be upon me. I quickly learned that my posting was contingent upon successful completion of the All Arms Commando Course, and this promised to be arduous. I did not delude myself that there had been exceptional reasons for selecting me in preference to other Depot staff who had expressed interest, but it was nevertheless good to be the candidate.

When I joined the Depot staff in the New Year, I learned that the posting would not be effected until March and I was meanwhile made a supernumerary instructor, assisting with various Basic Gunner courses. I had already renewed acquaintance with the airfield and I was putting in some serious training in order to be fit for the course. Instructing to basic courses served to refresh my memory of tradecraft and that was useful, although I soon noticed that I was 'filling in' for other instructors on a disproportionate number of exercises.

I set myself a fairly punishing programme of runs with a sand-weighted Bergen, aiming for six miles in sixty minutes and nine miles in ninety minutes, since these appeared to be the criteria for two of the commando tests. I also did some circuit training in the gym and spent time going over the assault course, being unpleasantly surprised to find that I seemed no longer confident on it. Better to discover that now, I thought, whilst there was time to address it.

Along with the fitness regime, I had begun to assess my drinking habits, perhaps really seriously for the first time. Periods of complete sobriety which lasted for months at a time notwithstanding, I was now feeling some alarm at a habit which placed me in the bar five and six nights in succession, routinely drinking eight or nine pints and sometimes following them with several brandies. Bells had begun to ring, although not quite loudly enough, and if I reduced my drinking very considerably for a time, then this was motivated entirely for reasons of short-term fitness than long-term health.

I found a break from the BG courses when a signals' instructor course came up light on students and I was allocated a space. Signals' expertise was not my forte and I soon began to struggle, especially where antenna theory was concerned. Nor were my studies assisted when I was asked to make an 'acquaint' visit to the Commando Centre about a month before my posting. I returned to the signal's course and made a complete hash of an exercise and it was all downhill from there. I failed the course, which was more than simply dispiriting, and by then I was under no illusions about the All Arms Commando, which promised to be tough.

Commando Training Centre, Royal Marines was at Lympstone, just above Exmouth in Devon, and I arrived there in the afternoon having left Catterick very early in the morning. I found a room, or cabin more correctly, in the Mess and the next morning I dressed in blue and went off to find the All Arms Wing. The camp at this time was in the latter stages of conversion to a modern, brick-built facility to replace the wooden huts that had housed and trained thousands of commandos during and since the war.

The largest of the new buildings was known as 'Puzzle Palace' for complexity and labyrinthine layout. I wandered about its corridors for some time and had just passed an open office door when a voice bellowed: **"WHAT ARE YOU DOING HERE?"** I turned around and saw that it was my great admirer from Brecon, Captain Chibnall. "I'm being posted here to teach you something about soldiering." I beamed. This inauspicious start was barely improved upon when I was ushered in to the WO2 PTI who ran the PT for the all arms courses. This was Maurice Logue and he regarded me in silence for a bit before asking me how old I was. "Thirty six." I responded. Another bit of silence, then: "We were expecting a young sergeant; you might find the course hard going." I thought about this for a few seconds then offered to race Maurice around the camp for a quid. Fortunately, he declined the challenge.

I spent a day at Lympstone being shown around by one of the sergeants and I returned to Catterick in a thoughtful mood. There was little time now to further improve my fitness, and I would pass or fail on that which I had acquired to date. The prospect of being the first member of the Regiment to undergo the exchange had been exciting; the chance of being the first to fail and RTU hardly bore thinking about.

My remaining time at the Depot evaporated and it ended upon the happy note of a send off at a country pub by the officers and SNCOs of II Squadron. I was genuinely sorry to leave their ranks, believing then, as now, that they contained some very considerable men. *Nunquam Non Paratus.*

I travelled down to Lympstone one Sunday at the end of March and sorted out my cabin. In the evening, I wandered down to the bar for a drink but drank alone since few were in and none of course that I knew. I noticed that a chap at the end of the bar bore a striking resemblance to Jack Charlton, the footballer, and that he moreover had a Geordie accent. Weeks later, I discovered that it had been Jack, who managed a football team and brought it to Lympstone now and again to put it over the assault course or whatever.

The commando course was preceded by a 'beat up' of two weeks, which was designed to eliminate the sort of dreamer who had made no attempt to get fit. These were normally conducted at Seaton Barracks, Plymouth or at Stonehouse in the Dockyard. Mine was conducted at CTC and I had a Royal Navy schoolteacher for company. He had volunteered for duty with a commando and thus had to undergo the course, although the training was intended for large numbers of soldiers serving with the artillery and engineers, Royal Marines-attached. There were no exceptions to the course which even naval Padres, wishing to serve with a Commando, had to complete. One such was issued with all the standard kit to include a rifle but he remonstrated at this, pointing out that he could not possibly carry a weapon. The training team had a think about the matter before coming up with an iron bar that weighed about nine pounds, equivalent to a rifle's weight. This was taken to a local blacksmith who fashioned it into a 'shepherd's crook' and welded a couple of swivels to it, in order that it might be carried with a rifle sling. The Padre ran with the 'flock' and duly passed the course.

The 'beat up', with the exception of some basic weapons training, was purely physical and we made early acquaintance of the Assault Course and the Tarzan Course. The latter placed great emphasis on the upper body and my arm and shoulder muscles were soon screaming, since I had mostly concentrated on building my legs up. We worked in ninety-minute slices and pretty soon all the other muscles were screaming as well. One evening in my cabin, I thought I might ease my stomach muscles by doing a few sit-ups, only to find that I could not complete one. If this was not sufficiently painful, I also got conjunctivitis for a day or two, making the daylight very painful on my eyes. That particular day we were due around the Tarzan course again, and I was reluctant to cry off in case this was misinterpreted. I went around the course badly in need of a guide dog and falling off just about everything. What preserved my morale was the sight of the 'Schoolie' who *did* fall off everything and his eyesight was 20/20.

We survived the beat up and in mid-April twenty-six other candidates joined us. A brief welcome address was offered, then we were doubled down to the Exe estuary, which at low tide was replete with stinking black mud. We doubled about this for some time, did a few press-ups and sit-ups, made some pretty patterns to the satisfaction of the DS, then trotted off looking like some Zulu tribe. This presumably was the 'fun' aspect of the course the welcome had referred to.

With five weeks of the course proper to push, we were walked around various of the final tests which would earn us either a green beret and a red dagger on the sleeve or a ticket home. One of these was the thirty foot rope climb, which I had already made a clandestine attempt at, failing to reach the top by about two feet. On this occasion, I made the top but then fell off the bottom twelve feet of the rope, bruising my back. I then fell off the Monkey Bars, getting soaking wet in the substantial water tank that lay below them. This was not a promising start and I noticed that I was being eyed by the mostly young candidates with a look that translated as: 'What is this old git trying to prove?'

There was as yet little evidence of spring and on day two we were introduced to the Endurance Course, which was spread over two miles of Woodbury Common, the local training area. The run began with a wade chest-deep through Peter's Pool and progressed to pitch-black tunnels of limited space, where pebbles dug painfully into knees, shins and elbows. There were several water obstacles and perhaps the most daunting of them was a concrete pipe wholly filled with opaque water. The course was no place to be for those with fears of water or confined spaces, and when the last of the obstacles was cleared the soaking candidate, with pack and rifle, faced a four mile run back to CTC. The course actually ended at the 25 Metre range, where proof that the weapon had been held clear of mud was required before the candidate put ten reasonably accurate rounds into his target. The bogey time for the Endurance Course was seventy minutes.

Each week of the course featured an exercise whose scenario changed each week, making this aspect very similar to Brecon. On day three we deployed to a three-day stint, got soaked in the first hour and stayed soaked for three days, other than when we slept off shift and changed into dry clothing to sleep in. It was not a new experience, but pulling on the soaking wet and freezing clothing after the warmth of the sleeping bag was something I would have forfeited a month's wages to avoid.

My great worry was that my left knee might let me down. I

already had some history of problems with it, especially when I was load-carrying in cold, wet weather. For the moment it was holding up, but another problem, and a literal pain in the arse, was piles with which I had lately been afflicted. I was also reluctant to advertise this problem, in case it meant being binned off the course, but I quietly arranged the supply of suppositories with a naval medic who was undergoing the training. For a time thereafter I was stuffing suppositories into one end of my body with much the same frequency that I stuffed Mars bars into the other.

The second exercise was defence-based and to no great surprise I found myself digging a battle trench in splendid isolation. My trench companion should have been a Sapper major, but he had been sent off to do something more vital. When I came off stag on the GPMG in the small hours of one morning, I returned to the bivvie we shared and found him reading a book of poetry by candlelight.

We spent a week at RM Poole, getting acquainted with small assault craft called rigid raiders. This was interesting, if wet, work, as was the training in larger boats of the landing craft variety. At Poole we also underwent the swimming tests, stepping off the top board in OGs, webbing and rifles to swim two lengths. I saw no problems with this, although I immediately sank in the deep end and did not appear to be getting to the surface at all quickly.

Some of the commando tests began when we returned to CTC and for the Fireman's Lift and hundred-metre carry I drew a real lardy arse who almost added a hernia to my piles problems. I was more careful in my selection for the rerun, telling 'lardy' to fuck off and find a forklift. The Assault Course and Tarzan Course had to be completed in five minute's each, and proved no problem. I hacked the rope climbs and the rope regain, watching with more than a degree of satisfaction as some of the young blokes failed to regain and plopped into ten feet of water below.

We did a patrols' exercise and during it we lined out for a night ambush on an old railway cutting which had very steep sides. The DS had insisted on the ambushers being linked together with D10, which was fine until some berk fell asleep. He slid down the bank, taking the entire ambush with him.

We resumed tests and I completed the Endurance Course with seven minutes to spare. It was my thirty-seventh birthday and there were moments in the tunnels when it had felt like my ninety-seventh. I reckoned that no remaining test could be as hard and I began to breathe a little easier. We ran the six and the nine milers and I had plenty in reserve. The final exercise was on Woodbury Common and I was required to lead a night patrol. I led it to a convenient hamburger van parked in a layby and we stoked up before continuing the patrol. The small victories were the best victories.

My last task was to organise an end of course piss-up in Exmouth, which was no problem at all. I drank my first pint in two months, then drank several more. The next day saw twenty survivors on parade to be presented with a green beret and as the sole representative of the junior service, I was the last man to receive the beret. I was the oldest man on parade and it wasn't a bad feeling at all.

All Arms Commando Course Royal Marines Lympstone 1978

23

The course was followed by a most welcome fortnight of leave, which I divided between Cheshire, Yorkshire and Uxbridge. The aches faded away and life was sublime. Returning to CTC, I devised a running route that would take me across four or five miles of Woodbury Common, and I prepared for my new duties. I was posted to Portsmouth Company which trained junior marines who enlisted at sixteen. Their syllabus, at thirty-two weeks, was six weeks longer than the adult recruit syllabus in order to develop their fitness over a longer period. A recruit troop assembled every fortnight and 'mine' was due to arrive in a few weeks. Meantime, I was attached as a supernumerary instructor to a troop that was entering its final weeks of training. This would serve to teach me the administrative ropes at Lympstone.

The core training team for each troop comprised a sergeant, who was the team leader, and four corporals whose specialist training was as PWs, meaning platoon weapons instructors. Other instruction was required, such as PT, Drill or Signals, but the instructors for these formed a pool and only joined a troop for specific periods. In addition to weapons, the PWs also taught minor tactics, navigation and various soldier skills, in addition to conducting the troop on a daily basis.

The TL was Brum Cleaver, who was about to leave the service, and he had a good team. This was a useful advantage to have, given that I was feeling my way to some extent. I joined the team and we got on with what remained of 233 Troop's training. Oddly enough, the troop included the son of a flight sergeant I knew in the Mob.

We proceeded almost immediately to an exercise on Dartmoor, where the team HQ was in a derelict farmhouse once infamous as a tryst for John Profumo and Christine Keeler in a Sixties political scandal. The building was rather basic by now, but it offered a degree of shelter in an environment where summer hardly seemed to reach. We underwent field-firing in the period and one of the ranges was disrupted by local gentry, passionate advocates for the closure of Dartmoor, a national park, to troops and training of any description.

We returned briefly to Lympstone then underwent an internal security exercise in the disused Wyvern Barracks in Exeter. For this we staged a 'bombing' which was so realistic that it attracted a police car, two ambulances, a fire engine, a TV external broadcast crew and a bollocking from the Training Major when we returned to CTC.

The troop completed the syllabus and passed off parade, but was held for a period in order to appear at a couple of military displays. These were to be held at the Royal Naval Air Stations at Yeovilton, in Somerset and Culdrose, in Cornwall. The team also was involved and I had to undergo a swift course of abseiling instruction, since the display involved abseiling two hundred feet from Wessex helicopters. This was exhilarating and as good a way as any of spending a couple of weeks as autumn approached. The troop was also required to provide a lining party in London for some ceremonial occasion, and it put us into the Union Jack Club for a couple of nights. This was infinitely better than holes in the ground. At the UJ I noted that a VC's gallery had been added since I had last visited, and 'Dasher' Wheatley's face was among them. 2 Battalion days, however, now seemed very distant.

My own troop, 239, formed early in September and it was sixty strong, although the chance of that number passing off parade was remote. Recruits had to remain until the sixth week of training, at which time they could opt out, and a further opportunity to do so was offered in the twelfth week. These two opt out periods accounted for more than fifty per cent of recruits, whilst injury or failure to pass tests accounted for a good many others. The fact, too, that each recruit represented four other applicants who never made it through the camp gates was testimony that the Royal Marines resolutely refused to budge from their high standards, at a time when there was pressure from on high to do so in the light of poor recruiting figures. My own Corps was one that did not resist the pressures and I would see some of the inevitable results later.

In the early weeks of the syllabus, the troop seemed to divide its time between the parade ground and the gymnasium, although we were concurrently busy teaching basic weapons. I used this relatively quiet time to study the programme and make my various preparations for it. Among my areas of ignorance was that of survival teaching, which was featured for a week at a later stage, and I began to research the subject.

With some exceptions, the week's training ended at lunchtime each Saturday and I developed the custom of assembling the troop on the stairs in the accommodation, to conduct a 'wash up' of the week past and a forecast of the coming week. I don't know if this served any real purpose, but I thought at the time that it at least balanced some of the pressures which recruits were subjected to from the day of arrival to the day of departure. Their day was indeed busy and did not end when lessons ceased. One of the early demonstrations showed them how to do their dhobi (laundry) in a bucket, and in the first weeks of training they were not permitted to use the camp laundrette. These were lessons in self-reliance that my own Corps might usefully have taught.

Lympstone sprang odd surprises. I strolled into the Mess ante-room one day and found the TV personality Jimmy Savill sitting there. He had some years before undergone elements of the commando course for a charity fund-raising effort and had remained in touch with the Corps. Some sixteen years after I left Lympstone, I returned to attend the dining-out of a former member of my team, and I was not greatly surprised to see the now Sir Jimmy Savill in the Mess.

The troop cleared the first hurdles of training and we went off to Snowdonia for a few days of adventurous training, of the hill-walking and canoeing variety. We stayed in a former forestry camp at Capel Curig and we took a cook with us to sort out the breakfast and the evening meals. PTIs from CTC were conducting the canoeing and Mountain Leaders were taking the hill-walking, but we had only one ML, Lenny. Rather that have him take an unwieldy number, I split the group with Lenny, reasoning that I had no pressing duties at Capel Curig. I had some knowledge of routes from the trips with pre-para and most of them in any case were well trodden.

The attached cook, having little to do after breakfast but prepare dinner, promptly went off to some local town and got pissed, a state he was still in when Lenny's group came down off the hill, somewhat cold and damp and looking forward to a hot wet of some description. The selection course for MLs was conducted by the Mountain and Arctic Warfare Cadre, and its standards were roughly those required by the Special Boat Service or the Special Air Service. Its successful candidates might easily be presumed to be pretty direct individuals, which is something the cook ought to have borne in mind when he responded to Lenny's complaint with a flippant remark. Lenny flattened the cook, who then was carried off to bed. I returned shortly after the event and went off to borrow a cook from an army unit we were sharing the camp with. The following morning, the cook confronted Lenny, whereupon Lenny flattened him for a second time. "Bloody hell, Lenny," I remonstrated, "you should have let him cook breakfast, first!" I then had to go off to borrow an army cook again.

Since corporals, ML or otherwise, are not supposed to strike marines, I had to interview the cook to see if he wished to make a formal complaint. The cook said he preferred to forget the whole thing and that was that. But only until the cook returned to Lympstone and formally complained to the catering officer. That put a whole bunch of us in front of the Commandant and I was left in no uncertainty that I had failed to uphold military discipline. It was one of those disappointingly one-way conversations that I simply had to accept, as apparently did Lenny. After a decent interval had elapsed, however, Lenny sought out the cook in a local pub and flattened him for the third time.

When we arrived at the week of training which featured survival techniques, I believed that I had done my homework. Among my chores as the troop shook out was the collection of a dozen live chickens, which would be given to the recruits, or 'Nods' as they were called.[1] Whilst the Nods were busy with some other instruction, I decided to practise wringing the neck of one of the birds, to ensure that I didn't botch the live demonstration. It worked, and apparently worked again when the Nods were seated before my pitch. I then laid the chicken on its back across my knees to demonstrate the plucking process. I had denuded the breast of about half the feathers when the chicken raised its head to fix its eye upon me with a clear message of: *'What the fuck is happening here?'* This did little for my credibility as a survival expert.

A member of the team, George Porthouse, had done the fishing demonstration and ensured success by tethering a fat fish he had bought in Exmouth from the fishmonger's slab. George also had a story of a commando unit he served on which was visited in Norway by the Duke of Edinburgh. One of the troop was demonstrating fishing through a hole in ice, and the inspecting officer on the dress

---

[1] Recruits, when not wearing steel helmets, wore a Cap Comforter which was a woollen sleeve folded in on itself to form a 'commando' hat. The exertions of the day invariably caused the top fold to flap open, rendering a good likeness of Enid Blyton's creation, Noddy.

rehearsal told him to have some fish on the line in case the Duke wanted proof of success. On the day, the Duke did in fact ask if the Marine was having any luck, and the Bootneck silently pulled up the line to reveal a packet of Birdseye frozen fish fingers.

Among my researches was the study of edible fungi, and I had filled a bag with some twenty different species in a quiet period between lessons. I had then begun to sort them out, referring to a pocket guide, but had to hand the task over when I went off to another lesson. The edible products went into our stew, which we had eaten when I asked the man how many he had eliminated. He shrugged: "I got well bored with that, so I tipped the lot in." I then spent some hours wondering if specimens of *Amanita* or *Fly Agaric* were already destroying my liver.

By the end of November, my troop strength was down to thirty-four and this was about par for the course. The company commander agonised about opt-outs and injuries, and CTC employed a full time psychologist, but when the going got tough some simply went. It was the price of excellence.

In December we had a week at RM Poole, undergoing the boats' work and generally enjoying the experience, although it was cold and wet. The week also provided the opportunity to visit the Royal Marines Museum, at Eastney and that was most interesting. I had lately begun to collect campaign medals and the Eastney museum had a very fine collection. There were several examples of medals that spanned generations of the same family.

The Xmas break arrived and I decided to put the time in at Uxbridge, drinking with Tom Jones and Ray Pelcot. On an earlier weekend we had been joined by Eddie Martin, who was undergoing a Rapier course at Larkhill. These were my only contacts with my own Corps for two years and I valued them.

I returned to Lympstone and the news that one of the Nods had tried to slash his wrists. The team believed that this was not a serious attempt, offering to draw a diagram for a more successful bid. Black humour abounded, in addition to a rich vein of ordinary humour among Bootnecks.

In the Mess I got chatting to an Australian SAS man who was on exchange to 22 SAS at Hereford and doing a round of visits. He knew Arch and had seen him more recently than me. Lympstone also had exchange personnel other than my slot. A United States Marine Corps gunnery sergeant was doing a two-year tour, as was a Dutch

Marine SNCO. There also was an SNCO of the Parachute Regiment and a Staff Sergeant from the Small Arms School Corps. The latter, Tom Astle, lived in and we became firm friends. Our excursions to the local drinking spotswas later accompanied by Dick Stuchbury, a Royal Marine posted in from Arbroath. These runs ashore became known to the Mess as 'Tom, Dick and Harry' runs.

The pubs in Exmouth were lively and we seldom ventured further afield to Exeter, although it was no great distance. The progression was usually from the Mess to the Park Hotel, the Ship, then on to the Heavitree Arms. These were also well attended by women and the aim was to attract one back to the Mess for a late drink, prior to a move upstairs. Earlier, I had been trying to cultivate the friendship of a petty officer WREN, but her drinking habits were worse than mine.

My drinking, other than when the demands of the syllabus were too great, was becoming excessive again, although I had ceased, for the moment anyway, to be anxious about it. Hard drinking simply seemed to go with the territory sometimes, and that was about the top and the bottom of it. My saving grace was that I did not swerve from the fitness training that took me out across Woodbury Common, irrespective of season.

Another break in the routine was offered by a few days of climbing near Penzance, in Cornwall. The MLs maintained a cottage there which, they told me, had been purchased for just £800 in 1957. It had been recently valued at £42,000 and would be worth God knows what by now. It proved a warm and cosy refuge at the end of the day, or after an evening pint. I had the feeling that the MLs had got life just about right.

In February we moved the troop up to Okehampton Camp on the north edge of Dartmoor to undergo six weeks of battle training and field-firing. This provided a refreshing change of training venue, and we were pretty much on our own as the training team. It paid, however, to remain on the ball with lesson preparation, since the Commandant was fond of pitching up quite unannounced and tacking himself on to a patrol. The Commandant had recently arrived from a Commando and his hard reputation preceded him. There was a story, perhaps apocryphal, that he had had three vacancies for corporals on his previous unit and had filled them by reducing three sergeants in rank.

Our initial training was hampered by severe snow and we

feared for a while that we would fall behind our syllabus. It led me to persevere on some occasion with a night patrol when the wind from the east was bitterly cold and there was already ten degrees of ground frost. One of my team ruefully admitted the next day that he had lost some cash, betting that I would scrub the patrol. My troop by this time had reduced to twenty-five, but there seemed no doubting the commitment of the remainder.

I had some problems with the troop commander at this time, feeling that his Orders were poor and that his preparation and execution of various tactical phases was unsound. I had been reluctant to criticise him, in view of the very professional corps he represented, but I was confident of my opinion and eventually confronted him. It was resolved amicably, with me preparing much of the action which he, nominally, led.

We returned to Lympstone harder and fitter and ready for the commando phase of the training syllabus, which was down to few weeks indeed. To no great surprise, I learned that it was among the TL's perks to demonstrate the water tunnel on the Endurance Course, so I ran as wet as anyone on the subsequent return to camp.

The Troop duly entered the commando tests that culminated in the thirty-mile tab across Dartmoor. The bogey time was eight hours and eight of the Troop failed to meet it. I reran them with the troop closest behind us in training and all passed at the second attempt. We were the King's Squad for a week that culminated in the Passing Off Parade. I had marked another birthday just days before it and another summer beckoned. I felt busy, fit and sublimely happy.

Thus severely denting my credibility as a Survival Instructor

24

After a break, we picked up a new troop of fifty-eight recruits, although we saw very little of them initially. The WREN psychologist had an early go at them, then she summoned the team to counsel us. She had our undivided attention, since she was lovely, but within hours I was storming at the troop for the disgraceful condition they had left the accommodation in, and I was presumably immune to the counselling. I also cancelled weekend leave planned for the troop later, in view of their continuing poor standard of accommodation turnout. This alarmed the company commander, but I refused to rescind the ban. He was even more alarmed when one of the recruits 'phoned home to complain to his mother of 'brutal' treatment. This was not substantiated and Lympstone remained free of the sorts of horror stories that occasionally featured in the Press about army recruit camps.

I became due for an award of the Long Service & Good Conduct Medal (Australian Army service having counted towards), and it was presented after the pass off parade of a recruit troop. The reviewing officer was an air vice marshal and he expressed some surprise at the sight of a Rockape under a green beret. After presentation, I was taken by the Adjutant to the Officers' Mess to drinks for an hour, then collected by the RSM and escorted to the Sergeants' Mess. The LS&GC attracted the payment of five pounds, and it was traditional to buy a round of drinks out of this sum, which had been set in 1920. The round of drinks cost me £17. Late in the afternoon, someone pressed a tankard of brandy upon me and that closed the proceedings so far as I was concerned. I lived on the third floor of the Mess and the next day I recovered my tunic, tie and medals from various of the stairs. I had also slept through a bomb scare. Bomb scares invariably were telephoned in on Friday nights, at about bar closing time. Every occupant of the camp had to muster on the parade ground, whilst the blocks were searched, and this procedure took an hour at least. No bomb was ever delivered and the popular theory was that the hoaxes originated from a woman who had a grudge against a Bootneck.

The news from home was that Mam and the Old Man planned a visit to England for Xmas. I decided that I needed a larger car for the visit and began to haunt the car sales. I was briefly tempted by a 4.2 litre Daimler, a snip at £1500, but reluctantly recognised that I could never afford the fuel for it. I went to the other extreme, buying a Polish-built Fiat, which was commodious and had quite good lines. It had minor faults and among them the fact that it had the steering agility of a steamroller, but I figured that I needed the upper body exercise anyway.

The troop was firing on the gallery ranges at the nearby facility of Straight Point, when it was visited by the Royal Marines Commandant, a general and one who later lost a leg to an IRA car bomb. The general, resplendent with glittering boots, red tabs, medal ribbons and gilt badges, approached a recruit to enquire: "Do you know who I am?" "No, Corporal." Was the lad's immediate response. Corporals had the status of God to recruits.

Less happy on Straight Point was the death of a recruit. His troop was preparing to fire a practice when a sudden shower enveloped them. The DS ordered the troop to shelter in the latrines and whilst in there one of the recruits fitted a charged magazine to his rifle. Spotting this, the senior recruit ordered him to clear the weapon, which was then cocked with the magazine still fitted, and fired. The 7.62mm round hit the clasp knife on the belt of another recruit, driving it into his spleen. He bled to death *en route* to hospital.

Three days later my troop was live-firing on Dartmoor when a recruit was hit by a ricochet. At his scream, I halted the practice and sprinted across the range, finding the recruit already being tended by George Porthouse. "It's okay," George was saying, "it's just a scratch." My incipient relief at this was just as quickly scotched when George, moving his head from the recruit's line of sight, silently mouthed: "Fucking big hole in his arm." No exaggeration there; the round had entered at the base of his thumb, leaving a hole no bigger than 7.62mm, but it had exited from the underside of his forearm, taking a large piece of flesh with it. Miraculously, it proved to have taken no bone, sinew or blood vessels with it, but for the moment we could only pack it with field dressings and get the lad away. I was required under range rules to quarantine the weapons and ammunition in use at the time of the incident, but I otherwise took a decision to continue firing. The fire and manoeuvre became somewhat pedestrian for a time, but I was keen to demonstrate that a single casualty stopped nothing. The decision proved controversial, but I was backed by the Training Major and that was that. A later court of enquiry confirmed a ricochet but it had been a worrying experience.

Block Leave intervened and CTC virtually closed down for three weeks. I was saving my leave for the visit by the folks and I was rostered to Duty Senior, or Orderly Sergeant, on a day on, day off basis for the period. This was quiet, not to say boring, and the Guardroom was shared by a single prisoner, the recruit who had fired the fatal round on Straight Point. His court martial had sentenced him to a period in cells, but allowed him to soldier on. I do not doubt that he became the safest marine in the world where live weapons were concerned. I shared the duties with Spike Kelly, who was my neighbour in the Mess and who had given me invaluable advice when I had first joined Portsmouth Company. The Mess itself at this time was deserted and we dined with the marines. There was also no hot water in the Mess and I suffered cold showers in a period of summer that was not especially warm. I later discovered that the Guardroom prisoner had hot showers each day.

The routine was broken by the IRA killing of Lord Mountbatten, blown up on his boat at his Irish holiday home. Mountbatten had been a consistent champion of the Royal Marines, who held him in a measure of esteem. It was decided that the Corps would handle the funeral and I spent some time calling out members of the drill staff who were required to put the ceremony together.

We resumed training and the first opt out reduced the troop strength to thirty-two. The recruiting trough had really begun to bite and it was likely that our troop would be combined with a troop one week behind it, in order to preserve a useful training strength. Not for the moment though, and we continued the training with the first of several exercises.

The matter of troop fitness began to pass more from PTI hands into those of the team - although a PTI corporal continued to work closely with the troop. When working on Woodbury Common, I would occasionally surprise the troop (and sometimes the team) by sending the wagons back empty and speed-marching the troop back to CTC. Team fitness was tested twice each year at Lympstone and I made sure that we were always up to it. I continued to train hard in my own time, however much my excessive drinking might militate against it.

Socially, a series of casual relationships struck up at the Ship,

'Tree and similar had not been entirely satisfying. I had also taken a lot of flak from my team during a team run ashore to a pub in Tavistock on some detachment. I had gone home with the black barmaid who weighed at least twenty stones. She had no bed but a mattress on the floor, which we had to share with her dog. I later developed a relationship with a bank clerk from Exmouth and we kept company for some months. Alarmingly, she developed thoughts of a permanent relationship and, even more alarmingly, I suddenly went off sex for some time.

The troop repeated the Okehampton phase and since the camp was no great distance from Lympstone I usually returned to the Mess each weekend. I had barely six months of my exchange remaining and wondered where the time had gone. I had also been quietly sounded by the Training Major as to whether I might wish to stay with the Corps. This provided food for thought, although I did not take up the suggestion, reasoning that the RM had little need of sergeants who were pushing forty.

In September, a letter from Arch revealed that the UK trip was postponed because of the Old Man suddenly being ill. It was thought that he had an ulcer, although my immediate worry was that it might be something much worse. I began to arrange for a trip home, although there was very little prospect of taking extra leave. Events moved rather more quickly however.

We deployed to another exercise and when the troop offended me with the amount of litter in the bivvie site, I put them into a river. This coincided with a surprise visit by the Commandant, who raised an eyebrow, said little and departed. The troop got out, got dry and got on with the exercise, doubtless more litter-conscious than previously. We were temporarily without a troop commander and I planned and wrote Orders for our attack on Scraesdon Fort, which was a 'Palmerston Folly' built near Plymouth in the nineteenth century. The Training Major accompanied the attack and he complimented the planning and the execution. My time at Brecon appeared not to have been entirely wasted.

The attack opened with an insertion by rigid raider, a small aluminium craft powered by an outboard motor. As dawn broke, we swept under the bows of the carrier, *Ark Royal*, recently decommissioned and awaiting a decision on whether she would be preserved or go to scrap. The 'Ark' was the last of the big carriers in the Royal Navy and I had been a guest aboard her in Singapore in '63.

She made a fine sight as we roared under the sweep of her forward deck, but she went for razor blades in the end.

At Scraesdon, the MLs were waiting to hoist us over the outer wall of the moat and we abseiled down to breach the wall into a gun gallery. The troop then fought in near-darkness up endless flights of stone stairs, into the central courtyard. An exhausting business but refreshingly different from Woodbury Common.

We redeployed to Okehampton Camp again and a letter from Arch caught up with me. The Old Man's illness was now confirmed as cancer of the stomach, and he would not survive it. I received swift permission from the company commander for a fast trip home but the Old Man was by now running to a different clock. Whilst travelling to Perth with Arch, he had taken very ill and was rushed into the hospital at Merredin. He had died there in the early hours of the morning with Mam at his side. The knowledge that this was the certain outcome of such illness proved wholly inadequate preparation for a moment of indelible pain, when the news came. Life went on but something of the light within mine was irrevocably dimmed.

"D'you know who I am," asked the General

25

For a couple of days I stood aside from training, allowing the team to run the troop. We were still at Okehampton Camp and I sought the solitude of the Tors, drawing some comfort spiritually although the days were raw. I felt badly about being half the globe distant at the time of the Old Man's death and Mam's grief. Jan and Arch had been in touch by 'phone, and Arch got in touch again with the news that Mam, with some courage, had decided to make the journey alone to England. She arrived at Heathrow early in December, looking vulnerable, but coping well. I drove her up to Cheshire to stay with Bess and Reg, who now lived in the Shavington lane where Mam and Bess were born. It was a brief visit for me, since the troop was entering a busy phase, but I had five week's leave to look forward to over Xmas.

The exercise I returned to was based on a former airfield at Dunkeswell and we had a frozen couple of days before returning gratefully to Lympstone. Less gratefully, we were also at the stage of commando training where frequent excursions to the Endurance Course featured.

When my leave began, I stayed with my cousin Jean, whose house also was in Shavington, and I established a routine which began each day with a six-mile run. The run took me through Wistaston and within sight of Uncle Arthur's house. He had bought it with a mortgage for £500 in 1938 to the derision of workmates who thought that borrowing such a huge sum of money was insane. A year later he was called up to service and he had to meet the mortgage repayments from a soldier's wage.

I mostly spent the time with Mam, but I also visited Arthur Podmore, the Old Man's oldest friend. He took me out to Minshull, quietly remarking that this was a trip he had planned for the Old

Man's visit. We both had little to say for a while after that. Mam was also discovering family whose existence I had not known, and we made a number of trips to the Waverton area, near Chester, where Gran'Ma Lindop's family had originated. We also visited old neighbours around Henry Street, although the houses of our particular row had long fallen to the developer.

Towards the end of January I returned to Lympstone to pick up the training, and within a few days Mam 'phoned with the news of Arthur Podmore's sudden death. He had been a few weeks younger than the Old Man and had died at almost exactly the same age.

The troop underwent the boats' week at Poole, which was another frozen experience, and returned to the speed march tests. The troop breezed through both and our extra training appeared to have paid a small dividend. Commando tests were well advanced by now and Pass-Off was no longer impossibly distant. We again attacked Scraesdon Fort and in leading a recce party up the hill upon which the fort stood, I grabbed hold of several electric fences. This was greatly to the mirth of George Porthouse, who had earlier assured me that all of the fences were deactivated.

We did the thirty-mile march across Dartmoor in teeming rain that made a torrent of even the minor watercourses. This inevitably slowed progress and only ten of our twenty-four made the bogey time. A week later we did the rerun in somewhat better weather and completed the distance in six and three-quarter hours. Late in February we again became the King's Squad and the drill instructor took over the troop to prepare for the passing off parade. It would be the last one for me since my time was quite simply running out.

In anticipation, I had applied for posting back to the parachute squadron, but PMC, at RAF Innsworth, got in touch with a mix of news. I had been selected for promotion to flight sergeant, but there was a three year waiting list in that rank for repeat tours on II Squadron. It briefly occurred to me to reject promotion and return as a sergeant, and I later regretted not having done so, since the picture was not quite as the Regiment desk at PMC had described it. I was now asked if I would accept a posting to QCS, and my instinct was to reject this out of hand, believing that I would not find the duties there congenial. I accepted though and it was the worst decision I ever made, insofar as postings were concerned.

249 Troop meanwhile went through the gates and my team was transferred to Chatham Company and adult recruits. I had the

team grot to myself for a couple of weeks, setting up the admin for a troop I would barely see. I was summoned by the Deputy Commandant for a chat more comfortable than a previous one at that end of the building, and he asked if I had any comments to offer about the exchange. I replied that the exchange service might be more usefully based at commando and squadron level, rather than merely between training depots, and this was actually taken up. My replacement, a friend from II, completed the commando course then served with 45 Commando at Arbroath. The Royal Marine did his time with No 1 Squadron, in Germany. When I stood to leave, the Deputy Commandant remarked that I was a good advertisement for the RAF Regiment. I prized his comment as much as I had prized the service at Lympstone, and I had the distinct feeling that no future posting would be quite so fulfilling. Worse than that, however, job satisfaction was about to become extinct for long months.

Tom Astle was concurrently returning to Warminster, and together we were paid the considerable compliment of being dined out by the Mess. Engraved tankards were presented at the dinner and mine was inscribed to 'King Plum' - a piece of libel that referred to my distinctly patchy performance with the local females. Tom's was inscribed 'The Rhinestone Cowboy', which celebrated Tom's line to females late at the Mess bar. "Would you like to come up to the room and listen to some music?" Tom would enquire, failing to point out that the only tape he had was of Glen Campbell. The familiar strains of Rhinestone Cowboy floating down the third floor corridor were evidence that Tom had 'trapped.' Two days later I left Lympstone and reported for duty with QCS.

It was early March and since the continuity season had yet to open, I was able to take a few days' leave. I drove to Shavington and learned that Mam was by now ready to go home. I thought that I might be able to arrange a month's leave from QCS to accompany her and we made a provisional booking for April. I went back to Uxbridge to organise the leave and I was promoted to flight sergeant on the tenth anniversary of my enlistment.

There were some familiar faces on the squadron and my neighbour in the Mess was John Todd, who had served on the squadron during my earlier tour. He had recently returned from a Rapier posting in Germany and was shortly posted to the Depot staff. QCS employed its SNCOs quite differently than conventional squadrons and mine was the sole post of flight sergeant. I soon discovered that, although my predecessors had been employed in a training role from time to time, I had no other function but administrative duties. Had I known this earlier I would certainly have rejected the posting, which now seemed to offer a daily routine no more demanding than presiding over the Orderly Room. The contrast between these and those of the previous two years was huge and I soon recognised that I had made a grave mistake. For the moment though I had to live with it.

I had also been transformed from being an 'old' SNCO in a young crowd, to being a 'youngster' in an elderly group. The Mess at Uxbridge appeared to have more than its quota of senior citizens; a fact which I remarked upon when I reported to the Mess Manager for a room. On his office wall was a large portrait of the Depot staff, taken in 1925. I nodded at it and asked: "How many of those are still serving here?" The manager, a warrant officer, saw no humour in my remark and we never got on after that.

I worked upon a brand-new pair of steel-shod boots and I bulled up a pace stick, although it was clear that this was a fairly redundant piece of equipment in my hands. I renewed acquaintance with the Grand Union towpath, running off some of the excesses of the excellent 'Pub Nights' which the Mess hosted. I was still drinking far too much but I was at last working towards an evaluation of my drinking habits.

The squadron still seldom worked beyond lunchtime, supposedly attending the gym in the afternoon. I made a random check and found the gym devoid of any but PT staff. I then rounded the blokes up from the block and took them for a five mile run, which seemed to shock many. I then established the runs on a daily basis, if no other duties intervened, and within a very short time there appeared to be some enthusiasm for them. A shop in the high street offered instant prints on T shirts and the runners mustered one afternoon with **HARRY'S HEALTH FARM** emblazoned on their chests. The running suddenly seemed popular, although it failed to find favour with the Warrant, who believed only in drill. We had some debate on the matter but his rank won all of these.

The squadron went to RAF St. Mawgan, in Cornwall, to participate in a Freedom parade and I ran across Ray Pelcot, who was serving on GDT at the station. I also renewed acquaintance with Phil Mutton, Gan running mate and a sergeant by now. We had arranged to have a drink in the Mess but a fight in the NAAFI between

Gunners and the resident US Marines required my presence instead.

Immediately after the return from St. Mawgan, I collected Mam from Shavington and we stayed overnight at Uxbridge before John Todd ran us out to Heathrow. We were met at Perth by Jan, since Arch was in the bush with an SAS selection course, and we spent a few days before taking the train up to the Goldfields. The house proved to be in a poor state and clearly lacking in basic maintenance, and it kept me busy for a few days. On Mam's first day home, Jack's wife brought her baby around and left her for some hours. This was bloody thoughtless and my relations with both of my younger brothers became strained for a time. A rather more serious breach developed between Jan and Jack's wife over even greater thoughtlessness in the aftermath of the Old Man's death, and this proved beyond repair. Family sadness seems often to beget even more of it.

Some work on the mine might have been a useful source of cash, but the leave was too short to justify it and I had, in any case, wanted to spend the time with Mam. She had made a good recovery but her health had not been good for a number of years, and England was a distant land.

My total time in Australia was just three weeks and I briefly stayed with Arch before flying out. At his house I met Danny Wright, again serving with the SAS and not seen in sixteen years. I flew back to England unenthusiastic about the duties I faced, wondering now what I might do to replace them with something more demanding.

The news on return was that a Gunner had been arrested for murder, and it transpired that he, a black lad, had been chased by a racist gang in Uxbridge. Backed into an alley, he had picked up a piece of wood and clouted one of his assailants with it, lethally. The charge was eventually reduced to manslaughter and he ultimately, and rightly, was acquitted.

Nothing so exciting existed in my day, which became a desperately slow progression to cease-work through mind-numbing duties. My hopes were briefly raised when I was given a training flight to run, but this proved to be a one-off and subsequent courses were given to the sergeants in rotation. Ironically, I was given full time training duties in respect of an 'RAF Regiment' cadet contingent from Harrow School. Whose brainchild this had been was anyone's guess (the product of Harrow School among the Corps was not noticeable), but it meant that Wednesday afternoons were mortgaged to weapon training, minor tactics, navigation or drill. I was assisted in these duties by a corporal and a Gunner, and on some occasion we were invited to the school for an open day. This visit afforded me no insights into the minds of public schoolboys, who seemed much the same as adolescents anywhere.

During a work's inspection of the block occupied by the Gunners, I found it in a filthy condition and I took on the responsibility of putting it right with night cleaning programmes and regular inspections. Just as this was having some effect, I was summoned by the Warrant and told not to concern myself with the block, which was strictly the province of the inventory holder, who actually was happy to accept the status quo. Concurrently, the canal runs had been stopped on the Warrant's orders for fear that injuries might leave us short of guardsmen, and my routines became utterly boring.

Socially, things were somewhat better. Within the station was an American communications unit that operated an old Nissen hut as a bar. 'Texas' or simply 'The Yankee Bar' (which perhaps is contradictory) offered Budweiser or Harvey Wallbangers at some ludicrously low prices, thus proving very popular with indigent Gunners, not to exclude flight sergeants. Its hours proved quite flexible and it was also a useful 'all ranks' facility where the Gunners had the chance to offer informal opinions that SNCOs might take up.

Uxbridge still had a fair complement of WRAFs and for a time I took up with a good-looking girl from the medical centre. She actually lived in a flat just beyond the camp gates and I visited on occasion, without getting seriously involved. Michelle's particular interests, it transpired, were in witchcraft and shopping at Harrod's. It was the latter which frightened me the most and I did not pursue the relationship.

I had been rather more interested in a WRAF driver I had first met some months before, whilst visiting Tom Jones one weekend. Joan lived in the WRAF block but actually was employed as a VIP driver, operating in London. I was attracted, but for the moment I did not act upon it.

In June I was despatched to the Brigade of Guards Depot, Pirbright to undergo six weeks of training as a drill instructor. This seemed nugatory to me, since I patently had no instructor duties with QCS, but it was a standard requirement for all squadron SNCOs. It was a sweltering summer and six weeks on the parade ground in full uniform promised to be sticky. We were forty-five strong, representing virtually the spectrum of regiments, and were divided into squads of eight or so for tuition and lesson practices. All of the DS were drawn from Guards regiments and my squad instructor was from the Coldstream Guards.

Each day began with a formal inspection of rooms and dress, and 'show cleans' were freely awarded for minor infringements. 'Show clean' simply meant showing clean the offending item at a given parade, usually after normal duty hours. I got an early show clean for a drop of water in my otherwise gleaming sink on the room inspection, and I learned from that. I bulled my sink to a gleam you could almost read by in the dark, and never again used it during the course. I shaved instead under the tap which served as a mop bucket sluice in the cleaning room; an idea which was enthusiastically embraced by all the other students on my floor, thus necessitating a bloody queue for it. At dress inspection by the squad instructor, a Greenfly landed upon the tunic of the infantryman standing alongside me. The squad instructor gazed at it in silence then tersely ordered: "Parade at 1700hrs. Show Greenfly removed from tunic." Mirth was not invited by such admonitions, since it was likely to result in: "Parade at 1700hrs. Show smile removed from face."

The instruction tended to end daily at 1530hrs, leaving us time to prepare two drill lessons and run them through on the parade ground with an imaginary squad. One day, I had memorised a lesson, which was saluting on the march with the SMG, and I went down to practise it. The parade ground was filled with students, however, all roaring orders, and I decided to go for a run instead. I had navigated a route of eight miles or so around the nearby Bisley Ranges, and when I returned the parade ground was empty. I decided to do the drill as I was, dressed in shorts and boots that dripped with sweat, and since the dummy weapons had been locked away, I did the drill with a broom which was lying about. The lesson proceeded nicely, until who should drive by but the RSM, Welsh Guards, and he ordered me to the Guardroom to be locked up for disgracing the parade ground. Being locked up was another familiar staple of the course on a day to day basis, and it normally meant 'bumpering' (polishing) the Guardroom floor for twenty minutes before being returned to (relative) sanity.

Each week of the course had a slightly different theme, although the student drill lessons simply worked the spectrum of drill with and without arms. One week we might prepare a Colour Trooping Ceremony, and the next might be a state funeral. We fitted in sword drill and pace stick drill between times, and the whole was intended to imbue us with a sense of presence on parade. For the Colour Ceremony, I drew the appointment of Colour Bearer and the 'Colour' was a blanket nailed to a broom handle. This nevertheless required the full respect due any battle honour-adorned silk job, as I swiftly discovered when I marched smartly off parade, dragging the 'colour' through some low-hanging chestnut branches. A howl from the RSM, Welsh Guards, preceded another fast visit to the Guardroom to bumper the floor again.

Escape from Pirbright and drill in full fig in eighty-degree heat was welcome, although the return to QCS brought no respite from the parade square. We were warned for Public Duties in September and the training for them was already in hand. Ray Pelcot was attached from St. Mawgan and, along with John Todd, we did a fair bit of drinking between training. Later, both were commissioned. Ray retired as a flight commander at the RAF College, and John was promoted to squadron leader during my final year of reservist service.

On 1 September we mounted the first guard, of forty-eight hours duration. The heat of summer had not faded and the bad news was that Wellington Barracks, where the guard formed for the short march to Buckingham Palace, was closed for renovation. (Actually, only the facade of the barracks was preserved and the rest gutted for new work) The guard now had to form at Chelsea Barracks and march through the city to Buck House. This march took forty minutes and by the time we arrived our tunics were black with sweat.

One of the very few justifications for the post of flight sergeant on QCS was the fact that PDs required a 'senior sergeant' for St. James's Palace Guard. This was a colour sergeant, or its equivalent. When New Guard and Old Guard faced each other across the Buck House forecourt, and had exchanged salutes, the senior sergeants of New and Old marched to the centre space for a piece of ritual which concerned the size of the guard and the state of the guardroom. I had meticulously rehearsed the script for this, only to find that the senior sergeant Old Guard was a Brecon acquaintance. We jettisoned the script and had an informal chat for a few seconds whilst the cameras at the railings clicked and whirred.

The formalities observed, we moved into respective guardrooms for forty-eight hours which were unrelieved by much other than routine. Ray and I alternated in twelve hour shifts, and I took the opportunity to go running in Hyde Park, where my boots and shorts (baggy) contrasted the smart designer wear of the many joggers, who seemed to me to be studies in suspended animation.

We had a series of guards, on a forty-eight on and forty-eight off basis, and these proved absorbent of time. We were also doing a fair bit of drinking between guards and on some occasion Ray and I left a party at 0200hrs, with an 0400hrs start for the guard preparation facing us. The march from Chelsea Barracks sweated most of that out, after a hamburger breakfast from a van on Chelsea Bridge.

When we dismounted for the last time, I went directly to 'Texas' and drank until closing, some six or seven hours later. When I left the bar I skidded on my studs and fell over, then repeated the fall after picking myself up. It was a defining moment and I knew then that my drinking was about to undergo a dramatic and permanent revision.

26

I made one more bid to develop a routine of field training for the plentiful occasions when the squadron was not ordered for drill. I submitted a programme that rotated the four flights and this found enthusiastic support from the Adjutant. Unfortunately, he lacked clout and when the Warrant pronounced against the scheme it quickly unravelled, save for a period at the close of the continuity season when we rehearsed the unit's war role. At this time the squadron's fitness for war was put nicely into perspective, for me anyway, by the (very) basic fitness test. Sixty per cent of the squadron failed it. I was shouting at the wind though and soon recognised the futility of it. The particular frustration lay in my recognition that sufficient time existed in most of the days to allow for both drill and field training; that the majority of the squadron would have welcomed a combination which would have fitted them for future service, and such training would have made the unit's field role far more realistic than it actually was. I was eminently qualified to assist such training, yet I presided instead over duties which any smart Gunner might have handled.

I was also more than aware by now that the drill-intensive routines of the squadron soon attacked the incentives of the Gunners to remain in touch with their chosen trade. Many of them arrived directly from basic courses at the Depot and thus never consolidated their tradecraft, whilst older hands from other squadrons simply wanted a life free of exercises and detachments. There was moreover a fair bit of dross floating about the Corps at this time; the result of lowered standards within recruiting offices in the later Seventies when recruiting began to dry up. Examples discovered on the conventional squadrons might soon find themselves posted to QCS when periodic trawls for volunteers were effected, and most of them would prove to be administrative burdens who were almost impossible to jettison. QCS was theoretically also a field squadron with a station defence war role, but no one was keen to put that to any test. Nor was the squadron all *that* good at drill, on occasion.

Joan and I began to keep company in a relationship that was oddly wary on both sides, yet mutually and instinctively trusting. Joan knew me as a drinker and apparently a committed bachelor, whereas I was cautious of her occasionally black moods. These, I believed, seemed mostly to stem from a brief and disastrous marriage, now dissolved. We shared an interest in museums and theatre and any drinking we did was extremely modest. I was avoiding the Mess by now and feeling much better for it. I might occasionally miss a genuinely convivial evening, such as 'pub night' in the Mess, but I was beginning to see that I had spent far too long in rooms full of empty people, and it was time to jettison that routine.

In November I attended a party held by II Squadron at RAF Hullavington, the unit's new location. It was an opportunity to renew acquaintance, although I was more interested in sounding out the CO for prospects of early return. These did not sound promising, although I did not entirely abandon hope. I was not to know then that my II Squadron days were entirely finished and that I would return only as a visitor. I am glad now that I did not know, for extinct hope in that direction might well have led me out of the service. *Apropos* of that, a letter from Arch revealed that he had retired and was now a civilian. I wondered idly about picking up the threads of life in Australia, although I had done rather too much of a pension term to lightly abandon the service.

The squadron exercised its war role by deploying to RAF Gutersloh in Germany. I went with a small advance party to sort out accommodation and quickly renewed acquaintance with Eddie Martin, now serving as a Rapier detachment commander on No 63 Squadron which defended Gutersloh. Another familiar face was that of Vic Eastman, undergoing a tour with Training Support Flight at Catterick, which was a supernumerary flight for the QCS exercise. Nor should I have been totally surprised to learn that Mick the Nutter, sometime bane of my life in Hong Kong and elsewhere, was currently in the Guardroom at Gutersloh. His chequered career had been remarked by a couple of lengthy absences, and he had just been returned to cells from the most recent of them. I went down to the Guardroom to see if he needed anything and we had a chat. He did not survive the court martial with which the Service returned him, with a sigh of relief, one suspects, to civvie street.[1]

Gutersloh had been built for the *Luftwaffe*, prewar, and it apparently had been a favourite call for Hermann Goering who had a suite of rooms there. Hermann, it seems, was an old bullshitter, whose favourite saying when he told some yarn was: "May the beams bend, if I don't tell you the truth." Between visits, a group of pilots rigged a beam in his room with a hinge and this beam duly 'bent' when a ring in the floor was pulled. This had been preserved and it was demonstrated for me by Flt Lt Chadwick, who was again the DSC on the Colour Squadron.

We proceeded to exercise, which passed uneventfully, and it was apparent that the RAF Regiment officers who formed the cadre of umpires did not greatly regard QCS as a unified fighting force. This was hardly surprising, on the basis of recruiting which was almost exclusively from basic courses at the Depot, and a field-training programme which lasted barely a month each year. We saw little of 63 Squadron in the period, although by one of those small ironies of life, in the drawdown of units and closure of RAF stations in the late Nineties, QCS *became* 63 Squadron.

I returned to Uxbridge with a 'jack' stereo headphone set for myself and a piece of Hummel porcelain for Joan, and we resumed our city round of entertainments. Dining out was usually a cheap meal of spaghetti bolognaise and a bottle of Valpolicella at '*Strikes*' cafes in the City, although an exceedingly good, and inexpensive, Greek restaurant had opened in the Uxbridge high street. The year was expiring and Joan had been promoted to corporal, with a posting to RAF St. Athan as a driving instructor to follow in the New Year.

In the second week of January Joan held her leaving party in the cricket pavilion on the station. I had just started a pint when an explosion caught our attention, and it swiftly proved to have been a

---

[1] Early in 1996 I received a clipping from a provincial Norfolk newspaper, sent by Eddie Martin. Beaming out from it was none other than Mick, resplendent in beret, regimental tie and blazer on the steps of some courthouse. His latest claim to fame/notoriety was in, as an 'old soldier', refusing to pay council tax.

bomb in Megiddo Block, about forty yards away. QCS was quickly pressed into duties to control access to the camp, which up until that time had been completely open to the public. It was a good stable door measure but we had to maintain it until the station was able to mount a permanent guard. It had been an IRA bomb, left in a haversack along with a gallon of petrol in a cider flagon. The bombers had chosen the block nearest to a particularly easy access and, as luck would have it, this was the Transit block, invariably empty. It had been so on this occasion, but the package had been spotted by someone and an MOD Policeman had actually removed the container of petrol. He had intended to remove the bomb, but thought better of this idea and merely quarantined the area until it shortly exploded.

A side effect of the bombing was that all entrances and exits to the station were sealed, exempt the main gate which was now subjected to a twenty-four hour sentry. John Todd and I had taken a stroll down for a quiet pint at the RAFA Club just outside the Band School entrance one evening, quite forgetting that the gate there was locked. Thoughtlessly, we then climbed over the wall and were apprehended by an MOD Policeman. This resulted in a short, one-way conversation with the CO, Nick Acons.

The news from Cheshire was that Aunt Bess and Aunt Jenny were planning a visit to Mam. Late in February, Joan and I drove up and stayed the night, then delivered Bess and Jenny to Heathrow. It turned out to be close run, since we hit a fair bit of snow and our speed was down to about ten miles per hour on odd stretches.

In March we took some leave and drove to Laarbruch where Tom Jones and his wife Sandy were serving. We actually missed Tom, who had been temporarily returned to England to undergo a course, but it was a pleasant visit.

My duties, or lack of them, were more than somewhat highlighted by the contrast of field training and deployment, with the empty routine of the office now that the continuity season was about to begin. I was earmarked as the squadron's representative on the station welfare committee, and an offshoot of this was appointment as editor of a monthly newsletter, which I called *'Pipeline'*. *Pipeline* depended very greatly upon plagiarism of any local guides I found at the Uxbridge library, since requests for contributions generally fell on deaf ears. I had to spike most of the offered jokes, since they tended to be racist, sexist or both, and when a risque joke which I failed to edit was published, it led to an uncomfortable interview with a man none too distant from the station commander's office, and where the chair on my side of the desk was conspicuous by its absence. At this point, I abandoned the unequal contest with *Punch* magazine and plundered the library guides ever more deeply.

My fortieth birthday approached and I sought a means of celebrating it appropriately, eventually signing up for the RAF Marathon, which was conducted annually at RAF Swinderby. I had intended to boost my training for it, yet somehow did little more than the standard runs along the Grand Union towpath most days. I drove to Swinderby, taking the station physical education officer and an Officers' Mess steward, also doing the run, with me and we found the changing room packed. I wedged myself between a couple of blokes who happened to be discussing the merits of running shoes, and a bit of a silence developed when I began to lace up my boots. "You're not going to run in *those*?" One of the blokes asked eventually. "Son," I responded, "I'm going to *win* in these." This could have been my finest hour, but I did not win. I was happy to finish the run in three hours and fifty minutes, although the drive back to Uxbridge was excruciating. The run also raised about £100 in sponsorship, which was passed to an old folk's home near the camp and which had served as an RAF hospital during the war. I passed the home on my runs and usually waved to the occupants when they sat out in the good weather, wondering when I would see a day when I could merely watch the runners go by. It arrived rather earlier than I might have expected.

Bess and Jenny had returned with the news that Mam appeared to be in good shape, and they had some good stories to relate as I drove them back to Cheshire. I returned to Uxbridge in time to attend a function at the Rugby Club, marking the retirement of a QCS sergeant. I drank nothing but lemonade, which was some sort of first or simply the past re-visited.

All units were liable for visits by establishment review teams, whose job was to decide if manning levels justified reduction or increase. Such a visit was received by QCS and I was warned that the team, comprising a group captain, a wing commander and a civilian, would be looking very hard at my post and that of the squadron Supply NCO. At interview, I gave honest answers to the few questions and when asked to describe my duties I did not embellish them. To no great surprise, the team recommended the disestablishment of my post, although, unfathomably, it also recommended increasing the sergeant posts by one in compensation. The decision was quickly confirmed and I was told that it would be implemented in October. I now began to look very hard at posting prospects.

With hindsight, I see now that this was the time when I should have pursued latent interest in commissioning, and I had in fact resurrected O Level studies via correspondence course. Forty was a watershed year and my present engagement was due to expire at the age of forty-seven, although service to fifty-five was possible. I dimly recognised the possibilities, but I procrastinated until the moment had passed.

By the middle of the year, the squadron SNCOs had begun to comment upon my continued absence from the bar, but I was not persuaded to resume the round of regular drinking. It was something that belonged to the past, and the past, as someone has pointed out, is another country.

The squadron deployed to Ramstein, in Germany, for a guard of honour, which we actually performed on a strip of an original Autobahn. The stay stretched into a couple of days, which was pleasant, but the unpleasant news upon return was that I was to be posted to GDT duties at RAF Honington. This was dispiriting, since I wanted most of all to return to Regimental duties after my now considerable absence from them. A lifeline was briefly extended by a former DSC of II Squadron, now the Senior Regiment Officer at the RAF College, Cranwell. He offered me a posting as an instructor, which I unhesitatingly accepted, but the Regiment desk at Innsworth was adamant that I go to Honington.

O Level studies continued and the mandatory reading for English Literature included *'Pride & Prejudice'*, which I noted in the diary as 'a barrel of laughs', and a copy of *'Macbeth'*, where the introduction was twice as long as the play. Some of these could be done to death by analysis, I thought.

The continuity season drew to another close and the squadron reverted to such bread and butter jobs as burying the remains of Hurricane or Spitfire pilots, which enthusiasts from preservation societies persisted in digging up. The last job for me was a Cenotaph parade on Guernsey to mark Armistice Day. I returned from the duty and handed in my ceremonial kit, did the blue card routine and left Uxbridge without fanfare. Driving to Honington, I had an engine problem that took the RAC two hours to respond to, and I arrived too late for dinner. I then discovered that I had been allocated a dirty room that took me two hours to clean. It was a depressing start to a posting I had not wanted.

27

Although it seemed to offer me a boring future, RAF Honington at least had an interesting history. Operational by 1937 as a part of the Expansion Scheme to meet the growing threat of war, it operated Wellington bombers and launched them on the first day of the war. For a time during the war the station passed into the hands of the American Eighth Air Force, and in later years it became a Royal Naval Air station, operating Buccaneer aircraft. The present Gate Guardian was a Buccaneer, but it proved to be something of a fraud, having served neither with the RNAS nor the RAF. Its entire working life had been at an aircraft test facility.

Day one began upon the note of a disagreeable conversation with the Mess Manager, a warrant officer, then I went off to accomplish the blue card routine, falling foul of the Chief Clerk when I inadvertently walked into the General Office on the wrong side of the counter, where I was presumably thought to be trying to read sensitive documents. At the Education Section I learned that the O Level subjects I had been studying could not be taken locally and I seemed to be back at square one in that respect. At the GDT Section, which was among a line of low huts shared with the RAF Police and a squadron of the Royal Auxiliary Air Force Regiment, I reported to a flight lieutenant of the RAF Regiment who headed the section, and he explained the current problems. The station was presently operated as a conversion unit for the Tornado aircraft that had recently entered service, and the raising of a Tornado squadron at Honington, No IX, was imminent. The station was some two and a half thousand strong in manning and about 20 per cent were out of date for annual ground defence training. The station also had a sizeable RAF Police flight that had specific defence duties that required them to range fire every twenty-eight days. Keeping abreast of this, I was told, had been something of a problem. Flight Lieutenant Owen knew of my aversion to the posting, and promised to do his level best to get me posted back to a squadron after just one year in the job, if I did my best to solve the training problems. This seemed fair.

The Section already employed a sergeant and two corporals and the flight sergeant post had recently been added to the establishment. There had been a flight sergeant Rock in the none too distant past and I later learned that his principal contribution had been to build himself a boat in the GDT lecture room. His peculiar solution to the knotty problem of securing attendance at, for example, range qualification had been to Tannoy 'range practice,' whereupon station personnel would simply report to the range, pick up a pre-loaded weapon and put a few rounds in the general direction of the target. 'Dangerous practice' would have been more descriptive of this.

Having already made myself unpopular with a couple of the middle-management types on station, I continued in that vein by reporting the inefficiency of other middle managers when it became apparent that the notification of defence training was routinely ignored. I put this complaint directly to the station commander's office. I also sent back to sections those who arrived late and I once put into the CS Gas chamber an NCO who had neglected to bring his respirator to the training. Flight Lieutenant Owen thought that my action was most unwise, but I reminded him that CS Gas was unpleasant but harmless, whereas Nerve Gas killed in about ten seconds.

When the RAF Regiment was formed in 1942, it was at least partially in response to the observations of Churchill at the fall of Crete. "Every Airman should be armed..." he declared, "...airfields should not be the abode of well-paid civilians in uniform, who, in the prime of their lives, are protected by detachments of soldiers." Uniformed civilians were pretty much in evidence forty years on, and perhaps still are.

It has to be admitted that blame lay also with some of the NCOs, senior and junior, who filled the GDT posts. Many welcomed the office- and lecture room-based routine which, usually, spanned no more than eight to five, Monday to Friday, and which precluded the inconvenience of lengthy detachments, frequent exercises, leave constraints and sundry other hardships which were part and parcel of squadron life. Another attraction of GDT was that its NCOs were annually assessed in relative isolation, rather than among a larger number of NCOs within squadrons, and the posts were therefore seen as offering promotion advantages. It is certain, too, that some were reluctant to leave GDT, and a number of Regiment NCOs attempted to found a career on it. In later years, I served on a squadron where a flight sergeant refused to soldier, unable to cope with the stress imposed by the job. It transpired that virtually all of his service since his first promotion to NCO rank had been on GDT posts. (He was subsequently detached as a supernumerary SNCO to the station GDT section until his engagement expired, and the squadron had to run light in the meantime.)

It was thus easy to see both sides of the coin, but I was not amused in the Mess when a warrant officer leaned across the table and announced: "You won't get *me* on GDT." Another proudly displayed his weapon card that revealed that the last weapon he had fired had been a Sten gun, obsolete for years. If these were typical of middle management, it was little wonder that the lower ranks had few enthusiasms for defence training.

I began by sitting in on weapon lessons, which I considered too casual, and looking at what else we taught to see what might be eliminated. Two days were allocated to each training group, to include range firing, and I believed that it could be reduced to a single day, thus making the package more attractive to station at large. I took a good look at our lecture room and realised that we could make much better use of it by turning the layout through ninety degrees, and cheaply arranging tiered seating by utilising some wooden pallets from the scrap compound. The storeroom and the instructors' rooms were a mess and a poor advertisement for efficiency, and I got the corporals busy. The sergeant was an affable sort of bloke where real drive was needed, and I tied him to a desk with the job of notifying courses and maintaining records. We began to make some early progress, although I had just one month to go at it before embarking upon a lengthy spell of leave over Xmas. Prior to notification of disestablishment, I arranged with QCS to take my entire leave entitlement of forty-two days in order to go to Australia. This arrangement had been honoured by Flight Lieutenant Owen and I flew out in mid-December.

The flight was via Damascus, Bahrein and Changi and the latter amazed me, being now the new international airport for Singapore and hugely expanded from the RAF airfield I had known in the early Sixties. Arrival at Perth was the usual early morning job and I hitchhiked through what remained of the night and the morning, securing a long lift with a chap who asked me to drive since he was tired. I did so, omitting to mention that I hadn't slept in about forty hours. I walked the last mile home from the Great Eastern Highway and I was met at the gate by Malc's dogs.

Mam's health was still not good, but she was uncomplaining and she still tried to do too much around the house and yard. We sat chatting most days and I had no particular interest in going much further afield. Although the temperature was in the Nineties early in the day, I did a run of about five miles each morning, and I usually took the dogs for a lengthy stroll in the heat of the afternoon. A friend of the Old Man took me for a drink to a club I hadn't visited before, and at some point I noticed that a portly, balding middle-aged bloke was staring at me. I assumed that he was merely noticing a club stranger, but as I turned away my memory suddenly produced a snapshot of the slim, raven-haired youth I had once attended night school with, a quarter of a century earlier. We had a drink and a brief chat, wondering where the years had gone.

Mam dished up a traditional Xmas Dinner just as the mercury in the thermometer rose above one hundred degrees. Some things did not change. I put another two weeks in at home then caught the modern train down to Perth. The 'Rattler' was retired and it was now possible to make the journey by day in about eight hours. I spent the remaining ten days of my leave with Jan and Arch, quietly sitting in the garden or strolling about the suburbs. The sunshine was welcome and I did not look forward to either the resumption of winter or duties at Honington.

It transpired, when I returned, that some angry letters had been flying about station on the subject of GDT attendance. Among them, in the file on my desk, was a specimen by one of the wing commanders in which he loftily dismissed ground defence training as coming 'a very long second to an airman's primary duties.' This seemed to encapsulate the RAF view pretty succinctly, and I preserved a copy of it. Some weeks later, the section was visited by an RAF Regiment wing commander from HQ Strike Command, and he expressed his anger at our poor training record. On the face of it at least, I had been in post for four months by then, and might have been expected to have sorted things out, and I was reluctant to offer reasons which sounded like excuses. I did, however, show the wing commander the letter and he seemed a bit more thoughtful later.

Mostly tied to my office, I contrived to escape each Wednesday afternoon by joining the cross-country league. Various of the East Anglian stations hosted the runs, which usually began at 1400hrs and sometimes finished as the light faded on the short winter days. I was plodding along in boots at these and presented no threat to the real runners. We ran at RAF Wyton one particularly bleak afternoon and I was actually the last man home. Even the marshals had buggered off.

Return from the runs was usually at about 1800hrs, by which time the dining room in the Mess was closed. I discovered that it was not possible to book a late, hot meal and the best that might be had was a plate of salad, which was left in the supper room. This was less than appetising on some February day, although on occasion even that had disappeared, apparently being scoffed as an early supper by some gannet. I went to see the Mess Manager again, tactlessly pointing out to him that he seemed to run his mess for the benefit of his staff, rather than the membership. He was not well pleased with this view, and it was clear that I was not about to win any popularity contests held within the Mess.

I *was* welcome at the police club, where the duty barman was usually Neil O'Brien, Swinderby mate last encountered at Aldergrove. I did not become a regular patron, but a pint with Neil each Friday evening made a pleasant break from the minor tribulations of dragging the GDT performance figures up to acceptable levels. I was at least satisfied that the section was pulling its weight and that the rest depended upon station. I was busy, although it seemed to have little effect upon the calendar on the wall. 1982 looked like being a slow year.

The relationship with Joan had so far survived some turbulence other than that offered by my posting and the Australia trip. Joan was still victim to black moods and these were not assisted by my defects of personality, which included bouts of arrogance that I seldom recognised until about three months after the event. When I had returned from the home visit, we spent a weekend in Bury St. Edmunds, which was the local town, but we mostly depended upon the mails and the telephone to keep in touch.

I chipped away at the training figures problem and I introduced the simple idea of sending the course notifications to section heads, rather than promulgate them in the Station Routine Orders which nobody appeared to read. None of the improvements, each of which saw our attendances rise, required either managerial or inspirational brilliance, and I wondered why the problem had been allowed to fester. The aggressive pursuit of recalcitrant airmen (to say nothing of their recalcitrant NCOs) gradually reduced our training debit, and if I was by now generally regarded as an objectionable bastard, I didn't much care. One angry visit from HQ Strike Command was one too many in my book. Attendances rose.

The NBC instructor qualification acquired for the Gan tour was no longer current, and in March I was required to attend another course at Winterbourne Gunner. I was actually reluctant to leave the section for three weeks, since we seemed to be humming along nicely, and beyond the days when two trainees out of twenty rostered might turn up for classes. I heavily briefed the team but they seemed keen by now to maintain the momentum.

I grabbed a couple of day's leave prior to the course and visited Joan at St. Athan, where she now rented a house in the village with another WRAF. I also called in on II Squadron at Hullavington, seeing Ray Pelcot among others and sounding the prospects for return. They still did not appear promising and actually were extinct.

The NBC course offered no surprises and I felt no especial need to devote much of the free weekends to study. I spent the time with Joan at Llantwit Major and we went down to Cardiff on one of them to trade the Polski-Fiat in on a '79 Morris Marina. The final week of the course featured nuclear and chemical prediction, for which I had developed neither liking nor ability. The instructor was a Royal Marine I had known at Lympstone and he told me to report early for the exam, showing me the answers sheet.

When I returned to Honington, I discovered that the sergeant had taken a fortnight's leave and had cancelled all the courses. I was furious, storming into Flight Lieutenant Owen's office but getting little sense out of him. I then rang PMC at Innsworth to ask about a posting - anywhere- but was not offered one. A day or so later, on 2 April, Argentina invaded the Falklands Islands and among the minor results of it was a faster move from Honington for me than had been intended.

The invasion fostered a good deal of national indignation, which was to degenerate occasionally into jingoism of the worst sort. Representation was made to the United Nations, but nothing more useful than a condemnatory resolution resulted and a round of shuttle diplomacy fostered by the USA, whose military clients included

Argentina. This diplomacy failed, but it was the failure of diplomacy prior to the invasion which produced more than a thousand broken bodies after it. A succession of British governments had been trying to off-load the Falklands, and the Argentine dictatorship clearly believed that only a purely token fuss would arise from their act of piracy.

The Task Force sailed as if it was a summer excursion, with bands and bunting to see them off at Southampton. The prospect of war seemed unrealistic, and perhaps it was until the cold waters of the South Atlantic closed over eight hundred sailors of the torpedoed Belgrano. There was no chance for peace after that sinking, which remains controversial. Because of all British governments' continuing belief that some truths are too strong for those who vote them into power, we shall not know the facts of the Belgrano affair for fifty years.

At Honington, life proceeded more routinely. We were finally up to date with training and preparing for a TACEVAL, which was a major examination of the station's operational effectiveness by external validation. This proved a useful stimulus to everyone and we had no problems now in maintaining attendances. I nevertheless found the time for some leave and took Joan to Ironbridge Gorge to view some preserved remnants of the Industrial Revolution, another incipient interest. We also visited Joan's folks in Worksop, but I quietly dropped my plans to attend the Review of the RAF Regiment by the Queen, planned at RAF Wittering to mark the fortieth anniversary of the Corps. Birthday parties, whilst some seven thousand servicemen sailed to war, and some of them to death, seemed just a touch inappropriate to me.

Runs through the woods at Honington were enlivened by sightings of deer and summer held much promise. The section was running smoothly and I had threatened to nail the sergeant's head to his desk if he ever cancelled a course again. We survived the TACEVAL more than comfortably, with all of the ticks in the right boxes for the separate phases, and if no queue formed at the Sergeants' Mess to shake my hand for having contributed to the success, then I was not losing sleep over it. In the second week of June I was shown a signal which ordered me to RAF Scampton within twenty-four hours, to await posting overseas. No details were given but it did not require genius to work out that the move was connected with the Falklands.

The news was only moderately exciting, since it was obvious by now that the Argentine surrender was likely, and it was in fact announced just one month later. I was not arguing with the posting, however. I reported to General Office for a blue card, expecting to complete only a temporary clearance, and was told to clear fully, 'in case you don't come back.' This was greatly cheering. I packed only the necessary kit then wrote a quick letter to Arch, explaining that I had nominated him as my next of kin, changing it from Mam. I did not believe that I was in any sort of danger, but if something did happen I preferred that any bad news should be filtered through Arch.

RAF Scampton proved almost to be a deserted airfield, having recently been run down when the last of the V-Bomber Fleet, the Vulcans, were declared obsolete and removed from service. Several examples of the type stood forlornly about the Scampton airfield, trailing wires under their cockpits where radar equipment had been stripped from the airframes, prior to scrapping. It was later alleged that Vulcan parts had to be hastily scavenged from such wrecks to support the Vulcans which were earmarked for the bombing of Stanley; operations which would prove enormously expensive and of very dubious value.

The station was famous as the original home of the 'Dambusters', the Lancaster aircraft which bombed the dams in the Ruhr Valley - another operation whose propaganda value exceeded the result of material damage or any impedance to the German war effort. An example of a Lancaster stood opposite the Guardroom, on loan from a couple of local farmers who had bought it after the war to commemorate their brother who had died in one. The station also preserved the grave of Wing Commander Gibson's Labrador, Nigger, complete with headstone. I am told that the dog's name has been posthumously changed recently to Digger.

I was interviewed by a wing commander of the administrative branch and told that all personnel who would form what was intended to become RAF Stanley, would arrive at Scampton for kitting, range qualification and some fitness training. My job was to demonstrate how '58 Pattern webbing was assembled, conduct the personal weapons firing on a gallery range and take the groups for some marches and runs. I was later joined by a Regiment officer from the nearby RAF Waddington. Flight Lieutenant Bruning was the man I would answer to and he was designate OC Regt, RAF Stanley. In passing, he mentioned that I had been selected for the job by Group

Captain Hawkins, who had been Squadron Leader Hawkins when I got lost on the Earls Court arena. I fleetingly wondered if the two events were connected.

Life became busy with the first of some five hundred personnel arriving to be processed. At some point I had seventy-five firers to conduct on a gallery range, zeroing and firing a practice at one hundred metres, when few of them had seen nothing except a 25 Metre range previously. Webbing assembly could usefully be done as a background activity to the ranges, and I was able to borrow some JNCOs from the GDT Section at Waddington. We also included advice on how to waterproof spare kit with polly bags, not knowing what the accommodation in the Falklands was likely to be.

It was intended that a squadron of Phantom aircraft would deploy to the Islands and the station commander at RAF Coningsby was presently preparing. Someone at Scampton decided that I should go to Coningsby to show the station commander how to assemble his webbing. Being at the time of this suggestion busier than the proverbial one-armed paper-hanger with a severe itch, I gritted my teeth and suggested that the Coningsby GDT section might just be more than competent to take this task aboard. This revolutionary idea was not taken up, and I was despatched one Saturday morning to do the job. Before leaving, I had also been given a very smart leather despatch case, which, it was thought, the station commander might find useful. The case was impressively fitted with brass locks and it was embossed in gold with the cypher **EIIR**. When I arrived at Coningsby, I reported to the Guardroom for precise directions and seemed to have arrived in the middle of a handover of duties. I waited patiently for some minutes but when it seemed that idle conversation had precedence over counter service, I rapped the desk and held the despatch case aloft. "Unless this is in the hands of Group Captain Wratten within the next ten minutes," I announced, "someone's career is likely to grind to a halt." This lie produced a satisfyingly swift response, and I was delivered to the station commander's door. He appreciated the webbing assembly and the tips on waterproofing, but declined the offer of the despatch case.

The programme at Scampton concluded in a few weeks, and we now merely awaited the word to move. I had the chance of some leave and visited Joan in Wales again, where she broached the topic of marriage. I thought the timing inopportune and we were at odds for a few days. We made a visit to Hullavington to stay with Cath and Ray

Pelcot. Ray had been on standby with II Squadron for the Falklands, but the unit had not been required and a stand down just announced. The hiatus in our move was irritating, especially since Flight Lieutenant Bruning had sailed with later elements of the Task Force, and it seemed that we might wait for another month.

I visited Joan's folks again then, at the end of July, I travelled with a group to Brize Norton. We flew in a VC10 to the Ascension Islands for an overnight stay and I had just missed Rocky Roxburgh who had been serving there for the duration. The fourteen-hour leg to Stanley was in a Hercules and I had my sleeping bag under my arm when we boarded it.

28

The C130 proved to be so crammed with kit that it was impossible to unroll the sleeping bag and seek a few hours of oblivion. That left just the box of sandwiches to look forward to as we climbed for height off the volcanic rock of Ascension, southbound. At least, we were able to land at Stanley, which was not guaranteed in the now midwinter weather. A blind landing system of sorts existed on the airfield, but it apparently required the pilot to see the runway before he committed himself to a landing. During the detachment, a number of Hercules made the fourteen-hour flight from Ascension, only to blindly circle the airfield before flying fourteen hours back again.

We deplaned and were met by Flight Lieutenant Bruning. It was cold and wet, with a bitter wind across the airfield and we did not loiter. We got a quick brief then were driven through the small township of Stanley to the wharf. There we waited briefly for a small vessel that would transfer us to floating accommodation. This proved to be *MV Rangatira*, dispelling my fears that the ship might be *HMS Maidstone*, and she had previously served as a ferry, plying between the North and South Islands of New Zealand. How she had come to be pressed into service with the Task Force was anyone's guess, but a fair bit of the mercantile fleet had been required, and some of it had been sunk. *Rangatira* was a crowded ship but a better-looking alternative than the vast encampment of twelve foot by twelve foot tents which were in use as accommodation on the airfield. Rangatira represented warmth, comfort and light, whereas few of those seemed evident at the future RAF Stanley.

The discomforts included crammed cabins and three of us were allocated to a cabin that looked suspiciously as if it had been designed for one. The bunks were tiered against one bulkhead and it was my misfortune to draw the top bunk. I could turn over in the bunk, but only just. My companions were a chief technician who worked on airframes and the RAF Regiment sergeant attached at Scampton to assist and who had volunteered for the tour. He swiftly confirmed my earlier guess that he was a whinger of Olympian performance.

We were given the next day off to settle in and I got a lift ashore to take a look at the town, which did not take long. It was home to about a thousand Falklanders, with a similar number living in the outlying districts, and I was immediately struck by the similarity of the town to the Boulder of the Fifties. The houses were mainly of timber frame and asbestos clad, with corrugated iron rooftops, painted either green or red. The citizens of Boulder, transplanted overnight, would only have wondered at the presence of the sea. On the seafront, I found the mizzen mast of Brunel's iron ship, the *Great Britain*, preserved as a memento of the years during which the ship had served as a storage hulk, before being beached off Sparrow Cove. There were half a dozen old ships, or hulls at least, serving some useful purpose in the harbour, and incidentally reminding of trade that was conducted under sail.

On the following day we joined the queue for a 4 Tonner that carried us the five miles to the airfield, and the sight of wreckage of a more modern sort. Hundreds of weapons had been left to rust when they were abandoned by the surrendering Argentines, who mostly had been mustered on the airfield prior to repatriation to the mainland. Self-loading rifles and M60 machine guns had simply been thrown into ditches, which also contained thousands of rounds of ammunition in every calibre from 9mm to 105mm. There even were Exocet missiles still lying about, although weapons of this order were soon rounded up for resale. A complete, and unfired, Tigercat missile system, sold to the Argentines by Britain, was recovered, refurbished and sold to some African country. Radar-directed antiaircraft guns built by Rheinmetal were also found in mint condition and these later equipped a squadron of the Royal Auxiliary Air Force Regiment raised especially for the role.

On the airfield itself were several wrecked examples of Aermacchi jets and Pucara turbojets, which apparently had been disabled by SAS teams that had operated covertly on the islands. Some wag had added a sign to the forlorn line. It read: **VISITING AIRCRAFT SERVICING FLIGHT**. Among the wrecked aircraft were several UH1B Iroquois helicopters, and the damage to these appeared to have resulted from postwar vandalism, rather than action. This was certainly true of the personal helicopter of General Menendez, the senior defending Argentine. It had few hours on its clock but had been comprehensively wrecked after the surrender.

The more pathetic detritus included steel drinking mugs, hundreds of them scattered everywhere and offering a useful and non-lethal souvenir. There were already concerns about some of the items that might be picked up innocently, and these included hand grenades that had a variable fuze setting from seven seconds down to instantaneous. Such finds could offer a nasty surprise to curious hands.

A small benefit of the freezing weather was that it at least suppressed, for the moment, a problem that had soon to be addressed. During their assembly at the airfield, thousands of Argentines had defecated quite randomly and the considerable evidence of it was everywhere in sight. The chief medical officer had warned of epidemics in the summer months, if a massive clean up was not effected, and it was the unhappy lot of the resident battalion to tackle this most unpleasant of tasks.

Thousands of boots over several extremely wet weeks had given the airfield the aspect of the Somme and Wellington boots were a necessity. Churned soil was everywhere and some of it courtesy the RAF. During the war, a decision was taken to bomb the airfield and it was for this reason that the Vulcan bombers had been hastily pressed back into service, although sound reasons for the bombing are hard to find. It was not simply a matter of denying the airfield to Argentine aircraft, for those which sank *HMS Ardent* and *Sheffield*, among others, had flown from mainland airfields. This was at extreme range and limited their time to a few minutes over the islands, but Exocets did their deadly work in seconds.

The Vulcan raids required a huge logistic effort, with a round trip of eight thousand miles, and air-to-air refuelling was not least among the problems. Another former V-Bomber, the Victor, was now employed as an airborne refueller, and it required a score of sorties by these aircraft to fuel a single Vulcan mission. A total of sixty-three bombs was aimed at the airfield, requiring three missions and more than a million gallons of fuel. Twenty-one bombs fell quite harmlessly, since they had not been armed, and of the remaining forty-two, only one just clipped the edge of the runway. The damage was repaired in a matter of hours by the Argentines, who artfully contrived some runway 'craters' for the reconnaissance flights, and the peat craters left by the others were left to fill with water. These, possibly the most expensive holes in history, now contained the floating evidence of the Argentine prisoners' most basic needs. It had not been the RAF's finest hour.

    The air traffic control tower was the only building of any size, apart from a servicing hangar from which all the corrugated iron cladding had been stripped by bomb blast. There was also a brick-built generator house and when we could not even locate a tent to work from, I suggested that we build our own facilities with sandbags, stacking against the back wall of the generator shed. This was agreed and took no more than a few days, during which we also scrounged timber and tin to roof the building. Runway cladding, with which the Argentines had clearly intended to extend the runway for fighter operation, made a fine roof, although we were in danger of losing it later. The same runway had now to be extended for the arrival of the Phantoms and all material was being looked at. In the event, sufficient cladding panels were brought in from elsewhere.

    The airfield was presently defended by the Harrier jump-jets which of course required no lengthy take off or landing run, and these would hold the fort until the present five thousand feet of runway was extended by three thousand feet. A horde of Sappers, including Ghurkhas, was presently engaged on the task.

    It was the task of our three-man section to try to sustain defence awareness among the RAF personnel as they went about their individual tasks, although I believed that we were very unlikely to inspire much enthusiasm for defence works. I proved to be absolutely right about that. We were provided with some labour from the Queen's Own Highlanders to prepare air raid shelters at a radar installation on Canopus Hill, which overlooked the airfield, and we worked laboriously for some days carrying filled sandbags up the hill. My indignation went into overdrive again when I discovered that the radar operators were devoting much free time to the building of a coffee bar from a huge packing crate, and were furthermore charging the Jocks who were toiling on their behalf for coffee which was supplied free to the site.

    Everyone appeared to be working a seven-day week and it was also a long day in bleak conditions, making return to the *Rangatira* welcome and not least for hot food and a hot shower. There were some water supply problems since the ship had mostly to desalinate sea water for its needs, and the showers were sometimes unavailable. When this was the case, I would strip naked at a sink and have a sponge bath. The idea did not catch on and my companions seemed to have a poor grasp of field hygiene.

Beer was available aboard, with a limit set at two cans per man but often exceeded in what passed for the Sergeants' Mess. My cabin companion, other than the inveterate whinger, often staggered in late at night. I did not drink at all and between dinner and an early night I usually wrote a 'bluey' (which was a free air mail letter) to Joan then listened to Paul Robeson or New Orleans jazz on the jack stereo. I had decided to save every penny of my wages for four months and that was easily achieved.

No 63 Squadron, from RAF Gutersloh, had accompanied the Task Force and they were still in theatre. They were not relieved until September and were, I think, the very last of the Task Force to go home. The squadron HQ and some of the fire units were also based on Canopus Hill and I found some time for a visit. Duncan Hood was a detachment commander and he and I had once provided the Escorts to the Colour on PDs. Canopus Hill had featured in an earlier Falklands War and a pair of six-inch guns remained on the hill. Duncan had acquired as his admin site the magazine that had served the guns, and although this was permanently a foot deep in water, it was five-star accommodation in comparison with anything else. A week or two later, a fact-finding team of cross-party MPs visited and they were appalled by the bunker. Duncan was obliged to move out and his admin site became a twelve foot by twelve foot tent, which was wet, draughty, prone to blow away and often did. Duncan expressed a pungent view of the MPs.

I addressed the matter of fitness by running up to the airfield each day, rather than ride in the 4 Tonner. It was usually a bleak prospect and the long hill that led out of the town was of about one in ten gradient. It certainly got the lungs working. I continued the runs even when I *got* the runs, a periodic bout of mild dysentery that swept the ship occasionally. It was locally known as 'Galtieri's Revenge', a reference to the unlovely Argentine dictator who, along with his cohorts, was now facing some hard times, questions and democracy in Argentina.

The sandbag section proved a useful shelter from time to time. We had run in an electrical cable from somewhere to provide light, and we added a paraffin heater that warmed the place and usefully boiled a kettle at the same time.

Late in August I was sent to Ajax Bay to assess the defence needs of the service element operating there. They were living within an abandoned refrigeration plant which had provided the field surgical facility during the war. Every casualty taken there survived the war. In my spare time I walked from Wreck Point, which overlooked the 'Green Beach' landings made by 3 Para and 42 Commando, to Ajax Bay and the 'Red Beach' landings by 45 Commando. On a cold but beautifully clear day, I sat high on the hill that overlooked the still waters of San Carlos Bay, watching the setting sun turn the water into syrup. It was difficult to imagine the horrors which had been enacted here just scant weeks before, but it was on the record. I waited until the sun had dipped completely out of sight, yielding swiftly to the darkness which seemed more appropriate, before I picked my way down the hill to unroll my sleeping bag and find sleep.

I completed my survey and made a report, although I believed by now that the next Argentine arrivals would be tourists, then I went in quest of a chopper ride back to the 'cab rank' that operated to and from the Stanley racecourse. Little had changed in my short absence; Sgt Hardaker was still whingeing for Britain and no one wanted to fill, carry or stack sandbags.

Joan was sending me copies of the *Observer*, which was a great treat, and I was not above reading copies of the *Daily Telegraph* that appeared from time to time. In one of them I read the obituary of Flight Lieutenant Alastair Gillan, who had been my first flight commander on II Squadron, and with whom I had served again on my second tour. He was a good 'un and his death, from cancer, was tragically early.

We began to run arrival courses, simply as the means of identifying labour, but it was useful also to show them a selection of the lethal ordnance lying about and to warn them off it. I was also required to teach helicopter emplaning and deplaning drills, since this was sometimes the means of returning aboard *Rangatira* when strong winds closed the harbour to light craft. Getting aboard a Chinook twin-rotor for such purposes could be a struggle when it kept the blades turning, and they were also ones to watch when they flew low over the airfield. The downwash from the blades was one hundred miles per hour and I once watched as a steel portacabin was hit by the 'wash and was bowled over several times, scattering a group of airmen like ants.

After two months on *Rangatira*, I had the great good fortune to secure a cabin for my sole use. It had *en suite* shower and toilet, which was indeed luxurious, although it took me nearly three hours to scrub the ingrained dirt from these facilities. It was another opportunity to ponder the hygiene standards of many aboard. I had by now noticed that many of the RAF personnel seemed to wear the same set of combat clothing perpetually, despite the facility aboard of a ship's laundry that was both efficient and free. Nor was there much attempt at smart movement by the RAF, which was greatly contrasted by the army units aboard, who invariably formed in three ranks and marched from the jetty to the transport. When I overheard two army officers discussing the RAF dress and bearing in appalled tones, I wrote a lengthy letter on the subject to the *RAF News*, which was then picked up by the national press. This resulted in a mixed bag of mail for me, to include the odd suggestion that I was 'letting the side down.'

The recent experience of service at an RAF station, where the presence of state-of-the-art fighter bombers indicated proximity to the Service's cutting edge, now closely followed by service at an arena where 266 British troops had died, had served to focus my thoughts very precisely on the subject of commitment to the Colours, and, not least, the absence of very ordinary routines which had traditionally underpinned such commitment - or discipline, to use an unfashionable term. Taxed by one or two SNCOs, I explained that, as a young soldier, every single working day of mine had begun by falling in with my platoon and rifle company upon a parade ground, and every single day concluded upon the same note. At the morning parade an inspection by either the platoon sergeant or platoon commander - sometimes the CSM or company commander - ensured that standards of dress, bearing, haircut, shave and weapon cleanliness were sustained, in addition to providing a simple demonstration of the chain of command. In winter we shivered a little and the sweat ran in summer and no one, so far as I recalled, ever considered this any great hardship. On the contrary, it was what set us apart from those who chose to work in factories and helped to make us what we were. Daily parades were by now virtually extinct in the RAF - with the exception of at training establishments - and were even under threat within the RAF Regiment, but we had not replaced them with anything more useful. The return argument suggested that the service simply had to reflect the changes in society at large, but I failed to see why, if we placed such great store by the 'willing volunteer'. I posited a theory that it had begun to go awry with the RAF at the demise of National Service at the close of the Fifties, when perhaps some bright progressive had believed that an all-volunteer force had little need for the tested methods of imposing and maintaining discipline. The volunteer, surely, would be a highly motivated and self-disciplined individual? The spectacle of the RAF at Stanley suggested otherwise, but I found few takers for my theory. I found myself now wondering if the RAF was intended to be a purely peacetime organisation.

RAF Stanley was very much in the peacetime mode when two Sea Harriers were flown off *HMS Illustrious* and headed for the airfield without prior notification. The alert was sounded and it was satisfying to view the flap that resulted in some quarters where total complacency towards defence works had prevailed.

Early in October, the first ever Stanley half-marathon was held and I entered for it. The race began in a blizzard at Moody Brook, then ran through the town and out to the airfield and back. Medals were promised to the first hundred to finish, and I was pleasantly surprised to finish at fifty-seven, with a time of ninety minutes. A few days later, Flight Lieutenant Bruning flew home and his replacement was my boss from Honington. Flight Lieutenant Owen's news was that my post had been filled in my absence and I tried to feel disappointed at this, but failed.

We were by now finding it difficult to be fully occupied and we began taking a day off in seven. I simply wandered about on mine, taking great pleasure in observing the rich variety of birdlife. I couldn't identify any of them, but that did not detract from the simple delight of viewing at close-quarters birdlife that seemed unafraid of human approach. There also were large gatherings of penguins, comic creatures which clustered about when one approached, as if curious at this sudden lack of uniformity. Walking towards a colony one day, I was about to step on a large rock, when closer inspection revealed that the 'rock' was in fact an elephant seal, basking in the watery sun. It had not moved at all, and I had only perceived its animate nature because it smelled like fourteen fish barrows.

Joan's birthday fell during the detachment and when she jokingly suggested that my location would not be an acceptable excuse for sending no present. I parcelled up ten pounds of compo boiled sweets and forwarded them. She consequently became very popular with neighbourhood children, although the effect on their teeth was probably dire.

The resident battalion was to do a live-firing exercise whilst retracing the Task Force route from San Carlos to Stanley, and they required safety supervisors. I volunteered and found myself trying to get ashore from *Rangatira* on a night when the winds blew and the harbour was closed to light craft. Since, however, Group Captain Wratten also needed to be ashore, a seagoing tug was despatched and it lay alongside, rising and falling about twelve feet in the swell. We had to time our leap and I prudently removed my webbing and threw that aboard first. From the jetty I made my way to the racecourse and got into my sleeping bag to await a morning lift to the exercise area.

I met A Company, Queen's Own Highlanders, on the side of some hill and I was attached to the mortar fire controller. My job would be to confirm his map references before he called in any live rounds. The blokes sportingly provided me with a brew, for my own rations had not yet been delivered, and towards nightfall we began the move out. The wind had gathered to forty knots by then and torrential rain followed when we headed up the steep side of a bald mountain. It promised to be a long night to precede the dawn attack that was the object of the night march.

As we toiled up the hill, the darkness began to be relieved by flashes of lightning as an electrical storm broke over us. The stark terrain was lit up impressively, and also lit up was a Jock, who was struck by a bolt of lightning. He survived it, apparently because he was so sodden that the charge went quickly to earth, but he was not a well man for a time. The rest of us simply felt miserable. At 2200hrs we were halted to get some rest before the dawn attack preparation and the absence of movement quickly turned us even colder than had seemed possible. There was no way of rigging a bivvie and our sleeping bags had remained in echelon somewhere down the mountain. I wrapped myself in the illusory warmth of my poncho and wedged myself in a narrow cleft in the rocks. It was without doubt the most wretched night I had ever spent.

We arose, stiff, cold and barely rested, before the first fingers of light touched the sky and moved into our attack positions. No mortar firing was planned and I was largely redundant, although I noted with interest that the Jocks seemed cheerful and untroubled by the hardships of the night. After the attack we were leapfrogged forward by Sea King helicopters to a new position, where the going was much easier. The rain eased and the sun came out, although there was no warmth in it.

We had been resting for a time, later in the day, when the MFC told me that he planned to call in some mortar fire, for practice. We compared maps to agree where the company position was and he then operated his radio to request an X-Ray tasking: "Two rounds, fire for effect, Over." The coordinates and the request were repeated for confirmation and we expectantly fixed our gaze on a spot about a thousand metres forward of our position, awaiting the black smoke and the report of the detonation. We heard the rounds passing overhead and were surprised, if not aghast, when the rounds exploded about two hundred metres in front of us. We exchanged alarmed looks then frantically grabbed at our maps, but even as we did so the radio was alive with urgent demands to cease firing. It transpired that as the mortars had fired, the shock of recoil had punched the baseplates through the peat crust the mortar line was established on. This had raised the angle of the barrels, thus greatly reducing the range. We were not culpable and no one was injured, but it was a sobering experience.

The advance to contact continued with platoon and company level attacks marking the progression. Each seemed more exhausting than its predecessor, although our job was relatively easy since we were not involved in the assaults. The hard graft was at section level where fire and manoeuvre over even short distances drains even the fittest. Here, the distances were long and the cover was poor.

A move forward in a Chinook helicopter (the only example of its type on the Islands, since the others sank with the *Atlantic Conveyer*) provided another welcome relief from tabbing, and the more so since we were climbing again. The move culminated in another company attack and this was the last occasion when mortars would be fired. I was wholly redundant now and I gave my spare rations to the MFC before catching a lift out with a Scout helicopter.

At Stanley, the news was that upon return to the UK I was posted to the RAF College, at Cranwell. This was welcome, although I had launched another fruitless enquiry into vacancies on II Squadron. I visited No 37 Squadron, which had recently relieved 63, and learned that they were about to send four Gunners back to England on a D Course. When I further learned that no revision was planned for them, I offered to run a cadre aboard *Rangatira* for a few days. This was accepted and it made a pleasant break in my routine. The days, meantime, were swiftly running out. I went down to the lighthouse end of the island to watch 37 Squadron fire off some time-expired missiles, and the same day I watched with greater interest than usual the arrival of a C130. It was the one that I was flying out on.

I had negotiated a month's leave and in mid-evening at Brize

Norton I was met by Joan. We returned to Llantwit Major where I anticipated a few quiet days and fresh newspapers. We discussed wedding plans, wondering whether to marry quickly in a simple register office ceremony, or to wait and try to make a more conventional affair of it. We opted for the quick wedding, but it actually assumed more convention than planned. We were invited, despite Joan's divorce and my Atheism, to wed at the Church of St. David, at St. Athan and this we did on 18 December. I dispensed with hymns and a Best Man, since Tom Jones was unavailable, but the witnesses to the registrar were Andy Ritchie and Ian Bellis, with whom I had served on II Squadron or QCS. Joan's folks arrived from Worksop and one of her brothers, Tony and his wife, Hazel, who were working in South Wales, also attended. Aunt Bess and Uncle Reg and Aunt Jenny and Uncle Arthur travelled down from Cheshire. The officer in charge of Joan's section provided a vintage Rover for the bridal car, and her colleagues provided a motorcycle escort. It was a grand day.

The organist played the Trumpet Voluntary and the reading was from Corinthians XIII. It concluded with the words:

Love is patient and kind; love is not jealous or boastful; it is not arrogant or rude.

Love does not insist on its own way; it is not irritable or resentful; it does not rejoice at wrong but rejoices in the right.

Love bears all things, believes all things, hopes all things.
Love never ends; as for prophecies, they will pass away, as for tongues they will cease; as for knowledge, it will pass away. For our knowledge is imperfect and our prophecy is imperfect; but when the perfect comes, the imperfect will pass away. When I was a child, I spoke like a child, I thought like a child, I reasoned like a child; when I became a man, I gave up childish ways. Now I know in part; then I shall understand fully, even as I have been fully understood.

So faith, hope, love abide. These three, but the

greatest of these is love.

RAF St ATHAN 18TH December 1982

Uncle Arthur & Aunt, Jenny Uncle Reg, & Aunt Bess, Tegwin &Ray

Service Ending
1983-1997

I wasted time and now doth time waste me

Richard II
Wm Shakespeare 1564-1616

1

The RAF College had derived from Trenchard's great plan for the new service, and built in the early Twenties closely to the design by Wren for the Chelsea Hospital. College Hall had four wings although the fourth was not completed until 1968. When it was, it was built identically to the other three. Three Kings of England had added pilots' wings to their tunics at the College, and a future fourth had done so. The long runway had been the setting for transatlantic bids in the Thirties, some of them ending in grief, and Frank Whittle's jet had flown for the first time from it, on the very day of my birth. Notable among others who had passed this way was TE Lawrence, who was perhaps aptly commemorated in the naming of an obscure lane on the station, although the substantial library in College Hall contained a whole rack of books about the man. I read somewhere that more books were written about Lawrence than any other man in history, and I could believe that. Although disappointed that my bid to return to II Squadron had failed, I looked forward to service at the College, believing that here at least was a bastion of service standards that elsewhere appeared to be in decline. This proved naive.

I knew that a large complement of RAF Regiment SNCOs was established and I wondered how many of them I might know. Most, as it happened, and I soon ran across Cath and Ray Hughes, who were surprised to learn that I had married. Rowley Watts and Graeme Curtis were two other QCS acquaintances, whilst Ron Smith and Dennis Allen I knew from the C Course, and Billy Little and I had shared some Depot duties with a BG course. The rest I knew at least on nodding acquaintance and I formed the early and optimistic view that such a team would work in especial harmony. This proved somewhat naive also.

I was posted to the Regiment Training Squadron that provided an inflated GDT package for each cadet squadron, at a fairly early stage of the eighteen-week course that took them to graduation. The syllabus covered the basics of weapons, NBC and First-Aid, but it also taught the essentials of tactical leadership to prepare cadets for the field exercises which punctuated their 'office' training. The package was conducted over two consecutive weeks, during which the cadets paraded only to RTS and were beyond the reach of the flight commanders who normally ran their day in fine detail. It was apparent that the cadets enjoyed this break, and equally apparent that few of the flight commanders liked the system, preferring our instruction to be delivered in smaller doses. The RTS syllabus had largely been developed by the previous Senior Regiment Instructor, now posted, and his successor seemed much less inclined to resist the changes for which the flight commanders now fought. For the moment, however, the system seemed secure.

There were four cadet squadrons and a graduation parade featured every six weeks. The squadrons accounted for eight Regiment posts at the rank of flight sergeant, leaving three flight sergeants, four sergeants, a corporal and four Gunners to run RTS courses. The SRI presided over our efforts, but was seldom seen on a day-to-day basis, whilst two flight lieutenants of the Regiment provided close supervision of RTS. These posts were known as Regt 1 and Regt 2.

There might be up to a hundred cadets on each of the squadrons and I was surprised to note that a third of them could be ex-rankers - those who had previously served in the RAF in any rank between airman and warrant officer, and now undergoing the commissioning process. I was also surprised to note that they followed exactly the same syllabus as the rest, and that ex-warrant officers lined the parade square to learn drill. This seemed pointless to me, but it was the system.

I settled to duties which included teaching the rifle, the light machine gun (which was a 7.62mm-modified Bren) and the Browning 9mm pistol, also teaching NBC and First-Aid and conducting practices on the station 25 Metre Range. Various of the instructors were required to accompany the three or four field exercises which were spread over eighteen weeks, and these exercises were of course multiplied by the four squadrons. It looked a busy syllabus and I had no complaint with that.

I was living in the Mess since Joan had no immediate chance of a co-location tour, and had also been advised by PMC that '84 was likely to provide the earliest date. Notwithstanding this, we had already been house hunting in the area, and during the Xmas leave and a visit to her folks we had spent much of my saved £1500 on furniture and appliances. We had quickly spotted an old cottage in the village of Ruskington, about five miles from Cranwell, and soon wanted it. The asking price was £30,000 that reduced to £28,500 on offer, and we were able to secure it, although the mortgage and endowment payments would account for seventy per cent of my wage. We were keen to move in but the wheels of conveyance proved slow and it was April before we finally got the keys.

For the moment, we had to be content with odd visits, although this led to the complaint by Joan that 'she hardly felt married.' My weekends proved not as free as they had at first seemed and I began to notice that the extra demands upon instructors were more adroitly dodged here and there. I visited Joan in Wales and we included a visit to Cath and Ray Pelcot, still serving at Hullavington. It was on this occasion that Ray told me that a vacancy existed for a flight sergeant, and I was annoyed to hear this in view of the very recent PMC insistence to the contrary. With my teeth into a new posting and a house purchase imminent, however, there was no question of applying for it. The door to II Squadron would now remain closed.

The final cadet exercises were of ten days' duration and the whole instructor team accompanied it for the first two or three days. An SNCO was then required to stay for the rest of the exercise, coordinating the 'enemy' injects. I was not surprised to catch this duty for the first exercise, but suspicious when rostered for the second and third. It transpired that my colleagues were entering excuses well in advance of the exercises, and that those who did not enter excuses were deemed content to go. I suggested to the coordinator that a simple roster be drawn up instead, but there was no enthusiasm for the idea and it was not adopted.

For the first exercise I was accompanied by the SRI and I assumed that he was vetting my ability. When we had deployed, he announced that he would lead one of the ambush serials, and he duly led us off. When he eventually put the group to ground, I checked the serial information against the map, wondering why we had gone to ground three kilometres from the ambush site. Time was pressing and I drew his attention to the error but he dismissed the view as inaccurate. We remained on the spot, quite uselessly, whilst, three Ks away, the patrol passed unimpeded. The following day he took the lead again and put us exactly in the ambush position, but unfortunately twenty-four hours too early. By this time, I was beginning to wonder where he had done most of his soldiering, and I was not greatly surprised to hear, at a later date, an anecdote by a mate serving at the Depot. The SRI, promoted to wing commander, had gone there as the Chief Instructor and was taken out to view a BG course, dug in on a defence exercise. The CI strode to the edge of a battle trench, which contained a recruit. "That's **very** good," Pronounced the CI, "did you dig it yourself?" If that was insufficient to bemuse the recruit, the CI then added: "Tell me, what do you **do** with all the soil you dig out of the trench?"

Before the year was much advanced, I was despatched to RAF Newton to undergo a fortnight's training as an instructor at the RAF School of Education. Regiment NCOs had to qualify as instructors during promotion courses, but the school reserved the right to teach the finer points of it. Newton was also the RAF Police school and it had an air of brisk efficiency. The Station Warrant Officer had a reputation for insistence upon standards and at a few minutes before 0800hrs each working day he positioned himself at the camp gates to monitor dress and bearing. My handlebar moustache was an early victim and had to be trimmed for the duration, but the SWO's act was one which I admired and one, moreover, which I would not see again.

Returning to Cranwell for one of the earlier exercises in the syllabus, I took a large group of cadets for NBC drills and became incensed by their laughing indifference to readiness for a chemical 'attack.' I put them into full NBC clothing to include respirators then doubled them about the area to make my point. Hearing of this, their squadron commander widely circulated a letter that condemned my 'act of mindless brutality.' This was prominently displayed on the instructor's notice board, and might have provided a good laugh, except that Regt 1 chose to accept the criticism, rather than reject it in robust terms for the nonsense it was. Other doubts surfaced about Regt 1, who apparently was in the running for promotion and obviously unwilling to jeopardize it.

Billy Little and I were required to invigilate at a GDT exam which took an hour or so. We briefed the cadets to check their paper when they had finished, then hand it in as they filed out independently. We usually ran a cursory eye over the papers as they landed on the desk, and Bill soon drew my attention to a couple. He had noted that the two cadets had shared a desk and the papers proved virtually identical, down to the order of answers and mistakes. I took them to Regt 1 expecting an enquiry but he shrugged off the suggestion. "It at least proves that they have initiative." was his comment and I was appalled by it. He shortly got his promotion.

We moved into the cottage in April and took some leave to effect it. I hired a vehicle to ferry our furniture from Worksop and soon discovered that the heat generated by moving the stuff in was not matched by anything in the cottage. Both the gas boiler and the immersion heater had quietly expired during the months of vacancy, and they proved expensive to replace. Rising damp was another costly problem, although we had been aware of it at the time of the survey on the property. The cure accounted for £1,000 and for about a year in the cottage we seemed to have no spare cash at all, despite two wages coming in. Joan haunted local auctions for various bits and I became adept at DIY, pointing brickwork, painting frames and papering walls.

The cottage was three centuries old, built by the Poyntell brothers, who were notable church builders in their day. The church opposite the cottage was built by them, and the land upon which the cottage stood had been granted by the church, as payment in kind. The village was pretty, with a stream running the length of the street and the whole aspect was like something off a chocolate box. Sadly, we had not looked much further than the street when we spotted the cottage, and soon found a possible reason for the cottage standing empty for two years.

Ruskington had a large council estate tucked behind the village and this was a centre of local unemployment. Some of the locally unemployed, who nevertheless seemed often to have the means for regular drinking, were in the habit of gathering at the church wall late at night and behaving offensively. I soon found myself in conflict with this crowd and among the results were a couple of bricks chucked through the kitchen windows in the early hours of one Sunday. This rather ended Joan's interest in the cottage and although some of the more offensive elements eventually went away to serve gaol terms and the village grew quieter, it was apparent that we would not be long-term residents.

The process of dismantling the RTS package was proceeding apace, to the point where cadets appeared for random lessons and returned to the squadron fold. This was less than satisfying and when I was asked by the College Warrant Officer if I would like a move to a squadron as a drill instructor, I agreed. In the meantime, I was due to undergo a management course, also conducted at RAF Newton.

The course dealt in the realms of files, critical path analysis and management structure and might have been utterly boring, except that the instructors, who represented several trades, presented their lessons with intelligence and humour. Of minor interest was the invited discussion of an article in a national newspaper that discussed standards in the service. It was based upon the letter I had written from Stanley. The two weeks passed easily enough and in the Mess I renewed acquaintance with Mick Tobin, whom I had last seen on II. His wife and he had bought a house not far from ours and we would see quite a bit of them.

When I returned to Cranwell I found that the squadron post had been filled by a newer arrival, and when I asked the Warrant why, he replied that he had been told that I was no longer interested in the job, although he would not specify who the informant was. I went back on the waiting list.

I was also required to re-qualify as a first-aid instructor and during the summer I went to RAF Halton. Tom Jones was also on the course and we found plenty of opportunity for a pint and a chat, also spending an evening at Uxbridge to drink with the QCS seniors. I offered to drive, which provided a useful opportunity to drink shandies all evening. Tom was a sergeant by now, but no less outrageous. Joan visited from St. Athan during the middle weekend and we stayed at the UJ Club in London, seeing Willy Russell's excellent *'Blood Brothers'* in the West End.

Among the good news was the fact that Joan would not have to wait until '84 for a posting to Cranwell. It may have had something, or nothing, to do with the fact that she had recently acted as the driver for the Commandant-General of the RAF Regiment, but she was posted to Cranwell MT in mid-September. In a less fortunate piece of timing, we got the bricks through the windows about two days later, after I had gone out to square off some idiot who was trying to set fire to a telephone box. For a time, I tried laying in ambush in the churchyard, but it seemed that this particular lightning was not about to strike again.

Worried about the occasions when Joan would be alone in the house, I suggested that we buy a German Shepherd, and we travelled out to a remote kennels in the Fens. We were directed to an old railway carriage, passing a large Shepherd which was trying to hurl itself at us through a barred window, passing another which was gnawing on a house brick, and the carriage door was slid open to reveal a recent litter of pups. These were feeding upon a cow's head that stared forlornly up at us and Joan rather lost interest in Shepherds at this point.

A few days later, Joan rang me from the MT Section. A dog had been found on the airfield and it would be delivered to the Sleaford pound, and destroyed in seven days if not claimed. She was a Labrador-Collie cross, about six months old and lately grown out of the cuddly pup stage. I surmised that she had been bought for kids on the married patch and turfed out when it became apparent that she was hyperactive. The dog, instantly named Gypsy, went home with us and immediately established herself as a member of the family.

"That's a *very* good trench," beamed the Chief Instructor

2

A particular burden during the Falkland's detachment had been the piles, which were especially troublesome when lumping sandbags about in the cold and wet conditions that prevailed. It had seemed frivolous to complain about them in the light of so many who were maimed or killed in the recent campaign, but I now determined to have them sorted out. Shortly prior to Xmas I was briefly booked into Ely Hospital and, in a job lot, I also had varicose veins in my left leg stripped out. I then had two weeks of convalescent leave, during which my left leg was merely sore and my rectum felt as if it had been treated with a hot poker. Goodbye suppositories, however.

Another course awaited my return to duty and I was sent off to Bicester, in Oxfordshire, to train for two days as a projectionist. I was supposed to secure this qualification for my Gan posting, but time had not permitted. I now caught it up, eight years on and, predictably, I was never required to put it to any use. I returned to Xmas leave and made the most of uncharacteristically fair weather by going out with Gypsy and an Ordnance Survey map to discover ancient footpaths. Most of them proved to have been ploughed under and I thought it just possible that the farmers did not find the estate people particularly congenial, either.

Some other part of Xmas I devoted to sorting out bills, which had multiplied with marriage. I reflected that at the end of '82 I paid just one - my Mess bill; now I paid a dozen and my account as the year closed stood at just £30. We were clearly still developing the cottage, but for a long time we seemed to have no spare cash at all.

The cadet exercises were mostly conducted on the Stanford Training Area a few miles from Thetford, in Norfolk. Someone once maligned Norfolk for being 'very flat', but the county possessed some outstandingly lovely countryside and fine forestry. STANTA itself, another area which had been acquired by the War Office for the duration of WW II and never given back, was a pleasantly rural setting that offered an equally pleasant stroll between exercise activities. There were five separate accommodation camps on the area, all of which dated from the war, with the ubiquitous Nissen huts predominating, and at some point Joan and I were at the same one. She had been detached to driving duties and I was running an 'enemy' group. We saw little of each other in the period though. During a recce, I ran across an Australian army captain on exchange to the School of Infantry. He happened to know Arch well.

The RTS package was all but dismantled by this time and it may have reduced the enthusiasms of the team as a result. At a routine training meeting I expressed my view that some of our recent work had a slipshod quality about it. This remark was not well received. Regt 1 and Regt 2 were both promoted and posted and the appointments were reshuffled. The flight sergeant who co-ordinated the training programmes now performed the duties of Regt 2, which seemed further proof that the contribution of RTS was somewhat diminished. I was developing an awareness of job dissatisfaction and did not resist when I found myself in the frame for a month's detachment to QCS to assist with Public Duties.

I was welcomed by the QCS Warrant, Andy Manson, who was long in post but shortly to leave the service. We had mostly disagreed during my tour on the subject of training other than drill, but there was no rancour in any of this. I joined the guard rehearsals as the Senior Sergeant and shared St. James's Palace guard duties with Rocky Roxburgh, attached from the Command School at RAF Hereford and not encountered in a few years. Also attached was Mick Austen, who had been a Gunner on QCS during my first tour. Faces simply cropped up, years later in some cases, and conversations were resumed as if we had been just out of the room. The PDs were not arduous and between them I rediscovered my routes along the Grand Union Canal. These were a change from long circuits of the Cranwell airfield, which had little to distinguish them.

The guard duties passed quietly and the best part of them was 'Captain's Rounds', when I would accompany the guard officer on a ritual visit to the night sentries. (We wore rubber soles for this duty, to avoid offence to Royal ears late at night). Afterwards, I would be invited to the Captain's Flat for a drink and the artefacts there included a snuffbox made from a hoof of Napoleon's charger at Waterloo, Marengo, named for a battle almost exactly fifteen years earlier and whose outcome had been a happier one for Bonaparte. Duties were otherwise dull and much of the night at Jimmy's was absorbed by laboriously copying out the Guard Report that was framed in archaic language and appeared not to have changed in a century or two. ('Sir, I humbly beg leave to report that there is nothing to report')

By the time I returned to the College, a vacancy existed for a drill instructor on C Squadron, and I accepted the offer, sharing duties with Jim Lavery with whom I had undergone pre-para years before. C Squadron was in its final weeks of training and we were therefore busy preparing for graduation parade. I would soon realise that, between the busy first weeks when the squadron formed, and the final weeks prior to graduation, there was not in fact a great deal for the flight sergeants to do. For the moment though I looked forward to the new duties.

After graduation, there was a six-week interval before the new squadron assembled and this might be regarded as 'free time', unless we were required to fill in with other duties. These might be in the form of assistance to the other squadrons, to the training of students who had been recoursed for some failure or other, to the 'special entry' courses, such as padres or medical staff who did not complete the entire syllabus, or even to parades which the station, rather than the College, might be contemplating. In addition to all of these were the familiar staples of Battle of Britain, Armistice Day and the Old Cranwellians. I soon made the slightly depressing discovery that there was no spirit of willingness among my colleagues to share in these duties. The fastest excuse tended to win the day here also, and I could not comprehend this, since there was no questioning the fact that our time off was more than ample. By the second month of the syllabus, we might be doing as little as two periods of drill *per week,* with little admin to otherwise fill the day.

I scarcely comprehended either why two flight sergeants worked with each of the squadrons, although this practice clearly derived from a time when there had been eight cadet squadrons at the College with one flight sergeant allocated to each. The requirement for two was great only in the opening and closing weeks of the training, and the whole matter of squadrons, special entry courses, recoursees, parades, etc. would have been more efficiently addressed with a pool of instructors, administered by the College Warrant. The latter was another seeming anomaly, for he had no direct authority over any of the Regiment staff, and was often reduced to requesting assistance from various of the training officers. This was the atmosphere that fostered the 'fast excuse.'

A new Warrant had arrived and he observed my group at

sword drill one morning, criticising the cadets' employment of the weapon on three different points, upon which he was incorrect in every respect. I gritted my teeth until we were off parade then walked into his office and dumped the AP818 (Manual of Drill and Ceremonial) on his desk, inviting him to defend his criticism by reference to the AP. He couldn't and didn't, but there was no admission of mistake and relations between us remained soured.

Between drill lessons there was more than adequate time to go for a run, usually taking Gypsy along since she had energy to burn, or for a swim in the fine pool that was adjacent to Whittle Hall. I also liked to wander about College Hall occasionally, studying the photographs of all the cadets who had passed this way since about 1925. Mostly they were undistinguished but not a few had perished during the war. Douglas Bader looked out from various sports groups and he was clearly a remarkable man even before the accident that launched his distinguished war service as a legless pilot. It was recorded somewhere that Bader boxed twenty times at Cranwell and won each fight by a knockout. The original Rockfist Rogan, perhaps.

Eddie Martin was also married by now and we invited Chrissie and him to the Mess Summer Ball. They also stayed at the cottage for a few days. Another visitor expected at this time was Mam, since we could see no easy way for both of us to make a visit to Australia. Mam arrived in June and came to us first of all, but, with her visit planned for six months or so, she also spent time with Bess and Reg in Shavington.

The village was quieter by now and the amenities were improved by the completion of a new library within it. (The bricks recently through our windows came from the building site). I was happy to pursue the quiet life when not at work and I did not miss the Mess, which perhaps had been most attractive to me at the height of my drinking.

Upon posting, Joan had brought her car, a '74 Triumph Toledo, and we continued to operate two, since Joan caught up a fair bit of night shift, which began in the late afternoon and lasted until 0800hrs. For a time we passed each other between camp going in different directions. I eventually bought a secondhand racing bike and used that for my travel, although we were slow to jettison the unnecessary expense of the spare vehicle.

Other than drill, the flight sergeants conducted a small amount of instruction in the realm of field living - showing cadets how to erect tents, maintain and operate pressure paraffin lamps and similar minutiae of field living. We also took part in the 'lat runs' that were a staple of fitness conducted by the flight commanders, whose 'flight' actually might be as few as seven or eight cadets. These runs were neither lengthy nor arduous, although some of the cadets appeared stretched by them. The cadets ran in CEFO, which was lightly weighted, and the flight commanders ran in clean fatigue. Jim and I would take turns, either running with the cadets or driving the safety vehicle, and it was another welcome opportunity to train in the Firm's time - not always possible in other postings by now.

We had been joined by a newish flight commander on some occasion and his 'encouragement' of his flight proved scathing and, in my view anyway, offensive. When we next paraded for the 'lat run', I quietly intercepted him and pointed out that he might have more credibility if he also wore CEFO. He clearly interpreted my suggestion as a challenge and he responded by offering to wear mine. I was happy to give it to him, having failed to mention that mine was sand-weighted up to forty-five pounds. Little was heard from the flight commander on this occasion, except for gasping breath.

I had by now begun to examine the flight commanders more closely, wondering just how willing I might be to work for one of them, should I persist with a commissioning application. Too many of them seemed to have too little experience of the RAF and it was not unknown for a 'second tourist' to be so employed. In other words, one tour somewhere since being a cadet then a return to the College to lead them. I was definitely seeing rather too much of a boorish or hectoring approach and this I believed alien to any forms of leadership which I had tried to emulate.

Within the RAF Regiment, leadership began at the rank of corporal, and the qualities of a leader were drummed into students at an early stage of promotion courses. The principles might vary, according to reference, but 'leadership by example' seemed consistent among them. I saw too little of this among the flight commanders, who perhaps regarded their role more as producing management trainees or, worse, 'members of the club'. I was astounded, too, that a flight commander might criticise a cadet for having worn the 'wrong sort' of a jacket at an informal Mess function, or that lessons in table etiquette formed part of the syllabus. Whilst this sort of thing represented excellence in a school for butlers, I could not see its relevance in a military training establishment in the late twentieth century. It occurred to me that the RAF was at pains to preserve some odious aspects of the class system.

Despite the presence of some undoubtedly fine officers on the squadrons, I noted too many examples of 'leaders' I would not have followed to a fire escape from a blazing building, and it was abundantly clear to me now that I was marching to a different drum. I had discussed commissioning and service to the age of fifty-five with Joan at some length, but recognised that I could sustain neither plan. We decided that I would leave the service when I was forty-seven, which by now was not at all distant.

If the sense of job satisfaction had seriously diminished, then the cottage life had plenty of appeal. We hosted Bess and Reg when Mam returned from Cheshire, and it was good to have the opportunity at last to reciprocate at least once the many occasions I had been provided with a 'home' in Crewe and Shavington. Sadly, Reg was by now in poor health and finding little opportunity to enjoy his early retirement from Royce's.

Towards the end of the year, the postings' NCO on the Regiment Desk at Innsworth got in touch with me directly. A vacancy for a flight sergeant on No 26 Squadron in Germany would shortly exist; did I want it? I accepted the offer without hesitation and went home to tell Joan. I had completed only a little more than eighteen months in the Cranwell posting, which more usually was a three-year tour, but the posting was approved, subject to completion of a Rapier Flight Commander's course. I was to do just one more exercise with C Squadron, deploying to the Catterick Training Area for a change. At an early stage of the exercise, the Training Officer sent me off to sort out about fifty Tilley pressure lamps which were no longer working, and I spent a couple of hours replacing smashed glass and broken mantles. Noticing that one of the lamps was made entirely of brass - a great rarity - I presented it to myself for services to light and understanding. It made a useful ornament to add to the shell cases.

My Rapier course was due to begin in the first week of January and I had no further duties with C Squadron from that point. I cleared my desk and was invited to a brief gathering of the Regiment staff, where a tribute was paid. I appreciated this, and said so, but I felt obliged to add that we somehow seemed to have lost the ability to work for each other. I remarked, too, that we seemed increasingly obsessed with working for ourselves, rather than towards common goals. This was sincerely meant, but silently received.

I wondered then where we were going wrong, but it took me some time to add a theory to it. That, I believed, concerned the way in which promotion had so greatly changed in the last decade and a half. National Service, with a regular intake and outflow of recruits, had kept promotion levels buoyant for years, but the demise of conscription at the end of the Fifties saw a reduction in manning and much reduced opportunities for advancement. In the Sixties and early Seventies, to remain at the rank of Gunner for five or six years was quite the norm, and a similar or longer time in the rank of corporal might precede promotion to sergeant. In a full service career spanning twenty-two years, the expectation might be to rise to flight sergeant, but there was no great expectation of it in the era of 'dead men's shoes.' Warrant officers, meanwhile, formed an august body and not a few of them wore WW II ribbons on their tunics.

Promotion had changed very dramatically with the arrival of the Rapier missile system, which expanded the sergeant posts on a squadron, thus opening up the trade. The second half of the Seventies was unprecedented for the scale and rapidity of peacetime promotion within the Corps, and I had been one of the beneficiaries. Perhaps, though, in this piece of good fortune for career Gunners, we had created not only the opportunity for promotion, but also a hunger and even a greed for it.

3

On 2 January I made a difficult leaving from Mam, whom Joan would deliver to Heathrow a few days later, and I drove to RAF West Raynham, which was no great distance from home. I arrived in midmorning and noted that a Gloster Javelin, the RAF's first all-weather fighter (exempting, naturally, Rockapes), stood guardian at the gate. It served to reinforce the image of a station that was frozen in time insofar as flying was concerned. On the far side of the airfield was a missile battery, whose obsolescent Bloodhounds awaited Soviet incursions, however unlikely their firing seemed, and the station portrayed a quiet aspect. The Rapier School product was far likelier to fire missiles in anger and it operated with an air of brisk purpose. Rapier results in the Falklands Islands were still classified information, but rumour had it that they were impressive. I completed the arrival procedure and found a room in the Mess, later having a drink in the bar with Mick MacGuire, last seen on II a few years before. Mick was now an Assistant Instructor Gunnery (AIG) to courses and he would in fact be my squad instructor.

The course was of seven weeks' duration and it was intended to make of its students reasonably proficient Rapier flight commanders, prior to a first tour with such squadrons. The course comprised mostly young officers, fresh from J Courses at the Depot, but I was one of two flight sergeants. Our inclusion was because the flight sergeant was deemed capable of flight command and on occasion had to deputise for his flight commander. Also on the course was Sqn Ldr Acons, previously served with on QCS, and undergoing the course because he was about to command one of the Germany squadrons, though unfortunately not the one I was bound for.

Prior to the course we had been provided with a pre-study package but I had made little sense of mine. It dealt mainly in the realm of radar characteristics and I would as soon have remained in ignorance of *how* it worked, provided that it *did* work. When the course opened, we would spend a day or two putting the kit into action and this was work analogous to weapon handling drills that I could understand. This handling, however, was at the level of detachment commander - a sergeant - and his crew, and we were not required to develop any real proficiency at it. What swiftly followed instead were long sessions in classrooms where 'pressure waveguides', 'frequency agility', 'planar arrays' and 'Doppler Theories' were the buzzwords. I was soon struggling with this and although our weekends were free and home no more than an hour's drive, I stayed on board to pore over my notes and manuals in a bid to remain abreast of the instruction.

I was happier with the Artillery Director, which essentially was a theodolite, when we did site surveys to select the optimum ground to locate the kits, but probably happiest when I went for runs around the airfield, despite the freezing winds. I was a steam soldier and 'electric bullets' were proving too radical by half. I noticed, too, that my signals procedure was very rusty and that something called 'Batco' - which secured speech over a net - had replaced Slidex and Griddle. Squadron practices had been quietly moving on since I had last served with any of them and it was time that I caught up.

The course wore on and at a weekly progress test I was alarmed when my score dropped to fifty per cent. I built it back to seventy per cent the following week, but took no delight in that, since it merely meant that thirty per cent of the subject was still eluding me. On a happier note, the Officer's Checks that were the bread and butter skills proved entirely practical and presented no difficulties. I scraped some sort of a pass in the final exams and was deemed qualified. I now had just days prior to departure to RAF Laarbruch and a new tour of duty.

Joan arranged a brief leave and we met Chrissie and Eddie Martin in London to take in the museums and the theatre. We then went to RAF Hereford to attend the christening of Jan and Rocky Roxburgh's son, and on this trip we also saw Cath and Ray Pelcot who by now were serving at Hereford. We had made the visits not least because we thought that the Germany tour would put us out of the service, and we were unsure what the later opportunities to see friends might be.

After some months of quiet, the yobbishness in the village

had broken out anew and this was both disappointing and slightly worrying, in view of my departure. Joan had again been warned that there seemed little prospect of a posting within a year, but almost on the eve of my leaving she was given a date in July. This was welcome news and we would not live in the cottage again.

I drove to Hull in the Morris, sailed overnight to Zeebrugge then drove through Belgium and Holland into Laarbruch. It was Sunday lunchtime when I arrived and the Mess bar was crowded. Among the attractions of Germany service was duty free beer and cigarettes and it sometimes looked as if the membership was trying to fit a lifetime's worth in. The posting also attracted a local overseas allowance, although this was not as generous as it had once been. The Pound, moreover, was doing none too well against the *Deutschmark*.

I reported to No 26 Squadron the next day and was greeted by the DSC since the CO was on leave. I then found my office in A Flight and spent an hour cleaning it, although it was not my intention to spend much time behind a desk. I had already realised that the way to learn Rapier was to get out on the ground with it. I met my flight commander and he gave me a rundown on the four sergeants and an equal number of corporals who comprised the command element. I was assured that no problems existed but this proved rather rosy. I met the AIG, who was John Steele from QCS and D Course acquaintance, but shortly to be posted, and the flight sergeant on B Flight. The other flight was the sizeable one of engineers who provided the first- and second-line servicing and repairs to the eight Rapier kits.

26 was momentarily quiet, with no exercises planned and the working week conformed to three days of Rapier training, followed by two of conventional training. The latter training was about all the flight commander or the FS had to programme, since much of the Rapier syllabus was dictated by the Instructor Gunnery (IG) or the AIG. I soon learned that my flight commander's preference was to sit in his office behind a closed door, and I just as soon went to him to enquire if he was familiar with the 'GOYA' principle of management. He wasn't and I explained that GOYA meant Get Off Your Arse and see what the flight was up to. His response to this suggestion was not good, but he actually was shortly due for posting and I did not press the matter, preferring to await his successor.

By the time he arrived, we were about to leave the Rapier for a fortnight and undergo a field-firing exercise on the ranges at Haltern.

We duly deployed and the ranges began badly simply because we had conducted no recce of them. This was inexcusable and we were subjected to a deserved roasting from the CO when we returned to Laarbruch. We rose no higher in the CO's estimation, either, when one of A Flight's sergeants failed to implement the correct NBC readiness on a station exercise a few days later. The CO succeeded in reducing the man to the rank of corporal and although I disputed some of the grounds upon which the charges had been levelled, I admired the example of punishment that actually meant something.

A reunion dinner was held annually for the five Regiment squadrons in Germany and it was hosted at RAF Bruggen, home to No 37 Squadron, shortly after my arrival. The principal guest was the Command Regiment Officer and he had clearly been briefed of my recent College tour. "How are we doing at Cranwell?" He asked me. "Great, Sir," I replied, "we've got nearly a dozen flight sergeants doing the job of six corporals." He was not pleased to hear this view and moved on, but it was the truth, if slightly stretched.

With evenings to fill until Joan arrived, I enrolled at the Education Section to top up my German, and on free weekends I cycled about the local area. In towns such as Weeze and Geldern I would order coffee and stollen in my execrable German from waitresses whose English was grammatically better than mine. An early trip to a Dutch town, just across the nearby border, revealed a war cemetery in which 25,000 German soldiers were buried. They had mostly been nineteen or twenty at the time.

A Flight was still failing to please the CO, but neither flight was much in favour after we had completed a major exercise, called '*Whirligig*.' This was army-sponsored and it consisted of deploying the fire units overnight to locations which would be defended by day. The overnight move was then repeated and this would be the scenario for a few days. We actually deployed very early in the day to RAF Gutersloh and had been operating in the field for two days before the exercise began. This put us into a degree of sleep debt, and on the second night of the exercise one of my fire unit vehicles left the road and hit a large tree. The one-tonne Land Rover was wrecked, and the Radar Tracker it was towing looked none too healthy (although it proved repairable), but the driver and passenger, although severely knocked about, survived. I patched up the passenger and awaited the German ambulance, generally losing contact with my flight in the process. For some reason, the maps, repeatedly requested at

Laarbruch, had been withheld from issue at the start of the exercise, and the new locations always seemed to be off the maps that I actually had. In one not easily forgotten episode, I scoured an area of Germany looking for my four kits in four different locations, with no better map than a photocopied fragment seized from the wall of the CP caravan. *'Whirligig'* was more snakes and ladders, for me. I had a long chat with the newly arrived flight commander when we returned to Laarbruch, remarking that our flight had to shine, and quickly. He was straight from the J Course, but bright and keen and I felt optimistic that we could pull the flight together. Happily, this proved to be the case.

4

We had returned from *Whirligig* to a station exercise and these frequently punctuated the normal training routine at Laarbruch. The station operated Tornado aircraft, whose thunder was familiar as they took off or landed on daily and evening exercises. Telephone calls were routinely suspended for a few seconds whenever a Tornado pair blasted along the runway, which was none too distant from the 26 Squadron Compound. These might have targets well to the East, if ever the Cold War deteriorated into armed aggression (to say nothing of Armageddon), and it was the task of the Rapiers to defend the airfield against preemptive strikes. There were more than thirty pre-selected sites around the station, at up to eight K's distance, and our deployment might be to any permutation of these with our eight fire units.

Exercise call out might be at the discretion of the station commander, and lasting no longer than it took to gauge the swiftness of response at all levels, or a wholly external validation team might present itself at station to declare TACEVAL, which was the ultimate test (in peacetime, anyway) of the station's readiness. Heads might roll with a poor TACEVAL result and the pressures to get it right were considerable. It was usual to see airmen *running* to their place of duty when the 'hooter' went, which offered a considerable and commendable contrast to exercise responses in the UK.

We were moving into summer and in July I took over a married quarter that was actually on the camp, in readiness for Joan's arrival. I had made just one trip to England since my own arrival, travelling via coach and ferry and using up about eighteen hours each way. When Joan arrived, we planned not to bother with UK visits, reckoning on seeing as much of Germany and neighbouring countries as possible. Joan's arrival was closely followed by that of Cath and Ray

Hughes, the latter now posted to our sister squadron at Laarbruch. No 1 Squadron operated light armour and although it 'lived' at the camp its role lay somewhere on the German Plain.

Also arriving, within a couple of weeks of Joan, were her folks, Tegwin and Ray, who brought Gypsy with them. We had very briefly considered finding a new home for the dog but rejected the idea, accepting that we would have to find the stiff quarantine fee a couple of years downstream. Not all dog owners felt the same, as was evident from frequent advertisements in the Forces' newspaper sadly requesting 'a good home required for....'

If my Rapier knowledge was not exactly advancing in quantum leaps, I was at least trying to make the conventional training as interesting and as varied as possible. An early attempt to teach GPMG SF foundered when the CO made it clear that he saw no useful application for the weapon, but I had rather more success in establishing a fitness programme which the blokes appeared responsive to. We would start a little earlier in the morning than usual, in order to justify taking some of the Firm's time each day, and as the weather got hotter I introduced a regime of morning swims at the open air pool. We succeeded in teaching a couple of non-swimmers to swim at such sessions and there was reward in that.

The CO still seemed very far from pleased with the collective training effort and some of our results on Rapier deployed exercises, whether at his behest or by station. The CO eventually mustered all of the SNCOs to itemise his concerns and it was quite an uncomfortable session. I was anxious to raise our status but floundered for a time in trying to get it right. I felt disadvantaged by having no depth knowledge of Rapier, and nor was it my particular job to drive the detachments. The kits and the Gunners who crewed them essentially belonged to the detachment commander - the sergeant - and it was my job to provide logistic support once we had deployed. I nevertheless felt that I should be more closely controlling, but I had no good, early ideas as to how I might implement this without vitiating the authority of my senior NCOs.

The Squadron Warrant Officer suddenly announced his retirement and for a time I was taken away from flight duties to occupy his chair. The station had in the past been granted the Freedom of Weeze and this was celebrated annually with a parade that was shortly due, and I was given the job of putting it together. This was no big deal, for there are few mysteries in the world of drill and ceremonial, but it proved time-consuming at a time when I particularly felt the need to be with the flight.

At much the same time, the CO decided to hold an Open Day for the families and we had to come up with some attractive ideas for keeping the kids amused. We established a 'minefield' where the kids detected 'mines' which actually were six-inch nails pushed into the turf. We had some pressure switches connected to a car horn for unwary feet and bags of sweets as prizes. I was running the stand when the putative father-in-law of one of the lads who was marrying a local girl approached. He examined the Mk V Mine Detector, remarking: "I could have done with one of those in 1944." As a nineteen-year-old member of the *Waffen SS*, he had lost a leg in the Ardennes campaign.

When we had settled in, I bought a bike for Joan and traded mine in on a new racer. It had taken me a mere forty-four years to acquire a brand-new bike. I also bought a trailer that Gypsy rode in, somewhat to her displeasure and to the surprise of the RAF Policeman on the main gate. "You don't half spoil that dog, Flight." He commented.

Whilst Tegwin and Ray were visiting, we joined a Sergeants' Mess trip to the Rhine. It was a long day, with a long coach journey at either end, but it was a start. We had already noticed how few bothered to travel beyond the camp gates, seeming to prefer their leisure time in the Mess or other of the numerous bars and clubs within the station. I later wondered if duty free drink was such a good idea, since it doubtless invited excess and perhaps also problems for the future.

The new Warrant was Mal Clouston, whom I already knew, and when he arrived he quickly divined that all was not well in the compound. He convened a meeting of the Seniors and I put the view that we no longer seemed able to execute our duties with a degree of humour. There was some agreement with this, although we came up with no useful suggestions for how we might improve our situation. Mal felt that things would get better when we deployed to the four-month detachment on the Falkland Islands, which was by now very close.

Weeze began a carnival week and attracted QCS, which performed a drill show and a Sunset Ceremony. Dave Bryant was the Warrant by now and Mick Austin was among his Seniors. We met after the ceremony and had a good chat over a litre or two of the local ale. On the following day, having preserved myself, just, from a hangover, we performed the Freedom Parade and it went off without a hitch. The CO was complimentary but it was his recognition for our Rapier training endeavours that I most sought. Drill was simple.

The sergeant demoted to corporal had now been posted and his successor seemed particularly keen. A second sergeant replaced another re-posting and we had a couple of changes at the rank of corporal. The flight commander was by now hitting stride and, in the absence of more pressing duties, I had ordered the equipment bays stripped out and thoroughly cleaned. I repeated the blitz on the flight offices, the crew room and the store and I felt that these improvements at least lent an air of efficiency.

Exercises continued and for a couple of them we were joined either by No 58 Squadron from Catterick, or by No 51 Squadron from RAF Wittering. Both of these units were light armoured squadrons, and both deployments tended to highlight the uncertainty attaching to the use of light armour within the RAF Regiment. Station commanders were perhaps rightfully nervous about seven tons of steel swerving about £18,000,000 worth of Tornado, but on the perimeter of the station and beyond the armour seemed to have no better function than a trench. The Scorpions were armed with a 76mm gun, but they had little indirect fire capability and we had surrendered a perfectly good indirect weapon, the 81mm mortar, when light armour was acquired.

September ran out and we prepared for the Falklands, flying out to the UK for a 747 flight down to Ascension. After a brief halt, the Boeing continued the journey, since the new airfield at Mt. Pleasant was now in operation and the 'air bridge' operated expensively by air-refuelled C130 aircraft was a thing of the past. We disembarked to an immediate lecture about unexploded ordnance that still existed in some quantity, and I was delighted to discover that the EOD man was a Geordie I had undergone the commando course with seven years previously.

We travelled by road to Stanley and were lodged for the night on a 'Coastel', which was one of several floating accommodations moored in proximity to the airfield. The original camp on the airfield pioneered by No 63 Squadron still existed, although much augmented now by Portacabins, but successive earlier detachments had occupied the relatively luxurious accommodation aboard the Coastel. We assumed that we would also do so, but the CO made very clear, very quickly his views that 'floating gin palaces' were no place for squadron personnel, and within days we were living on Black Eagle Camp (so named for the central motif of the 63 Squadron badge).

This created some grumbles, but it was academic insofar as the fire units' crews were concerned. The kits (which remained *in situ* and did not change with successive detachments), were strung the length of the land strip which projected some five miles east of the Stanley township. Each of the eight-man crews deployed to a kit and there they would remain, generally, for sixteen weeks.

Bill Mallinson, with whom I had undergone the C Course, was the flight sergeant on B Flight and we shared a room in one of the Portacabins. The accommodation was basic, but the kitchen looked good and there was abundant hot water in the showers. I did not grieve for lost social opportunities on the Coastel.

We had relieved No 37 Squadron and we spent a busy few days picking up the routine. A daily visit to each site was the staple activity, conducting Officer's Checks on the kit and delivering fuel, water and rations. Generators powered the Optical Tracker and the Radar Tracker, so fuel was used in some quantity with a routine of twenty-four hours' continuous operation. No roads other than rough tracks existed to any of the sites, and in finding a track it was common to sink to the axles in peat, thus necessitating a walk back to Black Eagle for assistance. This added time to an already tight schedule. Within days, the CO delivered a blistering attack on developing 'nine to five' mentalities, and I took exception to this, having worked a seventeen-hour day for the third day in succession. I wondered if this would set the tone of the detachment, but I was too busy to dwell upon it.

We nominally worked a seven-day week, although it was usually possible to take one day off in seven by arranging to cover the duties of our opposite numbers. The fire unit crews had a similar arrangement whereby a Gunner was stood down every seventh day and he usually spent the time in a reserved cabin on the Coastel. I had no particular wish for much time off in any case. Bill was a keen fisherman and went off with a rod at every opportunity, but I used the time to get some dhobi sorted and write a more thoughtful letter to Joan than the usual evening scribble on a 'bluey'. I was fitting in my runs okay, and I also took some strolls about the vicinity. I visited for the first time the lighthouse that stood adjacent to our Callsign One-One fire unit on the eastern tip of Pembroke Point. Made of iron and shipped out from England for assembly, it was long redundant and its light lenses had been comprehensively vandalised by moronic troops.

We were perched on one side of Canopus Hill and a shallow bay called the Canache lay to the other side. Canache, someone told me, was a corruption of 'careenage' that dated from when sailing ships were beached there at a low tide in order that marine fouling might be scraped from the hulls. This area formed the regular run, and I was hitting stride along the shore one day when I became dimly aware of shouts somewhere behind me. When the shouts grew urgent, I turned to see a huge German Shepherd closing upon me, clearly thinking: 'if it runs, it must be guilty.' It took me little time to work out that I would not outrun the dog, so I turned and shouted **"STAY"** with as much authority as I could muster - admittedly not much. The dog didn't, but it appeared to lose some momentum and when it grabbed me it caused no damage. By then it was also beginning to respond to the calls from its handler, who duly puffed up and collared the beast.

We marked the days towards Xmas without enthusiasm, since here it would be just another day, although one closer to relief, and we found the level of operation about right. We had some more aggravation from the CO, however, this time on the subject of F6442s, which were the annual assessments required on every Gunner. These were due, irrespective of location, and the detachment commanders had the task, among many others, of finding the time to write substantial narratives to back the numerical assessments of six Gunners. I became irritated to learn that some assessments were being sent back to the sergeants because of grammatical errors, which I thought might easily be rectified by the clerical staff who had accompanied the detachment, and who, generally, *did* work a 'nine to five' routine. I spoke to the DSC on the subject, without much result, and I eventually rewrote the assessments myself when it seemed that my flight commander stood to be redressed over them. It was not a happy time.

I never believed, however, that there would not be lighter moments, and just before Xmas we were roaring. Each of the fire units had a freezer and Mal Clouston had been doing the rounds, delivering a turkey to all of them, until it was unfortunately realised that the turkey ration was about six ounces per man, rather than the three or four pounds they currently had. Mal did the rounds again to confiscate the turkeys and promise a few slices in due course, with the possible joy of a Xmas raffle to decide the distribution of the legs. This was related in a letter written to home by one of the sergeants. His wife promptly got in touch with a British tabloid newspaper which was not noted for the accuracy of its reporting, and which splashed **SCANDAL OF THE XMAS TURKEYS FOR OUR BOYS IN THE FALKLANDS** across the front page. The CO was not amused, pulling the sergeant in for a withering interview, but was even less so by the appearance of a poster in the Black Eagle Canteen. This advertised a forthcoming video about the exploits of the SAS and the poster depicted a group of balaclava'd thugs administering a good kicking to some unfortunate on the ground. Someone had added a balloon issuing from one balaclava. "All right you bastard," It read, "where are the fucking turkeys?"

"All right, you Bastard, where are the turkeys?"

5

Unwanted, and perhaps unwarranted, minor aggravations such as bouncing F6442s quickly faded as we got the measure of the detachment. Breakfast at Black Eagle tended to be a hasty affair and unremarked by much social chat, before we launched anew at the routine of the day. Each of the fire units had to be visited, primarily for Officer's Checks of the kits, but also to deliver the staples of existence. Water was a particular problem, since it was required for washing, cooking and drinking in some quantity by eight men and every drop of it had to be carted out to the sites. This was merely half the problem, though, for the water jerricans first had to be filled at a standpipe close to the Stanley township and the water pressure was notoriously poor. There were many other users, inevitably, and water replenishment consumed an inordinate amount of time. We could be grateful that the Falklands summer never really amounted to very much, since heat would have magnified the problem greatly.

Eight kilometres only separated the furthest of the four fire units, and this would not normally have offered a time problem to the matter of daily runs. The problem arose from the terrain, which was a virtual moonscape in parts which had to be negotiated with great care even in a four-wheel drive vehicle, and a quaking bog elsewhere which sucked the wheels down to the axles. The MT fleet, which had seen, and suffered under, a succession of detachments was only kept alive at all with Herculean effort by our MT servicing staff, who sometimes worked in shifts around the clock to achieve it. We mostly used the familiar Series III Land Rovers or the 1 Tonne, V8-engined Land Rovers which were designed to tow the radar and optical trackers, a function which of course was not required here. The fleet additionally included a tracked vehicle, but its use was reserved for the worst of weathers since spares for the vehicle were not plentiful.

Officer's Checks could be done comfortably in half an hour, but it was necessary to get permission first from the Command Post, since the kit was effectively 'out of action' during the checks. It was frustrating, therefore, to arrive on site and radio for permission, only to learn that another crew's kit was down with a problem and that the remainder had to remain at readiness until the problem was rectified. Each of the detachment commanders was adept at faultfinding, and they moreover had a checklist to help them to identify problems, but when local resource failed an engineering team had to be summoned from Black Eagle. They of course faced the same travel delays and the whole thing tended to snowball. The agonising decision at the site picked for checks, meanwhile, was whether to wait in the hope of an early decision, or to defer the checks until later by continuing the round of visits.

Our furthest kit to the east, adjacent to the vandalised lighthouse, was Callsign One-One, and Callsign One-Four was at the western extremity of Pembroke Point. Between the two was Callsign One-Two, whose site looked like the surface of a dead planet, whilst Callsign One-Three was not on the mainland at all. It had been sited on the smaller of two islands called The Tussacs and was only accessible by helicopter. It was a stone dot in the approaches to Stanley Harbour and even the penguins appeared to shun it. It was known as 'The Landaway', although it was also sometimes called 'the eight Rocks on a rock site.' The Landaway was not visited daily, but weekly for checks and there might be a biweekly visit by a helicopter to drop off a cargo net or two filled with fuel, water and rations. If the comforts were few on the mainland kits, then they might have been supposed to be utterly Spartan on One-Three, but there were times, especially in the detachment early weeks, when the occupants of Tussac were much envied by the rest.

The helicopter chalks were also routinely used to replenish the mainland sites, and the preparation for these was usually conducted in the early evening, after dinner. Generator fuel had to be pumped from rubber reservoirs into forty-four gallon drums that were then netted for lift the next morning. Each site operated two small generators which had Hillman Imp engines to power the optical and radar trackers, whilst a much larger generator, diesel-engined, supplied power to the site for cooking and lighting. The kit generators, known as 'screamers' and well-named, as you discovered if you had to spend any time in close proximity to them, operated around the clock and they consumed a fair amount of petrol.

The generally long day was sometimes followed by an equally long night. The Command Post, or CP, was also continually manned and during the day it tended to be the province of the CO, DSC or

IG. Each of the flight commanders and the flight sergeants was a relief Watchkeeper and we normally drew the night shift when little was happening, save the hourly radio checks that ensued that the kits were keeping a listening watch. It was utterly boring in the CP, once the 'bluey' home had been written and the three-day-old newspaper read for the fourth time.

The CP ran exercises at a regular interval to keep the fire units practised. These would otherwise randomly track aircraft into the Stanley area, usually reporting that the aircraft IFF devices (Identification Friend or Foe) were not responding correctly. This, however, did not mean that the Argentine air force was launching a pre-emptive strike; it meant instead that we had yet another idle F4 Phantom pilot in the circuit. It happened all the time.

The station also held exercises periodically, but these offered us no inconvenience since we were perpetually at battle readiness, and we would watch, with a sense of smug superiority, as the 'Shinies' struggled in to their places of duty at an early hour of the day. It was supposed that the exercises maintained some sort of fighting edge, but the Argentines were long gone and a new invasion seemed hardly likelier than one from Mars.

Xmas arrived, bringing with it about six ounces of turkey but little festive cheer. A party was held in the canteen at Black Eagle but the 'two cans per man per day' rule held. I actually noticed that some of the Gunners made their ration last very well, and that they seemed unusually susceptible to the effect of so little alcohol. Perhaps they were tired. The rule did not affect me, since I was enjoying an alcohol-free detachment, with the exception of a night in the combined officers' and sergeants' portacabin. The DSC produced his Trivial Pursuit board and a couple of bottles of very decent red wine. My sobriety, apart from being a virtue, was also handy, especially on the occasion that I had to explain to my roommate that my locker was not in fact a urinal. On Xmas Day itself I trekked out to Callsign One-Four, to spend the day with Mick Sweeney and his crew. We dined well and, from somewhere or other, a roulette wheel was produced to provide a staple of entertainment. It swiftly accounted for my loose change.

Summer was so far amounting to very little and the strong winds that typified the climate continue to batter away at us. We had also a great deal of rain, which served to interrupt a weapons and ranges programme designed to maintain our more basic skills. We often found ourselves wondering why people would choose to live on the islands at all. The locals, for their part, were wondering when we would return the town of Stanley to them, for it had become something of a garrison town by now. I remembered that during my earlier tour, I had driven a 4 Tonner down to the harbour to collect some defence stores newly arrived, and while I waited at the dock I got chatting with a local. "I suppose you were glad to see the Argies go?" I had asked at some point. The old bloke nodded, then added: "Be just as happy to see your lot go, as well." I didn't feel then that he intended any ingratitude, although some of the British tabloids had recently accused the Falklanders of it. I think that the locals simply enjoyed their quiet life and wanted to return to it as speedily as possible. They certainly were not deserving of the troop epithet 'Bennies', which was a reference to some idiot in a UK soap opera.

My runs were something of an ordeal when the rain fell or the wind blew, or both, but I maintained the discipline to clear the brain as much as to preserve fitness. I was not unhappy with my duties, and the kits held fewer mysteries for me now, and nor did a long day - or night - especially bother me, although I continued to fret at time lost uselessly.

New Year's Day was finer than most and I took the opportunity to swim out to the *Lady Elizabeth*, a nineteenth century vessel lying a couple of hundred yards out in the waters of the Canache. Like the *Great Britain*, her sailing days had ended at Stanley and after some service as a storage hull she had been towed out to the Canache and holed at the waterline to anchor her against the tides. I had noticed that a ladder remained on her hull and decided to take a look aboard. Her iron hull, when I reached her, was tremendously scabbed with great flakes of rust, and so was the iron of her ribs, strakes and bulkheads. Her deck planking remained, bleached and rotting, but her masts, yards and sails were long gone. She nevertheless looked every inch the sailing ship she had once been, plying the Cape of Good Hope in some of the worst waters in the world. She was beautiful.

In January, the missiles that had been on their firing beams for some months, and were deemed to be now unreliable, were fired off. These mostly performed as they had been designed to do, but the odd 'rogue' performed some interesting stunts before being destroyed. It made a different day in those that were beginning to look somewhat the same.

In another minor aggravation, the occupants of Black Eagle were set to work painting the Portacabins. This was incomprehensible, not only since they had never been painted previously, but also because the days of Black Eagle were numbered. The building of the new airport at Mt. Pleasant was merely the first step in relocating the defence assets connected with the airfield at Stanley, which was now reverting to civil use. It was intended, too, to revert the Stanley airport to its original appearance, as far as was possible, and we found ourselves filling in some Argentine trenches as a consequence. On the north side of the runway a huge hole was being created by bulldozers, and it was intended to fill it with barbed wire, fuel drums and sundry other detritus. The huge piles of munitions left by the Argentines were now long gone, and mostly dumped into the sea.

Among the minor crises was the nervous breakdown of one of my Tactical Controllers - a corporal - on One-Two. I was especially concerned since I had sold him the Marina a few weeks before the detachment began, and it had gone wrong in a dozen different ways from the day that he bought it. It transpired, though, that this was not a contributory factor.

The Portacabin painting was followed by a programme designed to smarten up Black Eagle, and it was hard to fathom this also since the camp would be occupied for a few weeks only by the relief squadron, who would transfer the operation to Mt. Pleasant. Some members of the fire units were brought in for the clean up, and that did not sit too well with any of them. I began to speculate, perhaps uncharitably, that the CO and DSC had too little to do on the detachment and perhaps thought that everyone else was similarly underemployed. I thought also that maybe they both might have benefited by spending some time out on the kits, the better to understand what was important and what was not.

Opportunities for R&R existed but were somewhat limited. It was certainly not possible to go away for days at a time - opportunities that existed for the station personnel - but a day trip might be arranged. I took advantage of one to Sealion Island, and I reckon that about fifty elephant seals were lounging on the beach there. An impressive sight.

Early in February, a piece of paper arrived from RAF Laarbruch for me. It was an invitation to sign on to the age of fifty-five. I rejected the offer, having by now set my sights on ending my service at forty-seven, a little more than two years downstream. I also received a letter from the TC who had been sent home as a result of his breakdown. He blamed it on excessive drinking and this was a sudden worry; how was it possible, if true? It would be some weeks before I had further clues on this one.

Towards the middle of the month, the advance elements of No 63 Squadron arrived from Gutersloh and I was warned for the first chalk out, which would take half of the squadron. With just a couple of days before the flight, I woke up one morning feeling very groggy, and I collapsed on the floor as I tried to get dressed. Within a few hours the side of my face became very swollen, closing one eye, and it was as tender as a boil. I went sick and the MO quickly diagnosed Shingles. He was delighted to have a case since he was currently describing the condition with a medical class at the local hospital, and he asked if I minded being a demonstration patient. By this time, the symptoms were utterly eclipsed by a blinding headache and I felt as much like being a model as for being entered for the London Marathon. I told the MO this, civilly, and he nodded, dishing out some painkillers.

It had been considered turning me in at the hospital, but I resisted and the MO agreed that I could fly home as planned. I boarded the Tri-Star at Mt. Pleasant feeling completely wretched and just wanting the trip over. We landed at Dakar to refuel and the bloody aircraft promptly went sick with a nose wheel problem. We were met by the air attache, who gave us some cash and told us that we were to be accommodated in an Air France route hotel. We were to pay for nothing, the attache informed us, just sign a chit at the hotel. Through the red haze and a pounding skull, I noted the words and thought it just about the worst advice any officer could give to a crowd of Gunners. It was in my mind to say something, but I simply felt too ill and I went off to the hotel to find a bed.

We were delayed at Dakar for two days and I spent most of the time in a darkened room. I had little appetite but on the few occasions that I ventured out I noticed that the chalk appeared to be holding a continual party. I also noted a diminutive Gunner lurching about the lounge with a Jeroboam of champagne under each arm. Detachment pay hadn't been *that* good and I suspected that the 'chit system' was being milked for all it was worth.

Thus it proved. We were assembled in the hotel lounge at mid-evening and the chits were presented for payment. It may have been the fact of my confinement, but I had clearly missed meeting such Hollywood luminaries as D Duck and M Mouse, whilst a Washington resident, R Reagan, had obviously been doing a fair bit of drinking at the hotel. At some point, the DSC appeared to be under arrest but we were eventually allowed to leave for the airport. A bill for £7,000 followed us to Germany and I never did hear the outcome.

Detachment pay hadn't been *that* good

6

We completed the journey back to Laarbruch with a short hop from Brize Norton, finding that the wives had assembled at the squadron's canteen to meet us. Joan and Gypsy made a welcome sight, if only via monocular vision, for the shingles had by now affected the cornea of my right eye. We proceeded directly to leave and I went directly to bed, still feeling pretty wretched and plagued by headaches despite the painkillers I had in some quantity. I was sent to the RAF hospital at Wegberg and the specialist prescribed steroids, advising me that I was over the worst of it. That at least was welcome news. At Wegberg I met Di Bellis, wife of Ian the ex-Rock who had been one of the witnesses to the register of my marriage. Ian had remustered to MT from the Regiment because of a knee injury and he was now also serving at Laarbruch.

Earlier in the year, Joan had arranged a booking on a coach trip to Rome to coincide with the post-detachment leave, and we decided to go ahead with the holiday despite my being somewhat out of sorts. We travelled through Switzerland and stopped overnight at Lucerne, which proved to be tranquil, clean and expensive. We quietly removed ourselves from a restaurant during the evening of stay, having measured the price list. On the other hand, there was an extremely good aircraft museum where admission was free.

We arrived in Rome in mid-evening, immediately going in pursuit of food and finding a very cheerful place where the pasta was piled high and the carafes of red wine never seemed to empty. We were spending three days in the city and this seemed to be an excellent start. Less good were a couple of terrifying rides in taxis, piloted by demented Italians who seemed to consider it a point of honour to carve up at least six other motorists on the shortest of journeys. We quickly learned to use the railway and bus service instead.

The Vatican, which seemed entirely carved from marble, was an early visit and we completed the tours of the Sistine Chapel and the

Coliseum, which I considered a particular marvel. I marvelled no less at a group of English people who stood at the pavement within sight of a whole row of fine statuary, bemoaning the absence of a fish and chip shop. Pasta, clearly, was not to their liking. Despite feeling off-colour occasionally, it had been a good trip and when we made the return journey we spent a day in Florence, where our day was almost ruined by a sighting of Mrs Thatcher, English prime minister in town for some affair of state.

At the end of March, I returned to duty, feeling more or less normal and no longer wearing an eye patch. Among the less common duties was in having to escort a chief technician who was under open arrest for alleged offences of child molestation. He later had to be locked up since some of his 'escorts' were not averse to thumping him.

In April we began to train for the categorisation board which each of the Rapier squadrons were submitted to each year. It was a test of virtually every member of the squadron, exempt the engineering flight and a handful of the executives. The tests were conducted over three days and comprehensively examined the skills and knowledge of everyone who was subjected to them.

Free of the distractions of the Cat board, I resumed thinking about a matter that had been niggling at me since the return from the Falklands. I believed that we had incipient morale problems, as a flight if not as a squadron, and that I had to pursue the matter. I decided to put the flight, except all NCOs, into the crew room, where I pointedly removed my rank slides and invited frank comment. What I learned, after a hesitant start, was disturbing and disappointing. Several instances were quoted from the recent detachment where detachment commanders had exceeded the drinking rules, whilst nailing the Gunners firmly to them. This now chimed with the letter I had received from the returned corporal some weeks before, and I felt particularly responsible for having failed to spot the problem. This was the gravest of the complaints, and some of the others were trivial matters that I was able to deal with very quickly. I assembled a list of some twenty, noting that the various works at Black Eagle, which now appeared only to have been intended for a 'show' handover of the detachment, had been a particular aggravation among the fire units. I then went away to study the list and give it some deeper thought before confiding the meeting to my flight commander, who shared my sense of shock. We agreed that it was probably too late to discipline the errant detachment commanders, but that any future detachment would operate under very different rules and more structured overnight visits.

Since the CO had told me, shortly after my arrival, that his door was always open, I went through it and read off the complaints to him. His reply was that I had brought him a 'real horseshit list', and that appeared to be that. I reasoned that the squadron's morale was his problem and I went off to work at that of my flight.

Since Germany travel had been among our priorities for the tour, Joan and I now began to look for a camper van to facilitate such opportunities. At first, it seemed as if most new examples were beyond our purchasing power, until a local dealer persuaded us to accompany him to Cologne to view a range. He drove us down in his Mercedes, often hitting a hundred and fifty kilometres per hour on the autobahn. Joan's fingernails were imprinted in my wrist for some hours afterwards. The range of vans was staggering and varied between palaces on wheels to the small and strictly functional. We identified the Ford Econovan as the one that combined our needs with our means, and we returned to Laarbruch to arrange a bank loan. The van was delivered within a couple of weeks and our weekends were transformed. Di and Ian Bellis also had a van and we combined with them on an early outing to Cochem, on the Rhine, among others. The Friday routine swiftly became a matter of shoving a box of food and the dog in the back, then setting off for a site in Germany, Holland or Belgium. Among the perquisites of a Germany posting was subsidised fuel, which effectively meant half-price petrol. The German campsites offered me the chance to practise my German and the dog usually initiated the friendships by wandering into neighbouring vans to see if any food was on offer.

Travel also featured on the training calendar with another of the *Whirligig* exercises. Having known about this for some weeks and remembering the previous debacle, I had made careful preparations this time. I had acquired two dozen maps to show just about every square inch of Western Germany and would at least know where to go and how to get there on this occasion. Also, and bearing in mind the CO's criticism of the previous year that we had failed to meet every single RV time he had stipulated, I decided on a new approach to the matter of overnight deployments. Although it was implied that each of the fire units should proceed independently to the new sites, I instead corralled them each evening then led all of the vehicles to the new area. This had the added advantage of allowing some extra rest to the detachment commanders, who otherwise would have been navigating their own moves, and I thought this important since they were the ones most likely to be losing sleep. We missed no deadlines, performed at least competently throughout and we avoided the CO's ire on this occasion.

A few weeks after *Whirligig*, we deployed into Belgium for a brief exercise on a Belgian air force base, returning through the Ardennes region when it ended. It was a surpassingly beautiful day and as soon as we had been stood down from duty I loaded up the camper van for an immediate return to the area. By mid-evening we were camped on the Meuse, which Gypsy was splashing about in, and life was sublime.

Laarbruch was the setting for another families' day and I was handed the job of organising a police dog for a demonstration. I knew one of the RAF Police shift supervisors from Aldergrove detachments and he agreed to provide a dog. The CO was especially pleased with this piece of news, since 'live' events were a bit thin on the ground. On the eve of the day, however, the supervisor came to the door with bad news: "Sorry, Mate," He said, "the show's off; the dog died this morning."
"What d'you mean," I asked him, "you've got about a hundred dogs in the section, haven't you?"
"Yeah," He replied, "but they're all guard dogs. We only had one that runs up ladders and leaps through blazing hoops and rubbish like that. And that's the bugger that died." Since Gypsy wasn't into blazing hoops either, I had to report failure to the CO.

At the end of June I was summoned to interview by the CO and informed that I had been selected for promotion to warrant officer. This was a complete surprise and rather gratifying. The CO suggested that I might now reconsider my decision not to sign on to fifty-five. I went home and suggested to Joan that we dine out, announcing the news over dinner. She also suggested that I now sign on but I had already decided that I would remain with my decision to quit at forty-seven. In the meantime, we speculated on what the new posting might be, wondering if we might remain in Germany.

By way of demonstrating that good news and bad news are often passengers on the same train, the next day brought news from the station senior medical officer. For some months we had been aiming for Joan's pregnancy without a result and eventually submitted to tests to establish possible reasons. The tests proved my complete sterility and the impossibility of children. This was a crushing blow to Joan, who had wanted nothing more greatly. I felt wretched at my inability to provide.

Within the week I had learned that my posting was to RAF Honington, which now included a Rapier squadron among its assets. I was especially pleased to be getting a squadron warrant officer's post, since these were not guaranteed. Of forty-five warrants in the Corps, only fifteen of them could go to a squadron, and I had not liked the three to one odds of going to a GDT post or other extra-regimental duties again.

The squadron underwent field-firing ranges at Haltern again, and the act was much sharper on this occasion. The flight actually seemed happier and we appeared to be getting more things right than wrong. I actually now felt a twinge of regret to be leaving the flight at this time.

We took a fortnight's leave in August and drove the van down to Friedrickshafen. We were touring Bavaria and I had to work hard at my German since few of the locals spoke English - or at least affected not to speak it. I negotiated the site at some camp and also conveying the fact that I had a dog and making several other queries, learning later that the receptionist was actually Irish; a linguistics student. Possibly she thought I was a Serbo-Croat. It rained incessantly for the first three days, but got substantially better later. We took in one of Loony Ludwig's castles, built at a time when aeroplanes were being built elsewhere, and climbed modest mountains. We visited the Spa at Baden Baden, and I was struck by the number of amputees we saw. Heidelburg and Strasburg were on the visit list, although we had not realised that the latter was in France. Uncertain of French quarantine laws and with Gypsy in the back of the van, we quietly drove out again.

When I returned to duty my replacement had already arrived, and I began the handover process with him. He looked a keen man and he had already written me a lengthy letter prior to posting. A few days later I attended a farewell party with the flight, expressing a genuine regret that I was leaving in midstream.

7

We had spent a final touring weekend on the Zuider Zee then drove back to the UK. It was to be the briefest of visits for Joan since she had no indication of a posting to Honington, and was therefore returning to Laarbruch to continue her tour. This was a third such separation in just four years of marriage, but it simply went with the territory and it was, in any case, the final one.

RAF Honington appeared little changed since my brief tour on GDT, although the arrival of No 20 Squadron had occurred within that time. The squadron, now occupying a hangar that originally had housed Wellington bombers, had formed just one year earlier as the second of three units that were dedicated to the defence of American assets in Britain. The *quid pro quo* of Lendlease in WW II had been ninety-nine year leases on English soil and there were a number of bases in the country that flew the Stars and Stripes. Nominally, they were RAF stations, but they were American right down to the last 'burger in the bowling alley.

An attempt to sell the British Aerospace Rapier missile system to the US Air Force had resulted in a compromise. The Americans liked the system but preferred not to man it, and the task was handed to the RAF Regiment which now had three squadrons dedicated as 'USAAF RAPIER' - or 'Uncle Sam's SAMs', as it was less conventionally expressed by one of our sister squadrons. Each of the squadrons actually defended a spread of American bases, and those allocated to 20 Squadron were RAF Alconbury, in Huntingdonshire which operated F111 bombers, and the twin bases of RAF Bentwaters and RAF Woodbridge, in Norfolk which both operated the tank-busting A10s.

Upon arrival at 20, I underwent a three-day handover with the out-going warrant and we spent time at each of the three bases so that I could get a feel for them. Deployments to them, I learned, were frequent and 'Uncle Sam' clearly liked to see value for his cash.

I occupied a room in the Sergeants' Mess and discovered that a new mess manager had brought few changes and no improvements. The evening meal still ended at 1730hrs, sharp, and when I saw that there was little scope to be free of my office much before 1800hrs, I tried to institute meal times changes by canvassing the Mess membership with a form I had produced. This produced an incensed joint response from the mess manager and the chairman of the mess committee and nothing was done. They were good examples of the 'nine to five' mentality which was occasionally evident within the RAF and perhaps still is.

I was interviewed by the CO, who knew that my Rapier experience was limited, and he asked me if I had any particular problems. I honestly answered no, but remarked that if he was planning any CP exercises for the officers then I would like to join them. I knew that I had some watchkeeping responsibilities during exercises. I soon learned that the CO had a very detailed knowledge of Rapier and that he was a hard taskmaster in the field, but a very fair man. He seemed to thrive on exercises and I could live with that. I was also pleased to note that he insisted upon a full squadron parade each Friday, inspecting the flights himself, and I believed in the continuing usefulness of that, however extinct the practice may have been elsewhere.

The squadron had been operational for only a matter of weeks, but it seemed to run like a piece of well-oiled machinery. Exercise callouts, which might be initiated by any of the bases or by our own parent wing, were frequent and usually in the small hours of the morning. These responses worked to fine reporting times, which depended upon every member of the squadron going about his preparation unbidden in order to get the fire units at their respective bases and operating.

I was not asked to look for improvements, but I soon noticed that the large complement of squadron HQ Gunners, who in the field were employed as signallers, were usually in the 'gofer' role on a day to day basis. I suggested to the CO that they might more usefully train with the Rapier flights and he was happy to implement the idea. He also asked me about training the sizeable engineering flight in weapons and basic fieldcraft, and I suggested running such a programme each Friday morning. This usefully got me out of my office, although I was doubtless doing some bright corporal out of a job.

Out of hours, I pursued the quiet life. I rediscovered the local running routes, read voraciously and spent some time in the woodwork club restoring a percussion musket of American Civil War vintage. I also signed up for a correspondence course in short story writing, devoting much of the weekends to the assignments.

Joan returned to England briefly in October and we visited her family before travelling to Cheshire to see Bess and Reg. Reg was by now very ill with cancer but maintaining good spirits. The leave was altogether too brief and we returned to our respective stations.

Within days of return to Honington I received a 'phone call from Dave Armstrong, by now serving in the rank of captain with the Australian army and presently in England on an exchange visit. We arranged to meet on the following Saturday in Chelmsford and I travelled down by bike and train. We met, appropriately enough, in a pub called *The Rendezvous* and although we had not met in twenty-one years we recognised each other easily enough; grey hair and glasses notwithstanding.

At the end of the month I formed a small advance party, joining Tom Tomney, who was the squadron AIG, the MT JNCO and the squadron cook to travel to the Hebrides for the annual missile camp. We drove to Carlisle for an overnight stay, continued to Oban where we spent much of the day then sailed overnight on a ferry to Lochboisdale. No sleeping accommodation was provided on the ferry, which made it a long night. I had hoped that there might at least be a shower facility, but asking that question earned me a stony look from the crewman. I might as well have asked if there was a cruise director aboard.

The short journey from the jetty to the camp revealed a landscape uncannily like that of the Falklands. In view of the fact that successive British governments had, prior to 1982, sought ways of relinquishing the islands to Argentina, I wondered if it had occurred to anyone to build a couple of thousand luxury bungalows in the Hebrides and move the Falklanders into them *en masse*. After all, the British government had evicted the occupants of Diego Garcia, in the Indian Ocean, in 1967 to accommodate American defence assets in the area, and the Diego Garcians did *not* get luxury bungalows.

The camp we arrived at was army controlled and I paid a courtesy visit to the RSM before sorting out accommodation for Officers, SNCOs and the Gunners. It was neither a lengthy nor a difficult job and I was soon running a few miles about the local area, being battered by a ferocious wind which the locals doubtless regarded as no more than a light breeze. I was again struck by the similarity to the Falklands. The wind gathered overnight and the prospects for the squadron's arrival on time appeared slim. To a man, they were due to arrive in USAAF C130s but although it was nice to have a wealthy patron, even the Hercs had flying limits. When the first chalk circled overhead, the wind was gusting at eighty-five knots directly across the runway. The pilot made a dummy run but was so far off the centre-line at the runway threshold that he tucked his wheels and flaps up and returned to Mildenhall. We few of the reception party trudged head down to the accommodation, grateful for its shelter and warmth.

The squadron got in on the second day and quickly moved the kits out to the Rangehead for tests and adjustments before embarking upon the firing programme. I had little to do with any of this but went out most days since there were no duties either in the base camp. A fortnight had been allocated and each of the Gunners was due to fire at least one missile in that time. This programme might easily be accomplished in one week, but kit technical problems and poor weather often caused delays.

Sharing Rangehead was a Swiss unit. Rumour had it that the Swiss had managed to shoot down a target-towing aircraft when they first acquired the system, which must have impressed the pilot no end. On this occasion, they were not getting missiles away at anything since one technical problem was succeeded by another, which doubtless accounted for the absence of yodelling on the Swiss firing point. Since all of our kits were performing impeccably, our engineers offered a hand and they proved successful, although they returned notably unladen by either chocolates or cuckoo clocks.

The targets were almost invariably canvas drogues, which were towed a few hundred feet behind a Canberra bomber, but pilotless drones were also used. These apparently cost about as much as a Rolls-Royce Corniche and the radar-guided missile capability was not used against them. The tracking was done entirely by the Gunner seated at the Optical Tracker (which had been also the only technology available in the Falklands in '82) and among the incentives for a 'kill' was a bottle of Scotch from the CO. A 'kill' also raised a tremendous cheer from observers.

Sixteen missiles were fired on the first day and the tally mounted steadily as the weather held and few technical problems were encountered. I tended to my rations, kept an eye on the accommodation and NAAFI behaviour and otherwise found little to do. The missiles were 'shot out' within the first week and arrangements quickly put in hand to evacuate the squadron. The first chalks went fairly quickly and I found myself more or less in charge of a tail end group of about forty Gunners. The advance elements of 26 Squadron arrived from Laarbruch to acquire the accommodation, and I was pleased to have the opportunity of a chat with Russell Barnes, my former flight commander, and the chance of a pint with Mick Sweeney, who was still one of the A Flight DCs, but shortly himself to be posted to Honington.

On the eve of our anticipated departure I received a 'phone call from the CO. Upon return to Honington, one of the flight sergeants had gone to the CO with an allegation of misconduct by his flight commander. The gist of it was that the officer, and possibly other officers, had been mixing socially with Gunners and that there had been some unpleasant aspect to this. I decided to interview each of the Gunners still aboard and this process went late into the night. At the conclusion of it I did not know how much of a fire we had, but there was considerable smoke and I put it in writing for the CO. When we returned to Honington enquiries by the Special Investigation Branch of the RAF Police followed, since allegations of indecent conduct had also surfaced. Eventually, two of the squadron officers and a third officer who had recently been posted were cashiered, although one was reinstated after a lengthy appeal. Coincidentally, the recently posted officer had been my flight commander when I had first arrived at Laarbruch. It was a dispiriting episode and not least because one of the officers attempted to smear the CO. The attempt failed, although I later wondered if the affair had not cost the CO promotion.

On a less serious, if somewhat more frequent, scale, we had problems between Gunners and RAF Policemen on the station. The two branches, although combined within a single trade group, had the natural antipathy of poachers and gamekeepers and this usually found expression in the NAAFI late in the evenings, especially on disco nights. There was plenty of the fault among the Gunners, but situations were not helped when they were peremptorily ordered about for trivial reasons by RAF Policemen who were eighteen year old LACs with only the acting rank of corporal. Whatever the reasons, I was keen to improve our record and I paid a call to the RAF Police Warrant. I pointed out that I was living in the Mess and that his blokes could call me out at any time to sort a problem. I also asked him to ring me in the mornings if something untoward had happened, in the hope of defusing it somewhat. We established a good, working relationship and managed to deal with most of the problems at our level.

One such call advised me that two Gunners had been locked up in the Guardroom the previous night but released, so far, without charge. I interviewed both and it transpired that they were ordinarily mates, but one had tipped the other out of bed for not attending a flight party (which reminded me of something). I declined to charge the Gunner who had started the fight and merely sent him away with a flea in his ear. A few weeks later he was dead, murdered in his car outside a Dutch nightclub by an IRA gunman. The Gunner was just nineteen.

A month did not pass without the 'hooter' summons to exercise at our main operating bases, but these were both expected and prepared for. Our priority was to put the kits on the road then follow up with B Echelon, which was a combination of squadron HQ Flight and the engineering component. It was largely my responsibility to get B Ech rolling and our deployment was to a small copse within the wire at RAF Woodbridge. We halted, early one morning, at the Woodbridge main gate that was manned by a shapely American policewoman, who wore a gun at her hip with the easy panache of the late John Wayne. For a minute or two she compared our Identity Card photographs with the camouflage-painted faces underneath helmets which were covered with sacking and strips of Hessian. She then returned the cards and waved uncertainly: "Y'all have a nice day now." This was confusing. At the CO's Orders there had been no reference at all to having 'a nice day.'

In December an exercise was abruptly cancelled when a Tornado aircraft crashed whilst approaching for landing at Honington. Both crew ejected safely and the squadron was mobilised as the crash site guard for a few days, until all of the bits were collected to meet investigative requirements.

Xmas leave approached and a twelve-day grant was offered. This was quite generous, although I did not envisage a trip to Germany. A requirement of our declaration of assets to SACEUR meant that fifty per cent of the squadron had to be within call out range at all times. Six days seemed too slim for Germany. Hearing of this, the squadron DSC mentioned that he flew with a local club. If I was prepared to defray fuel costs, he would fly me to Laarbruch. This seemed too good to miss and we agreed. In the meantime, I had drawn the first six days of standby duty and on Xmas Day I went to the Airmen's Mess to serve dinner. Afterwards I went to quarters to have dinner with the CO and his wife.

I did some runs in the local woods but saw no wildlife. It was particularly bleak and there was no pleasure in being outdoors. Smoke rose from the quarters' chimneys and windowpanes were fogged with condensation. The Mess was all but abandoned and nothing disturbed my reading or the latest attempt at a short story.

On the twenty-ninth I met the DSC and we drove early in the morning to RAF Mildenhall, which actually was another American base. While he was doing the pre-flight checks on the small Cessna, we heard the roar of a departing jet and watched as an SR71 reconnaissance aircraft went like a rocket into the lightening sky. It was a spy plane and probably had no official existence.

It was a bad day for travel of any kind, but we got off, flying first to RAF Manston to clear Customs, then batting on to Monchengladbach. Snow was blanketing Germany and for a time it seemed that I might have to continue by train, but the weather cleared and we slipped into Laarbruch in the mid-afternoon. I turned up my collar and strode swiftly to the married quarters, discovering there that Joan was on call out for snow clearance on the runway.

8

Joan's snow clearance duties formed part of the same call-out criteria that I was subjected to, with the need to get Tornados quickly airborne if the Warsaw Pact countries decided to breach the Xmas spirit. She had to report in from time to time and I went off with Gypsy through the local woods that were about perfect for Xmas cards. I visited the 26 Squadron Compound and the quarter was visited in turn by several friends, including Denise and Mick Tobin who currently were serving at Gutersloh. We also found the time to shop for a new car, having been advised that a Ford which we had ordered in England could now not be delivered in time, despite the fact that the order had been placed in October. Among the attractions of the Germany tour was that a car could be purchased free of UK tax, but the purchase had to be made not less than six months before the tour ended. Joan's posting had been notified for July and we were keen not to miss the car opportunity, seeing little future use for a left-hand drive camper van. We approached the Volkswagen agent in the nearby town of Weeze and asked him how quickly we might be able to acquire a Golf Estate. "Would this afternoon be all right?" He asked. I thought of reporting this exchange to the manager of Ford UK for comment, but saved myself the stamp.

  Five days soon elapsed and I made the return to England via the Hook of Holland ferry and rail. It was utterly bleak and I spent four hours on the platform at Ipswich station in one of those little jokes that British Rail liked to play on its customers occasionally. A 'bus ride completed my journey to Honington, which was beginning to stir with life again. '87 had opened and doubtless it would be punctuated by a number of exercise deployments. The first of them was just two days later. Hello, Uncle Sam.

  Requiring a bank loan for the new car, but disliking debt, I had taken the loan over the shortest possible period in order to discharge it as quickly as I could. This enforced an even more frugal lifestyle for a while and I became something of a Mess hermit as a result. This was assisted by the fact that my drinking anyway had been very modest for quite some time now, and as the warrant officer there was a natural reserve in relations with the rest of the SNCOs. I attended and much enjoyed the periodic formal Mess functions, but I seldom went to the bar. To my few expenses I added the *Guardian* and the *Observer* to augment my library reading. The Mess took neither newspaper, the manager having resisted my suggestion that we add a quality broadsheet to the pile of tabloids that the ante-room sported.

Cash flow problems were slightly exacerbated when the rent from the cottage at Ruskington dried up. We had retained the property, for which Joan had arranged tenants upon her posting to Germany. These were reliable people from Cranwell but had moved on and were replaced by utterly unreliable occupants. We had visited the cottage in October and were fairly dispirited at the disorder we noticed. Rent payments became erratic then ceased and we eventually found ourselves with an empty cottage.

If I had feared that my duties would mostly confine me to office and desk, I was pleasantly surprised at the scope for external activity. The senior MT man was a corporal and I took on the responsibility of daily checks of the fleet to ensure that we remained at readiness to deploy. I also made a daily round of the flights and I kept an eye on the Gunner's accommodation, although one of the sergeants held the inventory. The accommodation was quite poor and harked to a day when single rooms were for officers and SNCOs only, and airmen were accommodated entirely within dormitories. All of the accommodation at Honington had been built to such acceptance but had gradually been updated over the years. Only the transit block still conformed to the 1937 design and this had been the only accommodation available when the squadron had formed. It was also incomplete, having been visited by the *Luftwaffe* in 1942. Built to an **H** block pattern, one wing had been entirely destroyed in the bombing raid and it had never been rebuilt.[1]

Visits at various levels occupied some of my time - or at least the preparation for them - and the accompanying officer on one of them was Paul Bruning, now a squadron leader. Hearing that I planned

---

[1] RAF Honington became the RAF Regiment Depot in 1993 and among the new works a replacement wing was belatedly added to the former Transit Accommodation.

to leave the service in the following year, he mentioned that the RAF Regiment auxiliary squadrons would shortly be recruiting full time staff as instructors, and that I might be interested. I was and he said that he would keep me in touch with developments.

In planning terms, my retirement was none too distant and Joan and I had begun to discuss our options for the future. For some years I had thought that running a teashop might be a pleasant way to earn a living, but I had developed the idea of acquiring a bed and breakfast business instead. Joan had some reservations until I had pointed out that, even if the business did not succeed, we still had the 'bricks and mortar' where our money was perfectly safe. I could not have been more wrong about that.

A new DSC arrived and he was a powerhouse of energy. I could live with that, and the fact that he expected his orders to be carried out to the letter. He knew what he was doing and, soon, so did everyone else. He perfectly complemented the CO, although the latter was shortly to be posted. Some years later, the DSC resisted a mugging on a South London street and was shot five times with a handgun. He fortunately survived.

In March I accompanied the DSC to a recce of the Sennybridge Ranges, where we were scheduled to hold our field-firing exercise in July. We learned that virtually all of the ranges we had bid for were available, but that no beds were spare in Sennybridge Camp. I pointed out that we could easily bivvie out on the area and that this would offer the bonus of time saved in transit to the ranges - which could take up to an hour to drive to in 4 Tonners. At the same time, I offered to run ranges myself, rather than simply run the camp, which required little effort. This offer was taken up and it was planned that the SNCO on the engineering flight would take care of the camp, assisted by a couple of HQ Gunners.

Back at Honington, I had one more disagreement with the Mess manager before giving it up as a hopeless job. The Mess served a snack meal at lunchtime and a three-course meal in the evening, but reversed this practice on Friday when large numbers went home for the weekend. I pointed out that my lunchtime run precluded a three-course meal, which I would prefer in the evening, but lunchtime runners were clearly a fitness-freak minority who might safely be ignored. The Mess manager later retired and became a butler to some local aristocracy. He already had the stuffed shirt.

'Hooters' regularly reminded us of our bread and butter

duties, but the deployment to the MOBs was slickly practised by now. The odd glitch could be counted upon and upon one move we found our way into the B Ech copse blocked by a rubbish skip that someone had thoughtlessly dumped. We were also learning that the Americans spoke a different language. I had to visit the USAAF Police to borrow some hand-held radios and the desk sergeant reported down the 'phone that I was there to 'interface' with someone I actually only wanted to see. On some other visit I was directed to a distant store and a corporal offered to run me across the airfield in his 'Pee-Oh-Vee'. 'Great,' I thought, wondering what exotic transport a Pee-Oh-Vee might be. It turned out to be a rather battered Datsun, a Privately Owned Vehicle. We could not fault American hospitality, however, and I can recall no unfriendliness from that time.

At Easter I considered a trip to Laarbruch but chose instead to visit Shavington. Reg was in very poor health by now and we simply sat out in the garden that he had created from nothing, but was now beyond his efforts. He spoke at some length about his time in the army during the war, and that was unusual. He was still in good spirits but I think that he knew his days were drawing in. His garden was alive with colour, offering sad contrast to pale illness and life ending.

I visited the empty cottage at Ruskington and found it in a depressingly dirty condition, recognising that I would have to address that before we put it on the market. We had decided to sell as soon as possible, in order to be free of the buyer/seller chain and thus able to make a quick purchase on a B&B prospect. I painted the cottage internally, top to bottom, then put it in the hands of an estate agent, hoping for an early offer and hoping also that the village remained quiet when prospective buyers viewed the property.

Routine at Honington was slightly relieved when one of the flight sergeants paraded himself to the CO with a refusal to soldier. Bemused, the CO asked for my advice and I recommended sending the flight sergeant to see the MO. He had already gone sick, however, and he was eventually diagnosed as suffering from stress and posted as a supernumerary SNCO to the station GDT flight. We were obliged to run light for a few months until a posting was arranged.

In mid-July we deployed to Sennybridge with half of the squadron, with the other half due to arrive for range firing in the second week. The range staff would remain for the fortnight, and I looked forward to that. We rigged a few twelve foot by twelve foot tents on the bivvie site, which included a shed we designated as the cooking area and a twelve-hole latrine. I recce'd my range, which was intended to be used for pairs fire and manoeuvre, and generally got on with it. We looked like getting a share of rain, which was a fact of life at any time at Sennybridge, and a local farmer gave me the good news. "If it rains on St. Swithin's Day," He announced (it had), "then it will rain for forty days and forty nights." This cheering forecast was not entirely accurate, but we got a fair soaking here and there. The farmer also told me that he had been moved off his farm during the war on seven days' notice, when the land was occupied by the War Office for 'the period of hostilities only'. Forty years on, he was still awaiting the return of it.

The ranges offered a hard day, day after day, but I thrived on it. Gunners and Engineers alike worked hard on them and whether we dripped with sweat or rain, it was obvious to me that we had a squadron that gave its best, whatever the job. When the ranges closed, I would travel initially with the 4 Tonner before dropping off a few miles short of the bivvie site to run in. I was sublimely happy at this time and if I had thought that I could preserve such conditions, then I would have very seriously considered signing on.

Before leaving Honington I had taken over a married quarter and whilst I was at Sennybridge Joan had moved into it, being now posted to the Honington MT Section. We had a little over a year left to serve and we were keen to begin looking for a B&B prospect somewhere. I had a few days of leave and we visited Joan's folks in Worksop, returning via a Kennels near Peterborough where Gypsy's six-month's quarantine had just expired. Joan had feared that the dog would forget us during her isolation, and her fears seemed justified when we addressed the plump Labrador at the end of a kennel line. The dog roundly ignored us and we belatedly realised that the frantic yapping behind us was in fact Gypsy, slimmed down by a strict diet. It took a long time to settle her before we were able to get in the car and drive home. The kennel Vet had advised against much exercise for the dog, in view of her long confinement to about eight feet of kennel and consequent 'low muscle tone', but I thought that I might take her on one of my routine runs to see how she was. Returning to the quarter, I was happy to sink to the kitchen step for a few minutes, but Gypsy appeared with a ball in her mouth, ready for additional exercise. 'Low muscle tone' like that I could have done with myself.

9

We took some leave and spent time in Worksop, coincidentally attending the christening of a nephew. I learned, in passing, that Methodists are pretty keen on long sermons and I felt grateful that I had not inherited a powerful strand of Methodism from the paternal line of my family. Within a week we were attending a religious service of a very different sort, Uncle Reg having finally succumbed to cancer after a protracted and painful illness. During his final weeks he had largely been nursed by my cousin Jean and her husband Ted, both of whom had to be trained to administer the Morphine which was vital to limiting Reg's pain. I found a quiet moment to talk to Jean, suggesting that we might subscribe together a fare to Australia for Aunt Bess, and this idea was supported by Jean and her brothers.

We had little time available for the visit but I found an opportunity to wander about the town, noting the now wholesale amputation of streets quite close to the town centre. The houses included those built by the railway companies a century before, and efforts were in hand to preserve a few of them in recognition of the industrial past. Market Street had virtually ceased to exist and a town bypass swept through the centre itself. The town was by now looking very different, and I thought that I might later find the time to make comparisons. Not during this visit, however.

In September we were again preparing for missile camp at Benbecula and I once more led a small advance party to set up for the main party's arrival by air. The weather was already poor and although the squadron landed as scheduled, we were delayed in firing until the second week of the camp. I again had few duties beyond those that were discharged very early in the day, and I soaked up some time with long walks along the beach and long runs wherever the mood took me. Our visit happened to coincide with some local 'Highland Games' in which we were invited to participate. Seeing little chance of even lifting a caber, much less tossing it, I volunteered instead for the half-marathon that was mapped along local roads. The night prior to the run, one of our sister USAAF Rapier squadrons arrived, No 19 from RAF Brize Norton, and I knew several of the seniors. I made the considerable mistake of remaining late in the Mess bar and was not in great shape for the morning run, which hurt.

We eventually 'shot out' and returned to Honington to prepare for a Sunset Ceremony that was to be performed in front of the Officers' Mess. I got my drill head on for a few days and put the guard together. The ceremony was actually being held at sunset, which was not always the case, and it happened to be a very spectacular one. A Tornado provided the flypast then it engaged reheat and went into the developing night sky like a rocket, the flames of its efflux reducing to a faint dot. The band played the lovely Evening Hymn and, standing off to one side during the display, I noted that ceremonial still had its moments.

The DSC had now departed on promotion and we also had a new CO. I felt little rapport with either of the new incumbents, which at least might soften the blow of leaving the squadron, and it was of much regret to note sharply changing priorities. Some months before, the CO's Land Rover, which was a three-quarter ton hardtop, had been equipped, with much effort and some expense, as a tertiary command post. The entire operation of the deployed squadron, including the engineering support, could be conducted from within the vehicle. The new CO took a look at the radios, the state boards and the replication, in miniature, of everything else in the CP Van then turned to the Squadron HQ Flight SNCO. "I want that lot out, and *this* in." He ordered. *'This'* was a basket for his Labrador. My fears about the CO's interest seemed to be confirmed on an exercise a week or two later, when he appeared just long enough to collect the squadron cook, who happened to be a cricketer of some ability and thus required for a team which the CO was leading. I handed the cooking job to a couple of off-duty Signallers, and it was no big deal, but I privately wondered what had happened to our priorities.

Conscious that the year was slipping away, Joan and I were examining B&B prospects along the east coast, but somehow failed to convince ourselves that Skegness, Felixstowe and similar offered quite what we were looking for. We were also looking for something which 'felt' right and by the time we realised that there is probably no such article, we had missed the market by a considerable margin. We decided to look at central and mid-Wales, but time off was beginning to be something of a problem and leave was never generous. Leave for the fire unit crews, in view of our call-out criteria, was quite literally raffled each year, and a fortnight of 'summer leave' might fall in April or September.

The squadron was approaching a Wing Evaluation exercise, which had to be right, and our deployment for it was complicated by very severe storms that hit the south and east of England in October. Thousands of trees were uprooted by the winds and among them were most of those within the B Ech copse at Woodbridge. The Americans offered generous help with gangs operating chain saws to clear access, but the net problem when they had done so was rather too little cover for the echelon's considerable complement of workshop vehicles. We had to find some other wood and begin the job of digging trenches all over again. We survived the WingEval and put the blisters down to experience.

Running was beginning to give me a problem with my knees, and I suspected that I might be developing cartilage wear. I saw the MO, who arranged for me to have X-Rays and see a specialist at RAF Ely Hospital. The subsequent good news was that my cartilage was in terrific shape, and the bad news was that I was probably developing osteo-arthritis. I was advised to pursue fitness in forms other than running, but I neglected to accept what doubtless was excellent advice.

We looked at a B&B in Scarborough and the owner explained that he had some tenants who were housed by the Department of Health and Social Security. We were shown around the rooms and two tenants proved to be an elderly couple who sat silently in theirs, surrounded by a few possessions which were in cardboard boxes. I suddenly felt more like a bailiff than a prospective buyer, and Joan and I later agreed that this was an aspect of B&B life which we were not at all keen to embrace.

Xmas passed quietly and we had Joan's folks down to visit. I went to the Airmen's Mess to serve dinner, realizing that it would be the last such opportunity. We did no house hunting in the period, but the goods news was that we had sold the cottage at Ruskington a few days before the Grant began. We now at least had a tidy deposit, should we find a place that appealed.

In January both Joan and I paraded at the Officers' Mess. She was receiving her Long Service and Good Conduct Medal, and I was receiving my Warrant. It was a pleasant afternoon and timely for Joan, who now planned to quit the service ahead of my own retirement date. In view of Bess' trip to Australia, which Jean had decided to accompany, I suggested to Joan that she also go, in order to meet the rest of my family. She liked the idea and we duly made the arrangements. I found myself wondering if Joan might enjoy Australia to the point of wanting to live out there. We made one other house-hunting foray to Bridlington but considered £42,000 a touch strong for a five-bedroomed property. We would remember that, later.

In March we visited Shavington and at the conclusion of the stay I delivered Bess, Jean and Joan to Manchester airport for the beginning of their three-month holiday. I returned to Honington and arranged to put Gypsy in the RAF Police kennels since the DSC and I were undertaking a recce to Germany for a June exercise. We travelled to the USAAF bases at Spangdahlem and Bitberg, sorting out the accommodation plot for the time on base and the exercise areas for the Rapier deployment. Working our way through the base HQ, I noticed again that the walls were fairly covered with the photographs of base personnel who had distinguished themselves that year, that month and, for all I know, that day. There is, I think, deep within the American psyche a very powerful desire for recognition. The photograph that seemed to say it all, however, hung behind the base commander's desk, as I noted when we paid a courtesy call. The photo was of John Wayne and it was signed in his real name, which I think was Marion Morrison.

Recce satisfactorily concluded, we returned to the UK with clinking luggage and I retrieved the dog and settled to the bachelor's existence for a few weeks. Since Arch's fiftieth birthday was to fall during the visit by Joan and Co., I had planned to make a surprise visit for the occasion, but it proved impossible to organise the necessary leave. Among other activities, the squadron faced the Annual Formal Inspection in April, so I was busy ensuring that the hangar was up to scratch, whilst also preparing the parade for the day.

I was entitled to a month of resettlement training and I had been combing out courses in the Education Section, eventually deciding upon *An Introduction to Building and Construction Trades*. This choice was not provoked by any desire to work on building sites, but by the thought that I might enhance my DIY capabilities. May was shaping up to be a quiet month for the squadron and I was able to book a course at the Catterick Garrison to coincide. I drove up via Worksop, leaving Gypsy with Tegwin and Ray.

About sixty servicemen, a mix from the three services, assembled on the Sunday, although only about two dozen of us were attending the building course. I went to the Mess bar for the first night, then decided to avoid it thereafter, noting that a good few of the course personnel went there early and stayed late. I could have lived in the Depot Mess, just six miles down the road, but I was avoiding that for the same reason.

The month of training was divided into four separate segments, to deal with bricklaying, plumbing, carpentry and decorating, and my squad began with the bricklaying. We had been told to take no uniform on the course and that ranks would be ignored whilst we were there. This seemed sensible, although we tended to be a bit deferential to the older student, who was thought to be a brigadier. This reserve soon wore off, and the more so when we discovered that the 'brigadier' was in fact a lance-corporal of the catering corps, long on service but short on promotion. The week was simply excellent. We laid and levelled bricks, we plastered walls and we tiled them. We cast concrete and picked up many useful tips from the instructor, who had about forty years in the trade. Every evening there was a presentation of some sort, ranging from advice on mortgages to house insulation. I attended all of them and the light evenings still allowed plenty of time for runs of eight or nine miles about the area.

Each of the trade instructors delivered advice with abundant humour, and none more so than the decorator, who was also a watercolourist of some distinction. He introduced us to the mysteries of marbling, graining and rag-rolling and invited us to be inventive. I discovered that I had some ability to simulate knot holes in my 'woodgrain' and students came from far and wide - well, across the room at least - to admire them. Wallpapering was also featured and as we stirred the paste one morning, the instructor came over to pronounce on it. "Looks a bit clarty." He said, and we nodded in wise agreement, privately wondering what the fuck 'clarty' might mean.

Out for a newspaper one Saturday morning, I ran across Bryn Davies, last seen on the Colour squadron where we shared Harrow School duties, and I went to his house for a visit. Bryn told me that Rocky Roxburgh was a neighbour and I was thus able to visit him, also not seen in some time. Before the course ended, I made a trip to the Depot to visit people I might not see again. I stayed late at the bar then left the vehicle and walked back to the Garrison. In the morning I ran back to the Depot to pick up the car.

On another weekend I drove down to York to visit the Railway Museum, which had a fine display of engines and carriages, whether you were a railway nut or not. I wasn't, but I had begun to develop an interest in Crewe's railway heritage. It was therefore very satisfying to discover that the museum preserved one of the early locomotives built in Crewe, in 1845.

Running putty, soldering joints, making picture frames, hanging doors, lagging pipes and a dozen other arcane subjects later, the course ended and I returned to Honington having first collected Gypsy. The grass in the back yard of the quarter was a foot high and I attacked it as soon as we were home. Two days later I drove to Heathrow to collect Bess, Jean, Joan - and Mam. During the visit, Joan had become concerned about the level of work that Mam insisted upon doing, and she thought that she might benefit from a few months with us. It was good to see Mam again, although it was apparent that she was becoming very frail.

We were now ready to resume our B&B quest in earnest after a three-month hiatus and we soon made the alarming discovery that the market had swiftly gone from mere buoyancy to positive volatility. We needed now to move quickly before we were priced out of the market entirely. Typically, this was also now a busy time for the squadron, leaving me with too few opportunities for the hunt.

The hunt for premises nicely combined with leisure interests on the occasion that we visited Portsmouth. My earlier interest in the restoration of the *SS Great Britain*, at Bristol, had recently been matched by the progress made on *HMS Warrior*, launched in 1860 as Britain's first armoured battleship. *Warrior* was an interesting amalgam of iron and teak, sail and steam, and had been all but forgotten as a floating platform for industrial purposes until someone recognised her historic importance. She now floated at Portsmouth, impressively and impeccably restored, and I had been keen to view her for some time. Also berthed at Portsmouth, albeit in dry dock, was *HMS Victory* and much-shrouded in canvas on this occasion, since she was undergoing major replacement of her timbers. *Victory* was actually now becoming more replica than original, being apparently only about ten per cent original, but she was nevertheless impressive. Another interesting preservation was that of the *Holland 1,* the Royal Navy's first submarine. She was also an accidental preservation, having parted her towline whilst bound for a South Wales scrap yard, circa 1910, and remaining on the sea bed until the Eighties. *Holland 1* was crewed by three, but she had a flush lavatory - a facility her bigger replacements would not acquire within the RN for a couple of decades.

Our visit to Portsmouth happened to coincide with Navy Week, which provided the opportunity to view ships both old and new. Among the new was the latest to carry the *Ark Royal* nameplate (there had been half a dozen), but she was dwarfed - in my memory, at least - by the carrier I had last seen whilst serving with the Royal Marines.

Accommodation was at a premium in the town, and we accepted the first offer of B&B rooms without troubling to check them. This proved unwise, although the quarters we got offered useful clues as to what sort of accommodation *we* might eventually provide. Our cramped room was on the third floor and it transpired that the nearest lavatory was on the ground floor. At a time of my life when I was making the unwelcome discovery that I now needed to urinate during the night, this additional discovery was also unwelcome. On the first morning of occupancy, the Landlady banged hard on the door at 0730hrs to 'remind us of breakfast', and since we were now wide-awake we dressed and went down. The information downstairs, however, was that breakfast was not served until 0900hrs. There being no shower, I had a bath later in the day and was admonished by the Landlady for not having booked such ablutions. I happened to have found the bathroom accidentally open, since it was normally securely locked. Guests were not encouraged to remain in the house after breakfast - memorable for its pots of industrial strength tea - and it was as well that Portsmouth had plenty to offer. We concluded our stay with a visit to the remains of Henry VIII's Flagship *Mary Rose*, recently recovered after four centuries on the sea bed. It had been an interesting weekend but we had not advanced our quest for B&B premises.

Concurrently, I had renewed my interest in auxiliary squadrons with the news that vacancies for weapons instructors in the rank of sergeant were being advertised in the *Services Resettlement Bulletin*. I found that the posts offered up to two hundred days per year and I reckoned that we could live on that, if the B&B took time to establish - assuming even that we would now find such a property. I knew that an auxiliary squadron existed at RAF St. Mawgan, in Cornwall and I got in touch with the CO, who invited me down for an interview. I could not go immediately, since the squadron was about to undergo the Germany exercise, but I arranged to visit when we returned.

At the end of May we embarked at Harwich for a ferry and road move, stopping overnight at Laarbruch. I spent the evening with Cath and Ray Hughes but returned to the Mess in time for late drinks, which probably was a mistake. We completed the journey the next day then had some days free before the exercise began. I joined a visit to Trier, where I noted Roman remains and a street busker playing Gershwin, then wandered about the local area. Adjacent to the base was a quiet village whose war memorial commemorated the dead of three conflicts, 1870, 1914 and 1939. It was a small village to have lost so many of its youth and I wondered if that loss contributed to the quiet.

When the exercise opened, B Echelon occupied the ground floor of a large barrack block which had been built for Hitler's *Wehrmacht*, but which had been successively occupied by Belgian, British and French troops. The Americans were currently making no use of it and our occupation was not resisted. We had barely moved in when a truck arrived, delivering a huge Coke dispensing machine. Things, military, clearly went better with Coke and I began to wonder if the firm formed part of the military-industrial complex in the USA. During the exercise I found myself slightly at odds with both the DSC and the CO over B Ech procedure. That which had been perfectly useful, if not gospel, for the past twenty months was no longer desirable. We also had some redeployment problems that stemmed from Orders that were delivered far too late, and I was gnawing at my lip on a few occasions.

When the exercise ended we had to stage home through a Belgian air force camp, owing to the German prohibition of heavy lorries on the roads at weekends. We drove to the camp on the Friday for an overnight stay and I noticed that the gate sentry wore '37 Pattern webbing and was armed with a Sten gun which looked as if it might prove most lethal to the firer. This, and the air of shabbiness that attached to the camp, seemed much closer to our own experience than the opulence of the American facilities we had so recently noted.

Within four days of return to England, we decamped for Scotland, intent on another missile camp and the last one for me. We got fourteen missiles away on the first day of firing and actually shot out by the end of the second day. I hoped that this meant an early return to Honington, for Joan and I were now writhing with impatience to secure a property. I had just two months of service remaining. We had a beach barbeque and invited fifteen WRACs who served on the island. Just one of them turned up and she was a Bessie Bunter lookalike who went directly to the scoff and did not budge from it.

In the first week of July I took some leave and we travelled to Newquay, staying in a B&B and now hoping to find one of our own. A trawl of the estate agents revealed a frightening rise in prices and when we worked our sums out we saw that very little property at our price was available. Our top price was £70,000. Meantime, I went up to St. Mawgan to see Sqn Ldr Addison, an ex-regular I knew slightly. He had been the regular CO of No 2625 Squadron at RAF St. Mawgan and since retirement he had been its reservist CO. He quickly told me that his real need was for a warrant officer, the last having left a year or so ago and the squadron having no obvious candidates for the job. In turn, I told him that I required an element of fulltime work, rather than simply reserve service, and I was offered three days per week, plus of course the training weekends. I accepted and went off to find Joan to resume the property search.

We found a B&B at £70,000 and offered to close on the price without any attempt to reduce it. I engaged a local solicitor in order to avoid further loss of time and we returned to Honington. Within a fortnight we were ready to exchange contracts, then it all went ominously quiet on the vendor's side. After some weeks of delay and hearing little from the estate agent, we decided to telephone the vendor directly to find out what the problem was. He calmly informed us that he now wanted an extra five thousand pounds. We did not have it and I would not have paid it on principle. We had agreed his price and he had agreed to sell to us. His avarice had cost us £350 in legal and survey fees and several wasted weeks. Had we been separated by a few streets instead of several counties, I would probably have gone around and separated him from his teeth.

I returned to duty and a deployment onto the Stanford Training Area for an exercise. I was prowling about B Echelon and spoke sharply to a Gunner who was moving around without his helmet on. Minutes later I was summoned to the CO's Orders Group, and he delivered them while sitting with his feet soaking in a bowl of water. Aggravations of the housing variety apart, it was very definitely time that I was moving on.

Back at Honington the entire squadron underwent the new annual physical fitness tests which had been introduced for the RAF

Regiment. They were comparatively tough, but we had few failures, thus proving that we had a fit squadron, in addition to a very proficient one. I do not think that, at this time, there was a more capable Rapier squadron within the Corps, and I deem it a great pity that the leadership of its first CO had not been maintained. I passed my fitness tests but took my pre-discharge medical a few days later, where I was informed that my hearing loss was bilateral and the standard was below acceptable Regiment criteria. Not that it mattered much now.

I began my twenty-eight days of terminal leave with no house purchase in prospect and we elected for a quick visit to Newquay to look anew at houses. We were shown two at our price, both with five bedrooms and neither presently trading as guesthouses. Both seemed in a poor state of repair, but we thought that one had some potential for conversion. We tried for a reduced price because of some fairly obvious damp in the house, but the owner would not budge. The market was still very much in the grip of the vendors and we agreed the purchase. We next went off to find a property we could rent in the town, correctly assuming that it might be some weeks before contracts were exchanged. I do not know who were the real villains of the boom and subsequent bust in the housing market at that time, but I know that we were among the victims of it.

We returned to Honington and I went back to the squadron for a couple of days to conduct a handover with my successor. He turned out to be a longtime GDT man whose face grew longer as the duties and deployment procedures were outlined for him. That, however, was his problem.

The Officers and the SNCOs held a Ladies' Guest Night in the Sergeants' Mess and Joan and I were dined out. It was a pleasant evening but in a speech of thanks I found it hard to contain the emotion I felt at my final departure from regular service. Whatever life held for me, it would never be quite the same again and there was much to be regretted in that. Earlier that week I had been walking the dog across local fields when I was startled at the sight of fire unit and B Ech vehicles deploying off the camp. For a moment I had wondered why I was not with them, until it dawned that there was no longer a place within the squadron for me. It was a powerful, and sad, recognition that my way of life was now irrevocably changed.

10

  Our departure from Honington was not as immediate as we would have preferred, since the rented accommodation in Newquay was largely a holiday flat and unavailable until the beginning of October. From my discharge date we had a couple of weeks to fill in and we remained at the married quarter. I had notified this to the Estates Office in plenty of time, but the Families Officer, a civilian, was pretty graceless about it and he seemed to regard me as some greasy squatter. Our quarters' rent was doubled for the brief overstay.

  All of the furniture and appliances that I had moved down from the cottage I now stored in Mick Sweeney's garage. Mick and Shirley had followed us from Laarbruch at much the same time of Joan's posting, although Mick was employed on defence duties at Honington, rather than with 20 Squadron. There was simply no room at the rented flat for our stuff and I would have to arrange a later collection when the house purchase was complete. The flat duly became free and we travelled down to Newquay.

  The flat was just yards from Porth Beach and although winter had begun to bite, it was pleasant to stroll the length of the beach every morning with the dog, before setting off to St. Mawgan, where the conditions of my employment had taken a disquieting turn. I had reported in as soon as we arrived in the town, in order to confirm which days of the week it was preferred that I should work, learning of very recent changes.

  RAF auxiliary units dated from 1925 and a dozen Regiment auxiliary squadrons had existed postwar until the late Fifties, when auxiliaries all but disappeared. In 1979, the auxiliary Regiment squadrons concept was resurrected and three were formed in various parts of England. Three more, including No 2625 Squadron, were formed in 1982 and a seventh was added a couple of years later. The seventh unit, No 2729 Squadron, at RAF Waddington was actually an anti-aircraft unit that was equipped with radar-directed Oerlikon cannons. These had been taken as prize from the Argentines at the end of the Falkland's campaign.

  The first six squadrons to be raised were field-equipped,

which is to say that they performed a broadly infantry role in defending their parent stations. I was entirely happy with such a role since infantry training was something I had been familiar with for thirty years. In my last four years of service I had understood Rapier only at the level of flight sergeant and warrant officer, when I would have preferred to have understood it in greater detail.

2625 Squadron was established at almost a hundred and thirty all ranks, to include a small cadre of regular personnel. These were mainly tradesmen, to conduct the armaments, MT, supply and clerical operation on a day to day basis, whilst the planning and execution of the weekend training was in the hands of two regulars of the RAF Regiment. These were the Adjutant, a flight lieutenant whose job actually was the equivalent of the DSC on a regular squadron, and the Training NCO, who was a flight sergeant. The squadron depended very greatly upon the combined effort of this pair, and I would quickly learn that the current team was something of a disaster.

During the development of the auxiliary squadrons, the regular Regiment staff had recognised that assistance with the training effort, beyond that which was made by the tradesmen, would be most useful, and it had become the practice to employ reservists on a semi-regular basis. After some years of *ad hoc* arrangements this had begun to form the basis of contract employment, and the advertisement that I had spotted some months earlier had been indicative of the intended direction. Unfortunately, questions had arisen over semi-regular employment and financial irregularities at one of the auxiliary squadrons that resulted in court-martial proceedings. The charges eventually were thrown out, but an immediate result was a drastic reduction in the numbers who might be employed on a daily basis. When I reported to the CO, he informed me that his upper limit of reservists working other than on weekends was now six - three SNCOs and three junior ranks - and that none of them would exceed a hundred and fifty days per year. Fag packet calculations suggested that I would gross £6,000 per year and this compared with the recent salary of £16,000 per year and a joint income of £25,000 per year none too distantly. Added to the wage was my service pension, from which I had borrowed to inflate my lump gratuity, yielding about £250 per month. It was a dose of financial reality, at a time when income from the B&B was no more than a distant possibility.

The house purchase was proceeding very slowly and we were not cheered when the survey painted a grim picture of rising damp and a leaking roof, both conditions which would have to be swiftly addressed as a condition of the mortgage offer. The repairs were estimated at between two and three thousand pounds. I had a mental image of rising damp and rainwater meeting somewhere on the middle floor of the house and we were briefly tempted to abandon the purchase, settling for jobs and a smaller property somewhere. I was trying to preserve an optimistic front for Joan's benefit, since she found this all a touch upsetting, but it was not an award-winning act.

On 12 October I took the 'Queen's Shilling' for the fourth time and attempted to get the measure of my new duties. I had a lengthy conversation with the CO and he identified a few of the problems for me. I saw it as my job to sort them out, although at the time I did not realise the true extent of the difficulties. They began, however, with the training team and it took no great wit to recognise that particular problem. The Adjutant and Training NCO barely acknowledged each other, much less worked together, and I wondered why one of them at least had not been posted. The Adjutant, a graduate, proved to be intelligent and a man of some ability, but he was simply lazy and clearly saw it as no part of his duties to work hard for reservists. He tended to stroll in after 0900hrs with his spaniel, compensating by strolling out early in the afternoon. His preferred activity was golf and he once cancelled his contribution to a weekend training programme in order to make up a team with some visiting chums from the Red Arrows flying display team. When he was posted, a year or so later, a senior officer threatened to send him back to the squadron to sort out the administrative mess he had left behind.

The flight sergeant was, if anything, an even greater disaster. He was grossly overweight, unfit and clearly preferred to spend his days in close proximity to the ashtray and the coffeepot. On the rare occasions when he might be required to teach a class the machine gun handling, he would use a demonstration man behind the weapon. Getting up and down behind the gun was clearly in the realms of higher acrobatics for this particular flight sergeant. He had left his family in the married quarters at a camp further up country and he mostly lived in the Sergeants' Mess, where he obviously did not resist the temptations of the bar. On several occasions he simply failed to appear for duty and it was apparent that he had a drink problem.

A consequence of our moves was that I had seen very little of Mam, who had mostly been staying with Bess since return. Joan drove up to Cheshire and brought both Mam and Bess down to stay for a few days at the flat, but the weather was too poor to permit much sightseeing. It appeared, too, that Bess was now in failing health. Mam wondered if she ought now to return to Australia, but I persuaded her to stay on and at least enjoy spring and early summer before going home.

In November the squadron moved up to Warcop Camp, in Cumbria to undergo a week of field firing. Most units did this a fortnight at a time, but 2625 preferred a week at both ends of the year. This purportedly was to accommodate those of the squadron who were seasonal workers, although there seemed no evidence that we had a significant proportion of Gunners who could not get away during the summer months. A 'summer' camp in November in the north of England was stretching it a bit. I looked forward to the camp, however, since field-firing ranges were what I most enjoyed and I thought that I would resolve any doubts I might harbour about reservists. Among my reservations when I had decided to seek auxiliary service was that I might possibly be joining some sort of 'ale and crisps' organisation.

The camp attendance was good, although this may have reflected nothing more than the fact that annual bounty payments were contingent upon annual training, and I found a good level of interest and effort on the battle ranges which I ran all week. I was less impressed by the regular staff, who only participated when directly ordered to, and I noted that they found reasons to avoid the reveille run which I organised for the squadron each morning. The regular staff also considered themselves above the midnight curfew that the CO imposed and I quickly saw that an 'us and them' attitude was among the unit problems. I thought that I might do something very quickly about that, which proved optimistic.

My return to Cornwall coincided with the house acquisition and I hired a 4 Tonner to drive up to Suffolk to collect our effects. Most of our stuff was in large boxes and it was destined to remain in them for a number of months whilst we wrestled with the house and its problems. This would occupy my efforts for four days each week in the foreseeable future, leaving me with three days to devote to squadron matters on a Wednesday to Friday basis. Xmas was rapidly approaching, although it looked anything but a cheerful prospect as we looked anew at our rotting, and expensive, abode, trying without notable success to visualise it as a warm and welcoming guesthouse.

11

December was marked by Trojan effort on the house as I tried to make sense of the ground floor at least. The two upper floors were more than depressing and we simply shoved numerous boxes in them to leave us room for manoeuvre, and to defer that problem for the moment. The skirting boards on the ground floor were nine-inch pine and I had fostered an illusion of carefully removing these with a view to stripping them back to bare board, which I would just as carefully varnish. This illusion was dispelled by the quick discovery that only several layers of paint were actually holding the skirting boards against the wall, since the rising damp had long since passed nine inches, rotting the pine in the process. This offered the tiny consolation of making their removal easy, and they went into the yard as the basis of the first of eight skip loads of rubble and renovation detritus. The yard and small garden quickly became a builder's yard with rubbish at one end of it and building material at the other. Pride of place was given to a cement mixer that I bought from the 'big boys' shelf at some local DIY outpost.

We had little working capital and building economies had to be employed. I had not liked the £1,000 quotation for damp-proofing and we shopped around until we got one which was substantially lower. Lower quotes, I swiftly learned, were dependent upon coin of the realm adroitly changing hands, rather than cheques, but my complicity in the black economy cost me no sleep. Working towards the damp-proofing, I now began to strip the rotten plaster and render back to the brickwork to the height of a metre, then went about one of a score of other tasks whilst the damp-proofer drilled holes and filled them with silicone. We had little option but to begin the work immediately, but the problems of major renovation in the depths of winter became apparent when we had to remove all the downstairs radiators from the walls. Additionally, about seven hours of daylight, and often quite poor daylight at that, proved less than useful for decorating.

A pile of sand appeared in the yard and I combined it with cement and lime in the mixer to render the walls. Joan viewed this process with some apprehension, as did I, but it stayed on the walls somehow. I had some difficulty in achieving level surfaces on the longer walls but it began to take shape. We had made a preliminary application to convert the house to business use and learned that we would have to fit fire alarms, emergency lighting, fire doors and a number of less expensive fittings. It was a pity about the doors for these were pine that had been sheathed in hardboard for ease of painting. They would have restored nicely but were too thin for fire retardation. During my forays to the DIY, I began to keep an eye open for doors of the required thickness.

The chap next door turned out to be a plumber and he offered to plumb in our extra sinks and showers at a competitive price, working on an opportunity basis. He also had an electrician friend who was willing to work on the same terms and this was something of a bonus. I briefly considered looking for acarpenter who might make up the trio, but reluctantly decided that our funding would not stretch to it. Much of the work we would simply have to tackle ourselves and, despite numerous frustrations, there was a degree of satisfaction in that.

The electrician soon uncovered a fair bit of dodgy wiring, which included a ring main that had not been routed through any fuse box, and the plumber uncovered a bath overflow which was not connected to any drain. I was meanwhile discovering rot every time I lifted old carpets or took wallpaper off the upstairs walls, and Joan was stripping paper off the top landing one day when the entire ceiling fell about her ears. The wood-chip paper and several coats of gloss paint had apparently been holding it together. I ordered more sand, cement and lime and added timber and plasterboard to the DIY shopping list. Some days, despite much effort, we seemed not to have progressed at all and the house became pretty depressing for a while.

We escaped very briefly to Cheshire for Xmas and brought Mam back with us. I had sorted out a bedroom for her and our front room was at least habitable by now, if not exactly ready for the pages of House & Garden. I was reluctant to subject Mam to such a mess but she took it in her stride and, given half the chance, would likely have weighed in with a paintbrush.

After the cycle of four days of very long hours on the house, it was almost a relief to report to the squadron and involve myself with either training matters or routine admin for the remaining three days of the week. I had been furnished with no specific brief, nor a job description, when I arrived and I simply tackled things that looked as if they might otherwise remain undone. The CO usually came in for one weekday in the winter months and I soon went to him with my concerns about the Training NCO. My opinion confirmed the CO's own doubts and he expressed the view that he should seek a posting for the man, who had been in post for more than two years and had in fact undergone an earlier tour with another of the auxiliary squadrons. Whether or not the SNCO got wind of this, I do not know, but he cleverly pre-empted it by submitting application for premature voluntary retirement to RAF Innsworth, requesting that it be effected in eighteen months. He had thus preserved himself from a posting, unless very strenuous efforts were made to get rid of him, and he now became totally disinterested in any form of activity. He continued to arrive late and not at all, and I once ordered him back to the squadron when I learned that he had simply gone home on leave to which he had no entitlement. He was a lost cause and his duties were absorbed by other staff. In the final year of his service he was wholly ineffective and an object of some derision among the reservists. He gave an excellent impersonation of a man in a coma, remaining a sad example of an RAF Regiment SNCO.

    I had noticed that only about fifty per cent of the effective strength consistently turned up for training venues other than the battle camps, and I wondered who 'drove' such training. It was clearly neither the Adjutant nor the Training NCO, and nor did we enjoy good experience levels among the full time reservists. One of the two SNCOs had served a full career as an MT mechanic and his last tour had been with 2625. Upon retirement he had remained on the squadron in a full time capacity as a Gunner whilst retaining the rank of sergeant. He had already served for two years thus but no attempt had been made to send him upon any courses that might make a *useful* SNCO of him.

    The other senior working full time was a flight sergeant who had about five year's service with the squadron, and he had acquired a couple of handy qualifications, but he seemed to deal only in the realm of recruiting and fiercely resisted any attempts to involve him in the training process. The three remainder of the full time staff seemed to work merely as 'gofers' and when I eventually suggested to the CO that the full time staff ought to be regarded as a training team, and qualified accordingly, he agreed, but his time was by then running out and the idea was slow to win acceptance by his successor.

Training problems extended to those reservists who only attended at weekends. The DSC was a former wing commander, retired after full service as a pilot. His previous service was admirable and, in particular, unique, but I privately wondered what particular gifts he brought to service with an RAF Regiment squadron. He may well have been recruited on the strength of his shooting activities, that included participation annually at Bisley, but this did not necessarily offer him great insight into battle shooting. He seemed completely unaware of the gulf between shooting competitively and shooting to kill, and resistant to suggestions that the difference was very great. Shortly after I joined the squadron we deployed to a gallery range to complete annual personal weapon practices under the DSC, and he succeeded in completing just two practices (one normally occupying about forty minutes) in the six hours that we spent at the range. I was further dismayed when all shooting ceased for a VIP visit from the reservist heirarchy, and I quietly fumed at the consequent waste of precious range-firing time that the lengthy visit imposed upon us, as all ranks were marshalled for the somewhat idle scrutiny of the long-retired in the VIP area, to the total exclusion of further firing.

After six years of existence, the squadron should not have lacked 'home-grown' talent - and it actually had some very good corporals - yet it continually sought service experience elsewhere. The classic, perhaps, was the appointment of a sergeant who reportedly had served in the Falklands with the Royal Marines. It later transpired that the sergeant had actually served in the artillery before deafness took him off the gun line. He had been briefly *attached* to the RM a good number of years before and his Falklands experience was long post-war as a mess manager. He proved not to have the first idea of basic weapons, minor tactics or anything at all useful and he simply wandered about on weekends until he got bored and left the unit. All of this ought to have told me something, but I continued to believe that the problems could swiftly be solved. The lord loves an optimist.

With the ground floor of the house something like straight, I ventured upstairs where the tasteful polystyrene tiles on the ceilings covered more problems, and wooden cladding in the lavatory covered rotten floorboards. I was practically on first name terms at the DIY by now, whilst the man who operated the rubbish skip hire doubtless had me at the top of his Xmas card list. The work required for fire certification required £1,000, and we later learned that it was not required at all if only three double bedrooms were being occupied. We had four doubles and a single. We also learned that houses that had been converted into holiday flats - two of which flanked our property - required no fire certification at all. Each of these flats had a potential chip pan fire - which caused about seventy per cent of domestic fires - in two or three rooms. It was hard to fathom equivalence in the regulations. I finished hanging the last of nine fire doors and we duly received our fire certificate. In a nice piece of timing, we received on the same day notice from the borough council that our application to convert to business premises had been refused.

12

Council objections to our trading as a guesthouse included the claim that ours was a residential only street and that we had insufficient parking spaces. In our appeal, which we had to take to the Department of the Environment, I was able to demonstrate that, of the nineteen houses in the street only one was a private dwelling, whether the council knew that or not, and that in addition to two parking spaces on our property to the front, I had just created two at the back by demolishing the garden wall and sending the garden away via my great friend, the skip hire owner. We won the appeal, which also won us the right to pay increased rubbish collection rates, enhanced water supply charges and, eventually, business rates. The New Year had aged and the house had aged me. It had taken about eight months and several thousand pounds to renovate and outfit the house, but we seemed to be ready to trade at least. At that point we knew nothing of the impending and deep recession, nor a succession of rotten summers, but the whole thing had rather been put into perspective in February. We received the news of Bess' death at Shavington and we made the sombre journey to Cheshire for the service. Her decline and death had followed with astonishing swiftness and during the brief visit I could not shake the conviction that I would meet Bess in the village.

Matters at the squadron were not improving. I had taken on the task of producing a training programme for the two weekends per month when the flights were expected to attend, but I was not enjoying unqualified success in getting the programmes implemented. I was most irritated by the degree of 'lobbying' which some of the regular and semi-regular staff resorted to whenever I tasked them with training duties that did not suit them. Among our problems, it seemed, were those of SNCOs who wished to soldier on their own terms and no one else's.

We had undergone another week of battle camp, this time at the familiar Sennybridge. I had accompanied the Adjutant to the range booking conference in January and had been pleasantly surprised to encounter Brum Cleaver. Brum had returned to service with the Royal Marines after a brief spell in civvie street, shortly after I had taken over his training team at Lympstone, and he was now in his final tour. I was not to meet him again, since he got a job as an instructor with an outward bound type of school and was killed in an abseiling accident.

The camp had again produced some pleasing examples of effort at the level of Gunner, and some displeasing examples of SNCOs who seemed reluctant to wear webbing or to get their feet wet. Three of the seniors were moreover exclusively employed for the week with a recruit course, and in my brief observations of it I noted little activity other than a lot of inappropriate shouting on the introductory battle ranges. Rather than reducing the list of training problems, I appeared to be constantly adding to them.

Spring approached and in April I was sent to the School of Infantry for a fortnight to undergo a course which would qualify me to conduct Stage V ranges. I had actually been conducting them for about twelve years but only on the CO's signature of authority, which I would no longer require with the qualification. I was accompanied on the course by two RAF Regiment SNCOs who also served at St. Mawgan, although in a defence capacity. I had previously served with both of them on II Squadron. These two made good running companions on what little free time we found between running ranges or acting as students, and I also devoted some time to drawing up a list of training problems which I intended to take to the CO on my return. The course meanwhile contained no surprises and it usefully began with a conversion to the L85, the new rifle that was just entering service.

Regrettably, the CO was by now not often to be seen. When leaving regular service he had set up a yacht-hire and day-skippering business, working out of Falmouth, and this had proved greatly successful. It meant, though, that the CO was seldom available during the summer months on either a daily or a weekend basis. The camp towards the end of the year would probably offer the best chance to discuss future training, since we also expected a new adjutant in post at about that time.

In May I had just £200 left in my bank account; the house having represented continual expense and much of it entirely unexpected. At least it was done and we were now up and running, although I had yet to tackle the backyard and make something of it. Some fears that the full time auxiliary posts might be altogether dismantled had receded and our days were actually expanded to a maximum of two hundred per year. This was then shortly increased to two hundred and fifty, then two hundred and seventy, which actually represented more than a five-day working week. I was happy enough with this, now that the house did not demand huge amounts of time, and still not knowing what our B&B earning potential might be.

RAF St. Mawgan underwent a TACEVAL in June and as many of the squadron who were able to secure time off work participated. It was undemanding stuff and I found myself working twelve-hour shifts in the Operations Centre. I could have been wrong, but I believed that there was not the slightest interest among the station executive staff in what the squadron was doing, although our Observation Posts on the perimeter detected every single attempt by the 'enemy' (No 58 Squadron, from the Depot) to infiltrate sensitive areas. I also noticed that the Adjutant carefully left himself off the Ops Centre shift roster and generally went home at night.

I had by this time ceased to bother the Adjutant with training problems, but I took to him my grave concerns about wage sheets which the full time flight sergeant reservist was submitting. It was no part of my remit, but I had taken a cursory interest that quickened when wage sheets began to be passed to me for a signature before being passed to the Adjutant. It was the practice at the time for each of the full time reservists to fill his wages' sheet in at the end of each month, and submit it for payment. I soon noticed that the flight sergeant was routinely claiming for twenty-six or twenty-seven days each month at a time when our average should have been no more than sixteen, and the regular staff working no more than twenty-two. It meant, obviously, that the flight sergeant was working often - assuming that he *was* working - when no one else was, and although this was possible, since he worked exclusively in the realm of recruiting, there seemed little justification for it. My suspicion, which I laid directly before the Adjutant, was that the flight sergeant was feathering his nest at the expense of the Taxpayer. The Adjutant proved typically offhand about the matter and did nothing. I took my concerns to the CO when he made one of his rare appearances and he looked a bit more thoughtful about it, asking me to monitor the wage sheets and keep him informed.

Summer brought a brief change with the presentation of a Colour to the Royal Auxiliary Air Force by the Queen, at RAF Benson. We spent a week in preparation for the parade, living in hutted accommodation at Bisley Camp, and it proved possible to bring both Mam and Joan down to the camp for a few days. Having gone with the advance party, I rang Joan to warn her about mosquitoes and advised her to bring some sort of repellent. She turned up with an electrical gadget which was not of great utility, since the huts had not been updated since Kitchener's days at the camp. The presentation saw several hundred reservists on parade and only one succumbed to the fierce heat. The week offered a very pleasant break from routine and problems and I encountered several colleagues who were now serving with other reservist formations.

Returning to the problems, I launched an assault on the training cell that had long ceased to function. Notionally under the control of the former MT sergeant, it represented seven filing cabinets stuffed with obsolete junk and I reduced the cabinets to just two. I then got in touch with the Depot and the RAF College to get hold of some lesson plans with a view to building a useful library for training use. I also spoke to the DSC at the time, since he was at least nominally the training officer and often appeared during the week, but it was apparent that his training interest lay exclusively in the sphere of competition shooting and it looked suspiciously as if he merely indulged a hobby at the Taxpayer's expense.

If my interest and morale was sustained by anything at all in this period, it was the recognition that the fifty per cent who regularly attended for training contained some very capable lads and some quite exceptional junior NCOs. These, at least, were worth working for and I began to be involved with a skills' team which trained on a weeknight. The principal competition annually was the Strickland Trophy, contested by the auxiliary squadrons at the Depot. 2625 had won the competition in the first two years it was held but had not been much in the running after staff changes saw a failure of interest in any forms of training, much less the additional effort required for such competitions. I was asked by the team if I might programme the training and I was happy to do so. For variety, I arranged a weekend at Woodbury Common, last visited during the Lympstone tour, and I managed to organise some team and section exercises against a Royal Marine Reserve troop from Bristol. Learning that the troop had a qualified PTI, I also managed to arrange a run on the Endurance Course for my team. We did the course towards midday on the Sunday morning and I elected to run it with them. I was pleasantly surprised to finish in just under the bogey time although, ominously, only one of the skills' team did.

I also found myself invited to join the Gig team, one of six rowers who were to contest the Newquay Rowing Club in craft which had originally been designed to put a pilot aboard sailing ships. The challenge had arisen from the town mayor, a keen rower in his youth, since he was a keen supporter of the squadron. Just prior to my arrival, the squadron had been formally affiliated to the town of Newquay and affiliation was a rare distinction for a reservist unit. This had largely been initiated by the mayor, who looked for ways to celebrate the union other than with formal parades. Each Tuesday evening, the team assembled at the harbour to put a gig into the water and practise for an hour. Our results were mixed but we could more than hold our own in the bar after the gigs had been returned to the boatshed.

In September we took Mam on a round of farewells to Worksop and Cheshire since she was going home in December. I had asked her if she might want to stay with us but Mam was ready for home and it was the right decision. She had a circle of friends in Boulder and her happiest memories were doubtless there also. And nor did she need the lengthy English winters any more. Following the visits, I took the Strickland Team up to the Depot and we were beaten into second place on just one per cent of the overall score. This was disappointing, although it seemed to prove that we were on the way back to form. I had no such hopes yet for the main training effort.

We had closed the door on the last guest in September, having made a modest beginning and hoping that 1990 might produce a better trade. With the rooms empty, I had to address some more renovation, having discovered rotten window frames. We briefly considered double-glazing and invited quotations. One chap displayed his wares, highlighted the technical superiority of the product, outlined the special savings plan, performed wizardry on his calculator and gave us the good news on his rock-bottom price. He could replace all of the windows for just £11,000. It was the best laugh I had had for quite some time.

In October we deployed the squadron to the Hythe and Lydd

ranges on the Kent coast for a week of mostly urban ranges. There being very little in the nature of dry-training areas, most of the evenings were free, and since the officers and seniors combined in the same mess, the CO began to take soundings on the training effort. The seniors spoke very frankly and not least about the quality of recruits who were being passed to the flights but soon terminating their service. I had already spoken to the CO about the recruit course, advertising my concern that there was no exemplar programme for it, and that there appeared to be no training objectives or objective assessment of the recruit. There were also no training tests, fitness tests or exercise phases. When the camp ended, the CO told me that I was to take over the running of the recruit courses in the New Year and I felt that I was getting somewhere at last. On the recent anniversary of my first year as a civilian, I had wondered if a single day had passed when I had not wished that I had stayed in regular service.

In mid-November I flew home with Mam. Finances did not allow Joan to accompany us and I had to finance my own ticket by unloading some gas shares and a unit trust I had acquired in more affluent times. Even this measure left me with little spending cash and life got a touch complicated when my stay became longer than the intended month. The Australian domestic airline pilots were on strike and a good number of West Australians who normally flew to the Eastern States for Xmas chose instead to fly to Singapore and Malaysia. This put a burden on the first leg of any UK flight and my stay stretched to six weeks.

We were met by Jan and Arch and spent a week with them before continuing to the Goldfields. My programme there was largely that of a run in the mornings before it became too hot, followed by a long walk in the afternoon. The TV programmes were pretty dreadful and I usually spent the evening with a book before having an early night. I occasionally went next door to share a bottle of beer with Lou Herll, former member of the armed Hitler Youth whose fortune it was to be captured by the American army, rather than the Russians, and former 'gun' miner on the Lake View & Star. Lou recalled the Old Man for me and he had some nice things to say about him. He also showed me a clipping from the obituary column of the Kalgoorlie Miner that he had preserved. There was a lengthy list of tributes to the Old Man from members of the RSL and the Mines & City Workers.

Farewells were getting no easier with age and I left Mam with Bea and Malc at the Kalgoorlie station as I boarded the train for Perth.

I had taken little luggage but my bag was heavy with diaries I had left at home for years. I had gathered them up on this trip, wondering how likely another visit might be.

Interlude

GIG RACING

The Newquay Rowing Club, prodded by the town mayor, issued a challenge to the squadron to contest a gig race on the local stretch of sea. We were assured that the club would field a purely novice team against us on the day, rather than some hearties whose idea of a day out was a quick row to the Isles of Scilly and home, but even so the volunteer list failed to grow. The single name on it for some time was that of the Adjutant, who possibly felt guilty at having done nothing for two years, and mine was mysteriously added whilst I was attending a course. The unknown hand perhaps believed I had a poor memory, but the idea was developing some momentum by the time I returned and I felt obliged to respond.

Although I had been stirred by the poetry of Masefield,('I must go down to the sea again, to the lonely sea and the sky; and all I ask is a tall ship and a star to steer her by'), no salt water flowed in the Foxley veins and, if asked, I might have ventured the guess that a gig was something that spotty musicians did to support their peculiar nasal habits. I had never considered parachuting half so dangerous as efforts afloat, which included such examples as the Mary Celeste, the Titanic and the raft Medusa, where, you may recall, the large survivors ate the small survivors.

Gigs sounded an extremely dodgy affair, and I speak with some authority on dodgy affairs, having run several squadron raffles in my time. Upon closer inspection at the harbour, the gig proved to be much the sort of craft that Fletcher Christian invited William Bligh to continue his naval career in. Viz: no engines, no stabilisers and clearly no entertainments' officer. It looked about as much fun as a ten-year posting to a Roman galley, as I stood gloomily on the harbour wall with the others of the hand-pressed crew, waiting for the Coxswain to arrive. He proved to be a gimlet-eyed individual whose specific brief, clearly, was to bring the boat back safely when all extraneous crew were washed overboard. He was not receptive to early questioning and my anxious enquiries about the possibilities of Teredo Worm were buried in an avalanche of recondite nautical terminology, delivered in an impenetrable accent. Scouse, I think.

Our initial outing was not a great success, apart from the fact that we appeared capable of completing circles faster than anyone else in the water, and the plan view of the gig was probably most reminiscent of some arthritic insect. The howls of laughter from the harbour wall we easily dismissed as emanating from ignorant Emmets (holidaymakers), except that the crowd seemed to include a fair proportion of the rowing club. We proved most adept at carrying the gig (and several others, come to think of it) back to the boat shed, where the only sensible thing I had heard all evening was that we might try the pint in the clubhouse.

It was at this point where we fell in with Digger, a retired carpenter and boatbuilder who was perhaps the senior member of the club. Digger's father, we learned, had rowed a pilot gig in the last days of their intended use, which was to put a Pilot aboard some ship which had to be guided inshore to safe anchorage. When the technology had moved on, hundreds of gigs fell into disuse. Some rotted on the beach, others, even more ignominiously, were sawn in half to provide garden sheds and a few, very few, survived.

The Newquay club had three gigs that dated from the first half of the nineteenth century. *Treffry* was built in 1838 (and had singly carried out an epic rescue from a foundering steamer a few years later), *Dove* was built in 1820 and the oldest of them all was the *Newquay*, built in 1812, which was the same year that Nelson's Flagship *Victory* was decommissioned. *Newquay* was the oldest gig in the world, in fact, although she might easily have rotted in Burma.

The gig was one of three built to ply the waters of the Irrawaddy in that country, but only two were taken and *Newquay* was bought by a Pilot. In 1928 *Dove* set the record for a measured mile, her crew completing it in six minutes and fifteen seconds, which is fairly scooting across the surface of the sea.

Gigs looked to be pretty sturdy affairs, and I was surprised when Digger told us that the planking seldom exceeded a quarter-inch in thickness. This was intended to keep the weight down and gigs were built to weigh no more than seven hundredweight, so that the crew might easily launch or beach the vessel. The crews were typically six in the days that they were a working boat, although gigs built for eight had featured for a time. These were eventually prohibited by an act of parliament, after complaints by the Revenue men that their sail cutters could not catch the 8-man gig that engaged in smuggling. The rowing gigs would simply turn upwind and draw away. Smaller gigs were also used on the smuggler's runs and one Cornishman was known to have completed at least a dozen trips to Roscoff, a round trip of two hundred and fifty miles. The gigs were clinker-built of elm on oak and instead of being fitted with rowlocks, the oars - or paddles as they were known - simply slotted between wooden pegs. In a rough sea, these would break rather than the hull planking.

Digger was a mine of information in the bar, where we were at least as successful as the club rowers, and he also cox'd for us a few times. The evening sessions of practice were notionally of two hour's duration, but we sometimes had difficulty in putting three vital components together. These were the gig (the club had seven, but *Newquay* was reserved for very special races), a Cox'n (since no club secretary in his right mind was about to entrust a gig to a bunch of landlubbers who didn't know a binnacle from a barnacle) and a set of paddles. A paddle, some twelve feet of it, cost about a hundred pounds and they were not indestructible in the hands of tyros who caught more crabs than a fishing fleet. The result of trying to assemble the kit sometimes saw us standing on the harbour wall for an hour or so, usually whilst the ladies' team skimmed effortlessly between the buoys, and we fretted at the lost, and much-needed, practice.

Paddles were sized according to station within the gig, and we seldom knew where we might be rowing until the Cox ran a practised eye over the assembly. The Cox sat in the stern, which was the blunt bit, and the rowers sat facing him with their backs to the bow, which was the sharp bit. Closest to the Cox was the Stroke oar, and he, Digger informed us, was the most vital man in the crew. Acquiring the rowing technique was important, but what won races was the Stroke responding to the cadence counted by the Cox ('One and Two and Three and Four and One and Two...') and the rest of the crew matching the Stroke.

Rowing began at the soles of the feet, continued up the legs and to the back which did the real work, whilst the arms had a relatively minor role in closing the paddle to the chest at the end of the stroke. The upper body had to move through nearly a hundred and eighty degrees to be fully effective on the paddle. Bare feet were recommended and the sparse wooden seat raised blisters on the arse. Padding was considered inefficient and effete. We toiled, caught crabs, lost the stroke, fucked up big time and carried all the gigs to the shed as a penalty. We also, rarely, worked in unison, using the paddles correctly, working the whole body and inwardly exulting as we skimmed across a lively sea. It was a marvellous feeling. The sea played its games occasionally and we had barely left the harbour some evening when the Cox shook his head and began to turn the gig. "I don't like the look of that sea." Was all he said, looking anxious. I was Stroke and caught his glance clearly, thinking: 'If he is looking anxious, shouldn't I be terrified?'

The gap in the harbour entrance was about eighteen feet wide and the Cox lined us up with it, saying, "Hold your paddles in the water until I shout, then row like buggery!" Then we saw the huge wave that was rolling up on us. The Cox shouted, we rowed like buggery, and then some and we shot through the harbour gap like a cork from a champagne bottle, recently shaken.

"How did you know that wave was coming?" someone asked, later. The Cox shrugged, noncommittally. "Bad ol' bastard, that sea sometimes." He said.

Practice continued and the prospect of being beaten by the ladies reserve team by about forty-seven lengths receded somewhat. We had distilled two gig's worth of 'volunteers' down to a single crew but we were working hard and were hungry for a win. This was not unnoticed by the club. It seemed incumbent upon the squadron to offer a trophy and we came up with a paddle from somewhere. (It perhaps fell off the back of a boat and we were anxious at the presentation that some club member might recognise it) The paddle was embellished with the rank badges of all participating crew and a suitably inscribed silver plate. We took a good look at it prior to the presentation, on the assumption that we might never see it again.

We developed a crew problem and the club sportingly offered to provide us with a Stroke; our enthusiasm for the offer only slightly diminishing when the individual reported to us. He had the build of a pipe-cleaner, the colouring of an egg tray and his spectacles were something you could have examined microbes with. 'Technique', we reassured ourselves, was the thing and brute strength counted for nothing. Moreover, Stroke did not actually need to see where he was going. We launched the gig and prepared to race over the two-mile triangular course. We wore rugby shirts and that was a mistake since they drew the sweat that dripped down to the benches and made a skating surface of them. We heaved on the paddles and the sea rushed beneath us. The Cox roared his cadences. We jack-knifed forwards then stretched full-length, dragging the last ounce of effort from the toenails upwards. Stroke suddenly bowed at the waist then stayed there, sobbing for breath as he produced a Ventolin inhaler from his pocket. Stroke, we learned, had a touch of asthma. We trailed the club crew in by some distance and got a nice wave from the ladies reserve team. We hauled the gig from the water and went in the quest of a pint and a commiserating word.

Digger was at the bar and he accepted a pint. "I expec' you'll be back?" he offered. "I expect so." I replied, adding that we might not be so reliant on a spare Stroke the next time, and nodding at the youth now recovered from his asthma attack. "Oh, 'im," said Digger, "'e's known around 'ere as 'Useless'."

"He's known around 'ere as 'Useless'"

13

I had spent the last few days in Australia with Jan and Arch, finding the long walks in the bright sunshine agreeable before the return to winter, and also taking the time to visit the construction of the replica *Endeavour*, Captain Cook's ship. This impressive project was taking place at Fremantle, a colonial town well worth a visit in its own right. Arch was also packing at this time; he had recently returned to fulltime service, had been promoted to major and was shortly posted to a training school in Queensland for what would be his last tour of duty. I saw Dave Armstrong again, now retired and living near Perth, and another guest at his house was Graham Hay, who had also served with 40 Air Supply. I hadn't seen him for twenty-five years, another reminder that the big wheel moved on. I eventually secured a flight which put me into Heathrow on Xmas Eve and I went home to find Joan preparing for guests, Mo and Vic Eastman, who currently were serving at the Regiment Depot.

With the Xmas Grant over, I reported to the squadron and was dispirited, if not entirely surprised, to discover that the training programmes had again collapsed. I cobbled one together for the imminent weekend and worked at a more measured pace on its successors, having to suspend my intention to draw up an exemplar syllabus for the recruit course which was due to begin fairly soon. The new Adjutant was in post and I had planned to approach him with a frank description of our training problems, but his manner proved distant and unwelcoming. I later surmised that someone may well have beaten me to his office and perhaps even advised that *I* was the problem.

Not least among the problems was that I by now had little faith in the integrity of the full time reservist flight sergeant, and matters ought to have been brought to a head when I noticed that his wages claim for February listed every single day of the month. This was demonstrably false and I summoned him to my office and challenged the claim. His revised claim was reduced by eleven days, representing some £350 in wages, but I had miscalculated my action and ought to have demanded an investigation, or, at the very least, have charged him. His claims became much more modest at this point and it was clear that he was alert to threat. I dug out the wages records and found that he had claimed forty-five consecutive days worked in my absence, and this despite having produced an excuse for not attending the recent Battle Camp. Had his claim for February passed without comment, his consecutive total would have risen to seventy-five days. This was outrageous and I again took the matter to the CO. The CO proved to have been harbouring doubts of his own for some time, although he was unsure of how we might resolve the matter. Events overtook him, however, for within two months he had relinquished his command of the squadron. This was so abrupt, and so much in contrast to the CO's recent enthusiasm for a resurrected training effort, that I became convinced that he had been asked to leave the unit because of his patchy attendance record. We had recently received a visit from the Honorary Inspector General (a retired air chief marshal) which the CO had not attended, and I think it probable that the CO's summer attendance record had been broadcast to the HIG during his visit.

In mid-March the recruit course assembled and it was working to the old syllabus, or, rather, no syllabus. I took the course off the flight sergeant on the third day, writing a new syllabus on the hoof and swiftly adding training objectives, tests and exercises to it. The Adjutant mildly queried the take over and it was clear that the flight sergeant was lobbying, but the course remained under my control.

I reposed no great faith in the Adjutant at even this early stage. He had been in post for three months but was yet to evince any interest in training programmes or the execution of them. He had made a grand address to the squadron on arrival, referring to the fact that he had 'been in several hot wars', although the single General Service Medal ribbon on his uniform offered other witness. He quickly proved to be entirely clueless in the training role and soon learned to remain in the world of administration, which seemed more to his liking.

On a slightly more promising note, the regular Training NCO - forgotten but not gone - was nearing demob, and I wrote to each of the warrant officers on the regular squadrons, advertising the post and emphasising the importance of a good man. There was some encouraging response to this and Eddie Martin was among the volunteers, but Innsworth chose its own candidate unilaterally, despite the promise of consultation with 2625. The replacement knew of his posting even before the squadron was informed, which was poor staff procedure, and although he had a useful training record he was in fact arriving under a disciplinary cloud and we would later learn that he apparently had something of a drink problem.

Nor were the problems confined to the job. In the house, we had not yet attended to the matter of the leaking roof and a severe storm put sufficient rain through it to collapse one of the bedroom ceilings. The storm also did little for TV reception, either, since the aerial sheared off the chimney then pendulumed down on its cable to smash the window of another bedroom. The aerial, the window and the ceiling were at least within my expertise to replace, but the last of the gas shares had to go to sort out new slates for the roof.

The squadron ran a promotion course over a couple of weekends (too few, in my opinion, but no one seemed interested) and any hopes I might have preserved that the Adjutant actually knew something of use to a field squadron were dispelled. He issued Orders which adhered to no recognisable format and his knowledge of even basic battle procedure was poor. His idea of night 'tactical' Orders was to put the course into the back of a 4 Tonner and have a second vehicle shine its headlights into it, and his most familiar mode was standing about, uncamouflaged and unencumbered by weapon or webbing, with fag in mouth and hands deep in pockets. It was painful to watch.

I was for a time taking too many of such problems home with me, and I resolved to leave them at the camp gates. I had lately been trying some of my short stories on the publishing market but they were returned without exception, often in suspiciously pristine condition. My market research had been confined to a perusal of the shelves at WH Smith's, revealing that the market was almost exclusively female. Men's magazines tended to the gynaecological only and short story success appeared to depend upon writing for the sort of women's magazines whose reader's lips moved as they read the words. When one of my stories was returned with the comment: 'Not enough romance', I decided to write a novel instead, and for some weeks worked out plot details as I walked the dog along the local cliff path. I noticed at some point that a central character underwent no less than three changes of name in the span of the narrative, but it was, I felt, a fine story of redemption which would bring tears to a glass eye. It actually proved a fine way of using up first-, then second-class stamps, and it now resides in the loft, awaiting discovery and critical acclaim late in the twenty-first century.

The DSC assumed command of the squadron in May and I could see no cause for rejoicing in his promotion. At interview he had not seemed enthusiastic about my view that robust training was essential, and nor did he share my concerns about the full time flight sergeant, with whom he had briefly administered a flight some years earlier. Nor was I greatly enthused by his instruction to parade the squadron in a hollow square for his initial address as CO. He directed that his Land Rover be arranged so that he might stand on the bonnet and speak to the throng. This was possibly something he had seen in wartime film footage of Montgomery or Mountbatten, but the squadron was considerably smaller than either the Eighth or the Fourteenth armies. I feared that our credibility was destined to slip a few notches further down the scale.

In July I intercepted another false wage claim submitted by the flight sergeant and I wheeled him straight in front of the CO. The flight sergeant blandly claimed to have made an error and this facile excuse was accepted by the CO. This was disappointing, as was the CO's continuing refusal to discourage the lobbying which still plagued our efforts. At my first interview with him, I had pointed out that the chain of command was sacrosanct on regular squadrons and ought to be on reservist units. The CO had nodded at this but he allowed the lobbying to continue, which actually was the least of our problems, when it became apparent that he was rather more a figurehead of the squadron, in contrast to a more active leader. Cockpit-management, however excellent, did not necessarily translate into efficient man-management or tactical leadership.

I was beginning to feel quite dispirited by a number of failures at this time, noting that I had for more than a year worked hard to rescue our effort in several areas, only to see them fail again as soon as I transferred my attention elsewhere. Without harbouring delusions of grandeur, I had sometimes wished that *I* was the CO and thus in a position to stop people avoiding their duties. I had no good reason for assuming that anyone else might.

I opened my copy of the *RAF News* one morning and spotted

an advertisement for contract employment in the Oman, discussing it with Joan when I went home. I had no especial wish to be serving in the desert, particularly as a drill instructor, for two years, when my home and my wife and dog were in Cornwall, but I could see nothing but frustration ahead with 2625 Squadron. I applied for the job, succeeded at the interview and was informed that I would likely be summoned in September.

14

I did not immediately advertise my intention to leave the squadron and life went on. The unit was visited by an establishment review team, whose remit was to ascertain the future of full time reservist posts, which might be justified on a contract basis. Each of the six full time auxiliaries was interviewed and during mine it was observed by the team leader, a group captain, that many of the duties I described seemed more properly the fiefs of the training officer or training NCO. I agreed that, without offering any amplification. At this time also we awaited the new Training NCO, whilst the recently arrived Adjutant was taking very little interest in the unit's weekend activities. It was possible that he was pining for another 'hot war' somewhere.

If we were meanwhile curious as to what form the new CO's innovations might take, then we were enlightened one Sunday when he insisted upon each flight laying out its entire complement of personal and section kit on the parade area for inspection. The inspection took two hours and was relieved only slightly when the Adjutant picked up a weapon and pronounced it filthy, demanding to know whose it was. It was his own. I dropped the production of training programmes out of curiosity to see who might pick them up, and when no one did so the flights paraded to no great purpose for a weekend or two. Officially, we were awaiting the arrival of the new Training NCO and he duly arrived from No 3 Squadron, which was permanently stationed in Northern Ireland. I had known John briefly at the Depot and he had some good service behind him, although he now appeared to have a drink-related medical problem, for which he was currently being assessed by the medical authority.

Towards the end of August I notified the CO that I would be leaving the squadron after the parade which would mark the fiftieth anniversary of the Battle of Britain, and to which I had been invited to contribute as the assistant parade warrant officer. This offer was extended by Nick Acons, by now a wing commander and largely responsible for putting the parade together, and I had been happy to accept. It seemed a good note upon which to end my service. Towards the day itself, I would spend a week at RAF Halton, where all training and rehearsals would take place. The CO expressed no regret at my intention to leave, but he staggered me by announcing his intention to appoint the full time reservist flight sergeant as the new warrant officer. This news was not received with unequivocal joy by the rank and file.

The somewhat bigger news at the time was the Iraqi invasion of Kuwait, and with the West's oil supplies thus threatened there was more than just an outside chance that armed intervention under the flag of the UN would result. I fleetingly wondered if reservists might be required, but could see little chance of it.

John established the new training regime and on a Saturday when one of the flights was completing the Combat Fitness Test, another was conducting a range practice and a third was training on the station, I found the Adjutant in the orderly room, playing computer games. On the following Monday, I went uninvited to his office to enquire if perhaps he was on an extended Cornish holiday, swiftly adumbrating several examples of his poor approach to training. He offered no defence but I later discovered that he had written a virulently one-sided account of the exchange and submitted it to the station commander. I thought this somewhat gutless at the time and still do. We had, and doubtless still have, some very sharp acts in the commissioned ranks of the RAF Regiment, but this dunce was not among them. Notwithstanding my poor opinion of him, however, he was promoted to squadron leader before the end of his tour and posted to the relative safety of the Ministry of Defence.

It was certainly my season for upsetting people, intentionally or otherwise. Upon arrival at RAF Halton, I was asked to take a particular interest in the reservist flights, one of which was armed and would be parading with the regular flights before the gates of Buckingham Palace. I learned that each of these flights totalled no more than forty-two, including Guides and Markers, and it was a matter of simple arithmetic to establish that we already had more reservists than spaces available, with more yet to arrive. I therefore paraded all of them to advise that they were competing for slots. Anyone who did not get one was free to RTU, thus preserving the time off work they had secured from employers, and anyone who chose to remain regardless might be found some other role on the day. I then turned to other duties, although I returned to monitor the drill standard from time to time, since that would form the basis for any exclusion.

Two corporals from the disciplinary branch were attached to train the flight daily and I had asked both to make notes for a couple of days. I then conferred with them, adding my own impressions, and reduced the flight to the select forty-two and a couple of spares. Whilst some of those excused elected to RTU, others decided to stay and one of them confronted me with the complaint that he had been unfairly excluded. I noted that he was a corporal with regular service, since his tunic bore the ribbon of the Long Service & Good Conduct medal, and that he was black. I told him that his drill and deportment had been eclipsed by others and that was that. Only it wasn't.

A day later I had a call from the full time reservist SNCO - a Rock I had known slightly at the Depot years before - at the complainant's unit, and he advised me that an official complaint was likely to be entered by the rejected corporal. I restated the facts and he said that he would advise his Adjutant accordingly.

I got on with the training and renewed some acquaintances. Jim Lavery had been borrowed from his present Germany squadron tour and we shared the drilling of some flights. Jim had a longtime reputation in the mob for fractiousness, but we rubbed along well enough. Graeme Curtis, last seen on QCS, was another familiar face and he was now serving as the training NCO with a sister auxiliary squadron. The parade warrant officer was Davy Munro, a II Squadron man, and Taff Price, who was the QCS warrant, I had last seen at the RAF College.

It was a blistering week and sweat pooled on the parade square. The flights worked uniformly hard at parade excellence but it was seldom matched by two dozen Colour and Standard parties, who would have pride of place on the day. The Colours and Standards were carried by a junior officer, who was flanked by a pair of SNCOs with a warrant officer in rear. None of them exuded either smartness or enthusiasm and most of the escorts appeared to be excused arm swinging. They were parading, limply, one day as I stood at the edge of the square and was joined by Air Commodore Hawkins, who had been my CO during the first QCS tour. "What d'you think, Mr Foxley?" He wanted to know. I had a ready answer: "I think they need an hour's extra drill, Sir, when everyone else is stood down." Later in the day, the flights were dismissed and I was despatched to pull the bearers and escorts off the coach for the extra drill. It was possibly my finest hour.

The Commonwealth and Dominions sent full flights, and both the Australian and the Kiwi contingents took a fair bit of keeping up with in the bar. I made it a point of honour to leave the bar last early one morning, consequently feeling very rough on the square. I was also thudding around the local lanes in boots after drill, which tended to develop a thirst.

I had been asked to sort out the business of getting markers onto parade, since it had so far been a complete shambles. This seemed a perfectly simple job and I identified each of the flights, then selected their tallest man. I explained the 'on parade' procedure in terms of the commands which would be issued, and the markers' response to it, believing that it would work first time. I then marched to parade centre, bellowed: **"RIGHT....MARKERS!"** and confidently awaited results. It all went to plan, except that two men stepped off from the Canadian flight and halted; one, large, Airman on the desired spot and a somewhat smaller Airman alongside him. Irritated by this development, I strode across and addressed a blunt question to the small Airman. "Who the fuck are you, Son?" The small Airman inclined his head towards the large Airman, replying, "I'm the interpreter, Sir. Pierre here don't speak English."

At 0300hrs one morning we were carted into London for a rehearsal outside the palace. It was the job of Jim Lavery and myself to dress the flights, before retiring to the flanking roads to sort out various other formations, and time spent in reconnaissance, as someone has pointed out, is seldom wasted. The parade was drawing close and scheduled for the Saturday morning.

I had no parade prominence on the day, and I was untroubled by that, but another who had no prominence was the Station Warrant Officer from Halton, who happened to be female. We heard that she had been intended to dress the parade, but that this had been forbidden by the Brigade of Guards, whose patch happened to include 'Buck House'. If true, this was distinctly odd in view of the gender of the principal observer of the parade from the palace balcony. It was also put into context, for me anyway, by a small episode prior to the parade. I had changed into uniform in the Guardroom at Wellington Barracks, when an elderly lady approached and asked if she might use the lavatories. I directed her and as she thanked me when she was leaving I noticed in her lapel the wings of the Air Transport Auxiliary. I asked if she had flown during the war and when she confirmed that, I asked her what types. "Nothing very unusual,"She replied, "Spitfires and Lancasters, mostly." Pilots of the ATA ferried 300,000 vital aircraft during the war and a hundred and fifty pilots, including the famous aviatrix Amy Johnson, died in crashes. Half a century on, there was no executive place on the parade for a serving Airwoman.

On the Saturday, we paraded early for the move to the city. Jim and I did our brief piece before the palace gates before retiring to our respective posts. I was on the road that led to Constitution Hill, stepping off the Observer Corps and various of the veterans' organisations, when the Flypast ended. This was led by a Spitfire, flown by the man whose webbing I had assembled some other Saturday. He was now an air vice marshal. With the last of the Veterans stepped off, I thought that I might as well march past too and I smartly fell in at the rear. As we rounded towards the 'Wedding Cake', which was the Victoria Memorial, an Australian warrant officer, in best blue, vaulted the railings and approached. "G'Day, Mate," He offered, "permission to join the parade?" I nodded him in and we marched past together. It wasn't a bad moment at all.

I returned to St. Mawgan on the Sunday and reported for duty the following day. Awaiting me was the news that I had been redressed on the grounds of racial prejudice.

"This is Pierre, Sir"

15

Having been invited to set out the facts of the parade exclusions and submit them to the Adjutant of the redressing corporal's unit, I did so, thinking that it might be the last of the matter. The Adjutant's response was to express a condemnatory opinion, which he circulated, and in which he admitted that he was not in possession of all of the facts. This gave me clear grounds for a redress of my own, but I withheld it, having no wish to protract a matter which should have been quickly resolved. I was obliged to restate my case in greater detail for the station commander of the corporal's parent unit, and the matter eventually went to the Inspector of the Royal Auxiliary Air Force for judgement. I had to appear before him some weeks later and the case was closed, but I was left with a sense of unease that the balance had been entirely wrong. The word of a warrant officer against that of a corporal, it seemed, meant little if the corporal happened to be black. Despite having explained my action repeatedly and to several pages, I had really expressed the truth of it all within a single paragraph: 'On my parade square I do not see black people or white people; I see those who perform their drill with a degree of effort and those who do not. Corporal A, in my view, was one of those who do not.' It had been a thoroughly disagreeable affair.

Almost as disagreeable, when I had returned to my desk, was the discovery that the full time reservist flight sergeant had circulated a lengthy memo that attacked the recruit syllabus that I had recently implemented. It was subjective, entirely offensive in tone and also insubordinate. I had presumably not been expected to see the memo, in view of my intended departure, and I went for the flight sergeant with some anger. The CO seemed anxious not to be involved and I began the business of clearing my desk, deciding that 2625's problems were now someone else's affair.

The affair, which later was incorrectly referred to as a 'feud', had become well known to the entire squadron by this time, and I had begun to receive tentative approaches which suggested that the flight-sergeant was not greatly admired, either for his soldier skills or personal qualities. These increased when the belief - also incorrect - surfaced that I was being forced to leave the squadron. This prompted some enquiries of my own and information from my predecessor in the job and that of three former SNCOs proved most revealing. It painted a distasteful picture, but there was little hard evidence in it all and it was mainly historical. I could advise the CO but since he appeared unwilling to accept the SNCO's dishonesty, there was little hope that he might proceed on the basis of hearsay, however damning it appeared to be.

I had a couple of days off and went for some thoughtful walks with the dog, wondering now if I wasn't merely abandoning the problem rather than fighting it. We sat to the evening meal during the week when my flight to the Oman was booked, and I told Joan that I was not going. She nodded, saying that she had believed all along that I should stay and do something about the situation, but had not said so, feeling that it had to be my own decision. I returned to duty, rescinded my notice and ordered the flight sergeant into my office, simply telling him that his days on the squadron were numbered. He predictably went directly from my office to that of the CO to enter a complaint in a sympathetic ear and I was subsequently interviewed by the CO. He made it clear that he would not back his warrant officer unreservedly and although it was disappointing to discover that no one stood in my corner, I at least knew where *I* stood.

I began another recruit course, working long hours with a very small team, rather than subject the course to incompetent instructors and assistants. Recruits, I had by now learned, were a scarce resource and not to be squandered. The Adjutant took no part at all, but we could safely discount his efforts by now. He had been selected for promotion and would leave the squadron early in the New Year. There was some hope that we might get lucky with his replacement.

Following the course I took an advance party to Warcop Camp for annual training, that by now was expanded to a full fortnight. I looked forward to the field firing again, although the weather was atrocious on that particular phase. There were also a couple of interesting incidents involving the flight sergeant. He had left a rifle negligently unattended in the accommodation one morning, and I paraded him to the CO for it. He was then involved in a drunken argument with an airman in the NAAFI, which was inconclusively investigated, and, finally, he was ordered off range duties (by the CO) when it was obvious he was under the influence of drink. On the third day of the camp he absented himself and returned to Cornwall. He would never return to duty after that, but it was far from the end of the matter.

I meanwhile renewed my unpopularity with the Adjutant by criticising, at the daily range debrief, his conduct of an introductory battle range which he had run in a wholly pedestrian manner. The Adjutant had been assisted on the range by the Adjutant from a sister squadron, and the latter felt so slighted by my remarks that he threatened to return to his unit. I privately felt that he was welcome to go since he was, if anything, even more useless than our own Training Officer, but I simply pointed out that battle ranges were supposed to advance our live-firing abilities, not return them to recruit standards. Apart from the quiet support of a few of the SNCOs, I was aware that I was quite isolated at this time, but I had burned my bridges by rejecting the contract employment in the Oman, and I felt sufficient anger to take on the rest of them if necessary.

When we returned to St. Mawgan, I went off to HMS Raleigh, near Plymouth but on the Cornish side of the Tamar, to assist teaching the new rifle to naval recruits. The squadron often got odd requests to help out neighbouring units and these made a pleasant break from desk routine.

Nothing having collapsed in the house for a while, I had begun the job of casting concrete in what had formerly been the bottom half of the garden to the rear of the property. I had the hardcore down and a frame assembled, but wondered if I would find any decent weather before spring. I had ordered the concrete from a local ready mix firm, telling them that I would take it if a break in the poor weather appeared. Early in December the 'phone rang at about 0700hrs and the firm advised me of a favourable forecast for the day, and would I like the concrete delivered? I accepted and it was still quite dark when the lorry dumped a yard and a half of wet mix at the back. It was still quite dark as I was spreading and the snow began to fall, and still not quite light when the wind began to howl and a blizzard developed. Joan ferried out mugs of hot tea, the dog watched in curiosity from the comfort of the dining room and my fingers turned blue as I levelled the surface and trowelled it off before it got dark again. There had been no mention of this in any of the DIY manuals.

In mid-December we were to break for the Xmas Grant,

which was of fourteen days. This was not particularly generous since full-time auxiliaries were paid only for the days they actually worked and nor were Public Holidays paid. It was nevertheless looked forward to with some relief, however, since it had been a difficult year. On the day that we ceased duty the CO made an appearance and he informed me that I had been again redressed, this time by the flight sergeant and on the grounds of victimisation. I was given a copy of the redress and told that my response would be expected when we resumed duty in the New Year. The redress statement was confined to a single sheet and when I read it the words 'previous submissions' leapt off the page. I asked the CO if I might be provided with copies of these and he refused, saying that they were irrelevant. Faint alarms sounded at this point and I wondered if I might be playing against a stacked deck. The Personal Files of all squadron personnel were held in a cabinet in the CO's office, and when everyone had gone home I went to the cabinet and retrieved the flight sergeant's file. The enclosures were a revelation and showed that the flight sergeant had been making written complaints about me since the moment of the CO's promotion to command of the squadron. These were lengthy, detailed and - like the recent memo - offensive. All were insubordinate in tone and I was additionally accused of dishonesty. There was also the implication that there was something very unpleasant in my private life. I was not especially surprised that the man would stoop to any of this, but I was puzzled and angry that the CO had chosen to allow all of it to remain on file without action. In my view, he had a clear duty either to refute the charges or to confront me with them. He had done neither and I wondered now just what my standing was. I photocopied the entire file and prepared for a somewhat less than Merry Xmas.

16

We spent much of the Xmas with Joan's folks and I devoted a fair bit of time to the redress, not merely rebutting it but also describing the extent of the flight sergeant's misconduct. We returned to Cornwall and I returned to duty, hearing nothing immediately, other than that the redress was to be investigated by the CO. I would have preferred independent arbitration but that did not appear to be within my right. I had, however, been wise to heed the faintest jangle of bells. The word of my redress had travelled beyond St. Mawgan and I received a 'phone call from a former flight commander now serving in Northern Ireland. He had, he said, a warning for me from his squadron commander, whom I had also served under in the past. The warning was quite explicit and I was advised to be very careful whom I chose to confide in. This chimed with my own discoveries.

The new Adjutant arrived in post and he made a calamitous beginning. The squadron deployed to weekend exercise on Dartmoor, where each of two flights spent the entire Saturday conducting recces for a night attack. After the evening Stand-To, the Adjutant assembled the Orders Group, at which he made the perplexing announcement that A Flight was now to attack the original B Flight objective and vice versa. There were some smiles and chuckles around the group at this rare piece of O Group humour, until it was realised that the Adjutant was perfectly serious. The flights set off in near-pitch darkness and deteriorating weather and utterly failed to find their objectives. Both flights became lost for a time, as did the enemy groups waiting at the objectives, and for some hours of a bleak February night the entire squadron fumbled its way back to the bivvie area. At the exercise debrief of the flight commanders and SNCOs in the CO's office back at St. Mawgan, I delivered a withering opinion of this farce (which caused the CO to abruptly terminate the debrief) and followed it with another uninvited visit to the Adjutant's office on the following Monday. He admitted that he had not liked the idea of the objectives' switch, explaining that it had been suggested by the CO as a means of 'testing the initiative of the flight commanders.' I told the Adjutant that this was nonsense, that he must have known it was nonsense and that it was his responsibility, as the training officer and specialist, to prevent such interventions by a CO who clearly knew plenty about cockpits, but perhaps too little about tactics.

The Adjutant accepted the criticism and invited me back into his office a day or two later to discuss training problems. We had two hours together and laid the foundations for the training effort for the immediate future. The Adjutant intended to operate the administrative and planning side of the house, leaving the Training NCO and me to assemble the nuts and bolts of specific programmes and courses. The Training NCO had already taken over the Training Cell from the full time reservist sergeant who had done little with it, and he was making swift improvements. I was given the job of producing an Orders package - formal Orders being among our weaknesses at all levels on the flights - in addition to programming a range coach's course and a patrol leader's course. All of this was well within my competence and I was happy to be fully employed.

The Gulf War was approaching the land-fighting phase and there had been considerable speculation as to whether reservists might be required to serve. There had certainly been some pressure for this, both within and beyond reservist formations, but the legal terms under which reservists had been formed proved an obstacle to any rapid use of auxiliaries. In a nutshell, reservists were formed to 'defend at Dover', since the lineage of the modern force dated to a French invasion scare in 1859, and a Queen's Order in Council was required before any wider application might be made. Meantime, a number of reservists of the non-serving and ex-regular variety were gaining a disproportionate amount of prime-time TV by *refusing* to serve in the Gulf, citing the amount of time elapsed since they had left the service. We had plenty of volunteers who were ready to serve, at home or abroad, and many of them had already secured unlimited time off work from their employers, but, as events proved, we were not even empowered to provide live-armed guards at the gates of our parent stations. A few reservists in specialist trades such as medical and air-photographic interpretation *did* serve in the Gulf, but the public perception was doubtless that of the unwilling volunteer. It was a sad failure of the reservist hierarchy to distinguish between the vocal few and the silent many on this account.

The manuscript of my novel by now having attracted sufficient rejection slips to paper a small room, I consigned it to the loft and began to research a no-smoking pamphlet. I had decided to rescue some 17,500,000 British people from the addiction of tobacco by writing and publishing a small booklet. The smoking world, I felt sure, would beat a path to my door, making them healthier and me wealthier. I await them still.

Riches beyond the dreams of avarice, or even modest wealth, would have been welcome. As we approached our third trading season with the B&B it was becoming apparent that we were unlikely ever to generate a primary income from the business, which had of course been the intention. Rotten summers were not helping, although it was probably more the case that we were too small, too late or both, but the real problem was the recession which was the worst since the Thirties. Least cheering of all, perhaps, was the crash of the property market and the rise of a new term: 'negative equity', which meant that some owners had houses which now were worth considerably less than the sums they had borrowed to buy them. We had kept our borrowing relatively small, and were at least not in that particular bind, but my earlier contention that, if the business failed to prosper we still had the bricks and mortar, was by now somewhat meaningless. Interest rates had risen again and the mortgage absorbed fifty per cent of my wage.

We had come to depend upon my wage from what had been intended as a part time job, and although I had been working a five-day week for some time now, the contract terms seemed as distant as ever. The collapse of the USSR and the dismantling of the Warsaw Pact had produced an MOD document called '*Options for Change*', which more than hinted at wholesale reductions in armed forces manning levels. Reservist units were not necessarily excluded and contracts were meanwhile on hold. In the meantime, a reservist was paid the same daily rate as his regular counterpart, with some allowance differential, but paid only for the days he worked, rather than three hundred and sixty-five days of the year. It effectively meant that a full time reservist earned sixty per cent of a regular's wage. Joan and I were not short of the staples of life and some of the trimmings, but holidays remained off the agenda for a while.

RAF St. Mawgan enjoyed the Freedom of Restormel, which

was the local borough, and entitled to parade from time to time with 'swords drawn, bayonets fixed and drums beating.' A parade was usually held biennially and we were invited to contribute a flight to the spring parade. We chose also to parade the Queen's Colour and ceremonial training supplanted more routine training for a couple of weekends. We had a glorious day for the parade, which beats standing in the rain by a good margin, and the band programme of incidental music included pieces from Duke Ellington. Standing at the rear of the Colour Party, I did not resist the temptation to tap a glossy toecap in time to *Mood Indigo*.

After the parade I took a dozen volunteers to North Wales for a week of hill walking, having discovered that reservists were as entitled to adventurous training pursuits as regulars. I had no formal qualifications to lead the climbs, but I could read a map and I had a brain. Later, such unqualified leadership would become difficult, if not impossible, thanks to a procession of fools who lost kids to hypothermia or drowning in easily preventable tragedies. Until that happened, I was able to repeat the expeditions and extend them to the Brecons and the Cairngorms.

The Military Skills Team continued to attract interest and on the May Bank Holiday weekend we travelled to a camp at Holcombe Moor, near Manchester to contest a competition against thirty-odd units of the Territorial Army. It was our first outing at the event, which had a poor reputation for the discipline of teams in the past, and would not have been staged at Holcombe at all unless the committee had appointed a warrant officer with disciplinary powers. That happened to be my job and I made it easy by ordering the bar closed at 2300hrs and by locking up someone who took exception to the order. The competition proceeded smoothly and the team ran third, which wasn't a bad result, first time out. Holcombe, I also discovered, had some history. It was formed as a militia camp early in the nineteenth century and the first of the 'Pal's Battalions'[1] had formed there during the Great War.

---

[1] National fervour and Jingoism having abated by the close of 1914, various recruiting ploys had to be implemented to replace the massive casualties suffered on the Western Front. The Pal's Battalions offered the promise that those men who had grown, lived and worked together would remain together during armed service. So they did, and in a final, chilling, uniformity they died together in their hundreds.

Our summer season began, if summer meanwhile failed to, and our bookings remained poor although there seemed plenty of visitors to the town. Possibly they were on the camping sites or in self-catering apartments. Less welcome were visitors at a house two doors from ours when they hosted a deafening 'rave' party throughout the night. The police were summoned but proved powerless to do anything other than request that the noise be kept down, which met openly with derision. At 0600hrs Joan, frustrated by a sleepless night and with guests to attend to, stormed around to protest anew and had beer thrown over her. I went in with fists and was briefly arrested when the police were summoned. I resolved that if it ever happened again, I would go in with a pick helve. I still have one handy.

I accompanied the Adjutant to Otterburn Camp, in Cumbria to recce ranges for our October annual training. Field firing was not much within his expertise but he happily took advice on what we should be seeking and we put together a reasonable package. Training was progressing reasonably efficiently at the time and if the Training NCO had a drink problem, he was at least able to separate it from duty. We had similar ideas on training and combined with a plan to create a better classroom facility than that which had sufficed for too long, mainly on the promise of a brand new build of facilities costed at a third of a million pounds. When it became apparent that this sum had gone away, never to return, we assembled some specialist talents from the squadron and converted an adjacent hut's worth of small rooms into a couple of reasonably spacious classrooms for weapon training. This cost the Taxpayer nothing whilst offering us fairly useful facilities.

A single line in Squadron Routine Orders alerted me to the fact that the full time flight sergeant had been quietly released from service, and I was left to assume that his redress had simply gone away. I was never debriefed, either formally or informally, by the CO on the matter, although I knew that he had not proceeded with the various counter-charges I had made. The crowning ironies were that the flight sergeant, despite having been formally reproved for falsely claiming wages, received a higher character assessment than I had in his annual confidential report for the period, and his 'outstanding achievements' were recognised by an award from the Lord Lieutenant of Cornwall, presumably upon the recommendation of the CO. It had been a disagreeable and a protracted affair and one, I believe, that could never have arisen in regular service.

Joan's mother had come down for a few weeks to help with the B&B and I concurrently decided on a break other than that offered by the squadron's twice-monthly outings. The Cornish coastal path had some appeal and on one of the four-day breaks which followed a working weekend, in August, I filled a Bergen with compo and dog food and set off with Gypsy to walk to Lands End.

Annual Camp loomed again and although we no longer preserved the fiction that we had to cater to seasonal workers, October was still an unlikely month for a 'summer' camp. If the previous CO had been busy yachting during the summer months, his successor was equally preoccupied by the shooting season at Bisley and elsewhere, and he preferred the late camp. Our sister squadrons went to the major training areas more sensibly in June, July and August, which offered a longer day and better conditions on ranges. It was already quite cold when we arrived at Otterburn, although the barrack heating was not yet turned on since, as the Quartermaster informed me, it was not yet 'officially' winter. We slept beneath small mountains of blankets until heat flowed through the pipes and otherwise accepted the fact of a cold, wet life on ranges. I was running field ranges throughout and happy with that. Happy also to be conducting the reveille run, which had an amusing moment at the first such outing. We had two German reservist officers attached for the camp and they were simply acting as Gunners with a section for most of the time. When the morning run lined up, I led it and the Training NCO ran at the rear to whip along any stragglers. We ran a mile or so across the Fell and throughout I could hear Training NCO giving some laggard a terrible time. When we were shaving after the run, Training NCO wanted to know: "Who is that big idle bastard recruit with the blond hair?" "Actually, John," I replied, "That's Captain Gummersbach of the German army."

The camp passed agreeably and I found some time to walk a stretch of Hadrian's Wall and inspect a preserved Roman fort. Exercises during annual camps seemed to have gone out of fashion and I regretted that, but it was beyond my influence. As the year drew to a close, I wondered, despite many improvements in our training effort, whether we were making any real progress. There seemed far too much emphasis on how things appeared, rather than how things were, and I considered this unhealthy.

In December Joan and I flew to Egypt for two weeks. It was our first holiday in five years and a good one. We cruised on the Nile for a week, which included daily trips to antiquities, and divided the remaining week between Luxor and Cairo. I had been fascinated by the pyramids as a boy and never dreamed then that I might someday see them. The antiquities were simply fantastic. In Luxor we spent a succession of days examining the Karnak Temples and each day that we walked to them we were importuned by a small boy, touting for trips on a *felucca*, the Arab craft. We had every intention of taking such a trip, but had reserved it for the last day, reassuring the boy every day we met him. On the final day of the visit we followed the boy, expecting to be met by his father, the *felucca* captain. As it happened, the boy was the captain, and a fine sailor, too.

A surprise birthday party at 2625 Squadron

Interlude

GYPSY

The four-day weekend that followed each of the working weekends was a fine opportunity to read the print off the *Guardian* and the *Observer*, or to repair the latest collapse in the house that was a memorial to DIY. The break also offered the chance of getting away briefly without having to take unpaid leave. The Coastal Path, that ran from the Devon border on the north coast from Bude to Land's End, then up the south coast to the Tamar river, had been attracting me for quite some time and during one of the August breaks I decided to walk the stretch down from Newquay to Land's End. Four days seemed adequate for a nominal distance of sixty miles, although the map appreciation revealed stretches when the plunge in and out of numerous coves might mean little forward progression for much vertical effort.

Nor did I know what the dog's abilities might be. She was eight years old now and therefore my senior in relative terms, but she had twice the number of legs and neither was she encumbered by the Bergen which held the food for both of us. This was reduced to the essentials of food, reserve water, a bivvie and a sleeping bag and had seemed unlikely to top fifty pounds, yet did so by a small margin. Joan had been perfectly happy about the idea when I first broached it (initial apprehension yielding to relief when she realized that she was not required on the walk), but I had not consulted the dog, who doubtless believed our morning stroll was merely taking a different route than the usual.

The navigation plot was beautifully simple - find the coast and turn left - and a fairly early start was prudent. Even as we negotiated the Gannel Estuary at no great distance from the house it was already quite hot, and an early start left the option of a rest in shade during the heat of the day, should the dog find it all a bit strong. At Pentire Point West, we spotted the first of the engraved acorns that signified the National Trust (custodians of the path) and also encountered the first of several dozen stiles that marked the route. The dog, roaming ahead, waited patiently at this until it became apparent to her that I was not about to lift her over (at eighty pounds a time), whereupon she took a successful leap at it. In the course of the walk she would become adept at going over, under, around or through a plethora of stile styles, and we encountered one which had a central stake which could be lifted to facilitate animal passage. Not all of the good ideas originate in the big city.

We gained Kelsey Head and Penhale Point in short succession, generally maintaining the high ground, and we wallowed along a good stretch of sand dunes that overlooked Perran Beach. The sea was serving up the waves in silver slices all along the frontage, and from our modest elevation the beach appeared to be billiard-table smooth with no holidaymaker yet doing a Man Friday on the sand. Notably absent also at this hour were other walkers on the path, although we encountered increasing numbers as the day wore on.

Below Perran, the path became somewhat less gentle for a time, as it descended steeply to sea level into silent coves before rising just as stiffly back to the high ground. This was a foretaste of much steeper climbs to follow and although modest enough on day one, I nevertheless felt the unaccustomed bite of Bergen straps on collarbones.

Steady climbs matched by the steadily climbing sun brought a measure of hardship to the day, whilst bringing to the dog some degree of understanding that this was no ordinary walk. Her zestful bounding ahead and off to the flanks had reduced to a more dutiful trailing astern, and shortly after midday I deemed it wise to rest her for a couple of hours. There being a nicely level and open piece of ground handy, but no obvious shade, I erected the bivvie and the dog, unbidden, vanished inside it whilst I put a brew together and checked our progress on the map.

By then we had passed a series of concrete blocks which were as mysterious as Stonehenge at first glance, but clearly were of wartime origin. The map soon revealed the unmistakeable cross of old runways and the name of the former airfield. Perranporth, I later discovered, had preserved its watchtower and a few of the perimeter buildings but otherwise had long been turned back to farmland. These were the first historic buildings we would sight, if not the earliest, and a part of the tragedy of the Cornish coast. Spitfires and Typhoons had operated over France from this forgotten airfield and many did not return. It was difficult to visualise on a benign summer's day, but the vanished aircrews are on the great record somewhere.

Rested by 1600hrs and finding the day slightly cooler, I evicted the dog, rolled up the bivvie, shouldered the Bergen and pressed on, pausing only in a re-entrant to fill the water bottles and allow the dog an impromptu bath. I was stoppering the bottles when an apparent stranger approached with a question: "Weren't you on II Squadron a few years ago?" He asked. I was and so was he, and as we shook hands and chatted we realised that it had been sixteen years since we last met. He was Taff Davies, who had been an MT mechanic, and it had been a pleasing encounter.

We rounded St. Agnes head and again found ourselves negotiating a succession of re-entrants that impeded the forward progress. A few Ks later, at 1900hrs, I selected our bivvie site for the night and broke out the rations. A few walkers continued to pass but the path soon grew quiet, leaving us in sole occupation. We ate and a last look at the map revealed that we had covered 26 Ks. By 2100hrs I was zipped inside the sleeping bag with the dog curled alongside me, her snores indicating that she had beaten me to sleep by a small margin.

The dog had grunted occasionally in the night, perhaps scenting rabbits, and she was sniffing the air experimentally when I awoke shortly after daybreak. Coastal fog surrounded us but had begun to clear when I finished breakfast and stacked the bivvie. By 0600hrs we were striding off and shortly in view of the extant Portreath airfield. It was another of the former wartime airfields but currently in use as a communications link. It was also controversial since chemical munitions had been dumped at the end of the war in the old mine shafts which dotted the airfield. Its perimeter fence parallelled our track for a good distance until we descended eighty metres or so to pass the village and cross a stretch of beach. The beach lavatories happened to be open so I afforded myself some Rolls-Royce ablutions whilst the dog kept an eye on the Bergen.

Progress became slow for a time, with numerous coves to cross and a steady pattern of descent-ascent-descent arresting the forward progress. Warm work, too, with the sun again appearing in some strength. One such cove presented us with the remains of a genuine shipwreck, well-reefed a hundred feet below us. This was no romantic clipper of course, but the rusting stern section of a coaster.

I could not make out her name but doubtless it was somewhere known. On Lloyd's Register, probably.

Towards midday we approached Hayle and the coastal path seemed to peter out. We tramped instead across sand dunes and after about five Ks of them I was beginning to feel like Beau Geste. We halted at the Hayle beach and I reckoned that it was time for a brew and a rest. The dog seemed to have no such need and for an hour she waded into the water to drag out large stones which appeared to be of interest to her. I belatedly studied the map and suddenly realised that we faced a lengthy detour around the town, unless we could ford the river that bisected the beach. Unfortunately, we had missed the tide and the remote pleasures of the path were traded for the monoxide fumes of dense traffic, and throngs of holidaymakers who blocked the pavements whilst deploring the price of the ice cream. The map made it clear that we needed also to clear Carbis Bay and St. Ives, if we desired solitude, and although I had planned on about eighteen Ks for the day, we had covered twenty-six by the time we found a suitably quiet spot. I was in the bag by 2100hrs, letting the aches ebb into the soil while I watched a spectacularly lovely sunset framed by the inverted vee of the bivvie, before drifting into a ten-hour sleep.

Excluding breakfast, the packing of kit and digging a small hole in which to defecate, the day began with a strafing attack by two seabirds whose swiftness on the wing defeated my admittedly limited powers of ornithological recognition. Presumably, we were in close proximity to a nest of fledglings and, notwithstanding the dog's indignation, we took the hint and moved on. The view was initially limited since a belt of fog clung to the coast, and through it we could hear the monotonous and mournful note of a fog horn, sounding at twenty second's interval. It seemed quite close but a morning of travel brought it little closer, and its gloomy peal had ceased by midday, the fog having dispersed.

Our checkpoint then was Gunnard's Head and we perched above a stone tower that overlooked a small beach. The map offered no clues to the structure, which may have been a fishermen's lookout, a minor fortification or even a folly, but it was in a good state of preservation. We had already encountered a number of old mine workings *en route* and these were mainly chimneys but occasionally including a selection of magazines and offices. The best examples were at the old Levant Mine, but that was yet some miles south.

The pause for a brew and a welcome rest from the Bergen

was undisturbed by other walkers and I reflected upon the fact that on this day, so far, we had seen very few of them. The path at this point probably offered the reason since, not only did it comprise a fair component of steep descent and climb, but it also picked a tenuous route through outcropping stone which had to be trodden with some care. The path was moreover almost completely enveloped in ferns which grew to waist-height, and this was soaked with dew or fog or both, ensuring a soaked lower half for me and a total soaking for the dog for the entire morning.

By now, however, we were gently steaming in the midday heat and life was sublime. We picked up the route again, noting with satisfaction that it yielded to gently undulating Downs for a good few Ks, allowing a more leisurely aspect to the enterprise. Our heading was due west again with just a few Ks to cover before reaching the point that would take us mostly south to our final destination. That point, which was Pendeen Watch and the location of the foghorn whose elusive note we had followed, had suggested itself as our final RV for the day, but a reappraisal of the map led me to reconsider. A point closer to Land's End seemed preferable, thus allowing a finish closer to midday and evacuation prior to the eastwards rush of holidaymakers. By mid-afternoon we had made the turn and again progress was slow with a series of ascents and a degree of rock-scrambling. The dog mostly chose her own route and she was invariably waiting for me at the top.

I noted with interest that ancient instincts were imposing themselves on Gypsy, who was a total town and house animal. At long halts, when I paused to ease the Bergen off or make a brew, she would occupy a piece of high ground, having first subjected it to a thorough inspection and sniffing, and only laying down when she had completely flattened and trampled the ferns. Having made a satisfactory bed, she would curl onto it and she seemed equally capable of instant sleep or instant alertness.

We noted a good number of benches provided along the more accessible reaches of the path and one such bore a plate which dedicated the bench to the memory of Denys Val Baker, Author, Editor and Seafarer. I knew neither Mr Baker nor his works, although I later looked for some of them in the local library. It would have been agreeable to discover that he had described this coast.

In the afternoon we encountered the Levant Mine and paused to inspect the old workings. These appeared to be in a most remarkable state of preservation, but I later learned that some restoration had taken place in recent years. The surface works had certainly been built in some style and the engine-house chimney was a fine example of what may be elegantly wrought in stone and brick. The area, once and long ago alive with miners, was thronged with tourists, whose camera lenses worked overtime and doubtless did wonders for Kodak shares.

The Levant opened in the 1820s and was first worked for copper, showing a profit of £200,000 in twenty years of operation - a tidy sum by contemporary standards. At the time of its closure after a century of continuous working it was being worked for tin, and had seen its share of tragedy. The main shaft ran far under the sea and in 1919 thirty-one miners were killed in a single accident when the shaft collapsed. The beam engine which raised ore for ninety years has happily been preserved, though elsewhere, and the shaft is still open, if filled now with sea water. The pumps are long silent, as are the miners they served.

We followed the path to St. Just and left it briefly to find a 'phone box to notify an RV time for Joan on the following day. The box was adjacent to a Chippy, whose product was sorely tempting, but we returned to the path and compo.   I noted that the narrow lanes of St. Just were already oversubscribed by tourists and we soon reduced the number by two. The shadows ahead of us began to lengthen and I reckoned that Cape Cornwall would do for the night. We had covered another 25Ks, some of them fairly wearing, and hot scoff and an early bag were welcome. We were stretched out in plenty of time to view the sunset, noting that light cloud, like cotton wool, had gathered on the western rim. It ignited like fire as the sun descended into it, flaring beautifully and spreading across the surface of the water until the sea inexorably and relentlessly extinguished it. It was a lovely and even an affecting moment.

Our final morning brought renewed fog and the visibility was down to ten metres. The foghorn sounded behind us and its frequency now was down to ten seconds, unless my watch was fast. We observed the routine of breakfast and packing then picked our way carefully across slippery outcrops of stone. It was a wet and slightly cold progression and I was glad that I had decided to end on a fairly modest distance. We could even afford to loiter a little, although the cool morning argued otherwise. We passed through Sennen Cove, last seen during the tour with the Royal Marines and now seeming a long time ago, and approached the bottom end of the A30. It was already well-plied with tourists who were heading for the old Customs buildings which now formed the centre of some 'theme park', and we were of brief curiosity to some of them as I brewed the tea and awaited Joan. We were an hour ahead of the RV time.

I had gratefully lowered the Bergen for the last time, although it had become progressively lighter as we consumed the food, and sat sipping tea, idly counting the cars until the dog recognised the one that mattered. Gypsy looked in pretty good fettle, if, like me, somewhat scruffy, but when we arrived home she sprang onto the bed and hardly moved off it for two days.

17

We had spent the Xmas with Tegwin and Ray again, facing laden plates which were hardly justified by a sedentary routine. We were at home in time for New Year's Eve, although we did not celebrate it with the locals who invariably paraded in fancy dress for the occasion. We spent some time discussing the future of the B&B, recognising at the close of the third season that this was not a winning idea, and that we appeared to be working rather more for the benefit of guests, tax man, council and tourist board than ourselves.

Our decision was to continue trading as long as we were in the house, but to put the property on the market and see if we might attract an offer. The only offer, in fact, was to swap for a new bungalow a few miles out of town, but we declined since we were principally aiming to reduce, if not lose, the mortgage. The house valuation invited us to write off some 20,000 pounds, thus providing sober reflection on the previously perceived wisdom of putting money into bricks and mortar.

I was at my desk on New Year's Day, since full time auxiliaries were still not paid for Public Holidays, and I had gone in on a matter of principle rather than in expectation of finding much to do. In considering the house, I had also been thinking about my remaining service with the squadron, feeling by now that even my best efforts on its behalf produced few lasting results, and that the hand on the tiller was pretty shaky. It was at this time that I abandoned my practice, carried over from regular service, of arriving thirty minutes early each day, having long noticed that everyone else preferred to open the day with a thirty-minute coffee break. I had not entirely lost my enthusiasms for training, and especially those of a robust sort, but I was beginning to wonder at the point of them in the present context.

I had recently turned fifty and this had been much more of a defining moment than reaching forty, which had not seemed very remarkable to me. At fifty, I wondered just how many 'good' years were left to me, by which I meant those when I could continue to run around the airfield or local roads when the mood took me, or set off for Snowdonia or the Brecons for a few days on the hills. Too few, I concluded, and the realisation emphasised the need to waste little of my time. My term of enlistment had about nine months to run and I wondered what I might replace it with. I briefly researched the prospects for contract employment as an NBC instructor in Saudi Arabia (having learned that, post-Gulf War, there was considerable Saudi interest in such facilities which might be provided by British Aerospace, which already had a multimillion pound defence contract with the Saudis.) The enquiries led to promising contacts then petered out. I was contacted instead by a former Regiment officer who had some sort of contract for weapons inspection in Eastern Europe, but the employment was very short term and with little prospect of renewal.

Meanwhile, training opened on the note of a Dartmoor exercise where the temperature overnight dropped to minus four degrees and there was fifteen degrees of wind chill with it. We remained fully dressed inside our sleeping bags but still rattled with cold. Dawn - such as it was- proved very welcome, if not quite as welcome as the mugs of steaming tea which took an age to brew in the wind conditions. The CO had wisely stayed at home, which at least preserved us from the latest of his 'tactical' brainwaves. In the same month we deployed to Bodmin Moor, which was somewhat closer to St. Mawgan if no less chill, and I had been tasked with running each of the section commanders through a blank-firing section attack stance. In order to preserve time which otherwise might be lost in orientation, I took each of the section commanders forward before the attack to show them the ground. They faced an open area, with high ground on the right, and a covered approach along a watercourse to the left. All opted for sending a gun under covering fire onto the high ground, then moving up the covered approach into an assaulting position. All except one. He moved his men to the Start Line, stood up and shouted: **"CHARGE!"** then led his section over three hundred yards of waterlogged wilderness. He had been reduced to the ranks by the previous CO for incompetence, but promoted anew by the present CO as soon as he took command. Baffling.

My anti-smoking booklet, '*ACT on FACT*', was printed but

I soon discovered that even the best idea in the world is useless until you can sell it. Local and national advertising produced few results and I eventually sent complimentary copies, with a covering letter, to some fifty environmental health officers up and down the country. These resulted in some letters addressed to 'Doctor Foxley' but few orders. I still have a couple of boxes full, should you be interested.

Having hungered for an opportunity to put my bricklaying 'skills' into practice - to say nothing of the trowel which I had bought in a fit of zeal when I underwent the Garrison course - I built a garage and a wall in what remained of the garden. The garage was a bit narrow, actually, since I was hemmed by the house next door and a drains inspection trap, and it proved too narrow to allow the doors of the Golf opening when inside. There was always the chance, though, that we might buy a thinner car. Or a motorcycle. The Golf was rapidly approaching a hundred thousand miles, and looked like going around the clock again. It was the first new car we had bought and very likely the last. I drove it to station in the winter and biked in during the summer months initially, but I eventually persuaded myself to bike in year-round, despite some truly rotten weather and a long hill of about 1:10 gradient. Joan replaced the racer with a mountain bike one Xmas, and it took some of the sting out of the hill.

The station had a small-bore indoor range which passed into the custody of the squadron, and I hit upon the idea of developing a projected target facility within it by slaving together some 35mm slide projectors, and backlighting cardboard screens which showed the fall of shot when firers aimed at the projections. This proved an effective use of the several thousands of rounds of .22in ammunition that we had seldom previously used, and the range attracted wide interest. Unfortunately, it attracted the wrong interest and some zealous Health & Safety functionary on the camp established that insufficient ventilation existed to deal with the lead levels. The range was condemned and turned into a locker room.

In April, II Squadron celebrated its seventieth anniversary of formation and I took a couple of days off to attend. RAF Hullavington was about to close and the squadron was returning to the Depot. In recognition of that it was decided to do a last run of the Eagle House March - one of the original pre-para selection tests. The squadron was to carry sixty-five pound Bergens and former members were invited to carry more modest weights, in return for a small levy to the local charity. I decided that I could hack the weight, not realising that it was intended to run all of the flat and the downhill bits. I went the distance but was severely dented by it, finding an early bed that night.

The Strickland Competition was held in May for a change and we sent a good team, which won the Trophy, in addition to the Marksmanship and Fitness prizes. The Strickland team had always seemed to me a microcosm of what the squadron might be, with the right sort of leadership and direction, but there was no early sign that we were about to get it.

I entered the three-mile run for the station commander's cup, with no expectation of coming anywhere, and met Phil Mutton, Gan running mate. He was by now commissioned and recently posted to the station. Gan also seemed a bit distant.

I spent a couple of weekends at RAF Mountbatten, at Plymouth, which was another station about to close. A Sunset Ceremony was planned and I had been asked to train the parade for it. Mountbatten had been a Sunderland flying boat base during the war and various of the wartime crews, including some Australians, attended the ceremony. A Sunderland flypast had been hoped for, since there was a sole flying example in private hands in England, but the asking price of £5,000 proved a bit steep for the organisers. Instead, a Spitfire from the Battle of Britain Memorial Flight was arranged, but on the day poor weather at its home base precluded takeoff. I stayed in the combined Officers' and Sergeants' Mess during the visits and noticed that the old photographs which adorned the walls included several of TE Lawrence. He had done valuable work on rescue boats at Mountbatten.

The School of Survival & Evasion was also at Mountbatten and we had frequently provided assistance to its courses, in the hope of slots on future courses. These never materialised and I was asked if I would put a course together for a score of volunteers. I dug out some old notes, researched new work and came up with a package of instruction for one weekend, followed by an escape and evasion exercise in Wales on another. My archive research produced the gem that 'Polar bear meat must be thoroughly cooked before eating.' I'd have thought that 'First catch your polar bear.' was better advice.

If experience had by now tempered my enthusiasms for the job, I was still in the habit of picking things up which had fallen over, and I now saw B Flight as in that category. Its commander was a recently commissioned corporal who showed much promise, but at this time he was greatly dependent upon his flight sergeant, whose attendances were tapering off. The flight commander then developed a domestic crisis which attacked his own attendances and on the first training weekend of each month the members of B Flight arrived to no organised programme. They were then usually invited to tack themselves onto A Flight or C Flight, which did nothing to foster flight spirit, and this soon reflected in falling attendances and applications to cease service. I put it to the Adjutant that I could take over as the flight commander for a few months, and he took this to the CO, who agreed. We were shortly due to attend the annual camp, which that year was being held in Germany and I looked forward to the change.

There were some strains at home by this time. We were in the tenth year of a marriage that had no weld of a child; a fact, I knew, which weighed upon Joan very considerably. We had recognised the failure of the B&B to provide any sort of a living, much less prosperity, and my job with 2625 had generated strains that I would scarcely have believed possible, and was just beginning to come to terms with. I was working as hard as and occasionally harder then I had in regular service and absences were frequent. Joan and I had lost our way a little and were groping uncertainly towards the future. It was a worrying time.

At the end of September, I accompanied a small advance party overnight from Sheerness to Holland, and we briefly staged through RAF Bruggen before continuing to Vogelsang Camp, which enjoyed a spectacularly lovely setting overlooking lake and forestry near the Belgian border. The ranges, we learned, were not exciting and they seemed to have been designed with Belgian conscripts in mind (the Belgiques ran the camp), but we thought that we might make something of them. The barracks were handsome edifices in stone and had been built for members of Hitler's civil service, undergoing training courses that had a strong element of physical pursuits. The camp looked battle-scarred here and there, but I learned that no fighting had taken place here; the damage was actually the result of American vandalism postwar.

Since there were few ranges that we recognised as 'field-firing' I requested that I be largely left off the range teams in order to run my flight, and this was agreed. I then wrote my programme, interviewed the flight members individually and collectively, and generally got on with it. There was some exasperation. We were not allowed to destroy 'blinds' on our ranges, despite qualification, and if the man dedicated to this job happened to have gone home for the day, then the range was simply closed. I was also less than amused when the CO summoned us to a range which he had set up, and which had not been advertised when we wrote our training programmes. Upon arrival I found that we were supposed to fire at targets across the lake at a distance of eight hundred metres, using iron sights. This was ludicrous and I promptly put my flight back onto the 4 Tonner and returned to my original programme. I was duly summoned to the DSC and the CO for a ticking off, but by then I had acquired a tally of scores from the flights which *had* fired the practice. Each of them had been allocated two thousand rounds to each section, and no section had scored more than forty hits. I drew attention to this utterly pointless waste of ammunition but neither the DSC nor the CO would concede the point.

The weather was terrific, if a touch hot for the more aggressive forms of training. The ranges lay within an eight-mile radius and at the end of the first day I sent the 4 Tonner off empty and speed-marched the flight home. We had a lad attached from another squadron and he seemed surprised that we should do this. When I repeated it the next day, I thought that he was going to burst into tears.

At the conclusion of the camp, the convoy move to Vlissingen was not well briefed and we had bits of the convoy in three different countries at some point. Mine was negotiating a roadworks diversion of some complication in a Dutch town and we suddenly found ourselves driving into the back yard of a supermarket. I actually had to leave the cab and move some trolleys in order to get the convoy out again, and this was very definitely not my finest hour. We arrived at the docks and pulled into a layby to await the other packets before boarding and were joined by the RAF Police escort, driving a BMW. This was headed by a WRAF flight lieutenant and the order, counter-order and disorder of the convoy had stretched her patience. She had, moreover, been stopped and fined for speeding and also had to refuel the BMW at her own expense as she chased errant packets. She expressed a pungent opinion of our leaders and drove off. I knew the feeling.

When we returned to St. Mawgan I wrote a report of the camp which was somewhat in contrast to the glowing account which appeared on the camp file. I noted that too many of the ranges had been conducted with little attempts at tactical realism, few opportunities for exercises at either flight or squadron level had been seized, and that the visit by the 'VIPs' had taken every precedence over useful work that day. I also made out a lengthy case to have one of my corporals reduced in rank (this being the 'up and at 'em' merchant) This the CO rejected on the curious grounds that 'you don't kick a man when he is down.'

    The utter failure of the convoy simply highlighted the fact that the squadron worked to no recognisable Standard Operating Procedures - the writing of which had been avoided by a succession of adjutants. I decided to write them myself, and did so but later experience suggested that these were merely gathering dust in office drawers.

    At the end of November Joan and I went to America for a fortnight, spending a few days initially in New York. Whatever the reputation for violence or menace, we found the city friendly and walked in Central Park and rode the Subway. When we were approached, it was not by muggers but people who wanted to know if we needed directions with the map we were studying. We viewed the city from a helicopter and the Empire State Building, and the harbour from the Statue of Liberty. I was particularly impressed by Ellis Island, where 12,000,000 immigrants had first landed until the middle of the twentieth century. The last had been processed here at much the time I was sailing to Australia, and the reception area had been accidentally preserved as a time capsule, with abandoned effects still littering the long dormitories. We saw *'Miss Saigon'* on Broadway at horrendous cost then flew to New Orleans, finding our hotel in the French Quarter. I had not really expected to find Jazz alive and well in its birthplace, other than in some entirely contrived manner, yet it proved so. There was plenty of sleaze along Bourbon Street, but also enough bars where cornets, banjos, clarinets and drums played fine music for no more than the price of the Budweiser at the bar. Street musicians were much in evidence and we sat at some pavement cafe when a strolling trumpet player held an incredibly long note. The cafe crowd burst into applause and the player acknowledged it with a bow. "Shore like tuh thank y'all for d' clappin'," He said, "an' now I'd like tuh thank y'all for d' givin'". New Orleans also featured a jazz museum, which was sited in the former Confederate Mint - a somewhat ironic choice. We saw the Mississippi from the deck of a paddle steamer and we viewed the battlefield where Andrew Jackson pasted Edward Pakenham. Within the space of thirty minutes Pakenham, obviously less successful in the same year as his brother-in-law Wellington at Waterloo, took 2,000 casualties, against 13 American losses. Pakenham was among the dead and, ironically, the war had ended a fortnight earlier with the peace treaty already signed.

After a few days of breakfasting on grits and being utterly charmed by the friendliness of New Orleans, we spent a week in Florida and found the Epcot Centre and Waterworld interesting. The day at the Paramount Studios was also of interest, but we avoided Disneyland, where we thought the risk of being mugged by someone dressed as Goofy or Mickey Mouse unacceptably high. The visit had been uniformly good, with the only slightly jarring note struck by the tour guide who had met us on the first morning in New York. An Englishman, he chose to lard his speech with Americanisms of the 'Y'all' variety. Charming enough from the natives, but, and like the accents affected by numerous disc jockeys in the UK, irritating on the ear when attempted by others. It was a fine fortnight and what remained in my memory was the courtesy of ordinary Americans. It was sadly contrasted by the loutish behaviour of the aircraft passengers when we disembarked at Manchester.

18

Blocked drains in the yard, whose rodding offered a chill and cheerless task, was the note upon which 1993 opened. This was such a common occurrence that the plumber next door occasionally called around to borrow *his* rods. The New Year brought also the expectation of a new Training Officer and a new Training NCO at an early point of it. I had extended my service with some misgivings, but for the simple reason that I could find no good alternative employment that might defray the mortgage and buy groceries. There was every possibility that the new training team might address some of our more serious deficiencies, but I had seen a couple of false dawns by now and I was no longer optimistic. It occurred to me to speak very frankly to the Adjutant when he arrived, but eventually I decided against. Unfortunately, neither the CO nor the DSC chose to brief him in any meaningful way, and the Adjutant was left to formulate his own training policy. This produced some later difficulties.

The Adjutant had previously served in the ranks with a Scottish regiment, then was trained and commissioned at Sandhurst before transferring to the RAF Regiment. He was a very fit man who clearly knew his stuff and I began to believe that his was the act that I had waited four years to see. The flight sergeant I knew from my final tour on No 20 Squadron, and although he had little field or training experience he was without doubt a useful administrator and thoroughly in charge of the Training Cell. The most immediate result of the new regime was that the full time auxiliary NCOs were now compelled to undergo courses of qualification, adding range management and weapons instructor skills to those held by the regular staff. I had been arguing the need for this almost since arrival on the squadron but the CO had turned a consistently deaf ear to it. The result of this neglect had been a sizeable auxiliary 'regular' component with too few instructor abilities to deploy during training weekends, recruit courses or at annual camp. The new Adjutant possessed a personality more forceful than that of three combined predecessors and training, clearly, was about to undergo dramatic change.

Weekend cadres were established and I began a GPMG SF

class that spread over two weekends. I still found the weapon interesting after a twenty-year acquaintance with it and I still believed that it was a much underrated weapon. The regular squadrons had long since abandoned SF, although they would rediscover its potential just a couple of years later, denuding the auxiliary squadrons of their SF kits in the process. The classes responded to the weapon and we soon had SF teams performing slick drills. The training pace was a cracking one, and heartening.

My relationship with the CO had been decidedly cool for quite some time, and it developed frost when a redress of complaint was mounted by a Squadron SNCO. The latter, a flight sergeant, had been working regular days for a number of months in anticipation of a full time post that had fallen vacant. It soon became apparent that the post was in fact being kept open for a JNCO who had been on extended leave of absence whilst working overseas. Not only did the corporal get the job, but he was additionally promised the rank of sergeant for the post, although he was not qualified in the rank, and nor were his recent assessments as a JNCO all that good. When the redress was entered, I was requested by the officer commanding the Administrative Wing on station to act as the adviser and point of contact for the complainant. The CO chose to interpret this as wilful exacerbation of the redress, which eventually was rejected – by the CO. When the complainant's file landed on my desk, I was alarmed to note that a retrospective entry appeared to have been made, seriously damaging the SNCO's case. When the redress was rejected, the complainant left the squadron. He was one of the fittest and most enthusiastic SNCOs we had ever had.

The business of the 'doctored' file was troubling and it recalled to me a late event in the matter of my own redress. When it had become apparent that the matter had closed without any attempt to investigate the questions I had raised, I had approached the CO and requested a formal investigation by the RAF Police. When I asked him a week or so later what was happening, he replied that 'Group' had rejected the idea. This was unsatisfactory and I was curious enough to see if I could generate enquiries on the basis of the former flight sergeant's file. It, however, had been removed and replaced with a new folder, whose single enclosure baldly recorded that the original file had been 'mislaid'. It remained mislaid.

At much the same time I had attended a conference of auxiliary warrant officers at RAF Marham, hosted by a squadron leader on the auxiliary desk at HQ Strike Command. Himself a former adjutant with an auxiliary Regiment squadron, he closed the meeting with the remark that he could be approached with any problems that we might feel unable to address locally. After due consideration, I spoke to him on the 'phone and was invited to a meeting at Strike. I did not sleep at all well on the night prior and not least because it seemed to me to be tremendously disloyal to refer Squadron problems externally. Against that, however, I had always believed that loyalty went sideways and down, in addition to up.

I was interviewed for two hours by the squadron leader and informed that the upward reporting would be to a group captain. Having very little proof of anything that underpinned my concerns, I wondered if I might shortly be invited to take my talents elsewhere, but it did not come to that. At the close of interview I was informed that I was being taken seriously because of *who* I was, and that was gratifying.

On the lengthy drive home, I paused at a Services to find a brew and a quiet corner to reflect a little on the exchange. I felt that I had discharged a moral obligation at least, and when I examined the question of integrity reckoned that mine at least was intact. On that basis, I believed, I could return to 2625 Squadron and simply immerse myself in training for what little now remained of my twilight service.

Having run recruit courses exclusively for two years, I was now eased out of them by the new training team, other than for drill instruction and assistance with exercises. This was of some regret to me, but I wholeheartedly agreed with the principle. Training was rightly the realm of the regular Regiment staff, as was the weekend programming which also was taking a quantum leap forward.

There was, however, a note of anxiety in the new thrust. Among the few things I had learned for myself in the service is that there is nothing more dangerous in the training environment than the unsupervised corporal. The same might be true of flight lieutenants, and ours was under no constraints from either the DSC or the CO, and for the now obvious reason that neither of our present incumbents had much of a clue about field training, and knew worryingly little about tactical leadership. It quickly became apparent that the new training programmes were very robust, and they proved a bridge too far for some of the weekenders. Exercises which went overnight on Saturday and aggressive training which extended late into Sunday took a great deal out of Gunners, who were then expected to report to their primary employment on Monday just as fresh as colleagues whose weekend had been that of relaxation. We observed no immediate fall in numbers, since the training was genuinely appreciated, but we were unable to sustain them in the longer term.

I was still running B Flight but I had to relinquish it before the year was much advanced. Its former commander had sorted out his domestic problems and a round of promotions provided him with a very capable flight sergeant. This was a pity from a personal point of view, but again absolutely right. Young Gunners needed a young commander to set the right sort of tone, although I had found it pretty much a tonic for the thick end of a year.

To our extracurricular training we added something called 'The Tough Guy'. This sounded naff, but it was an endurance run organised annually by some animal sanctuary in Shropshire. Our entry was organised by a full time auxiliary Gunner who was my age but who could run about twice as fast, and we succeeded in attracting a score of entrants. The run combined a long circuit of several fields with numerous obstacles that were nothing if not interesting. They included giant hay bales, tunnels fashioned from truck tyres and a huge dung heap which trapped legs to the knee. The dung heap was the only remotely warm item on a freezing January day, since any warmth generated by the running was dissipated by wading through endless stretches of water. I took about two and a half hours to complete the course and when I shared the 4 Tonner driving home with Ian, the organiser, I suffered agonies of cramp and it had probably not helped in that we had slept in a field the previous night. It was a bizarre way to spend one of our rare weekends off-duty. We decided to make an annual event of it.

I led another hill-walking expedition to Snowdonia, and we had learned by now to avoid the dedicated facilities at Capel Curig and elsewhere. The security situation had caught up with these and it was possible to spend as much time on gate guard as climbing, so we booked private facilities. The 'Bothy', upon inspection, looked suspiciously like a cow byre, with some evidence that the cows had only recently moved out. Indeed, it was very likely that they might move back in again at the end of the season. It was sparsely furnished with rusting iron two-tiered bunk beds, but it was all that we required. We had our own cooking equipment and there was a cheerful pub not ten minute's walk down the road.

The Strickland Competition was again held in May, again at

the Depot, but although the team had trained hard it relinquished the Trophy to the Highland squadron, retaining only the Fitness trophy. There was an especial affinity between the Jock unit and ours, which may have had something to do with Celtic origins, and we usually exchanged a bottle of Scotch with them, win lose or draw. We saw them only once each year but I got on well with their warrant officer. In conversation, we discovered that George had been serving with the unit in the Falklands that I had once accompanied as a safety supervisor during their tab from Carlos to Stanley. George also had a sharp memory of the night on the mountain.

From the competition I went directly to Worksop, where Joan was waiting with her folks. We had booked a narrowboat holiday for the four of us on the Leeds and Liverpool canal, intending to spend five days on the water. This was something I had wanted to do for quite some time. We embarked at Skipton on Swale, heading for Leeds, and the takeover of the boat had been remarkably rapid. I had been shown how to operate the engine, the bilge pump and the shower, but it seemed to be largely a matter of assumption that I knew how to steer the boat.

Early experience indicated that any change in direction had to be well anticipated and that gentle movements of the tiller were best. Anything else tended to produce a mad charge at the towpath, and more experienced users proved adept at getting out of my way. Dealing with locks was the subject of a leaflet in the cabin, and we were shortly to be put to the test of a 'stair', which was the famous Bingley 'five-rise'.

Travelling towards Leeds meant going down five locks grouped together, with a second grouping of three about a hundred yards further on. The locks were actually controlled by a Keeper and the idea was to work in tandem with him, floating the boat down (or up) the 'stair'. The Keeper was a Yorkshireman and he looked as jolly as Postman Pat, with red cheeks and bright blue eyes. His demeanour, however, was rather more Doubting Thomas. "'Ave you 'ad much experience of locks?" He wanted to know. "This is my first one." I told him, brightly. He groaned. "Bloody 'ell, I 'ad a boat sank 'ere last week. One o' they bloody tupperware cruisers." He put another question: "'Ow much narrow boating experience 'ave you 'ad, then?" I looked at my watch: "About forty-five minutes." He groaned more deeply and I could see that I was not exactly making his day perfect. We rode the stairs without difficulty however and continued our journey. The Keeper was no more cheerful when we made the return journey a few days later, and by that time I had been demoted from captain to cabin boy. Joan manned the tiller and I was despatched at the gallop along the towpath to heave aside numerous swing bridges. I removed bargee from my list of employment possibilities.

Tettenhall Animal Sanctuary 1993
(not actually leading the first three)

19

The RAF initiated a redundancy programme that accounted for both units and individuals, aiming to slim the service by 20,000 personnel in a fairly short period. Four of the RAF Regiment squadrons had been axed and the three USAAF Rapier squadrons were earmarked for disbandment. Post-Reagan, Uncle Sam was also counting the cost of his overseas bases and those to which USAAF Rapier had been dedicated were listed as superfluous. The British government appeared committed to the principle of larger reservist formations and a greater role for them, but there seemed no guarantee behind it. Not too long before, it had been intended to expand the auxiliary squadrons to twenty, but this was by now clearly off the agenda. Three defence flights at separate RAF stations, once believed likely to metamorphose into complete regiment squadrons, were disbanded, as was the ack-ack unit that had been equipped at RAF Waddington with the Argentine weapons. These had begun to require cash that had never been voted in the first place and the decision was taken to disband the squadron. The guns were doubtless polished up and sold on to some Third World country.

There was still no sign of the contract terms for full time auxiliaries and this had obviously been overtaken by more important concerns. There were only about forty of us affected, and even the entire auxiliary air force was pretty small beer in comparison with the Territorial Army. We totalled less than two thousand, compared with seventy-two thousand TA.

The Adjutant continued to make his mark and a signal contribution of his was in making all of the permanent staff get involved in training, irrespective of trade. This was something I had consistently argued for and occasionally had tried to implement, but without success. By the middle of the year the new programmes were beginning to bite and the attendance levels gave some cause for concern. The idea of orbatting the flights according to predicted attendance began to take hold, and the change was effected at the end of the year. Although I no longer ran the recruit courses, I had maintained a precise record of enlistments and further training and I continued to do so. I was eventually able to demonstrate, at the end of a four-year period, that no less than sixty per cent of all recruits who passed to a flight actually terminated their service prematurely, and most of them within the first year of service. I put all of this into a lengthy report, suggesting that it made a nonsense of contracting a volunteer for four year's service - signing legal documents and taking the Loyal Oath - if they could not be held to it. I had also known for some time that the service was loathe to prosecute those abstaining volunteers who refused to return several hundred pounds worth of kit which was held on the public charge.

At much this time, all reservists were circulated with a document which purported to show the way forward and it invited comment. I made a lengthy submission arguing that composite units were the answer, since any under-strength regular unit could make up its numbers from reservist formations, even if there was some gap in specialist skills. The flaw in this otherwise good case was that it left the auxiliary leadership out of the equation, and no enthusiasm was heard among the reserve hierarchy for the idea, although there would be a partial implementation of such a scheme a couple of years later.

Another recruit course featured towards the end of the year but I had little to do with it. I also noted that my input towards training weekends was by now very slight, although I still believed that the training was in the right hands. It did, unfortunately, make my weekends somewhat dull and of little contrast to the generally unexciting run of administrative duties during the week. The year largely ended upon the note of a two-week deployment to battle camp at Sennybridge, where I was disappointed in having no field ranges to conduct. The weather was harsh and we had more than half of the squadron in sick quarters at some time or other, as a virus did the rounds. (There was also the suspicion that at least some of the illnesses were notional, for the Adjutant was driving hard by now.) Sennybridge had one of the stiffest assault courses in the country and the entire squadron was divided into teams of four to contest for the fastest time. I was gratified to be on the winning team, although the win had depended much more on the effort of the other three than mine.

We again had two German officers attached and these,

according to established practice, were added to sections to act as Gunners. At some point in the final exercise, which was conducted during seventy-two hours of bitterly cold conditions, they reported to the CO and informed him that they would rather continue as observers at this time. A few hours later the CO sent for me and told me that the Germans now wished to withdraw from the exercise entirely and that I should organise a resting area for them. At this particular time I was preparing the B Echelon move, tactically, through a forestry block in pitch darkness to a new location some miles on the other side of the area. Illnesses had reduced an echelon crew that was invariably under strength anyway, and with one thing and another I wasn't at all happy to be distracted by trivia. I found the Germans and told them to get into their sleeping bags in the back of a 4 Tonner, until I had the time to sort them out. There was a short silence until one of the pair said: "We forgot to bring our sleeping bags with us." I thought about this briefly before replying: "D'you know, Sir, eleven thousand Germans froze to death at Stalingrad. Probably because they forgot to take their sleeping bags." This observation was not well received.

We concluded the camp on the note of annual fitness tests, although by then some thirty per cent of the squadron was excused training. The Combat Fitness Test was conducted over six miles of fairly stiff terrain, and I was looking to finish it in the allocated seventy minutes, rather than set any records. I had some back problems and my left knee was giving me some of its periodic gyp, but I made the time. We returned to St. Mawgan and the year had little left to run. I attended the cremation in Chester of my Uncle Archie, whose home in the country had been a magical place to visit when I was a boy, and I learned that Aunt Jenny had suffered a stroke, although she seemed to be making a good recovery. These events were useful, if sad, reminders of mortality and reminders too that job problems were actually pretty trivial things.

Of rather more anxiety to me was the deterioration in my handwriting, which had never been good but was now indecipherable - even to me. In the latter months of the year I had been attempting another manuscript and much of the careful attempt to print words simply resulted in a scrawl. I now wondered if this might be the very early symptom of some muscular degeneration and I arranged to see the MO. He quickly referred me to a specialist at the RAF Hospital at Wroughton, in Wiltshire and I travelled down on the eve of appointment, spending an anxious night in the Mess there and wondering if I was to be the recipient of some extremely shitty news the next day. To my considerable relief, I learned that the condition was localised to my left arm and it apparently offered no threat of spread. I had something called 'Writer's Dystonia' and it resulted from a garbling of the message from the brain to the muscles in the arm. 'Buy a typewriter,' was the specialist's advice. I already had one and I additionally began to learn to write with my right hand.

The Poll Tax, the most ludicrous levy since the Window Tax, had failed and a revised property rating system soon replaced it. The house was valued at £40,000 for rating, which was disturbing, but the real shock followed when the borough council advised us that we were now also assessed for rating as a small business. A bill for almost a thousand pounds was enclosed, and this was several months before we would even open the door to the first guest. It meant, too, that we would feed, bathe, bed and clean after almost a hundred guests simply for the council's financial benefit, and it was at this point that we decided to abandon the business. Ironically, the council now resisted our bid to de-register and an exchange of letters took place, with the incoming ones implying legal action. The matter was eventually dropped and we de-registered, with no intention of trading at any level.

The house meanwhile had attracted little interest and when the estate agent advised us to reduce our asking price to £50,000 we took it off the market. Joan had developed an ulcer and we were very thoughtful when we went off to her folks to spend Xmas with them. I was even more thoughtful when we returned in the New Year. Joan suggested that we should sell the house at any price and go our separate ways. 1994 was not beginning at all well.

20

I had no easy answer to Joan's shock proposal and no new thoughts on what factors might be contributing to the strains, other than those which I had been aware of for some time. There was, at least, no early prospect of jettisoning the house and therefore no reason to assume that we might very quickly be living apart. There seemed, nonetheless, a very real danger that our marriage was coming apart and I did not welcome it. I meanwhile wondered if we might benefit from a very short separation and I decided to go alone to Australia for the occasion of Mam's eightieth birthday, which would fall at the end of March.

Training continued and we had adjusted the flights to reflect attendance commitment. I had supported the idea when it was first mooted but it proved to have its problems. Prime among them was that we now appeared to be creating an elite flight, rather than training across the board to common skills, but I had long arrived at the conclusion that there were no easy solutions to the training problems that were wholly unique to reservist units. We simply had to make the best of it.

I attended another 'Tough Guy' endurance run and this time took nearly three and a half hours to complete the course. My left knee had been giving me some problems, particularly when we trained in the cold and the wet - which was pretty much all of the time between autumn and spring.

Early in March I flew from Gatwick and the cramped seats made the stops at Abu Dhabi, Bangkok and Jakarta more than welcome. I was flying with Garuda Airlines, having again shopped around for cheap flights, but would certainly not have, had I known then the Indonesian record of atrocities in Timor. I had lately joined *Amnesty International* and their periodic literature would shortly spell out the history of the twenty-year occupation of the former Portuguese colony.

I was met by Jan and Arch and I spent a few days with them before travelling on to Boulder. The heat was more than welcome and the temperature rose to forty degrees Celsius on a couple of occasions. I established a routine of morning runs and afternoon walks again, being joined by Arch for a run to Swanbourne beach one morning, where we alternately swam then walked a stretch. I again noted the tidy outer Perth suburbs and houses at realistic prices. Australia also had undergone a lengthy recession and it had its share of other problems, but the country seemed to be getting a lot of things about right.

I found Mam looking frail and with hip and back problems, but she was indomitably cheerful about them. She had suffered ill health for a number of years yet she was uncomplaining, bearing it all with the stoicism which seemed a family trait. My arrival was a surprise, as was the birthday party which Bea and Malc had arranged. They had quietly assembled as many of Mam's friends as they could and we celebrated with an evening barbeque. Malc had asked me to address the gathering with a few words and I was happy to have the opportunity of paying a public tribute to the early, and lean, years of Mam's arrival on the Goldfields.

My brother Jack was also present with his family, but Arch had made an earlier visit. Since retiring from the army he had been employed by the state court, and he was presently on circuit in the north-west with a judge. I planned to spend some more time with him before I returned to England and for the moment I was happy to potter about at home. It was actually the home of Bea and Malc by now, although Mam continued to live there, and Malc was making the most of his long service leave by virtually rebuilding the property. He was also developing his own business, repairing and rebuilding engines, and this was underpinned by something of a new boom on the Goldfields.

Malc had a racing bike that he seldom used and it became the means by which I took my first good look at the local area in nearly forty years. The town had grown and not merely back into the boundaries from which it had shrunk in the early Fifties, but well beyond them. The mines that had all but died had merely represented preserved wealth and ground was being broken at an unprecedented rate. I cycled along Burt Street and under the railway line towards the Boulder Block, where four hotels had once clung together on the same acre of land, and found an astonishing transformation. Poppet heads, machine sheds, ore treatment plants and mine offices had once stretched the three miles to Kalgoorlie and now there was no sign that they had ever existed. A huge hole had replaced it all and where solitary miners had once drilled and blasted in dim, isolated workings, machines with wheels twice the height of a man now gouged thousands of tons of ore from the ground. I tried to superimpose, in my mind's eye, the picture I recalled from the mid-Sixties, but it was not easy. Somewhere in that empty space had stood not just mines which had existed for almost a century, but the parks where the mines held their Xmas parties, and the pubs where I had sometimes slaked a thirst before walking the mile or so home. It was an unbelievable change in the landscape.

It occurred to me at this time that it would have been good to visit some of the gold towns that *had* died, and a good many years before. But it was simply too hot to contemplate cycling the sort of distances involved and I had to be content with a more modest radius of visits. One of them was to the Boulder graveyard, which I had not seen since we buried Gran'Ma Foxley in 1961. I rang the council offices to discover the plot number and I soon found the grave in the Anglican portion of the cemetery which divided Anglicans from Catholics for no good reason I could understand. The grave was partially mounded and partially collapsed and the red, dry soil was marked only by a rusting iron peg at its head. This was where Nell Foxley, born in a railway company house in Crewe, had been brought. Her son lay in a grave some two hundred miles to the south and her husband in the Crewe cemetery, oceans away. The Boulder cemetery was utterly quiet and no breeze stirred the ubiquitous gums marking its perimeter. The sun beat down as I walked back to the bike to uncap my water bottle and assuage the constant thirst, wondering the while at the random scatter of family down the years.

Whilst biking in the same area of the cemetery along a bush track, I unexpectedly came upon the Pioneer Cemetery, whose existence I had never even heard of. It was virtually overgrown with scrub, although a monument laid and dated a couple of years before by the Goldfields Historical Society was proof that the site was not entirely forgotten. I propped the bike and made a careful circuit of the couple of acres that were loosely fenced by some rusting cable, which very likely had once suspended cages on the mines. The cemetery, the monument told me, had been in use from 1899-1904 before presumably being replaced by the one where Gran'Ma Foxley lay. I found that it, too, was divided by faith, with separate plots for Catholic, Church of England, Presbyterian and Methodist. The graves that were marked by headstones were in a poor state and clearly had been visited by vandals, distant or recent. Many of the graves were simply mounds of earth, or slight depressions, with no markers at all, but sufficient fragments of headstones survived to offer a picture of death at the turn of the century. Here were the victims of the first mining accidents - 'John Campbell killed at Paringa Mine aged 20'- and victims of childbirth -Helen Mary Wills, Died 9 November 1901 aged 20. Her son survived her just 20 days. Margaret Hanna had died at 50 in the same year and she had been born in Co. Tyrone long before the division of Ireland. It is possible that her parents had fled the Great Famine that had devastated the population. A section of the cemetery had been reserved for infants and it seemed to reflect the infant mortality that was then a commonplace. 'Henry Noble, 15 months', 'Cassie Cairns, 3 Years' 'John Clancy, 3 Years and Kathleen Clancy, 12 Years'. Sweetly preserved in the quiet and mostly forgotten graveyard, some engraved lines which expressed such loss most poignantly:

> We love thee well, but Jesus loves thee best
> Good night Good night Good night

Interlude

HILL-WALKING

North Wales was the favourite location, although Brecon and the Cairngorms were not overlooked. The walks usually spanned three days, with Monday and Friday travel to bracket them. Working weekends every second week tended to preclude a longer stay, which was a pity, since we were usually hitting stride by day three. We only once stayed at dedicated facilities - these being at the former Forestry Camp at Capel Gurig - having decided that the comfort of them was at the price of gate guards and night security duties. We learned instead to find 'Bothies' which were off the beaten track. Pubs also had to be selected with some discrimination. An early mistake was to drink in one where everybody spoke like characters in a Noel Coward play, and the landlord was about as cheerful as a blind rivet catcher. There were better options and we soon found them. In the Cairngorms, we found a pub that was selling Bitter at just fifty pence a pint. I do not recall what the Bitter was, but we were faithful to it for the duration.

The North Wales climbs usually kicked off with a circuitous approach to the 1,000 metre summits of *Carnedd Llewellyn* and *Carnedd Dafydd*, both of which overlooked Lake Ogwen, where a great number of pre-para volunteers for II Squadron had camped in cold comfort during 'Wales' week. A long spur formed the initial approach to the peaks and at about 500 metres the grass underfoot yielded to crags. The broad path degenerated into a mere ribbon where it crossed a saddle between the two features, and the view down the steep sides was considerably superior to anything you might see through your office window. Higher still, and the fragment of mirror below was the reservoir with the unpronounceable name of *Ffynnon Llugwy*, whose paved track to the main road would form our escape route if we had problems. It was hard to visualise, on a perfect day, dire problems, but just three weeks prior to one of our visits a boy, his father and his uncle were found dead on the approach to *Llewellyn*. All were in different places and clearly the last to die had struggled on to seek help. The weather and the visibility might change very dramatically and it was prudent to plan alternatives.

When the visibility was at its best, the view across the basin to the northeast was stunning, and even moving. It was worth every inch of the climb, and a picture you could put in a frame, as the Irish say. The valleys might be alive with activity of another sort, and pilots from the flying school at RAF Valley, on Anglesea, were frequent visitors. Viewed from the heights, the Hawk trainers were mere toys as they dipped and banked below us. Their minimum height was supposedly 500 feet, but when viewed from lower on the slopes they seemed well under that. From 1,000 metres, the surface of Lake Ogwen was polished slate and the shifting patterns of cloud might move fingers of sunlight across the water, like spotlights seeking the entertainer on some vast stage. The views were mesmerising.

Descent from *Dafydd* was slow because there was a fair bit of scree on the Ogwen side of it. Footfalls had to be picked with some care to avoid a sudden lurch and a painful slide of ten feet or so. We might also be on the prismatic compass at that point, too, since a necklace of cloud at the summit was fairly common, whatever the season. The hills and the weather had long been catching out more than just unprepared climbers. I had descended *Daffyd* at one time and found four radial engines scattered in a small area, the silent witnesses to an aircraft crash. A hundred aircraft - a fifth of them being Avro Ansons - had crashed in these hills during WW II.

The village of Capel Curig offered the starting point for a wander over the *Glyders*; the ground rising steeply from the village and the earth swampily underfoot until nothing but dew clad the stone. Sweat cooled rapidly on the ridge where the wind increased its velocity, and loitering was not recommended. We might perspire or chill according to the vagaries of concealing cleft or exposed approaches, and a day-sack with extra clothing and waterproof clothing was essential. From the *Glyders* our route was to *Tryffan*, a black pinnacle which had looked utterly daunting when viewed from the other side of Lake Ogwen. It would not merit a second glance from the ice-axe and crampon crowd, but there were times when it felt like the north face of the Eiger. At the summit of *Tryffan* are two adjacent monoliths which have been named Adam and Eve, and it is a tradition among climbers to leap from one to the other. It is a tradition best tempered with caution on a windy day, for there is nothing much but space on the far side of Eve.

The North Wales climbs always culminated in a climb of Snowdon and seldom by the same route. The *Pyg Track* was a favourite, but an early meander from Pen y Pas around the waters of *Llyn Teyrn* and *Llyn Llydaw* was a nice way to get started. Old mine workings lay along this route, a reminder that such strenuous activity as hill-walking was merely a means of getting to work for generations of Welsh miners. Halfway up the side of one such approach, we noted a plaque that recorded the fact that the Prime Minister, Lloyd George, had once addressed miners at the spot. Hard to imagine any of the current crop doing that, and utterly impossible to see Mrs Thatcher ever attempting it.

The visibility might be down to ten metres and a scrutiny of the brown lines on the map would be necessary to check our progress, bets being offered as to where we might hit the spine of the summit approach. Even in spring the snow line might be encountered at 700 metres or so, and kicking snow purchases would alternate with some reasonably difficult rock scrambling. Frequent breaks to catch the breath and warm the fingers were recommended. Winds gusting to fifty knots at the exposed summit definitely precluded any hanging about, before leisurely strolling down the 'tourist route' which followed the funicular railway down to the town.

The Cairngorms offered gentler slopes, but no less scenic as we forayed out from the quiet village of Kincraig. It was a long haul from Cornwall, and we arrived punch-drunk with travel but keen to compare the walks. From Glasgow onwards the scenery on an autumn afternoon had been stunning and alone worth the journey. We had skirted Loch Ness for several miles then passed through quiet glens whose names rang with tragedy, distant and recent. Glencoe, Bannockburn and Lockerbie among them, but only the day was dying as we passed by.

We toiled through forestry up the slopes, startling deer and grouse and the latter squawking to divert our attention from a wild scatter of chicks. Not a soul in sight but ourselves, and that evening finding a pub which was almost as quiet, and agreeably so. The following day making a change by walking eighteen miles around Loch Laggan, and climbing again on the third day. I had also hoped to find one of the military roads built by General Wade in an unhappier era, but it eluded me. Some other time, perhaps. We did find the Commando Monument that commemorates the men who trained at Achnacarry, though, and I have a photograph of it somewhere. Bronze tribute to iron men who briefly trod this soil before melting irrevocably into it.

21

I had not intended the visit to be anything of a sentimental journey, but trundling about on the bike was greatly evocative of earlier years spent in the town. The bike itself recalled something of youth and when I considered how the immense mound of spoil from 'the Big Pit' dwarfed the earlier impressive slime dumps, I remembered how I had heroically (well, fairly) ridden down the acutely-angled sides of them in the adolescent pursuit of defeating boredom. I now cycled beyond the slime dumps to the satellite town of Lakewood, which had acted as a terminus for the wood gatherers, whose efforts stoked both the fires of industry and those of the tin houses. Sadly, it had vanished with virtually no trace, as had a line of rusting steam locomotives that had formerly stood on the redundant line. Untouched for years, it had presumably later found itself in the way of progress, unlike the Pioneer Cemetery that merely occupied a patch of unwanted scrub.

The Mount Charlotte shaft that had been the first to pull ore on a large-scale, was by now the last working shaft and it almost aligned with Hannan Street in Kalgoorlie. In its shadow was a shaft poppet head transplanted from elsewhere and now standing in the grounds of the Goldfields Museum, which represented a worthy attempt to preserve something of the past. The museum itself was a former hotel, called The British Arms. The museum was a stone's throw from where Paddy Hannan found the first gold, 35,000,000 ounces ago in the case of the Charlotte. Behind the mine was the hill that named the mine and also the reservoir atop it that held 1,000,000 gallons of water. The life-blood of the infant town, the water was piped three hundred and twenty miles from the Mundaring Weir, and the pipeline was the brainchild of the gifted engineer, O'Connor. He did not live to see his genius brought to fruition. Scorned for his ideas and beset with problems, he blew his brains out.

In 1956, I had paid ten shillings for a flight in a veteran

aircraft and what that flight had indelibly printed upon my mind - apart from the novelty of the flight itself - were two things. One was the aerial view of the slime dumps, grey and imposing above the town and seeming as if they would dominate the generally flat landscape forever. The other was the view of Hannan Street, a broad swathe that divided the town on a north-south axis. The street was two chains in width, since forty-four yards was deemed the necessary minimum in which a bullock team and cart might be turned. This had been virtually the sole means of providing heavy transport when the town was laid out, towards the close of the nineteenth century, and nor then was the street railed for trams - a means of transport which survived almost until my arrival as an adolescent migrant.

The airport was much newer and had been relocated about half a mile from its original setting. It was now possible to walk along the cracked tarmac where the daily DC3 had once added black strips to the runway, and where I had first flown in the Avro Anson. The DC3s I had watched as I biked home from work, following the perimeter fence. I had also biked home from night school and once was stopped by the Roads' Board traffic cop, for riding without lights. He had once also stopped the Old Man for driving at night on sidelights only; a practice which was legal in the UK but not in Australia. This resulted in a small fine. The former traffic cop was now in his eighties and he had been among the guests at Mam's party.

I hadn't seen the inside of the Mines & City Worker's Club since last drinking there with the Old Man, but Arch and I made a call and had a few pots. The club was much modernised and the stern portraits of past presidents and committeemen now no longer frowned down upon the drinkers. It may have been a faulty perception, or merely that we were in there too early, but I had the powerful impression that miners no longer predominated among the customers. Rumour had it, too, that women were now welcome, though we saw none as we quaffed the ice-cold lager. Hannans' Beer was a good brew, but the town brewery was also long gone and the beer was now brewed in Perth.

I opened each morning with an early run and upon one return I found Mam sitting out on the verandah. I joined her with a pot of tea and we chatted for an hour. I actually mostly listened, for she was recalling something of her first months in the town. It was an hour to preserve in memory for another day. The sad note of the visit was that Mam had been heard to remark that she wanted to see her four sons together again. We had not quite managed that and now seem unlikely to. My time was again running short and I returned Malc's bike to the shed and disuse, returning to Perth and a few more days with Jan and Arch.

We again visited the replica of Cook's collier *Endeavour*, built of the native wood, Jarrah, and now in the water and preparing for her maiden voyage. A fine sight. I was again content to wander about and feel the sun beating on my shoulders, although such exposure was no longer popular among Australians. Growing recognition of the dangers of skin cancer sent people early or late to the beaches, and skin creams or covering up was more the norm. I noted a hoarding whose message expressed the new view succinctly: 'A suntan is nothing more than proof that your skin is trying to protect itself'. I could accept that, but the sun just *felt* so good.

Arch had developed an interest in black powder firearms, spending time on a range with a Brown Bess replica and other pieces. I accompanied a couple of his visits and took some pleasure in loading, charging, priming and firing a cap and ball revolver. A lengthy process, which had never been apparent in the westerns screened at the Kino. Time again ran out and I boarded the aircraft at Perth, wondering on this beautiful autumn day if spring in England was amounting to much.

The disadvantages of cheap tickets became apparent at Bali, when I faced a six-hour wait for a connecting flight at a very early stage of the journey home. At Zurich we were stacked for some time and when we landed I had missed my connection to London. At Gatwick I had missed my courier ride to Cornwall and I spent seven hours awaiting another one. By the time I got home I had once again spent almost as much time on the ground as I had spent in the air.

Whatever had placed the strains upon our marriage appeared to have receded and we went cautiously forward. Ironically, I was now tentatively offered a job overseas, but this was no time to be contemplating lengthy separations and I turned the offer down. I had one day at home then returned to duty. Five weeks without pay was sufficient reason of itself, but the squadron was also about to undergo an evaluation exercise over a four-day period. The CO chose not to attend, but he did turn up on a couple of occasions at the tactical site, driving a bright blue van and wearing a flat cap and a Barbour jacket, offering useful advice on camouflage.

The squadron was tested in various ways and none of the

results was less than satisfactory. This mostly reflected the work that the Adjutant had put in, and it may not have been overlooked by the evaluation team that much of the leadership also had been generated by him. In the absence of the CO, nor was the DSC making a great deal of his leadership opportunities.

Spring had not amounted to much at all and we were cold and wet for much of the exercise, although there was nothing very novel in that. Three days after the exercise ended, I turned in early feeling ill, and I continued to feel ill, missing work. I eventually reported to my general practitioner and she told me to take Paracetamol. I might have told her that my pulse was twenty beats per minute higher than normal, but thought perhaps this was irrelevant. A week later I felt absolutely dreadful and another doctor diagnosed pneumonia, which then responded very quickly to antibiotic treatment. I remained off duty for a fortnight and felt fairly weak for a while.

I was hardly missed from the training programmes, having by now very little to do with them, although I spent my birthday assisting with a recruit selection course. The station then became a base 'somewhere in Europe' for a major exercise and we deployed some troops in the ground defence role. No 48 Squadron, from RAF Lossiemouth, provided the Rapier defence and I went off looking for familiar faces, finding several. The squadron was actually given very little to do on the exercise, which was a pity since it had developed something of a cutting edge by now.

It had been decided to run a pilot recruit course under our parent training wing at RAF Honington, and I saw my chance to accompany the course as an instructor. I also drove the 4 Tonner with the dozen recruits on the back, stopping only twice on the eight-hour journey. "Christ," Muttered a recruit, clambering off the back on the second stop, "I didn't know you had to have a bull's bladder to join the RAF Regiment!"

Whilst at the station, I learned that the warrant on the Highland squadron had been demoted to flight sergeant to create a vacancy for a retiring regular. Incensed at this cavalier treatment of a man who had served in the rank for five years without apparently giving cause for complaint, I wrote directly to the Inspector of the auxiliary air force. This ruffled a few feathers, not least those of my own CO who was buttonholed by the Inspector, and who professed ignorance of the affair despite there being a copy of the letter in his tray. Sadly, no redress was effected and it was allowed to stand as an example of a poor way to treat a good man. I wondered if this was a peculiarly reservist failing.

Weekend work came thick and fast for a while, which was ironic in view of the fact that abandonment of the B&B should have left Joan and me with plenty of time for weekends together. There were certainly plenty of occasions still when I was just as busy as I ever had been in regular service - if I sometimes still wondered where so much effort was taking us. Some of the work was in providing assistance to detachments of the Air Training Corps, whose cadets arrived from all over the country. Each detachment had its own instructors, but too few of these evinced any real interest or ability. It often seemed to me that once the morning drill was over, the majority of instructors were happy to swan about in Best Blue or hang about the Mess, rather than get their hands dirty with something really useful.

Weekend duties got in the way of a planned visit to the RAF Regiment Depot, at Catterick, which was about to close formally and whose closure was to be marked by a parade and a social gathering. The original Depot had been at Belton Park, in Lincolnshire but Catterick had been the spiritual home of the Corps since 1946. With almost half a century of service, the station was now to be handed over to the army, whose returning armoured assets from Germany would use the light armour facilities the Regiment no longer required. Some of us believed that a fair bit of tradition and a good slice of history had been too lightly yielded in the case of the transfer, and it was ironic that more money, probably, had been spent on the Depot in the last decade than in the six which had preceded it. The same some of us were accused of mere sentimental attachments to bricks and mortar, but RAF Catterick was also one of the oldest airfields in the country. I have not seen it since, although I may yet reside there. I intend to have my ashes scattered on Castle Hills, which is the Saxon fort overlooking the airfield. I spent enough time running around the airfield and the thought of my remains blowing about it is a pleasing one.

22

If I was not much busy with the principal training programmes for a while, I found plenty to do elsewhere. The military skills team trained mostly in the evenings and they were doing enough to do consistently well in the UK competitions, in addition to a couple of the European ones. There seemed no great support for the team within the squadron, which was a pity, but they at least experienced the satisfaction - quite apart from winning trophies - which is generated by belonging to a small and successful team.

Drill featured again when the squadron was asked to represent the station at a remembrance ceremony for the Allied air dead of WW II. It was held on the Plymouth Hoe where an imposing statue of Drake stared out into the Plymouth Sound, dwarfing the bronze figure of an Aircrewman that was the focus of our parade. It was a blistering day and we stood on parade for ninety minutes whilst endless tributes were read out. The arms that held rifles were numb when yet another figure stepped forward to the microphone, producing a sheaf of papers. "We are here today," Intoned the figure, "to remember the 55,000 who perished in the air war." "Bloody hell," Muttered a voice in the rear rank, "he's going to read out the names!"

I returned to the Hoe with a recruiting team to set up shop as part of the Armed Forces Week that featured in Plymouth annually. We were quartered at *HMS Drake*, which looked nicely historic and rewarded a casual stroll about its environs with views of fine buildings and a rare selection of cannon. The Senior Rates Mess had a fascinating collection of photographs taken at the turn of the century when the port was a forest of masts, with ships of every kind. I had a look at Union Street for the first time since the Royal Marines exchange, but whereas it had then appeared to retain much character, if slightly tacky here and there, it now exhibited the tackiness with no trace of character.

The weekend exercises were building steadily through the summer months into autumn and some of them stretched even the fittest. We worked quite solidly through one of them, with little opportunity for sleep, then tabbed six miles back to St. Mawgan carrying seventy-pound Bergens. I actually felt really stretched by this one and wondered, I think for the first time, if I was not trying to do a young man's job with a middle-aged man's body[1]. Also, my knees were giving me quite a bit of trouble by now.

I accompanied the skills' team to RAF Honington, which was now the RAF Regiment Depot, and whilst they went about a patrols-based competition I was asked to conduct a pistol shoot for the honorary air commodores on the 25 Metre Range. This seemed to pose few problems, although some of the HACs were unfamiliar with the Browning 9mm Pistol. I had anticipated that at least by conducting a quick lesson on the weapon, but the real problem was the HAC who also was a Marshal of the Royal Air Force. He had been a wartime Lancaster pilot and doubtless pistols would not have troubled him in his service years, but he now had arthritis in his hands so badly that when he aimed the weapon it tended to point at the firer alongside him. The cure, however, proved very simple for I turned the Marshal through ninety degrees on the firing point and he actually won the competition. This was a bit sad, because the HAC of 2625 Squadron came nowhere in the running.

---

[1]Another perspective on age was provided on the day off which followed such exertion: Joan's habit was to bring home various of neighbours' and friends' children from time to time, and through the back of the house she brought a young visitor as I sat with my newspaper in the lounge. "Go and see Harry," Joan suggested. The child's head appeared around the door and she gazed solemnly at me without responding to my greeting. "Did you see Harry?" Asked Joan when the child returned. "Yes," She replied, "isn't he *old?*"

The team also came nowhere on this occasion, simply being outclassed by teams who obviously were putting even more time in on ranges and dry-training areas. It was a difficult balance and all too easy to become the 'professional skills team' which devoted little time to routine activities.

In what little remained of my spare time in the period I was putting the mountain bike to good use by discovering the routes of railways which had closed in the Fifties and early Sixties. Cornwall seemed replete with them and the nature of the ground had preserved a few which might otherwise have vanished forever. These however tended to be in fairly inaccessible places marked by cuttings and embankments, but they were worth both searching for and the occasional topple off the bike. Fine bridges and viaducts, stone-built, were among the prizes. Nearer to the centres of occupation, the path of the railway was long obliterated and entirely replaced by something worthy. Council estates, perhaps.

Another year was running out and we deployed to Hythe and Lydd, in Kent for just a week of ranges. I had hoped that these might be the urban antiterrorist examples, and the mocked-up 'town' where patrols came under realistic fire and bomb attacks, but we had been booked into the more usual spectrum of gallery, crossing target and defence shoots. A disappointment. We had some free time and I took the opportunity of a day trip to Boulogne *sur* Mer, where I viewed Roman and other antiquities before sampling rather too much of the local brew. My souvenirs included two bottles of a reputedly excellent Beaujolais but, tragically, the carrier bag split when we returned to St.Mawgan and I lost both bottles, together with a bottle of Black Label Johnny Walker I had intended for Joan's dad. On another free day I had planned to walk the twenty-mile length of a military canal which had been dug to service the numerous Martello Towers which stood sentinel on the local coastline, but the weather deteriorated very badly and I abandoned the plan. The training week passed off quietly, but we had some JNCOs of the RAF Regiment attached to assist with ranges and they irritated me greatly with their patronising and condescending attitude to reservists - many of whom knew the score much better than they.

Joan and I had a quiet Xmas at home, preferring not to travel and generally relaxing. We were planning a spring cruise and intended to surprise her folks by taking them along, since their fiftieth wedding anniversary would fall in the period. When the New Year opened we should have been expecting a new Adjutant, but the incumbent had extended for an extra year and there was thus no dramatic change in programmes or policy. The robust training was getting to some of the reservists by this time however and our numbers steadily declined. This was probably of rather greater concern to the reservist hierarchy than to us, since the view from further up the tree appeared to be focused on quantity, rather than quality, but we were nonetheless keen to achieve and sustain our establishment figures. There was no perfect solution and each of the squadrons usually accepted some form of compromise.

My routine walks about Pentire Point and a stretch of the coastal path were now in company with two dogs. We had acquired Winston, a black Labrador about ten years old, from a friend of Joan's. The friend's husband had been working in Germany for some time, in the light of local unemployment, and Winston was rather missing out on exercise. I developed the habit of collecting him when I set off with Gypsy, and eventually found him waiting at the back gate. He somehow moved in and did not trouble to move out again. Gypsy seemed none too keen on sharing the mat with him, but he won her over by leaving some food in his bowl from time to time.

I did a third 'Tough Guy' run at the end of January but I had abandoned the boots by now and I ran in trainers. This was perhaps about thirty years too late and after a run along the coast a couple of weeks later I woke up with my left knee too sore and stiff to bend. When this failed to ease quickly, I reported sick and accepted painkillers. X-rays followed and the verdict confirmed the earlier diagnosis of osteo-arthritis. I was told to stop running, which of course I had, but the MO really meant *abandon* running. This I was reluctant to accept and I thought that I might pick up the routine after a few weeks, but although I would try at various times throughout the year, running was no longer an option. I would miss the regime very greatly.

I found myself putting pen to paper again to upset someone, this time on the behalf of the son of a friend on the squadron. The lad was enlisted in the Parachute Regiment, and in chatting to him whilst he was on leave I learned that his recruit platoon was being subjected to 'fines' by the corporals, who also insisted on expensive 'gifts' at various times. I addressed a letter to the Commandant but a subaltern replied and it became clear that nothing much was going to be done about it unless the platoon members made specific complaints. Their reluctance to do so was more than understandable, but I seethed with anger at the situation. I have remarked above that there is nothing quite so dangerous in the training environment as the unsupervised corporal, and here was a perfect example of it.

Joan had been looking for full time employment and I suggested that she return to driving with the RAF. She succeeded in application and was employed at RAF Portreath, which was about twenty miles to the south. She seemed much happier as a result, although the wages were not that grand.

On the contract employment front, the full time auxiliaries had now been waiting for six years and the whole thing was rather brought to a head when a full time auxiliary warrant officer elsewhere contracted cancer. His service wage stopped when he ceased to attend for duty, but the Department of Social Security proved reluctant to pay him benefit, since they regarded him as a serviceman. This was resolved and the warrant briefly survived his cancer, and we shortly learned that an interim measure would precede contracts. This measure was a short-term regular engagement for one year, with contracts to follow in 1996. One morning in March I drove up to Exeter and found the careers information office, where I confronted a bemused flight lieutenant with the news that I was enlisting. What he made of a fifty-three-year old recruit, he didn't divulge, but I duly took the 'Queen's Shilling' for the fifth and final time and I motored back to Cornwall. The other full time auxiliaries had even more fun, reporting to a Plymouth CIO which had no idea why they were being enlisted. With much theatrical glancing over their shoulders, the crew had probably left the impression that they were 'special forces'.

Being paid a hundred per cent of a regular's wage was a pleasant surprise, if limited to a year. My service pension was frozen for the duration and nor did I anticipate a return to the previous terms when the year ended. I firmly believed that the age of fifty-five was the time to go, although it was possible to serve on until sixty. Some did and they did not appear to understand how diminished their credibility became.

Paid leave was not only a great novelty after nearly seven years, but also quite timely. Within days of signing on Joan and I had driven to Worksop to collect her folks before flying from Manchester to Palma. We joined a cruise ship that evening and sailed the Mediterranean for a week, calling at Morocco, Tangier, Gibraltar and Portugal. It was a pleasantly balanced week of loafing about and looking at things of interest, and we recognised that we were happy again. It was also interesting to reflect that, in financial and material terms, we were pretty much back to the point we had entered 1988.

"Bloody Hell, he's going to read out all of the names!"

23

The squadron had at some time enjoyed the permission of local landowners to conduct low-intensity training on their land, and it was wondered if we might resurrect this facility. In spring, I was given the job of securing appointments with as many of the farmers as I could, and I arranged meetings. The intention was to try to secure an area that completely surrounded the twelve-mile perimeter of the station, and also a corridor to connect RAF St. Mawgan with the former airfield of St. Eval, a few miles to the north.

I was not greatly optimistic about this, perhaps remembering the survey I had undertaken in Northern Ireland some years before. We were baldly asking permission to turn up to a hundred Gunners loose on land which was devoted to crops and livestock, firing blank, using pyrotechnics and generally offering much potential for disruption and destruction, and for no fee. To my great surprise, the farmers proved welcoming of the idea almost without exception and I rapidly filled out the fields on a large-scale Ordnance Survey map with a coloured pen, closing the circle about the station. Not a few of the farmers invited me to stay for a meal, and all of them had some good stories to tell. Cattle rustling, it seemed, was not merely confined to western movies; a fair bit of it was happening in Cornwall. I put in a pleasant fortnight, surprised the Adjutant with the quick results and returned to my desk.

On the May Bank Holiday weekend I again accompanied the skills team to the major UK event and they won the trophy for the second year in succession. It was a glorious weekend and since the camp was no great distance from Cheshire, I nipped up to Wistaston to visit Aunt Jenny and Uncle Arthur. Jenny had made a good recovery from her stroke but both she and Arthur were in their eighties by now. Age did not appear to trouble Arthur, who still walked two miles for a haircut.

Another recruit course featured but I found that I was doing little with it, other than drill and the odd lesson on husbandry. I would have preferred to have been more involved, but I at least had the satisfaction of knowing that I had rescued the course some years before. Instruction was also escaping me on routine weekends, other than when a First-aid instructor was required. We had few instructors with that particular qualification, for some reason, although we were by now replete with weapons and NBC instructors, and range conductors.

In July I accompanied a recce to Cyprus, which was as pleasant a way to spend a week as any. Norm Alldis, who was the Training NCO, and I made a trio with one of the flight commanders who was temporarily unemployed and therefore available for the trip, and we were hosted by No 34 Squadron. 34 was permanently based at RAF Akrotiri, although soon to take up residence in the UK, and we were greatly dependent upon the unit for range bookings and training areas. Reservist units, we had long known, had virtually no priority for such bookings and there was great demand for those on Cyprus.

It was nicely hot and we went about our ranges and training areas recces for a few days, finding time also to explore some adventurous training possibilities and relax with the odd bottle of Keo, the local beer. The DSC of 34 was a former Gunner who had served on II Squadron and he also had undergone the exchange tour with the Royal Marines. He was more than helpful with our considerable 'shopping list' and by the close of the week we appeared to have everything we needed.

The summer months were mostly devoted to an intensive range programme, with much of the firing taking place at Tregantle Fort. Tregantle was one of 'Palmerston's Follies', built massively of stone and expensively so in the mid-nineteenth century to meet a supposed, but actually long-expired, French threat. We stayed overnight on a couple of occasions and the old gun galleries had been converted to sleeping quarters which were attractive and comfortable. I found the time to roam about the place, and I also tried to discover traces of a railway line which had once connected Tregantle with Scraesdon Fort and led from a jetty on the Tamar a couple of hundred feet below.

The deployment of the squadron to Cyprus brought an interesting problem. We were entitled to seats on the Air Trooper that flew from Brize Norton, but our low priority held out the prospect of being denied flights on the day. It was therefore decided to book a charter flight, out of the squadron budget, and this was done. Then, mere days before the flight, the travel agency collapsed. The firm was insured, which was the good news; the bad news being that it might take some time to recover the cash. The squadron then approached station for money from the station budget and the station commander agreed it without hesitation, thus confirming what we had already believed - that he was a fine chap.

I had gone ahead of the main party, with a small advance group, aiming to sort out accommodation, feeding arrangements and a dozen other trivial but important matters. My knees were getting quite brown again when the rest arrived, at about 0200hrs in the day, and the main party had a brief rest before embarking upon a round of presentations. One of these was by the medical staff, and it included the advice not to undertake strenuous activity for four to six weeks. Twenty-four hours later we were on exercise.

34 Squadron again pulled out the stops for us, providing facilities that we might not otherwise have enjoyed. The squadron operated rigid-hulled inflatable craft for patrol work in the local waters, and these were put to our use. We also had access to a much larger vessel, of the landing craft variety, to complete a beach landing on a later exercise, and helicopters for yet another.

A former Turkish village, at Paramali, was now used as a fighting in built-up areas facility, thus generating plenty of sweat on a boiling day, and it was clear that the village had been evacuated during the 1974 partition. It was quietly set on a hillside and the stone houses had clearly enjoyed few comforts, yet this had been home to generations of goat herders and crop growers. I wondered if there had been vengeance enacted here. Violence was at least not new to the island. I had been reading an account of the Crusades and mention was made of Cyprus. Almost the entire island population had been exterminated at one time by the 'Christians'.

Violence of an ugly sort had been enacted just weeks prior to our arrival, when three soldiers from the resident battalion of the Royal Green Jackets raped then beat to death with a shovel a Danish tour guide they had abducted. They claimed innocence and nearly walked free, despite undeniable forensic evidence, on a technicality but were found guilty. The lengthy trial cost the British Taxpayer one million pounds and the appeal was believed to cost the same. Additionally, one of the convicted men was reportedly planning to sue the British army for a large sum for having failed to recognise his drink problem, and counsel him. I do not doubt that he will receive a large amount of legal aid to facilitate his suit.

We enjoyed more than adequate free time for swimming, snorkelling or simply loafing about. I tried a few runs, believing that the hot weather might be kinder to the knees, but these were simply painful and I abandoned them. When the main party flew out, I remained with a small rear party to sort out stores and accommodation, and this provided a good opportunity to tour some of the antiquities. Roman ruins were being discovered regularly, and some of the more longstanding included a fine amphitheatre and a villa where the mosaic floors appeared as fresh as the day they had been laid, 2,000 years before. The opportunity to visit the unrecognised (other than by Turkey) area occupied by Turkish Cypriots, I did not take up. The border itself was usually the scene of nationalist strutting by both communities, and these episodes occasionally led to the death of a demonstrator. The Turkish Cypriots were generally held to be the villains of the 1974 partition, although it was seldom pointed out that the invasion by Turkey had been at least partially in response by an attempted coup by Greek Cypriot army officers, who presumably admired the then Greek military dictatorship in Greece. *'Enosis'*, or union, with Greece had of course been the backdrop to the violence on Cyprus during the Fifties, when Britain still owned the island. Nor was Britain's record that laudable; a British government had once offered the Island to Turkey as a bribe to remain neutral during the Great War. It is easy to imagine the fate of the Greek Cypriots, had Turkey accepted the offer.

Having had a month in strong sunshine and acquiring much the colouring of a nut, I returned to weather in the UK where the chances of displaying the tan were but remote. Winter had begun to bite early, but we had a plan to avoid at least some of it. We were spending Xmas in Australia.

Arch had written earlier in the year with the news that his daughter Lisa was to marry in December, and might we be over? I could think of no better way of ending the year and we flew out early in December, arriving at Perth in the small hours and being met by Jan and Arch. We had a couple of quiet days, losing jetlag and adjusting to the heat, and we attended the wedding on day that was relatively cool. The ceremony was held at Campbell Barracks, the home of the SAS near Perth, and it was in the grounds of a former nurses' home which had been acquired by former SAS men as an association club house. It was a fine old building, with immaculate Jarrah floorboards and a real flavour of another age. It was a pleasant day all around.

After a few days we travelled up to the Goldfields to spend time with Mam, Bea and Malc, and I dusted off Malc's bike again for another round of visits. I went to the Pioneer Cemetery again and was pleasantly surprised to find that some restoration had taken place. On the earlier occasion, I had written to the *Kalgoorlie Miner* to advertise the neglect, suggesting that it would not cost a great deal to effect at least some renovation. Whether the work had been undertaken as a result of the letter, or whether perhaps it had been routinely carried out by the local historical society, I do not know, but I was pleased to see the result of it.

We spent Xmas on the Goldfields then returned to Perth and saw the New Year in with Jan and Arch. I again accompanied Arch to the black powder range and added to my experience with the cap and ball revolver. I was hitting the target, but only just. I also spent a bit of time in the City, researching some facts in the Alexander Library by referring to microfiche of newspapers. I had become curious about the Goldfields at the time of my first arrival, and I was already contemplating autobiography. Joan and I additionally did the tourist bits, visiting Rottnest Island for the day, and we also accompanied Jan and Arch for a visit to the bush town where Lisa and her husband had gone to for work. This was Dalwallinu, about three hours drive to the north, and I had driven through the town, going south, at some time in the Sixties. We visited on a Sunday, and the small town was very quiet, but I reckoned that quiet probably best characterised the town at any time. It likely would have driven me mad at seventeen or so, but at fifty-four it had much to recommend it. In these most pleasant and pleasing of days our time ran out and we returned to cold, wet and noisy England. I was riding my bike to work year-round by now, and I did not best appreciate this toil for a good few days

24

I felt regenerated by the trip to Australia and time spent with family which was both old and new, but I had not concurrently generated fresh enthusiasms for what little now remained of my military service. I had already advertised my intention to quit service at the age of fifty-five, and not least among several factors which reinforced my decision to go was the fact of the duff knee which precluded battle fitness tests. Loathe to accept what the doctors had been patiently telling me, I had made further attempts to resurrect the fitness training, only to develop new pain, and I was now accepting the inevitable.

Of considerably more weight, however, was the continuing example of failed leadership and senior command at the top end of the squadron which allowed rather more power to be concentrated in relatively junior command hands than might be wise. The deputy squadron commander was by now promoted and theoretically running the squadron, but he had made very little of his leadership opportunities during his tenure as DSC, and now appeared quite content to continue leading the quiet life. In another (and the last) of my frank, uninvited and doubtless wholly unwelcome interventions, I had apprised the DSC some months earlier that his profile was poor and offering little promise for his future as the CO. My anxiety was that a new adjutant would arrive and, spotting the same leadership vacuum which his predecessor had noticed, would immediately occupy his post as *de facto* squadron commander. Which is pretty much what happened.

The question of contract employment terms for full time reservists was to have been resolved by 1 April but wasn't. We were advised instead that the short-term regular engagements would be extended for a further year, but that those who, like me, now faced their fifty-fifth birthday would be extended only until that date. Beyond 55th birthday and until the contracts were installed, some local arrangement would be reached. This seemed academic in my case, although I was requested to remain in service until April 1997, to which I agreed. I experienced a mild temptation to consider service beyond, since it had been very agreeable to draw regular rates of pay after six years of doing much the same job as a regular for about sixty per cent of regular salary, and to continue doing so would have been also agreeable. Against that, and leaving aside the question of unfitness, it became a matter of principle and no small one at that.

The squadron to which I belonged had formed to defend RAF St. Mawgan, but the defence picture had changed very substantially with the demise of the Warsaw Pact alliance and the dismantling of the former USSR. 'Options for Change' after the Gulf War was a government-inspired assessment of Britain's defence needs which produced deep cuts in regular manning levels, and a growing acceptance that Britain's reservists would need to shoulder some of the burden of tasking within UN and NATO commitments. Sharing regular duties in the former Yugoslavia, for example, would be part of the price of reservist units' survival, and anyone who might believe that such duties could lightly be undertaken would be seriously out of touch. There is plenty of scope for disaster in Sipovo and Split even without inept leadership, and these are not the sort of detached duties to risk lives on with just such failings.

Not that there has seemed, to date at least, much prospect of auxiliary regiment squadrons going into operations as formed units. At this time of writing, a dozen Gunners, drawn from the spectrum of reservist squadrons, are serving as volunteers with No 34 Squadron RAF Regiment in Bosnia, and this apparently token participation may be sufficient to satisfy the politicians that reservists usefully meet manning problems expressed by regular units. None of the volunteers is above the rank of corporal, although several SNCOs had volunteered, and the simple reason for that is the fact that 34 Squadron's manning gaps were at Gunner level. No problem.

The problems might begin with any future deployment that requires a formed auxiliary unit to be placed between Serbs and Croats or Hutus and Tutsis or whomever. In May 1996 a new Reserve Forces Act was introduced and it became law a year later. Formerly, reservists have been under no compulsion, however grave the situation, to serve overseas, but with effect from April 1997 such units may be called up and despatched anywhere. The detachment of a formed unit, under auxiliary leadership, is a very different proposition altogether.

On 2625 Squadron we had become accustomed to the fact of a CO who commanded but seldom led; who seemed to regard the unit as a shooting club with no operational purpose; and who apparently saw no good reason to acquire the qualities of tactical leadership which he so manifestly lacked. I had supposed, at the time of his appointment, that he was a 'caretaker' CO until a more suitable accession might be arranged and having no more than a year or so in the appointment. Caretaker or not, he lasted five full years and was close to his sixty-second birthday when he was finally (and reluctantly, one suspects) retired. The new CO was his protege, although he clearly had nothing useful to teach him, and another junior officer, a man of some ability, quietly resigned his commission when the succession was announced. We now had a young squadron commander, but one displaying no obvious leadership in a new era of reservist service which might well put his tactical abilities - or the absence of them - to tests upon which the lives of his men could depend. I was less than sanguine as to happy outcome of this.

I at least now know how such potential leadership disasters are arrived at. Leaving aside the fact of ex-regular officers who pass into auxiliary service and retain their rank, however ill-fitted they may be for new duties, it is a weakness of the system itself which allows the Peter Principle to flourish (meaning that, even within an ordered environment, a man may be promoted beyond the level of his competence). But the problems may begin much earlier.

Applicants for regular commissions are subjected to close scrutiny and put through severe tests of leadership potential that they must survive before even being accepted for further training. An applicant for the RAF Regiment will then undergo training for the better part of a year, and much of that training will be focused upon not only leadership, but *tactical* leadership. He will then be further and specialist trained before passing to his first unit, where he will be closely advised (and to some extent even controlled) by an experienced SNCO, and monitored by the CO and the DSC. Another year will pass before he is allowed much independent action, and during that time also he is likely to undergo further formal training at the School of Infantry at Warminster and Brecon - hard schools. His rise to the command of a squadron will be less than meteoric and not before he has undergone a variety of postings to broaden his experience. He will, moreover, be constantly in competition with some very sharp acts for too few promotion opportunities.

Consider, then, the auxiliary officer. If he has no previous regular service, he may have attracted notice on the grounds of promising performance as a JNCO, or possibly even as a Gunner. In the worst case - and it happens - he will have been selected on the basis of his civilian 'management' job and perceived social qualities. He will appear before a local board, which might be chaired by his own squadron commander (who selected him in the first place) and including junior officers from other branches who have little perception of the candidate's trade. If successful, the candidate will be duly despatched to the RAF College to undergo a ten-day course of initial officer training. This will doubtless introduce him to drill and the conventions of the dining-in night in the Mess, but it will not explore tactical leadership. A fortnight later, the newly-minted pilot officer might be commanding a flight; two years later, and with no formal training in the interim, he might still be commanding a flight and ten years later he might be commanding a squadron, still without formal training or any significant progress as a tactical leader. I might be persuaded to follow this man to a fire escape from a blazing building, but I may not be keen to follow his tactical lead, particularly if I know that his tactical knowledge is inferior to mine.

The future can only be guessed at, but the past may be studied. Britain's regular army in 1914 provided the BEF, which bled to death on the Aisne, the Marne and at Mons and Flanders. The total of British casualties in five months of war was 90,000. In 1915, Britain introduced territorial (reservist) units to the fight and in that year the total of British casualties rose to 285,000. An average monthly increase of 5,000 casualties just possibly resulted from inept reservist leadership at unit level, quite apart from the unimaginative generalship of the era, and we should not doubt that this piece of unhappy history could be repeated. Reservist units today are in dire need of the very best of leadership, not the bad nor even the indifferent. The Volunteer who sacrifices his weekends deserves better.

I formed the view that reservist units should be confined to just flight size and integrated with regular squadrons. This of course would leave auxiliary leadership out of the equation and doubtless would attract little favour among the reservist hierarchy. The latter, however, is simply a part of the problem, and until bold steps are taken to remove the dead hand of the long retired from spheres of reservist influence we shall simply fail to progress. Despite the fact that reservist Gunners have served in Banja Luka and Sipovo and earned the respect of those regulars with whom they served, reservists, generally, are not held in high esteem. They tend, instead, to be regarded as cowboys and incompetents, and sadly we have allowed into the reservist higher ranks those who foster just such false perceptions. Despite also the fact of armed service in the former Yugoslavia, we were still not permitted to bear loaded weapons on the gates of our parent stations. What message does this offer as to reservist competence?

In 1940, it took Hitler's armies only fifteen days to defeat those of Holland, Belgium and France and send a third of a million men of the British Expeditionary Force scrambling for a boat - any boat - at Dunkirk, scattering their equipment and weapons on the beaches. The conquest of Britain might swiftly have followed, had it not been for the Channel and the pre-requisite of air superiority by the *Luftwaffe* prior to a *Wehrmacht* sea-borne invasion. The Battle of Britain was narrowly won by the RAF at a time when there was a critical shortage of replacement aircraft, but a desperate shortage of trained pilots. A full third of those who were immortalised as 'the Few' were reservists; builders, bank clerks and businessmen who gave up their weekends to fly, and without whose contribution a victory in 1940 is impossible to imagine. Such history and fact, however, is soon forgotten. Those who forget the lessons of the past are condemned to repeat them, as someone has pointed out.

If such periodic thoughts were depressing, it was a matter beyond my influence and largely academic in view of the clock which was running against me. I began to prepare briefs for my successor, who was a good man already serving on the squadron and destined to become one of the very few 'home-grown' warrant officers, and I tried not to notice that the arrival of a new training officer had launched 'year zero' - again.

It was both disappointing and irritating that a new training officer might arrive and blithely ignore all that which had so recently been the gospel of his predecessor - and the more so if much of the gospel had been very soundly based. The defenestration of good practices was not heartening to witness, and within a few days of the new incumbent's arrival I predicted that we were about to be presented with the newly invented wheel. Thus it proved.

There was by now absolutely no hope that either the CO or the DSC would attempt to direct the training officer, and the ultimate expression of this was when both sat meekly receiving Orders from the new man on the first occasion that the squadron deployed to exercise. The Orders were moreover poorly prepared and delivered, and it was most definitely time that I moved on. I had no great wish to become accustomed to the sight of a training officer who stalked the training area in barrack dress and twirling a swagger stick, whilst all else carried their loads. Some months later the Adjutant was heard commenting that 'he was running his own train set', and the analogy was perfect: the components of 2625 Squadron whizzed about to no more useful purpose than the whim and the amusement of the Adj. You might define leadership as the art of getting the best out of blokes who might otherwise offer you their worst. The Gunners on 2625 often gave of their best, but they gave, I think, for each other rather than for the supposed leaders. When I had first enlisted with No 2625 Squadron, almost nine years earlier, I had quickly noticed that reservists at all levels were greatly admiring of the regular RAF Regiment staff, clearly seeing them as the 'professionals' from whom much might be learned by emulation. I now saw that such admiration had long evaporated, as a succession of dud acts had squandered their opportunity to preserve such regard. Reservists had become more knowing, and more cynical. It was depressing to consider that the Corps which had become my spiritual home and which I had long held in a measure of esteem appeared largely indifferent to reservists, placing no great emphasis upon the selection of the right men for auxiliary posts. That 'there are no bad soldiers; only bad leaders' is not new; it was of Roman coinage, yet it might have been newly-minted for 2625 Squadron. With the exception of a single training officer, the squadron remained poorly led for a decade and among the consequences was the steady exodus of useful lads who simply voted with their feet in the direction of the camp gates. It was difficult to defend the record of those of the Corps who were only too happy to occupy postings which otherwise would not have been open to them, and offering promotion prospects which would not have existed, and who suffered none of the hardships common to life on regular squadrons, but who saw little reason to work hard on behalf of reservists. Disappointing, too, that the very considerable scope for initiative and independent effort which auxiliary units offered to their regular staff was, if 2625 Squadron's experience was typical, often ignored altogether and wholly pedestrian attitudes allowed to hold sway. I wondered, too, if my own efforts on behalf of 2625 were more characterised by failure than success, and this was a particularly dispiriting thought as I faced the final weeks of service.

  I retained an interest in the Military Skills Team and during the May Bank Holiday we deployed to a camp near Liverpool in the hope of completing the hat-trick for the major UK Skills trophy. Heartbreakingly, although the team amassed the highest score of the thirty-odd teams competing, on the stance that we conducted our man neglected to deduct penalty points from a team that was pressing us very closely. By the time we uncovered the error, the results had been broadcast and there was simply no way that we could claim the victory. By way of compounding our gloom at this, we also came nowhere in the annual and prestigious mil skills competition which the RAF Regiment Depot hosted each autumn.

Elsewhere, I was peripherally involved with two basic gunner recruit courses, teaching drill and bayonet fighting for the last time and reminding myself that I would not include a pace stick among the souvenirs of service life, although I reserved space on a wall of the house for a polished bayonet. The bayonet, together with the infantry motto *Follow Me*, is wholly expressive of leadership and I regard it as a happy reminder of service. The year ticked on after my final discharge from regular service on the day prior to my 55th birthday and I could see that it was shaping up to be a swift one.

In October we deployed the squadron to the Kent ranges of Hythe & Lydd, intent upon a week of conventional ranges. I was given some ranges to conduct on this occasion, beginning with hand grenade, and this represented a welcome return to field activity after a number of recent camps where I had been required to do very little. I still had plenty of free time, however, although I again failed in my intention to walk a stretch of the military canal. I did find the time to stroll among the graves at the Shorncliffe Military Cemetery, which had provided the commital of broken soldiers for over two centuries. Here lay a soldier who at seventeen had won the VC during the Indian Mutiny in 1857, and here also the fourteen-year-old boy soldier killed in 1939. Shorncliffe offered a sobering reminder that those who choose the profession of arms may not survive to see the allotted three score years and ten. In one of life's sad ironies, I returned to the lines at St Martin's Plain Camp that night and to the shocking news that Mick Sweeney had died of a heart attack. Mick had retired just three weeks earlier and he was forty-two. I was able to secure time off during the second week of the battle camp, by which time we had redeployed to exercise in Norfolk, and I met Joan in Bolton for Mick's commital. The church was equally packed with Irish family and RAF uniform and I delivered a valedictory, as Shirl had requested. It was a difficult address on a bleak day.

In the anticipation of being on a much reduced wage - and possibly no wage - when my service expired, we looked anew at the question of the house which we simply rattled around in since we had abandoned the B&B prospects, and one which might be traded for a lower mortgage. The housing market appeared to be stirring again although the brightest forecasts typically came from the estate agents, who might have been less than objective in their assessments. We placed the house on the market and when it failed to attract a single viewer, much less an offer, in six months, we took a deep breath, slashed the asking price and tried again. This somewhat expensive ploy succeeded and by the close of the year we were looking at properties to buy, in the expectation of moving out of Newquay early in the New Year. We soon discovered that for all the received wisdom when we were offering ours that it was still very much a 'buyer's market', there was a markedly cool response to our suggestion that asking prices might be on the high side when we examined properties. Some you don't win. We did, however, managed to combine house, location and price fairly agreeably and with a month of service remaining we were painting and papering a bungalow on a snug estate a few miles down the coast from Newquay, and not missing the town at all. Not missing the service was the next hurdle.

Time simply ran out, and I suppose that may prove an apt metaphor for life itself. I returned my issues of clothing and equipment then assembled those bits and pieces that had been useful acquisitions down the years. These I auctioned at the close of a training day and passed the sum raised to a local charity. I bought some beer, shook a few hands and walked away, quelling the thought that I was bidding farewell to the unique brand of comradeship that had marked most of my days for the thick end of forty years. It really was that simple and relatively painless, although these things perhaps need a longer perspective. There was, in any case, little to be regretted since life is too short for that as well. There was nothing to be regretted in the house move, meanwhile. Sand dunes and the beach lay within a five-minute walk each morning and evening, with the dogs eager to chase rabbits whilst I appreciated the beauty of sunsets on the water; long moments which convinced me that I had found something just right in my life. Civil and friendly neighbours called at the door to say hello. (One such mentioned the neighbourhood watch scheme, and when I told him about my ever-ready pick helve he seemed alarmed, perhaps believing that Charles Bronson had moved into the street).

No more marking time. Time to move forward, find a job and see what the coming years hold. The first fourteen years of my life had not the remotest connection with matters military, and I suppose that will be the case for the next fourteen. I have few regrets about those years that intervened, although among them is spending barely sixty days in the company of my father in the last decade of his life. There is residual regret that I never made it back to the Australian army, too. 'Inclined to dream, could do better' is indelibly printed on my memory. Time to move forward. Time to regain the sense of humour that seems to me to have been somewhat under attack in recent years. Time to reflect. Time, finally, to grow old and die in a new century. Eventually.

****

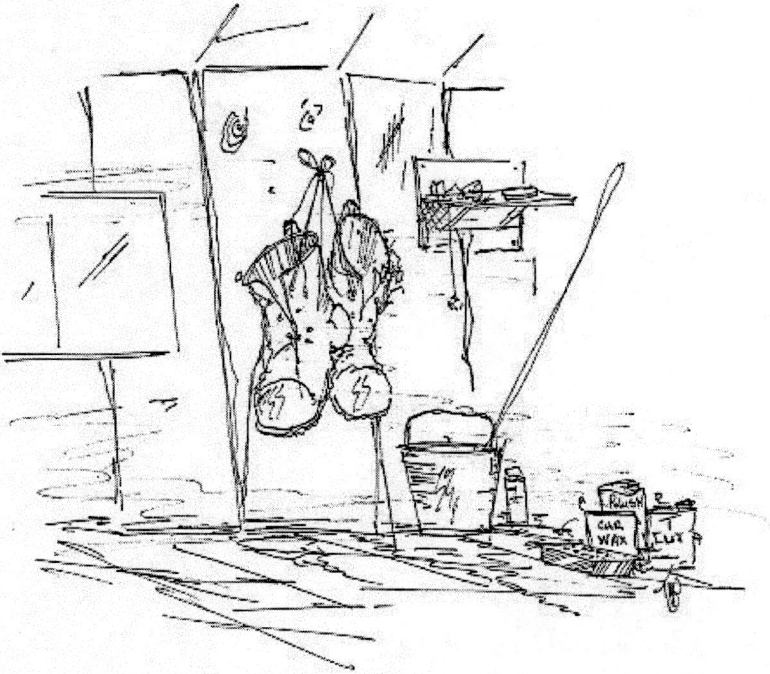
POLISH
CAR WAX

Epilogue

If a man will begin with certainties, he shall end in doubts, but if he will be content to begin with doubts, he shall end in certainties.

The Advancement of Learning
Francis Bacon 1561-1626

It has been said that the purpose of travel is to return from where you came and see it for the first time, and this aphorism was uppermost in my mind when I journeyed to Crewe one autumn afternoon in 1996. I had been back to the town perhaps a hundred times since I had left it as an adolescent migrant in 1955, but this was the first occasion when my purpose was to *study* the town. I had been attending an RAF Regiment SNCO's reunion at the RAF Regiment Depot in East Anglia, and little remained of the day when I drove along the quiet Sunday streets. I had a few days available to me for a protracted look, but I was impatient to learn if Richard Moon and Ramsbottom Streets, point of arrival perhaps for the Foxley and Emerton families, still existed, or whether, like the railwaymen they had been named for, they were long gone.

Ramsbottom Street, no more than two hundred yards in length, still led from West Street to the very entrance of the Works, but its houses were new and had never echoed the clatter of nailed boots on the paved road, as an entire shift responded to the steam whistle to be at their place of work at 0600hrs. I turned through ninety degrees at the Works' gate, locked and long-disused, to follow Richard Moon Street, which flanked the imposing north wall, noting the many gaps in what originally had been a continuous row of two up, two down houses. Towards the former technical institute, where the street met Flag Lane, I found Number 69 where William Foxley, sometime brick burner, casual labourer and, finally, indigent, had lived and raised his family. Among the sons and daughters, Arthur Malvern Foxley, born in 1880 within three months and two hundred yards of Mary Ellen Emerton, daughter of William's fellow Buckinghamshire migrant, David Emerton, mechanic and shopkeeper. The house could tell me little from its exterior, and the interior was doubtless much changed since its rooms were gas-lit, but it was pleasing to stand for a while and view, wondering about life four generations ago. I thought of William Foxley making a new life and I wondered if at some point in the nineteenth century he had ever considered migration to the American West. I wondered, too, what he would have thought of his grandson who, at fifty, would settle his family in West Australia. I then turned away and drove to the house of the cousin whose paternal line also descended from the south of England, and who also shared ancestry with the great-grandfather who lost his farm and his wife at the age of twenty-nine, and began anew as a farm labourer.

Early the next day I began where the Works had begun, on the site just south of the town centre, although little now remains. Engine repair that was subsidiary to the main effort at the new works on the Chester Line continued until 1960 and then forever ceased. By 1980, only the north wall of the Works, flanking Forge Street, remained and this was demolished by 1996 to create space for an MFI superstore. I was able to follow the course of the street by using a town map of about 1950 vintage, and I noted that a few dozen bricks of the original Works' wall remained embedded in new work, presumably by accident.

Lines still run through the former Works and a portion of the thirty acres is devoted to a Railway Heritage Centre, which was a mandatory visit. I viewed the complex signal box and various yard relics, whose pride was a locomotive in steam. The Duchess of Hamilton is a 4-6-2 built in 1938 and she would have been an impressive sight, at full throttle, in her day. Now, however, and despite her apparently pristine condition, she is confined to a couple of hundred yards of track, with not the remotest prospect of developing her power. With smoke curling from her stack and steam wreathing her pistons, she is doubtless a stirring sight for a real steam buff, but each time she panted along the short run I was minded of a powerful animal caged within some inadequate zoo.

At an indoor exhibition, a piece of jigsaw fell pleasingly into place when I noticed a painting of a loco named William Shakespeare. For years I had been reasonably certain that I had viewed the original loco at or near the Flag Lane Technical Institute, and the museum attendant, himself a retired railwayman, confirmed my memory. The William Shakespeare was exhibited in Crewe before being taken to London for the Festival of Britain, in 1951. Her buffers were chromed, the old chap told me, and her firebox was painted white. She was doubtless state of the art engineering, but the knell had already sounded for steam by then.

The houses first-built in the original town had long been demolished and the space they had occupied was now filled by a police station, the town library and a pedestrianised area. I walked through it to Market Street, once the principal thoroughfare but now dwarfed by a new road for by-pass traffic. Just off Market Street stood the Empire cinema, which ran its last reel at some time in the Sixties before becoming a bingo hall, but the building was later entirely demolished and a new pub stands on the site. The pub sign bears a fine representation of a steam loco and the pub itself is named The Grand Junction. Its clientele seemed mostly young and I fleetingly wondered how many of them knew the origin of the name, or if they are even curious about it.

The Borough School, built in 1908, still has pupils but only in the junior boy's building. They were at play when I passed and the selection of games on display looked a lot more technical than matchboxes and rubber bands. The senior boy's building, whose attractive red brick facade is adorned with various virtues ('Generosity' 'Friendship' 'Mercy' 'Reverence' 'Peace' 'Kindness'), is now the Brierley Business Centre, operated by the Cheshire County Council.

The 'Razza' has completely vanished, built upon by a large works of some sort at one end, and a sports' centre at the other. I wondered if the excavation for it all had turned up other 'dripping jars', and whether a few of them await the curiosity of later generations, as I headed for Henry Street to see what recent changes there had been. The allotments that flank the street are mostly neglected, with a few turned into detached gardens or garages. The Primitive Methodist Chapel, which stood fairly close to Number 4, has gone and a small cluster of new houses stands on the site. Speed ramps now exist on the street and these would have been wholly unnecessary for the pedestrian or bicycle-owning populace of forty and fifty years ago. Another concession to the age of common motor ownership was evident at the Cumberland Arms pub. The house of my boyhood friend has been demolished, along with several of its neighbours, and the space created now serves as the pub car park. To the town side of the pub is the Cumberland Bridge, built to carry the rolling stock of the Birmingham-Manchester Railway. The bridge is gaily painted and electric wires are suspended above the tracks, a reminder of steam's eclipse. Adjacent to the bridge a urinal once stood, made of iron, painted green and smelling badly. It has been removed and a cluster of copper beeches grows attractively on the spot.

In Middlewich Street, the small shop struggles gamely, if precariously, on. Dean's Bakery, Gunby's Newsagency and Dixon's the Butcher's have all become something else, but they survive. I was pleased to note the presence of a fish and chip shop and the product smelled good, although I did not buy any. In the town centre I had already seen that the site of the Odeon cinema, whose art deco facade contrasted oddly with the war memorial in the adjacent town square and which was the last of the six to close, had provided space for a beefburger outlet. (It occasionally is visited by a red-faced man wearing big boots, who calls himself Ronald MacDonald. I was fleetingly reminded of someone bearing the same description and a similar name, but not remotely connected with beefburgers.) Behind Middlewich Street, the allotments that included one which the Old Man had tended, had gone and a football pitch occupied the ground.

At Adelaide Street, I noticed lights on at the school that I had assumed was long closed. The door opened to my knock and I was invited in to learn that conventional classes had ended at the school a few years ago, before it was regenerated as a special needs unit. I met a couple of small pupils, generally uncommunicative, and was shown around the building. In the classroom where we had cheered the news of George VI's death - or at least the news of the day off - I noted that the gas fittings for the original lighting had never been removed.

Adelaide Street was among a dozen which ran off West Street and the area was densely populated by railway workers; those particularly from the Works. I understood now that it had been a tough area, rather than a rough one. West Street now is rather shabby, yet it preserves a friendly aspect and there is no air of menace which apparently has infected one of the housing estates elsewhere in the town.. I stopped an old bloke to enquire if he had any knowledge of the Works' bombing during the war (he had), and he was happy to stand and talk for twenty minutes or so. We stood adjacent to a roofed section of the Works and along the wall it was just possible to detect the faint outlines of 'windows' and 'doors' which had been painted on the bricks during the war, intended to camouflage the Works as a row of houses.

The westernmost edge of the Works lay opposite the gates of Rolls-Royce, from which the distinctive grilles of the famous car still emerge. Royces, however, went through a troubled period that followed the firm going into receivership in 1971, as a result of the astronomical development costs of the RB211 jet engine that was being produced for the Lockheed Aircraft Company. The aero engine and motor works were separated, with ownership of the latter changing twice in succeeding years. 1996 brought the news that Rolls-Royce would develop no new engines and it seems likely that the engines behind the Spirit of Ecstasy in the future will be made by the German company, BMW. The BMW badge represents a spinning propeller, because the company founded its fortune on aero engines, and there lies another of life's little ironies. As I stood before the Royce's gate I recalled with a smile that I once thought that the firm also made cutlery, since in the house at Henry Street several knives and forks had ROLLS-ROYCE stamped on the handles.

From Royce's I walked by the Webb Orphanage, another example of company paternalism which in more recent years was a technical college for British Rail Engineering Limited - the inheritor of the Works after the nationalisation of the railways. Since the demise of BREL, subsequent to de-nationalisation in the past couple of years, the function of the former orphanage is not clear.

An isosceles triangle frames the old Works and West Street, Wistaston Road and Flag Lane mark its perimeter. Walking towards Flag Lane along Wistaston Road, I noted a good deal of new building on the area of Park Place, where army huts served as housing for nearly four decades after the Great War, and more where slag heaps once rose, unlovely, adjacent to the gas works that was demolished in 1969. The slag heaps, by-product of an industry which once believed that it would extinguish travel by roads, were removed in the 1970s to provide in-fill for Britain's new arteries, the motorways. Another circle closed.

Predominant among the Flag Lane buildings is the former Technical Institute, another fine example in red brick, but forlorn now, empty and vandalised. It awaits a new owner and renewed purpose or, more likely, demolition. I crossed the bridge that will see no more trains, steam or otherwise, and called at the Crewe Baths, curious to know how much a slipper bath might cost. I was just days too late, however, since the baths, actually long disused, had been stripped out during the preceding week. I was advised that I could treat myself to the jacuzzi and the solarium, but chose not to. It seemed a far cry from a shilling bath whilst living in town digs.

I retraced my steps to view the Crewe Park, gift of the railway company to the town to mark the Diamond Jubilee of Victoria in 1897, and engendering the myth that the park was actually a bribe to keep Great Western Railway interests out of the town. The park is spacious, well laid out and preserving a clean and tidy appearance, with several employees busily at work as I strolled through. The boats on the lake seemed a touch neglected, but perhaps they reflected the end of the season and await restoration during the winter months. At fifty pence per half-hour, they represent good value at least. I found the point at which the Valley Brook enters the lake and I followed it briefly. It is much wider, deeper and more swiftly flowing than I could remember, and the water looked clean. The brook has long shed the indignity of being reduced to town sewer.

When I strolled to the town centre for a cup of tea, I passed 'Gaffer's Row', the houses built for railway foremen who had requested accommodation separate from lowlier employees. These houses have been preserved almost by accident, and they are the oldest railway houses in the world, built at the time of the Crimean War.

My final call was to the Crewe Cemetery, to find the grave of Grandad Foxley. A brief search of records at the gatehouse pointed me to the grave, which was unmarked other than by a plot marker. Arthur Malvern Foxley, son of the migrant William, was buried there in 1947, joining his brother William, who had died in 1945. Most surprising of all, the grave also contained the body of my cousin Betty, who had died of polio, aged thirteen, in 1949.

I had seen of the town that which I had most wanted to see, and I devoted what remained of my time to the Records section in the Crewe and Chester Libraries. But the images of the town remain, and I am able to superimpose upon them the descriptions from the pages of the books that recount the town's history. The era of the steam locomotive spanned a hundred and fifty years, during which time Crewe developed from migrant, railway and new town to industrial prosperity, becoming a by-word for rail travel. The Foxleys were a tiny fragment of that record; a migrant family from the south of England which in three generations became a migrant family in Western Australia. When I left Crewe in 1955, it was with no particular expectation of ever seeing the town again. I was instead focused upon a new life in a new country half a world distant. When I returned in 1969, it was without particular curiosity of Crewe, and not intended to be a lengthy stay. That length developed and with it a curiosity for the town of my birth and also my adoptive town. Both towns beckon me from time to time and I believe that I have not seen the last of either.

***

ISBN 141201587-1